OXFORD STUDIES IN EUROPEAN LAW

EU Values Before the Court of Justice

OXFORD STUDIES IN EUROPEAN LAW

The aim of this series is to publish important and original research on EU law. The focus is on scholarly monographs, with a particular emphasis on those which are interdisciplinary in nature. Edited collections of essays will also be included where they are appropriate. The series is wide in scope and aims to cover studies of particular areas of substantive and of institutional law, historical works, theoretical studies, and analyses of current debates, as well as questions of perennial interest such as the relationship between national and EU law and the novel forms of governance emerging in and beyond Europe. The fact that many of the works are interdisciplinary will make the series of interest to all those concerned with the governance and operation of the EU.

OTHER TITLES IN THIS SERIES

The Legislative Priority Rule and the EU Internal Market for Goods
A Constitutional Approach
Eadaoin Ní Chaoimh

The Jurisprudence of Constitutional Conflict in the European Union
Ana Bobić

Reflexive Governance in EU Equality Law
Emma Lantschner

Enhanced Cooperation and European Tax Law
Caroline Heber

Legal Pluralism in European Contract Law
Vanessa Mak

Europe's Passive Virtues
Deference to National Authorities in EU Free Movement Law
Jan Zglinski

Accountability in EU Security and Defence
The Law and Practice of Peacebuilding
Carolyn Moser

Accountability in the Economic and Monetary Union
Foundations, Policy, and Governance
Menelaos Markakis

Official Secrets and Oversight in the EU
Law and Practices of Classified Information
Vigjilenca Abazi

Risk Regulation in the Internal Market
Lessons from Agricultural Biotechnology
Maria Weimer

EU Health Law & Policy
The Expansion of EU Power in Public Health and Health Care
Anniek de Ruijter

The Horizontal Effect of Fundamental Rights in the European Union
A Constitutional Analysis
Eleni Frantziou

EU Powers Under External Pressure
How the EU's External Actions Alter its Internal Structures
Christina Eckes

Frontex and Human Rights
Responsibility in 'Multi-Actor Situations' under the ECHR and EU Public Liability Law
Melanie Fink

EU Equality Law
The First Fundamental Rights Policy of the EU
Elise Muir

Subnational Authorities in EU Law
Michèle Finck

Accessing Asylum in Europe
Violeta Moreno-Lax

National Parliaments after the Lisbon Treaty & the Euro Crisis
Davor Jančić

Environmental Integration in Competition and Free-Movement Laws
Julian Nowag

EU Agencies
Legal and Political Limits to the Transformation of the EU Administration
Merijn Chamon

EU Values Before the Court of Justice

Foundations, Potential, Risks

LUKE DIMITRIOS SPIEKER

Senior Research Fellow, Max Planck Institute for Comparative Public Law and International Law

OXFORD
UNIVERSITY PRESS

OXFORD
UNIVERSITY PRESS

Great Clarendon Street, Oxford, OX2 6DP,
United Kingdom

Oxford University Press is a department of the University of Oxford.
It furthers the University's objective of excellence in research, scholarship,
and education by publishing worldwide. Oxford is a registered trade mark of
Oxford University Press in the UK and in certain other countries

First Edition published in 2023

Published in the United States of America by Oxford University Press
198 Madison Avenue, New York, NY 10016, United States of America

British Library Cataloguing in Publication Data

Data available

Library of Congress Control Number: 2023932451

ISBN 978–0–19–887671–7

DOI: 10.1093/oso/9780198876717.001.0001

Printed and bound in the UK by
TJ Books Limited

Ich danke
meinem Doktorvater für Freiraum und Föderung,
der Dienstagsrunde für den geschützten Raum,
der Studienstiftung für die finanzielle Unterstützung
und M.

Αυτό το βιβλίο είναι αφιερωμένο στον παππού και τη γιαγιά μου

Series Editors' Preface

Since the enactment of the Treaty of Lisbon, Article 2 of the Treaty on European Union has proclaimed that the European Union is founded on the values of respect for human dignity, freedom, democracy, equality, the rule of law, and respect for human rights, including the rights of persons belonging to minorities. Despite the broad and declaratory language this provision of the Treaty has not remained purely symbolic but has begun to figure in the case law of the Court of Justice. Prompted by the rise of authoritarian and illiberal forces in various member states which saw national judiciaries coming under increasing political control, litigation has been brought before the Luxembourg court to challenge the compatibility with EU law of these illiberal moves, and the Court has drawn extensively on Article 2 in its rulings.

In this book, the author describes the case law of the Court dealing with the values in Article 2 and goes on to defend and justify the Court's operationalization and development of what many perceived to be a non-justiciable provision. He argues that the Court should review compliance with these values not only across the EU legal order but also within the legal orders of the Member States and develops an argument to this effect based on German scholarship concerning compound or composite constitutionalism (Verbund). The book explores how Article 2 could be developed and used to promote these values across the EU and its Member states. The author considers a range of criticisms from the perspective of judicial (over) empowerment, democracy, and pluralism, but argues that there are appropriately deferential strategies the Court could and should adopt to avert these risks.

At a time of increasing concern both about the authoritarian challenge to the rule of law and fundamental rights in the EU, and of interest in the appropriate role and limits of the Court of Justice in monitoring and promoting respects for these values, this book-length treatment of Article 2 TEU and its potential should be a welcome addition to the European legal literature.

Paul Craig
Gráinne de Búrca

Contents

PART IV RISKS AND RECALIBRATION

Detailed Contents

List of Abbreviations

AFSJ	Area of Freedom, Security and Justice
BVerfG	Bundesverfassungsgericht
CFSP	Common, Foreign and Security Policy
CJEU	Court of Justice of the European Union
CST	Civil Service Tribunal
EAW	European Arrest Warrant
EC	European Community
ECB	European Central Bank
ECHR	European Convention on Human Rights
ECJ	Court of Justice of the European Union
ECSC	European Coal and Steel Community
ECtHR	European Court of Human Rights
EEA	European Economic Area
EEC	European Economic Community
EP	European Parliament
ESCB	European System of Central Banks
EU	European Union
FRA	European Union Agency for Fundamental Rights
GC	General Court
IGC	Intergovernmental Conference
MEP	Member of the European Parliament
OSCE	Organization for Security and Cooperation in Europe
TEU	Treaty on the European Union
TFEU	Treaty on the Functioning of the European Union

Bibliographical Note

This book feeds in parts on previously published material. Chapters 1, 2, 9, and 13 partially draw on 'Defending Union Values in Judicial Proceedings. On How to Turn Article 2 TEU into a Judicially Applicable Provision' in Armin von Bogdandy et al. (eds), *Defending Checks and Balances in EU Member States* (Springer 2021) 237–268, 'Breathing Life into the Union's Common Values: On the Judicial Application of Article 2 TEU in the EU Value Crisis' *German Law Journal* 20 (2019), 1182–1213 as well as 'Protecting Fundamental Rights Beyond the Charter. Repositioning the Reverse Solange Doctrine in Light of the CJEU's Article 2 TEU Case Law' in Michal Bobek and Jeremias Adams-Prassl (eds), *The EU Charter of Fundamental Rights in the Member States* (Hart 2020) 525–546 (with Armin von Bogdandy) and 'Countering the Judicial Silencing of Critics: Article 2 TEU Values, Reverse Solange, and the Responsibilities of National Judges' *European Constitutional Law Review* 15 (2019), 391–426 (also with Armin von Bogdandy). Chapter 11 partially draws on 'Framing and Managing Constitutional Identity Conflicts: How to Stabilize the Modus Vivendi Between the Court of Justice and National Constitutional Courts' *Common Market Law Review* 57 (2020), 361–398.

Introduction

Article 2 TEU solemnly proclaims: 'The Union is founded on the values of respect for human dignity, freedom, democracy, equality, the rule of law and respect for human rights, including the rights of persons belonging to minorities. These values are common to the Member States ...' For some time, this provision played a rather marginal role in the jurisprudence of the Court of Justice of the European Union. Straddling between preamble and operative legal text, the provision was clouded by many uncertainties. In recent years, however, Luxembourg started to breathe life into this dormant provision. This step was triggered by unprecedented challenges to the Union's common values. During the past ten years, governing parties in Hungary and Poland, but also in other Member States, have started to openly reject the model of constitutional democracy enshrined in Article 2 TEU. Checks and balances of the political process, such as independent courts, have been the central target. Against this backdrop, the Court of Justice has mobilized the common values enshrined in Article 2 TEU. With a crucial breakthrough in *Associação Sindical dos Juízes Portugueses*, the CJEU has begun to operationalize the values of Article 2 TEU and scrutinize the Member States' internal structures against this yardstick.[1]

Even though the struggle over the Union's common values is far from over, the past years have been a critical juncture for the Court of Justice. After *ASJP*, it has stepped up its efforts to counter the resistance in the Member States. Pushed by the developments in Poland, Hungary, Romania, and Malta, the jurisprudence on Article 2 TEU has evolved at breakneck speed. According to Judge Marek Safjan such an intense concentration of case law in such a short period of time has been unprecedented in the Court's history.[2] Until recently, legal scholarship faced difficulties in catching up. After four years, however, the dust around the emerging case law has begun to settle and clear the view on an astounding, still growing jurisprudential edifice. While initially triggered by Member State contestations, the jurisprudence has spread to a variety of contexts and acquired overarching constitutional significance for the Union and its Member States. What we can observe today are the foundations of a veritable Article 2 TEU-based jurisprudence.

[1] Case C-64/16 *Associação Sindical dos Juízes Portugueses* [2018] EU:C:2018:117.
[2] Marek Safjan, 'Prawo do skutecznej ochrony sądowej' *Palestra* (5) (2020), 5, 25.

EU Values Before the Court of Justice. Luke Dimitrios Spieker, Oxford University Press.
DOI: 10.1093/oso/9780198876717.003.0001

I. Objectives

This study sets out to sketch a picture of this edifice and develop trajectories for its further development.[3] Even a brief glance into the book's bibliography makes clear that the growing relevance of EU values has not gone exactly unnoticed. Especially the 'rule of law crisis' in Member States like Poland or Hungary[4] and the Union's efforts to counter these developments are subject to an abundant literature.[5] So what sets the present book apart? Its title already indicates that this book is narrower and at the same time broader than the current debate. For one, it is narrower in that it concentrates only on the Court of Justice. It does not assess the Union's general toolbox and performance in monitoring and enforcing value compliance in the Member States. At the same time, this book is broader. As indicated above, the Court has divested the emerging jurisprudence of its initial rule of law context. Even though a large thrust of Article 2 TEU-related cases still concerns judicial independence in the Member States, a recourse to Article 2 TEU can now be found in a variety of contexts. This book will take this broader perspective and provide a first, fairly comprehensive study of this emerging jurisprudence.[6]

In doing so, it will be guided by three interrelated research objectives. Backward-looking, this book will systematize *what has happened so far*. It will trace the emergence of Article 2 TEU in the CJEU's judicial practice and anchor the jurisprudence in legal doctrine. By taking a more forward-looking perspective, the book will then explore *where we can go from here*. At its heart, this study will provide a conceptual framework for the judicial mobilization of Article 2 TEU, explore its potential and sketch trajectories for future development. As such, the second and third part of this book might read like a panoply of possibilities. Finally, this book will ask *whether these developments should be welcomed*. This will entail a critical reflection of the already existing case law and its prospective developments.

In this spirit, this book will sometimes shift its position between that of the Court's trainbearer, following and systematizing its emerging jurisprudence, and

[3] See aptly Ulrich Haltern, 'Europarecht und ich' JöR 68 (2020), 439, 456: 'Ist der institutionelle Kampf gekämpft und hat sich der Pulverdampf verzogen, kann geordnet werden'.

[4] From the plethora of assessments, see e.g. Tímea Drinóczi and Agnieszka Bień-Kacała, *Illiberal Constitutionalism in Poland and Hungary* (Routledge 2021); Wojciech Sadurski, *Poland's Constitutional Breakdown* (OUP 2019); Beáta Bakó, *Challenges to EU Values in Hungary* (Routledge 2023). From a broader perspective, see e.g. Ivan Krastev and Stephen Holmes, *The Light that Failed* (Penguin 2019).

[5] From the rich literature, see e.g. Armin von Bogdandy et al. (eds), *Defending Checks and Balances in EU Member States* (Springer 2021); András Jakab and Dimitry Kochenov (eds), *The Enforcement of EU Law and Values* (OUP 2017); Carlos Closa and Dimitry Kochenov (eds), *Reinforcing Rule of Law Oversight in the European Union* (CUP 2016); Werner Schroeder (ed), *Strengthening the Rule of Law in Europe* (Hart 2015). For monographs, see e.g. Matthias Schmidt, *Verfassungsaufsicht in der Europäischen Union* (Nomos 2021); Pablo J. Martín Rodríguez, *El Estado de Derecho en la Unión Europea* (Marcial Pons 2021); Mario Carta, *Unione europea e tutela dello Stato di diritto negli Stati membri* (Caducci 2020).

[6] For these two perspectives, contrast Lucia S. Rossi, 'La valeur juridique des valeurs. L'article 2 TUE' RTDE (2020), 639 with the rule of law-centred account provided by Dimitry Kochenov and Laurent Pech, *Respect for the Rule of Law in the Case Law of the European Court of Justice* (SIEPS 2021:3).

that of its torchbearer, shining possible ways ahead.[7] It should be stressed, however, that this study does not aim at developing a general doctrine or theory of EU values. Its objectives are more modest. Certainly, developing a broader conceptual framework for the emerging jurisprudence will require deeper insights and reflections into the nature of Article 2 TEU itself. Yet, these considerations are intended to serve the central theme of this book: EU values *before the Court*. As such, this study will limit more general reflections to those that yield consequences in the CJEU's judicial practice.

II. Focus

Before we follow the Court into this new edifice, it seems necessary to briefly delimit the object under investigation. This book will focus on the Union's founding values as enshrined in the first sentence of Article 2 TEU. By implication, several elements are excluded from the scope of this study. First, this book concerns neither the Union's ethic[8] nor other values beyond that provision, such as animal welfare.[9] Second, it is not about the Union's objectives in Article 3 TEU or other horizontal policy goals, such as those contained in Articles 8 to 13 TFEU. Although some understand these objectives as constitutional principles,[10] the Treaty drafters underlined the 'fundamental difference' between Articles 2 and 3 TEU. Article 2 TEU contains the requirements for the legitimate exercise of public authority, whereas Article 3 TEU provides the objectives justifying the common exercise of certain powers at the EU level.[11]

Third, the founding values treated in this book should not be confused with 'fundamental' or 'general principles' developed in the CJEU's jurisprudence.[12] The former qualification has been attributed to a rather heterogeneous cluster of principles, such as rights of the defence or even fundamental freedoms.[13] Article 2 TEU, by contrast, contains only the EU's *founding* principles.[14] It thus operates

[7] This picture is borrowed from Immanuel Kant, *The Conflict of the Faculties* (Univ. Nebraska Press 1992) 45.

[8] See e.g. Andrew Williams, *The Ethos of Europe* (CUP 2010). 242 ff; Markus Frischhut, *The Ethical Spirit of EU Law* (Springer 2019) 123 ff.

[9] On animal wellfare as a 'value', see Case C-336/19 *Centraal Israëlitisch Consistorie van België* [2020] EU:C:2020:1031, paras 41, 77. On further potential EU values beyond Art. 2 TEU, see Markus Frischhut, *The Ethical Spirit of EU Values* (Springer 2022) 33 ff, 118 ff, 227 f.

[10] Karl-Peter Sommermann, 'Article 3' in Hermann-Josef Blanke and Stelio Mangiameli (eds), *The Treaty on European Union (TEU): A Commentary* (Springer 2013) paras 2 f.

[11] See Praesidium, Draft of Articles 1 to 16 of the Constitutional Treaty, CONV 528/03, Annex II, Art. 3. See also Alain Pilette and Etienne de Poncins, 'Valeurs, objectives et nature de l'Union' in Giuliano Amato et al. (eds), *Genèse et destinée de la constitution européenne* (Bruylant 2007) 287, 302 f.

[12] Comprehensively Takis Tridimas, *The General Principles of EU Law* (2nd edn, OUP 2007).

[13] See e.g. Case C-609/13 P *Duravit* [2017] EU:C:2017:46, para 99 and Case C-591/17 *Austria v Germany* [2019] EU:C:2019:504, para 119.

[14] On the understanding of the values mentioned in Art. 2 TEU as legal principles see Chapter 2. On such 'founding principles', see already Armin von Bogdandy, 'Founding Principles' in von Bogdandy

on a much higher level of abstraction and significance. Fourth, Article 2 TEU contains *substantive* principles. Despite certain interplays, these can be distinguished from structural principles such as autonomy, primacy, direct effect, the principles of conferral, subsidiarity, mutual loyalty, or national identity. Finally, this study will be limited to the six values mentioned in the first sentence of Article 2 TEU. The second sentence features several elements—pluralism, non-discrimination, tolerance, justice, solidarity, and equality between women and men—that characterize 'a society' of the Member States (or the EU?). Yet, their legal nature and function is even less clear than that of the values mentioned in the first sentence. For that reason, these characteristics will be left aside.

III. Structure

With this focus, the book will proceed in three steps: providing foundations, exploring potentials, and assessing risks of the Court's mobilization of Article 2 TEU. The first part is devoted to the empirical, doctrinal, and theoretical foundations. After tracing the rise of Article 2 TEU in the Court's judicial practice (Chapter 1), the second chapter will provide a doctrinal basis for its judicial applicability by assessing, mitigating, and refuting often voiced objections. This concerns, in particular, the provision's legal normativity, its justiciability, and Luxembourg's jurisdiction. Chapter 3 unpacks two different dimensions of Article 2 TEU that will inform the structure of this book and provide a conceptual framework for the emerging jurisprudence. Flowing from its wording, Article 2 TEU reveals a *dual character* that resonates between an EU and a Verbund dimension. The latter comprises the common whole of the EU and the Member States' legal orders. A closer look into its drafting context suggests that these dimensions correspond to different forms of constitutionalism. While its EU dimension gives expression to a constitutive, thick constitutionalism, Article 2 TEU epitomizes a thinner, primarily restraining form in the Verbund. This justifies—in fact, requires—a different judicial treatment of Article 2 TEU depending on the dimension in which it is applied.

Building on these insights, the next two Parts set out to explore the potential of Article 2 TEU in the Court's jurisprudence. The second Part begins with the EU dimension. In this dimension, the Court should understand Article 2 TEU as a thick *constitutional core* that outlines the basic features of the Union's constitution (Chapter 4). The CJEU has already started to identify a set of Treaty provisions that form the Union's 'constitutional framework'. So far, however, it has neither followed

and Jürgen Bast (eds), *Principles of European Constitutional Law* (2nd edn, Hart 2009) 11; Karl-Peter Sommermann, 'Herkunft und Funktion von Verfassungsprinzipien in der Europäischen Union' in Hartmut Bauer and Christian Calliess (eds), *Verfassungsprinzipien in Europa* (Sakkoulas 2008) 15; Joël Molinier, *Les principes fondateurs de l'Union européenne* (PUF 2005).

an overarching idea nor drawn any specific conclusions from this step. This book suggests a different path. The Union's constitution, in substantive, not formal terms, could be composed of those provisions that give expression to a value enshrined in Article 2 TEU. This would imply a threefold, substantive hierarchization of primary law: Article 2 TEU at the top, provisions giving expression to an Article 2 TEU value at a second level, and the rest at a third one.

The subsequent chapters will spell out the potential of this proposal in three settings. With regard to the Treaties, the hierarchical division of primary law can provide a new tool to foster its coherence (Chapter 5). With regard to EU legislation, many have argued that the Treaties' extensive scope and the CJEU's strong institutional position overly constrain the space for legislative decision-making. To loosen its grip on the EU legislature, the Court could start distinguishing between the different levels of primary law. While retaining strict scrutiny concerning provisions that give expression to an Article 2 TEU value, the Court could relax the constraints flowing from the third level of primary law (Chapter 6). With regard to Treaty revisions, this study will tentatively explore whether the Court could derive substantive limitations for amendments of EU primary law from Article 2 TEU (Chapter 7).

The third Part zooms out to the level of the Verbund. In this dimension, Article 2 TEU should be reduced to a thin *constitutional frame* that secures a minimum of homogeneity between the EU and the Member States' legal orders. Indeed, a certain degree of constitutional homogeneity is an essential precondition for sustaining federal systems (Chapter 8). In this sense, the Verbund is permeated by various claims for homogeneity among the Member States and the EU, top-down, horizontal, and bottom-up, that form a system of mutual stabilization. Eventually, these claims converge in Article 2 TEU. Along these lines, the following chapters will demonstrate how the Union's judicial system can contribute to secure the constitutional homogeneity across the Verbund. Chapter 9 will concentrate on the top-down enforcement of EU values in the Member States. Drawing on recent experiences in the Union's rule of law crisis, it will assess how the Court has started to enforce value compliance in the Member States and sketch some trajectories for future development. Chapter 10, by contrast, will assess horizontal avenues for reviewing the value compliance of Member States, both directly before the Court of Justice (through Article 259 TFEU) and indirectly before national courts (through so-called mutual recognition regimes). Chapter 11 will examine the role that national constitutional courts can play—in tandem with Luxembourg—to stabilize the constitutional homogeneity across the Verbund. Many national legal systems contain certain constitutional principles, often summarized under the buzzword of 'constitutional identities', which must be respected at the EU level. In most Member States, these identities correspond to the values of Article 2 TEU. Voicing concerns in this regard before the Court and assessing the Union's compliance with these principles can therefore foster the constitutional homogeneity of the Verbund. This is especially the case if these concerns are addressed under the banner of Article 2 TEU.

The last Part provides a critical reflection. Placing an activated Article 2 TEU in the hands of the Luxembourg judges does not come without risks. By enforcing highly indeterminate values, especially against democratically elected Member State governments, the Court might overstretch its judicial function and transgress the lines drawn by the separation of powers. This might jeopardize the values of the rule of law and democracy (Chapter 12). At the same time, the federal balance is at stake. Many will object that the enforcement of EU values in the Member States risks violating the principle of conferral and national identity as well as the ideas of pluralism and diversity (Chapter 13). After assessing and mitigating these concerns, the last two Chapters will propose ways to recalibrate the Court's mobilization of Article 2 TEU.

IV. Method

Before diving into these issues, a brief note on the book's methodology should be provided. Despite some brief outliers (such as the quantitative assessments in Chapter 1), this study is at its heart a doctrinal work. To a large extent, this consists of systematizing the legal material on a meta-level (somewhere between the written law and theory) and providing orientation for a coherent application of the law.[15] However, doctrinal legal thinking not only has a systematizing function but can also aim at critical reflection, development, and innovation. Armin von Bogdandy aptly speaks of 'doctrinal constructivism'.[16] It is especially this latter perspective that will guide the exploration in Parts II and III.

Finally, this study is confronted with a twofold, seemingly opposite, challenge. On the one hand, many have lamented an increasing disconnect between EU legal scholarship as a genuinely transnational, 'Europeanised European law scholarship'[17] and the national doctrines of European law in each Member State. Today, EU legal scholarship seems to consist of 'concentric discursive circles' that seldom intersect.[18] On the other hand, a book such as this might be reproached for giving way to a twofold intellectual dominance in Europe. For one, the author employs an

[15] See e.g. Wolfgang Kahl, 'Dogmatik im EU-Recht' AöR 144 (2019), 159, 169 ff; Andreas Voßkuhle, 'Was leistet Rechtsdogmatik?' in Gregor Kirchhof et al. (eds), *Was weiß Dogmatik?* (Mohr Siebeck 2012) 111, 112.

[16] Armin von Bogdandy, 'The past and promise of doctrinal constructivism' I-CON 7 (2008), 364, 376 f. On this tradition, see Christoph Schönberger, *Der "German Approach"* (Mohr Siebeck 2016) 50 ff.

[17] Borrowing from Armin von Bogdandy, 'A Bird's Eye View on the Science of European Law' ELJ 3 (2000), 208, 238.

[18] Daniel Thym, 'The Limits of Transnational Scholarship on EU Law' EUI Working Paper LAW 2016/14 pp 8 f. See also Bruno de Witte, 'European Union Law: A Unified Academic Discipline?' in de Witte and Antoine Vauchez (eds), *Lawyering Europe* (Hart 2013) 101, 111 Gernot Sydow, 'Die Europarechtwissenschaft europäisieren?' JöR 68 (2020), 545.

approach strongly embedded in German legal scholarship ('Dogmatik').[19] At the same time, this book is not only written in English but also firmly embedded in a transnational discourse conducted almost exclusively in English. Both issues may foster intellectual dominance: the dominance of German legal thinking[20] as well as a linguistic, exclusionary dominance of English.

Countering this fragmentation and dominance requires a multilingual approach with respect to sources and literature that connects the transnational with national legal discourses.[21] As Daniel Thym noted, legal cultures are intricately linked to languages. Often, doctrinal conceptions cannot be translated without loss of meaning. Traduttore, traditore! Confining research to English sources from the transnational discourse might thus entail 'cultural costs'.[22] It risks missing interesting perspectives, reinventing the wheel, and drawing an all-too-narrow picture of the European legal landscape. As far as the author's capacities allow, this book will thus feed not only on English and German, but also on French, Italian, Spanish and, to a much narrower extent, on Polish and Hungarian sources (the little involvement of Eastern European perspectives is indeed a great shortcoming in this respect). Besides providing a broader outlook, this has the advantage of making debates accessible to readers from other legal cultures. At the same time, it hopes to increase the book's accessibility for readers not part of the transnational discourse by pointing to equivalent debates in their national legal contexts

[19] But see rather as a unifying element in European legal scholarship, Armin von Bogdandy, 'Vergleich' in von Bogdandy et al. (eds), *Handbuch Ius Publicum Europaeum*, vol 2 (C.F.Müller 2008) § 39, paras 26 ff.

[20] Some might even perceive a German hegemony, see on this Armin von Bogdandy et al., *German Legal Hegemony?* (MPIL Research Paper Series No. 2020-43). But see András Jakab, 'Warum verliert die deutsche Verfassungsrechtswissenschaft an internationalem Einfluss und was kann dagegen getan werden?' ZaöRV 82 (2022), 701.

[21] See e.g. Vassilios Skouris, 'Erwartungen der gerichtlichen Praxis and die Wissenschaft des Europarechts' in Armin Hatje et al. (eds), *Europarechtswissenschaft* (Nomos 2018) 149, 153 f. On the international plane, see Odile Ammann, 'Language Bias in International Legal Scholarship: Symptoms, Explanations, Implications and Remedies' EJIL 33 (2022), 821, 843.

[22] Thym (n 18) 8 f. See also Christian Tomuschat, 'The (Hegemonic?) Role of the English Language' NJIL 86 (2017), 196, 228; Matthias Ruffert, 'Eine Binnenperspektive auf die deutsche Europarechtswissenschaft' JöR (2020), 515, 521; Martina Bajčić, 'The Role of EU Legal English in Shaping EU Legal Culture' *International Journal of Language & Law* 7 (2018), 8.

I

FOUNDATIONS

1
Practice
The Rise of Article 2 TEU in the Court's Jurisprudence

I. Introduction

For a long time, Article 2 TEU was uncharted territory, a truly blank spot on the map of Union law. Subject to many uncertainties (see Chapter 2), Article 2 TEU and its predecessors played only a marginal role before the Court. Empirical evidence, however, suggests a growing engagement with the principles of democracy, the rule of law, and fundamental rights in the CJEU's jurisprudence. The following chapter will trace this rise both quantitatively and qualitatively, starting from the first judgments embracing these constitutional principles, over their codification in the Treaty of Amsterdam to today's Article 2 TEU (Section II). The judgment in *Associação Sindical dos Juízes Portugueses* (*ASJP*) constitutes the critical breakthrough for the judicial mobilization of Article 2 TEU. Under the pressure of illiberal developments in several Member States, the Court brought Article 2 TEU down from the sphere of lofty values to the realities of judicial practice (Section III). After this leap into uncharted territory, Article 2 TEU has been firmly anchored in the CJEU's case law and extended to very different contexts (Section IV).

II. Emergence

Seldom did the Court openly engage with the principles of the rule of law, democracy, and fundamental rights in its early jurisprudence. Despite the codification of these principles in Article 6(1) TEU-Amsterdam, it was not until Lisbon that the CJEU started to fully embrace Article 2 TEU.

A. From Rome to Amsterdam: Initial Neglect

Before Amsterdam, references to the rule of law, democracy, and fundamental rights *as such* were rather scarce. Even the rule of law, which lies at the very heart of

EU Values Before the Court of Justice. Luke Dimitrios Spieker, Oxford University Press. © Luke Dimitrios Spieker 2023.
DOI: 10.1093/oso/9780198876717.003.0002

European integration,[1] played a rather marginal role in the CJEU's jurisprudence. Certainly, the Court started early on to render rule of law-*related* judgments.[2] For instance, only five years after its establishment, the Court referred to the principles of legality, legal certainty, and legitimate expectations in *Algera*.[3] On the eve of Amsterdam, however, a reference to the principle of 'the rule of law' was employed in no more than a handful of cases. The first of these references appeared in the *Granaria* decision of 1979, in which the Court noted that 'although respect for the principle of the rule of law ... entails ... the right to challenge the validity of regulations by legal action, that principle also imposes upon all persons ... the obligation to acknowledge that regulations are fully effective so long as they have not been declared to be invalid by a competent court'.[4] *Les Verts* followed only a couple of years later, where the Court declared that the EEC is 'a community based on the rule of law, inasmuch as neither its Member States nor its institutions can avoid a review of the question whether the measures adopted by them are in conformity with the basic constitutional charter, the Treaty'.[5] However, the other language versions were semantically less connected to the rule of law *stricto sensu* and had, especially in German, a very specific connotation ('Rechtsgemeinschaft').[6]

A 'remarkably cautious jurisprudence' can also be observed with respect to democracy.[7] Starting in the 1980s, the Court introduced the democratic principle into the fabric of its jurisprudence with the so-called *Isoglucose* cases. According to the Court, the involvement of the European Parliament reflects 'although limited ... the fundamental democratic principle that the peoples should take part in the exercise of power through the intermediary of a representative assembly'.[8] For a long time, this was the only open reference to democracy. At the end of the 1990s, this was complemented with an emerging jurisprudence on public access to documents. The Court noted that such access aimed at 'strengthening the democratic character

[1] See Annex I: 'The Rule of Law as a foundational principle of the Union' to the Commission's Communication, 'A new EU Framework to strengthen the Rule of Law' COM/2014/0158 final. See already Walter Hallstein, *Der unvollendete Bundesstaat* (Econ 1969) 33 ff.

[2] For an overview, see Thomas von Danwitz, 'The Rule of Law in the Recent Jurisprudence of the ECJ' *Fordham Journal of International Law* 37 (2014), 1311.

[3] Cases 7/56 and 3–7/57 *Algera* [1957] EU:C:1957:7, p 55.

[4] Case C-101/78 *Granaria* [1979] EU:C:1979:38, para 5.

[5] Case 294/83 *Les Verts* [1986] EU:C:1986:166, para 23. See also Case C-2/88 *Zwartfeld* [Order of 13 July 1990] EU:C:1990:315, paras 16 f; Opinion 1/91 [1991] *EEA I* EU:C:1991:490, para 21; Case C-314/91 *Weber v Parliament* [1993] EU:C:1993:109, para 8.

[6] The other versions speak of a 'community of law' (communauté de droit, comunità di diritto, comunidad de Derecho) and not of préeminance du droit/Herrschaft des Rechts or État de droit/Rechtsstaat. As a very German concept, see Armin von Bogdandy, 'Ways to Frame the European Rule of Law' EuConst 14 (2018), 675, 677.

[7] Armin von Bogdandy, 'Founding Principles' in von Bogdandy and Jürgen Bast (eds), *Principles of European Constitutional Law* (2nd edn, Hart 2009) 11, 48. On the CJEU's case law, see Koen Lenaerts, 'The Principle of Democracy in the Case Law of the European Court of Justice' ICLQ 62 (2013), 300.

[8] Case 138/79 *Roquette Frères* [1980] EU:C:1980:249, para 33; Case 139/79 *Maizena v Council* [1980] EU:C:1980:250, para 34. See also Case C-300/89 *Titanium dioxide* [1991] EU:C:1991:244, para 20.

of the institutions'.[9] Advocate General Tesauro went even further by stating that 'the basis for such a right should be sought in the democratic principle, which constitutes one of the cornerstones of the Community edifice, as enshrined now in the Preamble to the Maastricht Treaty and Article F'.[10] Against this rather thin background, it seems surprising to see the General Court (GC) noting in 2001 that 'the principle of democracy is indeed a founding principle of the European Union'[11] and that preference should be given to the interpretation 'which best enables the full attainment of the democratic values of the Union'.[12]

Things are different with respect to fundamental rights. Here the jurisprudence unfolded relatively early and quickly. The prevalent narrative is well-known. Initially, the Court rejected review of Community acts against any kind of fundamental rights obligations.[13] It was only under the pressure of national constitutional courts that the CJEU changed course and developed a set of fundamental rights as general principles.[14] Beginning from *Stauder*, the Court quickly unfolded the basic tenets of its fundamental rights jurisprudence in cases like *Internationale Handelsgesellschaft*, *Nold* or *Hauer*. Already in 1986, the German Constitutional Court deemed this system to be 'essentially comparable' with the Member States' fundamental rights standards.[15] At the same time, Judge Pescatore noted with regard to his report at the 1986 FIDE congress that the fundamental rights developed so far amounted to 'une moisson relativement restreinte' (a relatively small harvest).[16] While it is true that the CJEU also advanced 'classic' rights like the freedom of expression,[17] the main thrust seemed to be rather inspired by the 'principes généraux' of French administrative law.[18] Tellingly, the seminal account by Takis Tridimas places fundamental rights behind the principles of proportionality, legal certainty, and legitimate expectations.[19]

What might explain this self-restraint? Some have argued that especially democracy and fundamental rights were simply 'not part of the original DNA of

[9] See e.g. Case T-174/95 *Svenska Journalistförbundet v Council* [1998] EU:T:1998:127, paras 65 ff. See also Case C-58/94 *Netherlands v Council* [1996] EU:C:1996:171, paras 35 f.

[10] Case C-58/94 *Netherlands v Council* [1995] EU:C:1995:409, Opinion of AG Tesauro, para 19.

[11] Cases T-222, 327 and 329/99 *Martinez and de Gaulle v Parliament* [2001] EU:T:2001:242, para 200.

[12] ibid para 196.

[13] See e.g. Case C-1/58 *Stork v High Authority* [1959] EU:C:1959:4, p 26; Cases 36, 37, 38 and 40/59 *Präsident Ruhrkohlen-Verkaufsgesellschaft and Others v High Authority* [1960] EU:C:1960:36, p 439.

[14] Contesting the accuracy of this narrative, see Giacomo Delledonne and Federico Fabbrini, 'The Founding Myth of European Human Rights Law' EL Rev 44 (2019), 178. But see William Phelan, 'The Role of the German and Italian Constitutional Courts in the Rise of EU Human Rights Jurisprudence' EL Rev 46 (2021), 175.

[15] BVerfG, Order of 22 October 1986, 2 BvR 197/83, *Solange II*, para 107.

[16] Pierre Pescatore, 'Les principes généraux du droit en tant que source du droit communautaire (1986)' in Fabrice Picod (ed.), *Études de droit ornization européen* (Bruylant 2008) 691.

[17] See e.g. Case C-260/89 *ERT* [1991] EU:C:1991:254, paras 41 ff; Case C-368/95 *Familiapress* [1997] EU:C:1997:325, paras 25 ff.

[18] On these, see e.g. Didier Truchet, *Droit administratif* (9th edn, PUF 2021), Part 3.I.4.

[19] Takis Tridimas, *The General Principles of EU Law* (2nd edn, OUP 2007).

European Integration.'[20] However, this argument cannot explain the Court's careful approach with regard to the rule of law, which has been at the heart of European integration from the very beginning. The rejection of Francoist Spain's accession further demonstrates that even the early Community was not indifferent to the values enshrined in Article 2 TEU today (see Chapter 3, III.B and Chapter 8, II.B). Nevertheless, it is true that the original Treaties provided not much textual material to anchor a rule of law, democracy, or fundamental rights jurisprudence. In this sense, Pierre Pescatore noted in 1981 that it was most difficult to draw a parallel between the Treaties and a constitution with regard to basic value questions.[21]

B. From Amsterdam to Lisbon: Growing Engagement

This fundamentally changed with Article 6(1) TEU-Amsterdam, which stated that '[t]he Union is founded on the principles of liberty, democracy, respect for human rights and fundamental freedoms, and the rule of law, principles which are common to the Member States'. Nevertheless, a jurisprudence embracing these provisions took off only slowly. The first significant steps were the decisions in *Gestoras Pro Amnistía* and *Segi* concerning a Council common position that imposed restrictive measures on persons allegedly involved in terrorism. Judicial protection against such measures was very limited. Article 35(1) TEU-Nice, for instance, explicitly mentioned the acts under the former third pillar subject to preliminary references, without featuring common positions. Nevertheless, the CJEU stated that '[a]s is clear from Article 6 EU, the Union is founded on the principle of the rule of law'.[22] Interpreted in this light, Article 35(1) TEU could not preclude references concerning acts not specifically mentioned in this provision.

Only one year later, the Court released a firework of constitutional semantics in *Kadi*. According to the CJEU, fundamental rights are 'constitutional principles' that form part of 'the very foundations of the Community legal order'.[23] Neither obligations imposed by international agreements nor primary law can 'authorise any derogation from the principles of liberty, democracy and respect for human rights and fundamental freedoms enshrined in Article 6(1) EU as a foundation of the Union.'[24] It remains unclear as to why the Court decided to embrace these

[20] See only Joseph H.H. Weiler, 'Deciphering the Political and Legal DNA of European Integration' in Julie Dickson and Pavlos Eleftheriadis (eds), *Philosophical Foundations of European Union Law* (OUP 2012) 137, 158.

[21] Pierre Pescatore, 'Die Gemeinschaftsverträge als Verfassungsrecht' in Wilhelm G. Grewe et al. (eds), *Festschrift zum 70. Geburtstag von Hans Kutscher* (Nomos 1981) 319, 330.

[22] Case C-354/04 P *Gestoras Pro Amnistía* [2007] EU:C:2007:115, para 51; Case C-355/04 P *Segi* [2007] EU:C:2007:116, para 51. See also Case C-303/05 *Advocaten voor de Wereld* [2007] EU:C:2007:261, para 45.

[23] Cases C-402 and 415/05 P *Kadi* [2008] EU:C:2008:461, paras 285, 304. See also with regard to democracy, Case C-518/07 *Commission v Germany* [2010] EU:C:2010:125, para 41.

[24] *Kadi* (n 23) para 303.

principles roughly around the same time the Constitutional Treaty failed. In any case, references to Article 6(1) TEU remained relatively scarce.

After Lisbon, the Court started to increasingly engage with the rephrased Article 2 TEU. Opinion 2/13 was a first step in anchoring the provision in Luxembourg's jurisprudence. The CJEU not only provided a comprehensive account of the Union's 'constitutional framework',[25] but also ascertained that '[t]his legal structure is based on the fundamental premiss that each Member State shares ... a set of common values on which the EU is founded, as stated in Article 2 TEU'.[26] The Court's increasing recourse to Article 2 TEU can be observed in several contexts that might be clustered in three groups.

To start with, the Court relied on the rule of law enshrined in Article 2 TEU when justifying an extensive reading of its jurisdiction in CFSP matters. If not explicitly provided otherwise, the Court lacks general jurisdiction over CFSP measures (Articles 24(1)(2) TEU and 275(1) TFEU). For instance, Article 275(2) TFEU allows the Court to review restrictive measures in actions for annulment. In *Rosneft*, however, the CJEU was confronted with a preliminary reference questioning the validity of such measures. By following the path taken in *Segi*, the Court referred to Article 2 TEU and recalled that 'one of the European Union's founding values is the rule of law'.[27] Against this backdrop, it construed Article 275(2) TFEU as not precluding references on the validity of restrictive measures. The General Court went even further by approaching the substantive content of the rule of law. In several cases, the General Court was called to assess the validity of restrictive measures against Ukrainian citizens.[28] According to the contested Council decision, these measures applied to persons responsible for the misappropriation of public funds. The applicants argued that this was inconsistent with that decision's overall objective, namely the consolidation of the rule of law. After noting that 'the rule of law is one of the primary values on which the European Union is founded', the GC assessed whether corruption is a threat to the rule of law by drawing on the ECtHR's jurisprudence, the Venice Commission, and relevant secondary legislation.[29]

Second, the Court started engaging with the value of democracy. In *Patriciello*, a case concerning the immunity of MEPs for opinions expressed in performance of their duties, the Court stated that the freedom of expression is 'an essential foundation of a pluralist, democratic society reflecting the values on which the Union,

[25] Opinion 2/13 *ECHR Accession II* [2014] EU:C:2014:2454, para 158.

[26] Ibid para 168.

[27] Case C-72/15 *Rosneft* [2017] EU:C:2017:236, para 72. See already Case C-455/14 P *H. v Council and Commission* [2017] EU:C:2016:569, para 41.

[28] See e.g. Case T-245/15 *Klymenko v Council* [2017] EU:T:2017:792, para 73; Case T-346/14 *Yanukovych v Council* [2016] EU:T:2016:497, para 97; Case T-340/14 *Klyuyev v Council* [2016] EU:T:2016:496, para 87.

[29] *Klymenko v Council* (n 28) paras 73 f.

in accordance with Article 2 TEU, is based'.[30] Further references to the Union's democratic foundations can be found in the General Court's case law. In cases concerning the independence of MEPs, it reiterated that 'as it appears from Article 2 TEU the Union is founded ... on the value of democracy'.[31] In other cases, the General Court stressed the importance of participatory elements for improving democracy at the EU level, which is 'one of the fundamental values of the European Union'.[32]

Third, the Court of Justice increasingly focused on the complex interplay of values, mutual trust, and fundamental rights. As seen above, the Court noted in Opinion 2/13 that the EU is based on the fundamental premise that all Member States share a set of common values. That premise, so the Court, 'implies and justifies the existence of mutual trust between the Member States that those values will be recognised'.[33] This has particular consequences for mutual recognition regimes such as the European Arrest Warrant, the Dublin system, or EU private international law. The fuel that keeps these mechanisms running is mutual trust, namely the presumption that EU law will be observed. As this trust relies on the premise that all Member States respect the values in Article 2 TEU, only a Member State's demonstrated non-compliance can lift said presumption. Thus, clarifying the limits of mutual trust always means engaging with Article 2 TEU. In this spirit, the Court concluded in *Aranyosi* that 'Articles 1 and 4 of the Charter ... enshrine one of the fundamental values of the Union and its Member States'.[34] In case of systemic deficiencies amounting to a real risk of inhumane or degrading treatment, mutual trust, and the implications flowing from it must be suspended (in detail Chapter 10, III).[35]

Where does this short tour leave us? Even after Lisbon, the values enshrined in Article 2 TEU did not feature much in the CJEU's judicial practice. And even if the Court employed a reference to this provision, its function remains elusive. This is also supported by the academic commentary at the time. For one, accounts of the principles and values enshrined in Article 2 TEU managed without any deeper analysis of the case law.[36] Conversely, accounts of the Court's jurisprudence on the Union's founding values did not concentrate on cases engaging with Article 2 TEU but more broadly on decisions concerning the rule of law, democracy, and fundamental rights in general.[37]

[30] Case C-163/10 *Patriciello* [2011] EU:C:2011:543, para 31. See also Cases C-203 and 698/15 *Tele2 Sverige* [2016] EU:C:2016:970, para 93.

[31] Case T-633/16 *Bilde v Parliament* [2017] EU:T:2017:849, para 54; Case T-634/16 *Montel v Parliament* [2017] EU:T:2017:848, para 58.

[32] Case T-754/14 *Efler v Commission* [2017] EU:T:2017:323, para 37.

[33] *ECHR Accession II* (n 25) para 158.

[34] Cases C-404 and 659/15 PPU *Aranyosi and Căldăraru* [2016] EU:C:2016:198, paras 81, 87.

[35] In detail, see e.g. Auke Willems, 'The Court of Justice of the European Union's Mutual Trust Journey in EU Criminal Law: From a Presumption to (Room for) Rebuttal' GLJ 20 (2019), 468, 490.

[36] See e.g. von Bogdandy (n 7) 22 (Fn. 70).

[37] See e.g. Koen Lenaerts, 'Die Werte der Europäischen Union in der Rechtsprechung des Gerichtshofes der Europäischen Union' EuGRZ 44 (2017), 639; Salvatore F. Nicolosi, 'The Contribution of the Court of Justice to the Codification of the Founding Values of the European Union' RDCE 19 (2015), 613.

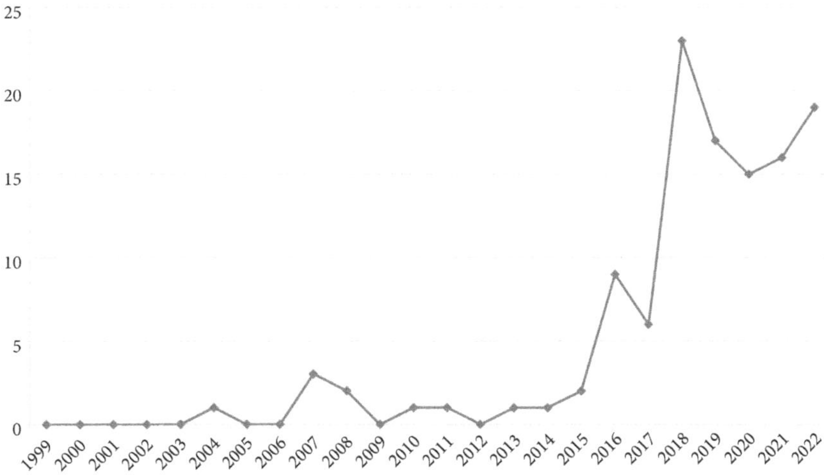

Figure 1.1 References to Art. 2 TEU-Lisbon and Art. 6 TEU-Amsterdam/Nice
This data was gathered by using the curia.europa.eu search form (Criterion: 'reference to case-law and legislation' = Art. 2 TEU-Lisbon and Art. 6 TEU-Amsterdam/Nice). It excludes cases, where Art. 2 TEU-Lisbon or Art. 6 TEU-Amsterdam/Nice were only mentioned by the parties and not in the CJEU's considerations. A table listing all identified decisions can be accessed here: https://www.mpil.de/s/spieker (Table 1).

This radically changed in 2018. Quantitatively, this shift is indicated by the Court's citation practice. As demonstrated with Figure 1.1, the references to Article 2 TEU exponentially increased in 2018.

The following Section argues that the decision in *ASJP* constitutes the central breakthrough. Before turning to a detailed analysis of this case, two further observations should be made. First, the emergence of Article 2 TEU in the CJEU's jurisprudence is part of a larger development. Empirical evidence suggests that the Court has increasingly displayed a more open and confident attitude towards the EU's constitutional foundations. In this sense, there has been a continuous rise in references to democracy or the rule of law without a mention of Article 2 TEU (see Figures 1.2 and 1.3). This rise cannot simply be explained by a general increase in cases.[38] Its foundations must lie deeper. It might be a sign of the CJEU's transformation into a fully-fledged constitutional court and eventually an expression of the EU's development towards a more mature constitutional order.

This leads to the second observation. Even after Lisbon, the CJEU continues to refer to the rule of law or democracy without anchoring it in Article 2 TEU. For

[38] In 2000, there were 873 cases pending before the ECJ and 786 before the GC, see Annual Report 2000, Press Release No. 12/2001. In 2020, there were 1045 cases pending before the ECJ and 1497 before the GC, see CJEU, *The Year in Review. Annual Report 2020*, pp 58, 61.

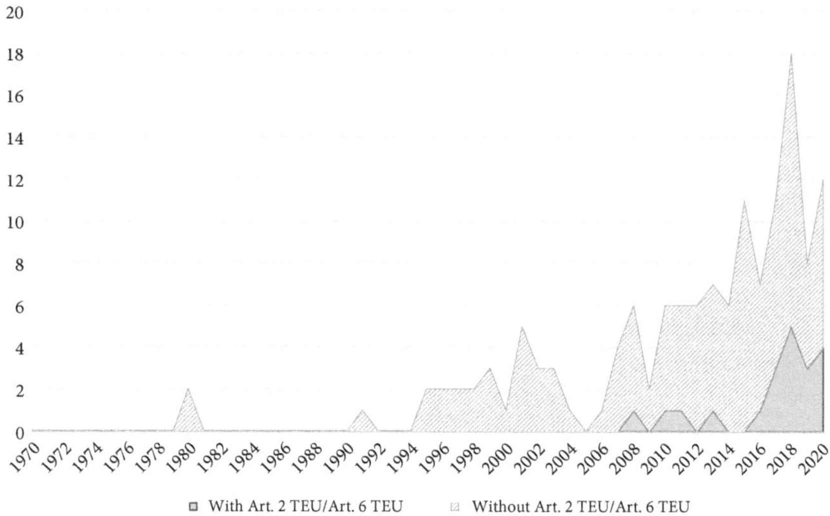

Figure 1.2 References to 'democracy' by the CJEU (incl. GC and CST)

This contains references to the 'democratic principle', 'democratic life' or 'democratic society'. A table listing all identified decisions can be accessed here: https://www.mpil.de/s/spieker (Table 2).

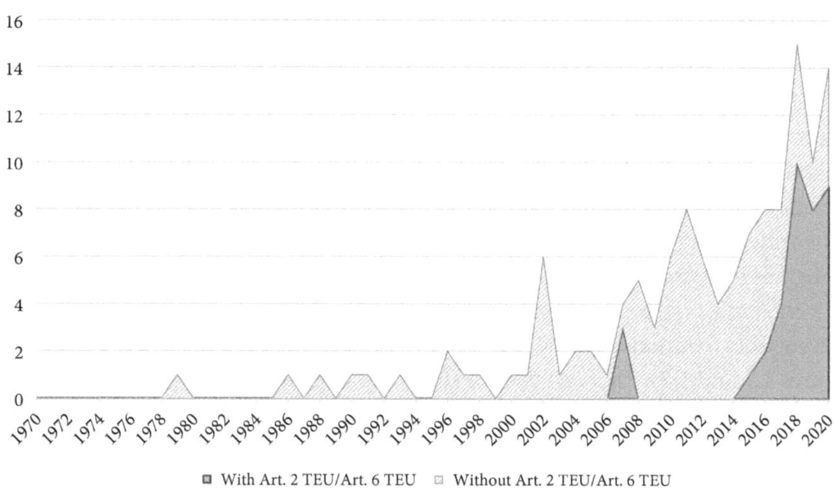

Figure 1.3 References to the 'rule of law' by the CJEU (incl. GC and CST)

This contains references to the 'Community' or 'Union based on the rule of law', see note 6. A table listing all identified decisions can be accessed here: https://www.mpil.de/s/spieker (Table 3).

instance, the Court still employs a free-floating 'principle of the rule of law'[39] and provides it with specific meaning, such as the separation of powers or effective judicial review.[40] Similarly, the CJEU refers to the 'principle of democracy'[41] when it engages with the participation of the European Parliament in the EU legislative process,[42] its budgetary powers,[43] but also participatory elements such as the ECI,[44] the freedom of expression,[45] and press.[46] Even in what has been qualified as 'value-related infringement proceedings',[47] the Court was hesitant to openly employ Article 2 TEU. In its verdict on the Hungarian NGO law, the Court referred to the freedom of association as 'one of the essential bases of a democratic and pluralist society' without mentioning Article 2 TEU.[48] This observation might question the focus on Article 2 TEU. However, the Court's citation practice equally suggests that references to the rule of law or democracy are increasingly provided with a textual anchoring in Article 2 TEU.

III. Breakthrough: *Associação Sindical dos Juízes Portugueses*

As indicated above, 2018 has been a turning point that propelled the Court's case law on Article 2 TEU into a completely new dimension. The founding stone for this new jurisprudential edifice was the decision in *ASJP*. This judgment constitutes a central breakthrough in two respects. First, the Court developed Article 2 TEU into an operational provision. Before 2018, it was far from clear to what end the Court referred to Article 2 TEU and its predecessors. With *ASJP*, it started to connect Article 2 TEU to more specific Treaty provisions that operationalize these values and render them subject to judicial application. Second, the CJEU applied Article 2 TEU to a Member State. Before 2018, the Court had mentioned the

[39] See e.g. Case C-316/19 *Commission v Slovenia (Archives de la BCE)* [2020] EU:C:2020:1030, paras 103 f.

[40] E.g. Cases C-924 and 925/19 PPU *FMS* [2020] EU:C: 2020:367, para 136; Case C-311/18 *Facebook Ireland and Schrems* [2020] EU:C:2020:559, para 187.

[41] See e.g. Case C-718/18 *Commission v Germany (Transposition des directives 2009/72 et 2009/73)* [2021] EU:C:2021:662, para 126.

[42] See e.g. Cases C-643 and 647/15 *Slovakia v Council* [2017] EU:C:2017:631, para 160; Case C-263/14 *Parliament v Council* [2016] EU:C:2016:435, para 70.

[43] See e.g. Case C-92/18 *France v Parliament (Exercise of budgetary powers II)* [2020] EU:C:2020:506, para 19; Case C-73/17 *France v Parliament (Exercise of budgetary powers)* [2018] EU:C:2018:787.

[44] See e.g. Case C-589/15 P *Anagnostakis v Commission* [2017] EU:C:2017:663, para 45.

[45] See e.g. Case C-719/18 *Vivendi* [2020] EU:C:2020:627, para 57; Case C-283/11 *Sky Österreich* [2013] EU:C:2013:28, para 52.

[46] See e.g. Case C-136/17 *GC and Others (De-referencing of sensitive data)* [2019] EU:C:2019:773, para 76; Case C-516/17 *Spiegel Online* [2019] EU:C:2019:625, para 73.

[47] See the document prepared by the Commission for the Council annexed to File 2018/0902 (COD) from 8 November 2018, 'The situation in Hungary. Information on values-related infringement proceedings'.

[48] Case C-78/18 *Commission v Hungary (Transparency of associations)* [2020] EU:C:2020:476, para 112.

provision primarily in EU contexts. With *ASJP*, it started to assess the Member States' very constitutional structures for their compliance with Article 2 TEU. The following section seeks to provide a 'thick' analysis of this decision. This concerns not only its legal thrust but also the multiplicity of actors and processes involved in achieving this breakthrough.[49] After sketching the context, from which the judgment emerged, this section will take a closer look at the central innovations advanced by *ASJP* and analyse its reception in EU legal scholarship and practice.

ASJP and the subsequent case law emerged in an extraordinary situation of unprecedented challenges to the values enshrined in Article 2 TEU. The basics of this story are well established (in detail, Chapter 9). In 2012, José Manuel Barroso already raised concerns with regard to 'threats to the legal and democratic fabric in some of our European states'.[50] These developments have become a larger illiberal turn. By 2018, judicial independence had become a central concern. The Polish and Hungarian governments especially had stepped up their efforts to dismantle the judiciaries. These measures included forcing judges into retirement, bringing appointment procedures under political control and threatening the remaining judiciary with disciplinary measures.[51] While the EU's toolbox to counter these developments has evolved over the last years,[52] the political process has nonetheless been beset by an astounding inertia. Both Article 7 TEU procedures launched against Poland and Hungary have been pending for years in the deadlocked Council. In these extraordinary circumstances, so the meanwhile prevalent narrative goes, the Court made a risky move. It ventured into uncharted territory and became the central forum to remedy violations of Union values in the Member States. As Judge Marek Safjan from the *ASJP* bench noted: 'Extraordinary situations call for extraordinary measures'.[53]

At the time of the decision, however, the CJEU's involvement was far from self-evident. Besides issues of institutional legitimacy, one key challenge was how to address value violations before the Court. Indeed, many developments seemed to escape the scope of EU law. Further, the Court's prior decision on the overhaul of the Hungarian judiciary had been criticized for being too narrow and ineffective.[54] While many creative proposals circulated in EU legal scholarship, such as *Reverse*

[49] For such an attempt, see also Michal Ovádek, 'The making of landmark rulings in the European Union: the case of national judicial independence' JEPP (2023) (forthcoming). On this research programme, see Antoine Vauchez, 'EU Law Classics in the Making' in Bill Davies and Fernanda Nicola (eds), *EU Law Stories* (CUP 2017) 21; Nele Yang, *Die Leitentscheidung* (Springer 2018) 13 ff.

[50] José Manuel Barroso, State of the Union (12 September 2012), SPEECH/12/596.

[51] For the status quo in this respect, see e.g. the Commission's 2022 Rule of Law Report, especially the country chapters on Hungary (SWD(2022) 517 final) and Poland (SWD(2022) 521 final).

[52] See e.g. Laurent Pech, 'The Rule of Law in the EU' in Paul Craig and Gráinne de Búrca (eds), *The Evolution of EU Law* (3rd edn, OUP 2021) 307.

[53] Marek Safjan, 'The Rule of Law and the Future of Europe' dUE (2019), 425, 435.

[54] See e.g. Gábor Halmai, 'The Case of the Retirement Age of Hungarian Judges' in Davies and Nicola (n 49) 471.

Solange or a bold application of the Charter beyond Article 51 CFR,[55] these must have sounded rather more like legal science fiction than a realistic option. Similarly, Kim Scheppele's suggestion to base infringement actions immediately on Article 2 TEU left many open questions, especially concerning the justiciability of Article 2 TEU (in detail, Chapter 2).[56] To avoid such a controversial step, some scholars proposed a combined reading of Article 2 TEU with other Treaty provisions.[57] Yet, these proposals hardly prevailed in academic circles, let alone in legal practice. Commissioner Reding, for instance, stressed the need to create 'a new specific procedure to enforce the rule of law principle of Article 2 TEU against Member States ... before the Court of Justice'.[58] This might also explain the Commission's self-restraint towards infringement proceedings against Member States like Poland or Hungary.

Without the necessary cases, however, the Court was in no position to get involved. 2017 seemed to herald a change in this regard. For one, the Court had 'shown teeth' against Poland in a case concerning the logging of a forest protected under several EU directives.[59] In its decision, the CJEU held that Article 279 TFEU allows it to impose not only interim measures but also penalty payments if those measures are not complied with. This seemed to indicate the Court's readiness to adopt a firm stance in face of Member State challenges and develop the necessary doctrinal innovations.[60] In this spirit, Judge Thomas von Danwitz noted in October 2017 that 'wherever Europe's values are abandoned, the moment of truth arrives for the judiciary' and that the Court 'will not hesitate to make its contribution to safeguarding the rule of law in Europe'.[61] Further, the Commission had initiated infringement proceedings against Poland concerning the lowering of retirement ages of ordinary court judges in July 2017.[62] Yet, even after the pre-litigation procedure had been completed in October, the Commission hesitated to lodge an application at the Court.

[55] See Armin von Bogdandy et al., 'Reverse Solange' CML Rev 49 (2012), 489; András Jakab, 'The EU Charter of Fundamental Rights as the Most Promising Way of Enforcing the Rule of Law against EU Member States' in Carlos Closa and Dimitry Kochenov (eds), *Reinforcing Rule of Law Oversight in the European Union* (CUP 2016) 187.

[56] Kim L. Scheppele, 'Enforcing the Basic Principles of EU Law through Systemic Infringement Actions' in Closa and Kochenov (n 55) 105.

[57] See already Carlos Closa, Dimitry Kochenov, and Joseph H.H. Weiler, 'Reinforcing Rule of Law Oversight in the European Union' EUI RSCAS 2014/25, pp 10 ff, 24.

[58] Viviane Reding, 'The EU and the Rule of Law—What Next?' (4 September 2013), SPEECH/13/677.

[59] See e.g. Ulrich Karpenstein, 'Europa zeigt Zähne' EuZW 29 (2018), 97.

[60] See especially the reference to Art. 2 TEU, Case C-441/17 *Commission v Poland (Białowieża Forest)* [Order of 20 November 2017] EU:C:2017:877, para 102. See e.g. Pål Wennerås, 'Saving a Forest and the Rule of Law: Commission v Poland' CML Rev 56 (2019), 541, 548, 554.

[61] Thomas von Danwitz, 'The Role of the Court of Justice in Safeguarding the Rule of Law in Europe' in von Danwitz et al. (eds), *12th Berlin Legal Policy Conference* (Konrad Adenauer Foundation 2018) 13, 16 f.

[62] European Commission, Press Release IP/17/2205 (29 July 2018).

A. Innovation

In this context, *ASJP* came as a surprise. Indeed, the facts of the case seemed rather innocent. A Portuguese court asked the CJEU whether salary reductions for judges adopted in the context of an EU financial assistance programme violated 'the principle of judicial independence, enshrined in the second subparagraph of Article 19(1) TEU, in Article 47 of the Charter and in the case-law of the Court of Justice'. Neither the Member States nor the EU institutions grasped the full potential of this reference. Only the Portuguese government and the Commission submitted observations. Moreover, both raised objections to the CJEU's jurisdiction on the grounds that the referring court had not sufficiently demonstrated the link between EU law and the national measures.[63] As the salary cuts were adopted in the context of an EU financial assistance programme, Advocate General Øe suggested grasping this thin link and applying the Charter.[64] Thus, he construed *ASJP* as a follow-up to the growing case law on the Charter's applicability to measures taken during the financial crisis.[65] In sum, the Court's immediate interlocutors were evidently not prepared for any ground-breaking innovations. Unlike cases such as *Van Gend en Loos* or *Costa/ENEL*, *ASJP* was not the result of a meticulous preparation by a whole community of 'legal entrepreneurs'.[66] Instead, it seems to have emerged primarily from within the Court.

To the legal community's surprise, the CJEU condensed the Portuguese reference to an interpretation of Article 19(1)(2) TEU, which stipulates that 'Member States shall provide remedies sufficient to ensure effective legal protection in the fields covered by Union law'. According to the Court, this entails the Member States' obligation to guarantee judicial independence. This obligation applies 'irrespective of whether the Member States are implementing Union law, within the meaning of Article 51(1)'.[67] Member States must ensure the independence of any court that '*may* rule ... on questions concerning the application or interpretation of EU law'.[68] For Article 19(1)(2) TEU to be triggered, it is not necessary that the respective court actually adjudicates a matter of EU law in the specific case. The potentiality of dealing with EU law suffices.[69] Considering the breadth of Union law today, this includes virtually the entire national judiciary.

[63] As noted by the AG, their observations concentrated on the scope of the Charter and left Art. 19(1)(2) TEU largely untouched, see Case C-64/16 *Associação Sindical dos Juízes Portugueses* [2017] EU:C:2017:395, Opinion of AG Øe, para 37.

[64] ibid paras 53, 58–67.

[65] Placing *ASJP* in this context, see Paul Dermine and Menelaos Markakis, 'Bailouts, the Legal Status of Memoranda of Understanding, and the Scope of Application of the EU Charter' CML Rev 55 (2018), 643.

[66] On this, see Antoine Vauchez, *Brokering Europe* (CUP 2015) 124.

[67] Case C-64/16 *Associação Sindical dos Juízes Portugueses* [2018] EU:C:2018:117, para 29.

[68] Ibid para 40 (emphasis added).

[69] See also Case C-619/18 *Commission v Poland (Independence of the Supreme Court)* [2019] EU:C:2019:531, para 51; Cases C-558 and 563/18 *Miasto Łowicz* [2019] EU:C:2019:775, Opinion of AG Tanchev, paras 878, 94, 125.

Two rationales seem to underpin this bold move. On the one hand, the Court refers to the functioning of the EU judicial system.[70] Despite some reforms (e.g. Article 263(4) TFEU), Lisbon largely retained the decentralized judicial system based on both the Court of Justice and Member State courts.[71] Already at the time of the Constitutional Treaty, the prevailing opinion was that this 'division of work' should not be profoundly altered.[72] As such, individuals are usually not provided with direct remedies in Luxembourg but are required to go through Member State courts in their function as first 'Union courts'.[73] However, this system can only work if national courts provide effective judicial protection. For this reason, the Court had started early on to review national provisions concerning judicial procedures and remedies.[74] Arguably, this case law was codified with Article 19(1)(2) TEU.[75] Although the far-reaching potential of this provision was soon noticed,[76] it played no significant role in the CJEU's jurisprudence.[77] In *ASJP*, however, the Court relied on Article 19(1)(2) TEU to justify an extension of its previous case law from procedural to institutional requirements of effective judicial protection, namely judicial independence. In this light, it could be read as an important step in strengthening the EU's diffused judicial system.

On the other hand, the Court employs an axiological rationale. In the crucial passage, the Court stated that 'Article 19 TEU ... *gives concrete expression* to the value of the rule of law stated in Article 2'.[78] Instead of applying Article 2 TEU in a self-standing manner, the Court refers to it through the intermediary of a specific provision. This nexus has a twofold effect. Interpreting Article 19 in light of Article 2 TEU justifies an extensive reading of the former (in detail, Chapter 9, III). At the same time, the Court operationalizes Article 2 TEU through a specific provision of EU law (in detail, Chapter 2, III). The Court had placed Article 2 TEU in the context of other provisions before *ASJP*. For instance, it referred to the rule of law enshrined in Article 2 TEU together with Article 47 CFR to justify a broad reading

[70] *Associação Sindical dos Juízes Portugueses* (n 67) paras 32–4, 43.

[71] See e.g. Takis Tridimas, 'Bifurcated Justice' in Allan Rosas et al. (eds), *The Court of Justice and the Construction of Europe* (Asser Press 2013) 367.

[72] Final report of Working Group II, CONV 354/02, p 16. See also Ricardo Passos, 'Le système juridictionnel de l'Union' in Giuliano Amato et al. (eds), *Genèse et destinée de la constitution européenne* (Bruylant 2007) 565, 579.

[73] See e.g. Opinion 1/09 *Agreement creating a Unified Patent Litigation System* [2011] EU:C:2011:123, para 80.

[74] See e.g. Case C-432/05 *Unibet* [2007] EU:C:2007:163, paras 40–3; Case C-213/89 *Factortame I* [1990] EU:C:1990:257, paras 19 ff; Case 33/76 *Rewe* [1976] EU:C:1976:188, para 5. For a detailed account, see Koen Lenaerts, Ignace Maselis, and Kathleen Gutman, *EU Procedural Law* (OUP 2014) 107 ff.

[75] Anthony Arnull, 'The Principle of Effective Judicial Protection in EU Law' EL Rev 36 (2011), 51, 56.

[76] See Koen Lenaerts, 'The Rule of Law and Coherence of the Judicial System of the European Union' CML Rev 44 (2007), 1625, 1629; Tim Corthaut, 'Plus ça change, plus c'est la même chose?' MJ 15 (2007), 21, 29.

[77] See e.g. Case C-682/15 *Berlioz Investment* [2017] EU:C:2017:373, para 44, where the Court referred to Art. 19(1)(2) TEU rather as a supporting annex of Art. 47 CFR.

[78] *Associação Sindical dos Juízes Portugueses* (n 67) para 32 (emphasis added).

of its jurisdiction in the CFSP.[79] However, *ASJP* is the first decision that establishes an immediate link between Article 2 TEU and a specific Treaty provision. Through this nexus, Article 2 TEU seems to leave the realm of lofty values and become subject to judicial application. Koen Lenaerts described this move with remarkable openness: 'For some time, it may have been assumed that the monitoring of those values would essentially be political in nature. *Juízes Portugueses* makes it clear that there is also scope for judicial monitoring'.[80]

B. Reception

ASJP was almost immediately put into practice both by the Court and its interlocutors. Although the Commission had initiated infringement procedures against Poland before *ASJP* in July 2017, it had mentioned Article 19(1) TEU and Article 47 CFR as potentially violated provisions in its reasoned opinion.[81] While the precise reasons for this choice remain obscure, it enabled the Commission to rely on the new doctrine established in *ASJP* when it lodged its application on 15 March 2018. All following procedures against Poland were based on *ASJP*. In this spirit, the Commission noted in 2019 that the Court 'has made an indispensable contribution to ... reaffirming the Union as a community of values'.[82] Further, *ASJP* triggered an unceasing wave of references from courts in Poland, Romania, Hungary, Malta, and even Germany concerning issues of judicial independence.[83] Also for the CJEU itself, the decision became a central point of reference. During the next two years, the Court (including its Advocate Generals) referred to *ASJP* in over seventy cases. To compare, *Achmea*, which was rendered only a couple of days later, was referenced in less than 30 cases. Besides some procedural limitations, the CJEU largely confirmed the decision's innovations. The central passage stating that Article 19(1)(2) TEU gives 'concrete expression' to the value of the rule of law was repeatedly used in cases on judicial independence and extended to other contexts (below III.A.).

[79] See above n 27.

[80] Koen Lenaerts, 'Upholding the Rule of Law through Judicial Dialogue' YEL 38 (2019), 3, 6.

[81] Press release IP/17/2161 (26 July 2017) and Press release IP/17/5367 (20 December 2017).

[82] European Commission, Further strengthening the Rule of Law within the Union, COM/2019/163 final, Fn. 7. On *ASJP* from within the Commission, see also Emmanuel Crabit, 'Upholding the rule of law for the future of Europe' in Wolfgang Heusel and Jean-Philippe Rageade (eds), *The Authority of EU Law* (Springer 2019) 261, 265; Karen Banks and Gregor von Rintelen, 'Infringement procedures and the Juncker Commission' EL Rev 45 (2020), 619, 631.

[83] From the plethora of Polish references, see only *A.K.* (Cases C-585, 624, and 625/18), *Miasto Łowicz* (Cases C-558 and 563/18), *A.B.* (Case C-824/18), *W.Ż.* (Case C-487/19), or *Getin Noble Bank* (Case C-132/20). From Romania, see e.g. *Asociația 'Forumul Judecătorilor din România'* (Cases C-83, 127, 195, 291, 355, 397/19), *DNA* (Case C-379/19) or *FQ* (Cases C-811 and 840/19). From Hungary, Malta and Germany, see *IS* (Case C-564/19), *Repubblika* (Case C-896/19) and *Land Hessen* (Case C-272/19). For an analysis, see e.g. Rafael Bustos Gisbert, 'Communicación transjudicial en Europa en defesa de la independencia de los jueces' *Revista de derecho constitucional europeo* 33 (2020).

Although taken by surprise, legal scholarship quickly discovered the centrality of *ASJP*. In retrospect, the decision permeated the scholarly discourse in four concentric circles. Within the narrowest circle, it seemed to provide a restrictive interpretation of the Charter's applicability to measures taken during the financial crisis.[84] Within the second circle, *ASJP* was read as 'bringing to life' the obligations enshrined in Article 19 TEU and was placed in one line with cases at the interface of effective judicial protection, the principles of effectiveness and equivalence, and the Member States' procedural autonomy.[85] While some observed the emergence of a European 'Justizverfassungsrecht', others interpreted *ASJP* in plain continuity with existing case law.[86] Within the third circle, the decision was understood as a response to the rule of law crisis, especially in Poland,[87] and as rendering the rule of law subject to judicial review.[88] For Laurent Pech and Sébastien Platon, it even constituted 'the most important judgment since *Les Verts* as regards the meaning and scope of the principle of the rule of law'.[89]

Within the fourth and most far-reaching circle, *ASJP* was embraced as a constitutional moment heralding the judicial activation of EU values.[90] This dimension was already emphasized by the first commentator of the case, who asked in surprise and wonder: 'Has the CJEU just Reconfigured the EU Constitutional Order?'[91] Others described the judicialization of Article 2 TEU as a significant step in the constitutionalization of the EU legal order and compared *ASJP*'s impact to that of *Van Gend* and *Costa/ENEL*.[92] In this sense, the judgment was perceived as

[84] See e.g. the disappointment of Francisco Pereira Coutinho, 'Associação Sindical dos Juízes Portugueses: Judicial Independence and Austerity Measures at the Court of Justice' *Quaderni costituzionali* 38 (2018), 510.

[85] Sacha Prechal, 'Effective Judicial Protection: Some Recent Developments' REAL 13 (2020), 175, 189. See also Matteo Bonelli, 'Effective Judicial Protection in EU Law: An Evolving Principle of a Constitutional Nature' REAL 12 (2019), 35; Thomas Jaeger, 'Gerichtsorganisation und EU-Recht' EuR 53 (2018), 611.

[86] Contrast, for instance, Klaus F. Gärditz, 'Europäisches Justizverfassungsrecht?' DRiZ (2019), 424 with Serena Menzione, 'Anything New under the Sun?' REAL 12 (2019), 219 and Ruairi O'Neill, 'Effet utile and the (re)organization of national judiciaries: A not so unique institutional response to a uniquely important challenge?' ELJ 27 (2021), 240, 244 ff.

[87] See e.g. Laurent Pech and Sébastien Platon, 'Judicial Independence under Threat: The Court of Justice to the Rescue in the ASJP Case' CML Rev 55 (2018), 1827; Matteo Bonelli and Monica Claes, 'Judicial Serendipity: How Portuguese Judges Came to the Rescue of the Polish Judiciary' EuConst 14 (2018), 623; Aida Torres Pérez, 'From Portugal to Poland' MJ 27 (2020), 105.

[88] Édouard Dubout, 'Integration Through the Rule of Law? La judiciarisation de l'État de droit dans l'Union européenne' RAE (2019), 51, 53 ff; Julie Teyssedre, 'La judiciarisation du contrôle de l'État de droit: la Court de justice au chevet des juges nationaux' RTDE (2020), 23, 26 ff.

[89] Pech and Platon (n 87) 1827, 1845.

[90] Armin von Bogdandy et al., 'A Potential Constitutional Moment for the European Rule of Law' CML Rev 55 (2018), 983, 985. See also José Martín y Pérez de Nanclares, 'La Unión Europea como comunidad de valores' *Teoría y Realidad Constitucional* 43 (2019), 121, 137.

[91] See the title of Michal Ovádek's blogpost on *Verfassungsblog* from 28 February 2018.

[92] Frank Schorkopf, 'Europäischer Konstitutionalismus oder die normative Behauptung des "European way of life". Potenziale der neueren Werterechtsprechung des EuGH' NJW 72 (2019), 3418, 3420 f.

a revolutionary and truly transformative step.[93] Although the challenges posed by Member States like Poland or Hungary are hardly overcome, some scholars have even started developing a narrative reminiscent of other critical junctures in the Court's history: faced with a paralysed political process, the Court stepped in to mobilize the Union's common values against unprecedented Member State challenges. In this spirit, the Court has been portrayed as 'the last soldier standing', *ASJP* and its progenies as a 'ground-breaking turn in the history of EU law' and as the key legacy of the Lenaerts court.[94]

This last perspective was actively supported by several judges involved in the case. In academic contributions, they repeatedly emphasized the established link between Article 19(1)(2) and Article 2 TEU.[95] To underline its centrality, *ASJP* was even placed in one line with foundational cases like *Van Gend*, *Costa/ENEL* or *Marbury v Madison*.[96] The remarks by Koen Lenaerts deserve to be quoted in full:

> 'I don't think, I exaggerate to say that the *Juízes Portugueses* Case has the same significance as cases like *Van Gend en Loos*, *Costa/ENEL*, *Simmenthal* or *ERTA*—it's a judgment of the same order and we were absolutely aware of that constitutional moment which we judicially fixed when we rendered that decision.'[97]

IV. Spread

As indicated above, empirical evidence suggests that the Court's engagement with Article 2 TEU has evolved with remarkable speed (see Figure 1.1). As the majority of these cases have been adjudicated by the Grand Chamber (nearly 80 per cent, excluding the General Court), the increasing recourse to Article 2 TEU does not appear to be a mere coincidence but a conscious choice supported by a majority within the Court. Nevertheless, the motivation behind invoking Article 2 TEU is

[93] See Kim L. Scheppele, Dimitry Kochenov, and Barbara Grabowska-Moroz, 'EU Values Are Law, after All' YEL 38 (2020), 3, 6 and Armin von Bogdandy, *The Emergence and Democratization of European Society* (OUP 2023) 4.6.C.

[94] Dimitry Kochenov and Petra Bárd, 'The Last Soldier Standing?' *European Yearbook of Constitutional Law* 1 (2020), 243, 249; Dimitry Kochenov and Laurent Pech, *Respect for the Rule of Law in the Case Law of the European Court of Justice* (SIEPS, 2021:3) 14, 19.

[95] From the bench, Lenaerts (n 80) 5; Safjan (n 53) 425; Thomas von Danwitz, 'Values and the Rule of Law: Foundations of the European Union—An Inside Perspective from the ECJ' RDUE (4) (2018), 263, 268; Egils Levits, 'Die Europäische Union als Wertegemeinschaft' in Thomas Jaeger (ed.), *Europa 4.0* (Sramek 2018) 239, 268. See also beyond the *ASJP* bench, Lucia S. Rossi, 'La valeur juridique des valeurs' RTDE (2020), 639, 650; François Biltgen, 'L'indépendance du juge national vue depuis Luxembourg' RTDH (2020), 551, 555.

[96] Koen Lenaerts, 'Upholding the Rule of Law within the EU' Speech held at the Reconnect Conference 'Democracy and the Rule of Law in the EU' (5 July 2019), <reconnect-europe.eu/elementor-3445/> (min: 28:25). See also Marek Safjan, 'Prawo do skutecznej ochrony sądowej' *Palestra* (5)(2020), 5, 25.

[97] Koen Lenaerts, 'Upholding the Rule of Law through Judicial Dialogue' Speech at King's College London (21 March 2019), <https://www.youtube.com/watch?v=qBOeopzvPBY&t=37s> [min: 19:23].

not always clear. Today, references to Article 2 TEU can be found in highly diverse contexts relating even to seemingly prosaic matters such as the EU's own resources, the internal market in natural gas, or trademarks.[98] Sometimes, the reference to Article 2 TEU seems to be merely a stylistic device. Leaving these cases aside, the following section will attempt to make sense of the Court's expanding case law.[99] In the decisions following *ASJP*, the Court has extended its jurisprudence both procedurally and substantively.

A. Procedural Extension

Procedurally, the CJEU seems to have developed the diffused and decentralized EU judicial system into a veritable value monitoring and enforcement mechanism. Today, violations of operationalized Union values can reach the CJEU not only via infringement proceedings initiated by the Commission (see *Commission v Poland I, II* and *III*) but also through preliminary references. On the one hand, such references can be launched by national courts within the affected Member State itself (see *ASJP*).[100] In *Miasto Łowicz,* however, the Court clarified that for a reference to be admissible there must be a 'connecting factor' between the dispute in the main proceedings and the provision whose interpretation is sought (Article 19(1)(2) and Article 2 TEU).[101]

On the other hand, judges may assess value compliance in *other* Member States within the context of mutual recognition regimes. To recall, these regimes operate under the presumption that each Member State respects the values enshrined in Article 2 TEU. To guarantee undisturbed cooperation, this relieves and precludes courts from assessing whether other Member States comply with EU standards. Only a Member State's demonstrated non-compliance with these values can refute said presumption and put cooperation on hold. For instance, European Arrest Warrants (EAWs) must be suspended if a surrender would amount to inhumane

[98] See e.g. Case C-310/16 *Dzivev* [2019] EU:C:2019:30, para 34; Case C-848/19 P *Germany v Poland* [2021] EU:C:2021:598, para 39; Case T-1/17 *La Mafia* [2018] EU:T:2018:146, para 36.

[99] For a first mapping, see Rossi (n 95); Schorkopf (n 92). From the rich literature focusing on the rule of law, see e.g. Kochenov and Pech (n 94); Thomas Giegerich, 'Die Unabhängigkeit der Gerichte als Strukturvorgabe der Unionsverfassung' ZEuS 22 (2019), 61; Ludovic Badet, 'À propos de l'article 19 du Traité sur l'Union européenne, pierre angulaire de l'action de l'Union européenne pour la sauvegarde de l'État de droit' CDE 56 (2020), 57; Manuel Campos Sánchez-Bordona, 'La protección de la independencia judicial en el derecho de la Unión Europea' RDCE 65 (2020), 11; Claudia Cinnirella, '"You cannot beat something with nothing"' dUE (2020), 361.

[100] On the plethora of references from Polish, Romanian, Hungarian, and Maltese courts, see above n 83.

[101] Cases C-558 and 563/18 *Miasto Łowicz* [2020] EU:C:2020:234, paras 48 f. See further Case C-564/19 *IS (Illégalité de l'ordonnance de renvoi)* [2021] EU:C:2021:949, paras 142 f; Case C-256/19 *S.A.D. Maler und Anstreicher OG* [Order of 2 July 2020] EU:C:2020:523, paras 44–6, 49; Case C-272/19 *Land Hessen* [2020] EU:C:2020:535, para 47 f. Critically, Sébastien Platon, 'Preliminary References and Rule of Law' CML Rev 57 (2020), 1843, 1855 ff.

and degrading treatment in the issuing Member State. To trigger this suspension, a two-pronged test must be satisfied (so-called *Aranyosi*-test). First, the applicant must demonstrate systemic deficiencies amounting to a real risk of inhumane and degrading treatment (systemic risk assessment). Second, there must be 'substantial grounds to believe that the individual concerned will be exposed to that risk' (individual risk assessment).[102]

In *L.M.*, the Court transformed this exception into a rule of law monitoring instrument. The Court extended the *Aranyosi*-test to systemic deficiencies affecting judicial independence and the essence of fair trial rights protected under Article 47 CFR.[103] This opened a new path for reviewing the value compliance of Member States issuing an EAW. Using the exceptions of cooperation under mutual recognition regimes as monitoring instruments bears considerable potential. It is therefore not excluded that this system will be extended to other fundamental rights and other mutual recognition regimes (in detail, Chapter 10, III).

B. Substantive Extension

As indicated above, the Court consolidated the nexus between Article 2 and 19(1)(2) TEU.[104] While some judgments combined both provisions into a cumulative yardstick,[105] the decision in *Repubblika* reversed their relationship and placed Article 2 TEU at the centre. The Court stressed that Member States are *generally* precluded from adopting measures that lead to 'a reduction in the protection of the value of the rule of law, a value which is given concrete expression by, inter alia, Article 19 TEU'.[106] Since *ASJP*, the Court's jurisprudence has expanded in three principal directions. First, there are signs that the Court has started to render the values in Article 2 TEU justiciable for individuals. Second, the Court has extended its jurisprudence horizontally by interpreting other Treaty provisions as 'giving specific expression to' these values. Finally, it seems that the Court has moved Article 2 TEU to the very heart of its constitutional jurisprudence.

[102] *Aranyosi and Căldăraru* (n 34) paras 89, 92.

[103] Case C-216/18 PPU *Minister for Justice and Equality (Deficiencies in the system of justice)* [2018] EU:C:2018:586, para 68. See also Cases C-354 and 412/20 PPU *Openbaar Ministerie* [2020] EU:C:2020:1033, paras 53–5.

[104] See e.g. *Commission v Poland (Independence of the Supreme Court)* (n 69) para 47; Case C-192/18 *Commission v Poland (Independence of ordinary courts)* [2019] EU:C:2019:924, para 98; Case C-791/19 *Commission v Poland (Régime disciplinaire des juges)* [2021] EU:C:2021:596, para 51. See also Cases C-585, 624 and 625/18 *A.K.* [2019] EU:C:2019:982, para 167; Cases C-357, 379, 547, 811, and 840/19 *Euro Box Promotion and Others* [2021] EU:C:2021:1034, para 217; Case C-430/21 *RS (Effet des arrêts d'une cour constitutionnelle)* [2022] EU:C:2022:99, para 39.

[105] See Cases C-748 to 754/19 *Prokuratura Rejonowa w Mińsku Mazowieckim* [2021] EU:C:2021:931, para 90; Case C-824/18 *A.B.* [2021] EU:C:2021:153, para 108 ff; Cases C-83, 127, 195, 291, 355, 397/19 *Asociația "Forumul Judecătorilor Din România"* [2021] EU:C:2021:393, para 186.

[106] Case C-896/19 *Repubblika* [2021] EU:C:2021:311, para 63.

The first dimension concerns the above-mentioned decision in *L.M.*, a case referred by the Irish High Court only two weeks after *ASJP*. The case dealt with the surrender of a Polish national who was arrested in Ireland based on a Polish EAW. The High Court had asked whether it could suspend the arrest warrant's execution due to systemic rule of law deficiencies in the Polish judiciary. The expectations for this carefully prepared reference were high. Yet, many found their hopes—ignited by *ASJP*—dashed by the realities of *L.M.*[107] The Court started by extending the grounds for the suspension of EAWs to systemic deficiencies that affect judicial independence and thus the essence of the rights protected under Article 47 CFR. At the same time, it rejected a general suspension of cooperation in case of such deficiencies and retained the requirement of an individual risk assessment.[108] Against this backdrop, some perceived *L.M.* merely as an 'intermezzo' in the Court's greater rule of law play.[109] A different reading is possible, though. Following the path laid out in *Aranyosi*, the Court seems to have rendered Article 2 TEU justiciable for individuals in the context of the EAW framework.[110]

As noted above, this regime is based on mutual trust, the presumption that all Member States respect the values enshrined in Article 2 TEU.[111] Only the issuing Member State's demonstrated non-compliance can refute that presumption and put cooperation on halt. By implication, the grounds that allow individuals to challenge the execution of an EAW must be connected to Article 2 TEU. To establish this link, the Court emphasized that the essence of fair trial rights under Article 47 CFR guarantee 'that the values common to the Member States set out in Article 2 TEU ... will be safeguarded.'[112] If an individual challenges the execution of an EAW on that basis, the Court can review whether the relevant policy areas in the issuing Member State (here: judicial procedures) violate the essence of Article 47 CFR and

[107] See e.g. Jean Paul Jacqué, 'État de droit et confiance mutuelle' RTDE (2018), 239; Michał Krajewski, 'Who Is Afraid of the European Council?' EuConst 14 (2018), 792, 810 f; Renata Uitz, 'The Perils of Defending the Rule of Law Through Dialogue' EuConst 15 (2019), 1, 9 f. On the difficult balance underlying the decision, see Luke D. Spieker, 'Breathing Life into the Union's Common Values' GLJ 20 (2019), 1182, 1195; Wojciech Lewandowski, 'Pomiędzy Scyllą zawieszenia wzajemnego zaufania i Charybdą fragmentaryzacji standardu ochrony prawa podstawowego' *Europejski Przegląd Sądowy* (2) (2019), 4.

[108] For criticism, see Krajewski (n 107) 805 ff; Mattias Wendel, 'Mutual Trust, Essence and Federalism' EuConst 15 (2019), 17, 29 ff; Petra Bárd and Walter van Ballegooij, 'Judicial Independence as a Precondition for Mutual Trust?' NJECL 9 (2018), 353.

[109] Matteo Bonelli, 'Intermezzo in the Rule of Law Play' in Armin von Bogdandy et al. (eds), *Defending Checks and Balances in EU Member States* (Springer 2021) 455, 469.

[110] Armin von Bogdandy, 'Principles of a Systemic Deficiencies Doctrine' CML Rev 57 (2020), 705, 728; von Bogdandy et al., 'A Potential Constitutional Moment for the European Rule of Law' in von Bogdandy et al. (n 109) 385, 396–9.

[111] This has been stressed over and over again, see e.g. Case C-483/20 *Commissaire général aux réfugiés and aux apatrides (Unité familiale—Protection déjà accordée)* [2022] EU:C:2022:103, para 27; Case C-665/20 PPU *X (Mandat d'arrêt européen—Ne bis in idem)* [2021] EU:C:2021:339, para 52; Case C-128/18 *Dorobantu* [2019] EU:C:2019:857, para 45.

[112] *Minister for Justice and Equality (Deficiencies in the system of justice)* (n 103) para 48. This formulation has become established jurisprudence, see e.g. *Repubblika* (n 106) para 52; *Commission v Poland (Régime disciplinaire des juges)* (n 104) para 51; Case C-562/21 PPU *Openbaar Ministerie (Tribunal établi par la loi dans l'État membre d'émission)* [2022] EU:C:2022:100, paras 45.

implicitly Article 2 TEU. In this highly specific context, individuals can thus invoke and remedy Member State violations of EU values. It remains to be seen whether the Court will go further down this path and render EU values justiciable even beyond this context.

In the second dimension, the CJEU extended its jurisprudence beyond the rule of law by connecting other Treaty provisions to Article 2 TEU. Such connections can be established in two degrees. Sometimes, Article 2 TEU is only loosely placed in context with the relevant provisions governing the case and serves as argumentative reinforcement. Following cases like *Patriciello*, the Court continued to connect the freedom of expression under Article 11 CFR with the value of democracy. For instance, the Court noted in *La Quadrature du Net*, *Privacy International*, and *Commissioner of An Garda Síochána* that the 'freedom of expression … constitutes one of the essential foundations of a pluralist, democratic society, and is one of the values on which, under Article 2 TEU, the Union is founded'.[113] Similarly, the Court has continued to interpret its jurisdiction in CFSP matters broadly by relying inter alia on Article 2 TEU.[114]

In other cases, Article 2 TEU is tightly connected to Treaty provisions 'giving specific expression' to a Union value. An illustrative example is the case of the Catalan politician Oriol Junqueras. Despite being elected in the 2019 European elections, Junqueras' name was not notified to the European Parliament by the Spanish authorities. As he was held in provisional detention for his role in the Catalan referendum, Junqueras was unable to appear in person to affirm his allegiance to the Spanish constitution (required under the respective national election legislation). The central question was whether he had acquired the status of MEP and thus gained immunity under Article 9 of Protocol (No 7). The CJEU interpreted the relevant provisions in light of the value of democracy and held that once the results have been declared, the elected person acquires the status of MEP. According to the principle of representative democracy enshrined in Article 10(1) TEU—'which gives concrete form to the value of democracy referred to in Article 2 TEU'[115]—the European Parliament's composition

[113] Cases C-511, 512 and 520/18 *La Quadrature du Net* [2020] EU:C:2020:791, para 114; Case C-623/17 *Privacy International* [2020] EU:C:2020:790, para 62; Case C-140/20 *Commissioner of An Garda Síochána* [2022] EU:C:2022:258, para 43. For a somewhat looser connection, see Case C-507/18 *Associazione Avvocatura per i diritti LGBTI* [2020] EU:C:2020:289, para 48.

[114] See e.g. Case C-134/19 P *Bank Refah Kargaran v Council* [2020] EU:C:2020:793, para 35; Case C-14/19 P *CSUE v KF* [2020] EU:C:2020:492, paras 58 f. See also in other areas, Case C-872/19 P *Venezuela v Council (Affectation d'un État tiers)* [2021] EU:C:2021:507, paras 48 f and Cases C-715, 718, and 719/17 *Commission v Poland, Hungary, the Czech Republic (Temporary mechanism for the relocation of applicants for international protection)* [2020] EU:C:2020:257, para 65.

[115] Case C-502/19 *Junqueras Vies* [2019] EU:C:2019:1115, para 63. See also Case C-629/21 P(R) *Puigdemont i Casamajó and Others v Parliament and Spain* [Order of 24 May 2022] EU:C:2022:413, para 250; Case C-207/21 P, *Commission v Poland (Protocole n° 36)* [2022] EU:C:2022:560, para 81; Case C-418/18 P *Puppinck and Others v Commission* [2019] EU:C:2019:1113, para 64. For similar connections between Art. 2 TEU and Art. 10(1)/(2) TEU, see e.g. Case T-624/16 *Gollnisch v Parliament* [2018] EU:T:2018:121, para 44; Case T-86/17 *Le Pen v Parliament* [2018] EU:T:2018:357, para 175; Case T-626/16 *Troszczynski v Parliament* [2018] EU:T:2018:270, para 163.

must 'reflect faithfully and completely the free expression of choices made by the citizens'.[116]

In its judgments on the rule of law conditionality regulation, the Court went even a step further by sketching a whole range of possible connections to Article 2 TEU. In an obiter dictum, it noted that Articles 6, 10 to 13, 15, 16, 20, 21, and 23 of the Charter 'define the scope' of the values of human dignity, freedom, equality, and respect for human rights, whereas Articles 8, 10, 19(1), 153(1), and 157(1) TFEU substantiate the values of equality, non-discrimination, and equality between women and men.[117] By outlining these paths of future development, the Court indicates its readiness to expand the approach developed in *ASJP* to other contexts. One thing seems abundantly clear: the operationalization of Article 2 TEU is far from completed.

Finally, Article 2 TEU has undergone an impressive evolution within the CJEU's constitutional jurisprudence. This refers especially to decisions that outline the EU's constitutional 'gestalt'. Starting with the seminal cases in *Van Gend en Loos* and *Costa/ENEL*, this jurisprudence has evolved over time into a full-blown account of the Union's constitutional features (in detail, Chapter 4, II.A). Today, these accounts read like a sort of constitutional narration for the EU legal order.[118] The beginnings of this jurisprudence remained rather thin, mentioning, for instance, the Community's institutional and federal setup[119] or the principles of autonomy, primacy, and direct effect as the 'essential characteristics of the Community legal order'.[120] As already noted above, substantive principles, such as the rule of law, democracy, and fundamental rights, entered the picture relatively late. It was especially in *Kadi* that the Court accorded a prominent place to the 'constitutional principles' enshrined in Article 6(1) TEU-Nice.[121]

A comprehensive account, however, was not provided until Opinion 2/13, where the Court unfolded a veritable 'constitutional blueprint for contemporary EU law'.[122] This blueprint comprises the Union's federal (Articles 4(1), 5(1) and (2) TEU) and institutional setup (Articles 13–19 TEU), as well as the principles of autonomy, primacy, and direct effect.[123] Importantly, '[t]his legal structure is based on the fundamental premiss that each Member State shares with all the other Member States ... a set of common values on which the EU is founded, as stated

[116] *Junqueras Vies* (n 115) para 83.

[117] Case C-156/21 *Hungary v Parliament and Council* [2022] EU:C:2022:97, paras 157 f; Case C-157/21 *Poland v Parliament and Council* [2022] EU:C:2022:98 paras 193 f.

[118] For a research agenda on judicial narratives, see generally Antoine Bailleux, 'Les récits judiciaires de l'Europe' RUE (2018), 5. For a general discussion, see the contributions to Claudio Franzius, Franz C. Mayer, and Jürgen Neyer (eds), *Die Neuerfindung Europas. Bedeutung und Gehalte von Narrativen für die europäische Integration* (Nomos 2019).

[119] Opinion 1/76 *European laying-up fund* [1977] EU:C:1977:63, para 12.

[120] Case C-106/77 *Simmenthal* [1978] EU:C:1978:49, para 18. See also Opinion 1/91 *EEA Treaty I* [1991] EU:C:1991:490, para 21; Opinion 1/00 *ECAA Agreement* [2002] EU:C:2002:231, para 21.

[121] *Kadi* (n 23) paras 285, 304.

[122] Takis Tridimas, 'The General Principles of EU Law and the Europeanisation of National Laws' REAL 13 (2020), 5, 12.

[123] *ECHR Accession II* (n 25) paras 164 ff.

in Article 2 TEU'.[124] Yet, the CJEU does not stop there but further adds to this list the Union's objectives and provisions relating to the fundamental freedoms, Union citizenship, the AFSJ, and competition policy.[125] This demonstrates that even though Article 2 TEU forms part of EU law's constitutional blueprint, it is only one among many other provisions. This is also reflected in the account provided in *Wightman*. As if emphasizing Article 2 TEU's secondary relevance, the Court deems it '*also appropriate* to underline the importance of the values of liberty and democracy . . .which are among the common values referred to in Article 2 of that Treaty . . . and which thus form part of the very foundations of the European Union legal order'.[126] This should change with Opinion 1/17, where the Court condensed the lengthy and convoluted account of Opinion 2/13 into a concise outline of the Union's 'constitutional framework':

> That framework encompasses the founding values set out in Article 2 TEU . . . the provisions of the Charter, and the provisions of the EU and FEU Treaties, which include, inter alia, rules on the conferral and division of powers, rules governing how the EU institutions and its judicial system are to operate, and fundamental rules in specific areas, structured in such a way as to contribute to the implementation of the process of integration.[127]

In this spirit, Article 2 TEU has moved to the very heart of the CJEU's constitutional jurisprudence. The provision's ascent seems to have reached its summit with the much awaited and politically highly salient decisions on the rule of law conditionality regulation. These judgments emphasize Article 2 TEU's centrality in unequivocal terms. In their crucial passages, the Court circumscribes—for the first time—the constitutional identity of the EU legal order by linking it to Article 2 TEU:

> The values contained in Article 2 TEU have been identified and are shared by the Member States. They define the very identity of the European Union as a common legal order.[128]

[124] ibid paras 168.
[125] ibid para 172.
[126] Case C-621/18 *Wightman* [2018] EU:C:2018:999, paras 62 f (emphasis added).
[127] Opinion 1/17 *CETA* [2019] EU:C:2019:341, para 110.
[128] *Hungary v Parliament and Council* (n 117) para 127; *Poland v Parliament and Council* (n 117) paras 145. On this rhetoric Matteo Bonelli, 'Constitutional Language and Constitutional Limits: The Court of Justice Dismisses the Challenges to the Budgetary Conditionality Regulation' EP 7 (2022), 507, 518 f; Ferdinand Weber, 'The Pluralism of Values in An Identity-Framed Verbund: Federal Belonging in the European Union after the Rule of Law Conditionality Judgments' EL Rev 47 (2022), 514, 524 ff; Vestert Borger, 'Constitutional Identity, the Rule of Law, and the Power of the Purse: The ECJ Approves the Conditionality Mechanism to Protect the Union budget' CML Rev 59 (2022), 1771, 1793 ff.

2
Doctrine
The Judicial Applicability of Article 2 TEU

I. Introduction

After tracing the rise of Article 2 TEU in the Court's jurisprudence, this chapter will take a step back and assess whether the increasing judicial application of Article 2 TEU is doctrinally sound. Indeed, a first glance at Article 2 TEU might suggest otherwise. To start with, Article 2 TEU seems to feature moral values, not legal obligations (Section II). And even if the provision were to contain legal obligations, they seem far too indeterminate to be justiciable (Section III). And even if Article 2 TEU contained justiciable legal obligations, the Treaties foresee specific political procedures for their enforcement and might thus exclude the Court's jurisdiction (Section IV). This chapter will consider all three of these objections and argue that they are, if not outright wrong, at least highly questionable. In conclusion, this part seeks to anchor Article 2 TEU firmly among the operative provisions of EU law.

II. Legal Normativity

The Treaty of Lisbon transforms the principles formerly enshrined in Article 6 TEU-Amsterdam/Nice into values. With this semantic shift, the Treaty drafters introduced a rather elusive notion in EU primary law. Values are widely used in very different contexts: ethics, philosophy, economics, political science, religion, sociology, psychology, etc. Uwe Pörksen even lists them as 'plastic words', empty formulas, clichés, and buzzwords that can mean everything and nothing.[1] As such, the notion of values is notoriously hard to pin down. This explains why their ontological nature, emergence, and mode of existence have been a persistent cause for headache and disagreement.[2] We will have to resist the temptation of exploring

[1] See Uwe Pörksen, *Plastic Words: The Tyranny of a Modular Language* (Penn. State Univ. Press 2004) 22, 26 placing 'values' in one line with notions like 'identity' or 'substance'.

[2] For an overview, see Hans Joas, *The Genesis of Values* (Univ. of Chicago Press 2000) 20 ff. For a concise historical introduction (from a German perspective), Herbert Schnädelbach, *Philosophy in Germany 1831–1933* (CUP 1984, repr. 2013) 161 ff.

EU Values Before the Court of Justice. Luke Dimitrios Spieker, Oxford University Press.
DOI: 10.1093/oso/9780198876717.003.0003

the rabbit hole of value theory and content ourselves with a rather purist definition. Put in most simple terms, values provide points of reference for evaluation. They help distinguishing whether something is 'good', desirable, and worth striving for.[3] In this sense, values guide human conduct and become normative. First-time readers of Article 2 TEU will probably stumble over the notion of values. Their first impression might be that values have to do with intuition not reason, sentiment not rationality, good intentions not legal obligations. Values, one might think, are the stuff of Sunday speeches, party manifestos, preambles but not operative legal texts. In short, values have *moral* but not *legal normativity*.

This leads us to the central question of this section: Has the shift to values altered or reduced Article 2 TEU's legal force? Such objections are usually raised in Member States accused of notoriously violating these values. According to the captured Polish Constitutional Tribunal, Article 2 TEU does not contain legal principles but only values of 'axiological significance'.[4] Still, reservations were harboured in the EU institutions as well. Tellingly, the Commission noted that '*beyond* its task to ensure the respect of EU law, [it] is also responsible ... for guaranteeing the common values of the Union'.[5] Even the reporting judge in *ASJP* advocated caution.[6]

Despite these doubts, understanding the values in Article 2 TEU as legal principles has become a widespread view among CJEU judges[7] and legal scholars.[8] Especially the Court's activity seems to have incited a shift from a 'general agreement' on the limited legal effects of Article 2 TEU to an 'overwhelming agreement' on its justiciability.[9] The judgments on the rule of law conditionality

[3] See Iwao Hirose and Jonas Olson, 'Introduction to Value Theory' (p 1) and Michael J. Zimmerman, 'Value and Normativity' (p 13) both in Iwao Hirose and Jonas Olson (eds), *The Oxford Handbook of Value Theory* (OUP 2015).

[4] See the press release accompanying the Judgment of 7 October 2021, K 3/21, para 19.

[5] European Commission, Reasoned Proposal in Accordance with Article 7(1) of the Treaty on European Union Regarding the Rule of Law in Poland, COM(2017) 835 final, para 1.

[6] Egils Levits, 'Die Europäische Union als Wertegemeinschaft' in Thomas Jaeger (ed.), *Europa 4.0* (Sramek 2018) 239, 262; Levits, 'L'Union européenne en tant que communauté des valeurs partagées' in *Liber Amicorum Antonio Tizzano* (Giappichelli 2018) 509, 521.

[7] See e.g. Lucia S. Rossi, 'La valeur juridique des valeurs' RTDE (2020), 639; Marek Safjan, 'Domestic Infringements of the Rule of Law as a European Union Problem' *Osteuropa Recht* (2019), 552, 553; José Martín y Pérez de Nanclares, 'La Unión Europea como comunidad de valores' *Teoría y Realidad Constitucional* 43 (2019), 121, 135.

[8] From the rich literature, see e.g. Armin von Bogdandy, 'Founding Principles' in von Bogdandy and Jürgen Bast (eds), *Principles of European Constitutional Law* (2nd edn, Hart 2009) 11, 22; Stelio Mangiameli, 'The Union's Homogeneity and its Common Values' in Mangiameli and Hermann-Josef Blanke (eds), *The European Union after Lisbon* (Springer 2012) 21, 22; Roberto Baratta, 'La "communauté de valeurs" dans l'ordre juridique de l'Union européenne' RAE (2018), 81, 89; Karl-Peter Sommermann, 'Die gemeinsamen Werte der Union und der Mitgliedstaaten' in Matthias Niedobitek (ed.), *Europarecht* (2nd edn, De Gruyter 2019) § 3, para 8.

[9] Contrast Carlos Closa and Dimitry Kochenov, 'Reinforcement of the Rule of Law Oversight in the European Union' in Werner Schröder (ed.), *Strengthening the Rule of Law in Europe* (Hart 2015) 173, 183 and Dimitry Kochenov and Laurent Pech, 'Monitoring and Enforcement of the Rule of Law in the EU' EuConst 11 (2015), 512, 529, with Kim L. Scheppele, Dimitry Kochenov, and Barbara Grabowska-Moroz, 'EU Values are Law, after All' YEL 38 (2020), 3, 67.

regulation provide an unequivocal statement in this respect. Sitting in full court, the Luxembourg judges emphasized that 'Article 2 TEU is not a mere statement of policy guidelines or intentions'.[10] Yet, many still question the legal normativity of Article 2 TEU.[11]

Among both proponents and sceptics, however, one often searches in vain for deeper justifications. Frequently, the legal normativity of Article 2 TEU is merely asserted without being grounded in a thorough interpretation.[12] Similarly unsubstantiated are many sceptical claims. Usually, a reference to the notion of values is deemed sufficient to cast doubts on Article 2 TEU's legal force.[13] The following Section seeks to complement the discussion by providing a comprehensive interpretation of Article 2 TEU.

Before starting with this endeavour, we should briefly outline our methodological approach. It seems commonplace that law is always the normative consolidation of certain evaluations.[14] Even the simplest traffic sign contains a decision based on value judgments (e.g. guaranteeing the road users' physical integrity is deemed more valuable than preserving their liberty). This trivial insight is not disputed even by resolute positivists. Yet, Article 2 TEU confronts us with a strange peculiarity. It is not a provision *based on* certain values, but a positivization of values—*as values*. Abstractly, there are two ways to approach this phenomenon.

One way is to understand Article 2 TEU as a gateway into the sphere of extra-legal, political, or societal morality. By implication, Article 2 TEU would have to be developed by means and methods of moral philosophy. Alternatively, one could argue that in the moment of their positivization, such ambiguous notions are translated into the language of law and become legal concepts.[15] In this sense, Ralf

[10] Case C-156/21 *Hungary v Parliament and Council* [2022] EU:C:2022:97, paras 232; Case C-157/21 *Poland v Parliament and Council* [2022] EU:C:2022:98, paras 264.

[11] See e.g. Matteo Bonelli, 'Infringement Actions 2.0: How to Protect EU Values before the Court of Justice' EuConst 18 (2022), 30, 45 ff; Peter Van Elsuwege and Femke Gremmelprez, 'Protecting the Rule of Law in the EU Legal Order' EuConst 16 (2020), 8, 13; Christoph Möllers, *The European Union as a Democratic Federation* (Bittner 2018) 124, 127.

[12] But see for brief assessments Armin von Bogdandy, 'Principles of a Systemic Deficiencies Doctrine' CML Rev 57 (2020), 705, 726–729; Enzo Cannizzaro, 'Il ruolo della Corte di giustizia nella tutela dei valori dell'Unione europea' in *Liber Amicorum Tizzano* (n 6) 159, 160 f; Christophe Hillion, 'Overseeing the Rule of Law in the EU' in Carlos Closa and Dimitry Kochenov (eds), *Reinforcing Rule of Law Oversight in the European Union* (CUP 2016) 59, 67–74.

[13] See e.g. Möllers (n 11) 127; Jan-Werner Müller, 'Should the EU Protect Democracy and the Rule of Law inside Member States?' ELJ 21 (2015), 141, 146; Thomas Oppermann et al., *Europarecht* (9th edn, C.H.Beck 2021) § 15, para 50. See also Martin Nettesheim, 'Kompetenzkonflikte zwischen EuGH und Mitgliedstaaten' ZRP 54 (2021), 222 ('pogrammatisch-axiologische Wertaussagen').

[14] See e.g. Christian Starck, 'Zur Notwendigkeit einer Wertbegründung des Rechts' *Archives for Philosophy of Law and Social Philosophy*, Supp 37 (1990), 47, 50; Christophe Grzegorczyk, *La théorie générale des valeurs et le droit* (LGDJ 1982) 265 f.

[15] See especially from Italian scholarship, Antonio D'Atena, 'I principi e i valori costituzionali' in *Lezioni di diritto costituzionale* (4th edn, Giappichelli 2018) 21 f. With regard to Art. 2 TEU, see Mangiameli (n 8) 22; Antonio Ruggeri, 'Valori e principi costituzionali degli Stati integrati d'Europa' *Teoria del diritto dello Stato* (2009), 292, 306.

Poscher refers to the 'Midas quality' of law. Just as whatever king Midas touched turned into gold, any concept taken up by the law turns into a legal concept.[16] In consequence such shared concepts must be developed by recourse to legal methodology. This study will follow the latter approach. Not only does it conform with the book's endeavour to assess the judicial applicability of Article 2 TEU; it also guarantees the provision's openness to divergent moral or philosophical understandings. Such an inclusiveness is key for a central constitutional provision like Article 2 TEU (see also Chapter 3).

Against this backdrop, the following chapter will approach Article 2 TEU with the toolkit of legal methodology.[17] Starting from the wording, neither legal theory, nor comparative considerations, not even the Treaty text itself can confirm a clear differentiation between legal principles and non-legal values. As such, the value semantics can hardly justify doubts with regard to the legal normativity of Article 2 TEU (Section A). In contrast, both systematic considerations (Section B) and the provision's drafting history (Section C) support the view that Article 2 TEU contains legal obligations. In particular, the *travaux* of the Constitutional Treaty, which introduced the notion of values in EU primary law, provide no indication that the value semantics were intended to weaken Article 2 TEU's normative relevance. To the contrary, they suggest that Article 2 TEU was drafted as a direct successor to the principles formerly enshrined in Article 6(1) TEU-Amsterdam. One could even argue that its denomination as values was intended to express a normative reinforcement of the principles enshrined in Article 2 TEU (Section D). Finally, some readers might have noticed that a central method is missing in the following account: teleology. However, making the teleological case for the judicial application of EU values (and thus their legal normativity) is a central aim of this book that would exceed the scope of this Chapter. Instead, it will be at the heart of the following parts.

A. Text

As seen above, the notion of values is a central argument against the legal normativity of Article 2 TEU. This section will demonstrate that textual considerations are probably not the best starting point. Legal theory has long grappled with the question of how to relate values to other legal concepts, such as rules and principles. In

[16] Ralf Poscher, 'The Hand of Midas' in Jaap Hage and Dietmar von der Pfordten (eds), *Concepts in Law* (Springer 2009) 99.

[17] For an overview of these methods in EU law, see e.g. Koen Lenaerts and José A. Gutiérrez-Fons, *Les méthodes d'interprétation de la Cour de justice de l'Union européenne* (Bruylant 2020) 13 ff; Gunnar Beck, *The Legal Reasoning of the Court of Justice* (Hart 2013) 147 ff; Sebastian A. E. Martens, *Methodenlehre des Unionsrechts* (Mohr Siebeck 2013) 329 ff.

this sense, it seems difficult to draw a clear line of legal normativity between values and other legal phenomena (Section 1). Further, a comparative outlook reveals that the notions of values and principles are used rather interchangeably in the constitutional law and jurisprudence of the Member States (Section 2). These semantic variations are also reflected by the Treaty text (Section 3).

1. Principles and values: The blurry lines of legal theory

In legal theory, values are usually juxtaposed with principles and rules. Intuitively, it seems that rules and values mark two extreme poles with principles allocated somewhere in between.[18] The various positions can be narrowed down to three camps. The first two translate the triad of rules, principles, and values into dichotomies, whereas the third perceives their relationship as one of degree. Jürgen Habermas, for instance, has reconstructed the triad as a dichotomy of *legal rules and principles as opposed to values*.[19] He argues that principles are higher-level norms of deontological character, whereas values express preferences of teleological nature that lack legal normativity. Legal norms command where values recommend. This leads to the following scheme:

Rules ≤ Principles ≠ Values

Thus, any positivization of values—as values—must seem to Habermas like a strange oxymoron. His distinctions are therefore of limited explanatory value with respect to Article 2 TEU.[20] The approach of Robert Alexy seems more promising. He argues for a *dichotomy of legal rules as opposed to legal principles and values*. For him, the only difference between principles and values is their deontological and axiological character.[21] However, it is 'not difficult to move from the idea that a certain solution is the best, constitutionally speaking, to the idea that it is required by the constitution'.[22] Statements about values can thus be formulated in terms of principles and vice versa without loss of meaning. After blurring the distinction between values and principles, Alexy categorically distinguishes both from rules. Importantly, rules operate in a binary manner (they are either fulfilled or not), whereas principles and values can be fulfilled to a greater or lesser extent. While conflicts among rules must lead to the invalidity of one, principles and values can

[18] See e.g. Gustavo Zagrebelsky, 'Diritto per: valori, principi o regole?' in *Intorno alla legge* (Einaudi 2009) 85, 99 f. For a comprehensive overview, see Luca Mezzetti, 'Valori, Principî, Regole' in Mezzetti (ed.), *Principî Costituzionali* (Giappichelli 2011) 1, 29 ff.

[19] Jürgen Habermas, *Between Facts and Norms* (Polity 1996) 255 ff.

[20] Indeed, Habermas' distinctions (and criticism) concern the *judicial* recourse to values.

[21] Robert Alexy, *A Theory of Constitutional Rights* (OUP 2010) 86 ff, 91 ff, 378.

[22] ibid 91. Similarly, Aleksander Peczenik, *On Law and Reason* (Springer 2008) 61 f; Klaus F. Röhl and Hans C. Röhl, *Allgemeine Rechtslehre* (3rd edn, Vahlen 2008) 290.

be balanced against each other. The precedence of one over the other does not affect their validity but only their application in the specific case.[23] Alexy's conception can thus be summarized as follows:

Rules ≠ Principles ≙ Values

Finally, a large group of authors questions the usefulness and accuracy of categorical distinctions between rules, principles, and values. As legal reality is much more nuanced, categorical distinctions might constitute a misleading oversimplification.[24] In this spirit, many propose to move from a *categorical or qualitative* to a *gradual or quantitative* distinction.[25] Instead of treating them as different legal phenomena, principles and rules can be distinguished based on their generality in content and impact.[26] Flowing from the generality in content, principles will usually require concretization and operate in a non-conditional manner (not an 'if-then' mode). Flowing from the generality in impact, principles are often transversal in application and usually not restricted to a certain area of law. Hence, it seems only consistent to apply a similar gradual distinction between values and principles. Put differently:

Rules ≤ Principles ≤ Values

An example might illustrate this gradual relationship. The starting point is a value relating to a certain interest or institution (e.g. 'equality'[27]); add a prescriptive dimension, such as a command, prohibition, permission, or right, and you transform the value into a principle (e.g. 'any discrimination based on ... shall be prohibited'[28]); place the principle into a conditional context and you end up with a rule (e.g. 'In the event of a violation of the prohibition of discrimination, the employer shall ... compensate the damage arising therefrom'[29]).

Of course, legal reality is much more complex than this brief example suggests. There can be many shades of grey that make transitions from one form to the other

[23] Alexy (n 21) 45 ff. Many distinguishing criteria between principles/values and rules are controversial and cannot be discussed here. On further distinctions, see Ronald Dworkin, *Taking Rights Seriously* (Bloomsbury, repr. 2013) 43 ff; Gustavo Zagrebelsky, *Il diritto mite* (Einaudi 1992) 147 ff.

[24] See e.g. Aulis Aarnio, *Essays on the Doctrinal Study of Law* (Springer 2011) 119, 122.

[25] See e.g. H.L.A. Hart, *The Concept of Law* (3rd edn, Clarendon 2012) 260; András Jakab, *European Constitutional Language* (CUP 2016) 368 ff; Ralf Poscher, 'Insights, Errors and Self-Misconceptions of the Theory of Principles' *Ratio Juris* 22 (2009), 425, 433 ff, 449. See also Riccardo Guastini, *Le fonti del diritto: Fondamenti teorici* (Giuffrè 2010) 201 ff, 207 ff; Jean-Louis Bergel, *Théorie Générale du Droit* (5th edn, Dalloz 2012) 104.

[26] Ralf Poscher, 'Theory of a Phantom' *Archives for Philosophy of Law and Social Philosophy*, Sup. 144 (2015), 129, 147; Franz Reimer, *Verfassungsprinzipien* (Duncker&Humblot 2001) 181 f.

[27] See Art. 2 TEU.

[28] See Art. 21(1) CFR or Art. 2(1) Directive 2000/78.

[29] See § 15 of the German General Act on Equal Treatment (AGG), which implements Directive 2000/78.

hardly discernible. As such, it seems impossible, arbitrary at the very least, to draw a firm line of legal normativity at a specific point on this scale. From the perspective of legal theory, one may therefore conclude that value semantics do not necessarily imply a lack of legal normativity.

2. Principles and values: Comparative considerations

Against this backdrop, it is not surprising that the notions of values and principles are often employed interchangeably in constitutional jurisprudence. In fact, a brief comparative outlook reveals that value semantics are no stranger to the Member States' constitutional law and jurisprudence. The German Bundesverfassungsgericht is probably one of the most elaborate examples. In an early line of cases, it began referring to the constitution as a system of values.[30] Similar semantics can be observed in other contexts. The Italian Corte Costituzionale, for instance, characterized the constitution as a 'quadro'[31] or 'tavola dei valori'.[32] After the fall of the Franco-regime, the new Spanish Constitution went even further by including a set of values in its very first Article. Under this impression, the Tribunal Constitucional has often referred to the 'sistema de valores' incorporated or established by the Constitution[33] and developed the 'valores superiores' to an important point of reference in its jurisprudence.[34]

After the upheavals of 1989, a similar reasoning can be traced in Eastern Europe. The Czech Constitutional Court stressed that the new constitution 'is not founded on neutrality with regard to values . . . rather it incorporates into its text also certain governing ideas, expressing the fundamental, inviolable values of a democratic society'.[35] Similarly, the Hungarian Constitutional Court stated that Article 2(1) of the former Constitution contains the 'basic values of the republic'.[36] Moreover, some constitutions, such as the Romanian, feature the notion of values explicitly in the constitutional text.[37]

Certainly, these doctrines are embedded in highly specific contexts. What they have in common, however, is that the notion of values usually refers to legal, not moral, concepts. Very often values and principles are used interchangeably. For instance, it seems relatively uncontroversial that, despite its

[30] BVerfG, Judgment of 15 January 1958, 1 BvR 400/51, *Lüth*, para 25. See also BVerfG, Judgment of 23 October 1952, 1 BvB 1/51, *SRP-ban*, para 37; Judgment of 1956, 1 BvB 2/51, *KPD-ban*, paras 246, 1432; Judgment of 1957, 1 BvR 253/56, *Elfes*, para 28.

[31] See e.g. Corte Costituzionale, 257/2006 (IT:COST:2006:257) para 2 (dir.); 202/2004 (IT:COST:2004: 202); 454/1993 (IT:COST:1993:454) para 2 (dir.).

[32] See e.g. Corte Costituzionale, 275/2016 (IT:COST:2016:275) paras 13 f (dir.). See further Giuseppe de Vergottini, *Diritto Costituzionale* (9th edn, CEDAM 2017) 14.

[33] See e.g. Tribunal Constitucional, STC 18/1981 (ES:TC:1981:18), FJ 2; STC 195/1983 (ES:TC: 1983:358A), FJ 2; STC 162/1999 (ES:TC:1999:162), FJ 8 b).

[34] Recently Tribunal Constitucional, STC 25/2019 (ES:TC:2019:25), FJ 7; FJ 3; STC 81/2020 (ES:TC:2020:81), FJ 12; STC 38/2022 (ES:TC:2022:38), FJ 9.

[35] Ústavní soud, Judgment of 21 December 1993, Pl. ÚS 19/93, *Lawlessness of the Communist Regime*.

[36] Alkotmánybíróság, Decision of 30 January 1992, 9/1992. (I. 30.), *Protest of illegality on appeals*.

[37] Art. 1(3) Constitution of Romania.

recourse to values, Article 1(1) of the Spanish Constitution unfolds legal effects.[38] While many scholars argue that principles and values are not distinct constitutional categories,[39] the Tribunal Constitucional seems to employ both notions synonymously.[40]

A similar fuzziness characterizes the jurisprudence in Italy and Germany. After 1945, legal positivism was perceived as the key reason for the shameful role of German jurists in the Third Reich. Thus, it was excluded from becoming a guiding theorem in the early days of the Bundesrepublik. With the notion of values the German Bundesverfassungsgericht managed to overcome—at least semantically—the scapegoated positivism without sliding into natural law.[41] As such, the Court's value-jurisprudence cannot be understood as referring to values beyond the constitutional text or as embracing any particular value philosophy.[42] It does not operate with an immediate reference to values, but with their manifestations in the constitution.[43] Though the Court continues to refer to the constitution as a 'system of values',[44] it has started to use principles and values interchangeably.[45] Similarly, the Italian Corte Costituzionale increasingly refers to 'principi e valori' without any distinction.[46] Some scholars, including constitutional judges, have criticized this equivalence as inaccurate, confusing, or even promiscuous.[47] In defence, former Constitutional Judge Antonio Baldassarre noted that the recourse to values does not refer to any metaphysical concepts but 'valori costituzionali *positivamente stabiliti*', meaning the values contained in or implied by constitutional provisions.[48]

3. Principles and values: The shifting Treaty semantics

All this might explain why the Treaties themselves do not employ a consistent terminology either. Indeed, the Treaty drafters used the notions of values and principles in a rather undifferentiated way. This becomes especially apparent in the

[38] Seminal Gregorio Peces Barba, *Los valores superiores* (Tecnos 1986) 41 f, 88 ff.

[39] For an overview, see Margarita Beladiez Rojo, *Los principios jurídicos* (Civitas 2010) 192.

[40] See e.g. Tribunal Constitucional, STC 103/2017 (ES:TC:2017:103), FJ 3 ('valores y principios constitucionales').

[41] See e.g. Michael Stolleis, *Public Law in Germany. A Historical Introduction* (OUP 2017) 137.

[42] Dieter Grimm, *Verfassungsgerichtsbarkeit* (Suhrkamp 2021) 190 ff; Gertrude Lübbe-Wolff, 'Die Verfassung als Wertordnung—Was heißt das?' *Merkur* 70 (801) (2016), 47, 51; Bernhard Schlink, 'The Dynamics of Constitutional Adjudication' *Cardozo Law Review* 17 (1996), 1231, 1234. But see Ernst-Wolfgang Böckenförde, 'Critique of the Value-Based Grounding of Law (1990)' in Mirjam Künkler and Tine Stein (eds), *Constitutional and Political Theory* (OUP 2017) 217.

[43] See e.g. Rainer Wahl, '*Lüth* und die Folgen' in Thomas Henne and Arne Riedlinger (eds), *Das Lüth-Urteil aus (rechts-)historischer Sicht* (BWV 2005) 371, 380 ff.

[44] See e.g. BVerfG, Judgment of 26 February 2020, 2 BvR 2347/15, *Assisted suicide services*, para 277.

[45] On human dignity 'as the essential constitutive principle, and as the supreme value, of the constitution', see e.g. BVerfG, Judgment of 15 February 2006, 1 BvR 357/05, *Aviation Security Act*, para 119.

[46] Illustratively Corte Costituzionale, 246/2019 (IT:COST:2019:246) para 9 (dir.); 206/2004 (COST:2004:206) para 3.2. (dir.); 1146/1988 (IT:COST:1988:1146) para 2.1 (dir.).

[47] See e.g. D'Atena (n 15) 19 f; Zagrebelsky (n 18) 94; Franco Modugno, 'Divagazioni su "principi" e "valori"' in *Scritti in onore di Antonio D'Atena*, vol 3 (Giuffrè 2015) 1995, 2026 f.

[48] Antonio Baldassarre, 'Una risposta a Guastini' *Giurisprudenza costituzionale* 52 (2007), 3251, 3270.

preamble to the TEU. While the Treaty drafters drew 'inspiration from the ... universal values of the inviolable and inalienable rights of the human person, freedom, democracy, equality and the rule of law', they confirmed 'their attachment to the principles of liberty, democracy and respect for human rights ... and of the rule of law'. Against this backdrop, some scholars have ascertained that the Treaties lack an overarching conception[49] and even warned against taking their misleading categorizations at face value.[50] Also in the Court's jurisprudence, shifts between values and principles are quite symptomatic. In *L.M.*, for instance, the Court referred to the 'values common to the Member States set out in Article 2 TEU'. One needs only to read a little bit further to witness the astonishing transformation from values to 'principles set out in Article 2 TEU'.[51] A similarly oscillating terminology can be found in *Hungary v Parliament*. With regard to democracy and equality, the Court noted that 'those two principles are values on which the European Union is founded, in accordance with Article 2 TEU.'[52]

Generally, one should not place too much weight on textual considerations in EU law. Certainly, the Court cannot ignore the clear and precise wording of a provision. Yet, the weight placed on the text is somewhat attenuated in the EU context. The Treaties are equally authentic in each of the twenty-four official languages (Article 55 TEU). Further, the drafting of EU law takes place in a unique multilingual and multi-cultural environment. It is faced not only with the challenge of expressing hard-won compromises, but also with the difficulty of connecting the legal text to equivalent legal concepts in all twenty-seven Member States. Such a connection, which is a precondition for the comprehensibility and acceptability of EU law in the Member States' legal orders, comes with a significant cost: ambiguity. These ambiguities, however, must be settled by recourse to the context and purpose of the provision.[53]

B. System

Starting with the context, systematic considerations provide a strong indication that Article 2 TEU contains legal obligations. First, this can be derived from the internal system of Article 2 TEU itself. Its second sentence ('These values are

[49] von Bogdandy (n 8) 21; Meinhard Hilf and Frank Schorkopf, 'Art. 2 EUV' in Eberhard Grabitz et al. (eds), *Das Recht der Europäischen Union* (75th edn, loose-leaf, C.H.Beck 2022)para 21.

[50] See e.g. Dimitry Kochenov, 'The *Acquis* and Its Principles' in Kochenov and András Jakab (eds), *The Enforcement of EU Law and Values* (OUP 2017) 9, 10; Rudolf Streinz, 'Principles and Values in the European Union' in Armin Hatje and Lubos Tichý (eds), *Liability of Member States for the Violation of Fundamental Values* (Nomos 2018) 9, 10.

[51] Case C-216/18 PPU *Minister for Justice and Equality (Deficiencies in the system of justice)* [2018] EU:C:2018:586, paras 70–3.

[52] Case C-650/18 *Hungary v Parliament* [2021] EU:C:2021:426, para 94.

[53] See only Lenaerts and Gutiérrez-Fons (n 17) 15.

common to the Member States ...') is systematically related to the first ('*These* values ...') and has been read as expressing not merely a description of the status quo but a legal obligation ('*are common*').[54] Such an understanding might emerge also from a comparison with the elements mentioned in the second sentence. These elements—pluralism, non-discrimination, tolerance, justice, solidarity, and equality between women and men—are not designated as values. They are referred to as features characterizing 'a society' of either the Member States or the Union. Although their precise nature and function remains unclear, it seems clear that they are even more indeterminate than the values mentioned in the first sentence.

Still, it should be noted that the Court seems to confer a certain legal value also to these elements. Recently, it started to increasingly rely on the notion of 'solidarity'.[55] Further, it stressed that if it were called upon to interpret the concepts contained in the second sentence of Article 2 TEU in an annulment action under Article 263 TFEU—and thus *as a legal yardstick*—'it would ... exercise only the powers conferred on it by the Treaties'.[56]

Second, arguments relating to the external system of the Treaties support the legal normativity of Article 2 TEU. The values are laid down not in the preamble but in the operative part of the Treaties.[57] In addition, the values mentioned in the first sentence are an explicit point of reference for other Treaty provisions. The EU institutions are under an obligation to promote (Article 13(1) TEU) and safeguard them (Articles 21(1)(a), 32(1), 42(5) TEU). Further, they form standards for the evaluation of Member or Candidate States' conduct under the sanctioning mechanism of Article 7 TEU and the admission procedure of Article 49 TEU. Unlike the Union's objectives, the breach or fulfilment of its values is thus linked to specific legal consequences, the suspension of Member State rights or admission to the EU. Accordingly, EU values are applied as yardsticks in legal procedures by public institutions and their disregard leads to sanctions, which are of a legal nature.[58]

C. History

As noted above, the semantic shift from principles to values was performed with Article I-2 of the failed Constitutional Treaty (CT). Even though the reasons

[54] Hilf and Schorkopf (n 49) para 40; Mangiameli (n 8) 22. But see Bonelli (n 11) 47.

[55] *Hungary v Parliament and Council* (n 10) para 129; *Poland v Parliament and Council* (n 10) para 157; Case C-848/19 P *Germany v Poland* [2021] EU:C:2021:598, para 38. On solidarity as a 'value', Koen Lenaerts and Stanislas Adam, 'La solidarité, valeur commune aux états membres et principe fédératif de l'Union européenne' CDE 57 (2021), 307, 314 f; Anne Joppe, 'EU Solidarity, Illustrated by the Covid-19 Crisis' *Utrecht Law Review* 17 (2021), 130, 132 f. As a legal principle, see Esin Küçük, 'Solidarity in EU Law: An Elusive Political Statement or a Legal Principle with Substance?' MJ 23 (2016), 965. Sceptical, see Marcus Klamert, 'Loyalty and solidarity as general principles' in Katja S. Ziegler et al. (eds), *Research Handbook on General Principles in EU Law* (Elgar 2022) 118.

[56] *Poland v Parliament and Council* (n 10) para 329.

[57] See von Bogdandy (n 12) 716; Streinz (n 50) 11.

[58] von Bogdandy (n 12) 716 f.

behind this choice remain unclear, the Convention's *travaux* provide ample evidence that weakening the provision's legal force was not the drafters' intention. The following sections will briefly trace the emergence of value semantics in EU law before engaging with the Convention's *travaux*. Due to their growing accessibility, *travaux* have become an important point of reference for the interpretation of EU primary law.[59] This applies especially to the Convention drafting the Constitutional Treaty.[60] In this spirit, the CJEU has started to rely increasingly on them when interpreting equivalent provisions in the Lisbon Treaty.[61]

1. The emergence of values in EU law

The notion of values emerges in official documents and EU legal scholarship in the early 70's.[62] The 1973 Declaration on European identity was the first document to explicitly affirm the Member States' intention 'to ensure that the cherished values of their legal, political, and moral order are respected' and to 'defend the principles of representative democracy, of the rule of law … and of respect for human rights.'[63] The preamble to the Single European Act[64] and Article F(1) TEU-Maastricht incorporated some of these principles into EU primary law. On the eve of Amsterdam, the notion of values slowly gained momentum. The Reflection Group preparing the 1996 IGC proposed to clearly proclaim, promote, and protect the Union's 'common values' in the Treaties.[65] Yet, the notion did not make it into the Treaties.[66] Instead, Article 6(1) TEU-Amsterdam proclaimed that the 'Union is founded on the principles of liberty, democracy, respect for human rights

[59] See e.g. Koen Lenaerts and Gutiérrez-Fons (n 17) 40 ff; Samuli Miettinen and Merita Kettunen, 'Travaux to the EU Treaties' CYELS 17 (2015), 145; Mattias Wendel, 'Renaissance der historischen Auslegungsmethode im europäischen Verfassungsrecht?' ZaöRV 68 (2008), 803.

[60] All *travaux* are accessible here: <european-convention.europa.eu>. For the verbatim reports of the plenary debates, see <www.europarl.europa.eu/Europe2004/compterendu/compterendu_en.htm>. Suggested amendments can be found here: <european-convention.europa.eu/EN/amendments/amendments3a7a.html?content = 2&lang = EN>.

[61] See e.g. Case C-583/11 P *Inuit* [2013] EU:C:2013:625, para 59; Case C-286/14 *Parliament v Commission*[2016] EU:C:2016:183, para 44; Case C-543/17 *Commission v Belgium* [2019] EU:C:2019:573, para 52.

[62] Hallstein was probably one of the first to explicitly define a set of 'Grundwerte' to be realized in the community framework, see Walter Hallstein, *Der unvollendete Bundesstaat* (Econ 1969) 43 ff. See also Pierre Pescatore, *Le droit de l'intégration* (Sijthoff 1972) 50 f.: 'à l'origine … de la supranationalité, est l'acceptation, par un groupe d'Etats, de valeurs qui leur sont communes'.

[63] Declaration on European Identity at the Copenhagen European Summit (14 December 1973), Bull EC. 12-1973, pp 118 ff. For an early appraisal, see Jean-Paul Jacqué, 'Cours générale de droit communautaire' *Collected Courses of the Academy of European Law* I-1 (1990), 237, 276. On the context, see Kiran K. Patel, *Project Europe* (CUP 2020) 155 ff.

[64] The preamble affirmed the Member States' attachment to 'the principles of democracy and compliance with the law and with human rights', see Single European Act [1987] OJ L169/1.

[65] IGC '96, Reflection Group Report, p 21. In similar terms European Commission, Reinforcing Political Union and Preparing for Enlargement, COM (96)90 final, para 8; European Parliament, Resolution on the Amsterdam Treaty [1997] OJ C371/99, Rec. H, para 11. See already Fernand Herman, Second Report of the Committee on Institutional Affairs on the Constitution of the European Union (9 February 1994), A3-0064/94, pp 11 f.

[66] The protection of 'common values' was only mentioned as CFSP objective in Art. 11 TEU-Amsterdam. See already Art. J.1(2) TEU-Maastricht.

and fundamental freedoms, and the rule of law, principles which are common to the Member States'. The year 2000 was a turning point. By the end of the year, the 'community of values' had become a central leitmotif in European discourse.[67] Two diametrically opposed developments determined the rather dramatic setting for this shift. While the Austrian Haider affair seemed to threaten the European value basis, the adoption of the Charter of Fundamental Rights presented an aspirational promotion of these values.

After devastating results in the 1999 elections, the Austrian Peoples' Party (ÖVP) negotiated with Jörg Haider, the highly controversial leader of the Austrian Freedom Party (FPÖ), to form a coalition government. Haider's FPÖ had attracted particular attention for its xenophobic election campaign and for sympathizing with authoritarian concepts.[68] This move raised serious concerns among the other EU Member States and led Portuguese Prime Minister António Guterres, who held the Council presidency, to issue the following press statement: 'The European Union is not only a single market ... It is also a Union based on a set of values ... All EU member states governments should clearly share those values ...'[69] This framing determined not only the reactions of the Member States and European institutions[70] but also the mandate of the three wise men who were tasked to assess the Austrian government's commitment to the common European values.[71]

At the same time, the European Convention drafting the EU Charter of Fundamental Rights made a huge leap in consolidating this value basis. Its preamble declares that the peoples of Europe are resolved to share a future 'based on common values' and further reaffirms that 'the Union is founded on the ... values of human dignity, freedom, equality and solidarity; it is based on the principles of democracy and the rule of law'. Jürgen Meyer, one of the driving forces behind the preamble's drafting, explained that the Charter's structure presents an interplay of values (in the respective Titles) and fundamental rights, which give more specific expression to each value.[72] This rhetoric might have been inspired by the Convention's mandate in the Tampere Presidency Conclusions[73] and by the

[67] For examples, see e.g. Jacques Chirac, 'Notre Europe' Speech at the German Bundestag (27 June 2000); Carlo Azeglio Ciampi, 'A proposito di una Costituzione europea' Speech at the University of Leipzig (6 July 2000); Joschka Fischer, Rede über die Zukunft Europas (Freiburg, 30 January 2001); Guy Verhofstadt, 'A vision of Europe' Speech at the European Policy Center (Brussels, 21 September 2001).

[68] For the whole context, see e.g. Konrad Lachmayer, 'Questioning the Basic Values. Austria and Jörg Haider' in Jakab and Kochenov (n 50) 436.

[69] António Guterres, Note to the press, Lisbon, 28th January 2000 (on file with the author).

[70] European Commission, Statement on Austria, IP/00/93; European Parliament, Resolution on the result of the legislative elections in Austria [2000] OJ C309/87, Rec. D.

[71] Martti Ahtisaari, Jochen Frowein, and Marcelino Oreja, Report on the Austrian Government's Commitment to the Common European Values (8 September 2000).

[72] Jürgen Meyer, 'Präambel' in Meyer and Sven Hölscheidt (eds), *Charta der Grundrechte der Europäischen Union* (5th edn, Nomos 2019) para 6. See further Justus Schönlau, 'New Values for Europe?' in Erik O. Eriksen et al. (eds), *The Chartering of Europe* (Nomos 2003) 112.

[73] Presidency Conclusions, Tampere European Council (15 and 16 October 1999) para 1: 'From its very beginning European integration has been firmly rooted in a shared commitment to freedom based

European Parliament, which welcomed the drafting of the Charter as a contribution 'to defining a collective patrimony of values and principles'.[74]

2. The Convention on the Future of Europe

The mandate for drafting a European constitution was issued under the impression of these two events. In the Laeken declaration, the Council explicitly asked the summoned Convention to debate the following question: 'What might the basic features of such a constitution be? The values which the Union cherishes . . . ?'[75] This was also stressed by the European Parliament. According to its rapporteur, Oliver Duhamel, both the Charter as well as the Austrian crisis confirmed that the Union is 'founded on a system of shared values . . . it is therefore only logical for them to be set in stone in a European Constitution and for this to be made a priority'.[76] Despite this explicit mandate, many proposals departed from Article 6(1) TEU-Amsterdam/Nice and continued to employ the notion of principles.[77] The Praesidium by contrast introduced the notion of values in its first draft of Article 2 (later Article I-2).[78] As the debate took place on the basis of this draft, the notion of values became somewhat the default position.

This did not go unnoticed. Some Convention members suggested modelling the wording more closely on Article 6 TEU-Nice.[79] Ernâni Lopes and Manuel Lobo Antunes, representatives of the Portuguese government, suggested that Article 2 should feature 'principles and not mere values' and added that 'only principles may be legally binding and . . . invoked before a Court'.[80] This critique found its expression also in the plenary debates. In the session of 27 February 2003, Ana de Palacio, representative of the Spanish government, called for more 'rigor jurídico'

on human rights, democratic institutions and the rule of law. These common values have proved necessary for securing peace and developing prosperity in the European Union.'

[74] European Parliament, Resolution on the drafting of a European Union Charter of Fundamental Rights [2000] OJ C377/329, V.1.

[75] Presidency Conclusions, Laeken European Council (14 and 15 December 2001) 24.

[76] Olivier Duhamel, Report on the constitutionalisation of the Treaties (12 October 2000), A5-0289/2000, Explanatory Statement, p 17. See also European Parliament, Resolution on the constitutionalisation of the Treaties [2001] OJ C197/186, M.1 and II.7.

[77] See Peter Hain, Constitutional Treaty of the European Union, CONV 345/1/02 REV 1, p 14; Robert Badinter, A European Constitution, CONV 317/02, Art. 2; Elena O. Paciotti, A draft constitution for the European Union, CONV 335/02, Art. 56; Freiburg Draft of a European Constitutional Treaty, CONV 495/03, Art. 2.

[78] Praesidium, Preliminary draft Constitutional Treaty, CONV 369/02, p 8; Praesidium, Draft of Articles 1 to 16 of the Constitutional Treaty, CONV 528/03, Annex I, Art. 2.

[79] Reactions to draft Articles 1 to 16 of the Constitutional Treaty, CONV 574/1/03 REV 1, p 17.

[80] To access the suggestions for amendment, see n 60. See also the suggestions by Meglena Kuneva (Gov. BG); Joschka Fischer (Gov. GER), Dominique de Villepin (Gov. FR) and Alberto Costa et al. (Parl. PORT). See further the early critique by Pierre-Yves Monjal, 'Le projet de traité établissant une Constitution pour l'Europe' RTDE (2004), 443, 454.

with regard to Article 2 and recalled that 'the ultimate outcome of the Convention is a legal text, justiciable before the courts'.[81]

Despite its continuing reliance on value semantics, it was never the Praesidium's intention to dilute the legal normativity of Article 2.[82] When presenting the initial draft, the Praesidium stressed the need for a short list of fundamental values that have 'a clear non-controversial legal basis so that the Member States can discern the obligations resulting therefrom'. Further, Article 2 was explicitly distinguished from the 'Union's "ethic" '.[83] After receiving a plethora of suggestions for expanding the list of Union values, Valéry Giscard d'Estaing, chairman of the Praesidium, felt the need to reiterate his call for restraint:

> on ne peut mettre dans cet article 2 que des valeurs qui sont définies juridiquement de façon suffisamment solide pour pouvoir permettre l'engagement de procédures contre les Etats membres qui ne les respecteraient pas. On ne peut donc pas mettre des valeurs indicatives ou respectables mais de caractère plus émotif que juridique... En effet, on ne voit pas bien une action juridique déclenchée vis-à-vis d'un Etat de l'Union à propos de la violation de telle ou telle de ces valeurs.[84]

Accordingly, the Praesidium was concerned to keep the first sentence of Article 2 concise and used the second sentence as a kind of collection basin.[85] Most of the seventy-two suggestions for amendments as well as the work of the responsible Working Group concentrated on the question of which values should be included in the provision.[86] These propositions were either accommodated within the short list already contained in Article 6(1) TEU-Nice or moved into the second sentence that was not supposed to feature legally enforceable obligations.[87] While this explains the second sentence's inflated and rather erratic character, it also

[81] Plenary Session of 27 February 2003, Debate on draft articles 1 to 3, 4-073—Palacio (Gov. ESP) (translation by the author). See also 4-018—Einem (Parl. AUT): 'wir treten dafür ein, lieber von Grundsätzen—principles—statt von Werten—valeurs—zu sprechen'; 4-083—Neli Kutskova (Gov. BG): 'we consider it preferable to keep the notion of principles typical of the acquis'.

[82] Giuliano Amato and Nicola Verola, 'Freedom, Democracy, the Rule of Law' in Giuliano Amato et al. (eds), *The History of the European Union: Constructing Utopia* (Hart 2019) 57, 60, 74; Clemens Ladenburger and Pierre Rabourdin, 'La constitutionnalisation des valeurs de l'Union. Commentaire sur la genèse des articles 2 et 7 du Traité sur l'Union européenne' RAE (2022), 231, 236.

[83] Praesidium, Draft of Articles 1 to 16 of the Constitutional Treaty, CONV 528/03, p 11.

[84] Plenary Session of 27 February 2003, 4-006—Giscard d'Estaing. See also Summary report on the plenary session—27 and 28 February 2003, CONV 601/03, para 5.

[85] From the Convention's secretariat, Alain Pilette and Etienne de Poncins, 'Valeurs, objectives et nature de l'Union' in Giuliano Amato et al. (eds), *Genèse et destinée de la constitution européenne* (Bruylant 2007) 287, 300 f; Ladenburger and Rabourdin (n 82) 239.

[86] For a comprehensive account, see Praesidium, Reactions to draft Articles 1 to 16 of the Constitutional Treaty, CONV 574/1/03 REV 1, pp 13–23. See also Final report of Working Group XI on Social Europe, CONV 516/1/03 REV1, pp 5–8.

[87] Pilette and de Poncins (n 85) 299 f. See also Laurence Burgorgue-Larsen, 'Article I-2' in Burgorgue-Larsen, Anne Levade, and Fabrice Picod (eds), *Traité établissant une Constitution pour l'Europe*, vol 1 (Bruylant 2007)paras 12, 15.

expresses the desire for continuity with Article 6(1) TEU-Nice.[88] Hence, we can state with some confidence that the values in the first sentence of Article 2 TEU (Article I-2 CT) were meant to reiterate the legal principles enshrined in Article 6(1) TEU-Nice.

D. Values as Normative Reinforcement?

In sum, there are no indications that the value semantics were meant to weaken the legal relevance of Article 2 TEU. Instead, Article 2 TEU was intended to codify the principles formerly enshrined in Article 6 TEU-Nice. Yet, this does not explain why the drafters chose this formulation. Here, we can only speculate. Some have suggested that the turn to values was even meant to *increase the provision's normative importance*.[89] The very notion of values might have been introduced to clearly distinguish the most important principles of the EU legal order from other non-foundational principles or objectives.[90] Sociological insights can support this claim. According to Niklas Luhmann, certain actions or choices can be justified by recourse to values. The values themselves, however, cannot be justified by referring to another level. They are—in the words of Nicolai Hartmann—'absolute, autonomous, and final instances'.[91] In this sense, the recourse to values relieves us from further justification and puts a 'halt on reflection'.[92] As will be discussed in the next chapter, it might have been exactly this expression of final authority that moved the drafters to address the EU's founding principles as values.

III. Justiciability

Acknowledging Article 2 TEU's legal normativity does not necessarily entail its justiciability. While there are no generally valid criteria for considering a provision of EU law justiciable, this is likely to be the case for all provisions that have direct

[88] See e.g. Kochenov (n 50) 9; Streinz (n 50) 11; Jean-Paul Jacqué, 'Art. 2 EUV' in Hans von der Groeben et al. (eds), *Europäisches Unionsrecht* (7th edn, Nomos 2015) para 1. See already Takis Tridimas, *The General Principles of EU Law* (2nd edn, OUP 2007) 15; Florence Benoît-Rohmer, 'Valeurs et droits fondamentaux dans la Constitution' RTDE 41 (2005), 261, 262; José Martín y Pérez de Nanclares, 'El proyecto de Constitución europea: reflexiones sobre los trabajos de la Convención' RDCE 7 (2003), 530, 539.

[89] See von Bogdandy (n 12) 717. See also Bertrand Mathieu, 'Le respect par l'Union européenne des valeurs fondamentales de l'ordre juridique national' *Cahiers du Conseil Constitutionnel* (18) (2005).

[90] See e.g. Susan Millns, 'Unraveling the Ties that Bind: National Constitutions in the Light of the Values, Principles and Objectives of the Constitution for Europe' in Jacques Ziller (ed.), *L'européanisation des droits constitutionnels à la lumière de la constitution pour l'Europe* (Harmattan 2003) 97, 100.

[91] Nicolai Hartmann, *Ethik* (4th edn, De Gruyter 1962) 19 ('absolute, autonome, letzte Instanz').

[92] Niklas Luhmann, *Gibt es in unserer Gesellschaft noch unverzichtbare Normen?* (C.F.Müller 1993) 18 f ('Reflexionsstopp').

effect. At first glance, three objections are likely to be raised against such an equation of justiciability and direct effect. First, one might object that direct effect is *too blurry in terms of conditions*. According to the standard textbook definition, a Treaty provision must be clear, precise, and unconditional.[93] Over time, however, the Court has applied these criteria in an increasingly relaxed manner.[94] Under this impression, many argued that direct effect should be assumed whenever EU law is capable of judicial application.[95] Some even suggest that direct effect should be presumed.[96] Admittedly, its conditions remain far from consistent. With regard Article 19(1)(2) TEU and Article 47 CFR, for instance, the Court noted that these provisions impose a 'clear and precise obligation as to the result to be achieved' and can therefore be regarded as directly effective.[97] At the same time, it considers Charter rights to be directly effective if the right at issue is 'sufficient in itself and does not need to be made more specific by provisions of EU or national law in order to confer on individuals a right'.[98] Even though the wording of each 'test' might vary, the conditions for direct effect nonetheless appears to revolve around one central criterion: specificity.

Second, direct effect might appear *too blurry in terms of consequences*.[99] Does it mean that EU law can be invoked by an individual before national courts?[100] Or that judges must set aside national law conflicting with EU law? Or does it simply mean that judges must take the respective EU law into consideration when interpreting and applying national law? The Court's recent case law seems to opt for the second path by linking direct effect to disapplication.[101] It differentiates

[93] See only Michal Bobek, 'The effects of EU Law in the national legal systems' in Catherine Barnard and Steve Peers (eds), *European Union Law* (3rd edn, OUP 2020) 143, 159.

[94] Robert Schütze, *European Constitutional Law* (3rd edn, OUP 2021) 159 ff; Ulrich Haltern, *Europarecht*, vol 2 (3rd edn, Mohr Siebeck 2017) paras 649 ff.

[95] Pierre Pescatore, 'The Doctrine of Direct Effect: An Infant Disease of Community Law (1983)' EL Rev 40 (2015), 135, 153. See also Daniele Gallo, 'Rethinking Direct Effect and Its Evolution: a Proposal' *European Law Open* 1 (2022), 576, 600 ff.; Robert Schütze, 'Direct and indirect effects of Union law' in Schütze and Takis Tridimas (eds), *Oxford Principles of EU Law* (OUP 2018) 265, 270; Bruno de Witte, 'Direct Effect, Primacy, and the Nature of the Legal Order' in Paul Craig and Gráinne de Búrca (eds), *The Evolution of EU Law* (3rd edn, OUP 2021)187, 192 ff.

[96] Christian Wohlfahrt, *Die Vermutung Unmittelbarer Wirkung des Unionsrechts* (Springer 2016).

[97] *Hungary v Parliament and Council* (n 10) para 162; Case C-487/19 *W.Ż.* [2021] EU:C:2021:798, para 159; Case C-824/18 *A.B.* [2021] EU:C:2021:153, paras 142–6.

[98] See e.g. Cases C-585, 624 and 625/18 *A.K.* [2019] EU:C:2019:982, para 162; Case C-556/17 *Torubarov* [2019] EU:C:2019:626, para 56; Case C-414/16 *Egenberger* [2018] EU:C:2018:257, para 78.

[99] David Edward, 'Direct Effect: Myth, Mess or Mystery' dUE (2002), 215, 219. More recently, Gallo (n 95) 578 ff. and Daniele Gallo, *L'efficacia diretta del diritto dell'Unione europea negli ordinamenti nazionali. Evoluzione di una dottrina ancora controversa* (Giuffrè 2018) 163 ff.

[100] Even as condition for direct effect, see Koen Lenaerts and Tim Corthaut, 'Of Birds and Hedges: The Role of Primacy in Invoking Norms of EU Law' EL Rev 31 (2006), 287, 311. Critical Gallo (n 95) 585 f.; Bobek (n 93); Olivier Peiffert, 'Un possible malentendu en droit de l'Union européenne: le droit subjectif comme condition de l'effet direct' RTDE 53 (2017), 665, 689 ff.

[101] Case C-573/17 *Popławski* [2019] EU:C:2019:530, para 62; Case C-282/19 *MIUR and Ufficio Scolastico Regionale per la Campania* [2022] EU:C:2022:3, para 120. See further Michael Dougan, 'Primacy and the remedy of disapplication' CML Rev 56 (2019), 1459, 1462 f; Dawid Miasik and Monika Szwarc, 'Primacy and direct effect—still together' CML Rev 58 (2021), 571.

between provisions of direct effect, which oblige judges to disapply conflicting national law, and other provisions, which must be taken into consideration by national courts. In this sense, the Court stressed that also a provision lacking direct effect 'places on national authorities an obligation to interpret national law in conformity with EU law'.[102]

This leads to the third objection. For some, the equation of justiciability and direct effect might be *too narrow* as it only focuses on a small part from the universe of judicial activity. Such an understanding seems to disregard the fact that constitutional principles, such as those enshrined in Article 2 TEU, have a strong interpretative function (see e.g. Chapter 5)—even if they lack direct effect. By implication, this chapter's focus on disapplication might appear too narrow. Instead, 'justiciability' could be perceived as a bundle of different judicial operations, ranging from taking a provision into consideration when interpreting the law to invoking it as an individual right before the courts.

Despite these legitimate objections, this section will concentrate on the direct effect of Article 2 TEU. For one, it remains unclear what level of specificity would suffice for EU law to be 'taken into consideration' when interpreting other provisions. Not any provision appears suitable for this exercise. Some basic degree of specificity will always be required. Further, directly effective provisions have the most far-reaching consequences in the Member States' legal orders. As such, assuming direct effect already incorporates—both in terms of specificity and consequences—other, less intrusive interpretative functions.

Against this backdrop, the following section will assess the direct effect and thus the justiciability of Article 2 TEU. At first glance, these values seem too indeterminate to fulfil the criterion of specificity. For that reason, a large part of EU legal scholarship questions or rejects the justiciability of Article 2 TEU.[103] As demonstrated in the previous chapter, this did not prevent the Court from engaging with that provision. The following section will briefly recall how the Court has coped with the indeterminacy of Article 2 TEU. Instead of applying Article 2 TEU in a freestanding manner, the Court has started to operationalize these values through more specific Treaty provisions (Section A). Yet, this approach does not answer the question whether Article 2 TEU could be developed—in the long-term—into a freestanding provision (Section B).

[102] *Popławski* (n 101) paras 72 ff; Case C-308/19 *Whiteland Import* [2021] EU:C:2021:47, para 30. The same applies—according to a well-established jurisprudence—also to directives lacking direct effect, see only *MIUR and Ufficio Scolastico Regionale per la Campania* (n 101) para 121; Case C-397/01 *Pfeiffer* [2004] EU:C:2004:584, paras 113 ff.

[103] Prominently Levits (n 6) 521. See also Bonelli (n 11) 47; Tom L. Boekestein, 'Making Do With What We Have: On the Interpretation and Enforcement of the EU's Founding Values' GLJ 23 (2022), 431, 437; Pekka Pohjankoski, 'Rule of Law with Leverage' CML Rev 58 (2021), 1341, 1345 f; Nina Wunderlich, 'Von der Wertegemeinschaft zur Verweigerungsunion?' EuR 54 (2019), 557, 575 f.

A. Current Practice: Operationalizing Article 2 TEU Through Specific Provisions

As indicated before, the Court considers a provision of EU law to be directly effective if it is 'sufficient in itself and does not need to be made more specific by provisions of EU or national law'.[104] Following this case law, Article 2 TEU could either be 'sufficient in itself' or in need of being rendered 'more specific' by other provisions. The latter approach can be construed in two ways. Article 2 TEU could be applied directly but informed by a more specific provision. Alternatively, one could apply a specific provision of EU law giving expression to a value enshrined in Article 2 TEU.

As analysed in the previous chapter, the Court opted for the latter approach. In *ASJP*, it stated that 'Article 19 TEU ... gives *concrete expression* to the value of the rule of law stated in Article 2'.[105] Article 2 TEU is thereby operationalized through a specific and directly applicable provision (here Article 19(1)(2) TEU). This reading was adopted early on by EU legal scholarship and publicly supported by several members of the Court (see Chapter 1, III). Ultimately, this operationalization consists of two interlocking systematic interpretations. While the specific provision is read in light of Article 2 TEU (which reinforces its importance), Article 2 TEU is read in light of the specific provision (which renders it more specific) (in detail Chapter 9, III).

As such, the Court remains on solid methodological ground.[106] Indeed, such an approach is not unprecedented. A parallel could be drawn to the case law on the objectives enshrined in Article 3 TEU. According to the Court, these objectives cannot impose legal obligations on the Member States or confer rights on individuals.[107] Instead, they 'are necessarily applied in combination with the respective chapters of the ... Treaty intended to give effect to those principles and objectives'.[108]

[104] See n 98.

[105] Case C-64/16 *Associação Sindical dos Juízes Portugueses* [2018] EU:C:2018:117, para 32 (emphasis added).

[106] For Christian Tomuschat the Court's solution is 'methodologically unassailable', see 'Kampf oder diplomatischer Ausgleich?' *Verfassungsblog* (15 July 2021). But see Richard Bellamy, Sandra Kröger, and Marta Lorimer, *Flexible Europe: Differentiated Integration, Fairness, and Democracy* (Bristol Univ. Press 2022) 79 ('weakly based judicial rulings'); Mark Dawson, 'How Can EU Law Respond to Populism?' OJLS 40 (2020), 183, 211 ('dubious legal grounding'). Sceptical, see also Peter M. Huber, 'Art. 2 EUV als Grundlage des Staaten- und Verfassungsverbundes der EU' *Alkotmánybírósági Szemle* (2020), 20, 21 ('technokratischer Trick'); Angelika Nußberger, 'Gefahr für das europäische Erbe' *Internationale Politik Special* (4) (2022), 4, 8 ('begründbar, aber gewagt').

[107] Case C-339/89 *Alsthom Atlantique* [1991] EU:C:1991:28, paras 8 f; Case C-260/89 *ERT* [1991] EU:C:1991:254, paras 39 f.

[108] Case C-484/08 *Caja de Ahorros* [2010] EU:C:2010:309, para 46. See also Case C-293/03 *My* [2004] EU:C:2004:821, para 29.

The Court's rulings on the rule of law conditionality seem to divide this operationalization into three steps. Article 2 TEU entails 'values which are given concrete expression in principles containing legally binding obligations for the Member States'.[109] As such, the process of thickening operates in a cascade from values (1) to principles (2) to legally binding obligations (3). The value of the rule of law, for instance, consists of a plethora of individual sub-principles, such as legality, legal certainty, effective judicial protection, or judicial independence.[110] The principle of judicial independence, as enshrined in Article 19(1)(2) TEU and Article 47 of the Charter, requires then further concretization into rules applicable to specific cases. Spelling out this 'fine print' in terms of judicial independence has occupied the Court during the past five years, especially when confronted with cases relating to the overhaul of the Polish judiciary.[111] Koen Lenaerts tried to illustrate this process of thickening with the an analogy to electricity:

> First, electricity is produced and transported at a high voltage—that high voltage can be compared to common values in their abstract form. Second, there are a whole range of transformers—those are the principles. Last, but not least, there is the supply of electricity at the voltage required for electrical appliances in a factory or in a household. Those are the rules.[112]

Eventually, the Court's approach could be extended to any specific provision of EU law that gives concrete expression to a value in Article 2 TEU.[113] This applies in particular to the Charter, which could be understood as a manifestation of several values. In fact, the Charter's structure presents an interplay of values, expressed in the Titles, and fundamental rights that give more specific expression to them.[114] Charter rights correspond to the values of human dignity (Title I), freedom (Title II), equality (Title III), democracy (e.g. Articles 10 to 12 and Title V), and the rule of law (Title VI). In this spirit, the Court has started to increasingly connect rights and values. In *La Quadrature du Net*, for instance, the Court emphasized the continuum between the freedom of expression under Article 11 CFR and the value

[109] *Hungary v Parliament and Council* (n 10) para 232; *Poland v Parliament and Council* (n 10) para 264.

[110] See e.g. the definition provided by Art. 2 lit. a Regulation 2020/2092 on a general regime of conditionality for the protection of the Union budget [2020] OJ L433I/1.

[111] On the evolving jurisprudence, see Dimitry Kochenov and Laurent Pech, *Respect for the Rule of Law in the Case Law of the European Court of Justice* (SIEPS 2021:3) or Rafael Bustos Gisbert, *Independencia judicial e integración Europea* (Tirant lo Blanch 2022).

[112] Koen Lenaerts, 'Concluding remarks' in CJEU (ed.), *EUnited in diversity: between common constitutional traditions and national identities* (Luxembourg 2022) 231.

[113] On the possible links, see e.g. the instructive charts by Boekestein (n 103) 451 and Markus Frischhut, *The Ethical Spirit of EU Values* (Springer 2022) 184, 190–193.

[114] On the drafter's awareness of this interplay, see Amato and Verola (n 82) 71; Meyer (n 72) para 6. On the intersections of values and Charter rights, see Fundamental Rights Agency, *Fundamental rights: challenges and achievements in 2013* (Luxembourg: EUR-OP, 2014) 10.

of democracy.[115] The judgment in *L.M.* established a similar nexus between the essence of Article 47 CFR and Article 2 TEU.[116] In its rulings on the rule of law conditionality regulation, the Court provided further possible connections between Article 2 TEU and other Treaty provisions. While Articles 6, 10 to 13, 15, 16, 20, 21, and 23 of the Charter 'define the scope' of the values of human dignity, freedom, equality, and respect for human rights, Articles 8, 10, 19(1), 153(1), and 157(1) TFEU substantiate the values of equality, non-discrimination, and equality between women and men.[117]

B. Future Outlook: Towards a Freestanding Application of Article 2 TEU?

This cautious approach hits two birds with one stone. It avoids the controversial, immediate recourse to Article 2 TEU and still translates EU values into justiciable obligations. However, the Court's strategy when introducing a new doctrine has often been that of a gradual development.[118] Usually, the CJEU operates step-by-step. It first introduces a new doctrine, albeit with qualifications or by refraining from applying it in the case. The Court can then assess the reactions and reaffirm, fine tune, restrict, or expand the doctrine. Such a strategy allows the Court to be experimental. In this sense, *ASJP* could present merely a first step. A further step could be the freestanding application of Article 2 TEU.

This could have several advantages, particularly in the face of illiberal developments in the Member States. For one, Article 2 TEU applies irrespective of the scope of other EU law and allows the Court to address upheavals in the Member States' internal constitutional structures (see Section IV). While an interpretation of specific provisions in light of Article 2 TEU might justify their extensive reading, this nexus still seems to curtail its overarching scope (but see Chapter 9, III). Moreover, addressing such developments under Article 2 TEU corresponds to the gravity of the situation. Instead of engaging in doctrinal contortions, invoking violations of Article 2 TEU seems to call a spade a spade.

[115] See Cases C-511, 512 and 520/18 *La Quadrature du Net* [2020] EU:C:2020:791, para 114. See also Case C-623/17 *Privacy International* [2020] EU:C:2020:790, para 62; Case C-140/20 *Commissioner of An Garda Síochána* [2022] EU:C:2022:258, para 43.

[116] See e.g. *Minister for Justice and Equality (Deficiencies in the system of justice)* (n 51) para 48; Cases C-354 and 412/20 PPU *Openbaar Ministerie* [2020] EU:C:2020:1033, para 39; Case C-791/19 *Commission v Poland (Régime disciplinaire des juges)* [2021] EU:C:2021:596, para 51. See also Cases C-83, 127, 195, 291 and 355/19 *Asociația "Forumul Judecătorilor din România"* [2020] EU:C:2020:746, Opinion of AG Bobek, para 225 noting that Art. 47 gives 'more precise expression' to the rule of law.

[117] *Hungary v Parliament and Council* (n 10) paras 157 f; *Poland v Parliament and Council* (n 10) paras 193 f.

[118] Davor Petrić, 'Game of Courts' ELJ 25 (2019), 273, 282 ff; Mark Dawson, 'How Does the European Court of Justice Reason?' ELJ 20 (2014) 423, 428; Trevor C. Hartley, *The Foundations of European Union Law* (4th edn, OUP 2014) 75.

Some understand the Court's judgment in *Repubblika* as a first step towards the self-standing application of Article 2 TEU (see also Chapter 1, IV.B).[119] The Commission's action against Hungarian violations of LGBTIQ rights (Case C-769/22) provides the Court with an opportunity to further move in this direction: for the first time the Commission invoked Article 2 TEU as a freestanding plea. Still, some members of the Court expressed scepticism in this regard. According to Advocate General Pikamäe, the value of the rule of law 'cannot be relied upon on its own.'[120] Similarly, Advocate General Tanchev argued that Article 2 TEU does not constitute a standalone yardstick for the assessment of national law.[121] Others seem more open to considering a freestanding application.[122] So far, the Court has been able to avoid this question. In the few procedures where it was asked whether courts can 'directly invoke and directly apply Article 2 TEU', it found the respective references inadmissible.[123]

Even though some scholars argue that the Court's recent case law has already put enough flesh on the bones of Article 2 TEU to render it justiciable,[124] this can hardly apply to all values. Certainly, Luxembourg is no stranger to interpreting and applying indeterminate provisions. Judge Pescatore even claimed that the justiciability of legal provisions depends less on their intrinsic qualities than on the goodwill of the deciding judges.[125] Yet there are limits to what the Luxembourg judges can do. To avoid being accused of inventing or fabricating praetorian principles, or even sliding into a European Freirechtsschule, the Court will have to employ 'recognised methodological principles' when transforming Article 2 TEU into a freestanding provision.[126] The following section will analyse two complementary, negative and positive, approaches for fleshing out the values enshrined in Article 2 TEU.[127]

1. Negative approach

Following a negative approach, Article 2 TEU would be interpreted as establishing merely red lines.[128] Instead of providing a full-blown, positive account of each

[119] See e.g. Ondrej Kadlec and David Kosar, 'Romanian Version of the Rule of Law Crisis Comes to the ECJ' CML Rev 59 (2022), 1823, 1837.

[120] Case C-457/18 *Slovenia v Croatia* [2019] EU:C:2019:1067, Opinion of AG Pikamäe, paras 132 f.

[121] Case C-824/18 *A.B.* [2020] EU:C:2020:1053, Opinion of AG Tanchev, para 35.

[122] See Rossi (n 7) 657; Marek Safjan, 'On Symmetry: In Search of an Appropriate Response to the Crisis of the Democratic State' dUE (2020), 673, 696.

[123] Case C-647/18 *Corporate Commercial Bank* [Order of 15 January 2020] EU:C:2020:13. See also Case C-505/13 *Yumer* [Order of 17 July 2014] EU:C:2014:2129, paras 21 ff and Case F-29/11 *BA v Commission* [2012] EU:F:2012:172, para 89.

[124] See e.g. Scheppele, Kochenov, and Grabowska-Moroz (n 9) 66–71; von Bogdandy (n 12) 727 f.

[125] Pescatore (n 95) 153.

[126] See e.g. BVerfG, Judgment of 5 May 2020, 2 BvR 859/15, *PSPP*, para 112.

[127] For an early systematization, see Frank Schorkopf, *Homogenität in der Europäischen Union* (Duncker&Humblot 2000) 79.

[128] Armin von Bogdandy et al., 'A Potential Constitutional Moment for the European Rule of Law' CML Rev 55 (2018), 983, 983. See also von Bogdandy (n 12) 705, 732 ff.

value, the Court would negatively determine what is not allowed. This negative approach could be coupled with a case-by-case reasoning. Rather than establishing positive standards on a jurisprudential meta-level,[129] which are stabilized to de-contextualized precedents, the Court could employ the technique of distinguishing practiced in common law[130] and concentrate on the specific case. Put differently, the CJEU would apply an 'I know it when I see it' approach.[131] A good point of reference for such an approach might be the ECtHR's jurisprudence on judicial independence protected under Article 6(1) ECHR. Due to the variety of systems for judicial appointments across Europe, the Convention does not impose any 'theoretical constitutional concepts' of separation of powers. Instead, '[t]he question is always whether, in a given case, the requirements of the Convention are met'.[132] The CJEU has already referred to this line of cases in its *A.K.* judgment.[133] Similarly, Advocate General Hogan noted in *Repubblika* that EU law does not impose 'any fixed, a priori form of institutional guarantees designed to ensure the independence of judges'. As long as the minimum of judicial independence is met, 'there is nothing in either Article 19 TEU or Article 47 of the Charter ... which seeks to impose uniformity in that regard.'[134]

However, leaving the precise content of EU values in abeyance has its limits. The proposed thin reasoning not only limits the decision's persuasiveness. It also reduces a judgment's predictability and puts legal certainty at risk. Eventually, it seems impossible to prevent the gradual sedimentation and consolidation of negative standards. Over time, the accumulation of negative standards will allow conclusions about the positive content of the values enshrined in Article 2 TEU to emerge. Even though the techniques proposed above may delay this process, the stabilization of standards on a meta level seems rather inescapable.

2. Positive approach

How then could Article 2 TEU be fleshed out in a positive manner? Abstractly, the content of a legal provision can be approached *deductively* or *inductively*. While a deductive strategy departs from general premises to reach a conclusion for a specific case, inductive reasoning operates in the reverse by extrapolating from specific cases to general rules. A deductive approach would allow the Court even greater

[129] On such meta-standards, see Mattias Wendel, 'Auf dem Weg zum Präjudizienrecht?' JöR 68 (2020), 113. From the German context, Oliver Lepsius, 'The Standard Setting Power' in Matthias Jestaedt et al. (eds), *The German Federal Constitutional Court: The Court Without Limits* (OUP 2020) 70.

[130] In detail, see Marc Jacob, *Precedents and Case-Based Reasoning in the European Court of Justice* (CUP 2014) 127 ff.

[131] In the same direction, Michel Waelbroeck and Peter Oliver, 'La Crise de l'État de Droit dans l'Union Européenne: Que Faire?' CDE 53 (2017), 299, 336.

[132] For recent expressions, see ECtHR, Judgment of 1 December 2020, App 26374/18 *Ástráðsson v Iceland*, paras 207, 215; Judgment of 7 May 2021, App 4907/18 *Xero Flor v Poland*, para 252.

[133] *A.K.* (n 104) para 130.

[134] Case C-896/19 *Repubblika* [2020] EU:C:2020:1055, Opinion of AG Hogan, paras 70, 76, 94.

leeway to flesh out the indeterminate values enshrined in Article 2 TEU and thus exacerbate the problem of lacking constraints. Thus, a deductive approach seems hardly advisable. Following an inductive approach, the Court could depart from sources *internal* or *external* to the EU legal order.[135]

The departure from internal sources strongly recalls the CJEU's approach outlined above. In this sense, the Court could derive the content of Article 2 TEU from those provisions of EU law that give concrete expression to these values. For instance, the value of 'respect for human rights' can be fleshed out by referring to absolute Charter rights or the essence under Article 52(1) CFR.[136] Whereas the former especially concerns human dignity (Article 1 CFR) or the prohibition of inhumane and degrading treatment (Article 4 CFR),[137] the essence of Charter rights is much more difficult to determine.[138] Although manifestations of this concept—such as essence or substance, *contenu essentiel* or *noyau dur*, *Wesens-* or *Kerngehalt*—can be found in practically all Member States,[139] the concept has remained relatively underexplored in the CJEU's jurisprudence. More recent case law, however, demonstrates a growing confidence to engage with the essence under Article 52(1) CFR (in detail Chapter 4, IV).

Further, the Court could rely on definitions provided by other EU institutions. To a certain extent, this would mean embracing the idea of 'interpretative pluralism'.[140] The Court would not monopolize the interpretation of Union values but share this responsibility with other EU institutions. For instance, the CJEU could consult definitions of the rule of law provided by the Commission[141] or Article 2(a) of Regulation 2020/2092 on a general regime of conditionality for the protection of the Union budget. Similarly, Advocate General Bobek argued that the benchmarks contained in the Cooperation and Verification Mechanism, a monitoring instrument for Romania and Bulgaria, 'specify the requirement of the rule of law of Article 2 TEU'.[142] Yet, the definitions provided in these materials reflect difficult

[135] Concerning the content of general principles, see Koen Lenaerts and José A. Gutiérrez-Fons, 'The Constitutional Allocation of Powers and General Principles of EU Law' CML Rev 47 (2010), 1629, 1655 ff.

[136] See already Armin von Bogdandy et al., 'Reverse Solange' CML Rev 49 (2012), 489, 509 ff.

[137] Fundamental Rights Agency, *Applying the Charter of Fundamental Rights of the European Union in law and policymaking at national level—Guidance* (Luxembourg: EUR-OP, 2020) 70 f.

[138] On the methodological uncertainties, see Orlando Scarcello, 'Preserving the "Essence" of Fundamental Rights under Article 52(1) of the Charter' EuConst 16 (2021), 647; Mark Dawson, Orla Lynskey, and Elise Muir, 'What Is the Added Value of the Concept of the "Essence" of EU Fundamental Rights?' GLJ 20 (2019), 763; Sébastien Van Drooghenbroeck and Cécilia Rizcallah, 'Art. 52' in Van Drooghenbroeck, Rizcallah, and Fabrice Picod (eds), *Charte des droits fondamentaux de l'Union européenne* (2nd edn, Bruylant 2020) 1249, 1254 ff.

[139] For a comparative overview, see Takis Tridimas and Giulia Gentile, 'The Essence of Rights: An Unreliable Boundary?' GLJ 20 (2019), 794.

[140] On this concept, see Gareth Davies, 'Does the Court of Justice Own the Treaties?' ELJ 24 (2018), 358, 362.

[141] See e.g. European Commission, 2021 Rule of Law Report COM(2021) 700 final, p 1; European Commission, A new EU Framework to strengthen the Rule of Law, COM(2014) 158 final, p 4.

[142] AG Bobek (n 116) para 151.

political compromises and offer rather unstructured accounts. As such, their practical usefulness seems rather limited.

Others have suggested reliance on the Copenhagen Criteria.[143] Under Article 49 TEU, a central requirement for accession to the EU is the adherence to the values enshrined in Article 2 TEU. The Copenhagen Criteria, already adopted in 1993,[144] have been understood as their concretization.[145] Unfortunately, these criteria seem a rather weak point of reference. Even though the Commission fleshed them out in considerable detail, they are spread over a vast array of documents—opinions on candidate countries, regular reports, strategy papers, or accession partnerships.[146] Dimitry Kochenov, for instance, criticized the 'complete lack of clarity about the standards that the candidate countries were expected to comply with.'[147] Indeed, it seems that these criteria have never been consolidated into one comprehensive list of conditions.[148] This makes them difficult to locate and apply.

In the second place, the Court could draw inspiration from external sources. To start with, Luxembourg could refer to standards developed by the Council of Europe. Its Strasbourg counterpart has been an important interlocutor for the Court of Justice since the very beginning of its fundamental rights jurisprudence.[149] The last decade, however, was marked by first cracks in this relationship. Since the Charter's entry into force, the Court has engaged much less with the Convention.[150] Even if Article 52(3) CFR expressly requires consistency among ECHR and Charter, this obligation finds its limits where it adversely affects the autonomy of Union law.[151] This emphasis on autonomy reached its peak with Opinion 2/13.[152] Against this backdrop, one could doubt whether the Convention is a likely point of reference for the interpretation of EU law, let alone its founding values. More recently, however, there were signs of rapprochement, especially in critical issues like mutual recognition.[153] Despite occasional frictions, both Courts should be perceived as standing in a relationship of mutual cross-fertilization.[154]

143 See especially Safjan (n 7) 559 and Hillion (n 12) 67–9.

144 Presidency Conclusions, Copenhagen European Council (21–22 June 1993), 7.A.iii).

145 Michael Rötting, *Das verfassungsrechtliche Beitrittsverfahren zur Europäischen Union* (Springer 2009) 167.

146 For a synthesis, see Ronald Janse, 'Is the European Commission a credible guardian of the values?' I-CON 17 (2019), 43, 62 f.

147 Dimitry Kochenov, *EU Enlargement and the Failure of Conditionality* (Kluwer 2008) 301.

148 A relatively general account is provided by European Commission, 2018 Communication on EU Enlargement Policy, COM(2018) 450 final, pp 2 ff and 2015 EU Enlargement Strategy, COM(2015) 611 final, pp 5 ff.

149 See only Case C-4/73 *Nold* [1974] EU:C:1974:51, para 13.

150 Jasper Krommendijk, 'The Use of ECtHR Case Law by the Court of Justice After Lisbon' MJ 22 (2015), 812, 832 f; Gráinne de Búrca, 'After the EU Charter of Fundamental Rights: The Court of Justice as a Human Rights Adjudicator?' MJ 20 (2013), 168, 174 ff. On possible reasons, see Síofra O'Leary, 'Courts, Charters and Conventions' *Irish Jurist* 56 (2016), 4, 21 ff.

151 Art. 52, Explanations relating to the Charter [2007] OJ C303/17, 33. This is regularly stressed, see e.g. Case C-481/19 *Consob* [2021] EU:C:2021:84, para 36.

152 See e.g. Daniel Halberstam, 'It's the Autonomy, Stupid!' GLJ 16 (2015), 105.

153 Koen Lenaerts, 'La Vie Après l'Avis' CML Rev 54 (2017), 805, 831–4. See also ECtHR, Judgment of 9 July 2019, App 8351/17 *Romeo Castaño v Belgium*, Concurring Opinion, Judge Spano.

154 See only Lucia S. Rossi, 'Autonomie constitutionnelle de l'Union européenne, droits fondamentaux et méthodes d'intégration des valeurs "externes"' (p 53) and Angelika Nußberger, 'La prise en compte

Some go even as far as describing them as two senates of *one* European constitutional jurisdiction.[155]

Of what help is the ECtHR's jurisprudence in order to flesh out the values in Article 2 TEU? Conceptually, the CJEU can take into consideration how the ECtHR has approached non-derogable rights (see Article 15(2) ECHR) and the core, substance, or essence of other rights.[156] Also substantively, both courts are faced with very similar challenges. A violation of Union values will not only be pursued before the Luxembourg court but is very likely to end up in Strasbourg too. Current threats to judicial independence, especially in Poland, illustrate this very well.[157] If the ECtHR ascertains, for instance, a flagrant denial of justice under Article 6(1) ECHR, this constitutes strong evidence that a red line under Article 2 TEU is equally crossed. Further, the CJEU could make use of the ECtHR's assessments of consensus among the Member States, especially when it relies on the common constitutional traditions. To justify an evolutionary interpretation of the Convention or to determine the margin of appreciation left to the Contracting States, the ECtHR establishes whether there is a consensus among them (in detail Chapter 13, III.B.2). Sometimes this amounts to comparative studies of considerable detail. In addition, the CJEU could consider opinions or studies by the Venice Commission.[158] While these documents are not legally binding, they express a common opinion of leading European experts. Some even perceive the Venice Commission as a constitutional 'standard-setter' in Europe.[159] They provide not only detailed assessments of the situation in individual Member States but also best practices and checklists.[160] The General Court has already referred to the Rule of Law Checklist to determine components of the value of the rule of law.[161]

de la Charte des droits fondamentaux de l'Union par la Cour européenne des droits de l'homme' (p 69) both in Anastasia Iliopoulou-Penot and Lamprini Xenou (eds), *La Charte des droits fondamentaux, source de renouveau constitutionnel européen?* (Bruylant 2020).

155 Armin von Bogdandy and Christoph Krenn, 'ECJ and ECtHR: Two Senates of Europe's Constitutional Jurisdiction' in Armin von Bogdandy et al. (eds), *The Max Planck Handbooks in European Public Law*, vol 4 (OUP 2023) § 118.

156 But see sceptical on the consistency of the ECtHR case law, Sébastien Van Drooghenbroeck and Cecilia Rizcallah, 'The ECHR and the Essence of Fundamental Rights' GLJ 20 (2019), 904.

157 See Robert Spano, 'The Rule of Law as the Lodestar of the European Convention on Human Rights: The Strasbourg Court and the Independence of the Judiciary' ELJ 27 (2021), 211, 223–6. See also Ben Smulders, 'Increasing Convergence between the European Court of Human Rights and the Court of Justice of the European Union in Their Recent Case Law on Judicial Independence: The Case of Irregular Judicial Appointments' CML Rev 59 (2022), 105; Rafael Bustos Gisbert, 'La influencia de los textos no vinculantes del Consejo de Europa sobre independencia judicial en el TEDH y en la UE' *Teoría y Realidad Constitucional* 47 (2021), 61.

158 As a 'useful source of information', see AG Bobek (n 116) para 170. See also AG Hogan (n 134) para 88.

159 Christoph Grabenwarter, 'Standard-Setting in the Spirit of the European Constitutional Heritage' in *Venice Commission. Thirty-year quest for democracy through law* (Juristförlaget 2020) 257.

160 See e.g. Venice Commission, Rule of law Checklist (18 March 2016), CDL-AD(2016)007; Parameters on the relationship between the parliamentary majority and the opposition in a democracy: A checklist (24 June 2019), CDL-AD(2019)015-e.

161 See e.g. Case T-290/17 *Stavytskyi v Council* [2019] EU:T:2019:37, para 61; Case T-240/16 *Klyuyev v Council* [2018] EU:T:2018:433, para 63.

The most likely point of departure are the common constitutional traditions of the Member States. According to Article 2 TEU, the founding values are common to the Member States. Thus, many argue for a structural link between common values and common constitutional traditions.[162] Highlighting this rootedness, Paul Kirchhof described Article 2 TEU as a 'constitutional tree rooted in a humus, which must be continually watered and recultivated if the tree is not to wither'.[163] Chapters 8 and 11 will demonstrate in detail that the constitutional identities of the Member States are a central point of reference for fleshing out the values of Article 2 TEU. Indeed, both encompass the same foundational principles: democracy, the rule of law, and the essence of fundamental rights.

Two objections are likely to be raised against this approach, namely that of *translatability* and *diversity*. Starting with translatability, critics might argue that the EU as an entity sui generis requires unprecedented thinking.[164] Some even perceive the quest for continuity with domestic concepts as an intellectual straitjacket.[165] While a truly unprecedented legal thinking seems neither possible nor desirable, domestic concepts can certainly not be transferred to the EU level in a blinkered fashion. This becomes especially apparent when considering the different manifestations of democracy at both levels. The second objection concerns the diversity among the Member States, which might render the identification of a common denominator difficult if not impossible. Take again the value of democracy. The Member States' legal orders and electoral systems cover almost any form of direct to representative democracy. It seems that the Court will have to choose. It can either go wide and stay shallow or go deep and stay narrow. The former approach implies reducing the content of the common values to a thin baseline that provides only little guidance in specific cases, whereas the latter might lead to more specific results but risk ignoring the Member States' autonomy and diversity.

Both objections are certainly not new. When developing general principles, the Court resolved these issues by employing an evaluative or critical legal comparison.[166] It does not draw on 'arithmetical "common denominators"' but

[162] Case C-62/14 *Gauweiler* [2015] EU:C:2015:7, Opinion of AG Cruz Villalón, para 61; Case C-127/07 *Société Arcelor Atlantique* [2008] EU:C:2008:292, Opinion of AG Maduro, para 16. From the plethora of contributions, see Levits (n 6) 518; Andreas Voßkuhle, *The Idea of the European Community of Values* (Bittner 2018) 110, 114; Koen Lenaerts, 'Die Werte der Europäischen Union in der Rechtsprechung des Gerichtshofs der Europäischen Union' EuGRZ 44 (2017), 639, 640. See already Vlad Constantinesco, 'L'intégration des principes constitutionnels nationaux dans le Traité: L'Article 6 § 1 du Traité sur l'Union' in Hélène Gaudin (ed.), *Droit constitutionnel, droit Communautaire. Vers un respect constitutionnel réciproque?* (Economica 2001) 299.

[163] Paul Kirchhof, 'Europa auf dem Weg zu einer Verfassung?' ZSE 1 (2003), 358, 369 (author's translation).

[164] On this issue, see Neil Walker, 'Postnational constitutionalism and the problem of translation' in Joseph H.H. Weiler and Marlene Wind (eds), *European Constitutionalism Beyond the State* (CUP 2003) 27. For a critical overview of these arguments, see Sebastian Unger, '"Präzedenzlos zu denken"?' in Armin Hatje et al. (eds), *Europarechtswissenschaft* (Nomos 2018) 191.

[165] Nico Krisch, *Beyond Constitutionalism* (OUP 2010) 68.

[166] Case C-550/07 P *Akzo Nobel Chemicals* [2010] EU:C:2010:229, Opinion of AG Kokott, para 94; Case C-282/10 *Dominguez* [2011] EU:C:2011:559, Opinion of AG Trstenjak, paras 94, 98. See already

chooses the solution that is best suited to the EU legal order.[167] With regard to Article 2 TEU, the CJEU could apply a similar approach.[168] By implication, this means that the common constitutional traditions are not only transferred to but also transformed at the Union level. The relationship between common values and common constitutional traditions is not one of unilateral rootedness but, rather, one of interaction (in detail Chapter 8, III.A). Admittedly, such an evaluative comparison reflects a deep but narrow analysis that might clash with the Member States' guaranteed autonomy and diversity. Yet, there are ways to remedy these concerns. Especially, Chapter 13 will explore judicial strategies to preserve the Member States' autonomy and diversity.

IV. Jurisdiction

Even if Article 2 TEU contains justiciable legal principles, it is not said that the Court of Justice has jurisdiction to assess and enforce them. Indeed, there is a strong case for the exclusivity of political procedures as far as the enforcement of EU values in the Member States is concerned. By implication, a substantive assessment of Article 2 TEU violations would be withdrawn from the CJEU's jurisdiction. This argument can be made in three degrees.

On a general level, the Court could be entirely excluded from reviewing Article 2 TEU compliance in the Member States. This might be justified by three considerations. To start with, one could argue that procedures before the Court, in particular Article 258 TFEU, are not capable of dealing with violations of Article 2 TEU (*argument from capacity*). Infringement procedures, so the argument goes, are designed to counter ordinary violations of EU law in the context of specific cases.[169] Article 258 TFEU mentions 'an obligation under the Treaties' in the singular, not large-scale deficiencies that would reach the thresholds of Article 2

Cases C-63 to 69/72 *Werhahn Hansamühle* [1973] EU:C:1973:95, Opinion of AG Roemer, p 1259 f; Case C-5/71 *Zuckerfabrik Schöppestedt* [1971] EU:C:1971:81, Opinion of AG Roemer, p 990.

[167] Case C-14/61 *Hoogovens v High Authority* [1962] EU:C:1962:19, Opinion of AG Lagrange, pp 283 f; Cases C-120 and 121/06 P *FIAMM* [2008] EU:C:2008:98, Opinion of AG Maduro, paras 55 f. For two competing visions of this exercise, see Koen Lenaerts, 'The constitutional traditions common to the Member States: the comparative law method' (pp 35, 39 f) and Peter M. Huber, 'The Constitutional Traditions Common to the Member States—Identification and Concretisation' (pp 55, 69 f) both in CJEU (ed.), *EUnited in diversity: between common constitutional traditions and national identities* (Luxembourg 2022).

[168] Christian Calliess, 'Art. 2 EUV' in Calliess and Matthias Ruffert (eds), *EUV/AEUV* (6th edn, C.H.Beck 2022) para 14.

[169] See e.g. Hermann-Josef Blanke, 'Article 7' in Blanke and Mangiameli (n 8) paras 7 ff. See also Claas F. Germelmann, 'Alternativen zum Rechtsstaatsverfahren nach Art. 7 EUV?' DÖV (2021), 193, 196; Alexandre Richard, *Procédure en manquement d'État et protection des droits fondamentaux dans l'Union européenne* (Bruylant 2021) 303 ff.

TEU.[170] Second, Article 7 TEU read together with Article 269 TFEU could be lex specialis for the enforcement of EU values, thus barring parallel procedures under Article 258 or 267 TFEU.[171] This boils down to an *argument from circumvention*. On the one hand, Article 7 TEU contains very high procedural and substantive thresholds. These demanding requirements have been put in place for a specific reason. As Article 2 TEU has an unrestricted scope of application covering any Member State act (see Section IV.B), it seems reasonable to make its enforcement subject to limitations. If the Court could reach the same conclusion in judicial proceedings, these high thresholds would be circumvented. On the other hand, Article 269 TFEU seems to limit the Court's review of acts taken under Article 7 TEU to procedural issues. If the Court cannot review the substantive outcome of this procedure, it should be excluded from reaching the same conclusion through different channels. Third, the Court could lack the legitimacy to unilaterally define and enforce the values enshrined in Article 2 TEU *(argument from legitimacy)*. Egils Levits argued that due to their high degree of abstraction and the countless ways of balancing them, these values are withdrawn from the Court's jurisdiction: 'Les valeurs fondamentales ... ne sauraitent être décrétée par les tribunaux.'[172] Determining violations of Union values is further a highly political exercise. Dragging the CJEU into such heated conflicts might politicize the proceedings and damage its credibility as a neutral arbiter.[173]

On a narrower level, the exclusivity of political procedures could be limited to issues *beyond the scope of EU law*. Lenaerts and Gutiérrez-Fons stressed that outside the scope of EU law the Treaties have entrusted the EU's political institutions with monitoring Article 2 TEU compliance. By pointing to Article 269 TFEU, they argue that in such situations the Court's role is limited to reviewing the procedural requirements of Article 7 TEU.[174] Moreover, such limitations might be an inbuilt feature of CJEU proceedings. Confronted with a potential violation of Article 2 TEU beyond the scope of other EU law, Advocate General Pikamäe noted that infringement procedures are 'linked to the fields that fall within the scope of EU law'.[175] This leads to a distinction between situations within and outside the scope of EU law. In the former, the Court could adjudicate violations of Article 2 TEU, whereas in the latter there is only Article 7 TEU and a procedural judicial

[170] On the high thresholds that should apply for invoking Art. 2 TEU, see Chapters 4, IV and 13, III.A.

[171] See e.g. Editorial, 'Safeguarding EU Values in the Member States' CML Rev 52 (2015), 619, 626 f. See also Bonelli (n 11) 47 f; Van Elsuwege and Gremmelprez (n 11) 9; Bernd Martenczuk, 'Art. 7 EUV und der Rechtsstaatsrahmen als Instrument der Wahrung der Grundwerte der Union' in Stefan Kadelbach (ed.), *Verfassungskrisen in der Europäischen Union* (Nomos 2018) 41, 45.

[172] Levits (n 6) 521.

[173] See Martenczuk (n 171) 45; Michael Blauberger and R. Daniel Kelemen, 'Can Courts Rescue National Democracy?' JEPP 24 (2017), 321, 331; Christoph Möllers and Linda Schneider, *Demokratiesicherung in der Europäischen Union* (Mohr Siebeck 2018) 107, 147.

[174] Koen Lenaerts and José A. Gutiérrez-Fons, 'Epilogue on EU Citizenship: Hopes and Fears?' in Dimitry Kochenov (ed.), *EU Citizenship and Federalism* (CUP 2017) 751, 774.

[175] AG Pikamäe (n 120) para 133.

review.[176] In this spirit, the Commission stated that infringement procedures can be launched only in case of

> a breach of a specific provision of EU law ... There are situations of concern which fall outside the scope of EU law and therefore cannot be considered as a breach of obligations under the Treaties ... For these situations, the ... mechanisms provided for in Article 7 TEU may apply.[177]

Recently, the European Parliament supported this view by stating that 'in contrast to Article 258 of the Treaty on the Functioning of the European Union, the scope of Article 7 of the Treaty on European Union is not confined to areas covered by Union law'.[178]

The Council Legal Service even went one step further. In its view, the enforcement of EU values beyond Article 7 TEU is excluded not only in a situation that exceeds the scope of EU law but also 'in a context that is not related to a *specific material competence*' of the EU. Apart from the procedures foreseen in Article 7 TEU, violations of EU values 'may be invoked against a Member State only when it acts in a subject matter for which the Union has competence.'[179]

These statements explain why German Chancellor Olaf Scholz suggested in 2022 the creation of 'a *new* way to launch infringement proceedings when there are breaches of what unites us at the very core: our fundamental values'.[180] However, there are strong arguments against these three lines of argumentation. The following Section will demonstrate that as far as the enforcement of Article 2 TEU compliance is concerned, there is neither a general exclusivity of political procedures (Section A) nor a partial exclusivity in situations beyond the scope of EU law or competences (Section B).

[176] See e.g. Leonard Besselink, 'The Bite, the Bark, and the Howl' in Jakab and Kochenov (n 50) 128, 141 f; Oliver Mader, 'Enforcement of EU Values as a Political Endeavour' HJRL 11 (2019), 133, 159, 162.

[177] European Commission, A new EU Framework to strengthen the Rule of Law (n 141) 5. See also Emmanuel Crabit, 'Upholding the rule of law for the future of Europe' in Wolfgang Heusel and Jean-Philippe Rageade (eds), *The Authority of EU Law* (Springer 2019) 261, 262.

[178] European Parliament, Resolution on the proposal for a Council decision on the determination of a clear risk of a serious breach by the Republic of Poland of the rule of law (17 September 2020), 2017/0360R(NLE), Rec. B (emphasis added).

[179] Council, Opinion of the Legal Service: Commission's Communication on a New EU Framework to Strengthen the Rule of Law: Compatibility with the Treaties, 10296/14, paras 16 f (emphasis added).

[180] Speech by Federal Chancellor Olaf Scholz at the Charles University in Prague (29 August 2022) (emphasis added). See also Viviane Reding, The EU and the Rule of Law—What next? (Brussels, 4 September 2013) (suggesting 'a new specific procedure to enforce ... Article 2 TEU against Member States by means of an infringement procedure') and the draft report by the LIBE Committee on establishing an EU mechanism on democracy, the rule of law and fundamental rights (5 April 2016), 2015/2254(INL) para 9 ('any future Treaty revision should include the following changes: Article 2 TEU to become a legal base for infringement procedures ... Enabling national courts under Article 2 TEU to bring before the CJEU actions on the legality of Member States' actions ...').

A. No General Exclusivity of Political Procedures

As noted above, assuming a general exclusivity of political procedures is essentially based on arguments from capacity, circumvention, and legitimacy. The argument from legitimacy touches upon complex institutional and substantive issues that cannot be assessed in this brief section and which will be discussed in Chapters 9, 12 and 13. The following section will concentrate on refuting the arguments from capacity and circumvention. Starting with the former, it is simply not true that infringement procedures (or preliminary rulings for that matter) are limited to ordinary and individual violations in specific cases. As Kim Scheppele convincingly demonstrated, there are no reasons why the Commission should not address structural issues beyond individualized breaches of EU law.[181] Neither the bundling of several infringements nor the addressing of general and persistent violations is revolutionary.[182] Moreover, the way in which the allegations are structured and framed is at the Commission's discretion.[183] Besides, the Court has already examined—also in preliminary rulings—the existence of systemic deficiencies in the Member States.[184]

Secondly, the arguments from circumvention can hardly convince. The high procedural and substantive thresholds of Article 7 TEU cannot justify the exclusion of parallel procedures before the Court. Both have completely different consequences.[185] Article 7 TEU may lead to the suspension of Member States' rights. The Court's sanctioning powers, by contrast, are limited to penalty payments under Article 260 TFEU. Thus, the judicial and political procedures are not identical. The high thresholds under Article 7 TEU are still justified by the much more severe legal consequences.

Further, two considerations advocate against the exclusionary nature of Article 269 TFEU. On the one hand, the Court has a general jurisdiction to interpret and assess the 'law' (Article 19(1)(1) TEU). This includes Union law in all its shapes, forms, and manifestations. While the former Treaties have kept the EU's foundational principles out of the Court's reach,[186] the Lisbon Treaty does not contain

[181] Kim L. Scheppele, 'Enforcing the Basic Principles of EU Law through Systemic Infringement Actions' in Closa and Kochenov (n 8) 105. See also Matthias Schmidt and Piotr Bogdanowicz, 'The Infringement Procedure in the Rule of Law Crisis' CML Rev 55 (2018), 1061, 1069 ff.

[182] See e.g. Luca Prete, *Infringement Proceedings in EU Law* (Kluwer 2017) 54 ff; Koen Lenaerts, Ignace Maselis, and Kathleen Gutman, *EU Procedural Law* (OUP 2014) paras 5.11 ff.

[183] See e.g. Luca Prete and Ben Smulders, 'The Coming of Age of Infringement Proceedings' CML Rev 47 (2010), 9, 14.

[184] See e.g. Cases C-411 and 493/10 *N.S.* [2011] EU:C:2011:865, paras 86, 89; Cases C-404 and 659/15 PPU *Aranyosi and Căldăraru* [2016] EU:C:2016:198, para 89; Case C-220/18 PPU *Generalstaatsanwaltschaft* [2018] EU:C:2018:589, para 60.

[185] Case C-619/18 *Commission v Poland (Independence of the Supreme Court)* [2019] EU:C:2019:325, Opinion of AG Tanchev, para 50. See also Vassilios Skouris, *Demokratie und Rechtsstaat* (C.H.Beck 2018) 50 f; Rossi (n 7) 655 f; Schmidt and Bogdanowicz (n 181) 1061, 1072 f.

[186] Under Art. 46(d) TEU-Nice the CJEU had only jurisdiction over then Art. 6(2) TEU but not the 'principles' in Art. 6(1). Nevertheless, the Court referred to them, see Chapter 1, II.B.

any comparable limitation with regard to Article 2 TEU. Instead, the CJEU enjoys 'jurisdiction by default'.[187] As Article 269 TFEU constitutes an exception to this general jurisdiction, it must be interpreted narrowly.[188] On the other hand, Advocate General Bobek made a compelling argument that Article 269 TFEU is not excluding but rather establishes the Court's jurisdiction.[189] The determinations under Article 7(1) and (2) TEU could easily constitute preparatory acts excluded from actions for annulment.[190] The function of Article 269 TFEU is to establish the Court's jurisdiction over these determinations, while decisions to impose sanctions under Article 7(3) TEU remain subject to full review under Article 263 TFEU.[191] This explains why the provision expressly refers only to 'determinations' and not to 'decisions'. Article 269 TFEU is further placed among the provisions conferring jurisdiction, not among the exceptions under Articles 274 to 276 TFEU, and uses the language of a positive attribution ('the Court ... shall have jurisdiction').[192] Despite these compelling arguments, the Court referred to Article 269 TFEU as a 'limitation' on its general jurisdiction.[193] Whether this implies a rejection of Bobek's reasoning remains to be seen.

B. No Partial Exclusivity of Political Procedures Beyond the Scope of EU Law

Shortly before Amsterdam, Advocate General La Pergola noted that '[t]he Community legal order is not all-embracing'.[194] Provisions overarching the entire system of EU and Member States were missing.[195] Article 6(1) TEU-Amsterdam fundamentally changed this configuration by reaching across the entirety of the EU and the Member States' legal orders.[196] This applies to Article 2 TEU as well. During the Convention's drafting process, the relatively short list of values was justified with the consideration that Article 7 TEU and thus the obligations under Article 2 TEU apply 'even if the breach took place in the field of the Member State's

[187] Case C-650/18 *Hungary v Parliament* [2020] EU:C:2020:985, Opinion of AG Bobek, para 35.
[188] *Hungary v Parliament* (n 52) para 31.
[189] AG Bobek (n 187) para 44.
[190] On the requirements, see e.g. Lenaerts, Maselis, and Gutman (n 182) paras 7.26–7.29.
[191] AG Bobek (n 187) para 64 ff, 73, 99.
[192] ibid paras 58 f.
[193] *Hungary v Parliament* (n 52) para 31.
[194] Case C-299/95 *Kremzow* [1997] EU:C:1997:58, Opinion of AG La Pergola, para 7.
[195] Armin von Bogdandy, 'The European Union as a Supranational Federation' CJEL 6 (2000), 27, 30.
[196] See e.g. Ingolf Pernice, 'Multilevel Constitutionalism and the Treaty of Amsterdam' CML Rev 36 (1999), 703, 726; Hélène Gaudin, 'Amsterdam: l'échec de la hiérarchie des normes?' RTDE 35 (1999), 1, 10 f. See further European Commission, Communication on Art. 7 of the Treaty on European Union COM(2003) 606 final, p 5 arguing that Art. 7 TEU (and thus implicitly Art. 2 TEU) is 'applicable in all areas of activity of the Member State'.

autonomous action (not affected by Union law)'.[197] Today, it seems uncontroversial that the values enshrined in Article 2 TEU are restricted neither to the scope of other EU law nor to the areas of competences transferred to the EU.[198] The same cannot be said about their enforcement. As noted above, many argue that Article 7 TEU is the only procedure for enforcing EU values beyond the *scope of other EU law* or *EU competences*. The following section seeks to refute these arguments.

Concerning the scope of EU law, three observations may challenge this view. In the first place, it seems odd to dissociate the scope of Article 2 TEU from the scope of EU law in general. Article 2 TEU is a provision of EU law containing obligations for the Member States. This fact should suffice to bring within the scope of EU law the behaviour of Member States not covered by other EU law. In other words, Article 2 TEU itself demarcates the scope of EU law. Any other view would necessitate a distinction between two scopes of EU law—one broad (Article 2 TEU), the other narrow (the rest).[199] Such a distinction, however, seems artificial and difficult to maintain.

Second, Article 2 TEU's unrestricted scope of application does not categorically distinguish it from other provisions of EU law. While there is only one scope of EU law, there can be different scopes of application for individual provisions.[200] Some provisions have an accessory scope such as Charter rights (Article 51(1) CFR) or Article 19(1)(2) TEU ('fields covered by EU law'). Other provisions are freestanding but nonetheless limited ratione tempore, personae, and materiae. Article 2 TEU applies irrespective of such limitations. Therefore, one could argue that it is categorically different from other EU law. Yet, many assert that the Court has gradually levelled these limitations. As it would go far beyond the chapter's scope to substantiate this bold claim,[201] cross-border requirements might provide a selective but illustrative example. It is established case law that the provisions on free movement do not apply to situations 'confined in all respects within a single member State'.[202] Nevertheless, the CJEU reduced the respective cross-border requirements to a mere potentiality test.[203] Similar approaches can be found in the

[197] Praesidium, Draft of Articles 1 to 16 of the Constitutional Treaty, CONV 528/03, p 11. See also Pilette and de Poncins (n 85) 300.

[198] In rare agreement, European Commission, A new EU Framework to strengthen the Rule of Law (n 141) 5; Council, Opinion of the Legal Service (n 179) para 17. See e.g. Marcus Klamert and Dimitry Kochenov, 'Article 2 TEU' in Manuel Kellerbauer et al. (eds), *The Treaties and the Charter of Fundamental Rights—A Commentary* (2nd edn, OUP 2023) para 5; Hilf and Schorkopf (n 49) para 18.

[199] In this sense, see e.g. Besselink (n 176) 128, 143.

[200] See e.g. Hélène Gaudin, 'Diversité et évolution des champs d'application en droit communautaire' RAE (2003–2004), 7; Clemens Latzel, 'Die Anwendungsbereiche des Unionsrechts' EuZW 26 (2015), 658.

[201] On this, see Amedeo Arena, 'The Wall Around EU Fundamental Freedoms: the Purely Internal Rule at the Forty-Year Mark' YEL 38 (2019), 153, 175 ff; André Lippert, *Der grenzüberschreitende Sachverhalt im Unionsrecht* (Mohr Siebeck 2013) 34 ff, 44 ff.

[202] See e.g. Case C-261/20 *Thelen Technopark Berlin* [2022] EU:C:2022:33, para 50.

[203] See e.g. Case C-293/02 *Jersey Produce Marketing* [2005] EU:C:2005:664, para 65; Case C-448/98 *Guimont* [2000] EU:C:2000:663, paras 20 f; Cases C-321 to 324/94 *Pistre* [1997] EU:C:1997:229, para 45.

context of the freedom of establishment,[204] the freedom to provide services[205] and especially the freedom of movement. This development reached its peak in *Ruiz Zambrano*, probably the most open and far-reaching waiver of cross-border requirements.[206] Against this backdrop, many have claimed a significant decrease in constellations that can be considered beyond the scope of fundamental freedoms.[207] The decreased importance of limitations in scope, however, largely levels the difference between Article 2 TEU and the free movement provisions.

Even if we distinguish between Article 2 TEU and the scope of other EU law, this does not necessarily mean that the Court has no jurisdiction beyond the latter. Admittedly, the CJEU stated in the context of preliminary references that 'in a purely internal situation the Court does not, in principle, have jurisdiction to rule on the question referred by the national court'.[208] In principle. Indeed, there is a growing jurisprudence assuming jurisdiction even in cases where the facts of the main proceedings do not fall within the scope of EU law.[209] The CJEU requires only a 'link' or 'connecting factor' between the subject of the dispute in the main proceedings and the provisions of EU law whose interpretation is sought—even when this link is extremely thin.[210] This jurisprudence has been explicitly extended to references concerning Article 19(1)(2) TEU.[211] As such, it is not inconceivable that preliminary references pertaining to obligations stemming from Article 2 TEU would have to be deemed admissible, even in situations beyond the scope of other EU law.

Similarly flawed is the second claim, namely that the CJEU can enforce Article 2 TEU values only when the EU has a competence in the respective field. As noted before, the Council Legal Service argued in 2014 that—except for Article 7 TEU—violations of EU values may be invoked against a Member State 'only when it acts in a subject matter for which the Union has competence based on specific competence-setting Treaty provisions'.[212] This conception was taken up by the

[204] See e.g. Case C-367/12 *Sokoll-Seebacher* [2014] EU:C:2014:68, para 10; Cases C-159 to 161/12 *Venturini* [2013] EU:C:2013:791, paras 25 f.

[205] See e.g. Case C-98/14 *Berlington Hungary* [2015] EU:C:2015:386, para 27; Case C-380/05 *Centro Europa 7* [2008] EU:C:2008:59, paras 66 ff.

[206] Case C-34/09 *Ruiz Zambrano* [2011] EU:C:2011:124. See e.g. Koen Lenaerts, '"Civis europaeus sum"' in Pascal Cardonnel et al. (eds), *Constitutionalising the EU Judicial System* (Hart 2012) 213.

[207] See e.g. Sara Iglesias Sánchez, 'Purely Internal Situations and the Limits of EU Law: A Consolidated Case Law or a Notion to Be Abandoned?' EuConst 14 (2018), 7; Pedro Caro de Sousa, 'Catch Me if You Can? The Market Freedoms' Ever-expanding Outer Limits' EJLS 4 (2011), 162; Niamh Nic Shuibhne, 'Free Movement of Persons and the Wholly Internal Rule: Time to Move On?' CML Rev 39 (2002), 731.

[208] See e.g. Case C-203/14 *Consorci Sanitari del Maresme* [2015] EU:C:2015:664, para 29.

[209] See only Case C-268/15 *Ullens de Schooten* [2016] EU:C:2016:874, paras 50–53. See also Jasper Krommendijk, 'Wide Open and Unguarded Stand Our Gates: The CJEU and References for a Preliminary Ruling in Purely Internal Situations' GLJ 18 (2017), 1359; Édouard Dubout, 'Voyage en eaux troubles: vers une épuration des situations "purement" internes' RAE (2016), 679.

[210] See e.g. *Ullens de Schooten* (n 209) paras 55–7; Case C-665/18 *Pólus Vegas* [2019] EU:C:2019:477, para 21; Case C-311/19 *BONVER WIN* [2020] EU:C:2020:981, para 23.

[211] See e.g. Case C-558/18 *Miasto Łowicz* [2020] EU:C:2020:234, para 48.

[212] Council Legal Service (n 179) paras 16 f.

captured Polish Constitutional Tribunal in its decision declaring the CJEU's jurisprudence based on Articles 19(1)(2) and 2 TEU incompatible with the Polish constitution. According to the Tribunal, Member State obligations under Union law can be enforced by the institutions, including the CJEU, only within the scope of EU competences.[213]

Such a condition, however, cannot be derived from the Treaties. There is no immediate connection between the Member States' obligations under EU law and the competences of EU institutions.[214] Any other view would require a considerable shift in the Court's jurisprudence. The Court would need to conduct a two-step assessment each time it reviews a Member State's compliance with EU law. Only after confirming that the Union has a general competence in the subject area under Articles 3, 4, or 6 TFEU could the Court proceed to assessing the Member State's compliance. Such a caveat cannot be derived from the Treaties. The Court has a general jurisdiction under Article 19(1)(1) TEU to ensure that 'the law is observed'. Further, Article 258 TFEU unequivocally states that the Court shall assess whether a Member State has failed to fulfil *any* 'obligation under the Treaties'. Accordingly, Union competences can delimit neither the obligations flowing from EU law nor the Court's jurisdiction.

This has been confirmed by the Court in the recent line of cases concerning the Polish judiciary. Although the organization of the judiciary in the Member States falls within the competence of the Member States, 'the fact remains that, *when exercising that competence*, the Member States are required to comply with their obligations deriving from EU law'.[215] It should be noted that this position is not limited to the organization of the Member States' judiciary, but has been applied consistently to most areas of sensitive Member State competences.[216] This includes matters such as nationality,[217] criminal law,[218] extradition,[219] direct taxation,[220]

[213] See the press release accompanying the Judgment of 7 October 2021, K 3/21, paras 18 f.

[214] Serena Menzione, 'The Organization of the National Judiciary: A Competence of the Member States within the Scope of EU Law' *Annuaire de droit de l'Union européenne* (2020), 361, 375.

[215] *A.K.* (n 104) para 75 (emphasis added). See further Case C-619/18 *Commission v Poland (Independence of the Supreme Court)* [2019] EU:C:2019:531, para 52; Case C-896/19 *Repubblika* [2021] EU:C:2021:311, para 48; Case C-487/19 *W.Ż. (Chamber of Extraordinary Control and Public Affairs of the Supreme Court—Appointment)* [2021] EU:C:2021:798, paras 74, 88.

[216] Loic Azoulai, 'The "Retained Powers" Formula in the Case Law of the European Court of Justice' EJLS 4 (2011), 192. See also Koen Lenaerts, 'L'encadrement par le droit de l'Union européenne des compétences des États membres' in *Mélanges en l'honneur de Jean Paul Jacqué* (Dalloz 2010) 421; Lena Boucon, 'EU Law and Retained Powers of Member States' in Loïc Azoulai (ed.), *The Question of Competence in the European Union* (OUP 2014) 168; Maria E. Bartoloni, *Ambito d'applicazione del diritto dell'Unione europea e ordinamenti nazionali* (ESI 2018) 119 ff.

[217] See e,g. Case C-221/17 *Tjebbes* [2019] EU:C:2019:189, para 32; Case C-135/08 *Rottmann* [2010] EU:C:2010:104, para 41.

[218] See e.g. Cases C-202 and 238/18 *Rimšēvičs* [2019] EU:C: 2019:139, para 57; Case C-203/80, *Casati* [1981] EU:C:1981:261, para 27.

[219] Case C-398/19 *Generalstaatsanwaltschaft Berlin* [2020] EU:C: 2020:1032, para 28; Case C-182/15 *Petruhhin* [2016] EU:C:2016:630, para 30.

[220] See e.g. Case C-35/19 *Belgian State* [2019] EU:C:2019:894, para 31; Case C-279/93 *Schumacker* [1995] EU:C:1995:31, para 21.

surnames,[221] social security,[222] civil status,[223] or the organization of education systems.[224] Against this backdrop, the applicability of EU law—including its enforcement by the Court of Justice—appears to be indifferent to the attribution of competences.[225] If this is the case, then it is simply not comprehensible why Article 2 TEU should be treated differently than other Treaty obligations.

221 See e.g. Case C-541/15 *Freitag* [2017] EU:C:2017:432, para 33; Case C-353/06 *Grunkin and Paul* [2008] EU:C:2008:559, para 16.

222 See e.g. Case C-179/18 *Rohart* [2019] EU:C:2019:111, para 14; Case C-158/96 *Kohll* [1998] EU:C:1998:171, paras 18, 19.

223 See e.g. Case C-673/16 *Coman* [2018] EU:C:2018:385, paras 37 f; Case C-267/06 *Maruko* [2008] EU:C:2008:179, para 59.

224 Case C-73/08 *Bressol* [2010] EU:C:2010:181, para 28; Case C-318/05 *Commission v Germany* [2007] EU:C:2007:495, para 86.

225 Bruno de Witte, 'Exclusive Member State Competences—Is There Such a Thing?' in Sacha Garben and Inge Govaere (eds), *The Division of Competences between the EU and the Member States* (Hart 2017) 59, 62.

3
Theory
The Dual Character of Article 2 TEU

I. Introduction

The previous chapters traced the judicial mobilization of Article 2 TEU and sought to establish its doctrinal soundness. The following chapter will develop a conceptual framework for this emerging jurisprudence that allows us to draw a conclusion not on *whether* but on *how* Article 2 TEU could be applied by the Court. The first section will set out two basic premises on which the next parts are built, namely a constitutional and a multidimensional approach to EU law (Section II). The latter approach boils down to a distinction between two dimensions with different scopes. While the first, narrower dimension is limited to the EU legal order (the EU dimension), the second one comprises the 'common whole' of EU and Member States (the 'Verbund' dimension). This chapter suggests that Article 2 TEU assumes a central, yet distinct role in these two contexts (Section III). In its EU dimension, it should be understood as a *constitutional core* of the EU legal order. Within the Verbund, Article 2 TEU should be reduced to a *constitutional frame* that secures a minimum of homogeneity between the EU and the Member States' legal orders. Insights from constitutional theory can provide a toolkit to better grasp this distinction. In fact, Article 2 TEU seems to draw on two distinct constitutional traditions at once. In its EU dimension, it tends towards a constitutive, thick form of constitutionalism. In the Verbund, it corresponds to a thinner, primarily restraining one. In consequence, Article 2 TEU reveals a *dual character*: its roles and rationales vary according to the context in which it is applied. Based on this dual character, the next parts will explore the potential of Article 2 TEU's judicial mobilization in its EU (Part II) and Verbund dimensions (Part III).

II. Premises

A. A Constitutional Approach

Readers might have already noticed that this chapter approaches Article 2 TEU from a constitutional perspective. At first glance, this seems hardly controversial. The Treaties have been perceived in constitutional terms since the very beginnings

EU Values Before the Court of Justice. Luke Dimitrios Spieker, Oxford University Press. © Luke Dimitrios Spieker 2023.
DOI: 10.1093/oso/9780198876717.003.0004

of European integration.[1] Even sceptics employ constitutional semantics when referring to the Treaties.[2] Then again, the constitutional question was one of the most fiercely debated issues of EU legal scholarship, in particular between Maastricht and the Constitutional Treaty.[3] Far from being settled, the Member States simply decided to abandon the 'constitutional concept'.[4]

Fortunately, the present chapter does not need to open this can of worms. As noted previously, this book concentrates on Article 2 TEU in the jurisprudence of the Court of Justice. At this narrower, judicial level, employing a constitutional perspective seems less prone to objections. Even though there is no official document formally adopted as the Union's 'constitution', the CJEU started long ago with the constitutionalization of the Treaties, meaning the development of effects (primacy) and constraints (fundamental rights) typically associated with constitutions. There is no need to reiterate this well-known story.[5] What is important for our purpose is that the Court perceives the Treaties in constitutional terms.[6] Accordingly, long before initiating the process towards a Constitutional Treaty, the EU already had some kind of substantive, 'judge-made' constitution.[7] This constitutional jurisprudence persisted even after the constitutional project was officially abandoned.[8]

Such a constitutional approach has real implications in the CJEU's judicial practice. First, it implies a specific *legal methodology*. It makes a difference whether the Court approaches the Treaties with the toolbox of treaty or constitutional

[1] See e.g. Anne Boerger and Morten Rasmussen, 'Transforming European Law. The Establishment of the Constitutional Discourse from 1950 to 1993' EuConst 10 (2014), 199, 201 ff; Antonin Cohen, 'Constitutionalism Without Constitution: Transnational Elites Between Political Mobilization and Legal Expertise in the Making of a Constitution for Europe (1940s–1960s)' *Law & Social Inquiry* 32 (2007), 109, 125 ff. For examples, see the explanatory memorandum by the German federal government on the EEC Treaty's ratification, BT-Drs. 2/3440, Annex C, pp 101, 108 ('Der Vertrag ruft … ein europäisches Gebilde verfassungsrechtlicher Gattung ins Leben') or Case C-6/64 *Costa v ENEL* [1964] EU:C:1964:51, Opinion of AG Lagrange ('the Treaty of Rome has, in a sense, the character of a genuine constitution').

[2] See e.g. BVerfG, Judgment of 30 June 2009, 2 BvE 2/08, *Lisbon*, para 231.

[3] For a critical overview, see e.g. Matej Avbelj, 'Questioning EU Constitutionalisms' GLJ 8 (2008), 1.

[4] Presidency Conclusions, Brussels European Council (21–22 June 2007), Annex I, para 1.

[5] See only Eric Stein, 'Lawyers, Judges, and the Making of a Transnational Constitution' AJIL 75 (1981), 1; G. Federico Mancini, 'The Making of a Constitution for Europe' CML Rev 26 (1989), 595; Joseph H.H. Weiler, 'The Transformation of Europe' YLJ 100 (1991), 2403, 2413 ff.

[6] See already Case C-294/83 *Les Verts* [1986] EU:C:1986:166, para 23.

[7] In this sense, see e.g. Jean-Paul Jacqué, *Droit institutionnel de l'Union européenne* (9th edn, Dalloz 2018) paras 177 ff. From the rich literature before the CT, see e.g. Jean-Claude Piris, 'Does the European Union have a Constitution?' EL Rev 24 (1999), 557, 559 ff; Jörg Gerkrath, *L'émergence d'un droit constitutionnel pour l'Europe* (Éd. de l'Université de Bruxelles 1997) 142, 201 ff; Maria L. Fernandez Esteban, 'La noción de Constitución Europea en la jurisprudencia del Tribunal des Justicia de las Comunidades European' *Revista Española de Derecho Constitucional* 40 (1994), 241.

[8] See, e.g. the continuing recourse to the 'constitutional charter' in Cases C-357, 379, 547, 811 and 840/19 *Euro Box Promotion and Others* [2021] EU:C:2021:1034, para 247; Case C-621/18 *Wightman* [2018] EU:C:2018:999 para 44; Opinion 2/13 *ECHR Accession II* [2014] EU:C:2014:2454, para 163; Cases C-402 and 415/05 P *Kadi* [2008] EU:C:2008:461, para 281.

interpretation.[9] Second, the very notion of a constitution implies certain *legal effects*. A constitution is not only formally superior but often permeates the entire legal order providing guidance and orientation (in detail, Chapter 4, IV). Finally, and related to the former, an underlying *constitutional theory* can have considerable implications on judicial practice. The way in which a judge understands a constitution (e.g. whether it has a stronger or weaker steering effect on the political process) has an impact on the way specific provisions are interpreted and applied (e.g. the level of detail that constitutional obligations impose upon the political process).

B. A Multidimensional Approach

At the same time, this chapter applies a multidimensional approach. As mentioned earlier, Article 2 TEU covers two different contexts: one relating to the EU legal system (including the Member States when acting within the scope of EU law) and a broader context comprising the entirety of both the EU and Member State legal orders. Like concentric circles, they take a close-up, micro perspective focusing on the EU legal order and a macro perspective that requires us to take a step back and perceive the EU and the Member States in their entirety (see Figure 3.1). As will be argued below, these contexts correspond to different dimensions of Article 2 TEU.

The broader dimension is especially difficult to grasp and requires some elaboration. Abstractly, it can be framed in two ways. To start with, one can follow a *spatial* approach. This path rests on the insight that the combined territories of the Member States are governed by several legal orders. Taken together, they establish a European legal space.[10] By implication, this concept is highly inclusive. If truly encompassing all provisions that take part in constituting, framing, organizing and legitimizing this space, it will not only include EU and domestic law but also the ECHR as well as international instruments.[11] In this sense, it seems too broad for our purpose. A different approach consists of taking the perspective of the *individual*. Due to the direct effect of EU law, individuals in the Member States are subject to several sources of public authority at once. From their perspective, it is often impossible to distinguish between the various legal orders. Instead, the EU's and

[9] See Giulio Itzcovich, 'The Interpretation of Community Law by the European Court of Justice' GLJ 10 (2009), 537, 557; Armin von Bogdandy and Jürgen Bast, 'The Constitutional Approach to EU Law' in von Bogdandy and Bast (eds), *Principles of European Constitutional Law* (2nd edn, Hart 2009) 1.

[10] See e.g. Armin von Bogdandy, 'European Law Beyond "Ever Closer Union"' ELJ 22 (2016), 519; von Bogdandy, 'Deutsche Rechtswissenschaft im europäischen Rechtsraum' JZ 66 (2011), 1, 2 f.

[11] With the formula 'European legal space = Law in Europe', see Rainer Wahl, 'Die Rechtsbildung in Europa als Entwicklungslabor' JZ 67 (2012), 861, 867. See also Christopher Harding, 'The Identity of European Law: Mapping Out the European Legal Space' ELJ 6 (2000), 128; Luzius Wildhaber and Johan Callewaert, 'Espace constitutionnel européen et droits fondamentaux: une vision globale pour une pluralité de droits et de juges' in Ninon Colneric et al. (eds), *Une communauté de droit* (BWV 2003) 61; Pedro Cruz Villalón, 'El espacio constitucional europeo' in *La Constitución inedita* (Trotta 2004) 13.

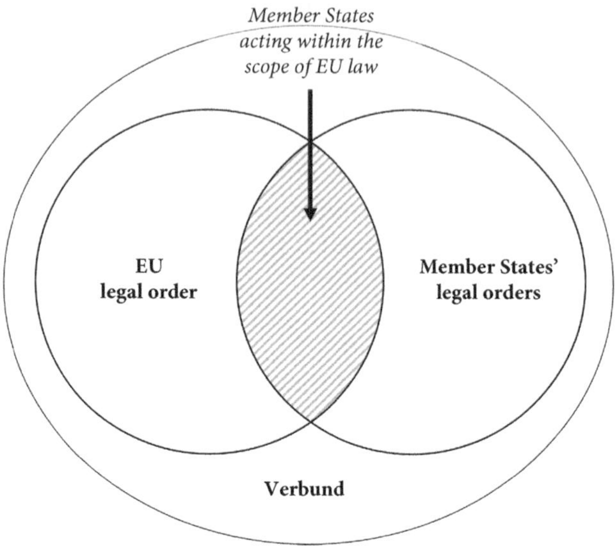

Figure 3.1 The Verbund of the EU's and the Member State's legal orders

the Member States' legal systems seem to form a mutually complementing whole. German legal scholarship has termed this 'whole' a 'Verbund'.[12] Like the European legal space, the Verbund builds on the premise that no single order represents the whole.[13] Its great advantage results from combining two seemingly opposite logics. While articulating the substantive and institutional complementarity of the respective legal orders, it still presupposes their autonomy.[14]

Nonetheless, the Verbund remains a rather elusive concept. On the one hand, its translations vary between association, compound, or composite without, however, fully expressing the gist of the idea. An example is the variety of translations for Ingolf Pernice's 'Verfassungsverbund', which has been (rather circumscribed than) translated as 'multilevel constitutionalism', 'composite European constitution', 'constitution composée', or 'costituzione integrata'.[15] On the other hand, the notion of Verbund is relatively open and remains agnostic towards concrete designs for the

[12] See Ingolf Pernice, 'Europäisches und nationales Verfassungsrecht (2001)' (pp 481, 507 f), 'Theorie und Praxis des Europäischen Verfassungsverbundes (2007)' (pp 625, 633 f) and 'Verfassungsverbund (2010)' (pp 663, 665 f), all in *Der Europäische Verfassungsverbund* (Nomos 2020).

[13] Armin von Bogdandy, 'The European Union as a Supranational Federation' CJEL 6 (2000), 27, 29.

[14] Pernice, 'Europäisches und nationales Verfassungsrecht' (n 12) 507.

[15] Ingolf Pernice, 'Multilevel Constitutionalism and the Treaty of Amsterdam' CML Rev 36 (1999), 703; Leonard Besselink, *A composite European constitution* (Europa Law Publ. 2007); Ingolf Pernice and Franz C. Mayer, 'De la constitution composée de l'Europe' RTDE 36 (2000), 623; Ingolf Pernice and Franz C. Mayer, 'La Costituzione integrata dell'Europa' in Gustavo Zagrebelsky (ed.), *Diritti e Costituzione nell'Unione europea* (Laterza 2003) 43.

relationship of the EU and its Member States. This distinguishes it from concepts such as Bund, union, or federation that aim at reconstruing the 'common whole' as a legal, institutional, or political entity.[16] Due to its openness, the Verbund can be coupled with very different, sometimes outright contrary conceptions.[17] Depending on the coupling, the notion may also relate to different aspects of the composite structure. For instance, the notion of Verbund has been employed to describe the integration of national constitutional courts into the EU judicial system or of national administrations into the EU's governance.[18]

For the purposes of this chapter, its openness—or better, its neutrality—is no shortcoming but rather an advantage. In its purest form, stripped from any specific coupling, the Verbund is simply an analytical tool that allows us to grasp the entirety of the EU's and the Member States' persisting legal orders.[19] Nevertheless, readers might ask why this study does not operate with a more accessible distinction. As seen in the previous chapter, Article 2 TEU entails obligations not only for EU institutions but also for the Member States. Accordingly, one could distinguish between an EU and a Member State dimension.[20] Yet, such a distinction will hardly yield clear-cut results. EU law essentially relies on the Member States' institutions, their governments (Article 10(2) TEU), parliaments (Article 12 TEU), courts (Article 19(1)(2) TEU), and administrations. These institutions are, to a large extent, integrated in the creation, application, and implementation of EU law. If the Member States act in this capacity, are they addressed by Article 2 TEU as Member States or rather as agents of the EU? One could avoid this ambiguity by drawing a dividing line between the EU institutions (including the Member States as far as they act within the scope of EU law) and the Member States acting beyond the scope of EU law. However, such a separation would neglect the role of Article 2 TEU as a constitutional basis for the *common* whole of EU and Member States. These drawbacks can be avoided with the Verbund concept.

[16] See e.g. Christoph Schönberger, 'Die Europäische Union als Bund' AöR 124 (2004), 81; Matej Avbelj, 'Theory of European Union' EL Rev 36 (2011), 818; Signe Rehling Larsen, *The Constitutional Theory of the Federation and the European Union* (OUP 2021) 5 f.

[17] Suffice to contrast Ingolf Pernice's 'Verfassungsverbund' with Paul Kirchhof's 'Staatenverbund'.

[18] Exemplarily BVerfG, Judgment of 5 May 2020, 2 BvR 859/15, *PSPP*, para 111. See further Andreas Voßkuhle, 'Multilevel Cooperation of the European Constitutional Courts: Der Europäische Verfassungsgerichtsverbund' EuConst 6 (2010), 175; Eberhard Schmidt-Aßmann, 'Introduction: European Composite Administration and the role of European administrative law' in Oswald Jansen and Bettina Schöndorf-Haubold (eds), *The European Composite Administration* (Intersentia 2011) 1.

[19] Pernice, 'Verfassungsverbund' (n 12) 679; René Barents, 'The Fallacy of European Multilevel Constitutionalism' in Matej Avbelj and Jan Komárek (eds), *Constitutional Pluralism in the European Union and Beyond* (Hart 2012) 153, 160.

[20] See, in this sense, Peter Van Elsuwege and Femke Gremmelprez, 'Protecting the Rule of Law in the EU Legal Order: A Constitutional Role for the Court of Justice' EuConst 16 (2020), 8.

III. The Dual Character of Article 2 TEU

Even if Article 2 TEU is relevant in both contexts, EU and Verbund, this does not necessarily mean that it always applies the same way. Indeed, its inner structure implies that Article 2 TEU fulfils a different function in each dimension. Flowing from its wording, the provision seems to have a *constitutive* function in the EU legal order ('The Union is founded on ...'). A comparison with other provisions that display a restraining tonality strongly indicates that Article 2 TEU goes beyond a *restraining* role.[21] The same does not apply in the Verbund. Here, the wording signals a much more limited function ('These values are common to the Member States ... '). Against this backdrop, it is suggested that Article 2 TEU displays a dual character. In its EU dimension, it should be read as a *constitutional core* that outlines the basic features of the Union's constitutional framework (in detail, Chapter 4).[22] In its Verbund dimension, however, Article 2 TEU should be understood rather as a *constitutional frame* securing only a minimum of homogeneity between the EU and the Member States' legal orders (in detail, Chapter 8). As we shall see, this distinction should be reflected in the Court's application of Article 2 TEU.

Ultimately, these two dimensions of Article 2 TEU seem to express different constitutional rationales. To better grasp this dual character, we might therefore resort to well-established concepts and distinctions from constitutional theory.[23] A common way of systematizing the varieties of constitutionalism is to situate them somewhere along a spectrum between thinner and thicker forms, in particular with regard to a constitution's *function* and *impact*.[24]

Concerning a constitution's function, scholars like Christoph Möllers distinguished between order-founding and power-shaping forms of constitutionalism.[25] Whereas the former concerns the founding of an entirely new system of government, the latter seeks to restrain an already existing public power. This distinction helps us understand two basic functions of a constitution, namely constituting and

[21] Compare e.g. Art. 4(2) TEU: 'The Union *shall respect* the equality of Member States before the Treaties as well as their national identities ...'

[22] For an early conception of Art. 2 TEU as constitutional core, see Daniel Sarmiento, 'The EU's Constitutional Core' in Alejandro Saiz Arnaiz and Carina Alcoberro Llivina (eds), *National Constitutional Identity and European Integration* (Intersentia 2013) 177.

[23] This chapter understands constitutional theory as seeking to reveal assumptions and rationales underlying the constitutional text on a higher level of abstraction, see Uwe Volkmann, *Grundzüge einer Verfassunsglehre der Bundesrepublik Deutschland* (Mohr Siebeck 2013) 2–5. On this programme, see Carl Schmitt, *Constitutional Theory* (1928) (Duke Univ. Press 2008) 54 [German vers.: p XII].

[24] See Joseph Raz, 'On the Authority and Interpretation of Constitutions: Some Preliminaries' in Larry Alexander (ed.), *Constitutionalism* (CUP 2001) 152.

[25] Christoph Möllers, 'Pouvoir Constituant—Constitution—Constitutionalisation' in von Bogdandy and Bast (n 9) 169. For a very similar reconstruction along the lines of a *negative* or *regulative* and *positive* or *constitutive* constitutionalism, see Nicholas W. Barber, *The Principles of Constitutionalism* (OUP 2018) 2–20; Cormac S. Mac Amhlaigh, *New Constitutional Horizons: Towards a Pluralist Constitutional Theory* (OUP 2022) 121 ff, 128 ff.

restraining public power. However, this tells us very little about the constitution's impact and the role of courts in the respective polity.

This is where a complementing dichotomy comes into play. This second pair is based on the impact a constitution exerts on the respective legal and political system. German scholarship distinguishes between the constitution as 'Grundordnung'[26] and the constitution as 'Rahmenordnung'[27]—as foundation and framework of public power.[28] Under the foundation paradigm, the constitution contains a steering blueprint for political decision making. Taken to the extreme, the entire legal system is just a concretization of decisions settled in the constitution.[29] Under the framework conception, by contrast, the constitution merely provides a procedural framework for the political process and contains rather negative delimitations than positive specifications.[30] Subsequently, this corresponds to a specific allocation of powers. While a constitution as *Grundordnung* favours a strong constitutional judiciary, the concept of *Rahmenordnung* seeks to free the political process from overly restrictive constraints.[31]

These conceptual pairs allow us to establish a very rudimental spectrum between thinner and thicker forms of constitutionalism (see Figure 3.2). Constitutions tending towards the thicker form will usually have a stronger constituting function and exert a higher impact on the legal system. By contrast, constitutions corresponding to a thinner form of constitutionalism will feature primarily a restraining function and exert a lower impact on the legal order, political processes, and society at large. It should be stressed that each of these pairs presents ideal types. Therefore, it comes as no surprise that no constitution will correspond entirely to one of these models. In addition, neither order-founding and power-shaping

[26] Konrad Hesse, *Grundzüge des Verfassungsrechts der Bundsrepublik Deutschland* (20th edn, C.F.Müller 1999) paras 17 f.

[27] Ernst-Wolfgang Böckenförde, 'Fundamental Rights as Constitutional Principles (1990)' in Mirjam Künkler and Tine Stein (eds), *Constitutional and Political Theory* (OUP 2017) 235, 264.

[28] See also Robert Alexy, 'Postscript' in Alexy, *A Theory of Constitutional Rights* (OUP 2010) 388, 390–4. For a related systematization, see e.g. Giorgio Pino, 'Costituzione come limite, costituzione come fondamento, costituzione come assiologica' *Diritto e Società* (2017), 91.

[29] See e.g. Mattias Kumm, 'Who is Afraid of the Total Constitution?' GLJ 7 (2006), 341. This issue is often addressed as 'constitutionalization' of the legal order, see e.g. Louis Favoreu, 'La constitutionnalisation du droit' in Bertrand Mathieu et al. (eds), *La constitutionnalisation des branches du droit* (Economica 1998) 181; Gunnar F. Schuppert and Christian Bumke, *Die Konstitutionalisierung der Rechtsordnung* (Nomos 2000) 32 ff; Riccardo Guastini, 'La "costituzionalizzazione" dell'ordinamento' in *Filosofia del diritto positivo* (Giappichelli 2017) 213. With regard to administrative law, see Luc Heuschling, 'The Complex Relationship Between Administrative and Constitutional Law' in Sabino Cassese et al. (eds), *The Max Planck Handbooks in European Public Law*, vol 1 (OUP 2017) 493, 523 ff.

[30] Böckenförde (n 27) 264 ff.

[31] This is also the gist of the distinction between *legal* and *political* constitutionalism, see e.g. Richard Bellamy, *Political Constitutionalism* (CUP 2007) 1–12. See also the distinction between *liberal* and *democratic* constitutionalism by Robert Schütze, 'Constitutionalism(s)' in Schütze and Roger Masterman (eds), *The Cambridge Companion to Comparative Constitutional Law* (CUP 2019) 40, 54 ff.

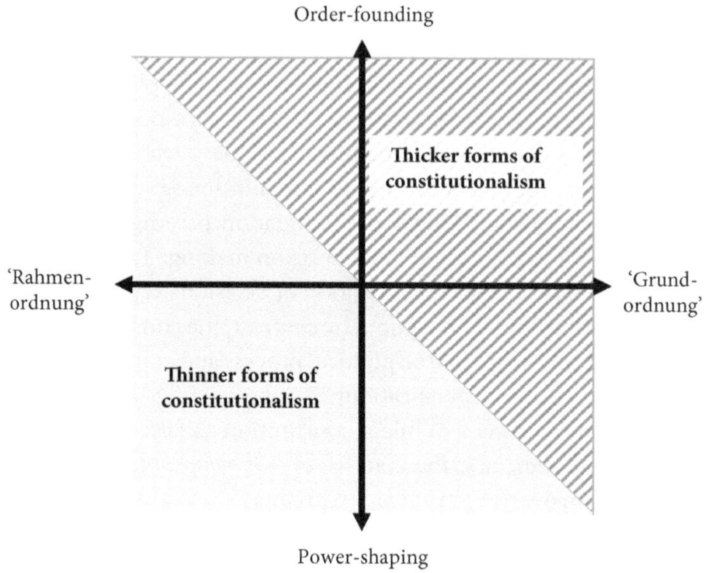

Figure 3.2 Thin and thick forms of constitutionalism

traditions nor *Grundordnung* and *Rahmenordnung* principally contradict one another. Indeed, most constitutions will reveal features pertaining to both.[32]

Finally, it should be stressed that there is no compulsory connection between the order-founding tradition and a constitution as *Grundordnung* (or power-shaping tradition and *Rahmenordnung*). Some might even argue the opposite. According to Möllers, the order-founding model tends structurally towards the politicization of law, whereas the power-shaping tradition aims at a juridification of existing political power.[33] This implies a more restrained role of law and courts in the order-founding tradition. However, this is no necessity. Certainly, a constitution, though constituting a new order, can act as a mere framework for the established public power (the U.S. or French constitutional tradition might be an example). Still it is very well possible that an order-founding constitution settles many political or societal issues in considerable detail and installs a strong constitutional judiciary (e.g. the German Basic Law).

As indicated above, Article 2 TEU seems to resonate between these thinner and thicker constitutional rationales. Its Verbund dimension appears to epitomize a thinner, restraining form of constitutionalism, while its EU dimension tends to

[32] Alexy (n 28) 394; Möllers (n 25) 177; Volkmann (n 23) 17 f. See also Dieter Grimm, *Constitutionalism* (OUP 2016) 364; Christoph Möllers, 'The Politics of Law and the Law of Politics' in Erik O. Eriksen et al. (eds), *Developing a Constitution for Europe* (Routledge 2004) 131, 132.

[33] Möllers (n 25) 170.

give expression to a thicker, constitutive one. The following sections will attempt to substantiate this intuition. Indeed, exploring the provision's drafting context reveals that the adoption of Article 2 TEU-Lisbon (respectively Article I-2 CT) and Article 6(1) TEU-Amsterdam was driven by very different motivations.

A. Verbund Dimension: Article 2 TEU as Manifestation of a Thin Constitutionalism

The Verbund dimension of today's Article 2 TEU can be traced back to Article 6(1) TEU-Amsterdam, which stated that '[t]he Union is founded on the principles of liberty, democracy, respect for human rights and fundamental freedoms, and the rule of law, principles which are common to the Member States.' This provision gave expression to a long-standing concern for constitutional homogeneity among the Member States (in detail, Chapter 8, II.B). A first attempt to include these concerns into the Treaty framework was the so-called Spinelli draft. In its Article 4(4), it stipulated that '[i]n the event of serious and persistent violation of democratic principles or fundamental rights by a Member State, penalties may be imposed' in accordance with Article 44 (very similar to today's Article 7 TEU).[34] However, it was not until the prospective eastern enlargement that these considerations found expression in hard law. After adopting the political Copenhagen criteria in 1993,[35] the most significant step came with the Treaty of Amsterdam that led to Articles 6(1), 7, and 49 TEU.

At first glance, Article 6(1) TEU-Amsterdam seems to go beyond a restraining function by proclaiming that the Union is 'founded' on a set of principles.[36] Some even read this as heralding the beginnings of a genuinely constitutive, European constitutionalism.[37] Yet, Amsterdam was hardly meant to be a constitutive step.[38] In light of the looming eastern enlargement, the Treaty makers seemed preoccupied with preparing for potential accessions rather than performing a constitutive act. The main driver for the adoption of Article 6(1) TEU was not the Union's refoundation but guaranteeing a certain homogeneity among the Member States.[39]

[34] See Draft Treaty establishing the European Union [1984] OJ C77/22, 37, 43.

[35] Presidency Conclusions, Copenhagen European Council (21–22 June 1993), 7.A.iii).

[36] This was less explicit in other language versions. The German ('Die Union *beruht* auf den Grundsätzen ...'), Spanish ('La Unión *se basa* en los principios ...'), Portuguese ('A União *assenta* nos princípios ...'), and Greek versions ('Η Ένωση *βασίζεται* στις αρχές ...') featured a formulation that corresponds rather to the 'the Union is based on ...'.

[37] Armin von Bogdandy, 'Founding Principles' in von Bogdandy and Bast (n 9) 11, 22. In this sense, see also Joël Molinier et al., *Les principes fondateurs de l'Union européenne* (PUF 2005) 28, 49 f; Hélène Gaudin, 'Amsterdam: l'échec de la hiérarchie des normes?' RTDE 35 (1999), 1, 6 ff.

[38] Amsterdam was broadly considered to be a limited and inconclusive step in the integration process, see e.g. Joseph H.H. Weiler, 'Bread and Circus' CJEL 4 (1998), 223; Jean-Victor Louis, 'Le Traité d'Amsterdam: Une occasion perdue?' RMUE 2 (1997), 5.

[39] In this sense, Wojciech Sadurski, *Constitutionalism and the Enlargement of Europe* (OUP 2012) 80 ff; Olivier de Schutter and Philip Alston, 'Introduction' in Schutter and Alston (eds), *Monitoring*

This is supported by the fact that Article 6(1) TEU was drafted in tandem with Article 7 TEU and the accession conditions in Article 49(1) TEU.[40] In this spirit, the Reflection Group preparing the IGC noted that

> in the run-up to enlargement, there is an urgent need to ensure full observance of fundamental rights, both in relations between the Union and the Member States and between States and individuals ... an Article should be inserted into the Treaty providing for penalties ... in the case of any State which commits a serious and repeated breach of fundamental human rights or basic democratic principles.[41]

Similarly, the Irish Presidency's first draft of Article 6(1) TEU stated that the '[t]he Union is composed of *States which are committed* to the principles ...'.[42]

Thus, the newly established Article 6(1) TEU-Amsterdam seemed to be directed, despite its wording, towards the Member States rather than the Union. In any case, this does not diminish its importance. Even if noticed by few, Article 6(1) TEU-Amsterdam was the first Treaty provision reaching across the entire Verbund and committing the Member States to a set of constitutional principles.[43] In this dimension, however, the provision was imbued with a thin, restraining constitutional rationale. Neither the Constitutional nor the Lisbon Treaty have altered this configuration. Indeed, the current Treaty set up provides strong indications that Article 2 TEU still corresponds to a thinner form of constitutionalism as far as it applies throughout the Verbund. Especially a systematic interpretation in light of Article 7 TEU suggests a restrained reading. Conceived as the central enforcement mechanism of EU values in the Verbund, its demanding procedural and substantive thresholds emphasize that Article 2 TEU was supposed to play an exceptional, limited role in this dimension. Further, the Member States' constitutional autonomy, pluralism, and diversity guaranteed by the Treaties (see only Article 4(1) and (2) TEU as well as Articles 5 TEU and 51(1) CFR) require that Article 2 TEU does not go beyond a thin framework within which the Member States can exercise their powers (in detail, Chapter 13).

Fundamental Rights in the EU (Hart 2005) 1, 7; Bruno de Witte, 'The Impact of Enlargement on the Constitution of the European Union' in Marise Cremona (ed.), *The Enlargement of the European Union* (OUP 2003) 209, 228 ff.

[40] See e.g. Pierre-Yves Monjal, 'Le traité d'Amsterdam et la procedure en contestation politique de manquement aux principes de l'Union' RMUE (1998), 69, 81 ff.

[41] IGC '96, Reflection Group Report (December 1996) 44.

[42] Presidency Introductory Note, CONF/3879/96 LIMITE (emphasis added). A later proposal tabled by Austria and Italy read: 'The Union and the Member States' systems of government are founded on the principles of ...', see CONF/3940/96 LIMITE.

[43] See in particular Pernice (n 15) 726; Gaudin (n 37) 10; von Bogdandy (n 13) 30.

All this supports the view that Article 2 TEU—as far as it applies across the Verbund—corresponds to a thinner constitutional rationale. In consequence, the provision draws a thin frame of constitutional constraints. It aims primarily at restraining the Member States' authority and exerts a more limited impact on their legal orders. This reflects also on the role of the judiciary when it comes to fleshing out, applying, and enforcing the principles of Article 2 TEU within the Verbund.

B. EU Dimension: Article 2 TEU as Manifestation of a Thick Constitutionalism

Even if Article 6(1) TEU-Amsterdam already displayed the first signs of a constitutive rationale, it primarily aimed at introducing constitutional constraints across the Verbund. With the Constitutional Treaty, the drafters sought to complement this thin rationale with a genuinely constitutive one. The following section will briefly outline the drafting context before exploring the central role played by Article 2 TEU (Article I-2 CT) in this respect.

With the new millennium, there was growing political support for a constitutional refoundation of the European Union.[44] A constitutional fever had seized Europe.[45] In this spirit, the Convention tasked with drafting the Constitutional Treaty seemed to operate *as if* it were elaborating a genuine constitution.[46] Yet, there was a central flaw. Though empirically and conceptually questionable, the necessity of a constituent power vested in the people—a 'We the People'—had a solid grip on the drafters' imagination.[47] Attributing a constitution to the people was perceived as a precondition not only for its normative justifiability but also for its social acceptability. Indeed, several Member State constitutions contain such a reference.[48] The statement of Jean-Claude Piris, Director General of the Council

[44] See e.g. Joschka Fischer, 'Vom Staatenverbund zur Föderation' Speech at Humboldt-University Berlin (24 May 2000) ('konstitutionelle Neugründung Europas') or Jacques Chirac, 'Notre Europe' Speech at the German Bundestag (27 June 2000) ('refondation'). For a critical discussion, Jean-Louis Quermonne, 'Le traité constitutionnel européen est-il un acte refondateur?' *Politique étrangère* 70 (2005), 245.

[45] Renaud Dehousse, *Une Constitution pour l'Europe* (Presses de Sciences Po 2002) 11. In retrospect, see Antoine Vauchez, *Brokering Europe* (CUP 2015) 198 ff.

[46] Convention member Klaus Hänsch considered the 'as if' approach the Convention's 'categorical imperative', see *Bulletin Quotidien Europe* 8154 (20 February 2002), 4. See also Marta Cartabia, 'Riflessioni sulla Convenzione di Laeken: "come se" si trattasse di un processo costituente' *Quaderni costituzionali* 22 (2002), 439, 440; Koen Lenaerts and Marlies Desomer, 'New Models of Constitution-making in Europe: The Quest for Legitimacy' CML Rev 39 (2002), 1217, 1237.

[47] See e.g. Joseph H.H. Weiler, 'A Constitution for Europe? Some Hard Choices' JCMS 40 (2002), 563, 567; Maurizio Fioravanti, 'Il processo costituente europeo' *Quaderni Fiorentini* 31 (2002), 273, 276 ff.

[48] 'Le peuple français proclame ...'; '... hat sich das Deutsche Volk kraft seiner verfassungsgebenden Gewalt dieses Grundgesetz gegeben.'; 'We, the people of Éire, ...'; '... decisão do povo português ...'; '... el pueblo español ratifica la siguiente ...'. See also 'We, the citizens of the Czech Republic ...'; '... the people of Estonia ... have adopted the following Constitution ...'; 'The Lithuanian nation ... by the will of the citizens ... adopts and proclaims ...'; '... we, the citizens of the Slovak Republic, have ... adopted this Constitution'.

legal service, aptly captured the gist of these considerations: 'it would be difficult for a "Constitution" which had not been directly adopted by the people concerned to be perceived as a "Constitution"'.[49]

Such a recourse to the constituent power of the people seemed barred at the EU level. Politically, the Member States would not have been ready to put their position as masters of the Treaties into question. Conceptually too, the idea of a constituent power at the EU level was met with scepticism. Some argued that the concept of constituent power was limited to a people or demos.[50] The peoples of the Member States, however, were widely considered to lack the necessary cohesion to form *one* European demos. Others advocated a democratically demanding or radically input-oriented concept of constituent power.[51] This required democratic participation of the people in the process of constitution making. Although the improvements of the Convention method were generally acknowledged, it fell short of a genuine constituent assembly.[52] Not only was the idea of a Europe-wide referendum rejected;[53] the draft had to pass the Member States' agreement in the following IGC. Of course, these views were far from being unanimously shared in the legal community.[54] From the outset, it was highly controversial, whether concepts from the state context, such as the constituent power of the people, could or should be transferred to the EU level.[55]

As such, the controversial step towards a European constitution could not feed on the legitimating potential of a single people's constituent power. Several proposals attempted to paper over these cracks. For instance, some delegates proposed allowing each Member State to formulate their own preamble recital and having recourse to its own people ('We the French people ... ', 'We the people of Germany ...').[56] Eventually, the final draft preamble referred to 'the will of the citizens and States of Europe'. There were only few enthusiasts, like the MEP Johannes Voggenhuber, who passionately remarked during the closing session: 'With this Constitution, European citizenship is constituted as the Union's sovereign ...'[57]

[49] Piris (n 7) 575 f.

[50] See e.g. Dieter Grimm, 'Does Europe Need a Constitution?' ELJ 1 (1995), 282; Olivier Beaud, 'Propos sceptiques sur la légitimité d'un référendum européen ou plaidoyer pour plus de réalisme constitutionnel' in Andreas Auer and Jean-Francois Flauss (eds), *Le référendum européen* (Bruylant 1997) 125, 144 ff.

[51] See e.g. Möllers (n 25) 185 ff.

[52] See e.g. Robert Badinter, 'A European constitution: Perspectives of a French delegate to the convention' I-CON 1 (2003), 363; John E. Fossum and Augustín J. Menéndez, 'The Constitution's Gift?' ELJ 11 (2005), 380, 399 f.

[53] See 'Referendum on the European Constitution' CONV 658/03; European Parliament, Resolution on the constitutionalisation of the Treaties, 2000/2160(INI), M. 21 and 22.

[54] See Paul Craig, 'Constitutions, Constitutionalism and the European Union' ELJ 7 (2001), 125, 136 ff; Anne Peters, *Elemente einer Theorie der Verfassung Europas* (Duncker&Humblot 2001) 360 ff, 699 ff; Sergio Dellavalle, *Una costituzione senza popolo?* (Giuffrè 2002) 263 ff.

[55] For an overview, see Neil Walker, 'Post-Constituent Constitutionalism?' in Walker and Martin Loughlin (eds), *The Paradox of Constitutionalism* (OUP 2008) 247.

[56] See Contribution by Alain Lamassoure, Elmar Brok, and Joachim Wuermeling, 'Testimonies of National Parliaments in the Constitution's Preamble?', CONV 467/02.

[57] European Convention, Plenary Session of 10 July 2003, 4-020.

The prevailing view was that the Constitutional Treaty was not the product of an autonomous constituent power.[58] For that reason, the Constitutional Treaty was widely regarded as sitting on the fence—a strange hybrid between international treaty and genuine constitution.[59] For others it remained a global amendment of the former Treaties,[60] for some even a deceiving 'treaty masquerading as a constitution'.[61]

How then could the Convention achieve the constitutional refoundation of the European Union? By entering more speculative ground, this section suggests that founding the Union on a set of common values was an attempt to compensate for the missing constituent power, a 'We, the people', at the EU level.[62] Article I-2 of the Constitutional Treaty was the central provision in this respect. Not only did it unmistakably proclaim that the Union is 'founded' on these values;[63] the drafters also moved the former Article 6(1) TEU-Amsterdam to the very head of the Constitutional Treaty. Further, the turn from principles to values might support this assumption. While the previous chapter extensively discussed how the notion of values found its way into the Treaties (without diluting the legal normativity of Article 2 TEU), it only briefly touched upon the reasons that motivated the drafters' choice for this wording. This section provides one possible answer: founding the Union on commonly shared values, rooted in the societies of the Member States, might have been driven by the desire to strengthen the constitutive rationale underpinning the Constitutional Treaty.

Quite surprisingly, the recourse to a constituent power and the reference to commonly shared values reveal strikingly similar features. First, both concepts can serve as *points of reference for identification* and establish a 'cadre d'appartenance'.[64] A recourse to 'We, the people' allows citizens to embrace the constitutional text as

58 See e.g. Miguel Maduro, 'The Importance of Being Called a Constitution' I-CON 3 (2005), 332, 352; Marta Cartabia, 'Ispirata alla volontà dei cittadini degli Stati d'Europa' *Quaderni costituzionali* 25 (2005), 9, 19–21; Gonzalo Maestro Buelga, 'Poder constituyente, principio democrático y continuidad en el Tratado Constitucional de la Unión Europea' *Teoría y Realidad Constitucional* (2004), 133, 146 ff. See also from greater temporal distance, Jürgen Neyer, *The Justification of Europe* (OUP 2012) 153 f.

59 On the uncertainties surrounding this distinction at the time, see e.g. Jean-Paul Jacqué, 'Le projet de traité établissant une constitution pour l'Europe. Constitutionnalisation ou révision des Traités?' in Paul Demaret et al. (eds), *Dynamiques Juridiques Européennes* (Lang 2005) 41; Dieter Grimm, 'Verfassung–Verfassungsvertrag–Vertrag über eine Verfassung' in Olivier Beaud et al. (eds), *L'Europe en voie de constitution* (Bruylant 2004) 279; Maurizio Fioravanti, 'Un ibrido fra "Trattato" e "Costituzione"' in Elena Paciotti (ed.), *La Costituzione europea* (Meltemi 2003) 17; Luis Díez-Picazo, '¿Qué diferencia hay entre un tratado y una constitución?' *Cuadernos de derecho público* 13 (2001), 85.

60 See even from within the Convention secretariat, Clemens Ladenburger, 'Towards a Post-National Constitution—Federal, Confederal or Genuinely "Sui Generis"?' ERPL 16 (2004), 75.

61 Joseph H.H. Weiler, 'On the Power of the Word: Europe's Constitutional Iconography' I-CON 3 (2005), 173.

62 I am indebted to Armin von Bogdandy for this thought.

63 This applies also to the formerly deviating German, Spanish, and Portuguese language versions ('gründet', 'se fundamenta', 'funda-se'). For their wording in Art. 6 TEU-Amsterdam, see n 36.

64 Günter Frankenberg, 'The Return of the Contract: Problems and Pitfalls of European Constitutionalism' ELJ 6 (2000), 257.

their own.[65] It can foster the identity of the established community and enhance the acceptance and legitimacy of the constitutional text. Article I-2 was supposed to fulfil an analogous function. Tasked to draw up proposals on 'how to bring citizens closer to the European design',[66] the Convention aimed at stimulating a European identity.[67] In this context, the Praesidium noted that Article I-2 contained 'the basic values which make the peoples of Europe feel part of the same "union" '.[68] Indeed, the recourse to highly abstract values appeared particularly well suited to stimulate a common identity. As they allow members of a community to bracket non-essential differences, they keep dissent hidden and enable parallel processes of identification.[69] Some even read Article I-2 as a basis for constitutional patriotism.[70]

Secondly, both concepts present *final grounds*. A specific legal act finds its legal basis in a law or statute, which again finds its legal basis in the constitution. But what about the constitution? How can we escape the infinite regress? The concept of constituent power answers this question by referring to an authority outside the legal system. As a 'Grenzbegriff' it demarcates the transition from factual political power (the 'is') to normativity (the 'ought').[71] Seen from within the legal system, it is a sort of closure concept or vanishing point. In addition, the concept produces a semantic cover for the messy historical realities of constitution making, which more often than not fall short of the democratic adoption by an identifiable, let alone homogenous people.[72] The use of value semantics might have been motivated by very similar considerations. In communication, values are usually referred to as final grounds. Actions or choices can be justified by recourse to values. The values themselves, however, cannot be justified by referring to another level. Thus, the recourse to values relieves us from further justification—they put a 'halt on reflection'.[73] Moreover, unlike truths, values are introduced into communication

[65] Alexander Somek, 'Constituent Power in National and Transnational Contexts' TLT 3 (2012), 31, 33.

[66] Draft Treaty establishing a Constitution for Europe [2003] OJ C169/1, Preface.

[67] Critically, see e.g. Armin von Bogdandy, 'The European Constitution and European Identity' I-CON 3 (2005), 295, 315; Dieter Grimm, 'Integration by Constitution' I-CON 3 (2005), 193, 204 ff; Ulrich Haltern, 'Pathos and Patina' ELJ 9 (2003), 14.

[68] Praesidium, Draft of Articles 1 to 16 of the Constitutional Treaty, CONV 528/03, Annex II, p 12.

[69] von Bogdandy (n 67) 307 f. Generally, see André Brodocz, 'Chancen konstitutioneller Identitätsstiftung. Zur symbolischen Integration durch eine deutungsoffene Verfassung' in Hans Vorländer (ed.), *Integration durch Verfassung* (VS Verlag 2002) 101.

[70] See e.g. Carlos Closa, 'Deliberative Constitutional Politics and the Turn Towards a Norms-Based Legitimacy of the EU Constitution' ELJ 11 (2005), 411, 423 ff. Sceptical, see Mattias Kumm, 'Why Europeans Will not Embrace Constitutional Patriotism' I-CON 6 (2008), 117.

[71] Ernst-Wolfgang Böckenförde, 'The Constituent Power of the People. A Liminal Concept of Constitutional Law (1986)' in Künkler and Stein (n 27) 169, 170.

[72] On such retroactive ascriptions, see Möllers (n 25) 185; Ulrich K. Preuß, 'Is There a Constituent Power in the European Union?' in Oliver Cayla and Pasquale Pasquino (eds), *Le pouvoir constituant et l'Europe* (Dalloz 2011) 75, 82 f; Hans Lindahl, 'Constituent Power and Reflexive Identity' in Loughlin and Walker (n 55) 9.

[73] Niklas Luhmann, *Gibt es in unserer Gesellschaft noch unverzichtbare Normen?* (C.F. Müller 1993) 19 ('Reflexionsstopp'). See also Niklas Luhmann, *Theory of Society* (Stanford University Press 2012) 205; Pierre Schlag, 'Values' *Yale Journal of Law and the Humanities* 6 (1994), 219, 222.

not by assertion but by presupposition. This exonerates us not only from further justification but also from entering upon the ground of rational explainability.[74] In this sense, values constitute a final ground that terminates, just like the recourse to a constituent power, a regress of justification.

Based on this (certainly limited) equivalence, the appeal to commonly shared values could be understood as the closest thing to invoking a constituent power, a 'We, the people', at the EU level. This strongly suggests that Article 2 TEU was supposed to fulfil a constitutive function in the EU legal order and supports the claim that Article 2 TEU epitomizes a thicker form of constitutionalism in its EU dimension.

IV. Summing Up

In conclusion, Article 2 TEU reveals a dual character resonating between two forms of constitutionalism. As noted earlier, this implies different functions, namely a constitutive one in its EU dimension and a restraining one in the Verbund. It should be emphasized that this is no academic glass bead game but yields very real consequences in judicial practice. A thick constitutional underpinning of Article 2 TEU in its EU dimension can justify a prevalent role in EU constitutional law, for instance as a focal point for the interpretation of primary law. By contrast, a thinner constitutional rationale in the Verbund must lead to a much more restrained function of Article 2 TEU. As such, the dual character of Article 2 TEU requires a different judicial treatment in each dimension.

One central objection might be raised against this reconstruction: the differential treatment of Article 2 TEU in both contexts seems prone to inconsistencies. Sceptics might question whether the Court will always be able to distinguish between the different dimensions without getting caught in contradictions. Such concerns are easily refuted. First, each dimension, the EU and Verbund, corresponds to relatively circumscribed procedural contexts. Article 2 TEU will primarily become relevant in its Verbund dimension if there is no other EU law applying to the case at hand. For instance, this might concern the Member States' value compliance beyond the scope of other EU law (in detail, Chapter 9). Thus, the Court should be able to clearly distinguish this dimension. Second, there are several judicial techniques to maintain diverging standards flowing from Article 2 TEU without creating inconsistencies or contradictions. To name but a few examples, the Court could show greater deference to national institutions or adopt a varying degree of specificity depending on the dimension in which Article 2 TEU is applied (in detail, Chapter 13).

[74] Luhmann (n 73) 18.

Ultimately, a bifurcated understanding of legal provisions is not unprecedented in EU law. The Charter provides a prime example in this regard. As Pedro Cruz Villalón noted, the Charter is a Janus-faced instrument—a 'deidad bifronte'—that reveals a different function, aim, and purpose corresponding to its addressee.[75] With regard to EU acts, the Charter was intended to be the primary bill of rights. It was a response to the increasing demand for legitimacy correlating to the Union's increasing scope of competences.[76] Concerning the Member States, however, the Charter's function might be different. The Member States already had mechanisms for the protection of fundamental rights in place. Applying these diverging fundamental rights standards to the national implementation of EU law would have jeopardized its coherent and uniform application. For the Court, the Charter's central aim vis-à-vis the Member States is therefore to secure EU law's uniform application, namely 'to avoid a situation in which the level of protection of fundamental rights varies according to the national law involved in such a way as to undermine the unity, primacy and effectiveness of EU law'.[77] Some went even further to suggest a layered system of EU human rights standards. According to Armin von Bogdandy, for instance, the density of EU standards should vary between acts of Union institutions and Member States when implementing EU law (highest normative density), the general human rights performance of the Member States (lesser normative density), and foreign States in the EU's foreign policy (minimally regulated).[78]

To sum up, Article 2 TEU constitutes a constitutional core of the EU legal order and a constitutional frame for the Verbund. This dual character finds support in the provision's wording, its inner structure, and drafting history. Importantly, Article 2 TEU epitomizes two diverging constitutional rationales. In its EU dimension, it gives expression to a thicker, constitutive form of constitutionalism, justifying a prominent role in the construction of the EU legal order. In the Verbund, it is reduced to a much thinner, primarily restraining, form. The notions of 'constitutional core' (EU) and 'constitutional frame' (Verbund) tried to grasp the gist of this distinction. Based on this conceptual framework, the following parts aim at developing the potential of Article 2 TEU in the Court's jurisprudence, both in its EU (Part II) and in its Verbund dimension (Part III).

[75] Pedro Cruz Villalón, 'El valor de posición de la carta de derechos fundamentales en la comunión constitucional europea' *Teoría y Realidad Constitucional* 39 (2017), 85, 91 ff.

[76] Cologne European Council, Presidency Conclusions (3–4 June 1999), Annex IV; Marta Cartabia, 'The Charter of Fundamental Rights of the European Union' in Giuliano Amato et al. (eds), *The History of the European Union* (Hart 2019) 113, 116.

[77] See e.g. Case C-198/13 *Hernández* [2014] EU:C:2014:2055, para 47; Case C-206/13 *Siragusa* [2014] EU:C:2014:126, para 32; Case C-399/11 *Melloni* [2013] EU:C:2013:107, para 60. Critically, see Eleanor Spaventa, *The Interpretation of Article 51 of the EU Charter of Fundamental Rights* (European Parliament, PETI-Committee 2016), 21.

[78] Armin von Bogdandy, 'The European Union as a Human Rights Organization?' CML Rev 37 (2000), 1307, 1318 f. See also for Art. 6(1) TEU-Nice and Art. 2 TEU-Lisbon, von Bogdandy (n 36) 40.

II

'THE UNION IS FOUNDED ON THE VALUES . . .'

Potential in the EU Dimension

4

Article 2 TEU as Constitutional Core of the EU Legal Order

I. Introduction

The previous chapter unpacked the dual character of Article 2 TEU. In its EU dimension, the provision epitomizes a thick, constitutive form of constitutionalism. On that basis, Article 2 TEU should be read as the constitutional core of the EU legal order. The following part seeks to explore the potential of such a reading. In particular, it will suggest a profound reorganization of primary law based on Article 2 TEU. In the Court's jurisprudence, the provision could serve as a starting point for the development of a genuine EU constitution—not in form, but in substance—and a hierarchical stratification of primary law.

Even though the EU lacks a formal constitutional document, this did not prevent the Court from perceiving the Treaties as 'constitutional charter' (see Chapter 3, II.A).[1] Yet, this undifferentiated understanding of the entirety of primary law as an EU constitution entails considerable drawbacks. First, over-inclusiveness can impede a constitution's coherence, challenge its capacity to serve as a yardstick for the legal system, and even weaken its constitutional value altogether. Second, overly detailed constitutions, especially if entrenched and subject to qualified amendment procedures, can remove many issues from the sphere of legislative decision-making.

These two challenges apply in particular to the EU context (see Chapters 5 and 6). Primary law is complex, sometimes confusing, and labyrinthine. Despite considerable attempts to streamline the Treaties, primary law still consists of not only two Treaties with overlapping contents, but also a myriad of protocols, reservations, and annexes of formally equal rank. Moreover, the Treaties regulate in considerable detail a broad range of matters that constitutions would usually leave to ordinary legislation.

Already in 1994, Fernand Herman noted with regard to the Treaty framework: '[t]here is a Constitution, but it is dispersed throughout texts which also

[1] See e.g. Cases C-357, 379, 547, 811 and 840/19 *Euro Box Promotion and Others* [2021] EU:C:2021:1034, para 247; Case C-621/18 *Wightman* [2018] EU:C:2018:999, para 44; Cases C-402 and 415/05 P *Kadi* [2008] EU:C:2008:461, para 281; Case C-294/83 *Les Verts* [1986] EU:C:1986:166, para 23. See already Opinion 1/76 *European laying-up fund* [1977] EU:C:1977:63, para 12 referring to the 'internal Constitution of the European Communities'.

EU Values Before the Court of Justice. Luke Dimitrios Spieker, Oxford University Press. © Luke Dimitrios Spieker 2023.
DOI: 10.1093/oso/9780198876717.003.0005

contain legal norms which are in no way "constitutional". There is a need to ... distinguish between those which have a genuine constitutional character and the others'.[2] Despite many proposals for a division of the Treaties,[3] such a distinction (let alone 'a pocket-size' EU constitution) never materialized. A narrower judicial reconstruction remains nonetheless possible. To recall, we are not looking at an EU constitution as a formal document but rather as a concept in the CJEU's jurisprudence. Against this backdrop, the following chapter will advance a narrower and arguably more consistent approach for the judicial construction of a substantive EU constitution.

Abstractly, the Court can employ two complementary approaches. On the one hand, many constitutional courts have identified—sometimes without any textual support—structuring constitutional principles or substantive hierarchies within the constitution aimed at reducing complexity and establishing coherence. Overarching conceptions like those of a constitutional core or identity, an 'invisible constitution' or a 'basic structure' provide vivid illustrations of these attempts. On the other hand, there is no reason why the Court should be required to equate its conception of a substantive EU constitution with the entirety of primary law. As there is no formal constitution at the EU level, it seems free to determine what parts of EU law feature constitutional value in the first place. Similar approaches can be observed even with respect to formal constitutions. As Pedro Cruz Villalón pointed out, there is no 'immediate relation between "basic structures" and "constitutional law" in the formal sense'.[4] Substantive constitutional value might often coincide with a formal constitution's content but can also be broader or narrower. One powerful example is the 'bloc de constitutionnalité' in France. In *Liberté d'association*, the Conseil Constitutionnel acknowledged the constitutional rank of the preamble to the 1958 constitution and thus, implicitly, of the texts to which the preamble refers, such as the 1789 Declaration of the Rights of Man and of the Citizen.[5] In doing so, the Conseil expanded constitutional value beyond the formal constitution and extended its yardsticks for judicial review.[6]

Both approaches are reflected in the CJEU's case law. Although the Court refers to the entire Treaties as 'constitutional charter', it has nonetheless started to

[2] Fernand Herman, Second Report of the Committee on Institutional Affairs on the Constitution of the European Union (9 February 1994), European Parliament, Session Doc. A3-0064/94.

[3] See e.g. European Parliament, Resolution on the constitutionalisation of the Treaties [2001] OJ C197/186, I. 4; EUI, *A basic Treaty for the European Union: a study of the reorganisation of the Treaties* (15 May 2000) 1; Jean-Luc Dehaene, Richard von Weizsäcker, and David Simon, *The Institutional Implications of Enlargement* (Brussels: 18 October 1999) 12 ff.

[4] Pedro Cruz Villalón, 'Grundlagen und Grundzüge staatlichen Verfassungsrechts: Vergleich' in von Bogdandyet al. (eds), *Handbuch Ius Publicum Europaeum*, vol 1 (C.F.Müller 2007) § 13, para 84 (author's translation).

[5] Conseil Constitutionnel, Décision no° 71-44 DC, *Liberté d'association*, para 2.

[6] For a detailed assessment, see e.g. Jean-Sébastien Boda, 'Bloc de constitutionnalité ou désordre constitutionnel?' RFDC (130) (2022), 393; Laurent Eck, 'Faut-il constitutionnaliser la décision du Conseil constitutionnel du 16 juillet 1971?' RFDC (130) (2022), 377.

distinguish a nuanced 'constitutional framework' from the plethora of Treaty provisions (Section II.A). Still, this jurisprudence is characterized by an expansive tendency and seems to lack an overarching conception. While approaches advanced in legal scholarship might lead to a more consistent vision of an EU constitution, they reveal considerable shortcomings too (Section II.B). The second section will propose a different path. As the constitutional core of EU law, Article 2 TEU outlines the basic tenets of the Union's substantive constitution. In consequence, this substantive constitution would consist of those Treaty provisions *that give expression to a value enshrined in Article 2 TEU* (Section III). Taking this idea one step further, the last section seeks to provide this Article 2 TEU-based constitution with (at least partially) constitutional effects. Usually, constitutions take formal and substantive precedence over ordinary law. Drawing on this insight, the chapter suggests introducing a substantive hierarchy between those Treaty provisions that give expression to an Article 2 TEU value and those that do not (Section IV). The following chapters will explore the potential of this hierarchical stratification in the Court's jurisprudence.

II. In Search of the Union's Constitution

A. Jurisprudence

Over the past decades, the Court has moulded a veritable constitutional framework from the vast array of Treaty provisions. In this process, the CJEU broadly distinguished between a *structural* and a *substantive* constitutional dimension.[7] Already in the 1970s, the Court referred to the Community's institutional and federal framework as the 'essential elements'[8] of its structure and to autonomy, primacy, and direct effect as the 'essential characteristics'[9] of this legal order. The substantive dimension, by contrast, was conceived in much thinner terms. An emphasis was placed especially on Community objectives that became the guiding star for the interpretation of the Treaties and the Community's tasks.[10] In *Kadi*, the Court complemented this structural dimension with a substantive one. According to the Court, fundamental rights are 'constitutional principles' that are part of 'the very foundations of the Community legal order'. Further, no provision of primary

[7] For this dichotomy, see Koen Lenaerts, 'Les fondements constitutionnels de l'Union européenne dans leur rapport avec le droit international' in *Liber amicorum Vassilios Skouris* (Bruylant 2015) 367, 370 ff.

[8] Opinion 1/76 *European laying-up fund* [1977] EU:C:1977:63, para 12.

[9] Opinion 1/91 *EEA I* [1991] EU:C:1991:490, para 21; Opinion 1/00 *ECAA* [2002] EU:C:2002:231, para 21. See also Case C-106/77 *Simmenthal* [1978] EU:C:1978:49, para 18.

[10] See e.g. Case 167/73 *Commission v France* [1974] EU:C:1974:35, para 18; Case C-126/86 *Giménez Zaera* [1987] EU:C:1987:395, para 10; *EEA I* (n 9) para 18. See also Hans P. Ipsen, *Europäisches Gemeinschaftsrecht* (Mohr Siebeck 1972) § 54, para 20.

law can 'authorise any derogation from the principles of liberty, democracy and respect for human rights and fundamental freedoms enshrined in Article 6(1) EU as a foundation of the Union.'[11] As will be discussed in Chapter 8, *Kadi* has been interpreted as creating a layer of hierarchically superior principles that form the EU's constitutional core or identity.[12]

More recent case law has consolidated both dimensions into a comprehensive account. Opinion 2/13 provides an especially detailed outline of the Union's 'constitutional framework'.[13] This framework encompasses the Union's 'constitutional structure' (its federal and institutional setup) and the 'specific characteristics arising from the very nature of EU law' (autonomy, primacy, and direct effect).[14] The substantive dimension comprises not only the EU's common values and fundamental rights but also the EU's objectives and those provisions that contribute 'to the implementation of the process of integration' (fundamental freedoms, citizenship, the AFSJ, and competition policy).[15] Opinion 1/17 streamlined this convoluted account to a 'constitutional blueprint' of contemporary EU law.[16]

> [T]he Union possesses a constitutional framework ... That framework encompasses the founding values set out in Article 2 TEU ... the general principles of EU law, the provisions of the Charter, and the provisions of the EU and FEU Treaties, which include, inter alia, rules on the conferral and division of powers, rules governing how the EU institutions and its judicial system are to operate, and fundamental rules in specific areas, structured in such a way as to contribute to the implementation of the process of integration ...[17]

In sum, the CJEU has developed a constitutional framework from the broad range of Treaty provisions that increasingly features Article 2 TEU at its centre (see also Chapter 1, IV.B). Still, the Court's approach is characterized by an expansive tendency and a sometimes confusing and inconsistent terminology. Importantly, it does not seem to be guided by any kind of overarching conception.

[11] *Kadi* (n 1) paras 285, 303 f.

[12] See e.g. Christina Eckes, 'Protecting supremacy from external influences: A precondition for a European constitutional legal order?' ELJ 18 (2012), 230, 241, 247; Giuseppe Martinico, 'Building Supranational Identity: Legal Reasoning and Outcome in *Kadi I* and Opinion 2/13 of the Court of Justice' *Italian Journal of Public Law* 8 (2016), 235, 249 ff; Myriam Benlolo-Carabot, 'La CJCE et la protection des valeurs fondamentales de l'ordre juridique communautaire' RMCUE (2009), 380, 385 f.

[13] Opinion 2/13 *ECHR Accession II* [2014] EU:C:2014:2454, para 158.

[14] ibid paras 165 f, 174–6.

[15] ibid para 168 ff.

[16] Takis Tridimas, 'The General Principles of EU Law and the Europeanisation of National Laws' REAL 13 (2020), 5, 12.

[17] Opinion 1/17 *CETA* [2019] EU:C:2019:341, para 110.

B. Scholarship

Legal scholarship offers several alternative paths in this regard. These can be regrouped according to formal, functional, and substantive approaches. Formally, two often mentioned characteristics of constitutions are their supremacy with respect to ordinary law and their entrenched status often expressed through qualified amendment procedures.[18] While there is no differentiation regarding the precedence of individual Treaty provisions over secondary legislation, primary law exhibits different amendment procedures. Article 48 TEU distinguishes between an ordinary and a simplified amendment procedure (Article 48(6) TEU). That simplified procedure concerns only the third part of the TFEU and thus especially what has been called the Union's 'economic constitution'. Along these lines, one could suggest that only those provisions falling within the ambit of the ordinary revision procedures feature a constitutional value.[19] However, such a distinction neglects an important concern linked to constitutional law: the focus on provisions that constitute and legitimize the exercise of public authority.[20]

Functionally, the Court could consider those Treaty provisions as constitutional that fulfil a constitutional function.[21] Yet, the functions ascribed to constitutions vary considerably from one author to another.[22] Further, many authors seem to simply take a set of constitutional functions from the national level and transpose it to the European one, which leads to the problem of translatability.[23] To avoid this translatability trap, one could either rely on an EU-specific conception of what functions an EU constitution should fulfil (which remains a desideratum) or depart from a highly abstract understanding (losing explanatory value). Methodologically too, the functional approach seems flawed. The fact that one institution fulfils the function of another does not necessarily mean that both should be described by the same term. To the contrary, a functional approach refers to

[18] For the classic treatment, see Hans Kelsen, *General Theory of Law and State* (Harvard Univ. Press 1945) 124 f. See also Dieter Grimm, 'Types of Constitutions' in Michel Rosenfeld and András Sajó (eds), *The Oxford Handbook of Comparative Constitutional Law* (OUP 2012) 98, 109 ff.

[19] See e.g. Matthias Herdegen, 'Vertragliche Eingriff in das "Verfassungsystem" der Europäischen Union' in Ole Due et al. (eds), *Festschrift für Ulrich Everling*, vol 1 (Nomos 1995) 447, 460 f.

[20] Armin von Bogdandy, 'Founding Principles' in von Bogdandy and Jürgen Bast (eds), *Principles of European Constitutional Law* (2nd edn, Hart 2009) 11, 14.

[21] See e.g. Koen Lenaerts and José A. Gutiérrez-Fons, 'A Constitutional Perspective' in Robert Schütze and Takis Tridimas (eds), *Oxford Principles of European Union Law*, vol 1 (OUP 2018) 103.

[22] From the variety of conceptualizations, see e.g. Kaarlo Tuori, 'European Constitutionalism' in Roger Masterman and Robert Schütze (eds), *The Cambridge Companion to Comparative Constitutional Law* (CUP 2019) 521, 533 ff; Anne Peters, *Elemente einer Theorie der Verfassung Europas* (Duncker&Humblot 2001) 76–91. More generally, see András Jakab, *European Constitutional Language* (CUP 2016) 144 ff; Dieter Grimm, *Constitutionalism* (OUP 2016) 143 ff.

[23] In detail, see e.g. Neil Walker, 'Postnational constitutionalism and the problem of translation' in Joseph H.H. Weiler and Marlene Wind (eds), *European Constitutionalism Beyond the State* (CUP 2003) 27; Sebastian Unger, '"Präzedenzlos zu denken"?' in Armin Hatje et al. (ed.), *Europarechtswissenschaft* (Nomos 2018) 191, 195

similar services of *different* institutions. By implication, not every legal structure that fulfils constitutional functions is therefore a constitution.[24]

Finally, many have argued that the Treaties are a constitution in the substantive, material, but not in the formal sense. The notion of 'material constitution' is highly ambiguous and has been theorized in different ways.[25] In its simplest form, it relates to the most important legal rules of a given legal order—irrespective of whether they are enshrined in a document designated as constitution.[26] A substantive constitutional content is ascribed, for instance, to provisions on institutions, competences, law-making procedures, the relation of the individual to public authority, and provisions on basic values and objectives.[27]At the EU level, many scholars avoid the theoretical baggage that comes with more demanding conceptions of a material constitution.[28] Instead, they identify principles and provisions that feature a typically constitutional or fundamental content.[29] Often, however, they do not engage with the underlying question of what distinguishes constitutions and is thus to be considered 'typically' constitutional. Further, the criteria for identifying what is fundamental, important, or significant are usually subjective. As such, it comes as no surprise that most accounts seem to be a product of the author's intuition rather than a systematic approach.[30]

III. Towards an Article 2 TEU-based Constitution

In sum, substantive conceptions of EU constitutional law have one central shortcoming. They largely rely on intuition when making the distinction between what is constitutional and what is not. Drawing on substantive approaches, this Chapter seeks to advance a new, arguably more consistent approach: deriving the Union's constitution from Article 2 TEU. The next sections will briefly outline the

[24] See the critique by Christoph Möllers, 'Pouvoir Constituant—Constitution—Constitutionalisation' in von Bogdandy and Bast (n 20) 169, 181.

[25] For an overview of the different concepts and meanings in the oeuvre of Carl Schmitt, Rudolf Smend, Herman Heller, Constantino Mortati, or Hans Kelsen, see e.g. Jakab (n 22) 151 ff.

[26] Fundamentally, see Georges Vedel, *Manuel élémentaire de droit constitutionnel (1949)* (Dalloz 2002) 112; Georg Jellinek, *Allgemeine Staatslehre* (3rd edn, Springer 1925) 505. More recently, see e.g. Louis Favoreu et al., *Droit Constitutionnel* (22nd edn, Dalloz 2020) 83 ff; Uwe Volkmann, *Grundzüge einer Verfassungslehre der Bundesrepublik Deutschland* (Mohr Siebeck 2013) 13.

[27] See e.g. Giuseppe de Vergottini, *Diritto Costituzionale Comparato* (10th edn, Cedam 2019) 263 ff; Markus Möstl, 'Regelungsfelder der Verfassung' in Otto Depenheuer and Christoph Grabenwarter (eds), *Verfassungstheorie* (Mohr Siebeck 2011) § 11.

[28] But see John E. Fossum and Agustín J. Menéndez, *The Constitution's Gift* (Rowman 2011) 20.

[29] Exemplarily, Manfred Zuleeg, 'The Advantages of the European Constitution' in von Bogdandy and Bast (n 20) 763, 765: 'it is not the legal form but rather the content that is decisive'.

[30] See e.g. Grimm (n 22) 299 who notes that '[t]here are no universally applicable principles for determining what belongs in a constitution'. See also Möllers (n 24) 189; Philipp Dann, 'Thoughts on a Methodology of European Constitutional Law' GLJ 6 (2005), 1453, 1458.

suggested approach (Section A) and provide some illustrations for how it might be applied (Section B).

A. Method

As articulated in the previous chapter, Article 2 TEU should be understood as a constitutional core that outlines the basic tenets of the Union's constitution. In consequence, the EU's constitution would be composed of those provisions that *give expression to the values enshrined in Article 2 TEU*. To distinguish the building blocks of the Union's constitution from the vast array of Treaty provisions, the Court would need to assess whether an individual provision gives specific expression to a value enshrined in Article 2 TEU. In this sense, Article 2 TEU becomes an analytic tool to identify manifestations of the 'constitutional' in EU law.

This proposal follows the path taken by the Court to operationalize Article 2 TEU through provisions that give specific expression to a Union value (see Chapter 2, III.A). At the same time, it expands on the principles-based approach developed, in particular, by Armin von Bogdandy.[31] According to this approach, primary law's constitutional character is expressed by the EU's founding principles.[32] Similar to the proposal at the core of this section, the founding principles are used to identify those Treaty provisions that feature a founding and legitimatory function.[33] Even though Article 6(1) TEU-Amsterdam/Nice (today Article 2 TEU) is considered the 'most important positive basis of European founding principles', this approach is not limited to the principles enshrined therein but extends to all principles located in the TEU's first title.[34] While this makes the principles-based approach more inclusive, it leads us right back to the alleged arbitrariness with which we tend to intuitively identify 'typically' constitutional functions or contents.

The proposal advanced in this section presents two key advantages when compared to the approaches considered in literature and jurisprudence. For one, it avoids the potentially controversial step of defining and subscribing to a specific constitutional concept (in contrast to functional approaches). Rather than operating in a deductive manner, it is suggested that the Court should proceed inductively from the letters of the Treaties. Instead of searching for the normatively

[31] von Bogdandy (n 20). For related principles-based approaches, see e.g. Jörg P. Terhechte, 'Prinzipienordnung der Europäischen Union' in Terhechte, *Europäische Verfassungsstudien* (Nomos 2020) 217; Karl-Peter Sommermann, 'Herkunft und Funktion von Verfassungsprinzipien in der Europäischen Union' in Hartmut Bauer and Christian Calliess (eds), *Verfassungsprinzipien in Europa* (Sakkoulas 2008) 15; Joël Molinier et al., *Les principes fondateurs de l'Union européenne* (PUF 2005).

[32] von Bogdandy (n 20) 13.

[33] ibid 21.

[34] ibid 19, 22. See also von Bogdandy, 'Constitutional Principles for Europe' in Eibe Riedel and Rüdiger Wolfrum (eds), *Recent Trends in German and European Constitutional Law* (Springer 2009) 1, 2: 'Neither Art 6 EU nor Art 2 CTConv (Art 2 CT-IGC) contain an exhaustive list of the founding principles. Of further significance—under current law—are in particular Art 2 EU and Arts 2, 5 and 10 EC.'

'right' constitutional model for the EU, we can concentrate on what has actually been agreed upon. At the same time, this approach provides a clear method for identifying constitutional provisions (in contrast to substantive approaches). In other words, it rationalizes the process of identifying the Union's substantive constitution.

As noted earlier, this chapter presupposes that Article 2 TEU contains a constitutional core that outlines the basic tenets of the EU's constitution. On the one hand, even a short glimpse at the content of Article 2 TEU seems to suggest that Article 2 TEU entails practically all substantive building blocks for a constitution (in detail, below III.B). As such, it comes as no surprise that Article 6 TEU-Amsterdam/Nice was perceived as the 'central European norm with substantive constitutional content'.[35] On the other hand, there are strong semantic, systematic, and historical arguments for such a reading (in detail Chapter 3, III.B). First, the provision states that '[t]he Union is founded' on these values—and *only* on them. Article 2 TEU's constitutive tonality becomes particularly apparent when contrasted with other Treaty provisions that are framed in restrictive terms (e.g. Article 4(2) TEU: 'shall respect'). Second, Article 2 TEU has been positioned at the very top of the provisions governing the Treaties and could thus be perceived as an overarching point of reference.[36] Third, its drafting history suggests that Article 2 TEU is a manifestation of a thicker, constitutive form of constitutionalism. Instead of founding the Union on the will of 'the people', it was founded on a set of values. Even though Article 2 TEU can certainly not remedy the lack of a popular constituent power at the EU level, one can nonetheless argue that both fulfil analogous functions. In this sense, the founding values in Article 2 TEU take the place of a final authority.

Finally, the proposed reading of Article 2 TEU is supported by comparative considerations. A short look into the Member States' constitutions reveals that many feature a more or less detailed provision outlining the central and guiding principles of the respective legal order. Article 20 of the German Basic Law, for instance, is generally understood as a 'Verfassung in Kurzform', a 'Verfassungskern',[37] 'Konzentrat', or 'Verfassung der Verfassung'.[38] In very similar terms, Article 1 of the Spanish Constitution is considered the 'constitución de la constitución',[39] and

[35] Peters (n 22) 349 ('zentrale europäische Norm mit materiell verfassungswürdigem Gehalt'). See also Cordula Stumpf, 'Art. 6 EUV' in Jürgen Schwarze (ed.), *EU-Kommentar* (2nd edn, Nomos 2009)para 1 ('zentrale materielle Norm des gesamten Unionsrechts').

[36] With regard to the former Art. I-2 CT, see e.g. Takis Tridimas, *The General Principles of EU Law* (2nd edn, OUP 2007) 16. On the importance of arguments sedes materiae in the Court's case law, see e.g. Giulio Itzcovich, 'The European Court of Justice' in Itzcovich et al. (eds), *Comparative Constitutional Reasoning* (CUP 2017) 277, 295.

[37] Karl-Peter Sommermann, 'Art. 20 GG' in Hermann von Mangoldt et al. (eds), *Kommentar zum Grundgesetz*, vol 2 (7th edn, C.H.Beck 2018)para 4.

[38] Markus Kotzur, 'Art. 20 GG' in Ingo von Münch and Philipp Kunig (eds), *Grundgesetz-Kommentar*, vol 1 (7th edn, C.H.Beck 2021)para 195.

[39] Angel Garrorena Morales, *El Estado español como Estado social y democrático de derecho* (Tecnos 1984) 13 ff.

Austrian constitutional law draws on the 'Baugesetze der Verfassung'.[40] Many constitutional courts read these provisions as a guiding star for constitutional interpretation. In this spirit, the Spanish Tribunal Constitucional noted that Article 1(1) of the Spanish Constitution 'represents the axiological foundation for the understanding of the entire constitutional order'.[41] Whereas some courts maintain a certain self-restraint with regard to these abstract principles,[42] others have fleshed out and refined them into specific, free-standing standards. In particular, the Bundesverfassungsgericht has used Article 20 of the Basic Law both as a catch-all standard for unregulated issues and as a point of reference for the interpretation of other constitutional provisions.[43]

B. Contours

To many, reconstructing the EU's constitution based solely on Article 2 TEU might seem overly simplistic, naïve, artificial, or underinclusive. To recall, under the proposed scheme, only those provisions form part of the EU's substantive constitution that give specific expression to a value enshrined in Article 2 TEU. As such, this proposal will inevitably lead to a narrow conception. Conversely, constitution-building *without* these elements—fundamental rights, democracy, and the rule of law—seems hardly possible either. Their relationship has been aptly compared to that of a three-legged stool: 'if one is missing the whole is not fit for purpose'.[44] In this sense, they are 'co-original'.[45] Although this does not allow the reverse conclusion that a constitution can be reconstrued *solely* on these three elements, it presents a promising start.

As seen in Chapter 2, the Court has already started to connect Article 2 TEU to a range of Treaty provisions, such as Article 19(1)(2) TEU, Article 10 TEU, as well as a range of Charter rights. Yet, the nascent jurisprudence is still at its very beginning. It would by far exceed the scope of this contribution to provide a precise and exhaustive assessment of all provisions giving specific expression to a value enshrined in Article 2 TEU. This ambitious programme must be left to further

[40] See e.g. Ludwig K. Adamovich et al., *Österreichisches Staatsrecht*, vol 1 (2nd edn, Springer 2011) 129 ff.

[41] Tribunal Constitucional, STC 12/2008 (ECLI:ES:TC:2008:12), FJ 4 (author's translation).

[42] With regard to Art. 1(1) of the Czech Constitution ('The Czech Republic is a sovereign, unitary, and democratic state governed by the rule of law, founded on respect for the rights and freedoms of man and of citizens'), see e.g. Ústavní soud, Judgment of 3 November 2009, Pl. ÚS 29/09, *Lisbon II*, para 112: 'the Constitutional Court does not feel authorised to formulate in advance, in an abstract context, what is the precise content of Article 1(1) of the Constitution'.

[43] Christian Bumke and Andreas Voßkuhle, *German Constitutional Law* (OUP 2019) para 1293.

[44] Sergio Carrera, Elspeth Guild, and Nicholas Hernanz, *The Triangular Relationship between Fundamental Rights, Democracy and the Rule of Law in the EU* (European Parliament, LIBE, 2013) 30.

[45] See e.g. Jürgen Habermas, 'On the Internal Relation Between the Rule of Law And Democracy' *European Journal of Philosophy* 3 (1995), 12.

research.[46] Instead, this section seeks to sketch in broad strokes how the proposed approach could work and where potential problems might arise. If we apply the proposed scheme, what could an Article 2 TEU-based constitution look like? Which provisions could give specific expression to the values enshrined in Article 2 TEU and thus form part of the Union's constitution?

First, this would include Article 6 TEU and the Charter as these provisions operationalize the value of 'respect for human rights'. Second, the proposed approach would cover the Union's institutional framework. The European Parliament (e.g. Articles 14 TEU and 223 ff. TFEU), citizen initiatives (Article 11(4) TEU), the recourse to national parliaments (Article 12 TEU), and the legislative process at the EU level give expression to the value of democracy. This includes the Council. Though representing the Member States' governments (Article 10(2) TEU), it is also a key feature in the Union's structure of dual legitimacy. The EU is directly connected to Union citizens via the European Parliament and indirectly via the democratically elected Member State governments in the Council.[47] For this reason, the Council could be understood as a manifestation of an EU-specific form of democracy. Further, the EU's institutional set up comprises the Union's judicial architecture. In this sense, provisions on the CJEU and national courts as 'EU courts' (Articles 19 TEU and 251 ff. TFEU) give concrete expression to the rule of law.

At first glance, the Union's competences seem difficult to square with this scheme. The same applies to the autonomy, primacy, and direct effect of EU law. Yet, a closer look reveals that even these issues feature links to Article 2 TEU. Jürgen Bast and Armin von Bogdandy have demonstrated that competences can be understood as a manifestation of the rule of law and, more precisely, the 'principle of constitutional legality'.[48] This principle has two sides. Negatively, every EU act must be consistent with higher-ranking law. Positively, any EU act must rest on a legal basis that can be traced back to the Treaties. The latter side especially relates to the Union's competences. Competence provisions in the Treaties may demarcate horizontally the competences of Union institutions and thus concern the separation of powers[49] or the institutional balance at the EU level.[50] Moreover, the

[46] For possible connections between Art. 2 TEU and other Treaty provisions, see Tom L. Boekestein, 'Making Do With What We Have: On the Interpretation and Enforcement of the EU's Founding Values' GLJ 23 (2022), 431, 451; Koen Lenaerts and Piet Van Nuffel, *EU Constitutional Law* (OUP 2021) para 5.004.

[47] Jelena von Achenbach, *Demokratische Gesetzgebung in der Europäischen Union. Theorie und Praxis der dualen Legitimationsstruktur europäischer Hoheitsgewalt* (Springer 2014) 300 ff; Jürgen Habermas, *Zur Verfassung Europas* (Suhrkamp 2011) 62 ff; von Bogdandy (n 20) 50.

[48] Armin von Bogdandy and Jürgen Bast, 'The Federal Order of Competences' in Bogdandy and Bast (n 20) 275, 278.

[49] See e.g. Christoph Möllers, *The Three Branches* (OUP 2013) 167 ff.

[50] For an overview, see e.g. Paul Craig, 'Institutions, power and institutional balance' in Craig and Grainne de Búrca (eds), *The Evolution of EU Law* (3rd edn, OUP 2021) 46; Sébastien Platon, 'The principle of institutional balance: rise, eclipse and revival of a general principle of EU constitutional law' in Katja S. Ziegler et al. (eds), *Research Handbook on General Principles in EU Law* (Elgar 2022) 136. As a manifestation of the rule of law, see e.g. Jean-Paul Jacqué, 'The Principle of Institutional Balance' CML Rev 41 (2004), 383. As a manifestation of democracy, see Koen Lenaerts and Amaryllis Verhoeven,

principle of positive legality entails that the EU may only exercise as much power as conferred on it by the Treaties. Hence, it encompasses the EU's vertical competences both as positive affirmation (generally in Articles 2–7 and specific e.g. in Article 114 TFEU) and negative delimitation (e.g. Articles 4 and 5 TEU).

The principles of autonomy, primacy, direct effect, as well as the effective and uniform application of EU law seem more difficult to connect to Article 2 TEU. On the one hand, one could reject the inclusion of these principles into the proposed scheme as they are either a premise or—concerning the latter three—an effect of EU law but not part of EU constitutional law *itself*. On the other hand, they might be derived from the rule of law and the value of equality. Indeed, one key consideration for their judicial development has been the equality of individuals in the EU legal space.[51] In *Costa/ENEL*, the Court stated that 'community law cannot vary from one state to another in deference to subsequent domestic laws, without ... giving rise to the discrimination prohibited by Article 7'.[52] In this sense, primacy and direct effect were never only a functional tool but justified by substantive considerations. Koen Lenaerts' recent attempt to ground primacy in the Member States' equality seeks to bring such substantive considerations to the fore.[53]

This leads to the limits of the proposed approach. Especially the Union policies contained in Part Three of the TFEU will not give expression to a value enshrined in Article 2 TEU. This includes not only policy areas, such as agriculture, transport, employment, education, health, consumer protection, energy, or environment but also the AFSJ and the so-called 'economic constitution'. While certainly an oscillating notion,[54] this concept comprises provisions pertaining to the internal market, such as fundamental freedoms, competition, or state aid law.[55] Others distinguish a micro-economic constitution that relates to the internal market and a macro-economic constitution that pertains to economic and monetary policy.[56]

'Institutional Balance as a Guarantee for Democracy in EU Governance' in Christian Joerges and Renaud Dehousse (eds), *Good Governance in Europe's Integrated Market* (OUP 2002) 34.

[51] Marcus Klamert, 'Supremacy, the Uniformity of EU Law, and the Principle of Equality' *Austrian Law Journal* 9 (2022), 82–92.

[52] See e.g. Case C-6/64 *Costa v ENEL* [1964] EU:C:1964:66.

[53] Koen Lenaerts, José A. Gutiérrez-Fons, and Stanislas Adam, 'Exploring the Autonomy of the European Legal Order' ZaöRV 81 (2021), 47, 70; Koen Lenaerts, 'L'égalité des États membres devant les traités' RDUE (2021), 7.

[54] On the origins and evolution of this notion, see e.g. Armin Hatje, 'The Economic Constitution within the Internal Market' in Bogdandy and Bast (n 20) 589; Herwig C.H. Hofmann and Katerina Pantazatou, 'The transformation of the European Economic Constitution' in Hofmann, Pantazatou, and Giovanni Zaccaroni (eds), *The Metamorphosis of the European Economic Constitution* (Elgar 2019) 2.

[55] See e.g. Peter-Christian Müller-Graff, 'Europäisches Wirtschaftsordnungsrecht: Das System' in Müller-Graff (ed.), *Europäisches Binnenmarkt- und Wirtschaftsordnungsrecht* (Nomos 2020) paras 25 ff, 73 ff; Julio Baquero Cruz, *Between Competition and Free Movement: The Economic Constitutional Law of the European Community* (Hart 2002) 29, 63 ff.

[56] Kaarlo Tuori, *European Constitutionalism* (CUP 2015) 23, 127 ff, 174 ff.

As a general rule, all these issues would not be part of an Article 2 TEU-based constitution. Admittedly, there are many grey areas. For instance, the policy areas mentioned above feature provisions delineating the competences of the EU and its institutions as well. This includes, for instance, those provisions that specify the ECB's mandate. At least in this respect, there is a connecting factor to the rule of law and, in particular, the principle of positive legality. Accordingly, such provisions could be understood as giving expression to the value of the rule of law.

This narrow conception will certainly raise objections. For many, the exclusion of the 'economic constitution' from the Union's constitutional framework will be difficult to digest. Indeed, both market freedoms as well as competition law guarantee individual autonomy and self-determination.[57] While the former protect individuals against constraining state power, the latter aims at limiting private power. Still, both are rooted in the individual's freedom to organize its economic life.[58] For that reason, they can be seen as giving specific expression to the value of 'freedom'. Article 2 TEU could thus provide the ultimate point of reference for the Union's entire 'economic constitution'.

However, there are several arguments against such a reading. Even if fundamental freedoms and competition law protect individual autonomy, it seems clear that these provisions have an objective beyond this function. According to the Court, these provisions 'must be understood as being *intended* to eliminate all barriers' to intra-Union trade. They are 'an indispensable instrument for the realization of a market without internal frontiers'.[59] In consequence, many perceive free movement rights and competition law rather as an instrument for the realization of a common market.[60] This corresponds to their respective titles in the TFEU. Their facet as guarantees for individual freedom is then better expressed through Charter rights such as Articles 15 and 16. Even if one takes the standpoint that market freedoms are lex specialis in cross-border situations,[61] Articles 15 and 16 of the Charter guarantee individual autonomy on a more general scale. As such, the value of 'freedom' or 'human rights' is mediated through these Charter rights

[57] See Carsten König, 'Zum Verfassungsrang der Grundfreiheiten und des europäischen Wettbewerbsrechts' EuR 57 (2022), 48, 62 ff. See further Hatje (n 54) 596 ff; David J. Gerber, *Law and Competition in Twentieth-Century Europe* (Clarendon 2001), 16 ff, 417 f.

[58] See only Guido Comparato and Hans-W. Micklitz, 'Regulated Autonomy between Market Freedoms and Fundamental Rights in the Case Law of the CJEU' in Ulf Bernitz and Xavier Groussot (eds), *General Principles of EU Law and European Private Law* (Kluwer 2013) 121.

[59] Case 112/00 *Schmidberger* [2003] EU:C:2003:333, paras 56 f.

[60] With regard to market freedoms, see e.g. Thorsten Kingreen, 'Fundamental Freedoms' in Bast and von Bogdandy (n 20) 515, 530; Francesco de Cecco, 'Fundamental Freedoms, Fundamental Rights, and the Scope of Free Movement Law' GLJ 15 (2014), 383, 385; Rufat Babayev, 'Private Autonomy at Union Level: On Article 16 CFREU and Free Movement Rights' CML Rev 53 (2016), 979, 988 f. With regard to competition law, see e.g. Rufat Babayev, 'Duality of Economic Freedom Protection in the Interplay of Art.16 CFR and Art.102 TFEU' EL Rev 45 (2020), 694, 698 ff.

[61] Matthias Ruffert, 'Art. 15 GRC' in Ruffert and Christian Calliess (eds), *EUV/AEUV* (6th edn, C.H.Beck 2022) paras 26 f.

before being further specified by fundamental freedoms (on the relationship of market freedoms and Charter rights, see Section IV).

It should be stressed that this chapter does not call into question the importance of the common market or the political salience of other excluded policy areas. Nevertheless, it is one thing to perceive a certain issue as politically salient and yet another to perceive it as constitutional. As will become clearer in the next section, this chapter proposes a *submission* of Union policies to the values enshrined in Article 2 TEU and the provisions that give specific expression to them.[62] Again, it should be emphasized that this is not meant to weaken the provisions pertaining to the individual policy areas. In fact, excluding them from the EU's constitution can even lead, if coupled with certain adjustments in the CJEU's case law, to their stronger politicization (in detail, see Chapter 6).

Eventually, this submission is not as revolutionary as it might sound. Such a relationship is already indicated by the Treaty framework. Article 2 TEU is placed before the Union's objectives, and even among these objectives, the promotion of its values stands—in Article 3 No. 1 TEU—above the AFSJ, the internal market, or the economic and monetary union. Further, the relationship between these policy areas and the values enshrined in Article 2 TEU has been the subject of debate for some time. In the context of the AFSJ, for instance, there is a longstanding, much criticized tension between EU fundamental rights and surrenders or transfers under the European Arrest Warrant or Dublin system. During the financial crisis, very similar tensions arose concerning EU instruments of macro-economic policy. Since then, these policy areas have been subjected—albeit slowly—to fundamental rights concerns. Even with regard to the very core of economic integration, some have advocated a 'constitutionally conditioned' internal market.[63] Ultimately, such an understanding might constitute a further step in the development of EU law into a more mature constitutional system.

IV. Effect: Substantive Hierarchies in EU Primary Law

Why does it matter what is part of the EU's constitution and what is not? As noted in the previous chapter, the notion of a constitution comes with certain effects in constitutional adjudication. Besides a specific constitutional methodology, constitutions usually imply a formal and/or substantive hierarchy with respect to ordinary law.[64] This means that constitutional provisions serve as yardsticks for the

[62] See also Armin von Bogdandy, *The Emergence and Democratization of European Society* (OUP 2023) 3.5.C. With regard to EU competition law, see e.g. Josef Drexl, 'Competition Law as Part of the European Constitution' in Bogdandy and Bast (n 20) 659, 665.

[63] Dagmar Schiek et al., *EU social and labour rights and EU internal market law* (European Parliament, EMPL, 2015) 78 ff.

[64] For a comparative assessment of this primacy, Vorrang, primauté, supremacía or supremazia, see Cruz Villalón (n 4) paras 72, 81 f. and Elena Bindi and Mario Perini, 'Legal Effect of Constitutions'

validity of ordinary law or, at the very least, as guidelines for its interpretation.[65] Drawing on these insights, the suggested reorganization of the Treaties in parts that feature constitutional value and parts that do not can be translated into a substantive hierarchy. This substantive hierarchy could have a considerable impact on the judicial practice of the Luxembourg court.

Many scholars assume that Article 2 TEU has a special place among the provisions of EU primary law. Its wording ('founded' and 'values' as final authorities), its place in the Treaties (at the top), its content (constitutional principles) as well as its unique form of protection under Article 7 TEU strongly support the thesis that Article 2 TEU transcends other Treaty provisions.[66] There was already an agreement among scholars that Article 6(1) TEU-Amsterdam/Nice and Article I-2 of the Constitutional Treaty should feature 'un rang essentiel dans la hiérarchie des normes du droit de l'Union'.[67] This chapter goes a step further and uses Article 2 TEU as a starting point for a hierarchical restructuring of the *entire* Treaties.

Twenty years ago, Anne Peters noted that the development of internal hierarchies within EU primary law, in particular between provisions that feature constitutional content and those that do not, would be a decisive step in the further constitutionalization of EU law.[68] The following approach could be an important step in this direction. As suggested above, the EU's constitution could be composed of provisions giving expression to the EU's founding values, which must be distinguished from the rest of primary law. This differentiation can be translated into a hierarchical structure (see Figure 4.1). At the top of this hierarchy stands Article 2 TEU. It contains the Union's founding principles and outlines the basic tenets of the Union's constitution. The second tier features those provisions that give expression to a value enshrined in Article 2 TEU. The rest of primary law, including large parts of what has been termed the EU's 'economic constitution', forms a third level.

This reconstruction cannot and does not suggest the establishment of *formal* but of *substantive* hierarchies. What distinguishes these notions? In principle, formal hierarchies present two key characteristics: superior law conditions the creation

in Rainer Grote et al. (eds), *Max Planck Encyclopedia of Comparative Constitutional Law* (OUP 2017) paras 69–89.

[65] See e.g. Thomas Möllers, *Legal Methods* (Hart 2020) 387 ff, 390 ff.

[66] See e.g. Allan Rosas and Lorna Armati, *EU Constitutional Law* (3rd edn, Hart 2018) 53 ff.

[67] With regard to Art. I-2 CT, see e.g. Marianne Dony, 'Les valeurs, objectifs et principes de l'Union' in Dony and Emmanuelle Bribosia (eds), *Commentaire de la Constitution de l'Union européenne* (Editions de l'Université de Bruxelles 2005) 33, 37; Laurence Burgorgue-Larsen, 'Article I-2' in Burgorgue-Larsen, Anne Levade, and Fabrice Picod (eds), *Traité établissant une Constitution pour l'Europe*, vol 1 (Bruylant 2007) 50, para 14; Tridimas (n 36) 16. With regard to Art. 6(1) TEU-Amsterdam/Nice, see e.g. Hélène Gaudin, 'Amsterdam: l'échec de la hiérarchie des normes?' RTDE 35 (1999), 1; Peters (n 22) 341 f.

[68] Peters (n 22) 349, 359. See also Peters, 'The Constitutionalisation of the European Union—Without the Constitutional Treaty' in Sonja Puntscher Riekmann and Wolfgang Wessels (eds), *The Making of a European Constitution* (VS Verlag 2006) 35, 40.

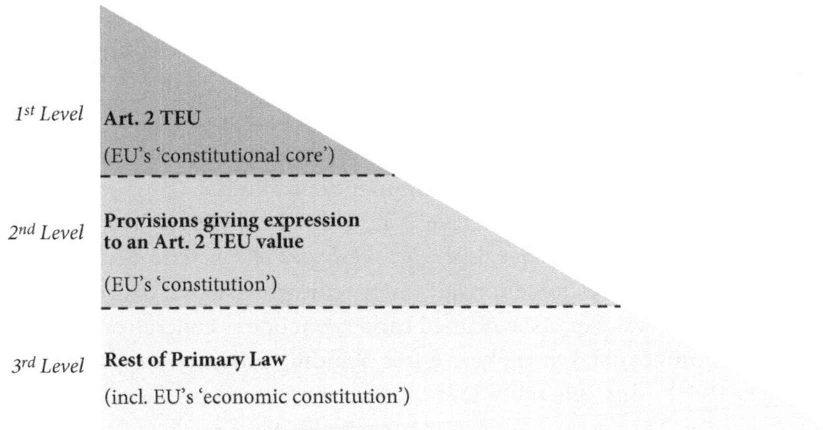

Figure 4.1 Substantive hierarchy of Treaty provisions

of other inferior provisions and has a derogatory effect in case it is contradicted.[69] Such formal hierarchies primarily regulate the relationship between constitutions and ordinary statutes. While formal hierarchies among constitutional provisions are not excluded per se,[70] this is usually the domain of substantive hierarchies. These are established according to the substance of legal provisions.[71] Some speak of axiological hierarchies.[72] The effect of substantive hierarchizations is softer and unfolds especially in constitutional adjudication. If two constitutional provisions of diverging substantive rank collide, this does not affect the validity of the inferior one. Instead, substantively higher-ranking provisions exert a stronger interpretative force and enjoy greater weight when balanced against other provisions.

The Treaties themselves do not establish any formal hierarchies between constitutional and other provisions. Nonetheless, Pierre Pescatore had already noted in the 1980s that 'a clear hierarchy of values emerges in the Court's case law, insofar as certain Treaty provisions are singled out as "essential"'.[73] The Court's first

[69] See Kelsen (n 18) 20. More recently Christoph Grabenwarter, 'Die Verfassung in der Hierarchie der Rechtsordnung' in Depenheuer and Grabenwarter (n 27) § 11, paras 5 ff.

[70] This might concern especially eternity clauses, which have a derogatory effect on constitutional amendments, see e.g. Art. 79(3) German Basic Law. However, this is controversial.

[71] Cesare Pinelli, 'Theories Concerning the Hierarchy of Norms' in Grote et al. (n 64) paras 9 ff; Volkmann (n 26) 93 ff; Véronique Champeil-Desplats, 'Hiérarchie des normes, principe justificatif de la suprematie de la constitution' in Michel Troper and Dominique Chagnollaud (eds), *Traité international de droit constitutionnel*, vol 1 (Dalloz 2012) 733, 739 f.

[72] Orlando Scarcello, 'On the Role of Normative Hierarchies in Constitutional Reasoning' *Ratio Juris* 31 (2018), 346, 349 ff; Riccardo Guastini, 'Gerarchie normative' *revus* 21 (2013), 57, 61; Giorgio Pino, 'La gerarchia delle fonti del diritto' *Ars interpretandi* (2011), 19, 34 ff.

[73] Pierre Pescatore, 'Die Gemeinschaftsverträge als Verfassungsrecht' in Wilhelm G. Grewe et al. (eds), *Festschrift zum 70. Geburtstag von Hans Kutscher* (Nomos 1981) 319, 331 (author's translation).

EEA opinion or *Kadi* have been read in this light.[74] Further, the establishment of substantive hierarchies is not unprecedented in constitutional adjudication. As we have seen before, many constitutional courts in the European legal space have been very active in restructuring their respective constitutions. Some have distinguished—at times even without textual support—a set of guiding constitutional principles or internal hierarchies within the constitution.

The three levels derived from Article 2 TEU can be distinguished in at least two respects. First, each level reveals a *different degree of concretization*. Whereas the second and third level contain relatively specific provisions, Article 2 TEU is an altogether different case. As explained earlier, it requires concretization and is difficult (if not impossible) to apply as a free-standing provision to specific cases (Chapter 2, III.B). This generality leads to specific functions of Article 2 TEU within this tripartite structure. For one, Article 2 TEU has a methodological function as a dividing line between the Union's constitutional framework and the rest of primary law. Substantively, it can function as a guideline for the Treaties' interpretation and application. Considering the difficulties in applying Article 2 TEU in a freestanding manner, it remains to be seen whether it can serve as an immediate yardstick. In any case, it would apply only in highly exceptional circumstances.

This leads to the second differentiation. Each level features *different scopes and different degrees of protection*. To provide a simple example: Fundamental freedoms protect certain conduct on the third level (e.g. the freedom to provide services). While the scope of protection afforded on this level is broad (including e.g. measures of equivalent effect), its degree of protection is comparatively weak (e.g. restrictions can be justified by relying on a broad range of grounds). On the second level, there are provisions corresponding to fundamental freedoms, such as Articles 15 and 16 CFR. According to the suggested scheme—and it should be emphasized that this is *not* the status quo[75]—the scope of protection under these provisions should be narrower. For instance, infringements of Articles 15 and 16 CFR could be restricted to direct discriminations while allowing other obstacles to market access.[76] At the same time, such infringements would be subject to

[74] On the general discussion of substantive hierarchies in primary law, see Rosas and Armati (n 66) 53 ff; Andreas von Arnauld, 'Normenhierarchien innerhalb des primären Gemeinschaftsrechts' EuR 38 (2003), 191; Herwig C.H. Hofmann, *Normenhierarchien im europäischen Gemeinschaftsrecht* (Duncker&Humblot 2000) 81 ff. Critically with regard to hierarchies in primary law, see Martin Nettesheim, 'Normenhierarchien im EU-Recht' EuR 41 (2006), 737; Markus Heintzen, 'Hierarchisierungsprozesse innerhalb des Primärrechts der Europäischen Gemeinschaft' EuR 29 (1994), 35.

[75] Pointing rather towards equivalence, see e.g. Art. 52(2) CFR and the Explanations to the Charter [2007] OJ C303/17 Art. 15. Similarly, the Court noted that 'Article 15(2) of the Charter reiterates inter alia the free movement of workers', see Case C-284/15 *ONEm and M* [2016] EU:C:2016:220, para 33; Case C-233/12 *Gardella* [2013] EU:C:2013:449, para 39.

[76] In this sense, see Nik J. de Boer, 'Fundamental Rights and the EU Internal Market' *Utrecht Law Review* 9 (2013), 148, 154 f; Sacha Garben, 'The "Fundamental Freedoms" and (Other Fundamental Rights)' in Garben and Inge Govaere (eds), *The Internal Market 2.0* (Hart 2020) 335, 345 ff.

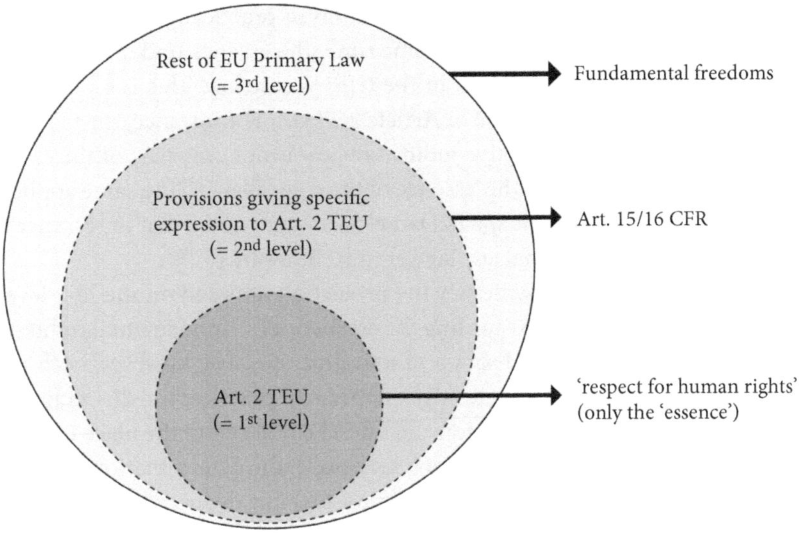

Figure 4.2 Substantive layering of Treaty provisions

stricter scrutiny. On the first level, the protection under the value of 'respect for human rights' should be even narrower. Article 2 TEU can only comprise a core or essence,[77] which is protected in an even stricter fashion. Many even understand Article 2 TEU as an untouchable core of EU law.[78] In consequence, the substantive hierarchization outlined before corresponds to a layered system of scope and protection from periphery to core (see Figure 4.2).

Certainly, the determination of core and periphery is inherently fuzzy. In particular, there are no clear-cut methods to determine what falls under Article 2 TEU and what pertains to the second and third layer. Similar concerns have already been raised with regard to the notion of essence.[79] Despite its fuzziness, however, manifestations of this concept—such as essence or substance, *contenu essentiel* or

[77] On the connection of essence of rights and Art. 2 TEU, see already Armin von Bogdandy et al., 'Reverse Solange–Protecting the Essence of Fundamental Rights Against EU Member States' CML Rev 49 (2012), 489, 509 ff. For a distinction between a 'Wertekern' (value core) and a 'Wertehülle' (value shell), see Till P. Holterhus and Daniel Kornack, 'Die materielle Struktur der Unionsgrundwerte' EuGRZ 41 (2014), 389, 397.

[78] See e.g. Marcus Klamert and Dimitry Kochenov, 'Article 2 TEU' in Manuel Kellerbauer et al. (eds), *The Treaties and the Charter of Fundamental Rights—A Commentary* (OUP 2019) para 1. See also Andreas Voßkuhle, *The Idea of the European Community of Values* (Bittner 2017) 116; Frank Schorkopf, 'Der Wertekonstitutionalismus der Europäischen Union' JZ 75 (2020), 477, 482.

[79] See e.g. Orlando Scarcello, 'Preserving the "Essence" of Fundamental Rights under Article 52(1) of the Charter: A Sisyphean Task?' EuConst 16 (2021), 647; Mark Dawson, Orla Lynskey, and Elise Muir, 'What Is the Added Value of the Concept of the "Essence" of EU Fundamental Rights?' GLJ 20 (2019), 763; Sébastien Van Drooghenbroeck and Cécilia Rizcallah, 'Art. 52' in Van Drooghenbroeck, Rizcallah, and Fabrice Picod (eds), *Charte des droits fondamentaux de l'Union européenne* (2nd edn, Bruylant 2020) 1249, 1254 ff.

noyau dur, *Wesens-* or *Kerngehalt*—can be found in practically all Member State jurisdictions.[80] Though neglected for some time, the essence under Article 52(1) CFR has become slowly operational in the CJEU's case law. This is a remarkable parallel to the increasing relevance of Article 2 TEU.[81] For instance, the Court has noted that the existence of effective judicial review is not only part of the essence of Article 47 CFR[82] but also of the 'essence of the rule of law'.[83] The same applies to judicial independence.[84] In this spirit, Daniel Sarmiento noted that the essence has become a 'relevant category that any lawyer must be aware of'.[85]

This raises the question of whether the protection afforded on the first level is absolute or relative in nature. Regarding the essence of EU fundamental rights, this issue is highly controversial.[86] From a practical perspective, however, both positions are not as irreconcilable as it might appear. In practice, the distinction between absolute and relative protection can often be reduced to the place of certain considerations in the judicial assessment. Generally, the determination of a right's essence or a value's content cannot be accomplished in a deductive fashion but requires conflicting values to be factored in.[87] In this sense, the balancing process is simply deferred to a stage preceding the proportionality assessment.[88] This conforms with the judicial practice of many constitutional courts. Often, they simply discuss conflicting rights and values when tailoring the scope of absolute rights.[89] As such, one could ask: what is the difference between 'This right/value does not apply or is not interfered with in the specific case' and 'The interference is justified'?

80 For a comparative overview, see e.g. Maja Brkan, 'The Concept of Essence of Fundamental Rights in the EU Legal Order: Peeling the Onion to Its Core' EuConst 14 (2018), 332, 339 ff; Takis Tridimas and Giulia Gentile, 'The Essence of Rights: An Unreliable Boundary?' GLJ 20 (2019), 794.

81 See also Romain Tinière, 'Le contenu essentiel des droits fondamentaux dans la jurisprudence de la Cour de Justice de l'Union européenne' CDE 57 (2021), 417, 436.

82 See e.g. Case C-245/19 *État luxembourgeois* [2020] EU:C:2020:795, para 66; Case C-311/18 *Facebook Ireland and Schrems* [2020] EU:C:2020:559, para 187; Case C-362/14 *Schrems* [2015] EU:C:2015:650, para 95.

83 See e.g. Case C-216/18 PPU *Minister for Justice and Equality (Deficiencies in the System of Justice)* [2018] EU:C:2018:586, para 51; Case C-64/16 *ASJP* [2018] EU:C:2018:117, para 36 Case C-72/15 *Rosneft* [2017] EU:C:2017:236, para 73.

84 See e.g. Case C-824/18 *A.B.* [2021] EU:C:2021:153, para 116.

85 Daniel Sarmiento, 'The Essential Content of EU Fundamental Rights' *Quaderni costituzionali* (2020), 851.

86 For an absolute protection, see Koen Lenaerts, 'Limits on Limitations: The Essence of Fundamental Rights in the EU' GLJ 20 (2019), 779, 786–8, 793; Brkan (n 80) 337, 359 ff; Tridimas and Gentile (n 80) 803. Against, see Scarcello (n 79).

87 See, e.g. the supposedly 'absolute' proposal by Brkan (n 80) 363: 'The essence of a fundamental right is interfered with . . . if overriding reasons for such interference do not exist'.

88 With regard to human dignity under the German Basic Law, see the—admittedly highly controversial—commentary by Matthias Herdegen, 'Art. 1 GG' in Günter Dürig, Roman Herzog, and Rupert Scholz (eds), *Grundgesetz-Kommentar* (99th edn, loose-leaf, C.H.Beck 2022) para 73 (see also paras 46 ff). See also Udo Di Fabio, 'Zur Theorie eines grundrechtlichen Wertsystems' in Detlef Merten and Hans-Jürgen Papier (eds), *Handbuch der Grundrechte*, vol 2 (C.F.Müller 2006) § 46, para 35.

89 With regard to the Bundesverfassungsgericht, see Manfred Baldus, 'Menschenwürdegarantie und Absolutheitsthese' AöR 136 (2011), 529, 536 ff; Michael Rosen, *Dignity* (Harvard Univ. Press 2012) 109 ff.

Further, it seems that absolute protection does not necessarily exclude proportionality or balancing assessments.[90] This applies especially to conflicts *among* supposedly absolute rights or values. At the same time, one could argue that a measure affecting the essence of a right or value is always disproportionate and thus simply the stabilized outcome of a certain balancing process.[91] Attributing 'absolute' protection to a set of values is certainly a powerful symbol.[92] Eventually, the claim for absolute protection should rather be understood as a warning sign and an indicator for stricter (in fact the strictest) scrutiny. With regard to Article 2 TEU, this could lead to a situation in which the values enshrined in Article 2 TEU could only be balanced with each other but not with other considerations. In all other cases, Article 2 TEU, including the essence of fundamental rights, takes substantive precedence (in detail, Chapter 5, III.B.2).

Finally, it should be stressed that there is no abstract hierarchy among the values enshrined in Article 2 TEU.[93] While they can be regrouped under the banners of 'respect for human rights', democracy, and the rule of law, none of these three takes abstract precedence (on their co-originality, see Chapter 4, III.B). Some statements of the Commission might be read as placing an emphasis on the rule of law. For instance, it stressed that '[c]ompliance with the rule of law is … a prerequisite for the protection of all fundamental values listed in Article 2 TEU'.[94] While the EU institutions seem to agree on this instrumental function, they nonetheless noted explicitly that 'there is no hierarchy among Union values … There can be no democracy and respect for fundamental rights without respect for the rule of law and vice versa.'[95]

The proposed threefold hierarchization could have a considerable impact on the CJEU's adjudication. The following chapters will explore its potential in three different settings. Substantively, these settings concern the interaction among Treaty provisions, their relationship with EU legislation, and, finally, Treaty revisions. Institutionally, the first setting relates to the jurisprudence of the Court itself, while the latter two focus on the relationship of the CJEU with the EU legislature and the Treaty makers. In the first setting, the suggested stratification could foster the coherence of primary law. The usual methodological tools, like systematic

[90] See e.g. Julian Rivers, 'Proportionality and Variable Intensity of Review' *Cambridge Law Journal* 65 (2006), 180, 186; Aharon Barak, *Proportionality* (CUP 2012) 498.

[91] See, e.g. Lenaerts (n 86) 781 ('automatically disproportionate').

[92] ibid 793.

[93] See, e.g. Egils Levits, 'L'Union européenne en tant que communauté des valeurs partagées' in *Liber Amicorum Antonio Tizzano* (Giappichelli 2018) 509, 515–7; Roberto Adam and Antonio Tizzano, 'Valori e obiettivi dell'Unione' in *Manuale di diritto europeo* (3rd edn, Giappichelli 2020) 387, 389; Meinhard Hilf and Frank Schorkopf, 'Art. 2 EUV' in Eberhard Grabitz et al. (eds), *Das Recht der Europäischen Union* (75th edn, loose-leaf, C.H.Beck 2022) para 48.

[94] European Commission, A new EU Framework to strengthen the Rule of Law (11 March 2014), COM/2014/0158 final, p 4.

[95] Regulation 2020/2092 on a general regime of conditionality for the protection of the Union budget, Rec. 3.

interpretation or balancing, reach their limits when faced with the multitude of potentially conflicting Treaty provisions. Further, perceiving all provisions as being of equal rank may lead to results that are hardly compatible with the achieved stage of integration. Against this backdrop, Chapter 5 will propose adding Article 2 TEU and the hierarchical division of primary law to the Court's toolbox. The second setting concentrates on the relationship of the Court and the EU legislature. As indicated above, the extensive scope of primary law and the CJEU's strong institutional position considerably reduce the space for legislative decision-making. Chapter 6 will demonstrate how the hierarchical division of primary law can help broaden this space. In particular, the Court could start distinguishing between the different levels of primary law. While retaining strict scrutiny of provisions that give expression to an Article 2 TEU value, the Court could relax the constraints imposed on the EU legislature by provisions from the third level of primary law. In contrast to the EU legislature, the Treaty makers seem entirely unconstrained. Accordingly, it is not excluded that future Treaty revisions could affect the constitutional core enshrined in Article 2 TEU. Chapter 7 will thus explore the potential of Article 2 TEU as a substantive limitation for Treaty amendments justiciable before the Court. This could help fortify the Union's constitutional core against changes in the Treaty framework that puts these values at risk.

5

The Court and the Treaties

Fostering Coherence

I. Introduction

It is generally accepted that legal orders should strive towards the ideal of consistency and coherence.[1] While consistency is understood as the absence of contradiction, coherence amounts to something more: provisions of a legal order should 'hang together' and 'make sense' as a whole.[2] In this spirit, the Court of Justice seeks to 'ensure consistency and uniformity in the interpretation of EU law'.[3] Primary law, however, poses a particular challenge in this regard. This chapter will argue that methodological tools such as systematic interpretation and balancing reach their limits if we perceive all provisions of EU primary law as being of equal rank. What is more, such an understanding may lead to results that are hardly compatible with the achieved stage of European integration (Section II). The Court has tried to remedy these issues by relying on the Union's objectives or general principles. Yet, these instruments have lost much of their appeal. Against this backdrop, this chapter will explore how Article 2 TEU and the hierarchical division of primary law can foster the Treaties' coherence (Section III).

Before diving into these issues, one brief disclaimer should be made. Today, the notions of consistency and coherence can be found in very different contexts throughout EU law.[4] For instance, several Treaty provisions impose requirements of consistency and coherence on EU action (e.g. Article 7 TFEU, Articles 13, 21(3) TEU).[5] Further, the Court has increasingly imposed consistency requirements on Member States when justifying free movement restrictions.[6] Finally, some have

[1] See e.g. András Jakab, 'Judicial Reasoning in Constitutional Courts: A European Perspective' GLJ 14 (2013), 1215, 1258. See also Lon Fuller, *The Morality of Law* (2nd edn, Yale Univ. Press 1969) 39, 63 ff.

[2] Neil MacCormick, *Rethoric and the Rule of Law: A Theory of Legal Reasoning* (OUP 2010) 189. See also Ken Kress, 'Coherence' in Dennis Patterson (ed.), *A Companion to Philosophy of Law and Legal Theory* (2nd edn, Wiley-Blackwell 2010) 521.

[3] See e.g. Opinion 2/13 *ECHR Accession II* [2014] EU:C:2014:2454, para 174; Case C-284/16 *Achmea* [2018] EU:C:2018:158, paras 35, 37; Opinion 1/17 *CETA* [2019] EU:C:2019:341, para 111.

[4] On their many facets, see e.g. Ulrike Schuster, *Das Kohärenzprinzip in der Europäischen Union* (Nomos 2017) 231 ff.

[5] For a short overview, see Marcus Klamert, 'Article 7 TFEU' in Manuel Kellerbauer et al. (eds), *The Treaties and the Charter of Fundamental Rights—A Commentary* (OUP 2019) paras 2 ff. In detail, see e.g. Christian N.K. Franklin, 'The Burgeoning Principle of Consistency in EU Law' YEL 30 (2011), 42, 58 ff.

[6] On the Court's respective case law in healthcare, tax, or gambling issues, see e.g. Jurian Langer and Wolf Sauter, 'The Consistency Requirement in EU Law' CJEL 24 (2017), 39, 53 ff; Tor-Inge Harbo, 'The

EU Values Before the Court of Justice. Luke Dimitrios Spieker, Oxford University Press.
DOI: 10.1093/oso/9780198876717.003.0006

employed the notion of coherence with regard to the compatibility of the EU and the Member States' legal orders.[7] The present Chapter will leave these issues aside and concentrate on the coherence of *EU primary law*.

II. Establishing Coherence in Primary Law

Despite many attempts to streamline the Treaties,[8] the Commission noted in 2002 that EU primary law is still a 'source of confusion and inconsistency'.[9] In this sense, several members of the European Convention argued for a leap from the 'jungle' or 'labyrinth' to a more concise and coherent primary law.[10] Since then, not much has changed. Instead, the Lisbon Treaty has still been described as a 'constitution "longe et obscure"'.[11] Indeed, primary law consists not only of two Treaties with overlapping contents but also a myriad of protocols, reservations, and annexes.[12] Further, the Treaties regulate in considerable detail a vast array of matters without differentiating between genuinely constitutional provisions and issues that would usually be regulated through legislation. This leads to a situation in which the Charter has the same *formal* rank as, for instance, Protocol (No 31) concerning imports into the European Union of petroleum products refined in the Netherlands Antilles. This does not mean that the Court *actually* accords the same weight to these two documents (on its current approach, see Section III.A). Nevertheless, this example illustrates the need for tools that allow the Court to differentiate between the broad range of Treaty provisions and establish coherence among them. The following Section argues that usual methodological tools like systematic interpretation or balancing are of limited help in this respect (Section A). Further, it is argued that perceiving all provisions as being of equal rank may lead to results that fall behind the EU's constitutional development (Section B).

Criterion of "Consistent and Systematic Manner" in Free Movement Law' in Mads Andenas et al. (eds), *The Reach of Free Movement* (Asser 2017) 205, 210 ff.

[7] See e.g. Eberhard Schmidt-Aßmann, 'Einheit und Kohärenz der europäischen Mehrebenenrechtsordnung' EuGRZ 43 (2016), 85.

[8] See Chapter 4, n 3.

[9] European Commission, A Project for the European Union (22 May 2002), COM(2002) 247 final, p 17.

[10] Plenary Debate of 13 September 2002, 5-023, López Garrido (Parl.-ES) ('Creemos que hay que ir a una Constitución breve, sencilla, corta, y a esa Constitución se tiene que adaptar lo existente hoy, no al contrario, es decir que la Constitución futura se adapte a la selva, a la jungla, al laberinto que tenemos hoy'). See further Plenary Debate of 24 May 2002, 5-028, Tiilikainen (Ch.E/G.-FI) ('The result of this process must be a clear and coherent constitutional treaty'). See also Claude Bluman and Louis Dubois, *Droit institutionnel de l'Union européenne* (6th edn, LexisNexis 2016) 121 ff.

[11] Franz C. Mayer, 'Die Rückkehr der Europäischen Verfassung?' ZaöRV 67 (2007), 1141, 1185 f.

[12] See only Editorial, 'Protocology' CML Rev 46 (2009), 1785.

A. Limited Instruments

Establishing consistency and coherence among constitutional provisions is by no means a specific problem under EU law, but a challenge faced by courts in practically every legal order. Usually, there are two ways for courts to harmonize provisions of equal rank or resolve conflicts among them. First, they can employ a systematic (systemic, contextual, or schematic) interpretation.[13] This tool has to be distinguished from textual, historical, or teleological interpretations that concentrate on identifying the meaning of a provision. A systematic interpretation, by contrast, seeks to harmonize a provision with its legal context. As other methods of interpretation are considerably weakened, this tool is of special relevance at the level of EU primary law.[14] Textual interpretations are rendered not only difficult due to the open texture and indeterminacy of many Treaty provisions but also by the fact that they are equally authentic in each of the 24 official language versions (Article 55 TEU).[15] Similar difficulties arise with regard to originalist methods of interpretation. While the drafter's intent plays an increasing role in the Court's reasoning, especially with regard to the Charter (see e.g. the Explanations) and secondary legislation,[16] the lack of openly accessible *travaux* for the Lisbon Treaty (except the European Convention) makes such an interpretative tool difficult to handle.[17]

Therefore, it comes as no surprise that the Court has put an emphasis on the method of systematic interpretation.[18] In this sense, it takes into account 'the general scheme' of the Treaties.[19] A Treaty provision 'must be placed in its context and interpreted in the light of the provisions of Community law as a whole'.[20] Yet, such a systematic interpretation encounters several difficulties. For one, this method does not entail criteria for selecting those provisions which should be taken into account.[21] Further, the more (potentially contradictory) provisions the Court has to take into account, the less helpful the systematic approach becomes.

[13] In detail Koen Lenaerts and José A. Gutiérrez-Fons, *Les méthodes d'interprétation de la Cour de justice de l'Union européenne* (Bruylant 2020) 27 ff.

[14] Jan Komárek, 'Legal Reasoning in EU Law' in Damien Chalmers and Anthony Arnull (eds), *The Oxford Handbook of European Union Law* (OUP 2015) 29, 37 ff.

[15] On these challenges, see e.g. Elina Paunio, *Legal Certainty in Multilingual EU Law: Language, Discourse and Reasoning at the European Court of Justice* (Routledge 2016) 20 ff.

[16] See e.g. Lenaerts and Gutiérrez-Fons (n 13) 40 ff; Giulio Itzcovich, 'The European Court of Justice' in Itzcovich et al. (eds), *Comparative Constitutional Reasoning* (CUP 2017) 277, 301.

[17] But see Chapter 2, n 56 f.

[18] Gunnar Beck, *The Legal Reasoning of the Court of Justice* (Hart 2013) 191 ff; Sebastian A.E. Martens, *Methodenlehre des Unionsrechts* (Mohr Siebeck 2013) 431 ff. See already Hans Kutscher, 'Methods of Interpretation as seen by the European Court of Justice' Judicial and Academic Conference (27–28 September 1976), I-16, I-36 f, I-40.

[19] See already Case C-26/62 *Van Gend en Loos* [1963] EU:C:1963:1; Case C-43/75 *Defrenne* [1976] EU:C:1976:56, para 7; Case C-294/83 *Les Verts* [1986] EU:C:1986:166, para 24.

[20] Case 283/81, *CILFIT* [1982] EU:C:1982:335, para 20. See also, Case C-561/19 *Consorzio Italian Management e Catania Multiservizi* [2021] EU:C:2021:799, para 46.

[21] See Martens (n 18) 406; Beck (n 18) 134.

Second, a usual way of reconciling conflicting provisions of the same rank is balancing. This method can be traced in different variations in nearly all European legal orders.[22] The CJEU is no exception in this regard. A usual location for such considerations is the last step of the proportionality assessment.[23] Although it often seems to gloss over this step, the Court does not entirely ignore such balancing considerations. Without going into detail, the CJEU has acknowledged the need to balance conflicting fundamental rights with each other,[24] but also with other interests protected by primary law, such as animal welfare, security, or transparency.[25] Similarly, the CJEU has engaged—at least on its face—in 'striking a fair balance' between conflicting fundamental freedoms and fundamental rights.[26] Yet, the method of balancing is not only highly contested with regard to its rationality (respectively, the lack thereof, in detail, Chapter 12, II.B);[27] it also becomes increasingly problematic with the extent of provisions that have to be taken into account. The logic is relatively simple: the more interests, guarantees, and policy choices gain constitutional status, the more trade-offs through balancing are required. This is likely to weaken the status of each constitutional provision and impede the predictability and clarity of judicial outcomes.

B. Outdated Outcomes

Further, perceiving all Treaty provisions as being of equal substantive rank can lead to results that are hardly compatible with the current stage of integration. As noted in the previous chapter, there has been a longstanding tension between the values enshrined in Article 2 TEU and specific EU policies, such as the AFSJ or economic and monetary policy (Chapter 4, III.B). Yet, these tensions arise primarily with regard to acts of EU institutions and not, strictly speaking, primary law. A more relevant example is the relationship of fundamental freedoms and fundamental rights. Already in the early 1990s, an influential article highlighted that there is no hierarchical relationship between fundamental rights and market freedoms. By

[22] For a comparative assessment, see e.g. BVerfG, Judgment of 5 May 2020, 2 BvR 859/15, *PSPP*, para 125.

[23] See e.g. Lenaerts and Gutiérrez-Fons (n 13) paras 161 ff.

[24] See e.g. Cases C-804/18 and 341/19 *WABE* [2021] EU:C:2021:594, para 84; Case C-283/11 *Sky Österreich* [2013] EU:C:2013:28, para 60; Case C-275/06 *Promusicae* [2008] EU:C:2008:54, paras 68, 70. See Xavier Groussot and Gunnar T. Petursson, 'Balancing as a Judicial Methodology of EU Constitutional Adjudication' in Sybe de Vries et al. (eds), *Balancing Fundamental Rights with the EU Treaty Freedoms* (Eleven 2012) 43.

[25] See e.g. Case C-336/19 *Centraal Israëlitisch Consistorie van België* [2020] EU:C:2020:1031, para 65; Case C-584/10 P *Commission v Kadi* [2013] EU:C:2013:518, paras 128 ff; Cases C-92 and 93/09 *Volker and Schecke* [2010] EU:C:2010:662, para 77.

[26] See e.g. Case 112/00 *Schmidberger* [2003] EU:C:2003:333, paras 77, 81.

[27] From the plethora of critique, see only Matthias Jestaedt, 'The Doctrine of Balancing–Strengths and Weaknesses' in Matthias Klatt (ed.), *Institutionalized Reason* (OUP 2011) 152, 159 ff.

implication, fundamental rights 'cease to be a "trump card" ... Instead, two norms of equal qualitative significance are balanced one against the other'.[28] In fact, legal reality turned out to be even more problematic. It seems there is an implicit hierarchy between fundamental rights and freedoms in *favour of the latter*.

This is inherent in the so-called *Schmidberger* constellation and has been perpetuated by cases like *Omega*, *Dynamic Medien*, *Viking*, and *Laval*. These cases concerned situations in which a Member State justifies the restriction of fundamental freedoms with the protection of fundamental rights. The Court usually proceeds as follows: after identifying a restriction of the respective freedom, it considers whether EU fundamental rights can justify this restriction. Putting the freedom in the default position has important legal consequences.[29] Fundamental rights considerations become an exception that must 'be interpreted strictly'.[30] The exercise of the right is subject to a proportionality test, whereas the exercise of the freedom is not.[31] Further, the argumentative burden as well as the burden of proof falls upon those advocating in favour of the right.[32] Finally, there seems to be a certain imbalance concerning the gravity in which the respected interests must be affected. While justifications based on fundamental rights are required to counter a 'sufficiently serious threat',[33] the Court is rather generous when assessing restrictions of fundamental freedoms. Though it has occasionally excluded measures for having a 'too uncertain and indirect' effect,[34] it rejected a de minimis rule and stated that 'any restriction, even minor', can trigger fundamental freedoms.[35]

Even though fundamental rights may eventually trump fundamental freedoms in a specific case, there is a 'fundamental asymmetry', 'structural bias', or 'architectural imbalance' in the Courts jurisprudence.[36] There seems to be an implicit hierarchy or priority between fundamental freedoms and rights.[37] The Charter's

[28] Jason Coppel and Aidan O'Neill, 'The European Court of Justice: Taking Rights Seriously?' CML Rev 29 (1992), 669, 689 ff.

[29] See also Agustín Menéndez, 'The Guardianship of European Constitutionality: A Structural Critique of European Constitutional Review' in Andenas et al. (n 6) 173, 183.

[30] See only Case C-36/02 *Omega* [2004] EU:C:2004:614, para 30. On whether fundamental rights are a free-standing justification or come under one of the Treaty exceptions, see e.g. Sybe de Vries, 'Balancing Fundamental Rights with Economic Freedoms According to the European Court of Justice' *Utrecht Law Review* 9 (2013), 169, 187 f

[31] See e.g. Mitchel Lasser, 'Fundamentally Flawed: The CJEU's Jurisprudence on Fundamental Rights and Fundamental Freedoms' *Theoretical Inquiries in Law* 15 (2014), 229, 247; Eleanor Spaventa, 'Federalisation versus Centralization: Tensions in Fundamental Rights Discourse in the EU' in Michael Dougan and Samantha Currie (eds), *50 Years of the European Treaties* (Hart 2010) 343, 358.

[32] See e.g. Case C-165/08 *Commission v Poland* [2009] EU:C:2009:473, para 53.

[33] *Omega* (n 30) para 30. More recently, see Case C-78/18 *Commission v Hungary* [2020] EU:C:2020:476, para 91.

[34] See e.g. Case C-674/20 *Airbnb Ireland* [2022] EU:C:2022:303, para 42.

[35] See e.g. Case C-15/15 *New Valmar* [2016] EU:C:2016:464, para 37.

[36] Lasser (n 31) 248; Menéndez (n 29) 185 ff. See also Stephanie Reynolds, 'Explaining the constitutional drivers behind a perceived judicial preference for free movement over fundamental rights' CML Rev 53 (2016), 643, 664 ff; Rufat Babayev, 'Private autonomy at Union level: On Article 16 CFREU and free movement rights' CML Rev 53 (2016), 979, 998.

[37] Case C-271/08 *Commission v Germany* [2010] EU:C:2010:183, Opinion of AG Trstenjak, para 183 f. This is rejected by important voices, see e.g. Vassilios Skouris, 'Fundamental Rights and Fundamental

entry into force did not remedy this issue.[38] Accordingly, some observed that the theory of fundamental freedoms does not reflect the evolution of the EU from an economic–political union to a constitutional system.[39] In a Union that has increasingly emancipated from its common market purpose, it seems justified to assume a substantive hierarchy between fundamental rights and market freedoms. As the Court stated, fundamental rights are 'at the heart' of the EU legal structure.[40] Therefore, it does not seem far-fetched to suggest a reversal of these implicit hierarchies or priorities between fundamental rights and freedoms.[41]

Some reject such a hierarchical relationship based on a supposed convergence between fundamental freedoms and fundamental rights.[42] Certainly, fundamental freedoms can be translated into the language of fundamental rights: discriminations based on nationality can be addressed under Articles 18 and 21, market freedoms under Articles 15 to 17 and the freedom of movement under Article 45 CFR. Yet, there are important differences between fundamental rights and fundamental freedoms. While EU fundamental rights have been introduced to strengthen supranational *legitimation*, free movement rules primarily serve transnational *integration*.[43] Even if fundamental freedoms constitute rights,[44] many have argued that the 'the vigilance of individuals concerned to protect their rights'[45] was primarily of instrumental value for the realization of the common market.[46] This explains why fundamental freedoms are subject to several preconditions, like a transnational and economic activity, whereas fundamental rights are not.

Freedoms' EBLR 17 (2006), 225, 237 ff; Takis Tridimas, *The General Principles of EU Law* (2nd edn, OUP 2006) 299, 337–41; Clemens Ladenburger, 'European Union Institutional Report' in Julia Laffranque (ed.), *Protection of Fundamental Rights Post-Lisbon* (Tartu Univ. Press 2012) 141, 200.

[38] Niamh Nic Shuibne, 'Fundamental rights and the framework of internal market adjudication: is the Charter making a difference?' in Panos Koutrakos and Jukka Snell (eds), *Research Handbook on the Law of the EU's Internal Market* (Elgar 2017) 215, 225 ff.

[39] See e.g. Menéndez (n 29) 193; Thorsten Kingreen, 'Fundamental Freedoms' in Jürgen Bast and Armin von Bogdandy (eds), *Principles of European Constitutional Law* (2nd edn, Hart 2009) 515, 531.

[40] *ECHR Accession II* (n 3) para 169.

[41] In this sense, see Dagmar Schiek et al., *EU social and labour rights and EU internal market law* (European Parliament, EMPL, 2015) 78 ff.

[42] See e.g. Verica Trstenjak and Erwin Beysen, 'The Growing Overlap of Fundamental Freedoms and Fundamental Rights in the Case-Law of the CJEU' EL Rev 38 (2013), 293, 309 ff; Vassilios Skouris, 'Das Verhältnis von Grundfreiheiten und Grundrechten im europäischen Gemeinschaftsrecht' DÖV 59 (2006), 89, 93.

[43] See in particular Kingreen (n 39) 530. More generally, see e.g. Philip Alston, 'Resisting the Merger and Acquisition of Human Rights by Trade Law' EJIL 13 (2002), 815, 823 ff.

[44] Even as 'political right', see Miguel Maduro, *We the Court* (Hart 1998) 166 ff.

[45] Case C-26/62 *Van Gend en Loos* [1963] EU:C:1963:1.

[46] See e.g. Damian Chalmers and Luis Barroso, 'What Van Gend en Loos stands for' I-CON 12 (2014), 105, 121 ff; Joseph H.H. Weiler, 'Van Gend en Loos: The Individual as Subject and Object and the Dilemma of European Legitimacy' I-CON 12 (2014), 94, 102; Johannes Masing, *Die Mobilisierung des Bürgers für die Durchsetzung des Rechts* (Duncker&Humblot 1997) 44.

III. The Potential of Article 2 TEU

As seen above, the usual methodological tools aimed at establishing coherence, such as systematic interpretation or balancing, reach their limits if we perceive all provisions of EU primary law as being of equal rank. Further, such an understanding may lead to results that are difficult to square with the achieved stage of integration. A usual response to such issues is for courts to rely on so-called second-order considerations.[47] These do not concern the meaning of a legal provision but the choices between different possible meanings established in applying first-order considerations (e.g. textual, historical, teleological interpretation). In this spirit, Neil MacCormick argued that legal texts can only be coherent *in relation to something* (e.g. underlying objectives, principles, or values).[48] This approach has also been employed in the Court's jurisprudence. The CJEU started early on to interpret and apply primary law in light of the EU's objectives and general principles. However, recourse to these instruments has become increasingly problematic (Section A). Against this backdrop, the last section will assess the potential and added value of the substantive hierarchies derived from Article 2 TEU (Section B).

A. The Court in Search for Coherence: Objectives and Principles

On the one hand, the CJEU's case law featured a strong preference in favour of interpreting Treaty provisions in light of (or even 'in conformity with'[49]) the EU's objectives formerly enshrined in Articles 2 and 3 EEC (today Article 3 TEU).[50] This blend of teleological and systematic considerations might be close to what some have described as meta-teleological or teleo-systemic interpretation.[51] Many perceived this as the guiding approach in the interpretation of primary law.[52] In this spirit, the Court stressed that former Articles 2 and 3 EEC are 'placed at the

[47] See e.g. Neil MacCormick, *Legal Reasoning and Legal Theory* (Clarendon 1994) 100 ff. In the EU context, see Neil MacCormick, Joxerramon Bengoetxea, and Leonor Moral Soriano, 'Integration and Integrity in the Legal Reasoning of the European Court of Justice' in Gráinne de Búrca and Joseph H.H. Weiler (eds), *The European Court of Justice* (OUP 2001) 43, 57 f.

[48] MacCormick (n 2) 193. See also Riccardo Guastini, *Le fonti del diritto* (Giuffrè 2010) 413 ff. distinguishing between 'axiological cohesion' (coherence) and 'logical cohesion' (consistency).

[49] See e.g. Case C-53/81, *Levin* [1982] EU:C:1982:105, para 15.

[50] See e.g. Case C-85/76 *Hoffmann-La Roche* [1979] EU:C:1979:36, para 125; Cases C-6 and 7/73 *Commercial Solvents* [1974] EU:C:1974:18, para 32; Case 6/72 *Continental Can* [1973] EU:C:1973:22, paras 22–6.

[51] Miguel Maduro, 'Interpreting European Law' EJLS 1 (2007), 1, 5; Joxerramon Bengoetxea, *The Legal Reasoning of the European Court of Justice* (OUP 1993) 250 f.

[52] See e.g. Pierre Pescatore, 'Les objectifs de la Communauté européenne comme principes d'interprétation dans la jurisprudence de la Cour de justice (1972)' in Fabrice Picod (ed.), *Études de droit communautaire européen 1962–2007* (Bruylant 2008) 383; Hans P. Ipsen, *Europäisches Gemeinschaftsrecht* (Mohr Siebeck 1972) 131.

head of the general principles which govern [the Treaty]',[53] thus according a 'paramount constitutional importance' to these provisions.[54] Yet, the EU's objectives no longer seem able to establish overarching coherence. First, this is due to the incorporation of highly disparate and vaguely outlined objectives into the Treaties. This multiplication considerably weakened their ability to provide guidelines for interpretation.[55] Second, the maturing of the EU legal order and the concomitant emergence of new normative manifestations (like principles and values) placed the Union objectives in a new context.

On the other hand, the Court understands the EU legal order as a 'structured network of principles'[56] and makes ample use of these principles in its jurisprudence. As indicated above, principles help in structuring and systematizing the body of law. They make it manageable and provide yardsticks, guidelines, or orientation for its coherent interpretation and application.[57] This also applies to principles in the CJEU's jurisprudence.[58] At the EU level, principles are either of a structural and functional (e.g. effectiveness and equivalence, sincere cooperation, subsidiarity, mutual trust ...) or substantive nature (e.g. fundamental rights, the rule of law, and democracy). In both capacities, however, they have what Takis Tridimas termed an 'enhanced interpretational authority'.[59] To recall but one example, in the *Titanium Dioxide* and *Isoglucose* cases, the CJEU was asked to determine the correct legal basis of an act of secondary legislation. The Court stated that if secondary legislation could be adopted on several legal bases, the legislature must follow the procedure which allows the greatest participation of the European Parliament. This interpretation was justified with a recourse to the 'fundamental democratic principle' of representative democracy.[60]

[53] Case 167/73 *Commission v France* [1974] EU:C:1974:35, para 18.

[54] Koen Lenaerts and José A. Gutiérrez-Fons, 'To Say What the Law of the EU Is' CJEL 20 (2014), 3, 31.

[55] Armin von Bogdandy, 'Founding Principles' in von Bogdandy and Bast (n 39) 11, 15 f; Jörg P. Terhechte, 'Art. 3 EUV' in Eberhard Grabitz et al. (eds), Das *Recht der Europäischen Union* (75th edn, loose-leaf, C.H.Beck 2022) para 14.

[56] Opinion 2/13 *ECHR Accession II* [2014] EU:C:2014:2454, para 167.

[57] Pierre Pescatore, *Introduction à la science du droit* (Centre Univ. de l'Etat, repr. 1978) 120; András Jakab, *European Constitutional Language* (CUP 2016) 38. From the international context, International Law Commission, Third report on general principles of law by Marcelo Vázquez-Bermúdez (18 April 2022) A/CN.4/753, p 50; Mads Andenas and Ludovica Chiussi, 'Cohesion, Convergence and Coherence of International Law' in Andenas et al. (eds), *General Principles and the Coherence of International Law* (Brill 2019) 9; Martti Koskenniemi, 'General Principles' in Koskenniemi (ed.), *Sources of international law* (Dartmouth 2000) 359.

[58] von Bogdandy (n 55) 17. See also Andreas von Arnauld, 'Harmonisation through general principles of law' in Katja S. Ziegler et al. (eds), *Research Handbook on General Principles in EU Law* (Elgar 2022) 40; Urška Šadl and Joxerramon Bengoetxea, 'Theorising General Principles of EU Law in Perspective' in Stefan Vogenauer and Stephen Weatherill (eds), *General Principles of Law* (Hart 2017) 41; Karl-Peter Sommermann, 'Herkunft und Funktion von Verfassungsprinzipien in der Europäischen Union' in Hartmut Bauer and Christian Calliess (eds), *Verfassungsprinzipien in Europa* (Sakkoulas 2008) 15, 29.

[59] Takis Tridimas, 'The General Principles of EU law and the Europeanisation of National Laws' REAL 13 (2020), 5, 8, 11.

[60] Case C-300/89 *Titanium Dioxide* [1991] EU:C:1991:244, paras 18–20; Case 138/79 *Roquette Frères* [1980] EU:C:1980:249, paras 33 ff.

Nevertheless, the CJEU's identification of free-standing principles has been challenged in recent times. Even though it seems uncontested that the creative judicial development of the law is an accepted feature of the Court's legal reasoning, this is not without limits. According to the Bundesverfassugsgericht, the judicial development in Luxembourg can only be accepted if the CJEU follows 'recognised methodological principles'.[61] The Court's approach to general principles always sat uneasily with this requirement. Generally, such principles can be inherent in the EU legal order and thus extracted from the spirit and system of EU law itself or derived from external sources, like the ECHR or constitutional traditions common to the Member States.[62] When referring to such external sources, the Court employs an evaluative or 'critical legal comparison'.[63] It does not draw on 'arithmetical "common denominators"' but chooses the solution best suited to the EU legal order.[64] Combined with the CJEU's succinct style of reasoning, such a liberty may severely undermine legal certainty. Unsurprisingly, many argue that there are no reliable criteria for the development of general principles in Luxembourg.[65] Advocate General Mazak even noted that general principles 'are to be sought rather in the Platonic heaven of law than in the law books'.[66] In consequence, the Court has often been accused of inventing or fabricating general principles. Some even go so far as to suspect the establishment of a European Freirechtsschule, in which legal methods do not play any role at all.[67]

A case in point is the notorious *Mangold* judgment in which the Court derived a general principle prohibiting discrimination based on age from 'various international instruments and in the constitutional traditions common to the Member States'.[68] At that time, however, only very few international instruments or Member State constitutions referred to non-discrimination on grounds of age. The way in

[61] See only BVerfG, *PSPP* (n 22) para 112.

[62] For an overview, see Chiara Amalfitano, *General Principles of EU Law and the Protection of Fundamental Rights* (Elgar 2018) 28 ff.

[63] See e.g. Case C-550/07 P *Akzo Nobel Chemicals* [2010] EU:C:2010:229, Opinion of AG Kokott, para 94; Case C-282/10 *Dominguez* [2011] EU:C:2011:559, Opinion of AG Trstenjak, paras 94, 98. See already Cases C-63 to 69/72 *Werhahn Hansamühle* [1973] EU:C:1973:95, Opinion of AG Roemer, p 1259 f; Case C-5/71 *Zuckerfabrik Schöppestedt* [1971] EU:C:1971:81, Opinion of AG Roemer, p 990.

[64] Case C-14/61 *Hoogovens v High Authority* [1962] EU:C:1962:19, Opinion of AG Lagrange, pp 283 f; Cases C-120 and 121/06 P *FIAMM* [2008] EU:C:2008:98, Opinion of AG Maduro, paras 55 f. See further Giuseppe Martinico, 'General Principles of EU Law and Comparative Law' in Katja S. Ziegler et al. (eds), *Research Handbook on General Principles in EU Law* (Elgar 2022) 82; Koen Lenaerts and Kathleen Gutman, 'The comparative law method and the Court of Justice of the European Union' in Mads Andenas and Duncan Fairgrieve (eds), *Courts and Comparative Law* (OUP 2015) 141; Hélène Ruiz Fabri, 'Principes généraux du droit communautaire et droit comparé' *Droits* 45 (2007), 127.

[65] See e.g. Stephanie Law, 'The Rationales, Reasoning and Methodology Underpinning the Judicial Recognition of Principles of Union Law' CDE 52 (2016), 11; Franz C. Mayer, 'Constitutional Comparativism in Action' I-CON 11 (2013), 1003, 1007; Matthias Herdegen, 'General Principles of EU Law: The Methodological Challenge' in Ulf Bernitz et al. (eds), *General Principles of EC Law in a Process of Development* (Kluwer Law International 2008) 343, 348.

[66] Case C-411/05 *Palacios de la Villa* [2007] EU:C:2007:106, Opinion of AG Mazák, para 86.

[67] Lüder Gerken et al., *"Mangold" als ausbrechender Rechtsakt* (Sellier 2009) 18.

[68] Case C-144/04 *Mangold* [2005] EU:C:2005:709, para 74.

which the Court pulled the said general principle out of the hat was subject to severe criticism, also from within the Court.[69] Some even perceived this decision as being ultra vires.[70] These challenges seem to have made an impression. Though continuing to apply free-standing general principles,[71] the CJEU has nonetheless started to follow a much more cautious approach.[72]

B. Fostering Coherence by Recourse to Article 2 TEU

As seen above, the methods employed so far have lost much of their potential. This section argues that Article 2 TEU and, in particular, the stratification of primary law derived from that provision could become a new structuring device in the Court's jurisprudence. There are two ways to make this argument. First, the turn to Article 2 TEU can be construed as a methodological shift. As discussed above, the CJEU's case law revealed a strong preference for an interpretation of primary law in light of the EU's objectives. The maturing of the EU legal order, however, has placed these objectives in a new context.[73] Importantly, Lisbon positioned the Union's common values before its objectives. According to Joris Larik, this symbolizes a paradigm shift. The EU matures 'from a legal entity that, in the first place, exists to strive for certain goals to one which, above all, expounds what it stands for'.[74] This shift should find its expression in the Court's methodology. Thus, it does not seem far-fetched to add a new device to the CJEU's toolbox: an axiological interpretation of primary law in light of Article 2 TEU.[75]

Second, one could understand Article 2 TEU as a successor of the EU's free-standing general principles. Despite the recent challenges outlined above, the need for principles has not lessened—it has just changed. While the proliferation of EU

69 For an overview, see Case C-427/06 *Bartsch* [2008] EU:C:2008:297, Opinion of AG Sharpston, paras 32–6. From the plethora of criticism, see Ján Mazák and Martin K. Moser, 'Adjudication by Reference to General Principles of EU Law: A Second Look at the Mangold Case Law' in Maurice Adams et al. (eds), *Judging Europe's Judges* (Hart 2013) 61, 76 ff.

70 See only Danish Supreme Court, Judgment of 6 December 2016, Case 15/2014, *Ajos*.

71 Takis Tridimas, 'The General Principles of Law: Who Needs Them?' CDE 52 (2016), 419, 426 ff.

72 Case C-354/13 *Fag og Arbejde* [2014] EU:C:2014:2463, paras 31–40 (no 'general principle of non-discrimination on grounds of obesity'); Case C-101/08 *Audiolux* [2009] EU:C:2009:626, paras 46, 62 f (no 'general principle ... relating to the protection of minority shareholders'); Case C-174/08 *NCC Construction Danmark* [2009] EU:C:2009:669, paras 41 ff (no 'principle of fiscal neutrality').

73 Kaarlo Tuori, *European Constitutionalism* (CUP 2015) 47.

74 Joris Larik, 'From Speciality to a Constitutional Sense of Purpose: On the Changing Role of the Objectives of the European Union' ICLQ 63 (2014), 935, 951. See also Giuliano Amato and Nicola Verola, 'Freedom, Democracy, the Rule of Law' in Giuliano Amato et al. (eds), *The History of the European Union: Constructing Utopia* (Hart 2019) 57, 60.

75 Luke D. Spieker, 'Breathing Life into the Union's Common Values' GLJ 20 (2019), 1182, 1209; Michael Potacs, 'Wertkonforme Auslegung des Unionsrechts' EuR 51 (2016), 164. Regarding Art. 6(1) TEU-Amsterdam/Nice, see already Stelio Mangiameli, 'La clausola di omogeneità nel trattato dell'Unione europea e nella costituzione europea' in Mangiameli (ed.), *L'ordinamento europeo*, vol 1 (Giuffrè 2006) 1, 7 f; Miguel Azpitarte Sánchez, 'Artikel 6 EU-Vertrag: Kodifizierung durch die Zeit, seine Bedeutung und Rechtsfolgen' JöR 51 (2003), 553, 566 f.

law diminishes the need to cover gaps in the written law, it reinforces the structuring and systematizing function of principles.[76] Yet, the progressing codification and consolidation of EU law may lead to an expectation and presumption of completeness, which leaves less room for free-standing principles (although these are expressly acknowledged in Article 6(3) TEU and Article 340 TFEU).[77] As such, many submit that general principles have to be derived in much closer interaction with the precept of the Treaties.[78] In this spirit, the focus could shift to the values enshrined in Article 2 TEU.

What justifies such an approach? To start with, an obligation to interpret and apply EU primary law in light of or in conformity with Article 2 TEU flows from Article 13(1) TEU. Pursuant to that provision, institutions of the EU 'shall aim to promote its values'. This includes the Court, which must take this obligation into account when discharging its mandate under Article 19(1) TEU. Further, the previous chapters suggested understanding Article 2 TEU as a constitutional core that radiates into the entire EU legal order. Such a reading finds support not only in the wording of Article 2 TEU, but also in its position in the Treaties (at its top), and in a comparative assessment of the practice of constitutional courts with regard to similarly worded provisions (see Chapters 3 and 4).

The previous chapter went even further and suggested that Article 2 TEU can serve as the basis for the EU's constitutional framework. Under this scheme, the Union's constitution would be composed of those provisions that give expression to an Article 2 TEU value. This gives rise to a threefold, substantive hierarchization of EU primary law: at the top stands Article 2 TEU. The second tier features those provisions that give specific expression to a value enshrined in Article 2 TEU. All other Treaty provisions are allocated to a third level. This hierarchical stratification bears two potentialities. First, Article 2 TEU can be established as a focal point for the interpretation of EU primary law. Second, the system of substantive hierarchies may become a tool to resolve conflicts among provisions of primary law.

1. Potential for interpretation

Starting with the former, Article 2 TEU can serve as a guiding star for the interpretation and application of EU primary law. Provisions of the second level not only give specific expression to the values enshrined in Article 2 TEU, but also have to be interpreted in light of and in conformity with them. If the Court interprets, for

[76] Tridimas (n 37) 10.

[77] See e.g. Matthias Knauff, 'Ungeschriebenes Primärrecht' in Peter-Christian Müller-Graff et al. (eds), *Europäisches Recht zwischen Bewährung und Wandel* (Nomos 2011) 127, 137 f; Wulf-Henning Roth, 'Verfassung und europäische Methodenlehre' *Rabel Journal of Comparative and International Private Law* 75 (2011), 787, 838.

[78] Observing a trend to a more 'positivist' approach, see Koen Lenaerts and José A. Gutiérrez-Fons, 'The Constitutional Allocation of Powers and General Principles of EU Law' CML Rev 47 (2010), 1629, 1655 ff; Constanze Semmelmann, 'General Principles of EU Law. The Ghost in the Platonic Heaven in Need of Conceptual Clarification' *Pittsburgh Papers on the European Union* 2 (2013), 1, 28 ff.

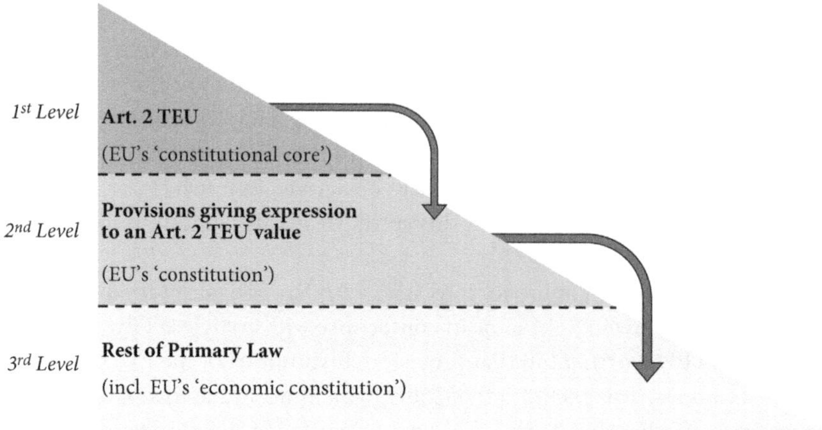

Figure 5.1 Interpretation cascade

instance, the provisions limiting its jurisdiction or the access of individuals to the Court, it must choose an interpretation that respects the rule of law. With regard to the third level, the effect of Article 2 TEU is mediated through provisions of the second level. Accordingly, fundamental freedoms should not be interpreted directly in light of Article 2 TEU but rather, for example, in light of Charter rights that give specific expression to the value of 'respect for human rights'. As such, second level provisions constitute the yardstick for the interpretation and application of third level provisions. This leads to an 'interpretation cascade', as illustrated with Figure 5.1.

The impact of Article 2 TEU on the interpretation of second level provisions can be illustrated by contrasting the decision in *Unión de Pequeños Agricultores* (*UPA*) with later rulings concerning the CJEU's jurisdiction in matters pertaining to the Common Foreign and Security Policy (CFSP). In *UPA*, the Court faced an action for annulment brought by individuals against a Council regulation. Under Article 263(4) TFEU (former Article 173(4) EC), individuals can challenge any EU act that is of direct and individual concern to them. The Court interpreted this provision in very narrow terms.[79] The rationale behind this narrow conception is that individuals should challenge EU acts primarily in national courts, which can then refer to Luxembourg.[80] As national judges have a large discretion in this regard (the parties

[79] See only Case 25/62 *Plaumann* [1963] EU:C:1963:17, p 107. On the state of the art, see Paul Craig and Gráinne de Búrca, *EU Law* (7th edn, OUP 2020) 548 ff; Koen Lenaerts, Ignace Maselis, and Kathleen Gutman, *EU Procedural Law* (OUP 2014) paras 7.97 ff.

[80] Case C-50/00 P *UPA* [2002] EU:C:2002:462, para 40. See also Athanase Popov, 'La complémentarité entre les recours en annulation formés par les particuliers et les renvois préjudiciels en appréciation de validité' CDE 48 (2012), 167.

have no 'right' to a reference),[81] this system sits rather uneasily with regard to effective judicial protection and the rule of law.[82] Nevertheless, the Court did not alter the demanding standing requirements but left it to the Member States to reform the system of legal remedies.[83]

Under the scheme of substantive hierarchies suggested in this book, *UPA* might have been decided differently. This intuition is supported by recent case law on the Court's jurisdiction in CFSP matters. Pursuant to Articles 24(1)(2) TEU and 275(1) TFEU, the CJEU generally lacks jurisdiction over CFSP measures except for those provisions explicitly providing otherwise. In this sense, Article 275(2) TFEU confers jurisdiction to review restrictive measures only under actions for annulment (Article 263(4) TFEU). In *Rosneft*, however, the Court received a preliminary reference questioning the validity of such measures. Instead of declining jurisdiction, it referred to Article 2 TEU and recalled that 'one of the European Union's founding values is the rule of law', which includes 'the very existence of effective judicial review'.[84] In this light, the Court interpreted Article 275(2) TFEU as not precluding references on the validity of restrictive measures.[85] It should be noted that Article 47 CFR alone could not justify this move, as Article 51(2) CFR specifically states that Charter rights cannot 'modify powers and tasks as defined in the Treaties'.[86] Thus, the Court had to find a different basis, namely Article 2 TEU.[87]

When contrasting *UPA* with *Rosneft*, it becomes apparent that an interpretation in light of Article 2 TEU can have a decisive impact. Recent case law indicates a further shift towards an axiological interpretation of standing requirements for individuals. In *Venezuela v Council*, the Court interpreted Article 263(4) TFEU as including actions brought by a third state against a regulation imposing restrictive measures (as a legal person under public international law). To justify this step, the Court recalled that '[i]t follows from Article 2 TEU that the European Union

[81] Under Art. 267(3) TFEU only courts of last instance are obliged to make a reference. Lower courts are only obliged to refer if they want to set aside EU law, see Case C-314/85, *Foto-Frost* [1987] EU:C:1987:452.

[82] See the fierce critique by Case C-50/00 P *UPA* [2002] EU:C:2002:197, Opinion of AG Jacobs, paras 102 ff. Of the prevailing criticism in academic circles, see Laurence W. Gormley, 'Judicial Review: Advice for the Deaf?' *Fordham Journal of International Law* 29 (2005), 655.

[83] *UPA* (n 80) para 41; Case C-263/02 P *Jégo-Quéré* [2004] EU:C:2004:210, para 36. See e.g. Dominik Hanf, 'Talking with the "pouvoir constituant" in Times of Constitutional Reform' MJ 10 (2003), 265.

[84] Case C-72/15 *Rosneft* [2017] EU:C:2017:236, para 72.

[85] On this 'audacious' interpretation, see e.g. Sara Poli, 'The Common Foreign Security Policy after Rosneft: Still Imperfect but Gradually Subject to the Rule of Law' CML Rev 54 (2017), 1799, 1813; Paz Andrés Sáenz de Santa María, 'Mejorando la lex imperfecta: tutela judicial efectiva y cuestión prejudicial en la PESC' RDCE 58 (2017), 871, 893; Thomas Henze and Jannika Jahn, 'Die Gemeinsame Außen- und Sicherheitspolitik der EU unter der Kontrolle des EuGH' EuZW 28 (2017), 506, 508.

[86] *Rosneft* (n 84) paras 74. See also Graham Butler, 'The Coming to Age of the Court's Jurisdiction in the Common Foreign and Security Policy' EuConst 13 (2017), 673, 691.

[87] For a similar approach, see also Case C-455/14 P *H. v Council and Commission* [2017] EU:C:2016:569, para 41; Case C-134/19 P *Bank Refah Kargaran v Council* [2020] EU:C:2020:793, para 35.

is founded on values, such as the rule of law' and interpreted Article 263(4) TFEU extensively.[88]

The approach outlined in this section could provide the Court with an opportunity to rethink its position in other fields as well. Indeed, the case law is far from consistent in questions concerning the Court's jurisdiction. For instance, the CJEU rejected actions brought under Article 263 TFEU against Member State acts taken 'by common accord' (see e.g. Article 48(4) TEU or Articles 253, 254, and 341 TFEU). Confronted with such decisions in highly controversial cases, such as the 'Sharpston affaire', the Court stressed that these acts were not adopted by 'bodies … of the Union' in the sense of Article 263(1) TFEU.[89] Admittedly, the respective acts do not emanate from a permanent body, which makes it difficult to determine a defendant.[90] Nevertheless, it seems hard to accept that such decisions should largely escape judicial scrutiny.[91] An interpretation in light of the principle of effective judicial protection—as a specific expression of the rule of law—could lead to different outcomes.

Another field of application for the approach sketched in this section could arise in the domain of monetary policy. Without going into detail, many lament that measures taken in this context, especially during the financial crisis, reveal considerable deficiencies in terms of effective judicial protection and fundamental rights.[92] Judicial review is not only limited due to the complexity of such measures,[93] but also due to the fact that many reactions to the financial crisis have taken place outside the EU's institutional framework.[94] Article 2 TEU could help the Court to interpret its jurisdiction in broader terms and close existing 'review gaps'.

88 Case C-872/19 P *Venezuela v Council (Affectation d'un État tiers)* [2021] EU:C:2021:507, paras 48 f.

89 Case T-180/20 *Sharpston v Council and Conférence des Représentants des Gouvernements des États membres* [Order of 6 October 2020] EU:T:2020:473, paras 30–2. See also Cases C-59 and 182/18 *Italy v Council (Siège de l'Agence européenne des medicaments* [2022] EU:C:2022:567, paras 106 ff; Case C-743/19 *Parliament v Council (Siège de l'Autorité européenne du travail)* [2022] EU:C:2022:569, paras 83 ff. Critically, see Eleanor Spaventa, 'Constitutional Creativity or Constitutional Deception? Acts of the Member States Acting Collectively and Jurisdiction of the Court of Justice' CML Rev 58 (2021), 1697; Ezio Perillo, 'Le decisioni collettive dei governi degli Stati membri e il rispetto dello Stato di diritto europeo: una competenza esclusiva della Corte di giustizia?' dUE (2021), 519.

90 Moritz Gabriel, 'Justizfreie Hoheitsakte und die Unabhängigkeit des EuGH' EuZW 31 (2020), 971, 974 ff.

91 The Commission could bring infringement proceedings against all Member States collectively under Article 258 TFEU. Further, it is possible to make such acts subject to preliminary references.

92 On these deficits, see e.g. Claire Kilpatrick, 'On the Rule of Law and Economic Emergency: The Degradation of Basic Legal Values in Europe's Bailouts' OJLS 35 (2015), 325; Andreas Fischer-Lescano, *Human Rights in Times of Austerity Policy* (Nomos 2015); Anastasia Poulou, 'Human Rights Obligations of European Financial Assistance Mechanisms' in Poulou and Ulrich Becker (eds), *European Welfare State Constitutions after the Financial Crisis* (OUP 2020) 24. On the gradual development of judicial review in this area, see e.g. Menelaos Markakis, *Accountability in the Economic and Monetary Union: Foundations, Policy, and Governance* (OUP 2020) 204 ff; Michalis Ioannidis, 'The judicial review of discretion in the Banking Union: from "soft" to "hard(er)" look?' in Chiara Zilioli and Karl-Philipp Wojcik (eds), *Judicial Review in the European Banking Union* (Elgar 2021) 130.

93 On the ESCB's 'broad discretion', see Case C-493/17 *Weiss* [2018] EU:C:2018:1000, para 73; Case C-62/14 *Gauweiler* [2015] EU:C:2015:400, para 68.

94 See e.g. Katerina Kalaitzaki, 'The Application of EU Fundamental Rights During the Financial Crisis' EPL 27 (2021), 331.

2. Potential for conflict resolution

The second potential relates to conflicts between Treaty provisions at different levels. Take, for instance, conflicts between the third and second level. Due to their connection to Article 2 TEU, provisions giving expression to the Union's founding values have an increased normative force. This leads to a substantive precedence of provisions giving specific expression to a value enshrined in Article 2 TEU. Therefore, they will have a greater weight when measured against conflicting provisions of the third level (see Chapter 4, IV). The effects of such a construction may be illustrated with two conflicting Treaty provisions, such as the free movement of goods and the freedom of assembly (constellation in *Schmidberger*).[95] Giving specific expression to the value of 'respect for human rights' and 'democracy', the freedom of assembly under Article 12 CFR is allocated at the second level. As such, there is a substantive hierarchy between Article 34 TFEU and Article 12 CFR, which entails interpreting the former in light of and in conformity with the latter. When considering the problematic relationship of fundamental freedoms and fundamental rights outlined above (Section II.B), this could lead to a reorganization of the way in which the Court assesses conflicts between them.[96]

Without going into detail, the CJEU should place Charter rights at the 'normative centre of gravity' when they conflict with fundamental freedoms.[97] There are many ways to put this into practice.[98] For instance, one could argue that in case the exercise of a fundamental freedom (e.g. cross-border trade) violates a fundamental right in a disproportionate manner (e.g. prohibiting a demonstration to secure cross-border trade), there is no legitimate exercise of (or no obstacle to) the fundamental freedom.[99] On a narrower scale, the Court could adapt the proportionality assessment of national measures that serve the protection of fundamental rights but restrict fundamental freedoms. For example, the CJEU could review the adequacy and necessity of the national measure in less demanding terms, reverse the burden of proof, or simply accord a greater weight to the conflicting right in the balancing assessment.[100]

[95] For a more recent example, see the 'clash' of the freedom of establishment and the Art. 11 CFR in Case C-719/18 *Vivendi* [2020] EU:C:2020:627, paras 57 ff.

[96] See e.g. Alberto Alemanno, 'À la recherche d'un juste équilibre ente libertés fondamentales et droits fondamentaux dans le cadre du marché intérieur' RDUE (2004), 709, 745: 'il s'agit de libérer la Cour ... de la cage des libertés fondamentales ... don't elle est inévitablement prisonnière'. See also Sacha Garben, 'The "Fundamental Freedoms" and (Other Fundamental Rights)' in Garben and Inge Govaere (eds), *The Internal Market 2.0* (Hart 2020) 335, 368.

[97] Menéndez (n 29) 183 ff.

[98] On the different options, see concisely Niamh Nic Shuibhne, 'The Social Market Economy and Restriction of Free Movement Rights: *plus c'est la même chose*?' JCMS 57 (2019), 111, 119 f. Suggesting a new 'interpretation framework' for the Court that is based on democracy, the rule of law, and fundamental rights, see Garben (n 96) 364 ff.

[99] In this sense, see already Alemanno (n 96) 745 f.

[100] See e.g. Christopher Brown, Case Note *Schmidberger*, CML Rev 40 (2003), 1499, 1507 f. See also—albeit rejecting any hierarchical relationship—Tamas Szabados, 'Conflicts Between Fundamental Freedoms and Fundamental Rights in the Case Law of the Court of Justice of the European Union'

Certainly, there are ambiguities and pitfalls attached to this scheme. Some might already wonder whether transitions among the levels are possible. Indeed, many interests can be articulated on all three levels. For instance, fundamental freedoms (third level) can be redressed as Charter rights—the freedom to conduct business under Articles 15 and 16 CFR (second level)—and thus give specific expression to the value of 'respect for human rights' as enshrined in Article 2 TEU (first level). In the *Schmidberger* constellation, we could thus end up balancing two highly abstract values—'respect for human rights' here, 'human rights' and 'democracy' there. If such a race to the top becomes too frequent, it could lead to a collapse of the proposed scheme. If any conflict among competing claims can transcend into the sphere of values, the substantive hierarchization derived from Article 2 TEU can no longer provide orientation.

For that reason, the previous chapter suggested that the substantive hierarchies derived from Article 2 TEU should go hand in hand with a layered scope of protection (Chapter 4, IV). While the scope of fundamental freedoms is extremely broad (including e.g. measures of equivalent effect), Articles 15 to 17 CFR could be interpreted as capturing only direct discriminations. The value of 'respect for human rights' could then be reduced to protecting only the essence of rights (Article 52(1) CFR). Such a layered scope would avoid a frequent regress to Article 2 TEU. What does this mean for the above example? A conflict between the freedom of assembly and the free movement of goods could only be articulated as a conflict between Article 12 and Articles 15 or 16 CFR if the restriction of the latter constitutes a discrimination (and not merely a measure of equivalent effect). In that case, we are faced with three options: first, both rights are not affected in their essence. Here, the usual rules of conflict apply (e.g. balancing). Second, if only one right is affected in its essence and the other is not, then the former takes substantive precedence. Only when both are affected in their essence is the conflict raised to the level of Article 2 TEU itself. Since the essence of a right is conceived in very narrow terms, conflicts among values at the level of Article 2 TEU should occur only in exceptional circumstances.

These considerations can be integrated into an abstract scheme of conflicts among Treaty provisions (see Figure 5.2). In the *first scenario* (A1), two provisions from the third level conflict with each other. If neither can be reframed as a second level-provision (e.g. a fundamental freedom as a Charter right), the usual methods of conflict resolution apply (A1, option 1). In case only one can be articulated as a second level-provision, it takes substantive precedence (A2/B1). If this is the case for both, the whole conflict transcends to the second level (B2). The *second scenario* departs from here. The central criterion is whether one of these colliding provisions is affected in its core or essence protected under Article 2 TEU. If this is not

European Papers 3 (2018), 563, 589 ff; Catherine Barnard, 'A Proportionate Response to Proportionality in the Field of Collective Action' EL Rev 37 (2012), 117, 129 ff.

Provision of...	3rd level	2nd level	1st level
3rd level	**A1** (1) None can be articulated on 2nd level: balancing/other way of conflict resolution (2) One articulated on 2nd level: **A2/B1** (3) Both articulated on 2nd level : **B2**	**A2** Substantive hierarchy	**A3** [does not occur]
2nd level	**B1** Substantive hierarchy	**B2** (1) None affected in its essence: balancing/ other way of conflict resolution (2) One affected in its essence: **B3/C2** (3) Both affected in their essence : **C3**	**B3** Substantive hierarchy
1st level	**C1** [does not occur]	**C2** Substantive hierarchy	**C3** Balancing

Figure 5.2 Template for conflict resolution among Treaty provisions

the case, the conflict must be resolved again with the usual methods of conflict resolution. If one provision is affected in its essence, it takes substantive precedence (B3/C2). In case both are affected in their essence, the conflict transcends to the first level (C3), where it has to be resolved through balancing.

This scheme has a twofold advantage. First, it is designed to keep collisions between Treaty provisions from turning into abstract value conflicts. As noted previously, Article 2 TEU is extremely vague and therefore difficult to handle. Even though the Court does not operate in a legal vacuum when interpreting Article 2 TEU, possible guidance might be scarce or—as far as the common constitutional traditions of the Member States are concerned—the outcome of a complex and challenging comparison (see Chapter 2, III.B.2). Second, the substantive hierarchization between different levels allows us to resolve more conflicts among Treaty provisions through substantive precedence rather than balancing. As such, this scheme seeks to enhance stability and predictability in the application and interpretation of EU primary law.[101]

[101] On this effect of hierarchies, see e.g. Roland Bieber and Isabelle Salomé, 'Hierarchy of Norms in European Law' CML Rev 33 (1996), 907, 909.

6
The Court and the Legislature
Encouraging Legislation

I. Introduction

The extensive scope of primary law is not only a challenge in terms of coherence. Many have argued that the Treaties in their current form excessively reduce space for legislative decision-making. This issue has been prominently addressed by Dieter Grimm as an 'over-constitutionalization' of EU law.[1] Although many of Grimm's observations express legitimate concerns, his claims require some attenuation. Thus, the first section will take a step back and explore the challenges to the EU legislative process at the Treaty and institutional level (Section III). Whereas Grimm and other scholars suggest a Treaty revision, cutting back primary law to its genuinely constitutional content and transferring the rest to the level of secondary legislation, this chapter will propose a less invasive and arguably more realistic path. It seems to have escaped the critics' attention that Luxembourg's judicial practice is already characterized by a remarkable responsiveness towards EU legislation (Section III.A). Building on these insights, the following chapter suggests a recalibration of the CJEU's jurisprudence. The Court could distinguish between the different levels of primary law outlined in the previous chapters. While retaining strict scrutiny of provisions that give expression to an Article 2 TEU value, the Court could relax the constraints imposed on the EU legislature by the third level of primary law. This would 'de-constitutionalize' large parts of the Treaties and broaden the space for legislative decision-making (Section III.B).

[1] Dieter Grimm, 'The Democratic Costs of Constitutionalisation: The European Case' ELJ 21 (2015), 460, 469 ff. See also Édouard Dubout, *Droit constitutionnel de l'Union européenne* (Bruylant 2021) 25 ff; Fritz W. Scharpf, 'De-Constitutionalization and Majority Rule: A Democratic Vision for Europe' ELJ 23 (2017), 315; Sacha Garben, 'Restating the Problem of Competence Creep, Tackling Harmonisation by Stealth and Reinstating the Legislator' in Garben and Inge Govaere (eds), *The Division of Competences between the EU and the Member States* (Hart 2017) 300, 323; Gareth Davies, 'Legislative Control of the European Court of Justice' CML Rev 51 (2014), 1579, 1591 ff.

EU Values Before the Court of Justice. Luke Dimitrios Spieker, Oxford University Press. © Luke Dimitrios Spieker 2023.
DOI: 10.1093/oso/9780198876717.003.0007

II. An Overly Constrained EU Legislature

Many scholars claim that, unlike national constitutions, EU primary law is not confined to those provisions that reflect the genuine functions or contents of a constitution. Instead, the Treaties regulate in considerable detail a vast array of matters that constitutions would usually leave to ordinary legislation. In this sense, EU law is 'over-constitutionalized'. This comes with a democratic cost: it reduces the EU legislature's scope of action and simultaneously reinforces the position of the Court of Justice. Dieter Grimm expresses his key concern as follows: 'more constitutional law means less democracy'.[2]

Before diving into the specifics, two disclaimers are required. Terminologically, the notion of 'over-constitutionalization' can be misleading. To start with, it may easily be confused with issues arising from the 'constitutionalization' of a legal order. The latter refers, irrespective of the length or detail of a constitution, to the practice of constitutional courts to expand the constitution's reach to administrative and private law.[3] Further, legal scholarship usually associates the 'constitutionalization' of the EU legal order with the CJEU's trailblazing jurisprudence providing the Treaties with direct effect and primacy. By contrast, the alleged 'over-constitutionalization' of primary law concerns neither the Treaties' radiation into the EU legal order nor their primacy or direct effect but their *extensive scope*.

Conceptually, the statement 'more constitutional law means less democracy' requires some attenuation. While Grimm explicitly acknowledges that constitutions not only constrain but also enable democratic decision-making,[4] his assertion is that too much constitutional law proves detrimental to the democratic process. Yet, demanding requirements for constitutional amendments do not withdraw constitutional law per se from the reach of democratic decision-making. Instead, it seems more accurate to ascertain that more constitutional law can mean less *ordinary political processes*.

Even if Dieter Grimm's critique is certainly not unfounded, it seems to require some reframing. The starting point for our argument is a twofold assumption. Any constitution faces the task of striking a balance between *stability and flexibility* at the level of the constitutional text and between *law and politics* on the institutional plane. As will be demonstrated in the following sections, the EU legal order presents two features that might upset this balance. First, the extensive reach of EU primary law reduces the legislature's scope of action. Second, the CJEU has an exceptionally powerful position vis-à-vis the EU legislature. Taken together, both factors risk overly constraining the space left to legislative decision-making.

[2] Grimm (n 1) 471.
[3] See Chapter 3, n 30.
[4] Grimm (n 1) 463 ff.

A. The Treaty Level: Extensive Primary Law

Constitutions are not only supposed to leave room for political processes, but also guarantee continuity, stabilize the political process, and relieve it from the burden of constantly rebuilding consensus on fundamental issues.[5] A stark imbalance between stability and flexibility, however, can lead to pathological results. An entrenched constitution that exhausts the political space risks becoming an 'asphyxiating straitjacket'[6] and impairing the system's adaptability to changing circumstances. An entirely flexible and deferential constitution might overburden day-to-day decision-making or allow governing majorities to dismantle constitutional checks and balances. This tension between stability and flexibility not only finds expression in the rules on constitutional change (i.e. amendment procedures) but also in the scope of the constitution itself.[7] As Paul Craig notes: 'By denominating an issue as "constitutional" we recognise that it is taken off the agenda of normal politics'.[8] Whereas the constitution's concrete interpretation or implementation may still be the subject of day-to-day politics, the constitution itself usually transcends these volatilities. That is the very function of its entrenchment.

Certainly, there is no universal way to strike the balance between stability and flexibility. Every legal order will find its specific answer corresponding to its specific context. An issue might be particularly controversial in a certain society and therefore enshrined in the constitution to stabilize the consensus reached. The status of churches and religious groups, electoral laws, affirmative actions, language arrangements ... whether and how these issues are laid down in the constitution may vary to a considerable extent. In consequence, constitutions can become lengthy and detailed. While this does not mean that such constitutions automatically prevent a meaningful political process, an overly inflated constitution *can* lead to the pathologies mentioned above. In this spirit, the following thumb rule has been suggested: 'the more stringent the amendment procedure is, the shorter the constitution should be' (and vice versa).[9]

The Treaty drafters do not seem to have followed this basic rule of reason. Primary law is not only 'fat' or 'over-materialized';[10] its extensive scope is also

[5] On the constitution's stabilizing or 'relief function', see e.g. Joseph Raz, 'On the Authority and Interpretation of Constitutions: Some Preliminaries' in Larry Alexander (ed.), *Constitutionalism* (CUP 2001) 152, 153, 174 ff; Dieter Grimm, *Constitutionalism* (OUP 2016) 217, 248.

[6] John E. Fossum and Augustín J. Menéndez, 'The Constitution's Gift?' ELJ 11 (2005), 380, 409.

[7] See e.g. Andreas Voßkuhle, 'Verfassungsstil und Verfassungsfunktion: Ein Beitrag zum Verfassungshandwerk' AöR 119 (1994), 35.

[8] Paul Craig, 'Constitutions, Constitutionalism and the European Union' ELJ 7 (2001), 125, 126. See also Joseph H.H. Weiler, 'A Constitution for Europe? Some Hard Choices' JCMS 40 (2002), 563, 571.

[9] Ruth Gavison, 'What Belongs in a Constitution?' *Constitutional Political Economy* 13 (2002), 89, 95.

[10] Craig (n 8) 127; Christoph Möllers, 'Pouvoir constituant—constitution—constitutionalization' in Armin von Bogdandy and Jürgen Bast (eds), *Principles of European Constitutional Law* (2nd edn, Hart 2009) 169, 194 f.

coupled with extremely demanding amendment procedures. One particularly problematic aspect is that the Treaties are not limited to stipulating the rules for political decision-*making* but to a large extent the decisions *themselves*.[11] This is especially the case with regard to the EU's 'economic constitution' that places matters of economic policy largely beyond the reach of day-to-day politics. Another example concerns 'purposive competences' that define an ultimate goal of action (e.g. Articles 114, 127, 151, 165, 166, 174, 191, 206 TFEU). Even though these objectives are relatively broad, they certainly do not cover any kind of measure. Monetary policy, for instance, is aimed at 'price stability' instead of fostering full employment (Article 127 TFEU), while common commercial policy is geared at free trade instead of ensuring a high level of consumer protection (Article 206 TFEU). This fixation of objectives reduces the EU legislature's discretion from making a choice of direction ('where should we go?') to merely selecting the means of implementation ('how do we get there?').[12] To make things worse, the extensive scope of primary law has been coupled with extremely demanding thresholds for Treaty amendments. Granted, the Treaties have been amended often since their creation. Yet, it will come as no surprise that the growing number of Member States makes future Treaty amendments, especially in politically controversial areas, increasingly difficult. In any event, the EU legislature is largely excluded from this process. Due to the institutional distinction between the EU legislature and the amending power (the Member States/the European Council), the amendment procedures at the EU level are disconnected from the ordinary political process.

B. The Institutional Level: A Strong Court of Justice

The second assumption is that democratic constitutions strive to connect, separate, and balance law and politics. The constitution politicizes the creation of laws by connecting it to the political process and juridifies said processes by submitting them to constitutional constraints.[13] The way in which this reciprocal relationship is institutionalized can differ considerably. Some legal orders might set up constitutional courts, others may rely on the self-discipline of their parliaments.[14]

[11] Grimm (n 1) 470; Scharpf (n 1) 316. See also Kaarlo Tuori, 'European Constitutionalism' in Roger Masterman and Robert Schütze (eds), *The Cambridge Companion to Comparative Constitutional Law* (CUP 2019) 521, 528.

[12] Gareth Davies, 'Democracy and Legitimacy in the Shadow of Purposive Competence' ELJ 21 (2015), 2, 3.

[13] See e.g. Niklas Luhmann, *Law as a Social System* (OUP 2004) 403 ff. From the rich literature, see e.g. Dieter Grimm, 'Types of Constitutions' in Michel Rosenfeld and András Sajó (eds), *The Oxford Handbook of Comparative Constitutional Law* (OUP 2012) 98, 124 f; Christoph Möllers, 'The Politics of Law and the Law of Politics' in Erik O. Eriksen et al. (eds), *Developing a Constitution for Europe* (Routledge 2004) 131, 137 f.

[14] On the various manifestations, see e.g. Armin von Bogdandy, Peter M. Huber, and Christoph Grabenwarter (eds), *The Max Planck Handbooks in European Public Law*, vol 3 (OUP 2020).

However, if a legal order opts for a system of constitutional adjudication, a certain distance between the respective court and the political process should be maintained. Interferences, let alone dominance, of one institution over the other may lead to practical malfunctions and legitimatory deficits.[15]

Without a doubt, drawing the line between both spheres is always controversial. Potential criteria are hardly clear-cut (e.g. specific methods, reasons, procedures, functions, see Chapter 12, III.B). In addition, constitutional courts are somewhat sitting on the fence: they are inevitably political and, to a certain extent, representative institutions.[16] Even though they might be considered counter-majoritarian, constitutional courts can play a crucial role in securing the functioning of democratic decision-making.[17] But there are limits. A constitutional court, for instance, that systematically assumes the function of a positive legislator might foster an overly constraining juridification of the political process and risk politicizing the court thus overstretching its legitimacy.

In light of these considerations, the relationship between the Court of Justice and the EU legislature seems particularly problematic. The Treaties have placed the EU judiciary and the EU legislature in a rather uneven playing field. While the EU legislature seems to be largely unable to *negatively* delimit or override the Court's jurisprudence, the Court has on many occasions *positively* assumed the function of a policymaker. Starting with the former, the CJEU operates—even compared to most constitutional courts in the Member States—in an 'unusually permissive strategic environment'.[18] In principle, a legislator may constrain a court *ex ante* by drafting rules which the court has to apply and *ex post* by reversing the court's jurisprudence through legislative (or constitutional) amendments. Both paths, however, are structurally weakened at the EU level.

From an *ex ante* perspective, the EU legislature is often unable to constrain the Court. Often, EU legislation is drafted in a form that reflects hard-won compromises between relevant stakeholders. Where this is necessary to secure agreement, it is likely to leave gaps and feature open or unwieldy formulations.[19] As such, EU

[15] See e.g. Christine Landfried, 'Constitutional Review in the European Legal Space: A Political Science Perspective' in Armin von Bogdandy, Peter M. Huber, and Christoph Grabenwarter (eds), *The Max Planck Handbooks in European Public Law*, vol 4 (OUP 2023). From a US perspective, John Ferejohn, 'Judicializing politics, politicizing law' *Law and Contemporary Problems* 65 (2002), 41.

[16] See e.g. Dieter Grimm, 'What Exactly Is Political About Constitutional Adjudication?' (p 307) and Mattias Kumm, 'On the Representativeness of Constitutional Courts' (p 281) both in Christine Landfried (ed.), *Judicial Power* (CUP 2019).

[17] See e.g. Rosalind Dixon, *Responsive Judicial Review* (OUP 2023); Christoph Möllers, *The Three Branches* (OUP 2013) 127 ff; Michel Troper, 'The Logic of Justification of Judicial Review' I-CON 1 (2003), 99, 109. Some argue that their activity should be reduced to this function, see e.g. John H. Ely, *Democracy and Distrust* (Harvard Univ. Press 1980) 73 ff, 105; Jürgen Habermas, *Between Facts and Norms* (Polity 1996) 264, 285.

[18] Alec Stone Sweet, 'The European Court of Justice' in Paul Craig and Grainne de Búrca (eds), *The Evolution of EU Law* (2nd edn, OUP 2011) 121, 127.

[19] For a colourful explanation of 'why EU legislation is the way it is', see Eleanor Sharpston, 'Legislating and Adjudicating' in Elizabeth Fisher et al. (eds), *The Foundations and Future of Public Law* (OUP 2020) 173.

legislation will usually constitute rather weak, negative *ex ante* constraints on the Court's activity. To the contrary, it will require further interpretation and elaboration. At the same time, by interpreting the Treaties, the CJEU defines the default conditions for legislative decision-making in the EU. Accordingly, the Court's jurisprudence circumscribes the space for policy making.[20] Many legislative acts even read like a codification of CJEU case law.[21] For instance, public procurement legislation, the Free Movement Directive, the Patient Mobility Directive, legislation on competition damages as well as much of the EU's anti-discrimination legislation have been understood as largely codifying prior case law.[22]

Ex post, there are rather limited opportunities to override, re-programme, or re-direct the CJEU's jurisprudence. The possibility of responding via secondary legislation is already reduced as there is a general discrepancy between the limited competences of the EU legislature and the CJEU's general jurisdiction to interpret the Treaties.[23] If the Court interprets, for example, a Treaty freedom as barring certain Member State regulations, the EU legislature does not necessarily have a competence to positively re-regulate these issues at the EU level. Further, legislative override becomes structurally difficult (if not impossible) when the respective jurisprudence is based on an interpretation of EU primary law. As some have observed, 'an interpretation of the Treaty effectively *becomes* the Treaty'.[24] Even if the EU legislature adopts acts 'overriding' CJEU case law,[25] it is at the Court's discretion to change its respective interpretation of primary law. The only way to force the Court is by amending the Treaties. Past experiences demonstrate, however, that the CJEU's jurisprudence has been codified rather than corrected by Treaty amendments.[26]

[20] Susanne K. Schmidt, *The European Court of Justice and the Policy Process* (OUP 2018) 10. On such a 'Vorwirkung' ('advance effect') of a constitutional court's case law, see Landfried (n 15).

[21] Gareth Davies, 'The European Union Legislature as an Agent of the European Court of Justice' JCMS 54 (2016), 846, 854; Anastasia Iliopoulou-Penot, 'Réflexions sur la codification de la jurisprudence par le législateur européen' in *Mélanges en l'honneur de Claude Blumann* (Bruylant 2015) 187. For examples of legislative codification, see Dorte Sindbjerg Martinsen, *An Ever More Powerful Court?* (OUP 2016) 241 ff.

[22] See e.g. Christopher H. Bovis, 'Developing Public Procurement Regulation: Jurisprudence and its Influence on Law Making' CML Rev 43 (2006), 461; Fabio Wasserfallen, 'The Judiciary as Legislator? How the European Court of Justice Shapes Policy-Making in the European Union' JEPP 17 (2010), 1128, 1136 ff; Stéphane de La Rosa, 'The Directive on Cross-Border Healthcare or the Art of Codifying Complex Case Law' CML Rev 49 (2012), 15; Jens-Uwe Franck, 'Striking a Balance of Power between the Court of Justice and the EU Legislature: The Law on Competition Damages Actions as a Paradigm' EL Rev 43 (2018), 837; Elise Muir, *EU Equality Law* (OUP 2019) 83 f.

[23] See e.g. Mark Dawson, 'The political face of judicial activism: Europe's law-politics imbalance' in Dawson et al. (eds), *Judicial Activism at the European Court of Justice* (Elgar 2013) 11, 13–17.

[24] Davies (n 1) 1582, 1583 f. See also Grimm (n 1) 470.

[25] For some examples, see e.g. Olof Larsson, 'Political and Constitutional Overrides: the Case of the Court of Justice of European Union' JEPP 28 (2021), 1932, 1940 ff.

[26] In this sense, Alain Ondoua, 'L'influence de la Cour dans l'elaboration des traités européens' in Antoine Vauchez and Pascal Mbongo (eds), *Dans la fabrique du droit européen* (Bruylant 2009) 199. For instances of override, see e.g. Giuseppe Martinico, 'Chasing the European Court of Justice: On Some (Political) Attempts to Hijack the European Integration Process' *International Community Law Review* 14 (2012), 243. For an empirical assessment of how Treaty amendments influence the CJEU, see Arthur

In addition to this structural imbalance, it has been claimed that the Court of Justice has assumed on many occasions the role of a 'direct policymaker'.[27] Arguably, judicial policymaking has become a veritable alternative to legislative policymaking in the EU context.[28] The way in which the Court propelled the integration process seems to support this observation. According to the prevalent narrative, the Union legislature was often deadlocked in the course of European integration requiring the CJEU to step in as an 'engine of integration'.[29] The classic, but by no means the only example, is *Cassis de Dijon*: when facing political inertia in constructing the common market, the Court stepped in with its doctrine of mutual recognition.[30] This does not mean that such steps were illegitimate. Being an EU institution, some suggest that the Court is under an obligation to 'promote [the EU's] values, advance its objectives, serve its interests' (Article 13 TEU) and thus foster the process of European integration.[31]

Yet, there are institutional and conceptual reasons that call this approach into question. Institutionally, the CJEU might be a hybrid, political and legal, and even a representative institution like other constitutional courts. Nevertheless, its democratic legitimacy is more fragile than that of a democratically accountable legislature. In addition, the EU legislature seems often better equipped than the Court to conduct complex and controversial balancing processes between different social interests and decide on the EU's course of action in an inclusive and transparent manner.[32] As such, there are arguments from legitimacy and from capacity in favour of the EU legislature.

Conceptually, the changing context of European integration might require a new framing of the relationship between the Court and the legislature. While their interaction was a subject of continuous debate throughout the integration process, the issue has acquired an increasing salience in the past decades. This might be

Dyevre et al., 'The Court of Justice and Treaty Revision: A Case of Strategic Leniency?' *European Union Politics* 19 (2018), 570.

[27] Thomas Horsley, *The Court of Justice of the European Union as an Institutional Actor* (CUP 2018) 156 ff.

[28] Schmidt (n 20) 123; Horsley (n 27) 156 ff; Grimm (n 1) 469. See already the critique by Hjalte Rasmussen, *On Law and Policy in the European Court of Justice* (Brill 1986).

[29] See e.g. Renaud Dehousse, *The European Court of Justice: The Politics of Judicial Integration* (Basingstoke: Macmillan, 1998) 70 ff; Koen Lenaerts, 'Some Thoughts About the Interaction Between Judges and Politicians in the European Community' YEL 12 (1992), 1, 2, 10; Pierre Pescatore, 'La carence du législateur communautaire et le devoir du juge (1983)' in Fabrice Picod (ed.), *Études de droit communautaire européen 1962–2007* (Bruylant 2008) 613.

[30] See only Karen J. Alter and Sophie Meunier, 'Judicial Politics in the European Community: European Integration and the Pathbreaking Cassis de Dijon decision' in *The European Court's Political Power* (OUP 2009) 139.

[31] Dominique Ritleng, 'The independence and legitimacy of the European Court of Justice' in Ritleng (ed.), *Independence and Legitimacy in the Institutional System of the European Union* (OUP 2016) 83, 104 ff.

[32] See e.g. Martijn van den Brink, 'Justice, Legitimacy and the Authority of Legislation within the European Union' MLR 82 (2019), 293, 307 ff.

due to several reasons, which will be formulated as intuitive hunches rather than substantiated observations. To start with, the political process at the EU level, and especially the role of the European Parliament, has been continuously strengthened and extended. Together with the growing amount of EU legislation, this has increased the potential points of friction between the CJEU and the legislature. At the same time, the idea of 'integration through law' seems to have lost much of its persuasiveness.[33] After the judicial constitutionalization of the EU legal order is largely consolidated, new challenges—especially in the Euro crisis—have arguably demonstrated the limits of this approach.[34] The challenge has therefore shifted from the Union's *judicial constitutionalization* to its *democratic politicization*. It goes without saying that the Court of Justice will continue to play a crucial role in this process—but its relation to other institutions might require adjustments.

III. The Potential of Article 2 TEU

This leads us to the central question of this chapter: How can we broaden the space for meaningful political processes at the EU level? In light of the extensive scope of EU primary law, scaling back the Treaties to their genuinely constitutional content has been proposed. All other Treaty provisions could be 'de-constitutionalized' by transferring them into the sphere of secondary legislation.[35] This would require a fundamental Treaty change. In addition, it is highly questionable whether the move towards a 'pocket size' EU constitution is desirable (let alone possible). Already in the past, several reform projects were guided by the ideal of a short and concise constitution.[36] Many proposals sought to divide the Treaties into a basic treaty featuring provisions of constitutional value and a separate text containing provisions for specific policies.[37] These aims never materialized. And indeed, there are good reasons to maintain the Treaties in their current shape. Importantly, their

[33] On this project, see e.g. Rebekka Byberg, 'The History of the Integration Through Law Project: Creating the Academic Expression of a Constitutional Legal Vision for Europe' GLJ 18 (2017), 1531.

[34] See e.g. Christian Joerges, 'Integration through Law and the Crisis of Law in Europe's Emergency' in Joerges, Damian Chalmers, and Markus Jachtenfuchs (eds), *The End of the Eurocrats' Dream* (CUP 2016) 299; Loïc Azoulai, '"Integration through law" and us' I-CON 14 (2016), 449. In this sense, see also Armin von Bogdandy, *The Emergence and Democratization of European Society* (OUP 2023). For its continuing relevance, Andreas Voßkuhle, 'European Integration Through Law' *European Journal of Sociology* 58 (2017), 145, 161 ff.

[35] Grimm (n 1) 473; Garben (n 1) 330 f. With regard to fundamental freedoms Martin Höpner and Susanne K. Schmidt, 'Can We Make the European Fundamental Freedoms Less Constraining?' CYELS 22 (2020), 182, 193 ff. With regard to economic and monetary policy Marco Dani, 'Deconstitutionalising the Economic and Monetary Union' in *Continuity and change—how the challenges of today prepare the ground for tomorrow. ECB Legal Conference 2021* (ECB 2022) 282, 302 ff.

[36] On the commonplace 'une constitution doit être courte et obscure', see e.g. Wolfgang Graf Vitzthum, 'Form und Stil der Verfassung' in Otto Depenheuer and Christoph Grabenwarter (eds), *Verfassungstheorie* (Mohr Siebeck 2011) § 10, p 384.

[37] See Chapter 4, n 3.

heterogeneous and detailed form expresses a compromise and the Member States' desire for control.[38] Against this backdrop, a 'pocket size' EU constitution might simply be an ideal out of reach.

On a much narrower level, Fritz Scharpf proposes to limit the judicial enforcement of some parts of EU primary law. He suggests the insertion of a provision at the head of Part Three TFEU stating that under Titles I–IV, VI, and VII, litigation and infringement proceedings may only be based on relevant secondary legislation. A similar clause might also be inserted in Articles 15/16 of the Charter.[39] Eventually, the present chapter aims to achieve a very similar result but in a less invasive manner. The relevant parts of the Treaties could be de-constitutionalized through a tailored jurisprudence of the CJEU.[40] The following section will start by assessing to what extent the Court is already responsive to legislative interventions. Building on these insights, the present chapter aims at a more profound recalibration of the CJEU's jurisprudence. Based on the hierarchical division of primary law derived from Article 2 TEU, the Court could differentiate between the levels of primary law. While retaining strict scrutiny for those provisions that give expression to an Article 2 TEU value, the Court could relax the constraints imposed on the EU legislature by provisions that do not feature such a link.

It should be emphasized that these suggestions are inherently limited. For one, the following section is restricted to the *horizontal* relationship between the Court and the Union legislature. Issues arising in the *vertical* relationship between the Court and the Member States, like the deregulation of national policies without any re-regulation at the EU level, will remain beyond the scope of this analysis. Further, the proposals presented below cannot render the EU political process *internally* more active, open, inclusive, or controversial. Instead, it is about relaxing and mitigating *external* ties placed on the political process by EU primary law and the Court of Justice. This is based on the hope that more space for legislative decision-making might encourage the EU political process.

A. The Court Between Responsiveness and Resistance

The Court has never been blind to the impact of its jurisprudence on the EU legislative process. Indeed, it seems to be part of the standard repertoire of a constitutional court to establish mechanisms easing the general tension with the political

[38] See e.g. Manfred Zuleeg, 'The Advantages of the European Constitution' in von Bogdandy and Bast (n 10) 763, 779 ff; Jacques Ziller, 'Une Constitution courte et obscure ou claire et détaillé?' in Giuliano Amato et al. (eds), *Genèse et destinée de la Constitution européenne* (Bruylant 2007) 957, 967 ff; Jean-Claude Piris, *The Constitution for Europe* (CUP 2006) 59.

[39] Scharpf (n 1) 422. See also Fritz W. Scharpf, 'De-constitutionalisation of European Law: The Re-empowerment of Democratic Political Choice' in Garben and Govaere (n 1) 284, 297 ff.

[40] In a similar direction, see Martijn van den Brink, 'The European Union's *Demoi*cratic Legislature' ICON 19 (2021), 914, 938 ff.

process. Such strategies can take many forms, like excluding constitutional amendments or laws adopted by way of referenda from judicial review (France), a system of legislative prerogatives and discretion (Germany), a political question (US), or margin of appreciation doctrine (ECtHR).[41] The Court of Justice is no exception in this regard. In the words of Koen Lenaerts:

> the ECJ moved onto a new paradigm. As the constitutional court of a more mature legal order, it now tends to be less assertive as to the substantive development of EU law ... overall it displays greater deference to the preferences of the EU legislator.[42]

In this spirit, the Court seeks to be more responsive towards the EU legislature. In general terms, the Court's jurisprudence seems to follow the logic of *compensating* and *encouraging* European legislation. According to Miguel Maduro, the Court has primarily relied on fundamental freedoms 'to compensate for the lack of Community harmonisation'.[43] When the respective area has been harmonized at the EU level, this rationale ceases to apply and the Court can defer to EU legislation. At the same time, Armin von Bogdandy has recently proposed to read this deferential attitude against the Court's rigorous review of national measures that potentially violate fundamental freedoms. Read together, both jurisprudential strands seem to serve the ultimate purpose of encouraging the Member States to adopt legislation at the EU level and strengthening the European political process.[44]

How does the Court's deferential attitude operate in practice? While Luxembourg has sometimes adjusted its case law to the express will of the EU legislature (even if it was based on primary law),[45] it seems to generally employ a deferential approach towards EU legislative acts.[46] Three strands of case law might serve

[41] See e.g. Peter M. Huber, 'Constitutional Courts and Politics in the European Legal Space' in von Bogdandy et al. (eds), *The Max Planck Handbooks in European Public Law*, vol 4 (n 15). On 'restraining' techniques, see Maartje de Visser, 'Constitutional Courts Securing Their Legitimacy: An Institutional-Procedural Analysis' in von Bogdandy et al. (eds), *The Max Planck Handbooks in European Public Law*, vol 4 (n 15).

[42] Koen Lenaerts, 'The Court's Outer and Inner Selves' in Maurice Adams et al. (eds), *Judging Europe's Judges* (Hart 2013) 13, 16.

[43] Miguel Maduro, *We the Court* (Hart 1998) 78.

[44] von Bogdandy (n 34) 4.3.B. The Court has also been described as 'agenda setter', 'catalyst', and 'idea giver' for legislation, see Dehousse (n 29) 82; Anne-Marie Burley, 'Democracy and Judicial Review in the European Community' *University of Chicago Legal Forum* (1992), 81, 90. Others refer to its 'impulse function', see Jürgen Basedow, 'The Judge's Role in European Integration' in Hans-Wolfgang Micklitz and Bruno de Witte (eds), *The European Court of Justice and the Autonomy of the Member States* (Intersentia 2012) 65, 72 ff.

[45] For a recent example, see Dorte Sindbjerg Martinsen and Michael Blauberger, 'The Court of Justice of the European Union and the Mega-Politics of Posted Workers' *Law & Contemporary Problems* 84 (2022), 29, 51 ff. See also Christopher Vajda, 'Democracy in the European Union: What Has the Court of Justice to Say' CJCIL 4 (2015), 226, 237 ff; Vasilis Hatzopoulos, 'Actively talking to each other: the Court and political institutions' in Dawson et al. (n 23) 102, 133.

[46] See convincingly Mattias Wendel, 'Auf dem Weg zum Präjudizienrecht?' JöR 68 (2020), 113, 122–4 who argues that the CJEU is much more focused on secondary legislation than Grimm tends to admit.

as illustrative examples. First, it is established jurisprudence that where a matter is the subject of exhaustive harmonization at the EU level, any national measure relating thereto must be assessed in light of the respective EU legislation (and not the Treaties).[47] Some even speak of a 'legislative priority rule'.[48] This is not limited to provisions that expressly defer to legislative concretization (e.g. Article 21(1) TFEU) but extends to the whole internal market context. For example, where a legislative act has exhaustively harmonized an area of law, Member States cannot appeal to the grounds of public morality, public policy, or public security under the fundamental freedoms to circumvent these legislative constraints.[49] In this sense, the Court applies the fundamental freedoms only if there is no fully harmonizing secondary law. Even independently from the degree of harmonization, the Court is often inclined to defer to legislation. In *Dano*, for instance, the Court stressed that the principle of non-discrimination (Article 18 TFEU) is 'given more specific expression' in Article 24 of the Free Movement Directive (Directive 2004/38) and decided the case exclusively on that basis.[50]

Second, the Court leaves a certain margin of discretion to the EU legislature when reviewing legislation.[51] The Court affirmed that 'the EU legislature must be allowed a broad discretion in areas in which its action involves political, economic and social choices and in which it is called upon to undertake complex assessments and evaluations'.[52] The legality of an act adopted by the EU legislature is only affected if the measure is manifestly inappropriate with regard to its objective.[53] A similarly broad discretion applies to highly complex economic, scientific, and technical facts.[54] While such a reduced standard of review has been subject to severe criticism concerning the ECB, these objections do not unfold the same power with regard to legislative processes (in detail, see the following section). To the contrary, a reduced review intensity broadens the space for political processes.

Third, the CJEU has even gone so far as to interpret provisions of primary law in light of secondary legislation.[55] One example is the relationship between Articles

[47] Case C-206/19 *KOB* [2020] EU:C:2020:463, paras 30–3; Case C-150/88 *Parfümerie-Fabrik 4711* [1989] EU:C:1989:594, para 28.

[48] Eadaoin Ni Chaoimh, *The Legislative Priority Rule and the EU Internal Market for Goods. A Constitutional Approach* (OUP 2022),

[49] Case C-78/18 *Commission v Hungary* [2020] EU:C:2020:476, para 88; Case C-5/77 *Tedeschi v Denkavit* [1977] EU:C:1977:144, para 35.

[50] Case C-333/13 *Dano* [2014] EU:C:2014:2358, para 61.

[51] For a general systematization, Alexander Fritzsche, 'Discretion, Scope of Judicial Review and Institutional Balance in European Law' CML Rev 47 (2010), 361; Oliver Dörr, 'Art. 263 AEUV' in Eberhard Grabitz et al. (eds), *Das Recht der Europäischen Union* (75th edn, loose-leaf, C.H.Beck 2022) para 188 ff.

[52] Case C-626/18 *Poland v Parliament and Council* [2020] EU:C:2020:1000, para 95; Case C-37/83 *Rewe-Zentrale* [1984] EU:C:1984:89, para 20.

[53] Case C-570/19 *Irish Ferries* [2021] EU:C:2021:664, para 151; Case C-331/88 *Fedesa* [1990] EU:C:1990:391, paras 14, 15.

[54] Case C-128/17 *Poland v Parliament and Council* [2019] EU:C:2019:194, para 95.

[55] Critically, Friedrich Müller and Ralph Christensen, *Juristische Methodik, Vol. II: Europarecht* (3rd edn, Duncker&Humblot 2012) paras 548–60.

20 and 21 TFEU and the Free Movement Directive. In particular, the Court started to apply the Directive by analogy to areas and situations that are not covered but nonetheless fall within the ambit of Article 21 TFEU.[56] This approach, however, is a two-edged sword. The extension of secondary law can undermine the intention of the legislature, who might have deliberately excluded certain situations from the respective act's scope.[57] Further, such an approach can lead to a legislative 'ossification' at the Treaty level.[58]

These last observations already indicate that not all is well with the Court's approach. Generally, there are three ways by which the CJEU can guard its jurisprudence against legislative intervention. First, the Court can interpret secondary legislation in conformity with primary law. Where it is necessary to interpret a provision of secondary law, 'preference should be given to the interpretation which renders the provision consistent with primary law'.[59] This has been justified with a protection of the EU legislature.[60] Instead of annulling the respective act, the CJEU interprets it as far as possible in conformity with the Treaties. At the same time, this allows the Court to align secondary legislation with its own conception of primary law and circumvent legislative attempts to override its jurisprudence.[61]

Second, the Court can conceive the scope of relevant secondary legislation narrowly (or as not being an exhaustive harmonization) and adjudicate the case on the basis of primary law. As already noted above, EU legislative acts can take the form of exhaustive or minimum harmonization.[62] In the latter case, the Member States retain the right to adopt more detailed or stricter standards than those provided for in the respective EU legislation. On the flipside, the Court can assess whether these standards are compatible with primary law. This is an important caveat. As the intensity or degree of intended harmonization is far from clear, the Court enjoys considerable leeway.[63] Without being able to provide a comprehensive empirical assessment, it seems to me that the CJEU frequently declares secondary legislation to constitute a non-exhaustive harmonization and therefore reviews national measures against obligations stemming from EU primary law.[64]

[56] See e.g. Case C-456/12 *O. and B.* [2014] EU:C:2014:135, para 50; Case C-133/15 *Chavez-Vilchez* [2017] EU:C:2017:354, paras 54–5; Case C-673/16 *Coman* [2018] EU:C:2018:385, paras 24–5.

[57] Davies (n 1) 1603. See also Thomas Horsley, 'Reflections on the Role of the Court of Justice as the "Motor" of European Integration' CML Rev 50 (2013), 931, 962.

[58] See Case C-282/10 *Dominguez* [2011] EU:C:2011:559, Opinion of AG Trstenjak, para 157.

[59] Case C-481/19 *Consob* [2021] EU:C:2021:84, para 50; Cases 201 and 202/85, *Klensch* [1986] EU:C:1986:439, para 21. See also Stefan Leible and Ronny Domröse, 'Interpretation in Conformity with Primary Law' in Karl Riesenhuber (ed.), *European Legal Methodology* (2nd edn, Intersentia 2017) § 8, p 181.

[60] See e.g. Lenaerts (n 42) 18 f.

[61] For examples, see Phil Syrpis, 'The Relationship Between Primary and Secondary Law in the EU' CML Rev 52 (2015), 461, 470 ff; Davies (n 1) 1598 ff; van den Brink (n 32) 313 f.

[62] On these distinctions, Paul Craig and Grainne de Búrca, *EU Law* (7th edn, OUP 2020) 661 f.

[63] Marcus Klamert, 'Altes und Neues zur Harmonisierung im Binnenmarkt' EuZW 26 (2015), 265.

[64] See e.g. from the internal market for electricity, Case C-573/12 *Ålands Vindkraft AB* [2014] EU:C:2014:2037, paras 56–64. Regarding the Parent-Subsidiary Directive (Directive 90/435/EEC), see

Finally, the CJEU can review whether secondary legislation complies with primary law (judicial review). The yardstick for the Court's judicial review contains aspects of genuinely constitutional value (like competences or fundamental rights) as well as Treaty provisions of the third level. The CJEU has expressly acknowledged that EU institutions are bound by these parts of the Treaties, especially with regard to fundamental freedoms.[65] Though admittedly a rare occasion, the Court has assessed and annulled EU legislation on that basis.[66]

B. From 'Over' to 'De-constitutionalization'

This leaves us with a rather mixed picture. Drawing on its responsive side, this section suggests a profound recalibration of the CJEU's jurisprudence. In essence, we will revisit the idea of countering the Treaties' 'over-constitutionalization' by 'de-constitutionalizing' large parts of primary law. Based on the hierarchical division of the Treaty framework, the Court could start differentiating between provisions that give expression to an Article 2 TEU value and those that do not. In particular, the Court could relax the constraints imposed on the EU legislature by the latter kind of Treaty provisions.

To recall, Chapter 4 suggested deriving a threefold, substantive hierarchization of primary law from Article 2 TEU. While Article 2 TEU stands at its summit, the second level features those provisions that give expression to the EU's founding values (the EU's substantive constitution). The crucial question is whether a provision of primary law gives specific expression to a value enshrined in Article 2 TEU. As seen previously, such an Article 2 TEU-based constitution would comprise not only Charter rights but also provisions concerning the Union's institutional framework, its legislative procedures, and its competences (in detail Chapter 4, III.B). All other provisions of EU primary law, including large parts of the Union's policies and the so-called 'economic constitution', would form part of a third level. On that basis, the Court could start differentiating between these three levels. With regard to the third level of primary law, this chapter suggests embracing the idea of 'interpretative pluralism'. Under such a conception, both the legislature and

e.g. Case C-6/16 *Eqiom and Enka* [2017] EU:C:2017:641, paras 15–7. Regarding Directive 94/62/EC on packaging and packaging waste, see e.g. Case C-198/14 *Visnapuu* [2015] EU:C:2015:751, paras 40–8.

65 Recently, see Case C-620/18 *Hungary v Parliament and Council* [2020] EU:C:2020:1001, paras 104–6; *Poland v Parliament and Council* (n 52) paras 87–9. Arguing that the fundamental freedoms do not apply to the Union legislator, see Thorsten Kingreen, 'Fundamental Freedoms' in von Bogdandy and Bast (n 10) 515, 543. For a very loose obligation, see Martin Höpner and Christine Haas, 'Ist der Unionsgesetzgeber an die Grundfreiheiten gebunden?' EuR 57 (2022), 165.

66 See e.g. Case C-457/05 *Schutzverband der Spirituosen-Industrie* [2007] EU:C:2007:576, paras 23 ff; Case C-363/93 *Lancry* [1994] EU:C:1994:315, paras 24 ff, 37–38; Case C-139/79 *Maizena v Council* [1980] EU:C:1980:250. For a comprehensive study, see e.g. Karsten Sørensen, 'Reconciling Secondary Legislation with the Treaty Rights of Free Movement' EL Rev 36 (2011), 344, 347 ff.

constitutional courts share the responsibility for constitutional interpretation.[67] In the words of Gareth Davies, this leads to 'an Escher-like arrangement, in which each arm of government is both above and below the other'.[68] What could this entail?

First, the Court should continue to defer as far as possible to acts adopted by the EU legislature. If the area of law is harmonized, the Court should apply and interpret the respective act of secondary legislation without any reference to primary law. This is already established practice in the Court's case law. If the area of law has not been harmonized by secondary legislation, the CJEU should emphasize that its interpretation of the respective primary law 'is subject to diverging legislation'. This would indicate its openness to change its jurisprudence in case the legislature decides to regulate the respective area differently.[69] This might provide an incentive and draw the legislature's attention to pressing social and political problems.[70] Of course, this presupposes that the EU legislature actually has a competence in the relevant area. If this is not the case, the Court could restrict its interpretation of the Treaties as far as possible and tailor it to the specific case at hand.

Second, the Court could adjust its standard of review when assessing the legality of secondary legislation. Abstractly, the Court could proceed in two ways. On the one hand, it could altogether reduce the yardstick of review to the second level of Treaty provisions. This would prevent the Court from reviewing secondary legislation (i.e. in the internal market context) against third level provisions (i.e. fundamental freedoms). Such a recalibration would lead to a review of EU legislation against genuinely constitutional standards. While the CJEU also fulfils the functions of an international, administrative, and Supreme Court,[71] the judicial review of legislation is one of its key constitutional functions. Accordingly, it is a widely shared perception both in scholarship[72] and the Court itself[73] that Luxembourg is in fact also the Union's constitutional court. Recent cases, in which the Court reviewed EU legislation against constitutional yardsticks (especially fundamental

[67] Gareth Davies, 'Does the Court of Justice Own the Treaties? Interpretative Pluralism as a Solution to Over-Constitutionalisation' ELJ 24 (2018), 358, 362 f, 368. See also van den Brink (n 32) 314; Mark Dawson, 'Constitutional Dialogue between Courts and Legislators in the European Union' EPL 19 (2013), 369.

[68] Davies (n 67) 362.

[69] See e.g. Case C-73/08 *Bressol* [2009] EU:C:2009:396, Opinion of AG Sharpston, para 153: 'I invite the Community legislator and the Member States to reflect upon the application of these criteria . . .'.

[70] Dawson (n 67), 381.

[71] See e.g. Dehousse (n 29) 34.

[72] See e.g. Pierre-Emmanuel Pignarre, *La Cour de justice de l'Union européenne, juridiction constitutionnelle* (Bruylant 2021) 743 ff; Federico Fabbrini and Miguel Maduro, 'Supranational Constitutional Courts' in Rainer Grote et al. (eds), *Max Planck Encyclopedia of Comparative Constitutional Law* (OUP 2016) paras 12 ff. But see Louis Favoreu, 'Les Courts de Luxembourg et de Strasbourg ne sont pas des cours constitutionnelles' in *Au carrefour des droits* (Dalloz 2002) 35.

[73] Through time, see e.g. José Luís da Cruz Vilaça, 'Reflections on Judicial Review of the Constitutionality of EU Legislation' in *EU Law and Integration* (Hart 2014) 44; Gil C. Rodríguez Iglesias, 'Der Gerichtshof der Europäischen Gemeinschaften als Verfassungsgericht' EuR 27 (1992), 225; Pierre Pescatore, 'La Cour en tant que juridiction fédérale et constitutionnelle (1963)' in Picod (n 29) 61.

rights), testify to this increasing function.[74] In this spirit, the Court would retreat to its function as a genuinely constitutional court in its relationship to the EU legislature.

On the other hand, the Court could operate with a flexible degree of discretion. As far as a review against third level Treaty provisions is concerned, the Court could leave a greater margin of appreciation to the Union legislature. This could especially concern the proportionality test and lead to relaxing the assessment of coherence, aptitude, or necessity of a certain Union act.[75] As far as Article 2 TEU and all provisions that give expression to it are concerned, the CJEU could apply strict scrutiny. This would imply a review that goes beyond assessing whether the respective acts are 'manifestly inappropriate'.

Either way, this proposal would deprive the third level of Treaty provisions of an important feature of constitutional law, namely being the yardstick for ordinary law and standard of review in constitutional adjudication. As such, this recalibration would lead to a judge-driven, soft 'de-constitutionalization' of the relevant Treaty parts. At the same time, such an adjustment would significantly expand the space left to legislative decision-making. This raises the question of whether such a profound shift and self-limitation is procedurally possible. And is it likely to occur?

From a procedural point of view, both Article 263 and 267 TFEU seem broad enough to allow for the proposed adjustments.[76] Article 19(1)(1) TEU defines the CJEU's central task vaguely as ensuring 'that in the interpretation and application of the Treaties *the law* is observed'. Similarly, Article 263(1) TFEU simply refers to the 'review of *legality*' (see also Article 267(1)(b) TFEU: 'validity'). A more detailed list of grounds for the review of secondary legislation can only be found in Article 263(2) TFEU, which refers to 'the lack of competence, infringement of an essential procedural requirement, *infringement of the Treaties* or of any rule of law relating to their application, or misuse of powers'. This could be read as a catch-all notion encompassing the whole range of primary law.[77] Yet, even the 'infringement of the Treaties' remains relatively vague. Hence, it does not seem excluded to read this ground narrowly as referring only to parts of the Treaties.

Nevertheless, referring courts and applicants in actions for annulment may still challenge the validity of EU legislative acts based on their incompatibility with third level Treaty provisions. Is the Court bound to follow these submissions? In

[74] See e.g. Case C-426/16 *Liga van Moskeeën en Islamitische Organisaties Provincie Antwerpen* [2018] EU:C:2018:335; Case C-362/14 *Schrems* [2015] EU:C:2015:650; Cases C-293 and 594/12 *Digital Rights Ireland* [2014] EU:C:2014:238; Case C-236/09 *Association Belge des Consommateurs Test-Achats* [2011] EU:C:2011:100; Cases C-92 and 93/09 *Schecke and Eifert* [2010] EU:C:2010:662.

[75] See e.g. Syrpis (n 61) 461, 484.

[76] See also Paul Craig, *EU Administrative Law* (3rd edn, OUP 2018) 266; Agustín Menéndez, 'The Guardianship of European Constitutionality: A Structural Critique of European Constitutional Review' in Mads Andenas et al. (eds), *The Reach of Free Movement* (Springer 2017) 173, 186.

[77] See e.g. Wolfram Cremer, 'Art. 263 AEUV' in Christian Calliess and Matthias Ruffert (eds), *EUV/AEUV* (6th edn, C.H.Beck 2022) para 96; Dörr (n 51) para 174.

preliminary references, the Court has ample space to reformulate the questions posed by Member State courts. Usually, the Court does not hesitate to limit or replace provisions indicated by the national court with provisions it deems to be actually relevant.[78] This is different in actions for annulment. According to a rather extensive interpretation of the ne ultra petita principle, the Court is limited not only to the subject of the respective application (the challenged EU act and the facts presented by the parties) but also by the mentioned grounds under Article 263(2) TFEU.[79] While this does not apply to the grounds of 'competence' and 'essential procedural requirements', which must be raised ex officio by the Court, pleas concerning the substantive legality of EU acts may only be considered if they are raised by the applicants.[80]

This could prevent the Court from reformulating pleas brought, for instance, based on fundamental freedoms as a fundamental rights case. Yet, this line of jurisprudence is by no means consistent and has been subject to criticism even from inside the Court.[81] In this sense, the General Court has indicated that 'it is for the EU judicature to identify the relevant provisions and to apply them to the facts put before it by the parties, even if the parties do not refer to the provisions in question or rely on different provisions.'[82] Given its jurisprudential nature, it would certainly be within the Court's power to revise the current setup.[83]

Comparatively, there are important parallels to the practice of other constitutional courts in the Member States. As explained above, the Court would redefine and limit its own yardstick of constitutional review and 'de-constitutionalize' large parts of the Treaties in its adjudication. Such a redefinition is not unprecedented in the European legal space. Indeed, most constitutional texts prove to be rather malleable. Though constitutional status is often equated with what has been enshrined in the formal constitutional document, it might equally reach beyond the text or be more restrained. One powerful example was already mentioned in Chapter 4. In its

[78] See e.g. Koen Lenaerts, Ignace Maselis, and Kathleen Gutman, *EU Procedural Law* (OUP 2014) para 3.23. Morten Broberg and Niels Fenger, *Preliminary References to the European Court of Justice* (3rd edn, OUP 2021) 371 ff.

[79] See also Article 127 of Rules of Procedure of the Court of Justice. Instructively Case C-122/16 P *British Airways v Commission* [2017] EU:C:2017:406, Opinion of AG Mengozzi, paras 82–92; Richard-E. Himmer, 'Die Geltendmachung der Nichtigkeitsgründe nach Art. 263 AEUV' *Neue Zeitschrift für Verwaltungsrecht* 41 (2022), 1512.

[80] See e.g. Case C-436/19 P *Abaco Energy v Commission* [Order of 21 July 2020] EU:C:2020:606, para 68; Case C-272/12 P *Commission v Ireland* [2013] EU:C:2013:812, para 28; Case C-367/95 P *Commission v Sytraval and Brink's France* [1998] EU:C:1998:154, para 67. See further Lenaerts, Maselis, and Gutman (n 78) para 7.146.

[81] See e.g. Case C-210/98 P *Salzgitter AG v Commission* [2000] EU:C:2000:172, Opinion of AG Jacobs, paras 125–50. See also René Barents, 'EU procedural law and effective legal protection' CML Rev 51 (2014), 1437, 1452, 1460 ff; Ulrich Everling, 'Überlegungen zum Verfahren vor den Gerichten der Europäischen Gemeinschaften' (pp 537, 542) and Bo Vesterdorf, 'Le relevé d'office par le juge communautaire' (pp 551, 560) both in Ninon Colneric et al. (eds), *Une communauté de droit* (BWV 2003).

[82] Case T-124/13 *Italy v Commission* [2015] EU:T:2015:690, para 36.

[83] See in this sense also Michał Krajewski, 'The Many-Faced Court' EuConst 15 (2019), 220, 231.

decision in *Liberté d'association*,[84] the French Conseil Constitutionnel expanded constitutional value beyond the formal constitution[85] and defined its yardsticks for judicial review.

The proposed 'de-constitutionalization' of large parts of the Treaties operates in the reverse. The CJEU should not *expand* constitutional value beyond the formal Treaties but *restrict* it to those Treaty provisions that give expression to a value enshrined in Article 2 TEU. While this might be a more contentious step than the one undertaken by the Conseil, it is equally true that the CJEU has considerably more leeway to define the limits of what has constitutional status in EU primary law. As there is no formal constitutional document at the EU level, the Union's substantive constitution is largely a product of judicial interpretation (Chapter 3, II.A). By implication, constitutional status can, but does not have to, be equated with EU primary law.

Three objections are likely to be raised against the proposals advanced in this chapter. The first one is to question the *added value* of this approach. As noted in previous chapters, it is possible to reformulate third level provisions (e.g. fundamental freedoms) on the second level (e.g. Articles 15 to 17 of the Charter). If the same legal interest can be rearticulated at the second level, limiting the constitutional features of third level provisions makes no difference at all. Yet, this objection misses an important element of the substantive hierarchization developed in the previous chapters—it goes hand in hand with a layered scope of protection (see figure 4.2). Thus, it should make a difference whether the Court assesses secondary legislation for its conformity, for instance, with fundamental freedoms or Article 16 CFR.

Second, one could argue that the proposed turn is highly unlikely to occur as the Court *lacks incentives* to adjust its jurisprudence. An external motivation of the Court is hardly possible as the options of political influence are very limited.[86] In particular, court curbing (e.g. interfering with appointments, capping salaries, political override, or just non-compliance) is structurally difficult at the EU level.[87] In any case, the idea of pressuring the CJEU into responding to political arguments should be met with extreme caution. In light of threats against judicial independence in several Member States, any such step at the European level would openly undermine the EU's efforts to counter these developments. Further, it is rather questionable whether such political 'incentives' are needed to convince the

[84] Conseil Constitutionnel, Décision no° 71-44 DC, *Liberté d'association*.

[85] Namely, the preamble to the 1958 constitution and the texts to which the preamble refers: the 1789 Declaration of the Rights of Man and of the Citizen, the preamble of the 1946 constitution, and, cited in the latter, the 'fundamental principles recognised by the laws of the Republic'.

[86] Scharpf (n 1) 321 f.

[87] See e.g. Dawson (n 67) 390 ff; Marcus Höreth, 'Warum der EuGH nicht gestoppt werden sollte—und auch nicht gestoppt werden kann' in Ulrich Haltern and Andreas Bergmann (eds), *Der EuGH in der Kritik* (Mohr Siebeck 2012) 73, 102 ff; R. Daniel Kelemen, 'The Political Foundations of Judicial Independence in the European Union' JEPP 19 (2012), 43.

Court. Indeed, the CJEU has performed remarkable U-turns in its jurisprudence without such pressure. A case in point is its citizenship case law. The Court's readjustment, construing the citizen's right to equal treatment in increasingly narrow terms,[88] was to a large extent an implementation of the legislative decisions taken in Directive 2004/38. Even though one can legitimately criticize the Court's restrictive approach, it seems responsive to the legislature.

Finally, the proposed relaxation of judicial review of EU legislation seems to consolidate the alleged *double standards* in the review of EU and Member State acts. A common but rather sweeping accusation of the CJEU's review practice runs as follows: EU institutions are protected from extensive judicial review, their competences are interpreted broadly, and their discretion tends to be enhanced. Member State measures, by contrast, are rigidly reviewed against obligations arising from EU law. Though sharply rejected by members of the Court,[89] many see this as one expression of the Court's greater bias in favour of European integration.[90] The recent *PSPP* decision of the German Constitutional Court can be read in this context. In fact, the Bundesverfassungsgericht called for a more stringent proportionality assessment by the Court of Justice.[91] The Luxembourg Court had limited its review of some ECB acts to manifest errors.[92] According to Karlsruhe, this self-restraint is not only 'objectively arbitrary', 'untenable', and 'incomprehensible';[93] it also poses an essential problem for the Union's federal balance and democracy. Even if the Court's insistence on a proper proportionality assessment has been described as 'painfully German',[94] there is a grain of truth in it. There are manifold examples of the EU's reliance on independent, technocratic institutions to achieve highly

[88] See e.g. Case C-333/13 *Dano* [2014] EU:C:2014:2358; Case C-67/14 *Alimanovic* [2015] EU:C:2015:597; Case C-308/14 *Commission v UK* [2016] EU:C:2016:436. See on this Eleanor Spaventa, 'Earned Citizenship' in Dimitry Kochenov (ed.), *EU Citizenship and Federalism* (CUP 2017) 204, 208–21. For possible explanations of this turn, see e.g. Michael Blauberger et al., 'ECJ Judges read the morning papers' JEPP 25 (2018), 1422.

[89] 'EU's top judge defends ECJ against charges of integration agenda' *Financial Times* (22 November 2016). See also Juliane Kokott, 'Der *pouvoir neutre* im Recht der Europäischen Union' ZaöRV 69 (2009), 275, 281.

[90] On the various manifestations of this argument, see e.g. Michal Bobek, 'Legal Reasoning of the Court of Justice' EL Rev 39 (2014), 418, 424 ff. For an attempt to prove this bias empirically, see Michal Ovádek, 'Supranationalism, Constrained?' *European Union Politics* 22 (2020), 46.

[91] BVerfG, Judgment of 5 May 2020, 2 BvR 859/15, *PSPP*, paras 123 ff.

[92] Case C-493/17 *Weiss* [2018] EU:C:2018:1000, paras 56, 78, 91; Case C-62/14 *Gauweiler* [2015] EU:C:2015:400, paras 68, 69.

[93] BVerfG, Judgment of 5 May 2020, 2 BvR 859/15, *PSPP*, paras 118 f, 153.

[94] Franz C. Mayer, 'To Boldly Go Where No Court Has Gone Before' GLJ 21 (2020), 1116, 1123. With regard to the question of proportionality, see also the criticism in Editorial, 'Not Mastering the Treaties' CML Rev 57 (2020), 965, 972 f; Mattias Wendel, 'Paradoxes of *Ultra-Vires* Review' GLJ 21 (2020), 979, 985 ff; Toni Marzal, 'Making Sense of the Use of Proportionality in the Bundesverfassungsgericht's PSPP Decision' RAE (2020), 441.

political results.[95] In this light, *PSPP* could be read as a call for more control and accountability.[96]

But does this mean that the approach proposed in this section might clash with these requirements? Probably not. *PSPP* concerned measures taken by the ECB, a particularly independent part of the EU executive, and not the EU legislature. Further, the proposal outlined above does not mean that the CJEU would relax its review entirely. With regard to genuinely constitutional yardsticks that give expression to a value in Article 2 TEU, the Court would continue to apply strict scrutiny. This concerns, in particular, fundamental rights and questions of competence. As a result, there should be no dissonance between the Bundesverfassungsgericht's stance in *PSPP* and the approach proposed in this chapter.

[95] See only Michael A. Wilkinson, *Authoritarian Liberalism and the Transformation of Modern Europe* (OUP 2021) 203 ff; Jürgen Habermas, *The Lure of Technocracy* (Polity 2015) 3 ff. With regard to the ECB, see Nik de Boer and Jens Van 't Klooster, 'The ECB, the Courts and the Issue of Democratic Legitimacy after Weiss' CML Rev 57 (2020), 1689, 1700 ff, 1721 ff.

[96] In this sense Isabel Feichtner, 'The German Constitutional Court's PSPP Judgment: Impediment and Impetus for the Democratization of Europe' GLJ 21 (2020), 1090, 1099 ff; Ulrich Haltern, 'Ultra-vires-Kontrolle im Dienst europäischer Demokratie' NVwZ 39 (2020), 817, 820 f.

7

The Court and the Treaty Makers

Constraining Treaty Revision

I. Introduction

The previous chapters have demonstrated how the Court can use the substantive hierarchies derived from Article 2 TEU to foster the coherence of primary law and broaden the space for legislative decision-making at the EU level. The following Chapter will focus on Article 2 TEU itself, the top tier of this substantive hierarchy, and explore whether the EU's founding values are open to revision. Put differently, does Article 2 TEU constitute a substantive limitation on Treaty amendments? And if so, are these constraints amenable to judicial review?

The idea of substantive limitations on constitutional amendments is not new. Eminent but highly controversial thinkers like Carl Schmitt, Maurice Hauriou, or Costantino Mortati devoted seminal parts of their scholarship to this question.[1] Since then the issue has been continuously on the agenda of constitutional scholars.[2] In recent years, however, the 'doctrine of unconstitutional constitutional amendments' seems to have gained support in many jurisdictions[3] and increasing attention in comparative constitutional scholarship.[4] Even though there is no common position among EU Member States with regard to such constraints (or their judicial review), one can nonetheless detect a trend towards placing constitutional amendments under certain constraints.[5]

[1] See e.g. Carl Schmitt, *Constitutional Theory* (1928) (Duke Univ. Press 2008) 67 ff, 75 ff, 140 ff; Maurice Hauriou, *Précis du droit constitutionnel* (2nd edn, Sirey 1929) 276, 336, 357–60; Costantino Mortati, 'La Costituente' in *Raccolta di Scritti I: Studi sul potere costituente e sulla riforma costituzionale dello stato* (Giuffrè 1972) 3, 316 ff and Mortati, 'Studi sulla costituzione e sulla revisione costituzionale' in *Raccolta di Scritti II: Scritti sulle fonti del diritto e sull'interpretazione* (Giuffrè 1972) 3, 43 ff.

[2] For instance, Claude Klein, *Théorie et pratique du pouvoir constituant* (PUF 1996) 123 ff; Benito Aláez Corral, *Los límites materiales a la reforma de la constitución Española de 1978* (Boletín Oficial del Estado 2000); Marcello Piazza, *I limiti alla revisione costituzionale nell'ordinamento italiano* (Cedam 2002).

[3] Yaniv Roznai, 'Unconstitutional Constitutional Amendments—The Migration and Success of a Constitutional Idea' AJCL 61 (2013), 657.

[4] See e.g. Yaniv Roznai, *Unconstitutional Constitutional Amendments* (OUP 2017); Richard Albert and Bertil Emrah Oder (eds), *An Unamendable Constitution?* (Springer 2018); Silvia Suteu, *Eternity Clauses in Democratic Constitutionalism* (OUP 2021).

[5] Danielle Azébazé Labarthe, 'À la recherche d'un patrimoine constitutionnel européen de la révision constitutionnelle' RFDC (108) (2016), 769.

EU Values Before the Court of Justice. Luke Dimitrios Spieker, Oxford University Press. © Luke Dimitrios Spieker 2023.
DOI: 10.1093/oso/9780198876717.003.0008

As the Hungarian case illustrates, this issue can be of great political salience. In the last elections, the governing party secured a two-thirds majority, thereby allowing it to circumvent rulings of the Hungarian Constitutional Court, in case it strikes down legislation, by simply amending the constitution.[6] Such a misuse weakens checks and balances and leads to the constitution's increasing trivialization. Admittedly, the degradation of constitutional amendments to instruments of everyday politics is no issue at the EU level. The complete opposite is the case. As seen in the previous chapter, the demanding amendment procedures can reduce political space. Thus, the idea of unconstitutional constitutional amendments seems more like legal science fiction than a realistic concern in the EU context.

Still, such developments can take very different forms. To provide some (not so hypothetical) examples: imagine the restructuring of the EU in the face of a financial crisis. Such a restructuring might lead to the creation of entities that are neither democratically accountable nor subject to constitutional constraints. Sounds familiar? Or imagine a Treaty amendment that allows the European Council to overturn a CJEU ruling that seriously affects a Member State.[7] Still legal science fiction? As these examples demonstrate, there can be a legitimate interest in shielding some central constitutional principles against Treaty amendments.

The debate on substantive limitations on Treaty amendments is not without precedent. After some enigmatic statements in the Court's first EEA opinion, there was a short-lived discussion concerning such constraints.[8] Despite manifold Treaty amendments since then (Maastricht, Amsterdam, Nice, Lisbon, and Article 136 TFEU), the Court had still no opportunity to clearly position itself. However, in light of the increased judicial and doctrinal interest in 'unconstitutional constitutional amendments', the idea of substantive limitations to Treaty amendments has resurrected silently.[9] The following sections will jump into the slipstream of that trend and explore how this idea could help protect the EU's founding values against potential encroachments by Treaty revision. At first sight, the lack of any textual anchoring and the CJEU's rather thin and ambiguous case law may cast doubt on the existence of such constraints (Section II). Despite these challenges,

[6] According to Art. 24(5) of the Hungarian Fundamental Law, the Constitutional Court cannot review constitutional amendments. See e.g. Pál Sonnevend, András Jakab, and Lóránt Csink, 'The constitution as an instrument of everyday party politics: The basic law of Hungary' in Armin von Bogdandy and Pál Sonnevend (eds), *Constitutional Crisis in the European Constitutional Area* (Hart 2016) 33.

[7] For such a proposal, see Fritz W. Scharpf, 'Legitimacy in the Multilevel European Polity' *European Political Science Review* 1 (2009), 173, 199 f.

[8] For some key protagonists, see Ulrich Everling, 'Zur Stellung der Mitgliedstaaten der Europäischen Union als "Herren der Verträge"' in Ulrich Beyerlin et al. (ed.), *Festschrift für Rudolf Bernhardt* (Springer 1995) 1161, 1169 ff; José Luís da Cruz Vilaça and Nuno Piçarra, 'Y a-t-il des limites matérielles à la revision des Traités instituant les Communautés européennes' CDE 29 (1993), 3; Roland Bieber, 'Les limites matérielles et formelles à la revision des Traités établissant la Communauté européenne' RMC (1993), 343.

[9] See e.g. Reijer Passchier and Maarten Stremler, 'Unconstitutional constitutional amendments in European Union law' CJICL 5 (2016), 337.

this chapter will demonstrate how implicit substantive limitations could be derived from Article 2 TEU and even rendered justiciable before the Court (Section III).

II. Unconstrained Treaty Makers?

A. Explicit Procedural but Implicit Substantive Constraints?

Abstractly, constraints on Treaty amendments can be of procedural or substantive nature. Article 48 TEU contains detailed procedural rules for an amendment of the Treaties. Nevertheless, some argue that the Member States can even bypass the revision procedure laid down in the Treaties by pointing to public international law.[10] Despite Article 40(1) of the Vienna Convention on the Law of Treaties (VCLT),[11] it has been submitted that parties to an international treaty may unanimously bypass specific amendment procedures.[12] If the parties remain free to terminate a treaty by mutual consent (Article 54(b) VCLT), they must retain—maiore ad minus—the right to amend or modify it. In the EU context, this view can hardly convince.[13] EU law governs the relations between Member States within its scope in an exclusive manner shielding them from international law.[14] Moreover, the procedures involve third parties, such as the European and national parliaments.[15] The Treaties therefore provide for a procedural corset when it comes to Treaty change.[16] In this sense, it is well-established jurisprudence that rules on Treaty amendments are not at the Member States' disposition.[17] This was recently confirmed in *Pringle*.[18]

[10] See e.g. Trevor C. Hartley, *The Foundations of European Union Law* (8th edn, OUP 2014) 91 f; Andreas Haratsch, Christian Koenig, and Matthias Pechstein, *Europarecht* (11th edn, Mohr Siebeck 2018) para 97. This claim has already been advanced in Marguerite Deliège-Sequaris, 'Révision des traités européens en dehors des procédures prévues' CDE 16 (1980), 539, 542 ff.

[11] Art. 40(1) VCLT: '*Unless the treaty otherwise provides*, the amendment of multilateral treaties shall be governed by the following paragraphs . . .'.

[12] See Robert Jennings and Arthur Watts, *Oppenheim's International Law*, vol 1 (9th edn, OUP 2008) § 624, p 1255; Paul Reuter, *Introduction au droit des traités* (3rd edn, PUF 1995) paras 210 ff; Alfred Verdross and Bruno Simma, *Universelles Völkerrecht* (3rd edn, Duncker&Humblot 1984, reprint 2010) 505. Differently, when the established institutions are involved, see Henry G. Schermers and Niels M. Blokker, *International Institutional Law* (6th edn, Nijhoff 2018) § 1163.

[13] See e.g. Koen Lenaerts and Piet Van Nuffel, *EU Constitutional Law* (OUP 2021) para 3.009; Marcus Klamert, 'Article 48 TEU' in Manuel Kellerbauer et al. (eds), *The Treaties and the Charter of Fundamental Rights* (OUP 2019) para 4; Christoph Ohler, 'Art. 48 EUV' in Eberhard Grabitz et al. (eds), *Das Recht der Europäischen Union* (75th edn, loose-leaf, C.H.Beck 2022) para 26.

[14] See e.g. Achilles Skordas and Luke D. Spieker, 'Supranational Law' in Anne Peters (ed.), *Max Planck Encyclopedia of Public International Law* (OUP 2021) para 4.

[15] Jean-Paul Jacqué, *Droit institutionnel de l'Union européenne* (9th edn, Dalloz 2018) para 909; Werner Meng, 'Art. 48 EUV' in Hans von der Groeben et al. (eds), *Europäisches Unionsrecht* (7th edn, Nomos 2015) paras 36 f; Bruno de Witte, 'Treaty revision in the European Union' *Netherlands Yearbook of International Law* 25 (2004), 51, 62 f.

[16] Klamert (n 13) para 4.

[17] See e.g. Case 43/75 *Defrenne* [1976] EU:C:1976:56, paras 57–8; Case 68/86 *United Kingdom v Council* [1988] EU:C:1988:85, paras 24, 38; Opinion 2/94 *ECHR Accession I* [1996] EU:C:1996:140, para 35.

[18] Case C-370/12 *Pringle* [2012] EU:C:2012:756, paras 30–7.

The construction of substantive limitations, however, is much harder to justify. At first glance, one could argue that such a far-reaching restriction of the Member States' sovereign powers should be explicitly anchored in the Treaties to be legally comprehensible and convincing.[19] As the Treaties *explicitly* refer to *procedural* requirements for Treaty amendments, it seems difficult to accept the *implicit* existence of far more intrusive *substantive* limitations. Further, one could conclude a contrario that these explicit constraints were supposed to be conclusive. Still, many argue that the content of national eternity clauses is merely declaratory and derives implicitly from the constitution itself.[20] One pertinent example for such implicit limitations can be found in Italy. While the Italian Constitution contains an explicit eternity clause protecting the republican form of government (Article 139), the Corte Costituzionale has elaborated a system of substantive limitations going far beyond this clause. According to the Corte, the 'principi supremi' on which the Italian Constitution is based, cannot be subverted or modified even by constitutional revision.[21] Despite the implied character of these supreme principles, the Corte nonetheless established its power to review constitutional amendments against this yardstick.[22] This example vividly illustrates the large discretion that constitutional courts enjoy in this respect. As such, the lack of explicit provisions does not per se exclude the existence of such limitations or their judicial review.

B. The Court's Enigmatic Position

Many have read the Court's first opinion on the EEA Agreement as a confirmation of substantive limitations. In that opinion, the CJEU had to assess the compatibility of the court system envisaged in the EEA Agreement with the Treaties. The Court stated that

> Article 238 of the EEC Treaty [Art. 217 TFEU] does not provide any basis for setting up a system of courts which conflicts with Article 164 of the EEC Treaty [Art. 19 TEU] and, more generally, with the very foundations of the Community. For the same reasons, *an amendment of Article 238 … could not cure the incompatibility with Community law*.[23]

[19] See Rudolf Bernhardt, 'The sources of Community law: the "constitution" of the Community' in Commission of the European Communities (ed.), *Thirty years of Community Law* (Office for Official Publ. of the EC 1983) 69, 75.

[20] See e.g. Schmitt (n 1) 152 f [pp 105 f]; Roznai (n 4) 150 ff; Suteu (n 4) 125 ff.

[21] See Corte Costituzionale, 1146/1988 (IT:COST:1988:1146) para 2.1. For a concise overview, see e.g. Gustavo Zagrebelsky and Valeria Marcenò, *Giustizia costituzionale, Vol. I: Storia, principi, interpretazioni* (Mulino 2018) 187–95; Tania Groppi, 'Constitutional Revision in Italy' in Xenophon Contiades (ed.), *Engineering Constitutional Change* (Routledge 2013) 203, 210.

[22] Davide Paris and Raffaele Bifulco, 'The Italian Constitutional Court' in Armin von Bogdandy et al. (eds), *The Max Planck Handbooks in European Public Law*, vol 3 (OUP 2020) § 9, pp 447, 462.

[23] Opinion 1/91 *EEA Treaty I* [1991] EU:C:1991:490, paras 70, 71 (emphasis added).

For many, this enigmatic passage appeared to be 'an electrifying hint that the Court will review the constitutionality of purported Treaty revision'.[24] The opinion was read as recognizing a hard core of principles and values that can be neither modified nor abrogated.[25] Others read the opinion in much narrower terms as merely rejecting the *implicit* amendment of fundamental Treaty provisions, namely through the backdoor of revising Article 238 EEC.[26] If the Member States want to fundamentally revise the EU's judicial system, they would have to do so openly and according to the amendment procedure foreseen in the Treaties (Article 236 EEC at that time).

The discourse was fuelled again by *Kadi*, which concerned obligations stemming from a UN Security Council resolution. According to Article 351(1) TFEU, pre-accession international law obligations of the Member States should, in principle, not be affected by the Treaties. This seems to allow derogations from the Treaties. In *Kadi*, however, the CJEU clarified that Article 351(1) TFEU (and potential derogations from primary law) 'may in no circumstances permit any challenge to the principles that form part of the very foundations of the Community legal order'.[27] It further stressed that a provision of primary law, such as Article 351(1) TFEU, cannot 'authorise any derogation from the principles of liberty, democracy and respect for human rights and fundamental freedoms enshrined in Article 6(1) EU as a foundation of the Union'.[28] These statements have been interpreted as creating a new layer of untouchable core principles that is hierarchically superior to the rest of EU primary law.[29]

[24] Stephen Weatherill, *Law and Integration in the European Union* (Clarendon 1995) 221.

[25] See e.g. Carlo Curti Gialdino, 'Some Reflections on the Acquis Communautaire' CML Rev 32 (1995), 1089, 1110 f; Everling (n 8) 1170; da Cruz Vilaça and Piçarra (n 8) 3, 24–7; Bieber (n 8) 343, 345 ff. See further Jacqueline Dutheil de la Rochère, 'L'Espace économique européen sous le regard des juges de la Cour de justice' RMC (1992), 603, 607; Deirdre Curtin, 'The Constitutional Structure of the Union' CML Rev 30 (1993), 17, 63 ff; Chiara Cattabriga, 'Limiti materiali alla revisione comunitaria' *Rivista di diritto europeo* 34 (1994), 245, 256 ff; Matthias Herdegen, 'Vertragliche Eingriff in das "Verfassungsystem" der Europäischen Union' in Ole Due et al. (eds), *Festschrift für Ulrich Everling*, vol 1 (Nomos 1995) 447, 457.

[26] See e.g. Noreen Burrows, 'The Risks of Widening without Deepening' EL Rev 17 (1992), 352, 360; Astrid Epiney, 'La Cour de justice des Communautés européennes et l'Espace économique européen' *Swiss Review of International and European law* 2 (1992), 275, 301–3; Markus Heintzen, 'Hierarchisierungsprozesse innerhalb des Primärrechts der Europäischen Gemeinschaft' EuR 29 (1994), 35, 39.

[27] Cases C-402 and 415/05 P *Kadi* [2008] EU:C:2008:461, para 304.

[28] ibid para 303.

[29] See e.g. Christina Eckes, 'Protecting supremacy from external influences' ELJ 18 (2012), 230, 241, 247; Nikolaos Lavranos, 'Protecting European law from International Law' EFAR 15 (2010), 265, 269 ff; Myriam Benlolo-Carabot, 'La CJCE et la protection des valeurs fondamentales de l'ordre juridique communautaire' RMCUE (2009), 380.

III. The Potential of Article 2 TEU

Despite these bold readings of the EEA opinion and *Kadi*, the case law is far from clear. Thus, many have criticized reading the acceptance of substantive limitations on Treaty revision into these thin and ambiguous passages. To them, such an interpretation seems not only highly speculative but—without any textual support in the Treaties—also legally dubious.[30] The following section will start from scratch and explore how substantive limitations on Treaty amendments could be construed. It is submitted that Article 2 TEU plays a crucial role in this regard (Section A.1). Nevertheless, the mere existence of substantive limitations does not necessarily imply their justiciability. As such, the CJEU's jurisdiction to review Treaty amendments as well as its standard of review (only procedural or also substantive) will have to be established separately (Section A.2). Finally, this section will engage with likely objections (Section B).

A. Article 2 TEU as a Justiciable Limit of Treaty Revisions?

1. Substantive limitations

Abstractly, there are two possible, albeit not mutually exclusive, ways to construe substantive limitations at the EU level.[31] On the one hand, substantive limitations could be derived from heteronomous sources, *external* to the EU legal order, such as (regional) jus cogens or Member State constitutions. On the other hand, substantive limitations could originate from *internal* sources, meaning intrinsically from the Treaties themselves. This is where Article 2 TEU comes into play.

a) External sources

First, substantive limitations for the amendment of EU primary law could be found in the realm of the supra-positive, in particular, in the limits set by international jus cogens. Pursuant to Article 53 VCLT, a treaty and its amendment are void if they conflict with a peremptory norm of international law. On that basis, it has been suggested that the EU institutions cannot be exempted from the ties to fundamental human rights.[32] Yet, there are several objections to such an approach. The theoretical basis for the peremptory character of jus cogens is highly controversial and varies between natural and positive law conceptions.[33] As a result, there

[30] See e.g. Bruno de Witte, 'International Agreement or European Constitution?' in Jan A. Winter et al. (eds), *Reforming the Treaty on European Union* (Kluwer 1996) 3, 17. In this sense, see also Martin Nettesheim, 'Normenhierarchien im EU-Recht' EuR 41 (2006), 737, 743.

[31] With regard to constitutional amendments, see also Olivier Beaud, *La puissance de l'État* (PUF 1994) 336 who distinguishes between 'limites *autonomes*' and 'limites *hétéronomes*'.

[32] Anne Peters, *Elemente einer Theorie der Verfassung Europas* (Duncker&Humblot 2001) 447.

[33] See e.g. ILC, First Report on jus cogens, UN Doc. A/CN.4.693 (8 March 2015) paras 50 ff.

seems to be no generally accepted framework to identify jus cogens.[34] Moreover, international jus cogens only provides for an extremely low level of protection.[35] A higher protection could only be achieved by relying on some kind of regional jus cogens. Indeed, some argue that the non-derogable rights under Article 15(2) ECHR manifest such a common minimum.[36] The existence of a regional jus cogens, however, is far from being generally accepted.[37]

Second, substantive limitations could arise from the constitutions of the Member States.[38] Some constitutions contain explicit or implicit limitations on further European integration, which are often summarized under the banner of constitutional identities. In case these confines are reached, Member State legislatures are precluded from adopting a consent act to a new Treaty or its amendment. In some Member States, these limitations can be overcome by constitutional amendments.[39] The German Basic Law, by contrast, stipulates in Article 23(1) that '[t]he establishment of the European Union, as well as changes in its treaty foundations … shall be subject to paragraphs (2) and (3) of Article 79.' Hence, even constitutional amendments approving, ratifying or implementing Treaty amendments will be measured against the eternity clause in Article 79(3) Basic Law. Thus, some Member States face substantive limitations stemming from their own constitutions when amending the Treaties. As will be demonstrated in Chapter 11, these limitations are often congruent with the values enshrined in Article 2 TEU. In addition, the principles that form the Member States' constitutional identities will usually provide the building blocks for their interpretation and concretization. As such, Article 2 TEU becomes, albeit in form of a reflex, a substantive limit to Treaty amendments.

b) Internal sources

Implicit substantive limitations could also be derived from the Treaty framework itself. This is the case with regard to the simplified revision procedure. Pursuant to Article 48(6) TEU, the European Council can only decide to amend the Third Part of the TFEU. By implication, amendments of other Treaty parts are excluded.

[34] See e.g. Ulf Linderfalk, *Understanding Jus Cogens in International Law and International Legal Discourse* (Elgar 2020) 110 ff.

[35] ILC (n 33) para 71.

[36] See e.g. Erika De Wet, 'The emergence of international and regional value systems as a manifestation of the emerging international constitutional order' LJIL 19 (2006), 611, 617; Fausto de Quadros, 'La Convention Européenne des Droits de l'Homme: un cas de *ius cogens* régional?' in Beyerlin et al. (n 8) 555.

[37] In favour, see e.g. Robert Kolb, *Peremptory International Law—Jus Cogens* (Hart 2015) 97 ff; Stefan Kadelbach, *Zwingendes Völkerrecht* (Duncker&Humblot 1992) 203 f. But see ILC, Fourth Report on jus cogens, UN Doc. A/CN.4/727 (31 January 2019) paras 21–47.

[38] See e.g. Bieber (n 8) 348; Heintzen (n 26) 43, 45.

[39] For France, see e.g. George Vedel, 'Schengen et Maastricht' RFDA 8 (1992), 173. On the discussion, see Édouard Dubout, 'Les règles ou principes inhérents à l'identité constitutionnelle' RFDC (83) (2010), 451.

According to Advocate General Kokott, this is not only a formal restriction concerning the text of the amended provision. It also implies that the respective amendments may not *substantively contradict* other parts of the Treaties.[40] Otherwise the European Council could circumvent the restrictions of Article 48(6) TEU by amending the Third Part of the TFEU in a way that leads to spill-over effects or an implicit modification of other parts.[41] In this sense, Kokott ascertains a 'certain hierarchy' between provisions of the Third Part and the rest of the Treaties.[42]

The construction of substantive limitations on the ordinary amendment procedure (Article 48(2) to (5) TEU) is far more complicated. The starting point for such an approach could be the distinction between an *amendment* of the Treaties and the adoption of a *new* Treaty. This is not just a textual distinction but rests on deeper theoretical foundations. Its corollary is the differentiation between an original or primary constituent power (*pouvoir constituant originaire*) and a derived, delegated, or secondary constituent power authorized to amend the constitution (*pouvoir constituant derivé, institué, constitué,* or *pouvoir de révision*).[43] Carl Schmitt, in particular, stated that 'constitution "*making*" and constitutional "*change*" ... are *qualitatively* different.'[44] The authority to amend the constitution is not the authority to abrogate the current and establish a new constitution. But where should we draw the line? According to Schmitt, the secondary constituent power can only amend the constitution 'under the presupposition that the identity and continuity of the constitution as an entirety is preserved.'[45] Two clarifications should be added. For one, the distinction does not depend on the scope of changed provisions. While revising the entire constitution can constitute an amendment (as long as the constitution's identity is maintained), the modification of a single provision can reach the critical threshold. Second, these substantive limitations do not originate from natural or supra-positive law but are inherent in the constitution.[46]

The distinction between amendments and the adoption of a new constitution finds expression in many constitutional texts. Today, several constitutions explicitly distinguish between a total revision and amendments.[47] Similarly, the German

[40] Case C-370/12 *Pringle* [2012] EU:C:2012:675, View of AG Kokott, para 29 (see also paras 27 f).

[41] See e.g. Stanislas Adam and Francisco J. Mena Parras, 'The European Stability Mechanism through the Legal Meanderings of the Union's Constitutionalism: Comment on Pringle' EL Rev 38 (2013), 848, 854.

[42] AG Kokott (n 40) para 60. See also Florence Giorgi, 'Le pouvoir constituant européen, "l'Arlésienne" du constitutionnalisme européen? Quelques réflexions à propos de l'arrêt *Pringle*' in Vincent Kronenberger et al. (eds), *Mélanges en l'honneur de Paolo Mengozzi* (Bruylant 2013) 275.

[43] For an overview of these distinctions, see Roznai (n 4) 113 ff, 120 ff; Beaud (n 31) 310 f, 314 ff; Arnaud Le Pillouer, 'Le pouvoir de révision' in Michel Troper and Dominique Chagnollaud (eds), *Traité international de droit constitutionnel,* vol 3 (Dalloz 2012) 34, 56 f.

[44] Schmitt (n 1) 80 [pp 25–7], p 145 [pp 98 f]. See also Beaud (n 31) 310. Critically, Georges Vedel, 'Souveraineté et supraconstitutionnalité' *Pouvoirs* 67 (1993), 79, 90; Martin Loughlin, 'The Concept of Constituent Power' *European Journal of Political Theory* 13 (2014), 218, 232.

[45] Schmitt (n 1) 150 [p 103]. See further Beaud (n 31) 351; Roznai (n 4) 144 ff. On such a 'change of identity', see also BVerfG, Judgment of 30 June 2009, 2 BvE 2/08, *Lisbon*, para 179.

[46] See Beaud (n 31) 348 f.

[47] See e.g. Art. 44 Austrian BV-G and Art. 168 Spanish Constitution. See also Roznai (n 4) 154 ff.

Basic Law distinguishes between an amendment under Article 79 and the adoption of a new constitution under Article 146 Basic Law. Eventually, such a distinction can also be traced in the Treaties. Article 48 TEU speaks only of an 'amendment' of the Treaties but not of a total revision, not to mention their termination and the adoption of a new Treaty. This textual differentiation is also reflected by the other language versions, which only refer to *Änderung* and *Änderungsverfahren*, *modifications* and *révision*, *modifiche* and *revisione*.[48] Suppose there is a distinction at the EU level between the mandate to amend and the authority to abrogate the current and adopt new Treaties,[49] where should we draw the line? Where does a change of the EU's constitutional identity begin?

Abstractly, such a change will affect the foundational principles on which the EU is based.[50] Before the adoption of Article 2 TEU (and Article 6(1) TEU-Amsterdam), it was far from clear what should be identified as foundational. Most scholarly accounts seemed to flow from the respective author's intuition rather than an underlying theory. Some even went so far as to establish comprehensive lists of unamendable principles stretching from primacy, direct effect, democracy, and fundamental rights to essential elements of the Community's economic constitution.[51] Even though these principles were only supposed to be protected 'in their essence of values and not the actual ways in which they are expressed',[52] it seems clear that such accounts are far too expansive.

If we accept that there are substantive limitations to an amendment of the Treaties, Article 2 TEU seems like a plausible starting point for their identification. In this spirit, many have argued that Article 2 TEU constitutes the Union's constitutional identity,[53] its untouchable core,[54] or even an eternity clause of the EU.[55] This conception was openly embraced by the Court of Justice in its decisions

[48] With regard to Art. 236 EEC and Art. N TEU-Maastricht, see da Cruz Vilaça and Piçarra (n 8) 33; Bieber (n 8) 347.

[49] On the feasibility of such a transfer, see Section III.B.

[50] With regard to national constitutions, see Roznai (n 4) 141 ff; Schmitt (n 1) 77 f [pp 28 f].

[51] See e.g. Curti Gialdino (n 25) 1112 ff; da Cruz Vilaça and Piçarra (n 8) 33–5; Werner Schroeder, *Gemeinschaftsrechtssystem* (Mohr Siebeck 2002) 380 ff.

[52] Curti Gialdino (n 25) 1114.

[53] See e.g. Gerhard van der Schyff, 'Constitutional Identity of the EU Legal Order' *Ancilla Iuris* (2021), 1, 11; Lucia S. Rossi, 'Fundamental Values, Principles, and Rights After the Treaty of Lisbon: The Long Journey Toward a European Constitutional Identity' in Frédérique Berrod et al. (eds), *Europe(s), Droit(s) européen(s)* (Bruylant 2015) 511, 512; Fausto de Quadros, 'L'identité constitutionnelle de l'Union européenne et les valeurs communs' in Laurence Potvin-Solis (ed.), *Les valeurs communes dans l'Union européenne* (Bruylant 2014) 165. See also with regard to the judgment in *Kadi*, Benlolo-Carabot (n 29) 385 f; Giuseppe Martinico, 'Building Supranational Identity' *Italian Journal of Public Law* 8 (2016), 235, 249 ff.

[54] Marcus Klamert and Dimitry Kochenov, 'Article 2 TEU' in Kellerbauer et al. (n 13) para 1; Andreas Voßkuhle, *The Idea of the European Community of Values* (Bittner 2017) 116.

[55] Lenaerts and Van Nuffel (n 13) para 3.010; Passchier and Stremler (n 9) 356 ff; Frank Schorkopf, 'Der Wertekonstitutionalismus der Europäischen Union' JZ 75 (2020), 477, 482. With regard to Art. 6(1) TEU-Amsterdam/Nice, Bieber (n 8) 348; Miguel Azpitarte Sánchez, 'Artikel 6 EU-Vertrag: Kodifizierung durch die Zeit, seine Bedeutung und Rechtsfolgen' JöR 51 (2003), 553, 567; Stelio Mangiameli, 'La clausola di omogeneità nel trattato dell'Unione europea e nella costituzione europea' in Mangiameli (ed.), *L'ordinamento europeo*, vol 1 (Giuffrè 2006) 1, 14.

on the rule of law conditionality regulation. In their crucial passages, the Court circumscribes—for the first time—the constitutional identity of the EU legal order by linking it to Article 2 TEU: 'The values contained in Article 2 TEU ... define the very identity of the European Union as a common legal order.'[56] At the same time, the Court seems to leave this identity open for further elements by stating that the values are 'an integral part' of it.[57] As such, there might be other 'parts' beyond Article 2 TEU.

For some, conceiving the values in Article 2 TEU as the Union's constitutional identity may appear at odds with the prevalence of economic considerations in the founding days of the European integration project. Many argue that the identity of the European project, as envisaged by the founding Member States, was a purely economic union with the purpose to secure peace and enhance prosperity.[58] The values of Article 2 TEU, by contrast, were incorporated into the Treaties much later with the Treaty of Amsterdam, which was an amendment to the existing Treaties following the respective procedure. Then again, the fact that the values enshrined in Article 2 TEU became relevant and were made explicit with increasing political integration does not exclude that they were implicitly at the heart of European integration since its very beginnings.[59] Any other view seems to seriously disregard the context from which the European project emerged. Even if the EU may have been originally construed as an economic endeavour, it was never destined to remain that.[60] Further, the Member States' commitment to a set of common values can be derived from the circumstances of the founding period. Some Member State constitutions would have barred participation in an organization, which, irrespective of its object, does not adhere to the values of the rule of law, democracy, and fundamental rights.[61] Moreover, all founding Member States were parties to the Council of Europe and therefore officially committed to these values. This implicit commitment was also reflected by the process of enlargement. It was only after Greece, Spain, and Portugal found their way to democracy that they were welcomed in the Communities (see Chapter 3, III.B) Eventually, the common core was made explicit in the Declaration on European Identity of 1973, in which the Member States

[56] Case C-156/21 *Hungary v Parliament and Council* [2022] EU:C:2022:97, paras 127; Case C-157/21 *Poland v Parliament and Council* [2022] EU:C:2022:98, paras 145.

[57] *Hungary v Parliament and Council* (n 56) para 232; *Poland v Parliament and Council* (n 56) para 264.

[58] See e.g. Daniel C. Thomas 'Constitutionalization through enlargement: the contested origins of the EU's democratic identity' JEPP 13 (2006), 1190.

[59] See only Pierre Pescatore, *Le droit de l'intégration* (Sijthoff 1972) 50 f: 'à l'origine ... de la supranationalité, est l'acceptation, par un groupe d'Etats, de valeurs qui leur sont communes'.

[60] On the 'messianic' character of the founding Treaties, see Joseph H.H. Weiler, 'Deciphering the Political and Legal DNA of European Integration' in Julie Dickson and Pavlos Eleftheriadis (eds), *Philosophical Foundations of European Union Law* (OUP 2012) 137.

[61] On the debate concerning a 'structural congruence' of the Treaties and the German Basic Law, see Bill Davies, *Resisting the European Court of Justice. West Germany's Confrontation with European Law, 1949–1979* (CUP 2012) 53 ff.

emphasized their determination 'to defend the principles of representative democracy, of the rule of law, of social justice—which is the ultimate goal of economic progress—and of respect for human rights. All of these are fundamental elements of the European Identity.'[62]

2. Justiciability

Accepting substantive limitations on Treaty amendments, however, does not necessarily imply that the CJEU has the responsibility to police them. This raises the question whether the Court has jurisdiction to assess Treaty amendments in the first place and, subsequently, what kind of limitation it can review.

a) Jurisdiction

In the past, the Court has often refused to assess the validity or legality of primary law.[63] Yet, this does not mean that *decisions to amend* primary law are withdrawn from the Court's jurisdiction.[64] Some argue that a distinction has to be made between simplified (Article 48(6) TEU) and ordinary revision procedure (Article 48(2) to (5) TEU).[65] Under the former, amendments are adopted by the European Council. As such, they constitute an act of an EU institution and are generally subject to review both under Article 263(1) TFEU as well as under the preliminary ruling procedure (Article 267(1)(b) TFEU).[66] A recent example for the latter is the decision in *Pringle*, where the CJEU assessed the validity of Council Decision 2011/199 amending Article 136 TFEU.[67]

Establishing the Court's jurisdiction for amendments adopted under the ordinary revision procedure proves to be more problematic, especially with regard to actions for annulment. In principle, amendments adopted in the form of treaties between Member States are not acts of the institutions and thus not reviewable by the Court under Article 263 TFEU.[68] In the context of Treaty revision, the final decision is taken by 'common accord' in a 'conference of representatives of the governments of the Member States' (Article 48(4) TEU). Though highly controversial, the Court has repeatedly stated that such acts cannot be challenged before the Court

[62] Declaration on European Identity at the Copenhagen European Summit (14 December 1973), Bull EC. 12-1973, pp 118 ff.

[63] See Case C-264/94 P *Jacques Bonnamy v Council* [Order of 13 January 1995] EU:C:1995:5, para 11; Case C-253/94 P *Roujansky v Council* [Order of 13 January 1995] EU:C:1995:4, para 11. See also Case T-113/96 *Dubois v Council and Commission* [1998] EU:T:1998:11, para 41.

[64] For this distinction, see *Pringle* (n 18) paras 33.

[65] Steve Peers, 'The Future of EU Treaty Amendments' YEL 31 (2012), 17, 80.

[66] See e.g. Klamert (n 13) para 25; Claude Blumann and Louis Dubois, *Droit institutionnel de l'Union européenne* (6th edn, Lexis Nexis 2016) para 616 (pp 482 f).

[67] *Pringle* (n 18) paras 31 ff.

[68] See e.g. Peers (n 65) 81; Jacqué (n 15) para 908. This applies, for instance, to acts of accession, which are concluded between the Member States and the applicant State (Art. 49(2) TEU), see Cases 31 and 35/86 *LAISA* [1988] EU:C:1988:211, paras 17 f; Case C-313/89 *Commission v Spain* [1991] EU:C:1991:415, para 10; Case C-445/00 *Austria v Council* [2003] EU:C:2003:445, para 62. Critically, see Cases 31 and 35/86 *LAISA* [1987] EU:C:1987:516, Opinion of AG Lenz, para 19.

through Article 263 TFEU (see Chapter 5, III.B.1). However, it is the European Council, an EU institution, that decides to summon a Convention elaborating on a proposal submitted by the Commission, the European Parliament, or a Member State (Article 48(3) TEU). Since Lisbon, acts of the European Council fall within the scope of Article 263 TFEU if they are 'intended to produce legal effects vis-à-vis third parties'. In this light, the respective decision of the European Council could be perceived as a mere preparatory act excluded from review.[69] Yet, the case law has never been absolute in this regard.[70] For instance, the Court ruled that Council decisions authorizing the opening of negotiations for international agreements between the EU and third countries produce legal effects between the EU and the Member States.[71] In fact, the situation here is quite similar: the European Council summons a Convention for the elaboration of a revision proposal.

Besides actions for annulment, it seems possible to initiate infringement procedures under Article 258 TFEU directed against all Member States together adopting an amendment under Article 48(4) TEU.[72] An indirect review of the amendment within the context of preliminary references seems far more realistic. The Court could not only review the validity of the decision of the European Council but also interpret the new provision in conformity with Article 2 TEU after the adoption of the respective amendment (see Chapter 5).

b) *Yardstick*

Accepting that the CJEU has jurisdiction to review Treaty amendments does not necessarily imply that the Court can control substantive limitations. Three positions are possible in this respect. First, the Court might only be able to assess amendments on procedural grounds. This would mean that judicial review would primarily serve the purpose of preventing the Member States from bypassing the cumbersome Convention procedure.[73] Second, the Court could be empowered to review Treaty amendments with regard to their substance only if they have been adopted under the simplified revision procedure.[74] The Court's decision in *Pringle* especially seems to indicate such a substantive review. As noted above, Advocate

[69] See e.g. Andreas von Arnauld, 'Normenhierarchien innerhalb des primären Gemeinschaftsrechts' EuR 38 (2003), 191, 215. But see Jacqué (n 15) para 908.

[70] For a comprehensive account, see e.g. Case C-62/14 *Gauweiler* [2015] EU:C:2015:7, Opinion of AG Cruz Villalón, paras 71 ff; Koen Lenaerts, Ignace Maselis, and Kathleen Gutman, *EU Procedural Law* (OUP 2014) para 7.28.

[71] See e.g. Case C-425/13 *Commission* v *Council* [2015] EU:C:2015:483, para 28; Case C-114/12 *Commission* v *Council* [2014] EU:C:2014:2151, para 40; Case 22/70 *Commission v Council (EATR)* [1971] EU:C:1971:32, paras 34 ff.

[72] See e.g. Lenaerts and Van Nuffel (n 13) para 3.011; Bieber (n 8) 348 f; Matthias Niedobitek, 'Vertragliche Grundlagen, rechtliche Gestalt, Institutionen der Union' in Niedobitek (ed.), *Europarecht* (2nd edn, De Gruyter 2020) § 1, para 103.

[73] With regard to the simplified revision procedure, see Bruno de Witte and Thomas Beukers, 'The Court of Justice Approves the Creation of the European Stability Mechanism Outside the EU Legal Order' CML Rev 50 (2013), 805, 827. See also Ohler (n 13) para 27; Meng (n 15) paras 36 f.

[74] Klamert (n 13) paras 25–7.

General Kokott interpreted Article 48(6) TEU as preventing the Member States from amending the text of Part Three of the TFEU in a way that is 'incompatible' with other primary law.[75] The CJEU seemed to follow this suggestion.[76] Finally, one could go even further and submit that the Court could review Treaty amendments adopted under the ordinary revision procedure against the values of Article 2 TEU.

What speaks in favour of such an approach? Positively, the Court has the task to 'ensure that in the interpretation and application of the Treaties the law is observed' (Article 19(1) TEU). The procedure provided for in Article 48 TEU constitutes an 'application of the Treaties'. As demonstrated earlier, Article 2 TEU not only contains ethical convictions and moral aspirations. The Union values are 'law' in the sense of Article 19(1) TEU. Negatively, there is no provision like Article 269 TFEU that might be read as excluding a substantive review of the Court. In case of Treaty amendments, there are no similar provisions. A contrario, these matters come under the CJEU's general jurisdiction. Comparatively, the European legal space offers many precedents for substantive reviews of constitutional amendments.[77] The German Bundesverfassungsgericht, for instance, has reviewed constitutional amendments in several instances.[78] Similarly, the Czech Constitutional Court has derived limitations from an explicit eternity clause[79] and confirmed its competence to review constitutional amendments.[80] Such review powers are not confined to explicit eternity clauses but extend to implicit limits as well. As mentioned above, the Italian Corte Costituzionale has claimed the authority to review constitutional amendments against the yardstick of supreme constitutional principles. Admittedly, there are many counterexamples. Most prominently, the French Conseil Constitutionnel has explicitly rejected review of constitutional amendments despite having an explicit eternity clause in place (Article 89(5) of the French Constitution).[81] Further, most courts exercise this power in a very self-restrained

[75] AG Kokott (n 40) para 29.

[76] *Pringle* (n 18) para 36. See also Adam and Parras (n 41) 854; Augusto A. Calahorro, 'La decisión Pringle en el proceso de constitucionalización de la Unión Europea' *Revista Española de Derecho Constitucional* (101) (2014), 337, 346–9.

[77] For an empirical assessment, see Michael Hein, 'Do Constitutional Entrenchment Clauses Matter? Constitutional Review of Constitutional Amendments in Europe' I-CON 18 (2020), 78. Looking also beyond Europe, see e.g. Gábor Halmai, 'Unconstitutional Constitutional Amendments: Constitutional Courts as Guardians of the Constitution?' *Constellations* 19 (2012), 182; Sabrina Ragone, 'El control material de las reformas constitucionales en perspectiva comparada' *Teoría y Realidad Constitucional* 31 (2013), 391.

[78] See e.g. BVerfG, Judgment of 3 March 2004, 1 BvR 2378/98, *Großer Lauschangriff*, para 54; Judgment of 14 May 1996, 2 BvR 1938, *Sichere Drittstaaten*, paras 208 ff; Judgment of 1970, 2 BvF 1/69, *Abhörurteil*, para 85.

[79] Ústavní soud, Judgment of 26 November 2008, Pl. ÚS 19/08, *Lisbon I*, para 196.

[80] Ústavní soud, Judgment of 10 September 2009, Pl ÚS 27/09, *Melčák*. See further Yaniv Roznai, 'Legisprudence Limitations on Constitutional Amendments?' *ICL Journal* 8 (2014), 29.

[81] See e.g. Conseil Constitutionnel, Décision no° 2003-469 DC, paras 2 f. See further Louis Favoreu, 'L'injusticiabilité des lois constitutionnelles' RFDA 19 (2003), 792; Susan Wright, 'The Self-restraint of the French Conseil Constitutionnel in 2003 and 2004' EPL 11 (2005), 495. Critically, Olivier Beaud, 'Le cas français: l'obstination de la jurisprudence et de la doctrine à refuser toute idée de limitation au pouvoir de révision constitutionnelle' *Jus Politicum* 18 (2017), 93; Guy Carcassone, 'Un plaidoyer résolu en faveur d'un tel contrôle sagement circonscrit' *Cahiers du Conseil Constitutionnel* 27 (2010).

manner (see also below). In this sense, neither the German nor the Italian constitutional courts have ever declared a constitutional amendment to be unconstitutional.[82] Though this restraint is certainly justified, this does not mean that such review powers should, in principle, not exist.

B. Potential Objections

Most certainly, the suggested construction will raise objections. First, one may question whether it is possible to transfer the distinction between primary and secondary constituent power (the crucial justification for substantive limitations of constitutional amendments) to the EU level. Second, the approach proposed above might be perceived as yet another empowerment of an overly activist EU judiciary at the expense of political processes, in this case the Member States.

1. Primary and secondary constituent power in the EU

From the outset, it is highly controversial whether the concept of constituent power can be transferred to the EU level.[83] To start with, this relates to the question of whether the EU does, can, and should have a constitution. As noted in previous chapters, this book operates on the assumption that the EU already has a substantive constitution (see Chapter 3, II.A). Nevertheless, 'constitution-making' at the EU level took place primarily through intergovernmental decisions of the Member States.[84] While the General Court has sometimes referred to the Member States as the 'founding authority of the Union',[85] it is questionable whether the Member States can be perceived as the EU's primary constituent power. One cannot underestimate the part played by the Court of Justice in the constitutionalization of the Treaties.[86] Likewise, the evolutionary character of this process will make it particularly difficult to pinpoint a specific foundational moment.

[82] See National Report—Germany, XVIIth Congress of the Conference of European Constitutional Courts (2017), www.confeuconstco.org/reports/rep-xvii/allemand_EN.pdf, pp 41–2; National Report—Italy, XVIIth Congress of the Conference of European Constitutional Courts (2017), www.confeuconstco.org/reports/rep-xvii/italy_EN.pdf, p 33.

[83] See e.g. Neil Walker, 'Post-Constituent Constitutionalism? The Case of the European Union' in Walker and Martin Loughlin (eds), *The Paradox of Constitutionalism* (OUP 2008) 247.

[84] Jürgen Neyer, *The Justification of Europe* (OUP 2012) 152 ff.

[85] The other language versions are more explicit ('pouvoir constituant', 'verfassungsgebende Gewalt' and 'Verfassungsgeber', 'potere costitutivo'), see Case T-289/16 *Inox Mare v Commission* [Order of 21 June 2017] EU:T:2017:414, para 41; Case T-28/03 *Holcim (Deutschland) v Commission* [2005] EU:T:2005:139, para 34; Case T-172/98 *Salamander v Parliament and Council* [2000] EU:T:2000:168, para 75.

[86] Arguing for a 'judicial constituent power', see e.g. Chris Thornhill, 'The European Constitution and the *pouvoir constituant*' in Jiří Přibáň (ed.), *Self-Constitution of European Society* (Routledge 2016) 13, 16. See also Gaëlle Marti, *Le pouvoir constituant européen* (Bruylant 2011) 269 ff, 335 ff; Peters (n 32) 401 ff.

Eventually, perceiving the Member States as the primary constituent power seems almost impossible if one subscribes to more demanding theories that link the concept of constituent power to peoples' sovereignty and democracy.[87] Many argue for such a democratically demanding, 'radically input oriented' concept of primary constituent power.[88] This requires certain minimum standards for democratic participation of the people. Under these conditions, it will be difficult to argue for a constituent power at the EU level (see also Chapter 3, III.B). This is not only the case if one accepts the so-called no demos-thesis, meaning the lack of European people.[89] In light of the missing popular participation, the founding Treaties (e.g. the Treaty of Rome or, even before that, the ECSC) can hardly constitute an act of primary constituent power in the democratic sense.[90]

Yet, such a democratically demanding conception is not imperative. Throughout history, constituent power has emerged in various shapes and manifestations. In the words of Carl Schmitt, it is the 'formlos Formende'.[91] In fact, accounts referring to the primary constituent power as an identifiable, let alone homogeneous, people adopting a constitution in a participatory and inclusive manner, are often historically inaccurate fiction, imagination, or ascription.[92] As Daniel Innerarity notes, 'the "us" gathered in the foundational act masks an original heterogeneity.'[93] Moreover, it has been submitted that the exercise of primary constituent power is only recognizable *retroactively*, when a constitution has come into existence.[94] Accordingly, there is a fine line between the acceptance of an entity as primary constituent power and a failed revolution or coup d'état—it is largely based on its

[87] See e.g. Ernst-Wolfgang Böckenförde, 'The Constituent Power of the People: A Liminal Concept of Constitutional Law (1986)' in Mirjam Künkler and Tine Stein (eds), *Constitutional and Political Theory* (OUP 2017) 169, 172.

[88] See e.g. Christoph Möllers, 'Pouvoir constituant—constitution—constitutionalization' in Jürgen Bast and Armin von Bogdandy (eds), *Principles of European Constitutional Law* (2nd edn, Hart 2009) 169, 185 ff. See further Markus Patberg, 'Constituent Power' *Constellations* 24 (2017), 51; Andrew Arato, 'Forms of Constitution Making and Theories of Democracy' *Cardozo Law Review* 17 (1995), 191.

[89] See especially Dieter Grimm, 'Does Europe Need a Constitution?' ELJ 1 (1995), 282, 290 ff. Critically, see e.g. Daniel Innerarity, *Democracy in Europe* (Palgrave Macmillan 2019) 97 ff; Cormac S. Mac Amhlaigh, *New Constitutional Horizons: Towards a Pluralist Constitutional Theory* (OUP 2022) 156 ff.

[90] See e.g. Ulrich K. Preuß, 'Is there a constituent power in the European Union?' in Oliver Cayla and Pasquale Pasquino (eds), *Le pouvoir constituant et l'Europe* (Dalloz 2011) 75, 84.

[91] Schmitt (n 1) 129 [p 81] ('formless formative capacity'). Against any normative concept of original constituent power, see e.g. David Dyzenhaus, 'The Politics of the Question of Constituent Power' in Loughlin and Walker (n 83) 129.

[92] On the variety of sometimes dubious historical practices, see Jon Elster, 'Deliberation and Constitution Making' in Elster (ed.), *Deliberative Democracy* (CUP 1998) 97, 105 ff. See also Richard Albert, Xenophon Contiades and Alkmene Fotiadou, 'Imposition in Making and Changing Constitutions' in Albert, Contiades, and Fotiadou (eds), *The Law and Legitimacy of Imposed Constitutions* (Routledge 2019) 1.

[93] Innerarity (n 89) 105.

[94] See e.g. Hans Lindahl, 'Constituent Power and Reflexive Identity' in Loughlin and Walker (n 83) 9. See also Beaud (n 31) 321 ff; Möllers (n 88) 185; Preuß (n 90) 82 f.

success and thus a contingent criterion.[95] This demonstrates the flexibility characterizing the notion of primary constituent power.

But even if we accept a transfer of the concept of *pouvoir constituant* to the EU level, it might be argued that both—primary and secondary constituent power—are *one*: the Member States.[96] The Member States adopted the Treaties in the first place and therefore exercised their authority as the primary constituent power. At the same time, the Member States decide on the amendment of the Treaties. Two rejoinders might be advanced in this regard. Institutionally as well as procedurally, there are important differences between the Member States coming together diplomatically to adopt a new Treaty and the Member States following the procedures of Article 48 TEU. As already indicated above, the procedures envisaged in the Treaties include several EU institutions. Pursuant to the ordinary revision procedure, the European Parliament and the Commission may submit proposals to the European Council for the amendment of the Treaties. Both (and on some occasions even the ECB) must be consulted. Also, it is the European Council that decides to summon a Convention to elaborate a proposal. Even though it is eventually a conference of representatives of the Member States' governments that adopts the amendment, Article 48 TEU constitutes a juridification of the procedure. This mirrors a crucial difference between the primary and secondary constituent power: 'Le premier relèverait de la *politique*, le second du *droit*'.[97]

In addition, there are reasons to hold that the Member States are not the Union's primary constituent power *anymore*. According to Carl Schmitt, the primary constituent power is not consumed by the act of adopting a new constitution but continues—albeit latently—to exist.[98] Under this postulate of permanence, however, it seems plausible to perceive the primary (post-founding) constituent power not as a static entity but as subject to change. Put differently, the primary constituent power might be understood as a dynamic, evolving concept.[99] This is already the case for a 'people', which is not a stable point of reference but constantly evolving both in empirical (with each generation) and conceptual terms (with changing social identities).[100] In the EU context, Ulrich Everling observed that 'it is questionable what is to be regarded as the *pouvoir constituant* of the community

[95] This renders the concept prone to abuses, see only Hannah Arendt, *On Revolution* (Penguin 1965) 163.

[96] See e.g. Heintzen (n 26) 42; Nettesheim (n 30) 741; Markus Sichert, *Grenzen der Revision des Primärrechts in der Europäischen Union* (Duncker&Humblot 2005) 596 ff; Herwig C.H. Hofmann, *Normenhierarchien im europäischen Gemeinschaftsrecht* (Duncker&Humblot 2000) 88.

[97] Beaud (n 31) 314.

[98] See e.g. Schmitt (n 1) 140 [pp 91 f].

[99] Note, however, that for Carl Schmitt the change of primary constituent power entails concomitantly a change of constitution, see Schmitt (n 1) 142 [p 94].

[100] See also Walker (n 83) 249.

today. The founding act can no longer be decisive, but the overall character of the Community thus created and developed further until *today* is important.'[101]

In this spirit, it has been suggested that the constituent power in the EU should no longer be equated with the Member States. Instead, there are many proposals on the table, like a transnational European demos, the peoples of the Member States as *pouvoirs constituants* (in plural), or a *pouvoir constituant mixte* comprising both the peoples of the Member States and EU citizens.[102] Such accounts do not refer to the realities of a founding moment but are in essence reconstructive or a retrospective attribution of constituent power.[103] They are not genetic or historical claims but *normative* concepts underpinning the authority of the EU's constitution.[104]

2. The dead hand of the past

The second objection boils down to the reproach that demanding amendment requirements are one way by which the 'dead hand' of the past imposes itself on the present. Preventing future generations from amending certain parts of the constitution may obstruct social development and turn a democracy into a 'necrocracy'.[105] For our purposes this has a twofold implication. On the one hand, EU law is by definition subject to a dynamic process (see especially Article 1(2) TEU). Hence, it seems particularly difficult to reconcile the diametrically opposed concepts of unamendability and the evolutionary character of European integration. On the other hand, it restricts the space for political processes and usually strengthens the constitutional judiciary. As the 'dead hand' of the past is usually led by constitutional judges who interpret and enforce substantive limitations to constitutional amendments, they can effectively shield their interpretations against political contestation. This seems to squarely contradict the claims made in the previous chapter. To recall briefly, it was suggested that the constraints of primary law on the EU legislature could be relaxed thus broadening the space for meaningful political processes. Placing substantive limitations on Treaty amendments, however, seems to achieve the exact opposite. Not only do they constrain the space for political processes; they also strengthen the Court's position with regard to the other branches of power.

While these are certainly legitimate concerns, they can be mitigated to some extent. As regards the dynamic character of EU law, this does not exclude the process

[101] See already Ulrich Everling, 'Sind die Mitgliedstaaten der Europäischen Gemeinschaft noch Herren der Verträge?' Rudolf Bernhardt (ed.), *Festschrift für Hermann Mosler* (Springer 1983) 173, 189 (translation by the author, emphasis added).

[102] For the different conceptions, see Markus Patberg, *Constituent Power in the European Union* (OUP 2020) 63 ff.

[103] See e.g. Markus Patberg, 'A Systematic Justification for the EU's *Pouvoir Constituant Mixte*: Principles of Constitutional Politics in Supranational Polities' ELJ 23 (2017), 441, 442.

[104] For this clarification, see George Duke, 'European Constitutionalism and Constituent Power' EL Rev 44 (2019), 49, 54, 58 f.

[105] Roznai (n 4) 188 ff. See also Yaniv Roznai, 'Necrocracy or Democracy? Assessing Objections to Constitutional Unamendability' in Albert and Oder (n 4) 29, 32 ff.

of European integration being based on a firm set of values. Similarly, allowing broader space for political processes at the EU level—in particular with regard to issues pertaining to the third level of Treaty provisions—does not mean that there is no legitimate interest in shielding some central constitutional principles against encroachments. This holds true as long as these principles are reduced to an absolute minimum and handled with outmost restraint. In this spirit, most constitutional courts operate with caution. The Bundesverfassungsgericht, for instance, interprets the German eternity clause as an exceptional provision that must be interpreted strictly.[106] It prohibits only a 'prinzipielle Preisgabe'[107] and may not prevent the legislator from modifying even fundamental constitutional principles.[108] Similarly, appeals to constitutional identities—irrespective of whether they pose limits to EU intervention or the secondary constituent power—aim at protecting essential core guarantees[109] and are triggered only in exceptional situations.[110] Accordingly, the Court will be required to adopt a highly restrained reading of Article 2 TEU as far as Treaty amendments are concerned.

Finally, it should be noted that the idea of unamendability does not oppose the adoption of a new Treaty. Since the substantive limits apply only to amendments, the primary constituent power is free to constitute a new constitutional order.[111] Admittedly, opening up the entire constitution for re-negotiation is not only costly but might also trigger strategic bargaining. Thus, unamendable provisions might serve the exact opposite of their key purpose: guaranteeing stability.[112] Nevertheless, the adoption of a new constitution or Treaty has an 'expressive function'.[113] The clear break with the former legal order does not only enhance transparency; it also constitutes a clear and unequivocal warning sign.

[106] See e.g. BVerfG, *Großer Lauschangriff* (n 78) para 11.

[107] See e.g. BVerfG, *Abhörurteil* (n 78) para 99.

[108] ibid para 100. See also BVerfG, *Sichere Drittstaaten* (n 78) para 209; Judgment of 23 April 1991, 1 BvR 11/70, *Bodenreform I*, para 131; Judgment of 7 October 2014, 2 BvR 1641/11, *Art. 91e GG*, para 84.

[109] See e.g. BVerfG, Order of 14 January 2014, 2 BvR 2728/13, *OMT*, para 27 ('inviolable core'); Judgment of 30 July 2019, 2 BvR 1685/14, *European Banking Union*, para 124 ('core principles'); Ústavní soud, *Lisbon I* (n 79) paras 93 f, 110; Judgment of 3 November 2009, Pl. ÚS 29/09, *Lisbon II*, para 112 ('material core'). But see the detailed and much criticized catalogue of identity-relevant issues in BVerfG, *Lisbon* (n 45) paras 252 ff.

[110] See e.g. BVerfG, Order of 15 December 2015, 2 BvR 2735/14, *Identitätskontrolle I*, para 45 ('in exceptional cases and under narrowly defined conditions'); Ústavní soud, *Lisbon I* (n 79) paras 84, 120, 139.

[111] Roznai (n 4) 190.

[112] See e.g. Stephan Michel and Ignacio N. Cofone, 'Credible commitment or paternalism? The case of unamendability' in Albert and Oder (n 4) 123, 138.

[113] Borrowing the term from Richard Albert, 'The Expressive Function of Constitutional Amendment Rules' *McGill Law Journal* 59 (2013), 225.

III

'THESE VALUES ARE COMMON TO THE MEMBER STATES . . .'

Potential in the Verbund Dimension

8
Article 2 TEU as Constitutional Frame of the Verbund

I. Introduction

Having explored the potential of Article 2 TEU in the EU legal order, the following part will shift to its Verbund dimension. As argued previously, Article 2 TEU reaches across the entire Verbund of the EU and its Member States. In this second dimension, the provision corresponds to a thinner form of constitutionalism: it does not fulfil a *constitutive* but rather a *restraining* function (see Chapter 3, III.B). Against this backdrop, Article 2 TEU can be read as an outer frame guaranteeing only a minimum of constitutional homogeneity throughout the Verbund. This chapter will start by briefly outlining why a certain degree of constitutional homogeneity is a key prerequisite for the functioning of federal systems. This applies especially to looser forms of federalism, such as the EU (Section II). Within the Verbund, this homogeneity is assured through a complex web of vertical and horizontal homogeneity claims that converge in Article 2 TEU (Section III). The next chapters will concentrate on the role of the CJEU and national courts in guaranteeing the Verbund's constitutional homogeneity. A particular focus will be placed on judicial responses to recent Member State contestations of democracy, the rule of law, and fundamental rights. Before diving into these issues, this chapter is subject to an important caveat. As will be demonstrated below, the Verbund's constitutional homogeneity can be guaranteed both externally and internally. The former aspect concerns, in particular, compliance with Article 2 TEU as accession criterion under Article 49(1) TEU. The following chapter, however, will concentrate on the *internal* dimensions of constitutional homogeneity and only briefly touch upon its external implications.

II. What Holds a Federal System Together?

Despite its ambiguity, homogeneity has become a key concept of federal thinking. The homogeneity of the federal entities' constitutional structures seems to be a particularly important prerequisite to hold a federal system together. Indeed, the concept seems well suited to balance the tension between autonomy and unity that is at the heart of any federal system (Section A). On that basis, it is suggested that Article 2

EU Values Before the Court of Justice. Luke Dimitrios Spieker, Oxford University Press. © Luke Dimitrios Spieker 2023.
DOI: 10.1093/oso/9780198876717.003.0009

TEU lays down a requirement of constitutional homogeneity for the Verbund. Yet, the constitutional homogeneity imposed and guaranteed by Article 2 TEU cannot go as far as equivalent requirements in federal states. Instead, it needs to be adapted to the particularities of the Verbund as a looser federal system (Section B).

A. Constitutional Homogeneity in Federal Systems

Since the very beginning of federal thinking, a certain degree of congruence, convergence, compatibility, or homogeneity among federal entities has been perceived as a key element for the successful formation, functioning, and sustainability of federal systems.[1] Montesquieu was one of the first to notice that 'la constitution fédérative doit être composée d'états de même nature'.[2] This similar nature can relate to two different aspects. On one hand, it can refer to economic, cultural, religious, linguistic, national, or ethnic homogeneity. On the other hand, it can mean the congruence of fundamental constitutional structures. The former aspect is highly controversial—especially as a general precondition for democracy[3]—and empirically questionable.[4] In contrast, it seems undisputed that a federal system can only function when there is a certain congruence of constitutional values, structures, and institutions—in short: a constitutional homogeneity.

This latter requirement can be traced like a red thread throughout the development of federal thinking. From Montesquieu it made its way into the writings of James Madison, thus influencing the formation of the United States (Federalist No. 43, para 6). Much later, the idea was at the core of both Carl Schmitt's and Kenneth C. Wheare's seminal conceptions of federal systems.[5] Although difficult to substantiate in empirical terms, it has become generally accepted that the functioning of federations depends on a certain degree of constitutional homogeneity.[6] In this sense, it constitutes an inbuilt feature of many federal constitutions.[7] Its most

[1] In detail, see Giacomo Delledonne, *L'omogeneità costituzionale negli ordinamenti composti* (Editoriale scientifica 2017); Holger Hestermeyer, *Eigenständigkeit und Homogenität in föderalen Systemen* (Mohr Siebeck 2020).

[2] Montesquieu, *Esprit des Lois* (Garnier 1777) 265 (Liv. IX Chap. 2).

[3] Arguing for its necessity, see e.g. Carl Schmitt, *Constitutional Theory* (1928) (Duke Univ. Press 2008) 259, 261 ff, 392 ff [pp 228, 231 ff, 375 ff]; Ernst-Wolfgang Böckenförde, *Staat, Nation, Europa* (Suhrkamp 1999) 109 ff; Chantal Mouffe, *The Democratic Paradox* (Verso 2000) 37 ff. Critically, see e.g. Jürgen Habermas, *Between Facts and Norms* (Polity 1996) 500; Felix Hanschmann, *Der Begriff der Homogenität in der Verfassungslehre und Europarechtswissenschaft* (Springer 2008) 140 ff, 296 ff; Daniel Innerarity, *Democracy in Europe* (Palgrave Macmillan 2019) 97 ff.

[4] With regard to the US-experience, see e.g. Manfred Zuleeg, 'What Holds a Nation Together? Cohesion and Democracy in the United States of America and in the European Union' AJCL 45 (1997), 505.

[5] Schmitt (n 3) 392 f [p 375 f]; Kenneth C. Wheare, *Federal Government* (4th edn, OUP 1963) 42, 46.

[6] See e.g. Olivier Beaud, *Théorie de la Fédération* (2nd edn, PUF 2009) 366 ff; Christian Starck, 'Idee und Struktur des Föderalismus im Lichte der Allgemeinen Staatslehre' in Ines Härtel (ed.), *Handbuch Föderalismus*, vol 1 (Springer 2012) § 1, paras 12–17.

[7] See e.g. Francesco Palermo and Karl Kössler, *Comparative Federalism* (Hart 2017) 130–6, 321 ff; Raffaele Bifulco, 'Federalism' in Roger Masterman and Robert Schütze (eds), *The Cambridge*

visible manifestations are so-called homogeneity clauses, like those enshrined in the constitutions of the U.S., Germany, or Switzerland.[8] Some go even further to argue that real federal diversity can only be achieved if all entities have not just a *similar* but a *democratic* structure. According to Christoph Möllers, for instance, only democratic conditions guarantee the necessary degree of freedom and tolerance that allows diverse political preferences to emerge and coexist.[9]

It should be noted that homogeneity is a relative concept. In contrast to uniformity or identity, homogeneity operates in degrees and does not require complete equation.[10] Accordingly, homogeneity characterizes a relation of objects that generally preserve their respective autonomy. At the same time, it presupposes a tertium comparationis, a point of reference in relation to which two or more objects can be perceived as homogeneous.[11] The way in which this point of reference is framed—in broader or narrower terms—is a decisive question. This flexibility turns homogeneity into a useful concept for any federal system. In very general terms, sustaining a federation requires a careful balance between two antagonistic claims: keeping centripetal forces from turning the federal entity into a unitary one, while preventing centrifugal forces from exploding the system into separate parts.[12] As a relative concept, homogeneity seems ideally suited to navigate between these claims and mediate the tension.

B. Constitutional Homogeneity in the Verbund

In this flexible sense, the concept of constitutional homogeneity can be applied to any kind of federal context, including the Verbund of EU and Member States. Since the early days of the European Communities, the integration project has been envisioned along federal lines.[13] Irrespective of the specific conception, it seems widely acknowledged that the EU and its Member States form a federal system. While the EU has often been compared and juxtaposed with federal states,[14] many

Companion to Comparative Constitutional Law (CUP 2019) 312, 329; Giuseppe de Vergottini, *Diritto Costituzionale Comparato* (10th edn, Cedam 2019) 451 ff.

[8] See e.g. Art. IV, Section 4 US Constitution, Art. 28(1) German Basic Law, Art. 51 Swiss Constitution. See also Arts. 95 ff Austrian Constitution and Art. 152 Spanish Constitution.

[9] Christoph Möllers, *The European Union as a democratic federation* (Bittner 2018) 120.

[10] On this distinction, see with regard to the German homogeneity clause, BVerfG, Judgment of 27 April 1959, 2 BvF 2/58, *Bremen Civil Servant Case*, para 61: 'The Basic Law ... does not aim at conformity or uniformity, but only at a certain homogeneity through adherence to guiding principles'.

[11] Hanschmann (n 3) 4.

[12] Daniel Halberstam, 'Federalism: Theory, Policy, Law' in Michel Rosenfeld and András Sajó (eds), *The Oxford Handbook of Comparative Constitutional Law* (OUP 2012) 577, 602.

[13] See only Michael Burgess, *Federalism and the European Union. The Building of Europe, 1950–2000* (Routledge 2000) 55 ff.

[14] Trailblazing, Mauro Cappelletti, Monica Seccombe and Joseph H.H. Weiler (eds), *Integration through Law. European and the American Federal Experience*, vol 1 -3 (De Gruyter 1986). See now

have sought to pinpoint its federal gestalt somewhere between national and international law.[15]

This chapter will not commit to one of these ambitious conceptions. Instead, it will depart from a broader, less demanding understanding of federalism that fits with the Verbund. To recall, the Verbund is neither an amalgamated legal order nor a political entity. It is an analytical tool that allows us to grasp the entirety of the EU and the Member States' persisting legal orders (see Chapter 3, II.B). A very similar distinction can be drawn between federalism as an analytical framework and federalism as a form of political organization.[16] Subscribing to the former, Pierre Pescatore noted that federalism is a 'philosophy which adapts itself to all political contexts on both municipal and the international level, wherever and whenever two basic prerequisites are fulfilled: the search for unity combined with a genuine respect for the autonomy and legitimate interests of the participant entities.'[17] This fundamental tension between unity and autonomy also characterizes the Verbund of EU and Member States.

As such, it is not surprising that the necessity of a certain form of constitutional homogeneity across the Verbund is widely acknowledged.[18] A sense for this requirement developed slowly and hand in hand with the accession process. Indeed, one can observe a close interaction and even 'constitutional synergies' between the Union's enlargement and its constitutionalization.[19] Without going into detail, the enlargement of the Communities (and later the Union) made the need for constitutional homogeneity visible. A first step was the Community's refusal to open negotiations for association with Francoist Spain in 1962. The European Parliament,

also in reverse, Ernest A. Young, 'What Can Europe Tell Us About the Future of American Federalism' *Arizona State Law Journal* 49 (2017), 1109.

[15] From the plethora of conceptualizations, see e.g. Signe Rehling Larsen, *The Constitutional Theory of the Federation and the European Union* (OUP 2021) 11 ff; Robert Schütze, *From Dual to Cooperative Federalism* (OUP 2009) 69 ff; Armin von Bogdandy, *Supranationaler Föderalismus als Wirklichkeit und Idee einer neuen Herrschaftsform* (Nomos 1999) 61 ff. For conceptions as a 'Bund' or 'Union', see e.g. Christoph Schönberger, 'Die Europäische Union als Bund' AöR 124 (2004), 81; Matej Avbelj, 'Theory of European Union' EL Rev 36 (2011), 818.

[16] On this distinction, see John E. Fossum and Markus Jachtenfuchs, 'Federal Challenges and Challenges to Federalism. Insights from the EU and Federal States' JEPP 24 (2017), 467, 471 ff. See also Tim Koopmans, 'Federalism: The Wrong Debate' CML Rev 29 (1992), 1047.

[17] See the foreword by Pierre Pescatore to Terrance Sandalow and Eric Stein (eds), *Courts and Free Markets. Perspectives from the United States and Europe*, vol 1 (Clarendon 1982) ix f.

[18] Through time, see e.g. Giacomo Delledonne, 'Homogénéité constitutionnelle et protection des droits fondamentaux et de l'État de droit dans l'ordre juridique européen' *Politique européenne* 53 (2016), 86; Roberto Miccù, 'Il principio di omogeneità nel processo di costituzionalizzazione dell'Unione' in Miccù and Vincenzo Atripaldi (eds), *L'omogeneità costituzionale nell'Unione Europea* (Cedam 2003) 49; Hans-Peter Ipsen, 'Über Verfassungs-Homogenität in der Europäischen Gemeinschaft' in Hartmut Maurer (ed.), *Festschrift für Günter Dürig* (C.H.Beck 1990) 159. For a similar claim, albeit avoiding the notion of 'homogeneity', see Vestert Borger, 'Constitutional Identity, the Rule of Law, and the Power of the Purse' CML Rev 59 (2022), 1771, 1794. Critically concerning the notion of 'homogeneity', see e.g. Armin von Bogdandy, 'Founding Principles' in von Bogdandy and Jürgen Bast (eds), *Principles of European Constitutional Law* (2nd edn, Hart 2009) 11, 40 f.

[19] Wojciech Sadurski, *Constitutionalism and the Enlargement of Europe* (OUP 2012) 205 ff.

in particular, insisted that 'l'existence d'une forme d'Etat démocratique, au sens d'une organisation politique libérale, est une condition à l'adhésion'.[20] But even after Greece, Spain, and Portugal found their way to democracy, the Commission noted that the Community 'will have lost much of its homogeneity' with their accession[21] and emphasized that adherence to democracy and fundamental rights are 'essential elements of membership'.[22] In response, the European Parliament proposed in 1979 to commit the Member States to fundamental rights and democracy and to enforce these obligations through the Court of Justice.[23] Though these attempts were pushed even further in the 1984 Spinelli draft, it was not until the fall of the Iron Curtain and the looming eastward enlargement that concerns for constitutional homogeneity across the Verbund found expression in positive law. After adopting the political Copenhagen criteria in 1993, Amsterdam established Article 6(1) TEU as the Verbund's central homogeneity clause.[24]

Since Amsterdam, the Verbund's constitutional homogeneity has been assured in two main ways: *external and preventive* as well as *internal and reactive*.[25] In both dimensions, Article 2 TEU serves as the central point of reference.[26] Externally, compliance with Article 2 TEU has become—over Article 49(1) TEU and the political Copenhagen criteria—a basic requirement for membership. As such, these

[20] Willi Birkelbach, Report on behalf of the Political Affairs Committee on the political and institutional aspects of accession or association to the Community (19 December 1961), European Parliamentary Assembly, Doc. 122, para 24 ff. See further Valentina Volpe, 'Realizing European Identity. The Role of the Enlargement Process' in Immacolata Amodeo et al. (eds), *Why Europe?* (Steiner 2017) 71, 74; Víctor Fernández Soriano, 'Las Comunidades Europeas frente al franquismo' *Cuadernos de Historia Contemporánea* 32 (2010), 153, 160 f.

[21] European Commission, The Transitional Period and the Institutional Implications of Enlargement (20 April 1978), COM (78) 190 final, Bull. EC, Suppl. 2/78, p 5.

[22] Commission Opinion of 23 May 1979 on the application for accession to the European Communities by the Hellenic Republic [1979] OJ L291/3. See also Commission Opinion of 31 May 1985 on the applications for accession to the European Communities by the Kingdom of Spain and the Portuguese Republic [1985] OJ L302/3. See further Ronald Janse, 'The Evolution of the Political Criteria for Accession to the European Community, 1957–1973' ELJ 24 (2018), 57; Kiran K. Patel, *Project Europe* (CUP 2020) 155 ff.

[23] European Parliament, Resolution on the prospects of enlargement of the Community, Part One: political and institutional aspects [1979] OJ C39/47, Rec. 2. See also Jochen A. Frowein, 'The European Community and the Requirement of a Republican Form of Government' *Michigan Law Review* 32 (1984), 1311.

[24] Seminal, see Frank Schorkopf, *Homogenität in der Europäischen Union: Ausgestaltung und Gewährleistung durch Art. 6 Abs. 1 und Art. 7 EUV* (Duncker&Humblot 2000). See further e.g. Stelio Mangiameli, 'La clausola di omogeneità nel trattato dell'Unione europea e nella costituzione europea' in Mangiameli (ed.), *L'ordinamento europeo*, vol 1 (Giuffrè 2006) 1; Olivier Beaud, 'La question de l'homogénéité dans une fédération' *Lignes* 13 (2004), 110, 128.

[25] In detail Delledonne (n 1) 237 ff. See also Édouard Dubout, *Droit constitutionnel de l'Union européenne* (Bruylant 2021) 183 ff.

[26] On Art. 2 TEU as central homogeneity clause, see e.g. Stelio Mangiameli, 'The Union's Homogeneity and its Common Values in the Treaty on European Union' in Mangiameli and Hermann-Josef Blanke (eds), *The European Union after Lisbon* (Springer 2012) 21; Marcus Klamert and Dimitry Kochenov, 'Article 2 TEU' in Manuel Kellerbauer et al. (eds), *The Treaties and the Charter of Fundamental Rights—A Commentary* (2nd edn, OUP 2023) para 4; Meinhard Hilf and Frank Schorkopf, 'Art. 2 EUV' in Eberhard Grabitz et al. (eds), *Das Recht der Europäischen Union* (75th edn, loose-leaf, C.H.Beck 2022) para 9.

provisions aim at establishing homogeneity before accession. After accession, the Treaties contain various instruments to guarantee the Verbund's internal homogeneity. This includes not only the mechanism of Article 7 TEU but also judicial procedures. In both these dimensions, the Court's role, however, is still developing and far from consolidated. For instance, it is highly controversial whether the Court may review accession conditions.[27] As noted above, the following chapters will leave these external issues aside and concentrate on how the Verbund's homogeneity can be guaranteed internally post accession by the CJEU and its national counterparts.

The constitutional homogeneity in the Verbund features several differences to equivalent requirements in other federal polities. These concern the required degree of homogeneity, the relevance of its protection and enforcement as well as the direction of homogeneity claims. To start with, the EU cannot warrant the same level of homogeneity that is needed to sustain a federal state. As established in previous chapters, this assumption rests on deeper considerations. Article 2 TEU corresponds to a thinner form of constitutionalism in its Verbund dimension (Chapter 3, III.A). Confronted with the pre-existing public authority of the Member States, Article 2 TEU can only take part in restraining, not constituting, this authority. Moreover, to protect the Member States' autonomy and diversity, it cannot go beyond a very thin frame within which their legal orders can unfold. Thus, Article 2 TEU will necessarily establish a thinner common baseline and impose less demanding requirements on the Member States.

Second, even if the degree of required homogeneity is lower in looser federal systems, the relevance of its protection seems to increase. At first sight, this may seem counterintuitive. As James Madison observed during the formation of the United States: 'The more intimate the nature of … a union may be, the greater interest have the members in the political institutions of each other; and the greater right to insist that the forms of government under which the compact was entered into should be substantially maintained' (Federalist No. 43, para. 6). This chapter proposes a reversed reasoning: the higher the autonomy of a federation's individual parts, the greater the necessity for an enforceable common core of constitutional principles. Although there are certainly exceptions in this respect, the balance of autonomy and unity in federal states will usually tip towards the latter. The individual entities are not only subject to stronger constraints under the federal constitution; their scope for autonomous decision-making might also be narrower. As such, deviations from the common baseline are unlikely to occur or can be remedied at an earlier stage and through less conflictual channels. This explains the little practical relevance of homogeneity clauses in many federal constitutions. In

[27] See Christophe Hillion, 'Enlargement' in Paul Craig and Grainne de Búrca (eds), *The Evolution of EU Law* (2nd edn, OUP 2011) 187, 212 ff; Dimitry Kochenov, *EU Enlargement and the Failure of Conditionality* (Kluwer 2008) 15 f; Juli Zeh, *Recht auf Beitritt?* (Nomos 2002).

the U.S., for instance, the justiciability of the guarantee clause in Article IV, Section 4 is highly disputed.[28] The Supreme Court has persistently rejected claims brought under this provision as political questions.[29] Either way, the Supreme Court can enforce core constitutional principles through other channels. *Baker v Carr*, a case on malapportionment of election districts, illustrates this well. Though falling into the guarantee clause's scope, the issue was resolved by the Supreme Court under the equal protection clause.[30] This is different in looser federal systems, such as the EU. Due to their comparatively high degree of autonomy, the Member States have more space for independent decision-making. This increases the possibilities for deviations from common constitutional principles. In addition, there are fewer options for federal intervention at earlier stages. This applies especially when the Member States' very constitutional structures are concerned (see Chapter 9). For that reason, preserving a baseline of constitutional homogeneity across the Verbund acquires an increased relevance in the EU (see further Section III.B).

Finally, constitutions of federal states usually establish vertical homogeneity claims from the federal to the state level. Individual states must comply with a set of constitutional principles defined at the federal level without, however, formulating reciprocal claims with regard to the federal constitution. The situation in the EU is quite different. It not only features unilateral, vertical claims from the EU to the Member states but is characterized by a veritable interaction.[31] As will be outlined in the following, Article 2 TEU unites several claims that reinforce the overall constitutional homogeneity within the Verbund.

III. Article 2 TEU as a Framework for Constitutional Homogeneity Claims

The following sections aim to unpack the complex web of homogeneity claims that converge in Article 2 TEU (Section A) before turning to the specific functions of these claims in the Verbund of EU and Member States (Section B).

[28] See e.g. Ryan C. Williams, 'The "Guarantee" Clause' *Harvard Law Review* 132 (2018), 602. For the main positions, see Erwin Chemerinsky, 'Why Cases Under the Guarantee Clause Should Be Justiciable' (849) and Louise Weinberg, 'Political Questions and the Guarantee Clause' (887) both in *University of Colorado Law Review* 65 (1994).

[29] For a concise overview, see Erwin Chemerinsky, *Constitutional Law* (6th edn, Kluwer 2019) § 2.8.3 (pp 145 ff).

[30] *Baker v Carr*, 369 U.S. 186 (1962).

[31] See already Francesco Palermo, 'La prescrittività circolare dell'assetto ideologico. Le clausole di omogeneità e integrazione' in Palermo and Roberto Toniatti (eds), *Il processo di costituzionalizzazione dell'Unione europea* (Univ. Trento 2004) 115, 173. See also Francesco Palermo, 'Annäherungen an den "Verfassungskern" der Europäischen Union. Die Homogenitäts- und Integrationsklauseln im integrierten Verfassungsrecht des Europäischen Verfassungsgsraumes' in Karl Weber and Norbert Wimmer (eds), *Festschrift für Peter Pernthaler* (Springer 2005) 295.

A. Three Claims

Three strands of constitutional homogeneity claims can be distinguished.[32] First, Article 2 TEU establishes the requirement of *horizontal constitutional homogeneity among the Member States*. Article 2 TEU states that 'these values are common to the Member States'. Hence, the Member States' constitutional orders must be—among each other—homogeneous with regard to their basic constitutional features. Second, there are *vertical requirements for constitutional homogeneity emerging from the Member States and directed to the Union*. These vertical claims find their expression at both the EU and the Member State level.

On the one hand, this is inherent in Article 2 TEU itself, which entails obligations not only for the Member States but also for the Union institutions. The content of these values is determined, in particular, by having recourse to the common constitutional traditions of the Member States (see Chapter 2, III.B.2).[33] Accordingly, Article 2 TEU might come close to what some have described as provisions of 'shared normativity'.[34] Although formally part of one legal order (the EU), such provisions present a permeability towards another.[35] They allow access to legal principles or incorporate the content of norms, which emanate from separate legal sources. It should be noted, however, that the common constitutional traditions are not only transferred to but also transformed at the EU level. The common constitutional traditions in their entirety, not a single tradition, serve as the basis for interpreting Article 2 TEU. In this sense, the respective value develops a life of its own and reveals an emancipated substance before it reflects back to the Member States' legal orders. The content of Article 2 TEU is thus the product of an *interaction* between legal orders. In the words of Andreas Voßkuhle, one could also speak of a 'system of communicating vessels'.[36]

On the other hand, implicit homogeneity requirements can also be found at the Member State level. As Christian Tomuschat observed, any constitution reveals to some extent an 'egoistic character' leading to requirements of homogeneity for inter- or supranational organizations, whose decisions will later reflect back into

[32] For a first systematization, see Schorkopf (n 24) 42 ff. For a reconstruction as a 'omogeneitá "biunivoca"', see Delledonne (n 1) 272 ff.

[33] See e.g. Egils Levits, 'L'Union européenne en tant que communauté des valeurs partagées' in *Liber Amicorum Antonio Tizzano* (Giappichelli 2018) 509, 518; Koen Lenaerts, 'Die Werte der Europäischen Union in der Rechtsprechung des Gerichtshofs der Europäischen Union: eine Annäherung' EuGRZ 44 (2017), 639, 640; Christian Calliess, 'The Transnationalization of Values by European Law' GLJ 10 (2009), 1367, 1377. See also Case C-62/14 *Gauweiler* [2015] EU:C:2015:7, Opinion of AG Cruz Villalón, para 61; Case C-127/07 *Société Arcelor Atlantique* [2008] EU:C:2008:292, Opinion of AG Maduro, para 16.

[34] In detail, Dana Burchard, *Die Rangfrage im europäischen Normenverbund* (Mohr Siebeck 2015) 199 ff, 351 f.

[35] Mattias Wendel, *Permeabilität im europäischen Verfassungsrecht* (Mohr Siebeck 2011) 7.

[36] Andreas Voßkuhle, *The Idea of the European Community of Values* (Bittner 2018) 110. As 'dialectic', see Takis Tridimas, 'The general principles of EU law and the Europeanisation of national laws' REAL 13 (2020), 5, 7, 30.

the national legal sphere.[37] Such claims can be found in the Member States' constitutions or in the jurisprudence of their apex courts. Starting with the former, several constitutions make EU membership conditional upon the Union's compliance with a set of constitutional principles.[38] Pursuant to Article 23(1) of the German Basic Law, for instance, Germany shall participate in a 'European Union that is committed to democratic, social and federal principles, to the rule of law and to the principle of subsidiarity and that guarantees a level of protection of basic rights essentially comparable to that afforded by this Basic Law.' By making German participation conditional upon these requirements, Article 23(1) Basic Law is implicitly addressed to the EU.[39] This does not mean, as claimed by several commentators in the 1950's, that the institutional order at the EU level must be 'structurally congruent' to the national one.[40] Instead, the Bundesverfassungsgericht opted for a broader approach requiring a homogeneity only in relation to fundamental constitutional principles.[41] Moreover, these requirements are adapted to the nature and function of the Union, thus acquiring a genuinely European meaning.[42]

At the same time, there can be an indirect push for homogeneity by the national judiciary. Several courts claim jurisdiction to review EU acts (or their domestic acts of implementation) against a set of constitutional principles. Initially, this concerned fundamental rights standards. Today, the focus has shifted to a more general set of constitutional principles and values often summarized under the catchphrase of constitutional identity.[43] While they cannot invalidate EU acts or formulate requirements binding upon Union institutions, national constitutional courts can nonetheless decide to suspend EU law's direct effect in the domestic legal order. To prevent such an open confrontation, Luxembourg will have to align its position with that of the respective constitutional court. As such, these

[37] Christian Tomuschat, 'Der Verfassungsstaat im Geflecht der internationalen Beziehungen' VVDStRL 36 (1978), 38.

[38] On these clauses, see e.g. Leonard Besselink et al., *National Constitutional Avenues for further EU Integration* (European Parliament, Legal Affairs, 2014) 28 ff. In detail, see Stefan Griller, Lina Papadopoulou, and Roman Puff (eds), *National Constitutions and EU Integration* (Hart 2022).

[39] Reading the provision as a homogeneity clause, see e.g. Frank Schorkopf, 'Art. 23 GG' in Wolfgang Kahl et al. (eds), *Bonner Kommentar zum Grundgesetz* (211th edn, loose-leaf, C.F.Müller 2021) paras 78–82; Robert Uerpmann-Wittzack, 'Art. 23 GG' in Ingo von Münch and Philip Kunig (eds), *Grundgesetz-Kommentar* (7th edn, C.H.Beck 2021) para 17.

[40] In the context of the European Defence Community, see Herbert Kraus, 'Das Erfordernis struktureller Kongruenz zwischen der Verfassung der Europäischen Verteidigungsgemeinschaft und dem Grundgesetz' in *Der Kampf um den Wehrbeitrag*, vol 2 (Isar 1953) 545. Critically, Peter Badura, 'Bewahrung und Veränderung demokratischer und rechtsstaatlicher Verfassungsstruktur in den internationalen Gemeinschaften' VVDStRL 23 (1966), 34, 38 ff. On this debate, see Bill Davies, 'Resistance to European Law and Constitutional Identity in Germany: Herbert Kraus and *Solange* in its Intellectual Context' ELJ 21 (2015), 434, 441.

[41] BVerfG, Judgment of 30 June 2009, 2 BvE 2/08, *Lisbon*, para 266. See also Rudolf Streinz, 'Art. 23 GG' in Michael Sachs (ed.), *Grundgesetz* (8th edn, C.H.Beck 2018) paras 20–3.

[42] With regard to democracy, BVerfG, *Lisbon* (n 41) paras 227, 262 f.

[43] See e.g. the studies in Christian Calliess and Gerhard van der Schyff (eds), *Constitutional Identity in a Europe of Multilevel Constitutionalism* (CUP 2019). For a systematization, see e.g. Luke D. Spieker, 'Framing and Managing Constitutional Identity Conflicts' CML Rev 57 (2020), 361.

constitutional identity claims exert an indirect form of pressure.[44] As will be demonstrated in Chapter 11, these constitutional identity claims can and should be channelled through Article 2 TEU, brought before the CJEU, and thus influence the interpretative development of the Union's common values.

Finally, Article 2 TEU is not only a gateway for domestic constitutional law into the EU legal order. It also entails a *vertical claim from the EU to the Member States*. It has been argued that such a claim can only constitute a reflex of the horizontal homogeneity among the Member States. Especially, Frank Schorkopf argued that there is no original EU claim for homogeneity directed to the Member States.[45] The Union has just taken up the task of policing the horizontal homogeneity between the Member States. Even though there are vertical enforcement mechanisms by Union institutions, the enforced *standards* are still those of a horizontal homogeneity.[46] Yet, there are strong arguments suggesting an autonomous EU claim for constitutional homogeneity.

To start with, Union institutions not only protect the values enshrined in Article 2 TEU but are also deeply involved in determining their substance. Certainly, these values are rooted in the Member States' common constitutional traditions. Still, defining this common heritage will always require compromises. When striking such compromises, the CJEU will likely conduct an evaluative or critical legal comparison (see Chapter 2, III.B.2). It seems highly artificial to assume that this creative assessment will merely reflect the horizontal homogeneity between the Member States and keep EU-specific understandings out of consideration. As noted above, the common constitutional traditions are not only transferred to but also transformed at the EU level. This is even more so, should the CJEU decide to flesh out Article 2 TEU by relying on other sources, such as the ECHR or the Copenhagen criteria for accession.

Further, the requirement of constitutional homogeneity not only stabilizes the relationship among the Member States but will necessarily encompass specific features to sustain the proper functioning of the EU itself (see Section III.B). To provide an example, the EU's judicial architecture relies on a certain level of homogeneity with regard to issues of judicial independence. To serve as first 'Union courts' and maintain dialogue with Luxembourg, national courts and tribunals must be sufficiently independent. This criterion of independence, however, cannot be understood as merely reflecting the horizontal homogeneity between the Member States. It is a requirement adapted to the specificities of the EU judicial architecture.

[44] Arguably, this pressure was made visible in the BVerfG's decision in *Identitätskontrolle I* and the CJEU's reaction in *Aranyosi*, see Matthias Hong, 'Human Dignity, Identity Review of the European Arrest Warrant and the Court of Justice as a Listener in the Dialogue of Courts' EuConst 12 (2016), 549.

[45] See e.g. Schorkopf (n 24) 67–8 (paras 77–8).

[46] ibid 67 f, 102 (paras 77 f, 147).

Admittedly, not all values can be realized in the same manner at the EU and the Member State level. This applies especially to the value of democracy. The EU has a complex polycentric character that is difficult to square with democracy at the national level.[47] Yet, such differences do not necessarily preclude claims for homogeneity. Even in federal states, democracy can take very different forms. In Germany, for instance, most Länder constitutions contain a wide range of participatory elements like plebiscites and referenda, whereas these elements are almost completely absent from the federal level. Despite these considerable differences, Article 28(1) of the federal constitution requires the Länder to conform to the democratic principle 'within the meaning of this Basic Law' and contains detailed criteria for their elections (general, direct, free, equal, and secret). Thus, diversity does not seem to exclude homogeneity claims. It only affects their scope and intensity. In this spirit, the Bundesverfassungsgericht has noted that Article 23(1) of the Basic Law does not require the realization of democratic self-determination at the EU level 'in the exact forms prescribed by the Basic Law'.[48] The same could apply to genuine homogeneity claims emanating from the EU.

In sum, the claims for homogeneity sketched above form a complex web:

1) *vertical* from the EU to the Member States (top-down)
2) *horizontal* among the Member States,
3) *vertical* from the Member States to the Union (bottom-up)
   a) through anchoring Article 2 TEU in the Member States' constitutional traditions
   b) through requirements in national constitutional law and jurisprudence

Whereas claim (3b) derives from national constitutional law,[49] claims (1), (2), and (3a) are amalgamated in Article 2 TEU and cannot be separated. This has an important implication at the institutional level. As will be demonstrated in the next chapters, most of these claims can be voiced through the EU judicial system (the CJEU and its national counterparts). Accordingly, these different claims for homogeneity correspond neither to specific legal provisions nor specific institutions responsible for their realization. Abstractly, there are three avenues of enforcement: top-down (from the EU to the national level), horizontal (among the Member States), and bottom-up (from the national to the EU level). Admittedly, if we disregard diplomatic sanctions by the Member States, such as those against

[47] As a 'democracy of many mediations', see Armin von Bogdandy, *The Emergence and Democratization of European Society* (OUP 2023).
[48] BVerfG, *Lisbon* (n 41) paras 227, 267.
[49] On how to articulate these claims under Art. 2 TEU, see Chapter 11.

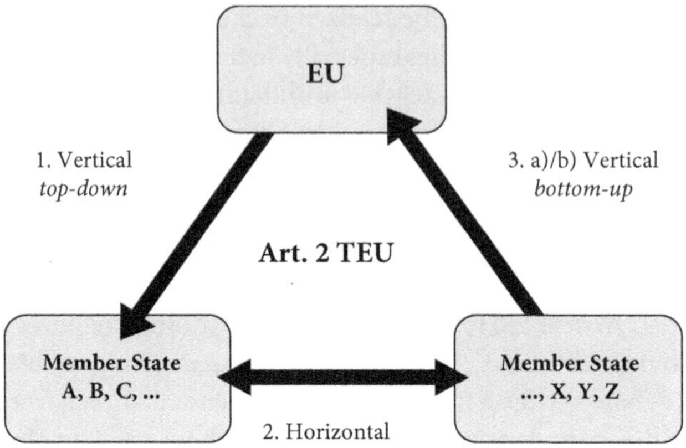

Figure 8.1 The web of constitutional homogeneity claims in the Verbund

Austria in the Haider affair, there are no *genuinely* horizontal enforcement mechanisms in the Verbund. Article 7 TEU, for instance, constitutes a top-down enforcement from the Council, an EU institution, against a Member State. The same holds true for infringement proceedings under Article 259 TFEU or the review by national courts of Article 2 TEU compliance in other Member States e.g. through the European Arrest Warrant framework (in detail, Chapter 10). In the former context, it is the Court of Justice that decides. In the latter one, the respective national courts police substantive EU standards and act—institutionally—as first 'Union courts'. This shifts these particular situations into more vertical channels.[50] Nevertheless, for the sake of clarity this book will refer to these channels as horizontal.

B. Three Functions

In any case, these three claims for homogeneity lead to a system of reciprocal constitutional stabilization and fertilization.[51] Within the Verbund, the European level not only receives impulses from the national level; it equally sends such impulses back to the Member States.[52] Article 2 TEU is placed at the centre of this system and could be understood as a platform for a dialectic relationship between national constitutions and Union values. In this sense, the Czech Constitutional Court has acknowledged that Article 2 TEU and the Member States' constitutions 'support

[50] See Luke D. Spieker, 'Breathing Life into the Union's Common Values' GLJ 20 (2019), 1182, 1194.

[51] Christoph Grabenwarter, 'National Constitutional Law Relating to the European Union' in von Bogdandy and Bast (n 18) 83, 128. See already Ingolf Pernice, 'Multilevel Constitutionalism and the Treaty of Amsterdam' CML Rev 36 (1999), 703, 726 f.

[52] Egils Levits speaks of a 'situation circulaire', see (n 33) 518.

each other'.[53] Besides this stabilization, the outlined claims for constitutional homogeneity assume various functions.

First, they fulfil a *safeguarding function*. In entering the European Union, the Member States simultaneously accepted an openness towards the developments and decisions taken by other Member States. The EU not only extends the transnational reach of each Member State but also creates a situation of mutual vulnerabilities.[54] Internal developments in one Member State can lead to spill-over effects in all other Member States. The complex network of cooperation created by the EU is not only enabling, but also transmitting and intensifying these effects. An example of this intensification is mutual recognition as an increasing mode of EU governance.[55] In the internal market, but also in many other fields like the European arrest warrant or the recognition of judgments under EU private international law, Member States must accept decisions taken by other Member States. Similarly, majority voting in the Council leads to a situation in which all Member States are governed not only by their own government but also to a certain extent by governments in other Member States. As such, the internal developments in one Member State indirectly affect all others.[56] Eleanor Sharpston described this situation with a short parable:

> A group of men are travelling together in a boat. Suddenly, one of them takes out an auger and starts to bore a hole in the hull beneath himself. His companions remonstrate with him. 'Why are you doing that?' they cry. 'What are you complaining about?' says he. 'Am I not drilling the hole under my own seat?' 'Yes', they reply, 'but the water will come in and flood the boat for all of us'.[57]

The acceptance of such mutual vulnerabilities requires a minimum of constitutional homogeneity among the Member States from which they cannot derogate as long as they are Member States of the Union.

[53] Ústavní soud, Judgment of 26 November 2008, Pl. ÚS 19/08, *Lisbon I*, para 209.

[54] For an analysis, see Alexander Somek, 'The Argument from Transnational Effects I' ELJ 16 (2010), 315. Critically, see also Somek, 'The Darling Dogma of Bourgeois Europeanists' ELJ 20 (2014), 688.

[55] Instructively, see Cecilia Rizcallah, 'The Challenges to Trust-Based Governance in the European Union' ELJ 25 (2019), 37. See also the overviews by Clemens Ladenburger, 'The Principle of Mutual Trust between Member States in the Area of Freedom, Security and Justice' ZEuS 23 (2020), 373 and Eugene Regan, 'The Role of the Principles of Mutual Trust and Mutual Recognition in EU Law' dUE (2018), 231.

[56] On this 'all affected principle', Carlos Closa, 'Reinforcing EU Monitoring of the Rule of Law' in Closa and Dimitry Kochenov (eds), *Reinforcing Rule of Law Oversight in the European Union* (CUP 2016) 15, 18 f. See also European Parliament, Resolution on the proposal for a Council decision on the determination of a clear risk of a serious breach by the Republic of Poland of the rule of law (17 September 2020), Rec. C: 'a serious breach by a Member State of the values referred to in Article 2 ... does not concern solely the individual Member State where the risk materialises but has a negative impact on the other Member States'.

[57] Cases C-715, 718, and 719/17 *Commission v Poland, Hungary, and Czech Republic* [2019] EU:C:2019:917, Opinion of AG Sharpston, para 255.

Similar vulnerabilities emerge in the vertical relationship between the Union and its Member States. With progressing integration, the EU has acquired unprecedented powers and competences in a wide range of policy areas. Further, primacy, direct effect, and the establishment of national courts as 'Union courts' extend the reach of EU law deep into the Member States' domestic structures. Such a far-reaching opening of domestic constitutional structures requires a safety net. In this sense, the EU's adherence to a common constitutional core is a crucial safeguard for the Member States. At the same time, the Union is no less vulnerable. Being a community of law and not of coercion,[58] it essentially depends on the domestic implementation of EU law. While the set of coercive measures has considerably developed,[59] Member States' compliance with EU law is still ultimately voluntary.[60] Unlike many federal states, the EU does not have a national guard[61] or instruments of a Bundeszwang.[62] Therefore, implementation is conducted by State institutions and especially by national courts. If a Member State ceases to adhere to the values enshrined in Article 2 TEU and threatens, for instance, the independence of its judiciary, national courts cease to be a reliable partner in guaranteeing the coherent and uniform application of EU law.

Second, the vertical homogeneity claims between the Member States and the Union assume a *conflict-preventing function*. Some authors consider this as the core function of constitutional homogeneity in federal systems.[63] With regard to the predecessor of Article 2 TEU, Advocate Maduro noted that 'Article 6 TEU ... indicates how best to prevent any real conflict ... in particular by anchoring the constitutional foundations of the European Union in the constitutional principles common to the Member States. Through this provision the Member States are reassured that the law of the European Union will not threaten the fundamental values of their constitutions.'[64] The same could be said in reverse.

Third, the constitutional homogeneity claims have a *legitimizing function*. The democratic legitimacy at the EU level springs from a dual source. The Member State governments represented in the Council derive their legitimacy from the national level (Art. 10(2) TEU), whereas the European Parliament is directly elected by the Union citizens.[65] The elections of a Member State government are

[58] See Walter Hallstein, *Die Europäische Gemeinschaft* (Econ 1973) 348.

[59] See e.g. Stefano Montaldo, Francesco Costamagna, and Alberto Miglio (eds), *EU Law Enforcement. The Evolution of Sanctioning Powers* (Routledge 2021); Stephan Bitter, *Die Sanktion im Recht der Europäischen Union* (Springer 2011) 121 ff.

[60] Roland Bieber and Francesco Maiani, 'Enhancing Centralised Enforcement of EU Law: Pandora's Toolbox?' CML Rev 51 (2014), 1057, 1060 f.

[61] Max Steinbeis, 'The EU has no National Guard' *Verfassungsblog* (31 January 2020).

[62] See Art. 37 German Basic Law, Art. II, Section 3 US Constitution, Art. 79(2) No. 1(a) and 146(2) Austrian Constitution, Arts. 49(2), 173(1)(e), 182(2), 186(4) Swiss Constitution or Art. 155 Spanish Constitution.

[63] See Schmitt (n 3) 392 [p 376]. See also Dubout (n 25) 47 ff.

[64] Case C-127/07 *Société Arcelor Atlantique* [2008] EU:C:2008:292, Opinion of AG Maduro.

[65] On the Union's structure of dual legitimacy, see von Bogdandy (n 47); Jelena von Achenbach, *Demokratische Gesetzgebung in der Europäischen Union. Theorie und Praxis der dualen*

a domestic matter. Similarly, the elections to the European Parliament are partially governed by national provisions[66] and take place, to a great extent, within the public sphere of the Member States.[67] Therefore, the democratic legitimacy at the EU level largely depends on the situation in each Member State. If there are no free, fair, and democratic elections at the national level (e.g. due to undemocratic party financing rules or undue government influence on the media), this has an immediate impact not only on national elections (and thus the composition of the Council) but also on elections to the European Parliament. The participation of non-democratically legitimized governments and deputies in Council and Parliament, however, risks tainting the legitimacy of the whole decision-making process at the EU level.[68] Hence, there is not only 'a shared interest in the public life of all the Member States'[69] but also a vital interest in their adherence to essential democratic standards.

Moreover, majority voting has been subsequently strengthened in the Council. This leads to the question, under what conditions an outvoted minority will accept the majority's decisions? While there is relatively little research on why and under what conditions States accept the shift from unanimity to majority voting,[70] the acceptance of majority decisions among citizens has been the subject of ample scholarly reflection. Admittedly, a direct transfer of these insights might be accused of being methodologically flawed. They may, nevertheless, serve as a reference point for our reflection. Generally, a minority seems more likely to accept majority decisions if there is a non-controversial, common basis not subject to debate and change.[71] This corresponds to sociological insights. According to Niklas Luhman, democracy can only work if the opposition is acknowledged as legally and morally permitted.[72] Yet, this presupposes a very basic understanding of what is legally and morally permitted in the first place. In this spirit, Herman Heller has noted already, in 1928, that the very basis of parliamentary democracy was 'the belief, not in public discussion as such, but in the existence of a common foundation for

Legitimationsstruktur europäischer Hoheitsgewalt (Springer 2014) 300 ff; Peter M. Huber, 'Art. 10 EUV' in Rudolf Streinz (ed.), *EUV/AEUV* (3rd edn, C.H.Beck 2018) para 25.

66 Art. 8 of the Act concerning the election of the representatives of the Assembly by direct universal suffrage. See also Case C-502/19 *Junqueras Vies* [2019] EU:C:2019:1115, para 69.

67 For this claim, see also BVerfG, *Lisbon* (n 41) para 251.

68 See also Christoph Möllers and Linda Schneider, *Demokratiesicherung in der Europäischen Union* (Mohr Siebeck 2018) 6-8.

69 See Case C-78/18 *Commission v Hungary (Transparency of associations)* [2020] EU:C:2020:1, Opinion of AG Campos Sánchez-Bordona, para 124.

70 On this development, see Luuk van Middelaar, *The Passage to Europe* (Yale Univ. Press 2013) 72 ff. On homogeneity as condition for majority voting, see Liesbet Hooghe, Tobias Lenz, and Gary Marks, *A Theory of International Organization* (OUP 2019) 107 ff.

71 See e.g. Ernst-Wolfgang Böckenförde, 'Conditions for European Solidarity' in Krzysztof Michalski (ed.), *What Holds Europe Together?* (CEU Press 2006) 30.

72 Niklas Luhmann, 'Participation and Legitimation' in Luhmann, *Political Theory in the Welfare State* (De Gruyter 1990) 219, 228.

discussion'.[73] Further, a common political identity seems to foster acceptance of the majority's will. As Daniel Innerarity argues, the majority must be made up of something the minority can still recognize as part of itself.[74] This does not necessarily hark back to the controversial discussion of economic, cultural, religious, national, or ethnic homogeneity.[75] Arguably, political identity can also be constituted on the basis of common values and principles.

IV. Guaranteeing Constitutional Homogeneity Through the EU Judicial System

In conclusion, a certain level of constitutional homogeneity is indispensable for the functioning and legitimacy of the EU. This explains the dense web of homogeneity claims throughout the Verbund of the EU and its Member States. As a constitutional frame of the Verbund, Article 2 TEU is the central provision that brings these claims together. As long as the Member States are part of the Union, it defines an outer constitutional frame they may not breach. Ultimately, this obligation extends to the Member States' constitutional or national identities under Article 4(2) TEU, which may not contradict the Union's values.[76] At the same time, this chapter reiterated the reasons for a restrained understanding of Article 2 TEU in its Verbund dimension. As a mere constitutional frame, it cannot impose more than a minimum of constitutional homogeneity (in detail Chapters 3, III and 12, III).

The rest of this part will explore the role of the EU judicial system in guaranteeing this homogeneity across the Verbund. Corresponding to the avenues of enforcement outlined above, such a guarantee can be facilitated *top-down, horizontal,* and *bottom-up*. Starting with the former, the next chapter will analyse how the CJEU can—in fact already does—review value compliance in the Member States. Indeed, under the pressure of illiberal developments in Poland, Hungary, Romania,

[73] Herman Heller, 'Political Democracy and Social Homogeneity (1928)' in Arthur J. Jacobson and Bernhard Schlink (eds), *Weimar* (Univ. California Press 2001) 256, 260.

[74] Innerarity (n 3) 101.

[75] See the discussion mentioned in n 3.

[76] Case C-156/21 *Hungary v Parliament and Council* [2022] EU:C:2022:97, paras 233 f. There is a broad agreement on this point, see e.g. European Parliament, Resolution on the situation of fundamental rights: standards and practices in Hungary (3 July 2013), 2012/2130(INI), Rec. M; Case C-62/14 *Gauweiler* EU:C:2015:7, Opinion of AG Cruz Villalón, para 61; Case C-490/20 *Stolichna obshtina, rayon "Pancharevo"* [2021] EU:C:2021:296, Opinion of AG Kokott, paras 73, 116 ff; Case C-430/21 *RS (Effet des arrêts d'une cour constitutionnelle)* [2022] EU:C:2022:44, Opinion of AG Collins; Case C-391/20 *Boriss Cilevičs and Others* [2022] EU:C:2022:166, Opinion of AG Emiliou, para 87. From the bench, see also Koen Lenaerts, 'Concluding Remarks' in CJEU (ed.), *EUnited in Diversity: Between Common Constitutional Traditions and National Identities* (Luxembourg 2022) 231, 234; Marek Safjan, 'On Symmetry: In Search of an Appropriate Response to the Crisis of the Democratic State' dUE (2020), 673, 681 f; Lucia S. Rossi, '2, 4, 6 (TUE) … l'interpretazione dell'"Identity Clause" alla luce dei valori fondamentali dell'Unione' in *Liber Amicorum Antonio Tizzano* (n 33) 858, 866. See also Voßkuhle (n 36) 117.

or Malta, the Court of Justice has become the central forum to address violations of EU values in the Member States. Chapter 10, by contrast, will assess horizontal avenues for reviewing the value compliance of Member States, both directly before the Court of Justice (through Article 259 TFEU) and indirectly before national courts (through so-called mutual recognition regimes). Finally, Chapter 11 will explore how constitutional courts can assert—in tandem with Luxembourg—the Union's own value compliance. Currently, such a bottom-up review takes especially place within the framework of constitutional identity claims. This book suggests articulating constitutional identity concerns under the banner of Article 2 TEU. This might help turn heated identity conflicts into a productive dialogue that stabilizes the constitutional homogeneity in the Verbund.

9
Top-Down Review

I. Introduction

The following chapter will focus on the CJEU's role in preserving the constitutional homogeneity in the Member States. Confronted with illiberal developments in several Member States and the lack of political responses, the Court has already started to review their compliance with the Union's common values. However, involving Luxembourg raises institutional (Why the Court? see Section II.A) and substantive questions (Which legal basis? see Section II.B). One crucial problem is that upheavals of the Member States' constitutional structures do not necessarily feature any link to EU law. This challenge is certainly not new. Indeed, academia and practice have developed several approaches to protect Union values, even in situations that seemingly escape the scope of EU law. The *Reverse Solange* doctrine is probably one of the most sophisticated examples. Yet this approach reveals several shortcomings. As such, this chapter will explore a different path: operationalizing Article 2 TEU itself.

So far, the Court has refrained from applying Article 2 TEU as a self-standing provision. For good reasons, it operationalizes Article 2 TEU through other Treaty provisions that give specific expression to these values (for a recap, see Chapter 1, III and IV, Chapter 2, III). At first glance, this construction seems to curtail the unlimited scope of Article 2 TEU (namely to that of its operationalizing provision). This would leave its potential as a standard for the entire Verbund untapped. In *Associação Sindical dos Juízes Portugueses (ASJP)*, however, the Court found a way to operationalize Article 2 TEU without limiting its scope. This chapter suggests that the interplay of Article 2 TEU and its operationalizing provision can lead to their mutual amplification. While the specific provision translates the values enshrined in Article 2 TEU into applicable legal obligations, Article 2 TEU justifies an extensive reading of the specific provision (Section III).

II. Countering Illiberal Developments in the Member States

During the last decade, some Member States started to increasingly test the limits established by Article 2 TEU. These challenges have consolidated into a larger illiberal turn. Governing parties in Poland, Hungary, Romania, or Malta started dismantling checks and balances of the political process, such as independent

EU Values Before the Court of Justice. Luke Dimitrios Spieker, Oxford University Press.
DOI: 10.1093/oso/9780198876717.003.0010

courts, free media, academia, or civil society organizations.[1] Other achievements, such as LGBTIQ rights, are also at stake.[2] In Hungary and Poland, national constitutions seem no longer apt to shield against attacks on fundamental rights, democracy, and the rule of law. While Viktor Orbán secured a majority sufficient for constitutional amendments, the Polish Constitutional Tribunal—once the constitution's guardian—has been captured by the government. These developments severely threaten the constitutional homogeneity of the Verbund and strongly suggest an EU intervention.[3]

Much has been written on how to address these issues institutionally and procedurally.[4] Even if the EU's toolbox has considerably evolved during the last years,[5] the political process has nonetheless been beset by an astounding inertia. Both Article 7 TEU procedures launched against Poland and Hungary have been pending in the Council for years. As Poland and Hungary are watching each other's backs, this is not likely to change in the near future.[6] Further, neither are willing to change course or to withdraw from the Union. In this deadlocked situation, some heads of state have started to speculate openly about a possible reestablishment of the EU—without Poland and Hungary.[7]

As noted earlier, this political paralysis resembles a well-known pattern of European integration: in times when the necessary actions have not been pursued in the realm of politics, the CJEU stepped in to safeguard the European integration agenda (see Chapter 1, III.B). When it comes to countering the illiberal turn in several Member States, a similar inertia seems to beset the political plane, and

[1] See the analysis by the Commission in its 2022 Rule of Law Report, especially the country chapters on Hungary (SWD(2022) 517 final) and Poland (SWD(2022) 521 final).

[2] European Parliament, Resolution on breaches of EU law and of the rights of LGBTIQ citizens in Hungary (8 July 2021), 2021/2780(RSP).

[3] On the EU's legitimacy to act, see e.g. Anastasia Iliopoulou-Penot, 'La justification de l'intervention de l'Union pour la garantie de l'Etat de droit au sein des pays membres' RAE 24 (2019), 7; Armin von Bogdandy, 'Principles of a Systemic Deficiencies Doctrine' CML Rev 57 (2020), 705, 711–15; Miguel Maduro and Benedita Menezes Queiroz, 'A Hard Law Approach to States Systemic Violations of Article 2 of the Treaty of the European Union' in Elizabeth Fisher et al. (eds), *The Foundations and Future of Public Law* (OUP 2020) 363, 370 f.

[4] For comprehensive accounts, see the individual contributions to András Jakab and Dimitry Kochenov (eds), *The Enforcement of EU Law and Values* (OUP 2017), Carlos Closa and Dimitry Kochenov (eds), *Reinforcing Rule of Law Oversight in the European Union* (Cambridge: CUP) and Werner Schroeder (ed.), *Strengthening the Rule of Law in Europe* (Hart 2016).

[5] On the development of the toolbox, see e.g. Laurent Pech, 'The Rule of Law in the EU' in Paul Craig and Gráinne de Búrca (eds), *The Evolution of EU Law* (3rd edn, OUP 2021) 307.

[6] On the weaknesses of this procedure, see Dimitry Kochenov, 'Article 7: A Commentary on a Much Talked-About "Dead" Provision' PYIL 38 (2018), 165.

[7] On this proposal by the Dutch Prime Minister, see Merijn Chamon, 'Re-establishing the EU. Dissolution, Withdrawal or Succession' *EU Law Live* (10 October 2020). On the option of expelling Member States, see Michael Dougan and Christophe Hillion, 'The EU's Duty to Respect Hungarian Aovereignty: An Action Plan' CML Rev 59 (2022), 181; Tom Theuns, 'The Need for an EU Expulsion Mechanism: Democratic Backsliding and the Failure of Article 7' *Res Publica* 28 (2022), 693 ; Zachary Sanfilippo, 'United, We Stand: Expelling Autocratic States from the European Union' *Duke Law Journal* 72 (2022), 675.

especially the Council as key decision-maker under Article 7 TEU.[8] Even though the rule of law conditonality regulation seems to be an instrument with much bite, it still remains to be seen how its activation will play out.[9] Accordingly, many argued for concentrating on judicial mechanisms, to employ the infringement procedure under Article 258 TFEU,[10] or to interact with national courts via the preliminary reference procedure.[11]

Against this backdrop, the Court of Justice has become the main arena to challenge violations of EU values in the Member States. In an act of judicial bravery, so the prevalent narrative runs, it has taken on the task of countering the illiberal turn. This story has been told in Chapter 1 and will not be reiterated here. Instead, the following section touches upon two central issues. First, it will assess whether and why the CJEU is the right institution to remedy violations of EU values in the Member States (Section A). Second, it will explore how to address these issues before the Court substantively. The Charter or provisions from the internal market context can hardly counter upheavals of the Member States' internal constitutional structures. The second Section will assess how the *Reverse Solange* doctrine allows the Court to review such developments and then turn to its shortcomings. Ultimately, these considerations confirm the need to engage with Article 2 TEU itself (Section B).

A. Institutionally: Why the Court?

Despite the apparent risks of entrusting Luxembourg with the protection of EU values (see Chapter 12), there are solid arguments for involving the Court of Justice. These boil down to four considerations. First, addressing violations of Article 2 TEU in judicial proceedings might help depoliticize, rationalize, and eventually de-escalate the conflict (*argument from de-escalation*). Compared to other political

[8] For fierce criticism, see European Parliament, Resolution on the proposal for a Council decision on the determination of a clear risk of a serious breach by the Republic of Poland of the rule of law (17 September 2020), para 3; Laurent Pech, Patryk Wachowiec, and Dariusz Mazur, 'Poland's Rule of Law Breakdown: A Five-Year Assessment of EU's (In)Action' HJRL 13 (2021), 1, 17 ff; R. Daniel Kelemen, 'Appeasement, ad Infinitum' MJ 29 (2022), 177; Gráinne de Búrca, 'Poland and Hungary's EU Membership: On not Confronting Authoritarian Governments' I-CON (2022), 13. For the potential reasons, see Carlos Closa, 'Institutional Logics and the EU's Limited Sanctioning Capacity under Article 7 TEU' *International Political Science Review* 42 (2021), 501, 510 ff.

[9] For its activation with regard to Hungary, see Council Implementing Decision (EU) 2022/2506 of 15 December 2022 on measures for the protection of the Union budget against breaches of the principles of the rule of law in Hungary.

[10] See e.g. Kim L. Scheppele, Dimitry Kochenov, and Barbara Grabowska-Moroz, 'EU Values are Law, after All. Enforcing EU Values Through Systemic Infringement Actions' YEL 38 (2020), 3; Matthias Schmidt and Piotr Bogdanowicz, 'The Infringement Procedure in the Rule of Law Crisis' CML Rev 55 (2018), 1061, 1073.

[11] See e.g. Michael Blauberger and R. Daniel Kelemen, 'Can Courts Rescue National Democracy?' JEPP 24 (2017), 321, 325 f.

institutions, the Court enjoys an image of neutrality and is less vulnerable to accusations of political or ideological bias (*institutional argument*). In contrast to sanctions taken under Article 7 TEU, judicial proceedings guarantee a certain fairness (*procedural argument*). Finally, enforcing values before the Court has proven, at least for now, to be more efficient than the largely deadlocked political procedures (*outcome-related argument*).

To start with, governments in recalcitrant Member States often try to shift the debate on their value compliance into the sphere of political, moral, or ideological differences. Orbán's verbal attacks against the 'moral judgement' passed by the EU over some Member States are evidence of this rhetoric.[12] In this sphere, however, value conflicts turn particularly heated. Perceived as an imposition of ideological convictions, the defence of Union values might acquire a paternalistic dimension, trigger antagonism, and ultimately deepen the cleavage between the EU and non-compliant Member States.[13] Addressing such violations in judicial procedures implies a 'change of arena'. Brought before a court, conflicts on political, moral, or ideological issues are subjected to the substantive and methodological constraints of legal discourse.[14] As such, judicial procedures can rationalize and depoliticize conflicts.[15] Unlike value conflicts in the political, moral, or ideological sphere, they can even unfold an integrating potential—if they are conducted in open- and fairness.[16]

Institutionally, the Court enjoys considerable authority and the appearance of neutrality, especially when compared to the Commission. Indeed, it was one of the Commission's top priorities to become a more political actor.[17] At the same time, this makes it vulnerable to accusations of political or ideological bias.[18] Such claims are difficult to extend to the Court of Justice. Admittedly, the Luxembourg judges have often been reproached for zealously following a pro-integrationist stance to the detriment of the Member States. Nevertheless, the CJEU is an independent court that enjoys considerable trust from both national judges and the

[12] Address by Prime Minister Viktor Orbán in the debate on the so-called Sargentini Report (Strasbourg, 11 September 2018).

[13] See e.g. Armin von Bogdandy, 'Towards a Tyranny of Values?' in von Bogdandy et al. (eds), *Defending Checks and Balances in EU Member States* (Springer 2021) 73, 75.

[14] See e.g. Dieter Grimm, 'What Exactly is Political about Constitutional Adjudication' in Christine Landfried (ed.), *Judicial Power* (CUP 2019) 307, 309.

[15] On exactly this need to 'keep it juridical', see Filipe Marques, 'Rule of Law, National Judges and the Court of Justice of the European Union: Let's Keep It Juridical' ELJ 27 (2021), 228, 238 f. Generally, see Christoph Möllers, *The Three Branches* (OUP 2013) 92 ff, 96 ff.

[16] On the CJEU's capacity to resolve or mitigate crises, see e.g. Ulrich Everling, 'Justizielle Krisenbewältigung' in Armin Hatje (ed.), *Verfassungszustand und Verfassungsentwicklung der Europäischen Union* (Nomos 2015) 86.

[17] See e.g. Daniel Sarmiento, 'The Juncker Presidency—A Study in Character' EJIL 31 (2020), 727, 729.

[18] See e.g. Orbán's defamation of Frans Timmermans as an 'ideological warrior', 'They want to make Soros's man the President of the Commission' (2 July 2019), <www.miniszterelnok.hu/they-want-to-make-soross-man-the-president-of-the-commission/>.

general public.[19] In this spirit, opinion polls show that a majority of Polish citizens consider the Court's intervention to protect judicial independence in the Member States as legitimate.[20]

Procedurally, requesting value compliance before the Court guarantees a certain fairness. The fairness of European responses is key to assure their acceptance by citizens in the respective Member State.[21] Judicial proceedings provide the defendant Member State with a full set of procedural rights and guarantees. The political avenues, by contrast, reveal severe shortcomings in this respect. This became most apparent during the Haider affair and the sanctions of fourteen Member States against Austria. Besides the questionable legality of these actions, it was especially the lack of reasons and a fair hearing that raised concerns.[22] The procedure under Article 7 TEU seems equally problematic.[23] Although highly controversial, Article 269 TFEU seems to limit judicial review of acts taken under Article 7 TEU to procedural grounds (see Chapter 2, IV.A). Without any substantive control, however, Article 7 TEU sits uneasy with one of the Union's fundamental principles: 'the very existence of effective judicial review'.[24]

Finally, judicial proceedings have been a rather efficient response. Certainly, Court rulings cannot eliminate the roots of the current crisis.[25] Yet, their effect should not be underestimated. Unlike political avenues, judicial procedures allow for the enforcement of legal principles without compromise. Further, authoritative judgments by the CJEU assert pressure on non-compliant Member States. For one, the appearance of legality is crucial for governments in backsliding Member States. This is evidenced by the particular attention that these governments pay to law as a tool of power consolidation.[26] A verdict from Luxembourg would unmask the abuse of legal institutions.[27] Moreover, any non-compliance with these judgments

[19] In 2012, the CJEU was 'the only European institution that is trusted by a majority', see Standard Eurobarometer 78, p 73 (after 2012, the Eurobarometer does not include data on trust in the CJEU anymore).

[20] See e.g. Piotr M. Kaczynski, 'Half of Poles Consider EU Institutions "Too Weak" Over Rule of Law Conflict' *Euractiv* (25 November 2021) and Anna Wójcik, 'Większość uważa, że TSUE ma prawo cofnąć zmiany w polskim sądownictwie' *OKO.press* (7 October 2021).

[21] See von Bogdandy (n 3) 739.

[22] See e.g. Eugene Regan, 'Are EU Sanctions Against Austria Legal?' ZÖR 55 (2000), 323; Frank Schorkopf, *Die Maßnahmen der XIV EU-Mitgliedstaaten gegen Österreich* (Springer 2002) 53, 78 ff.

[23] See e.g. Matthias Niedobitek, 'Right and Duty to Pursue the "Wrongdoer" and a Possible Abuse of Art. 7 TEU' in Armin Hatje and Lubos Tichý (eds), *Liability of Member States for the Violation of Fundamental Value* (Nomos 2018) 233, 241.

[24] See only Case C-64/16 *Associação Sindical dos Juízes Portugueses* [2018] EU:C:2018:117, para 36. On Art. 269 TFEU as 'unconstitutional constitutional law', see Thomas Giegerich, 'Die Unabhängigkeit der Gerichte als Strukturvorgabe der Unionsverfassung' ZEuS 22 (2019), 61, 88.

[25] See among many others, Bojan Bugaric, 'The Populist Backlash against Europe: Why Only Alternative Economic and Social Policies Can Stop the Rise of Populism in Europe' in Francesca Bignami (ed.), *EU Law in Populist Times. Crises and Prospects* (CUP 2020) 477, 493 and Werner Schroeder, 'An Active EU Rule of Law Policy' in Allan Rosas, Juha Raitio, and Pekka Pohjankoski (eds), *The Rule of Law's Anatomy in the EU* (Hart 2023).

[26] See e.g. Kim L. Scheppele, 'Autocratic Legalism' *University of Chicago Law Review* 85 (2018), 545.

[27] Mark Dawson, 'How Can EU Law Respond to Populism?' OJIL 40 (2020), 183, 210.

would not only damage the façade of legality but also lead to a new stage of escalation. The EU essentially depends on the domestic implementation of EU law as interpreted by the Court. For that reason, a Member State's non-compliance with CJEU judgments is extremely rare[28] and entails also costly consequences, not only under Article 260 TFEU but now also under Article 279 TFEU.

Indeed, the Court has stepped up the pressure on non-compliant Member States by developing interim orders under Article 279 TFEU into an instrument with actual bite. In what can be considered an audacious step, the CJEU developed a two-stage procedure. In a first step, the Commission can request interim measures under Article 279 TFEU. If the respective Member State does not comply with the interim order, the Court can—and here lies the novelty—order daily penalty payments.[29] The full potential of such penalty payments was revealed in the Commission's fourth infringement procedure against Poland. After announcing a daily penalty payment of 100.000 Euro against Poland in the *Białowieża forest* case and ordering one of 500.000 Euro in the *Turów mine* case,[30] the Court broke its record by imposing a daily penalty payment of 1.000.000 Euro until the Polish government complies with its interim order.[31] In conclusion, the Court seems to have provided the instruments at its disposal with actual bite.

At first sight, however, one might argue that hefty penalty payments are well intended but eventually useless if Poland refuses to pay. Such doubts are hardly convincing. Indeed, it is well-established that the Commission can off-set and thus deduct the respective amount from payments due to Poland.[32] While offsetting was a controversial issue for some time,[33] this possibility is now codified. Under the Financial Regulation, EU institutions are authorized to recover amounts receivable from debtors through offsetting.[34] With regard to lump sums and penalty payments ordered by the Court of Justice, this has been put in practice by a

[28] If this is any indication, the Court delivered no judgment under Art. 260(2) TFEU in 2021, see European Commission, Monitoring the application of European Union law, 2021 Annual Report, General Statistical Overview, SWD(2022) 194 final, p 30.

[29] Case C-441/17 R *Commission v Poland (Białowieża Forest)* [Order of 20 November 2017] EU:C:2017:877, paras 97–108. For critical assessments, see Pål Wennerås, 'Saving a Forest and the Rule of Law: *Commission v Poland*' CML Rev 56 (2019), 541, 545–8; Laurent Coutron, 'La Cour de justice au secours de la forêt de Białowieska' RTDE 54 (2018), 321, 326; Luca Prete, 'Infringement Procedures and Sanctions under Article 260 TFEU' in Stefano Montaldo et al. (eds), *EU Law Enforcement* (Routledge 2021) 71, 83.

[30] Case C-121/21 R *Czech Republic v Poland (Turów Mine)* [Order of 20 September 2021] EU:C:2021:752.

[31] Case C-204/21 *Commission v Poland* [Order of 27 October 2021] EU:C:2021:878.

[32] In detail, see Pekka Pohjankoski, 'Rule of Law with Leverage: Policing Structural Obligations in EU Law with the Infringement Procedure, Fines, and Set-Off' CML Rev 58 (2021), 1341, 1358 ff.

[33] On this discussion, see Giuseppe Tesauro, 'La sanction des infractions au droit communautaire' *Rivista di diritto europeo* (1992), 477, 488; Rolf Wägenbaur, 'Zur Nichtbefolgung von Urteilen des EuGH durch die Mitgliedstaaten' in Ole Due et al. (eds), *Festschrift für Ulrich Everling*, vol 2 (Nomos 1995) 1611, 1621 f.

[34] Arts. 101 and 102 of Regulation 2018/1046 of the European Parliament and of the Council of 18 July 2018 on the financial rules applicable to the general budget of the Union [2018] OJ L193/1.

Commission decision.[35] Its current wording seems to apply equally to daily penalty payments ordered for the non-compliance with interim measures under Article 279 TFEU.[36]

This leads to the question of whether this financial pressure will have any deterrent effect on Member State governments. Here we are leaving the terrain of legal scholarship and venture into the realm of politics, sociology, and psychology. Some might argue that there is a risk that Member States like Hungary or Poland will use penalty payments to 'purchase' continued non-compliance. Still, unprecedented fines are difficult to communicate to voters—especially if a majority perceives the current CJEU interventions as legitimate. Moreover, the Court of Justice has demonstrated its willingness to elevate the penalty payments with each step of further non-compliance. It should be added that any threats of the affected governments to suspend the national contributions to the EU budget are hardly credible. As Member States like Hungary or Poland are by far the biggest net recipient of the Union's budget,[37] the Commission could easily recover the respective amounts through offsetting.

Admittedly, all this can go terribly wrong. The Court could be dragged into a heated political conflict. This might politicize the proceedings and damage the CJEU's credibility as neutral arbiter.[38] In particular, national governments could try to blame and discredit the Luxembourg judges. In this spirit, the Polish Minister of Justice criticized the CJEU's ruling on the Supreme Court's disciplinary chamber[39] for being a 'political judgment made on the political orders of the European Commission'.[40] Further, the impact of CJEU judgments on the ground presents a rather mixed picture. The Court's stance on judicial independence triggered a wave of preliminary references by Polish courts and several successful infringement procedures (see Chapter 1, III.B). Initially, the Polish government seemed responsive to these decisions. After interim measures were ordered in 2018,[41] it immediately

[35] Art. 29(2) and 31 of Commission Decision of 3 August 2018 on the internal procedure provisions for the recovery of amounts receivable arising from direct management and the recovery of fines, lump sums and penalty payments under the Treaties, C(2018)5119 final. See also Bernd Schima, 'Article 260 TFEU' in Manuel Kellerbauer et al. (eds), *The Treaties and the Charter of Fundamental Rights—A Commentary* (OUP 2019) para 17; Ulrich Karpenstein, 'Art. 260 AEUV' in Eberhard Grabitz et al. (eds), *Das Recht der Europäischen Union* (75th edn, loose-leaf, C.H.Beck 2022) para 76.

[36] On 25 May 2022, the Polish government filed an application against the Commission's decision to offset penalty payments imposed in the *Turów mine* case (interim order in Case C-121/21 R) before the General Court (pending as Case T-314/22).

[37] For an instructive chart, see e.g. Katharina Buchholz, 'Which Countries are EU Contributors and Beneficiaries?' *Statista* (13 January 2020), <www.statista.com/chart/18794/net-contributors-to-eu-budget/>.

[38] See e.g. Blauberger and Kelemen (n 11) 331; Christoph Möllers and Linda Schneider, *Demokratiesicherung in der Europäischen Union* (Mohr Siebeck 2018) 107, 147.

[39] Case C-791/19 *Commission v Poland (Régime disciplinaire des juges)* [2021] EU:C:2021:596.

[40] Press Statement, 'Polityczny wyrok TSUE segreguje państwa Unii Europejskiej' (15 July 2021), <www.gov.pl/web/sprawiedliwosc/polityczny-wyrok-tsue-segreguje-panstwa-unii-europejskiej>. See also 'EU court involved in "coordinated assault" against Hungary, Orbán says' *Politico* (15 May 2020).

[41] See the orders of 19 October and 17 December 2018 in Case C-619/18 *Commission v Poland*.

reversed parts of its reforms that violated judicial independence.[42] More recent developments cast doubts on this responsiveness. While the Polish government indicated its readiness to make concessions in the conflict on the disciplinary regime for judges (only, however, under massive political pressure[43]), it continues to pit the captured Constitutional Tribunal against Luxembourg. It comes as no surprise that the Tribunal followed suit. For one, it declared the CJEU's interim order[44] that suspends the activities of the disciplinary chamber to constitute an ultra-vires act.[45] In a second ruling, the Tribunal went even further by stating, among others, that the CJEU's interpretation of Articles 2 and 19(1)(2) TEU is incompatible with the Polish constitution insofar as it confers on Polish judges the power to review the independence of other courts.[46] As such, it seems that the real acid test is yet to come.[47]

B. Substantively: What Legal Basis?

This leads to the following question: What happens when a case, in which Union values are at stake, reaches the CJEU? A first intuition is to stick to well-established instruments, such as the Charter or provisions relating to the internal market.[48] Unfortunately, this approach can hardly counter upheavals of the Member States' internal constitutional structures. From the outset, these instruments are *too narrow in scope*. Many provisions pertaining to the internal market, such as fundamental freedoms, require a cross-border element. The Charter is an equally limited tool. Pursuant to Article 51(1) CFR, it applies to the Member States only when they act 'within the scope of European Union law'.[49] But even if their scope is triggered, these instruments are *too narrow in substance*. Provisions from the internal market context usually require some sort of economic activity. Further, not all dangers to democracy and the rule of law are depictable as fundamental

[42] See Press Release, President Signs Bill Amending Law on Supreme Court (17 December 2018), <www.president.pl/en/news/art,926,president-signs-bill-amending-law-on-supreme-court.html>.

[43] On the dissolution of the discplinary chamber of the Supreme Court in exchange for releasing funds from the EU recovery plan, see critically Daniel Tilles, 'Poland Closes Judicial Disciplinary Chamber at Heart of Dispute with EU' *Notes from Poland* (15 July 2022).

[44] Case C-791/19 R *Commission v Poland* [Order of 8 April 2020] EU:C:2020:227. This order has been reiterated in Case C-204/21 R *Commission v Poland* [Order of 14 July 2021] EU:C:2021:593.

[45] Trybunał Konstytucyjny, Judgment of 14 July 2021, P 7/20.

[46] Trybunał Konstytucyjny, Judgment of 7 October 2021, K 3/21.

[47] The Polish government brought a further case regarding the constitutionality of penalty payments imposed by the Court of Justice for non-compliance with its interim orders, see K 8/21.

[48] On this 'get Al Capone on tax evasion strategy', see Blauberger and Kelemen (n 11) 325 f. In detail Mark Dawson and Elise Muir, 'Hungary and the Indirect Protection of EU Fundamental Rights and the Rule of Law' GLJ 14 (2013), 1959.

[49] Case C-617/10 *Åkerberg Fransson* [2013] EU:C:2013:105, paras 18 f. For a systematization of the case law, see Sara Iglesias Sánchez, 'Article 51: The Scope of Application of the Charter' in Michal Bobek and Jeremias Adams-Prassl (eds), *The EU Charter of Fundamental Rights in the Member States* (Hart 2020) 401; Sacha Gourdet, *Europäischer Grundrechtsschutz* (Nomos 2021) 149 ff.

rights violations.[50] And even if the respective developments in the Member States were covered, these provisions are *too narrow in impact*. Indeed, experience shows that this strategy leads to rather limited results.[51] Though contributing to defuse the conflict, it conveys an image of business-as-usual and risks marginalizing the erosion of European values. Nevertheless, the Commission continued on this path and situated the infringement proceedings against the Hungarian foreign-NGO and higher-education laws firmly in the internal market context.[52]

Compared to these instruments, relying on Article 2 TEU presents several advantages. It features an unrestricted scope of application and captures developments threatening fundamental rights, democracy, or the rule of law in their entirety. Yet, the value semantics, its indeterminacy, and the CJEU's contested jurisdiction placed a question mark on the justiciability of Article 2 TEU (Chapter 2). For some time, engaging directly with Article 2 TEU might thus have seemed excluded. Under this impression, legal doctrine developed strategies for remedying violations of EU values—even if they seemed to escape the scope of EU law. The most sophisticated construction is probably the *Reverse Solange* doctrine.

It departs from the CJEU's decision in *Ruiz Zambrano*. In this case, the Court held that Article 20 TFEU precludes national measures that deprive Union citizens of the 'substance of the rights conferred by virtue of their status as citizens of the Union'.[53] Accordingly, a Union citizen can challenge any Member State act before national courts on the ground that the substance of its Union citizenship is violated—even in purely internal situations.[54] A team headed by Armin von Bogdandy suggested interpreting this substance as comprising the essence of EU fundamental rights protected under Article 2 TEU.[55] This proposal was then articulated in the form of a *Reverse Solange* doctrine: beyond the scope of Article 51(1) CFR, Member States remain autonomous so long as they secure the essence of EU fundamental rights protected under Article 2 TEU.

[50] On the lacking equivalence of Charter rights and the values of Art. 2 TEU, see Fundamental Rights Agency, *Fundamental rights: challenges and achievements in 2013* (EUR-OP 2014) 10. See also Dimitry Kochenov and John Morijn, 'Le rôle de la Charte dans la lutte pour l'État de droit au sein de l'Union européenne' Anastasia Iliopoulou-Penot and Lamprini Xenou (eds), *La Charte des droits fondamentaux, source de renouveau constitutionnel européen?* (Bruylant 2020) 173, 184.

[51] On the limited impact of infringement proceedings based on Directive 2000/78 against Hungary for lowering the retirement ages of judges, see Gábor Halmai, 'The Case of the Retirement Age of Hungarian Judges' in Fernanda Nicola and Bill Davies (eds), *EU Law Stories* (CUP 2017) 471, 482 f.

[52] Case C-78/18 *Commission v Hungary (Transparency of associations)* [2020] EU:C:2020:476; Case C-66/18 *Commission v Hungary (Enseignement supérieur)* [2020] EU:C:2020:792. For a critique, see Luke D. Spieker, 'Werteverteidigung im Binnenmarkt?' EuZW 31 (2020), 854, 856.

[53] Case C-34/09 *Ruiz Zambrano* [2011] EU:C:2011:124, para 42.

[54] See e.g. Koen Lenaerts, '"Civis europaeus sum"' in Pascal Cardonnel et al. (eds), *Constitutionalising the EU Judicial System* (Hart 2012) 213.

[55] See von Bogdandy et al., 'Reverse Solange' CML Rev 49 (2012), 489, 508.

Besides (largely anticipated) doctrinal critique,[56] the proposal reveals two major shortcomings. First, the doctrine does not reflect the current jurisprudential outlook anymore. In the early 2000s, there was a trend towards strengthening the normative status of Union citizenship. Since 2012, however, the jurisprudential landscape has radically changed. In an almost reactionary phase,[57] the Court began to construe the substance of citizens' rights[58] and their right to equal treatment in increasingly restrictive terms.[59] Thus, the *Zambrano* detour, the doctrine's essential twist for addressing purely internal situations, seems barred.[60] Second, linking citizenship and fundamental rights seems conceptually problematic. Citizenship is an exclusionary concept that sits uneasily with the universal character of human rights.[61] For that reason, fundamental rights have been progressively decoupled from the status of citizenship and extended to foreigners in many jurisdictions.[62] It would seem counterintuitive to seek a different development in the EU context.

III. The Potential of Article 2 TEU

This chapter argues that *Reverse Solange*'s central aim can be better achieved by following a different path: operationalizing Article 2 TEU itself. Besides the unrestricted scope of its application, Article 2 TEU presents two features that qualify it especially for countering illiberal developments in the Member States. First, unlike *Reverse Solange*, it captures developments threatening the rule of law, democracy, or fundamental rights in their entirety. Second, a justiciable Article 2 TEU could be invoked not merely by Union citizens before national courts but in virtually any judicial proceeding.

[56] See prominently Koen Lenaerts and José A. Gutiérrez-Fons, 'Epilogue on EU Citizenship: Hopes and Fears?' in Dimitry Kochenov (ed.), *EU Citizenship and Federalism* (CUP 2017) 751, 771 ff. But see von Bogdandy et al. (n 55) 514 ff.

[57] Eleanor Spaventa, 'Earned Citizenship' in Kochenov (n 56) 204. See also Adrienne Yong, *The Rise and Decline of Fundamental Rights in EU Citizenship* (Hart 2019) 113 ff, 143 ff.

[58] See e.g. Case C-434/09 *McCarthy* [2011] EU:C:2011:277; Case C-82/16 *K.A. and Others (Family reunification in Belgium)* [2018] EU:C:2018:308, paras 63 ff; Case C-836/18 *Subdelegación del Gobierno en Ciudad Real (Spouse of a Union citizen)* [2020] EU:C:2020:119, paras 56 ff. See also Martijn van den Brink, 'Is It Time to Abolish the Substance of EU Citizenship Rights Test?' *European Journal of Migration and Law* 23 (2021), 13. For its potential, however, see Delia Ferri and Giuseppe Martinico, 'Revisiting the Ruiz Zambrano Doctrine and Exploring the Potential for Its Extensive Application' EPL 27 (2021), 685.

[59] See e.g. Case C-333/13 *Dano* [2014] EU:C:2014:2358; Case C-67/14 *Alimanovic* [2015] EU:C:2015:597; Case C-308/14 *Commission v United Kingdom* [2016] EU:C:2016:436. See also Charlotte O'Brien, 'Civis Capitalist Sum' CML Rev 53 (2016), 937.

[60] For a 'repositioned' version, see Armin von Bogdandy and Luke D. Spieker, 'Protecting Fundamental Rights Beyond the Charter. Repositioning the *Reverse Solange* Doctrine in Light of the CJEU's Article 2 TEU Case Law' in Bobek and Adams-Prassl (n 49) 525, 532.

[61] Samantha Besson and André Utzinger, 'Towards European Citizenship' *Journal of Social Philosophy* 39 (2008), 185, 190.

[62] In detail Martijn van den Brink, 'EU Citizenship and (Fundamental) Rights' ELJ 25 (2019), 21, 28.

Against this backdrop, it is surprising how little Article 2 TEU has been invoked as a self-standing ground before the Court.[63] Recent developments seem to indicate a shift in this respect. In particular, the Commission has started to rethink its approach to infringement proceedings. As noted previously, 'value-related infringement proceedings' against Hungary were largely anchored in the internal market context.[64] The recent procedures concerning the Hungarian and Polish violations of LGBTIQ rights finally call a spade a spade. The Commission based its case not only on specific provisions of EU law (e.g. fundamental freedoms, Charter rights, Audiovisual Media Services Directive): 'Because of the gravity of these violations, the contested provisions also violate the values laid down in Article 2 TEU'.[65]

As demonstrated in Chapter 2, it is possible to construe the judicial applicability of Article 2 TEU. Despite the misleading value semantics, its indeterminacy, and the CJEU's contested jurisdiction, relying on Article 2 TEU in procedures before the Court is legally possible. This applies even in situations beyond the scope of other EU law. Yet, developing Article 2 TEU into a freestanding provision would be controversial and provide the Court with a large discretion to flesh out the highly indeterminate values (on this, see Chapter 12). For now, the CJEU seems to follow a more cautious approach. In a seminal line of cases beginning with *ASJP*, the Court started to review the Member States' constitutional structures for their compliance with EU values. Instead of relying on Article 2 TEU alone, the Court resorted to specific Treaty provisions that give concrete expression to these values.

At first glance, however, this strategy seems to curtail Article 2 TEU's unrestricted scope. To provide a hypothetical example: if the value of democracy was operationalized by the freedom of expression protected in Article 11 CFR, its reach would be limited to the scope of the Charter under Article 51(1) CFR. This would reduce the full potential of Article 2 TEU as a standard for the entire Verbund of EU and Member States. This section argues that the case law suggests otherwise. In *ASJP*, the Court seems to have found a way to operationalize Article 2 TEU without curtailing its unrestricted scope. In this sense, it killed two birds with one stone. The following sections will outline the CJEU's approach (Section A) before exploring how it could be extended beyond the specific case (Section B).

[63] But see the (inadmissible) references in Case C-647/18 *Corporate Commercial Bank* [Order of 15 January 2020] EU:C:2020:13, para 43; Case C-505/13 *Yumer* [Order of 17 July 2014] EU:C:2014:2129, paras 21 ff. See also Case F-29/11 *BA v Commission* [2012] EU:F:2012:172, para 89.

[64] See the account prepared by the Commission for the Council, 'Values of the Union—Hungary—Article 7 (1)' 2018/0902 (COD).

[65] European Commission, EU founding values: Commission starts legal action against Hungary and Poland for violations of fundamental rights of LGBTIQ people (15 July 2021), IP/21/3668. The case against Hungary is currently pending before the Court of Justice (Case C-123/22).

A. *ASJP* or How to Kill Two Birds with One Stone

As demonstrated in Chapter 1, *ASJP* constitutes the central breakthrough for the Court's mobilization of Article 2 TEU. Briefly, the decision concerned salary reductions for Portuguese judges adopted in the context of an EU financial assistance programme. The referring court asked whether these cuts violated judicial independence. In this context, the CJEU resorted to Article 19(1)(2) TEU, which stipulates that 'Member States shall provide remedies sufficient to ensure effective legal protection in the fields covered by Union law'. According to the Court, this entails an obligation to guarantee judicial independence,[66] which applies 'irrespective of whether the Member States are implementing Union law, within the meaning of Article 51(1) of the Charter'.[67] Instead, they must ensure the independence of any court that '*may* rule ... on questions concerning the application or interpretation of EU law'.[68] Considering the breadth of Union law today, this includes de facto the entire Member State judiciary.[69]

Two rationales justify this extremely broad scope. On the one hand, the Court refers to the functioning of the EU judicial system.[70] National courts as first 'Union courts' are an inherent part of the EU judicial system. That system cannot function if national courts are not independent. Concerning their independence, there is no way to distinguish between a national court's 'European' and 'domestic' function. Judges are not Janus-faced creatures that can split in half. Either they are independent, or they are not. Hence, the Member State judiciary must comply in its entirety with EU standards of judicial independence (in detail Chapter 1, III.A).

On the other hand, the Court provides a justification based on Article 2 TEU. In the crucial passage, it emphasized that Article 19(1)(2) TEU 'gives concrete expression to the value of the rule of law stated in Article 2'.[71] As argued previously, this statement lays the groundworks for the judicial applicability of Article 2 TEU (see Chapter 2, III.A). The Court operationalizes Article 2 TEU through a more specific Treaty provision. At first glance, however, this construction seems to limit Article 2 TEU's full potential. In particular, Article 2 TEU would be limited to the scope of its operationalizing provision (here, Article 19(1)(2) TEU: 'the fields covered by Union law'). Yet, the case law suggests otherwise. In *ASJP*, the Court established

[66] *Associação Sindical dos Juízes Portugueses* (n 24) para 36.

[67] ibid para 29.

[68] ibid para 40 (emphasis added).

[69] Thus, some argue that *ASJP* established a 'quasi federal standard', see Laurent Pech and Sébastien Platon, 'Judicial Independence under Threat' CML Rev 55 (2018), 1827, 1847; Stanislas Adam and Peter Van Elsuwege, 'L'exigence d'independance du juge, paradigme de l'Union européenne comme union de droit' JDE (2018) 334, 341. On the provision's broad scope, see also Koen Lenaerts, 'Upholding the Rule of Law through Judicial Dialogue' YEL 38 (2019), 3, 5; Thomas von Danwitz, 'Values and the Rule of Law' RDUE (4) (2018), 263, 269; Egils Levits, 'Die Europäische Union als Wertegemeinschaft' in Thomas Jaeger (ed.), *Europa 4.0* (Sramek 2018) 239, 268.

[70] *Associação Sindical dos Juízes Portugueses* (n 24) paras 32–4, 43.

[71] ibid para 32.

standards not only for those courts that actually operate in the 'fields covered by Union law' but for the entire Member State judiciary.

This chapter argues that the operationalization of Article 2 TEU is no one-way street. Article 19(1)(2) TEU translates Article 2 TEU into a specific legal obligation. At the same time, Article 2 TEU has an impact on Article 19(1)(2) TEU as well. In particular, interpreting that provision in light of Article 2 TEU justifies an extensive reading of its scope that reaches beyond the 'fields covered by Union law'. In this sense, both provisions reinforce each other. Their interplay leads to a *mutual amplification*.[72] In very similar terms, Judge Rossi noted that it is especially the anchoring in Article 2 TEU that has given Article 19(1)(2) TEU a reach that would have been difficult to imagine before *ASJP*: 'Il s'agit donc d'une "concretisation" au moins réciproque.'[73] In consequence, the idea of mutual amplification kills two birds with one stone. It allows for the judicial applicability of Article 2 TEU through a specific Treaty provision without curtailing its unrestricted scope of application. As will be discussed below, this approach could be extended to any provision giving specific expression to a value enshrined in Article 2 TEU.

Such a reading of *ASJP* leads to a considerable development of the law. Even if it is uncontroversial that EU law requires a creative judicial development,[74] this does not mean that anything goes. According to the BVerfG, such a development can only be accepted if it preserves the order of competences between the EU and its Member States (in detail Chapter 13) and if the Court applies 'recognised methodological principles'.[75] Even without the suggested twist, some perceive the Court's recent jurisprudence as having a 'dubious legal grounding'.[76] While certainly creative, there are two ways to anchor the idea of mutual amplification in established methods of legal reasoning.

To start with, the suggested approach can be construed as two interlocking systematic interpretations. First, the Court performs a systematic interpretation of Article 2 TEU *in light of a more specific Treaty provision*. This is aimed at rendering

[72] See Spieker (n 50) 1204 ff; Spieker and Armin von Bogdandy, 'Countering the Judicial Silencing of Critics: Article 2 TEU Values, *Reverse Solange*, and the Responsibilities of National Judges' EuConst 15 (2019), 391, 413 ff.

[73] Lucia S. Rossi, 'La valeur juridique des valeurs. L'article 2 TUE' RTDE (2020), 639, 650.

[74] See already BVerfG, Judgment of 8 April 1987, 2 BvR 687/85, *Kloppenburg*, paras 58–60. See also Robert Lecourt, *L'Europe des Juges* (Bruylant 1976, repr. 2008) 236; Ulrich Everling, 'Richterliche Rechtsfortbildung in der Europäischen Gemeinschaft' JZ 55 (2000), 217; Koen Lenaerts and Kathleen Gutman, '"Federal Common Law" in the European Union' AJCL 54 (2006), 1, 7.

[75] BVerfG, Judgment of 5 May 2020, 2 BvR 859/15, *PSPP*, para 112. See also BVerfG, Judgment of 21 June 2016, 2 BvE 13/13, *OMT*, para 161; Order of 6 July 2010, 2 BvR 2661/06, *Honeywell*, paras 62, 64.

[76] Dawson (n 27) 211. See also Richard Bellamy, Sandra Kröger, and Marta Lorimer, *Flexible Europe* (Bristol Univ. Press 2022) 79 ('weakly based judicial rulings'); Peter M. Huber, 'Art. 2 EUV als Grundlage des Staaten- und Verfassungsverbundes der EU' *Alkotmánybírósági Szemle* (2020), 20, 21 ('technokratischer Trick'); Angelika Nußberger, 'Gefahr für das europäische Erbe' *Internationale Politik Special* (4) (2022), 4, 8 ('begründbar, aber gewagt').

these indeterminate values more specific.[77] The Court then complements this first step with a systematic interpretation of the specific provision *in light of Article 2 TEU*. As noted above, the operationalization of EU values is no one-way street. Article 2 TEU exerts an impact on the specific provision too. As established in the previous part (in detail Chapter 5, III.B), EU primary law must be interpreted in light of and in conformity with the founding values enshrined in Article 2 TEU.[78] Conversely, this implies that EU primary law must not limit the impact and reach of Article 2 TEU. Provisions that give specific expression to these values are no exception in this regard.

Abstractly, there are two ways to preserve the full effectiveness of Article 2 TEU. With regard to Article 19(1)(2) TEU, the Court could interpret 'the fields covered by Union law' either extensively (as applying to all fields covered by Article 2 TEU) or narrowly (as not precluding the provision's application as far as Article 2 TEU is concerned). Methodologically, this approach oscillates between a teleological extension (of its scope) and a teleological reduction (of its restriction in scope).[79] In both variants, this method concerns provisions that require an extension/restriction against their literal meaning but in accordance with the law's telos. In this case, we are dealing with an overarching teleology detached from the interpreted provision—the preservation of the common values enshrined in Article 2 TEU.[80]

The second way to justify the Court's approach concerns only those provisions that feature an accessory scope of application, such as Article 19(1)(2) TEU (or the Charter for that matter). Article 19(1)(2) TEU applies to the 'fields covered by Union law'. Like the Charter, some kind of Union law must trigger its scope.[81] Article 2 TEU is part of 'Union law'. By implication, Member State violations that reach the demanding thresholds of Article 2 TEU could trigger these 'fields' and lead to an application of Article 19(1)(2) TEU even beyond the scope of other EU law. Ultimately, this is very close to what András Jakab proposed with regard to the Charter.[82] He suggested that Article 2 TEU could trigger the Charter's scope under Article 51(1) CFR and render EU fundamental rights generally applicable in the Member States. Still, Article 2 TEU has not been applied as a self-standing

[77] On such a concretization as methodologically sound endeavour, see Thomas Möllers, *Legal Methods* (Hart 2020) 259 ff; Sebastian A. E. Martens, *Methodenlehre des Unionsrechts* (Mohr Siebeck 2013) 515 ff.

[78] See also Michael Potacs, 'Wertkonforme Auslegung des Unionsrechts' EuR 51 (2016), 164, 167.

[79] On these methods, Möllers (n 77) 234 ff.

[80] On such a 'teleosystemic' interpretation in light of EU objectives, see already Chapter 5, n 51.

[81] On such 'triggering rules' in the context of Art. 51(1) CFR, see Daniel Sarmiento, 'Who's Afraid of the Charter?' CML Rev 50 (2013), 1267, 1279. But see on Art. 19(1)(2) TEU rather as self-standing provision, Pech and Platon (n 69) 1838, 1848; Pál Sonnevend, 'The Responsibility of Courts in Maintaining the Rule of Law' in von Bogdandy et al. (eds), *Defending Checks and Balances in EU Member States* (Springer 2021) 155, 166.

[82] András Jakab and Lando Kirchmair, 'Two Ways of Completing the European Fundamental Rights Union: Amendment to vs. Reinterpretation of Article 51 of the EU Charter of Fundamental Rights' CYELS (2022), 1; Jakab, 'Application of the Charter of Fundamental Rights by National Courts in Purely Domestic Cases' in Jakab and Kochenov (n 4) 252, 255.

provision and requires further concretization. This casts doubt over its capability to serve as a triggering rule. For instance, the Charter's scope under Article 51(1) CFR is triggered in case EU law imposes a '*specific* obligation' on the Member States.[83] Article 2 TEU lacks exactly that specificity. Against this backdrop, neither Article 2 TEU (due to its indeterminacy) nor the specific provision (due to its limited scope) would be applicable beyond the scope of other EU law. The only solution is to read them together.

In fact, such an interaction is not unprecedented in the CJEU's case law. An apt example is the interplay of directives and Charter rights in horizontal situations. If individuals seek to challenge a national provision in judicial proceedings against another private party on the basis of relevant EU directives and Charter rights, they face a twofold problem. Directives do not apply horizontally.[84] EU fundamental rights apply horizontally.[85] Yet, they apply only in case the Charter's scope is triggered by other EU Law (e.g., by a directive). Thus, taken in isolation, neither of them is applicable. The Court, however, found a creative solution. The directive, though not directly applicable, has 'the effect of bringing within the scope of European Union law the national legislation at issue'.[86] Once its scope is triggered, the Charter right applies horizontally in the case at hand. In this sense, Article 2 TEU could have the effect of 'bringing within the scope of European Union law' violations of democracy, the rule of law, or respect for human rights in the Member States.

B. Beyond *ASJP*: Operationalizing the Values of 'Human Rights' and 'Democracy'

In sum, *ASJP* could be interpreted as laying the groundworks not only for the judicial applicability of Article 2 TEU but also for its protection beyond the scope of other EU law. These doctrinal innovations concerned primarily the Polish overhaul of the judiciary. While the situation in Hungary seems even more entrenched, the Court has approached these developments much more hesitantly. Many argue that Hungary has ceased to be a fully-fledged democracy.[87] The OSCE mission, for instance, noted that the 2022 election campaign was marked by an 'an absence

[83] Case C-609/17 *TSN* [2019] EU:C:2019:981, para 53; Case C-152/17 *Consorzio Italian Management* [2018] EU:C:2018:264, para 34; Case C-198/13 *Hernández* [2014] EU:C:2014:2055, paras 34 f.

[84] See e.g. Case C-122/17 *Smith* [2018] EU:C:2018:631, paras 42–4.

[85] See e.g. Case C-684/16 *Max-Planck-Gesellschaft* [2018] EU:C:2018:874, paras 75–9; Case C-569/16 *Bauer* [2018] EU:C:2018:871, para 79–90; Case C-414/16 *Egenberger* [2018] EU:C:2018:257, para 76.

[86] Case C-555/07 *Kücükdeveci* [2010] EU:C:2010:21, para 25. See also *Max-Planck-Gesellschaft* (n 85) para 50; *Bauer* (n 85) para 53.

[87] Listing Hungary and Poland under the top-5 'autocratizing countries' and Hungary even as 'electoral autocracy', see V-Dem Institute, Democracy Report 2022, pp 33, 45. See also Freedom House, Nations in Transit 2022.

of a level playing field' as media bias and campaign financing regulations constricted genuine political debate.[88] At the same time, the space for civil society is shrinking. In response, the Commission brought various value-related infringement proceedings against Hungary. These concerned not only measures such as the Hungarian transparency requirements for foreign funded NGOs, but also the oppression of academic freedom. Unlike its decisions concerning the Polish judiciary, both the Commission and the Court refrained from mobilizing the Union's values in these cases.

The judgment concerning foreign-funded NGOs illustrates this point. In 2020, the Commission brought an action against a Hungarian statute that imposed duties of registration, reporting, and disclosure on civil society organizations which receive funding from abroad.[89] The Court addressed the Hungarian measures mainly as a violation of the free movement of capital under Article 63 TFEU, not under Article 2 TEU. As such, the case was settled on the uncontested ground of the internal market.[90] Admittedly, the Court also relied on EU fundamental rights by stressing that 'the right to freedom of association constitutes one of the essential bases of a democratic and pluralist society'.[91] In this sense, the judgment constitutes an improvement when compared to the first timid cases on the overhaul of the Hungarian judiciary.[92] Still, fundamental rights remain a rather meek accessory to the internal market. For sure, abstaining from the highly politicized value rhetoric can contribute to de-escalating the conflict. As previously noted, however, it marginalizes the erosion of European values (see Section II.B).

To safeguard democratic processes in Hungary, the Commission and the CJEU should take bolder steps towards the judicial activation of Article 2 TEU. The ongoing attacks on the freedom of press and media pluralism could become a springboard for such a reinforced approach.[93] In June 2021 the Commission

[88] OSCE, Hungary, Parliamentary Elections and Referendum, 3 April 2022: Statement of Preliminary Findings and Conclusions. See already OSCE, Hungary, Parliamentary Elections, 8 April 2018: Statement of Preliminary Findings and Conclusions; European Parliament, Resolution on a proposal calling on the Council to determine, pursuant to Article 7(1) of the Treaty on European Union, the existence of a clear risk of a serious breach by Hungary of the values on which the Union is founded (12 September 2018), 2017/2131(INL), Rec. 10.

[89] *Commission v Hungary (Transparency of associations)* (n 52).

[90] On this approach, see n 48. A very similar strategy can be observed in the CEU case, see Case C-66/18 *Commission v Hungary (Enseignement supérieur)* [2020] EU:C:2020:792. In detail, Vasiliki Kosta and Darinka Piqani, 'Where trade and academic freedom meet: Commission v Hungary (LEX CEU)' CML Rev 59 (2022), 813.

[91] *Commission v Hungary (Transparency of associations)* (n 52) para 112.

[92] As promising decision, see Matteo Bonelli, 'European Commission v Hungary (Transparency of associations) (C-78/18): the "NGOs case": on how to use the EU Charter of Fundamental Rights in infringement actions' EL Rev 46 (2021), 258, 268; John Morijn, 'Separate Charter invocation as a new enforcement method: The Lex NGO case' CML Rev 59 (2022), 1137.

[93] European Parliament, Resolution of 12 September 2018 on a proposal calling on the Council to determine, pursuant to Article 7(1) of the Treaty on European Union, the existence of a clear risk of a serious breach by Hungary of the values on which the Union is founded (2017/2131(INL)), Annex, paras 27–32; Venice Commission, Opinion of Media Legislation of Hungary, No. 798/2015.

announced an infringement procedure against Hungary for rejecting an application by Klubrádió—Hungary's last outspoken opposition channel—to use the national radio spectrum.[94] Regrettably, the Commission only relied on the European Electronic Communications Code (Directive 2018/1972), even though such an action could have equally been based on the essence of media freedom protected by Article 11(2) CFR, which gives specific expression to the value of 'human rights' in Article 2 TEU.

Generally, the approach developed in *ASJP* could be extended to other provisions that give expression to the values in Article 2 TEU. This concerns especially the Charter of Fundamental Rights. In fact, Charter rights give expression to the values of human dignity (Title I), freedom (Title II), equality (Title III), democracy (Articles 10 to 12 and Title V), and the rule of law (Title VI).[95] In this sense, the Court has already started to connect Article 2 TEU and Charter rights. In *Patriciello* and *Tele2 Sverige*, it established a continuum between the freedom of expression under Article 11 CFR and the value of democracy.[96] This was reemphasized in *La Quadrature du Net*, *Privacy International*, and *Commissioner of An Garda Síochána* where the Court stressed that 'freedom of expression … is one of the values on which, under Article 2 TEU, the Union is founded'.[97]

In taking this nexus a step further, the Court could start reviewing violations of the essence of Charter rights even *beyond the scope of other EU law*. As seen above, this could be achieved either by interpreting Article 51(1) CFR in light of Article 2 TEU or by conceiving the latter as a triggering rule for the Charter's scope. It should be stressed, though, that this cannot lead to an application of the full fundamental rights acquis beyond the confines of Article 51(1) CFR. Article 2 TEU comprises only a qualified part, namely the essence of fundamental rights (in detail, Chapters 4, IV and 13, III.A). Beyond the Charter's scope, EU fundamental rights could apply only as far as their essence, protected under Article 2 TEU, is concerned.[98]

Yet, fundamental rights do not address all threats to democracy in Hungary. The curtailing of opposition rights, unfair electoral laws, gerrymandering, party financing and campaigning rules largely escape the Charter's scope. Still, such practices might violate the value of democracy, which can be operationalized under the suggested scheme. With regard to the composition of the European Parliament,

[94] On the status quo, see European Commission, Media freedom: The Commission calls on Hungary to comply with EU electronic communications rules (2 December 2021).

[95] Case C-156/21 *Hungary v Parliament and Council* [2022] EU:C:2022:97, paras 157 f.

[96] Case C-163/10 *Patriciello* [2011] EU:C:2011:543, para 31; Cases C-203 and 698/15 *Tele2 Sverige* [2016] EU:C:2016:970, para 93.

[97] See Cases C-511, 512 and 520/18 *La Quadrature du Net* [2020] EU:C:2020:791, para 114; Case C-623/17 *Privacy International* [2020] EU:C:2020:790, para 62; Case C-140/20 *Commissioner of An Garda Síochána* [2022] EU:C:2022:258, para 43. For a somewhat looser connection, see Case C-507/18 *Associazione Avvocatura per i diritti LGBTI* [2020] EU:C:2020:289, para 48.

[98] See also von Bogdandy and Spieker (n 60) 531 f.

the Court noted that the principle of representative democracy in Article 10(1) TEU 'gives concrete form to the value of democracy referred to in Article 2 TEU'.[99] Though Article 10 TEU seems to primarily concern democracy at the EU level, the latter cannot function if democratic decision-making in the Member States falters.[100] As outlined in Chapter 8, democracy at the EU and the national level are essentially intertwined. Elections to the European Parliament are partially governed by national provisions and take place within each domestic public sphere.[101] At the same time, the Member State governments represented in the Council derive their legitimacy from the national level. Article 10(2) TEU specifies that they must be 'democratically accountable either to their national Parliaments, or to their citizens'.[102] In consequence, the democratic legitimacy at the EU level depends to a great extent on the situation in each Member State.

This logic mirrors the one underpinning Article 19(1)(2) TEU, which integrates the national judiciaries into the EU system of judicial protection. As noted above, it is impossible to separate the 'European' and 'domestic' functions of national courts. Thus, the obligations derived from Article 19(1)(2) TEU in combination with Article 2 TEU apply to the Member State judiciary even in cases not related to EU law. In a very similar way, national democracy is tied into the European one. It is impossible to distinguish between the 'European' and 'national' facets of democracy in the Member States. A government cannot be 'democratically accountable' at the European level if it governs autocratically at home.

Based on these insights, a combined reading of Article 10 and 2 TEU can result in imposing essential democratic requirements on the Member States.[103] This would not be confined to the 'European' dimensions of democracy in the Member States (e.g. the elections to the European Parliament), but would apply to the domestic state of democracy. For instance, the Court could review, under Articles 10(1) and (2) TEU in combination with Article 2 TEU, issues such as the curtailing of opposition rights, unfair electoral laws, gerrymandering, party financing and

[99] Case C-502/19 *Junqueras Vies* [2019] EU:C:2019:1115, para 63. See also See also Case C-629/21 P(R) *Puigdemont i Casamajó and Others v Parliament and Spain* [Order of 24 May 2022] EU:C:2022:413, para 250; Case C-207/21 P, *Commission v Poland (Protocole n° 36)* [2022] EU:C:2022:560, para 81; Case C-418/18 P *Puppinck and Others v Commission* [2019] EU:C:2019:1113, para 64.

[100] On the EU's structure of dual legitimacy, see Armin von Bogdandy, *The Emergence and Democratization of European Society* (OUP 2023).

[101] Art. 8 of the Act concerning the election of the representatives of the Assembly by direct universal suffrage. See also *Junqueras Vies* (n 99) para 69.

[102] On this 'remarkable' interference in the Member States' constitutional autonomy, see Martin Nettesheim, 'Art. 10 EUV' in Grabitz (n 35) para 74.

[103] See John Cotter, 'To Everything There is a Season: Instrumentalising Article 10 TEU to Exclude Undemocratic Member State Representatives from the European Council and the Council' EL Rev 46 (2021), 69, 77 ff. For first tentative sketches David Krappitz and Niels Kirst, 'An Infringement of Democracy in the EU Legal Order' *EU Law Live* (29 May 2020); Thomas Verellen, 'Hungary's Lesson for Europe: Democracy is Part of Europe's Constitutional Identity. It Should be Justiciable' *Verfassungsblog* (8 April 2022).

campaigning rules, or the abuse of public media.[104] States of emergency of unlimited duration could equally be challenged.[105]

Eventually, democratic standards can be invoked even by individuals against national measures. Article 10(3) TEU stipulates the citizens' 'right to participate in the democratic life of the Union'. Many understand this as establishing an individual right to democratic participation.[106] As such, Article 10(3) TEU fulfils even the most demanding conception of direct effect, which requires a provision to contain a right that can be invoked by an individual before courts (see Chapter 2, III). Such a right would not only concern democratic standards at the EU but also at the national level. As previously explained, the democratic life *of the Union* presupposes a democratic life *in the Member States*. Therefore, Article 10(3) TEU could become a provision that translates the value of democracy into obligations justiciable by individuals. Since *Van Gend en Loos*, 'the vigilance of the individuals concerned to protect their rights' has been a central instrument in assuring that the Member States observe EU law.[107] Hence, this proposal follows a well-trodden path of European integration.

Admittedly, reviewing the Member States' internal constitutional structures for their compliance with Article 2 TEU will not only strengthen the constitutional homogeneity in the Verbund but also lead to a considerable shift in power. This is especially the case if the enforcement takes place beyond the scope of other EU law. Even if methodologically sound, the creative reading of *ASJP* suggested in this chapter bears the potential of severely disrupting the federal balance between the EU and its Member States. These concerns will be assessed and mitigated in Chapter 13. To preserve the federal balance, that chapter will develop strategies of judicial restraint that could be applied when the Court sets out to enforce Article 2 TEU values in the Member States.

[104] On these practices, see only Kim L. Scheppele, 'How Viktor Orbán Wins' *Journal of Democracy* 33 (2022), 45, 50 ff.

[105] See e.g. the country chapters on Hungary in the Commission's Rule of Law Report from 2021 (SWD(2021) 714 final, pp 20 f) and 2022 (SWD(2022) 517 final, p 25).

[106] See in particular Matthias Ruffert, 'Art. 10 EUV' in Ruffert and Christian Calliess (eds), *EU-Vertrag* (C.H.Beck 2022) para 12; Marcel Haag, 'Art. 10 EUV' in Hans von der Groeben et al. (eds), *Europäisches Unionsrecht* (7th edn, Nomos 2015) para 12. But see skeptically Thomas Kröll and Georg Lienbacher, 'Art. 10 EUV' in Jürgen Schwarze et al. (eds), *EU-Kommentar* (4th edn, Nomos 2019) para 16.

[107] Case C-26/62 *Van Gend en Loos* [1963] EU:C:1963:1.

10
Horizontal Review

I. Introduction

The Member States have a considerable interest in guaranteeing a certain level of constitutional homogeneity among each other. As noted in Chapter 8, entering the European Union means accepting spill-over effects. EU membership not only extends the transnational reach of each Member State but also creates a situation of mutual vulnerabilities. The complex network of cooperation created by the EU, for instance under mutual recognition regimes like the European Arrest Warrant, intensifies these effects. Accepting such vulnerabilities requires a minimum of constitutional homogeneity among the Member States. Such an active interest should correspond to the Member States' equally active participation when it comes to policing respect for this minimum. At present, however, the Member States are little involved in this task. This chapter will explore ways that allow national institutions to participate in securing constitutional homogeneity across the Verbund. The EU judicial system provides two avenues for such 'horizontal review'.

First, national governments can launch infringement procedures before the Court of Justice under Article 259 TFEU (Section II). This leads to a *direct* assessment of whether the Member State concerned complies with EU values. As the legal basis for such a review has been previously discussed (Chapters 2 and 9), this chapter will concentrate only on the institutional issues arising from the involvement of national governments. Second, national courts can *indirectly* assess a Member States' value compliance through the gateway of so-called mutual recognition regimes (Section III). These mechanisms are based on mutual trust among the Member States, which itself builds on the premiss that the Union's common values will be respected. In consequence, national courts are generally not permitted to check the legality of acts originating from another Member State, which they are supposed to execute or recognize. Over the years, the Court has developed exceptions to this 'duty to trust'. In judgments like *Aranyosi* and *L.M.* it clarified that cooperation must be put on hold in case of demonstrated non-compliance with the Union's common values. This has far-reaching implications. Exceptions to mutual recognition allow national courts to review whether other Member States comply with EU values. This turns mutual recognition regimes into horizontal instruments for detecting and countering systemic deficiencies in other Member States.

EU Values Before the Court of Justice. Luke Dimitrios Spieker, Oxford University Press.
DOI: 10.1093/oso/9780198876717.003.0011

Before diving into this chapter, one short disclaimer seems required. Readers might have already noticed that these two paths are not strictly horizontal. Substantively, they do not empower Member State institution to check whether their peers comply with their *own* essential guarantees, but with those of a *third*, the EU legal order. Also institutionally, the Court of Justice remains at the centre of both scenarios. Operating in a triangle, the instruments studied in this chapter resemble so-called 'bank shots' on a billiard table. Sometimes, players cannot target a ball directly. In this case, most players will resort to more indirect techniques. They may aim at another ball which subsequently pushes the one aimed at into the table's pockets. The same applies to the horizontal approaches outlined in this chapter.

II. Direct Review Through Infringement Actions

There are three main ways on the political level to police and sanction value compliance among the Member States: diplomatic sanctions, the Article 7 TEU-procedure, and, on a narrower level, a more or less formalized dialogue in the Council. It becomes immediately apparent that these approaches suffer from severe shortcomings in terms of legitimacy and efficiency (Section A). As such, this section will concentrate on a different path: the infringement procedure under Article 259 TFEU. Even if not strictly horizontal, this procedure may nonetheless allow individual or groups of Member States to take the lead in policing the value compliance of their peers. Hence, this mechanism might become an important tool in securing constitutional homogeneity in the Verbund (Section B).

A. Involving Member States in Policing Value Compliance: The Shortcomings of Political Procedures

Even though this may seem hard to believe given the Council's persistent inaction, peer pressure to uphold common values is by no means unprecedented in the history of integration. The highly controversial sanctions by fourteen Member States against Austria during the so-called Haider affair constitute the most far-reaching horizontal measures applied so far. By threatening to suspend diplomatic relations with Austria, the Member States prevented a coalition government with Jörg Haider's Freedom Party, which had attracted particular attention for its xenophobic election campaign.[1] While being highly effective, these actions were

[1] See Martti Ahtisaari, Jochen A. Frowein, and Marcelino Oreja, 'Report on the Austrian Government's Commitment to the Common European Values (The Wise Men Report)' *International Legal Materials* 40 (2001), 102. See further Konrad Lachmayer, 'Questioning the Basic Values. Austria and Jörg Haider' in András Jakab and Dimitry Kochenov (eds), *The Enforcement of EU Law and Values* (OUP 2017) 436.

criticized for taking place outside the EU framework, for falling short of the duty to provide reasons, and for not granting a fair hearing. The sanctions were imposed on Austria without specifying the charge and without providing its government with an opportunity to respond. For that reason, many considered these actions as 'fatally flawed' and reflecting very badly on a community based on the rule of law.[2]

In any case, such a concerted Member State action seems impossible in the Union of today. This is evidenced by the still pending Article 7 TEU-procedures against Hungary and Poland. Currently, the Council has not even succeeded in mustering the four-fifths majority required for completing the first step of this procedure, namely, to determine whether there is a real risk of a serious breach of Article 2 TEU. On top of that, Article 7 TEU suffers from severe procedural shortcomings as well. Despite its improvements when compared to unconstrained diplomatic sanctions, the procedure under Article 7 TEU still does not seem to provide sufficient procedural guarantees (see Chapter 2, IV.A and Chapter 9, II.A). In consequence, the Article 7 TEU-procedure seems deficient both considering it efficiency and its legitimacy.

Finally, there have been attempts to introduce forms of peer review in the Council. Already in November 2014, the Council stated its intention to conduct a 'Rule of Law Dialogue'. These dialogues were supposed to take place once a year in its General Affairs configuration and aimed at launching debate on thematic subject matters. It was clear from the outset, however, that this format would constitute only a 'complementary' tool.[3] Today, many perceive these dialogues as a disorganized discussion forum that amounts to nothing more than a 'façade action'.[4] Following a proposal advanced by the German, Belgian, and Dutch governments,[5] these dialogues have developed from thematic into periodic, country-specific debates. Still, being a soft-law instrument, even this proposal specifically excludes the possibility of sanctions.[6] As such, peer-review procedures can be considered only as complementary tool, not as alternative for legal actions against Member States that disregard EU values.[7]

[2] See e.g. Eugene Regan, 'Are EU Sanctions Against Austria Legal?' ZÖR 55 (2000), 323, 333 ff; Ludwig Adamovich, 'Juristische Aspekte der "Sanktionen" der EU-14 und des "Weisenberichts"' EuGRZ 28 (2001), 89, 90; Lucia S. Rossi, 'La "reazione commune" degli Stati membri dell'Unione europea nel caso Haider' *Rivista di diritto internazionale* (2000), 151, 153 f.

[3] Conclusions of the Council of the European Union and the member states meeting within the Council on ensuring respect for the rule of law, General Affairs Council meeting, Brussels, 16 December 2014.

[4] Ramona Coman, *The Politics of the Rule of Law in the EU Polity: Actors, Tools and Challenges* (Palgrave Macmillan 2022) 179 ff, 184. See also Matthias Schmidt, *Verfassungsaufsicht in der Europäischen Union* (Nomos 2021) 538 ff.

[5] Michael Roth, Didier Reynders, and Stef Blok, 'Fundamental Values Check-Up: Let's Intensify Our Dialogue!', German Federal Foreign Office (20 March 2019).

[6] On its further shortcomings, see Thomas Conzelmann, 'Peer Reviewing the Rule of Law? A New Mechanism to Safeguard EU Values' EP 7 (2022), 671, 691 ff.

[7] In this sense, Ernst Hirsch Ballin, 'Mutual Trust: The Virtue of Reciprocity—Strengthening the Acceptance of the Rule of Law Through Peer Review' in Carlos Closa and Dimitry Kochenov (eds),

B. Peer Pressure Beyond Political Procedures: Article 259 TEU

Instead of pushing for political approaches, determined Member States could make use of the EU judicial system and advance infringement proceedings under Article 259 TFEU.[8] Such procedures could be based on Article 2 TEU in combination with provisions that give specific expression to these values (in detail Chapter 2, III.B and Chapter 9, III). In this sense, the Member States would operate as the 'horizontal trigger' for a vertical procedure. Before a Member State can bring its action it must take the matter to the Commission, which delivers a reasoned opinion after each State has been given the opportunity to submit its views. If the applicant State disagrees with the Commission's opinion or prefers to act in its own capacity, it is not prevented from bringing the case before the Court by itself.[9]

So far, the Article 259 TFEU procedure has been little used in practice.[10] This can be explained by various factors. On the one hand, the Commission can decide to take the matter to the Court in which case there is little need for the Member States to further pursue their claim under Article 259 TFEU. On the other hand, the procedure seems to be strangely out of place in the current set up of EU law. Since the Treaty of Rome, the provision has remained nearly unchanged. It appears as a left-over from a different time, in which the European integration project was still situated on the terrain of public international law and thus characterized by inter-state relations. Yet, even back in the early days, this mechanism was rarely used. Instead, the evolution of EU law took a very different path. With *Van Gend en Loos*, the Court of Justice interpreted many Treaty provisions as conferring rights on individuals enforceable before domestic courts. As such, it turned the 'vigilance of individuals concerned to protect their rights' into a tool of 'effective supervision'. The enforcement by national courts and private parties diminished the need for inter-state retaliation.[11]

Reinforcing Rule of Law Oversight in the European Union (CUP 2016) 133, 146; Roberto Baratta, 'Rule of Law "Dialogues" Within the EU: A Legal Assessment' HJRL 8 (2016), 357, 370.

[8] For such proposals, see Guillermo Íñiguez, 'The Enemy Within? Article 259 TFEU and the EU's Rule of Law Crisis' GLJ 23 (2022), 1104; Schmidt (n 4) 531 f; Monica Parodi, 'Il ruolo degli Stati membri nella tutela dei valori dell'Unione europea: il ricorso agli strumenti giurisdizionali' *Diritti umani e diritto internazionale* (2021), 671; Kim L. Scheppele, Dimitry Kochenov, and Barbara Grabowska-Moroz, 'EU Values Are Law, after All: Enforcing EU Values through Systemic Infringement Actions by the European Commission and the Member States of the European Union' YEL 38 (2020), 3, 95 ff. See already Dimitry Kochenov, 'Biting Intergovernmentalism: The Case for the Reinvention of Article 259 TFEU to Make It a Viable Rule of Law Enforcement Tool' HJRL 7 (2015), 153.

[9] Luca Prete and Ben Smulders, 'The Coming of Age of Infringement Proceedings' CML Rev 47 (2010), 9, 27; Nina Wunderlich, 'Art. 259 AEUV' in Hans von der Groeben et al. (eds), *Europäisches Unionsrecht* (7th edn, Nomos 2015) paras 11, 15.

[10] Graham Butler, 'The Court of Justice as an Inter-State Court' YEL 36 (2017), 179; Ulrich Karpenstein, 'Art. 259 AEUV' in Eberhard Grabitz, Meinhard Hilf, and Martin Nettesheim (eds), *Das Recht der Europäischen Union* (75th edn, loose-leaf, C.H.Beck 2022) para 7.

[11] See only Cases 90 and 91/63 *Commission v Luxembourg and Belgium* [1964] EU:C:1964:80. In detail William Phelan, 'The Troika: The Interlocking Roles of Commission v. Luxembourg and Belgium, Van Gend en Loos and Costa v. ENEL in the Creation of the European Legal Order' ELJ 21 (2015), 116,

This might be slightly different in the logic of the Verbund dimension, where Article 2 TEU establishes only a thin framework for the Member States' internal structures. Here, the pull for constitutional autonomy and pluralism exerts a particularly strong force. This places considerable constraints on any action by EU institutions (see Chapters 9 and 12). Accordingly, Member States might take a stronger lead in guaranteeing the constitutional homogeneity throughout the Verbund. The Article 259 TFEU procedure could be a useful tool in this respect. Two main arguments advocate for such a use of Article 259 TFEU.

By triggering the pre-litigation phase under Article 259 (2) to (3) TFEU the Member States can push the Commission to accelerate its actions. Indeed, the past years have demonstrated that value-related infringement procedures launched by the Commission take an extremely long time.[12] The proceedings against the Polish 'muzzle law', which prevents judges from assessing the independence of their peers, illustrate this point.[13] That law entered into force in February 2020. Though a flagrant violation of EU law, the Commission referred the matter to the Court of Justice no earlier than April 2021. Such a delay is hardly understandable given the serious and obvious infringements at stake. The deadline between the letter of formal notice and the Member State's observations as well as between the Commission's reasoned opinion and the Member State's compliance is usually set at two months.[14] Even 'very short periods may be justified in particular circumstances, especially where there is an urgent need to remedy a breach'.[15]

When bringing a case before the Court, Member States are moreover less vulnerable to accusations of power-grabbing. The Commission can easily be accused of pursuing an expansion of the Union's powers to the detriment of the Member States and of transgressing the lines drawn by the principle of conferral. This argument has become an integral part of the Polish or Hungarian government's rhetoric (see Chapter 13, II.A). As far as the defence of EU values is concerned, the Commission has thus been extremely careful to remain within the limits of the Union's competences and the scope of EU law. As demonstrated in the first chapter, it needed a doctrinal push by the Court to turn infringement proceedings into an instruments with bite against Member States that violate EU values.

130 ff; William Phelan, *In Place of Inter-State Retaliation: The European Union's Rejection of WTO-style Trade Sanctions and Trade Remedies* (OUP 2014) 135 ff.

[12] This has been repeatedly stressed, see only Laurent Pech, Patryk Wachowiec, and Dariusz Mazur, 'Poland's Rule of Law Breakdown: A Five-Year Assessment of EU's (In)Action' HJRL 13 (2021), 1, 22 f.

[13] On this law, see e.g. Luke D. Spieker, 'The Conflict Over the Polish Disciplinary Regime for Judges—An Acid Test for Judicial Independence, Union Values and the Primacy of EU Law' CML Rev 59 (2022), 777.

[14] See e.g. Bernd Schima, 'Article 258 TFEU' in Manuel Kellerbauer et al. (eds), *The Treaties and the Charter of Fundamental Rights—A Commentary* (OUP 2019) paras 21, 23.

[15] See Cases C-715, 718, and 719/17 *Commission v Poland, Hungary and the Czech Republic (Temporary mechanism for the relocation of applicants for international protection)* [2020] EU:C:2020:257, para 92.

Such arguments by national governments run empty once these procedures are advanced by their peers. In this sense, Member States can be bolder and more experimental than the Commission.

Certainly, the Member States are usually not considered to be the drivers of centripetal developments in the EU legal order. Often, they take the opposite position. In addition, the little use of Article 259 TFEU demonstrates that Member States are usually prepared to take such action when it concerns 'classic' neighbourhood disputes and if the domestic political pressure or public attention is particularly high.[16] Though none of these factors has been prominent in the current value crisis, there is a growing number of Member States that seems ready to increase its efforts. In the infringement proceedings against the Polish disciplinary regime for judges, Belgium, Denmark, the Netherlands, Finland, and Sweden intervened in support of the Commission.[17] In the actions brought by Hungary and Poland against the rule of law conditionality regulation, ten Member States—Belgium, Denmark, Germany, Ireland, Spain, France, Luxembourg, the Netherlands, Finland, and Sweden—intervened in support of the Parliament and Council. The Dutch Parliament went even further by adopting a resolution that specifically requested the government to consider the use of Article 259 TFEU.[18]

In his response, the Dutch minister of foreign affairs noted that there was 'no inclination among like-minded Member States to seriously consider the option of a state complaint at this time.'[19] Three main arguments were advanced to justify this hesitation. The fist and least convincing one is that the individual Member States lack the Commission's expertise and capacity to study another Member State's internal systems in depth. Second, there is supposed to be a risk of undermining the Commission's role as guardian of the Treaties. As Advocate General Bobek observed, 'effective protection of something tends to dramatically decrease if everyone is made responsible for it.'[20] Where responsibility is scattered among many people, the individual responsibility of each one diminishes proportionately.[21] Hence, *sharing* may eventually result in *diffusing* responsibility. However, it corresponds much more to the logic of the Verbund to distribute the responsibility for guaranteeing the necessary degree of constitutional homogeneity among all its actors. Hence, a more 'pluralistic view' of the values' guardianship seems

[16] In this sense, see Schmidt (n 4) 532.

[17] See Art. 40 of the Court's statute and Art. 129 to 132 Rules of Procedure of the Court of Justice [2012] OJ L265, 1.

[18] Motie van het lid Groothuizen c.s. over onderzoek om Polen voor het Europese Hof van Justitie te dagen (26 November 2020), 35570-VI-58.

[19] S.A. Blok, Reactie op de motie van het lid Groothuizen c.s. over onderzoek om Polen voor het Europese Hof van Justitie te dagen (Kamerstuk 35570-VI-58), 21501-02-2264 (1 February 2021).

[20] Case C-40/17 *Fashion ID* [2018] EU:C:2018:1039, Opinion of AG Bobek, para 92.

[21] On this phenomenon, see André Nollkaemper, 'The Duality of Shared Responsibility' *Contemporary Politics* 24 (2018) 524, 529 ff.

appropriate.[22] Moreover, it is clear that the Commission remains the principal guardian of the Treaties. Member State actions will very probably remain a complementary tool. Ultimately, these observations help to overcome also the third counterargument. The use of Article 259 TFEU against another Member State is perceived as seriously undermining the bilateral dialogue with the Member State concerned. Admittedly, each government must assess for itself, whether it is ready to take the heat and bear the political costs of such a step. Yet, it should take into account that sharing responsibility equally leads to burden sharing. Member States can therefore reduce the political costs of infringement proceedings by cooperating with like-minded peers.

III. Indirect Review Through Mutual Recognition Regimes

A Member States' value compliance cannot only be reviewed by the Court of Justice but also before national courts. A consolidated line of jurisprudence, starting with *Aranyosi* and developed by *L.M.*, has turned so-called mutual recognition regimes into a veritable review mechanism. These regimes facilitate cooperation between autonomous Member State policies without harmonization at the EU level. While the recent case law evolved in particular around the European Arrest Warrant ('EAW'),[23] the Common European Asylum System ('CEAS')[24] and judicial cooperation in civil matters[25] are also examples for mutual recognition. Through the gateway of these regimes, national courts (and, in case of a reference, the Court of Justice) can review whether other Member States adhere to the values of Article 2 TEU and put cooperation on hold. Starting with the EAW framework as an illustrating example (Section A.1), the chapter will demonstrate how this horizontal review can be theorized in terms of a *horizontal Solange* doctrine (Section A.2). Still, the current practice under the EAW regime reveals several shortcomings (Section B.1). The past years further suggest that suspending individual EAWs does not exert much pressure on Member States that disregard EU values. For that

[22] In this sense, Íñiguez (n 8); Kochenov (n 8) 163 f. On this 'collective assessment', see also Chapter 12, III.B.2.a.i.

[23] See Council Framework Decision 2002/584/JHA on the European Arrest Warrant [2002] OJ L190 1.

[24] See e.g. Regulation 604/2013 establishing the criteria and mechanisms for determining the Member State responsible for examining an application for international protection (Dublin III) [2013] OJ L180/31.

[25] See e.g. Regulation 593/2008 on the Law Applicable to Contractual Obligations (Rome I) [2008] OJ L177/6; Regulation 864/2007 on the Law Applicable to Non-contractual Obligations (Rome II) [2007] OJ L199/40; Regulation 1215/2012 on Jurisdiction and the Recognition and Enforcement of Judgements in Civil and Commercial Matters (recast) (Brussels I bis) [2012] OJ L351/1; Regulation 2201/2003 concerning jurisdiction and the recognition and enforcement of judgments in matrimonial matters and the matters of parental responsibility (Brussels II bis) [2003] OJ L338/1.

reason, the last section will explore whether this approach could be extended to other regimes with potentially more bite (Section B.2).

A. *Horizontal Solange*

1. Mutual recognition regimes: Gateways for rule of law and fundamental rights considerations

The fuel that keeps cooperation under mutual recognition regimes running is mutual trust.[26] Generally, the principle of mutual trust requires each Member State to presume that all other Member States are complying with EU law, including fundamental rights.[27] This presumption is based on the 'premiss' that all Member States share and respect the values enshrined in Article 2 TEU.[28] The way this principle works can be illustrated with the EAW framework. Generally, a Member State triggers its own human rights responsibility if it surrenders a person to a Member State where it would be subject to human rights violations. Accordingly, the surrendering State must examine the conditions in the issuing State. This is where the principle of mutual trusts kicks in. To facilitate an automatic cooperation among Member States and allow 'an area without internal borders to be created and maintained',[29] the executing State can rely upon the presumption that the issuing State complies with all EU standards. However, the principle of mutual trust does not stop there. It also entails an obligation for the executing Member State to refrain from *assessing* whether the issuing Member State complies with EU standards.[30] Put differently, it prescribes a 'duty to trust'.

The grounds for refusing to execute an EAW were initially limited to the ones explicitly listed in the Framework Decision.[31] Yet even besides these explicit grounds, national judges can make cooperation under mutual recognition regimes subject to fundamental rights and rule of law considerations. That is the case in two kinds of situations. First, judges can determine whether the conditions for a request for cooperation or recognition have been validly formed in the first place. Under the

[26] In detail Andrea Miglionico and Francesco Maiani, 'One Principle to Rule Them All? Anatomy of Mutual Trust in the Law of the Area of Freedom, Security and Justice' CML Rev 57 (2020), 7; Cecilia Rizcallah, *Le principe de confiance mutuelle en droit de l'Union européenne* (Bruylant 2020), pp 247 ff; Elena Kullak, *Vertrauen in Europa* (Mohr Siebeck 2020) pp 155 ff. For a theoretical underpinning, see Michael Schwarz, 'Let's Talk About Trust, Baby! Theorizing Trust and Mutual Recognition in the EU's Area of Freedom, Security and Justice' ELJ 24 (2018), 124.

[27] Case C-216/18 PPU *Minister for Justice and Equality (Deficiencies in the system of justice)* [2018] EU:C:2018:586, para 36.

[28] ibid para 35. For an overview of its different legal foundations, see Luc von Danwitz, 'Der Grundsatz des gegenseitigen Vertrauens zwischen den Mitgliedstaaten der EU' EuR 55 (2020), 61, 76 ff.

[29] Opinion 2/13 *ECHR Accession II* [2014] EU:C:2014:2454, para 191.

[30] ibid para 192. More recently, Cases C-562/21 PPU and C-563/21 PPU *Openbaar Ministerie (Tribunal établi par la loi dans l'État membre d'émission)* [2022] EU:C:2022:100, para 41.

[31] See Case C-237/15 PPU [2015] *Lanigan* EU:C:2015:474, para 36; Case C-396/11 *Radu* [2013] EU:C:2013:39, paras 35 f.

EAW Framework, an executing judge can check whether the arrest warrant has been issued by a 'judicial authority' in the sense of Article 6(1) of the Framework Decision. According to the Court, the concept of 'judicial authority' is an autonomous notion of EU law referring to an entity independent from the executive.[32] As such, the EAW allows for the assessment of the issuing or rendering authority's independence and can lead eventually to a denial of cooperation. Still, the room for rejecting execution on this basis is very narrow. The CJEU clarified that systemic deficiencies with regard to the independence of a Member State's courts—'however serious'—do not suffice on their own to question their status as judicial authority.[33]

Second, after the EAW or the respective judgment has been validly issued or rendered, national judges can determine whether they must deny cooperation due to the risk of systemic deficiencies in the issuing Member State. Realizing the potential for conflict and inconsistencies with the ECHR and the Union's own Charter—and probably pushed by national constitutional courts[34]—Luxembourg began clarifying that mutual trust should not be confused with blind trust. As previously mentioned, mutual trust requires national courts to presume that EU law will be observed in other Member States. That presumption is based on the 'fundamental premiss' that the values in Article 2 TEU will be respected. In other words: the presumption of compliance for Union law hinges on the deeper presumption of respect for its values.[35] Conversely, a Member States' demonstrated non-compliance with these values can lift said presumption and put cooperation on halt. In consequence, mutual trust can be lifted in 'exceptional circumstances'.[36]

In *Aranyosi*, the Court started to operationalize this exception with regard to Articles 1 and 4 CFR 'that enshrine one of the fundamental values of the Union and its Member States'.[37] The decision established a two-step examination: the

[32] Case C-477/16 PPU *Kovalkovas* [2016] EU:C:2016:861, para 36. See also Case C-452/16 PPU *Poltorak* [2016] EU:C:2016:858, para 35; Cases 508/18 and 82/19 PPU *OG (Parquet de Lübeck)* [2019] EU:C:2019:456, para 74. See also Valsamis Mitsilegas, 'Autonomous Concepts, Diversity Management and Mutual Trust in Europe's Area of Criminal Justice' CML Rev 57 (2020), 45, 63–70; Tricia Harkin, 'The Case Law of the Court of Justice of the European Union on "Judicial Authority" and Issuing European Arrest Warrants' NJECL 12 (2021), 508.

[33] Cases C-354 and 412/20 PPU *Openbaar Ministerie (Independence of the issuing judicial authority)* [2020] EU:C:2020:1033, paras 34–50. Critical, see Agnieszka Frackowiak-Adamska, 'Trust Until It Is Too Late! Mutual Recognition of Judgments and Limitations of Judicial Independence in a Member State: L and P' CML Rev 59 (2022), 113, 130 ff.

[34] See e.g. Mathias Hong, 'Human Dignity, Identity Review of the European Arrest Warrant and the Court of Justice as a Listener in the Dialogue of Courts: Solange-III and Aranyosi' EuConst 12 (2016), 549.

[35] On the fragility of this reasoning, see Rizcallah (n 26) 424 ff; Kullak (n 26) 176 f; Lukás Boháček, 'Mutual Trust in EU Law: Trust "In What" and "Between Whom"?' EJLS 14 (2022), 103.

[36] *ECHR Accession II* (n 29) paras 191, 194. See also Georgios Anagnostaras, 'Mutual Confidence is Not Blind Trust!' CML Rev 53 (2016), 1675; Koen Lenaerts, 'La vie après l'avis: Exploring the Principle of Mutual (Yet Not Blind) Trust' CML Rev 54 (2017), 805; Auke Willems, 'The Court of Justice of the European Union's Mutual Trust Journey in EU Criminal Law: From a Presumption to (Room for) Rebuttal' GLJ 20 (2019), 468.

[37] Cases C-404 and 659/15 PPU *Aranyosi and Căldăraru* [2016] EU:C:2016:198, paras 81, 87. In the CEAS context, see also Case C-483/20 *Commissaire général aux réfugiés and aux apatrides (Unité familiale—Protection déjà accordée)* [2022] EU:C:2022:103, para 27

applicant must substantiate the existence of systemic deficiencies amounting to a real risk of inhumane and degrading treatment in the issuing Member State (systemic step) and present substantial grounds that he or she will be exposed to that risk (individual step).[38] In *L.M.*, the Court extended this test to the essence of fair trial rights under Article 47 CFR and thus to deficiencies in the Member States' judiciaries (see Chapter 1, III.A).[39]

This decision paved the way for national courts to review whether other Member States observe judicial independence. As mutual trust can only be shaken by non-compliance with the Union's common values, the Court had to establish a link between the essence of Article 47 CFR and the values in Article 2 TEU. This underlying consideration seems to surface when the Court emphasizes that 'the requirement of judicial independence forms part of the essence of the fundamental right to a fair trial, a right which is of cardinal importance as a guarantee … that the values common to the Member States set out in Article 2 TEU, in particular the value of the rule of law, will be safeguarded.'[40] Moreover, it stressed that the very existence of effective judicial review 'is of the essence of the rule of law'.[41] In this sense, the Court seems to operationalize the value of the rule of law through the essence of Article 47 CFR.

These exceptions have far-reaching implications. Through the gateway of mutual recognition regimes, national courts (and, in case of a reference, the CJEU) can increasingly review whether issuing Member States comply with the values in Article 2 TEU. As far as the first prong of the *Aranyosi*-test is concerned, mutual recognition regimes become a tool to *detect* systemic deficiencies in the Member States. While the notion of 'systemic deficiencies' remains remarkable under-theorized (in detail, Chapter 13, III.B), the Court provides some indications of what this first step might entail. The executing court is required to conduct a 'general' or 'overall assessment'.[42] In order to identify systemic deficiencies, it must rely on 'material that is objective, reliable, specific and properly updated',[43] such as the information contained in the Commission's reasoned proposal under Article 7(1) TEU, information provided by courts in the issuing Member State (i.e. through preliminary references concerning the deficiencies at issue), case law from the Luxembourg and Strasbourg courts as well as decisions, reports, and other documents produced by bodies of the Council of Europe or under the aegis of the United Nations.[44]

[38] *Aranyosi and Căldăraru* (n 37) paras 88 f, 92.
[39] *Minister for Justice and Equality* (n 27) para 68.
[40] ibid para 48.
[41] ibid para 51. On this link, see also Mattias Wendel, 'Mutual Trust, Essence and Federalism' EuConst 15 (2019), 17, 27–9; Catherine Dupré, 'The Rule of Law, Fair Trial and Human Dignity: The Protection of EU Values After LM' in Armin von Bogdandy et al. (eds), *Defending Checks and Balances in EU Member States* (Springer 2021) 431, 433.
[42] *Openbaar Ministerie (Tribunal établi par la loi dans l'État membre d'émission)* (n 30) paras 67, 74.
[43] ibid para 52.
[44] ibid paras 78 f. See also *Aranyosi and Căldăraru* (n 37) para 89.

At the same time, this approach allows national courts to *support* EU responses against Member States that have been found to violate EU values. According to the Court, the EAW system must be generally suspended, when there is a serious and persistent breach of Article 2 TEU determined by the European Council under Article 7(2) TEU.[45] In the absence of such a determination, national courts can only suspend individual EAWs under the *Aranyosi*-test. The systemic deficiencies required by its first prong, however, could also be determined by the Court of Justice in parallel infringement proceedings. In this case, national courts can support and assist the CJEU in enforcing its rulings by subsequently freezing their cooperation with the issuing Member State. Vertical rulings in infringement proceeding are then reinforced—in other words: their effects are potentiated—by horizontal rulings suspending cooperation with non-compliant Member States.

In sum, national courts can use mutual recognition regimes in two phases: to detect systemic deficiencies in the first place and, second, to support the Union's response once such deficiencies have been established. Such an involvement of national courts follows a well-trodden path of European integration.[46] The development of EU law has always been advanced through its application by domestic courts as first 'Union courts'.[47] Up to now, they were considered the CJEU's partners in guaranteeing the rule of EU law in their respective jurisdiction. The jurisprudence evolving around mutual recognition regimes adds another layer to this function. It raises national courts to partners in Luxembourg's greater struggle to assure the constitutional homogeneity in the Verbund.

2. The far-reaching effects of *horizontal Solange*

Ultimately, this approach can be articulated in terms of the well-established *Solange* doctrine.[48] This judicial tool aims at facilitating smooth cooperation between interconnected but autonomous legal orders without giving up essential guarantees. By combining these two objectives, *Solange* doctrines establish the presumption—in legal order A—that acts emanating from legal order B generally comply with standards that are 'equivalent', 'substantially similar', or 'essentially

[45] *Openbaar Ministerie (Tribunal établi par la loi dans l'État membre d'émission)* (n 30) para 64; *Openbaar Ministerie (Independence of the issuing judicial authority)* (n 33) para 57; *Minister for Justice and Equality* (n 27) paras 69–72.

[46] See Karen J. Alter, *Establishing the Supremacy of European Law* (OUP 2003).

[47] See Case C-294/83 *Les Verts* [1986] EU:C:1986:166; Opinion 1/09 *Unified Patent Litigation System* [2011] EU:C:2011:123, para 80. See also Nial Fennelly, 'The national judge as judge of the European Union' in Allan Rosas et al. (eds), *The Court of Justice and the Construction of Europe* (Asser 2013) 61.

[48] On *Solange* as a judicial tool, see e.g. Andreas Voßkuhle, 'The Cooperation between European Courts: The Verbund of European Courts and its Legal Toolbox' in Rosas et al. (n 47) 81, 92–4. Antonios Tzanakopoulos, 'Judicial Dialogue in Multilevel Governance: The Impact of the Solange Argument' in Ole K. Fauchald and André Nollkaemper (eds), *The Practice of International and National Courts and the (De-)Fragmentation of International Law* (Hart 2012) 185.

comparable' to those in legal order A.[49] This presumption holds as long as essential guarantees are met or as long as the underlying substructures correspond to each other. As the judgments in *Solange II* (Member State-EU), *Kadi* (EU-UN Security Council), or *Bosphorus* and *Avotins* (ECHR-EU) indicate, the doctrine can be applied to any cooperation between different jurisdictions.

The same logic applies to mutual recognition regimes. Cooperation will be maintained 'as long as' the presumption holds that the other Member State adheres to the Union's values. As this doctrine applies in the horizontal setting between two Member State courts, some have described this mechanism as *horizontal Solange* doctrine.[50] Yet, it should be stressed again that its horizontality is limited. National courts can review the compliance of other Member States only with essential standards *emanating from EU law*. Accordingly, this review involves a horizontal (Member State-Member State) and a vertical axe (EU-Member State). The EU legal order acts—both concerning the relevant standards and institutionally once the Court of Justice is involved—as a hinge linking and regulating the relationship between the Member States. In this sense, the doctrine rather operates in a triangular setting.

Horizontal Solange is striking in at least two respects. On the one hand, these exceptions allow executing authorities (and the CJEU) to review policy areas in the issuing Member State that would otherwise escape the scope of EU law.[51] Although the surrender itself is clearly within its scope, this is not necessarily the case for what is scrutinized under the *Aranyosi*-test. To briefly recall, *Aranyosi* concerned an EAW issued by Romania that was challenged based on systemic deficiencies in Romanian detention conditions. These conditions do not reveal any link with EU law but were nonetheless reviewed against EU standards (Article 4 CFR). Before *ASJP*, the same would have applied to the issue of judicial independence and the organization of the national judiciary which was at the heart of the judgment in *L.M.*

On the other hand, the exceptions sketched above can exert an implicitly harmonizing effect even in fields for which the EU has no competence.[52] This is striking as mutual recognition regimes are specifically designed to coordinate

[49] ECtHR, Judgment of 30 June 2005, Appl. No. 45036/98 *Bosphorus v. Ireland*, para 155 as well as BVerfG, Order of 22 October 1986, 2 BvR 197/83, *Solange II*, para 132; Order of 7 June 2000, 2 BvL 1/97, *Bananenmarkt*, para 57.

[50] Iris Canor, 'Suspending Horizontal Solange' in von Bogdandy et al. (n 41) 183. See already Iris Canor, 'My Brother's Keeper? Horizontal Solange' CML Rev 50 (2013), 383.

[51] Canor (n 50) 395 f.

[52] Suzanne A. Bloks and Ton van den Brink, 'The Impact on National Sovereignty of Mutual Recognition in the AFSJ' GLJ 22 (2021), 45, 59 ff. As an 'informal harmonisation', see Sara Iglesias Sánchez, 'The Scope of EU Fundamental Rights in the Area of Freedom, Security and Justice' in Sánchez and Maribel González Pascual (eds), *Fundamental Rights in the EU Area of Freedom, Security and Justice* (CUP 2021) 21, 35. On the harmonizing effect of the CJEU's interpretation of autonomous concepts in mutual recognition regimes, see Mitsilegas (n 32) 63 ff; Leandro Mancano, 'Judicial Harmonisation Through Autonomous Concepts of European Union Law' EL Rev 43 (2018), 69.

independent Member State policies without harmonization.[53] Compared to other modes of integration, mutual recognition is considered a better safeguard for the Member States' sovereignty, diversity, and political autonomy. Admittedly, establishing deficiencies in the issuing Member State leads only to an obligation for the executing authority (namely to put the EAW on hold). In *Aranyosi*, the CJEU could not order the issuing State (Romania) to change its prison conditions but only state under what conditions the executing German authorities had to suspend Romanian EAWs. In *L.M.* it could not oblige Poland to respect the independence of the judiciary and re-establish its judicial system in line with EU values. Instead, it could only establish the requirements under which the referring Irish court would have to suspend the EAW issued by Poland. Still, the issuing Member State is indirectly affected—in the form of a reflex—via the suspension of cooperation. If it wants to participate in these enhanced cooperation mechanisms, it must align its policies with the requirements set out by the Court. Hence, exceptions to mutual recognition can exert a harmonizing pressure on Member States.

B. Making Better Use of Mutual Recognition Regimes

While *horizontal Solange* constitutes a useful instrument to address internal developments in the Member States that violate Article 2 TEU values, it remains a complementary tool rather than the central path for guaranteeing value compliance throughout the Verbund. Going through mutual recognition regimes inherently limits the *horizontal Solange* doctrine to the review of rule of law and selected fundamental rights issues. Threats to democracy or the other Union values remain largely beyond its scope.[54] In addition, the current practice does not only reveal several shortcomings; it seems also highly questionable whether suspending European arrest warrants will pressure Member States into compliance with Article 2 TEU. For that reason, the final section will assess possible trajectories for expanding the *horizontal Solange* doctrine to mutual recognition regimes with more bite.

1. Current shortcomings

Since *L.M.*, the Court has been urged to reduce the *Aranyosi*–test to its first prong concerning structural rule of law deficiencies, to assess the situation in Poland in a centralized manner, and to generally suspend the EAW framework with regard

[53] See e.g. Susanne K. Schmidt, 'Mutual Recognition as a New Mode of Governance' JEPP 14 (2007), 667, 671 f; Annika Suominen, 'The sensitive relationship between the different means of legal integration: mutual recognition and approximation' in Chloé Brière and Anne Weyembergh (eds), *The Needed Balances in EU Criminal Law* (Hart 2018) 165, 168 ff.

[54] Arguing for an expansion of the exceptions to social rights, see e.g. Neža Šubic, 'Resisting a European Arrest Warrant: A Social Rights Perspective' NJECL 11 (2020), 299.

to Poland.[55] So far, these calls have not been answered by the Luxembourg court. Indeed, the current jurisprudential outlook points into a different direction. The Court rejected a general suspension of the EAW regime, maintained the second, individual step of the *Aranyosi*-test, and eventually ended up with a decentralized case-by-case approach. Even if the decision against a general suspension can be justified with convincing arguments, the individual and decentralized assessments reveal several shortcomings in terms of practicability and desirability.

The Court's central argument for refusing the EAW framework's general suspension flows from the Framework Decision's preamble. According to its 10th recital, such a far-reaching move is only possible in case of a determination by the European Council under Article 7(2) TEU.[56] Although this is admittedly a weak argument,[57] there are further reasons advocating against a general suspension. First, it must be stressed that mutual trust among the Member States has been elevated to a 'constitutional principle', even the Union's 'raison d'être', in the jurisprudence of the Court of Justice.[58] In this sense, the free movement of judgments within the Union is often described as a 'fifth freedom'.

Second, the rationales governing mutual recognition regimes advocate for a cautious approach. One of their central aims is swift and undisturbed cooperation. In addition, the EAW framework aims at combatting impunity, which also affects the rights of third parties in criminal proceedings.[59] The framework's general suspension runs counter to both aims. Moreover, mutual recognition regimes are supposed to merely coordinate autonomous Member State policies. As seen above, exceptions that justify putting cooperation on hold can exert a harmonizing pressure. To respect the legislative decision for mere coordination and against harmonization at the EU level, the Court must therefore interpret these exceptions narrowly.

Third, keeping the EAW system alive with regard to Member States like Poland, allows the Court to keep this kind of inter-Member State cooperation within its reach. Luxembourg can continue to set and define relevant standards for cooperation among Member States and thus to indirectly force the issuing Member States to comply with them. This prevents also unintended spill-over effects. As the Court noted, suspending the entire EAW framework due to systemic deficiencies in a Member State's judiciary could affect the preliminary reference procedure under

[55] Michał Krajewski, 'Who is Afraid of the European Council?' EuConst 14 (2018), 792, 805–7; Petra Bárd and Walter van Ballegooij, 'Judicial Independence as a Precondition for Mutual Trust?' NJECL 9 (2018), 353; Wendel (n 41).

[56] See the cases cited in n 45.

[57] See only Krajewski (n 55) 806 who points to the inconsistency of interpreting the limits of primary law in conformity with a non-binding preamble of an act of secondary legislation.

[58] *ECHR Accession II* (n 29) para 167 and Cases C-411 and 493/10 *N.S.* [2011] EU:C:2011:865, para 83.

[59] *Openbaar Ministerie (Tribunal établi par la loi dans l'État membre d'émission)* (n 30) para 61; *Openbaar Ministerie (Independence of the issuing judicial authority)* (n 33) para 64. In this sense, see also ECtHR, Judgment of 9 July 2019, App No. 8351/17 *Romeo Castaño v. Belgium*, para 85.

Article 267 TFEU—with the undesirable consequence that references from within that Member State are inadmissible.[60]

Still, the individual prong of the CJEU's two-step test proves difficult in practice, especially when judicial independence is concerned.[61] In *L.M.*, the Court stressed that the executing authority must determine not only whether there are systemic deficiencies in the issuing State's judiciary, but also whether the applicant runs a real risk of being tried by a court that is not sufficiently independent.[62] How should the executing authority get this information? By asking their Polish colleagues under Article 15(2) of the Framework Decision?[63] Would a court under political pressure or influence admit its lack of independence? It is hardly surprising that this requirement has caused considerable irritation among national courts. In consequence, reactions to Polish EAWs have varied between execution[64] and rejection.[65]

Despite these inconsistencies, the CJEU has confirmed the necessity of the individual step.[66] Recent case law demonstrates moreover how narrowly the individual assessment is conceived. To start with, the burden of proof lies on the person challenging the EAW.[67] He or she must specify to what extent the systemic deficiencies have an impact at the level of the courts with jurisdiction over the proceedings.[68] Concerning EAWs issued for executing custodial sentences it does not suffice to show that members of the court that heard the respective case were appointed in procedures that violate EU requirements. Instead, the individual concerned must provide substantial grounds that the court's composition affected his or her fundamental rights under Article 47 CFR.[69] In the context of EAWs issued for conducting a criminal prosecution, the judges called to hear the case will usually be unknown. Here, the specific risk must be substantiated by relying on the personal

[60] *Openbaar Ministerie (Independence of the issuing judicial authority)* (n 33) para 44. This question was also at the heart of Case C-132/20 *Getin Noble Bank* [2022] EU:C:2022:235. See also Charlotte Reyns, 'Saving Judicial Independence: A Threat to the Preliminary Ruling Mechanism?' EuConst 17 (2021), 26.

[61] See Stanisław Biernat and Paweł Filipek, 'The Assessment of Judicial Independence Following the CJEU Ruling in C-216/18 LM' in von Bogdandy et al. (n 41) 403, 423 ff; Bárd and van Ballegooij (n 55) 360 f; Krajewski (n 55) 797–9; Wendel (n 41) 44 f.

[62] *Minister for Justice and Equality* (n 27) paras 60, 70 f.

[63] This is suggested by the Court, see ibid paras 77 f.

[64] See e.g. Irish High Court, Judgment of 19 November 2018, *The Minister for Justice and Equality v. Celmer No.5*, [2018] IEHC 639, para 123; OLG Karlsruhe, Order of 7 January 2019, Ausl 301 AR 95/18, paras 18–21; OLG Düsseldorf, Order of 14 June 2019, 4 AR 38/19; OLG Braunschweig, Order of 21 March 2022, 1 AR (Ausl.) 3/22, paras 24–5; Rechtbank Amsterdam, Judgment of 27 January 2021, ECLI:NL:RBAMS:2021:179, paras 5.4.1 ff.

[65] See e.g. OLG Karlsruhe, Order of 17 February 2020, Ausl 301 AR 156/19, paras 33 ff; Rechtbank Amsterdam, Judgment of 10 February 2021, ECLI:NL:RBAMS:2021:420, para 5.3.4.

[66] *Openbaar Ministerie (Tribunal établi par la loi dans l'État membre d'émission)* (n 30) para 51; *Openbaar Ministerie (Independence of the issuing judicial authority)* (n 33) para 63.

[67] *Openbaar Ministerie (Tribunal établi par la loi dans l'État membre d'émission)* (n 30) para 83.

[68] ibid para 53; *Openbaar Ministerie (Independence of the issuing judicial authority)* (n 33) para 55; *Minister for Justice and Equality* (n 27) paras 74–7.

[69] *Openbaar Ministerie (Tribunal établi par la loi dans l'État membre d'émission)* (n 30) paras 88 f.

situation of the prosecuted individual, the nature of the offence, and the factual context in which that arrest warrant was issued.[70]

This leads to the second issue. In *L.M.* and its progenies, the CJEU has left the two-step assessment in the specific case to the referring courts. Thus, the Court seems to have opted for a decentralized case-by-case review. At first sight, this approach seems to flow from the domestic courts' integration into the EU judicial system, a system built upon a division of labour and burden sharing between national and European courts. It therefore seems inevitable that Member State courts become involved in vindicating the common values across the Verbund.[71] In addition, this decentralized approach allows for interactions, communication, and cooperation not only at the level of the highest courts but also at the level of lower courts. Such a dialogue might bring familiarity with the other legal orders and draw domestic courts closer together, which helps the aim of 'an ever closer union'.[72]

Nonetheless, a decentralized review contains some considerable risks. For one, it might provoke diverging or incompatible decisions throughout the EU judicial space. Even a brief look at the inconsistent national practices suffices to confirm this intuition.[73] As currently practised, *horizontal Solange* entails a risk of fragmentation that is hardly desirable. Especially regarding the existence of systemic deficiencies, a uniform stance appears essential. The Court of Justice should therefore decide at least on the systemic part of the *Aranyosi*-test.[74] Under the preliminary reference procedure, the Court might not be able to directly assess the factual situation within a Member State. Still, it can apply a high degree of specificity that clearly suggests the outcome of a case.[75] This is hardly revolutionary.[76] Taking the proceedings to Luxembourg becomes even more important as it is the only way for the 'accused' Member State to defend itself (by submitting an observation). In national proceedings, a foreign Member State has practically no possibility to intervene. While the Court tries to attenuate this defect by requiring the issuing Member State to provide the necessary evidence, there is no possibility of actually countering allegations concerning systemic deficiencies in the respective national proceedings. For that reason, the decentralized approach seems to be at odds with

[70] ibid paras 96 f. See also the criticism by Frackowiak-Adamska (n 33) 137.

[71] Armin von Bogdandy et al., 'A Potential Constitutional Moment For The European Rule of Law—The Importance of Red Lines' CML Rev 55 (2018), 983, 991.

[72] Canor (n 50) 199.

[73] See the cases cited in n 64 and 65.

[74] Canor (n 50); Wendel (n 41) 41 ff.

[75] Takis Tridimas, 'Constitutional Review of Member State Action: The Virtues and Vices of an Incomplete Jurisdiction' I-CON 9 (2011), 737, 739 ff.

[76] The Court already assessed the existence of systemic deficiencies in several cases, see *N.S.* (n 58) paras 86, 89, 94, 106 or Case C-220/18 PPU *Generalstaatsanwaltschaft (Conditions of detention in Hungary)* [2018] EU:C:2018:589.

a central component of the rule of law: a fair hearing, audiatur et altera pars, and the equality of arms.[77]

2. Beyond the European Arrest Warrant: Increasing the stakes for non-compliant Member States

Certainly, detecting systemic deficiencies is important. It calls certain Member States out and can lead to a naming and shaming. Nevertheless, suspending cooperation under mutual recognition regimes unfolds its full potential for the Verbund's constitutional homogeneity only if it presents an incentive for Member States to actually comply with EU values. Currently, it appears highly unlikely that Poland's or Hungary's isolation from the EAW system would exert enough pressure for their governments to change course.[78] As such, it might be useful to expand the *horizontal Solange* doctrine to other mutual recognition regimes and increase the pressure.[79] Yet, not all mechanisms seem equally suitable in this respect. For instance, suspending cooperation with Poland or Hungary under the Dublin system could be perceived as a courtesy.[80]

Mutual recognition regimes that could provide serious leverage concern the cooperation in civil matters, such as the recognition of judicial decisions. Regulations covering this field are equally underpinned by mutual trust. Similar to the EAW framework, this trust is not blind but subject to control in exceptional situations. Accordingly, such mechanisms could provide two avenues for reviewing the independence of bodies issuing judicial decisions. The Brussels Ibis Regulation may illustrate these paths. First, the executing authority might consider, whether the respective decision whose enforcement is sought constitutes indeed a 'judgment'.[81] Article 2 of the Regulation defines judgments as decisions 'given by a court or tribunal of a Member State'. Read in conformity with Articles 2 and 19 TEU as well as Article 47 of the Charter, this can mean only an independent tribunal established by law. In this spirit, the Court stated in *Pula Parking* that only entities that offer guarantees of independence and impartiality could be considered 'courts' within the meaning of the Brussels Ibis Regulation.[82] However, in light of the judgment

[77] On these sub-principles of the rule of law, see e.g. Case C-219/20 *Bezirkshauptmannschaft Hartberg-Fürstenfeld (Délai de prescription)* [2022] EU:C:2022:89, para 46.

[78] See differently Canor (n 50) 203.

[79] See e.g. a reference from the Landgericht Aachen (Case C-819/21) concerning a refusal to recognize the judgment of another Member State and to enforce the sentence enforced by that judgment based on Article 3(4) of Council Framework Decision 2008/909/JHA of 27 November 2008 on the application of the principle of mutual recognition to judgments in criminal matters imposing custodial sentences or measures involving deprivation of liberty for the purpose of their enforcement in the European Union.

[80] Further, recent case law seems to indicate a departure from the notion of systemic deficiencies in the Dublin related jurisprudence. See e.g. Case C-163/17 *Jawo* [2019] EU:C:2019:218, para 87; Case C-578/16 PPU *C. K. and Others* [2017] EU:C:2017:127.

[81] Magdalena Ličková and Crístian Oró Martínez, 'Mutual Recognition in Civil and Commercial Matters: On Certified Mutual Trust' in Iglesias Sánchez and González Pascual (n 52) 179, 189.

[82] Case C-551/15 *Pula Parking* [2017] EU:C:2017:193, para 54.

in *Openbaar Ministerie*, it seems highly unlikely that Luxembourg will go further down that path (see Section III.A.1).

Second, most regimes facilitating cooperation in civil matters contain public policy exceptions.[83] Article 45 of Brussels Ibis, for example, states that 'the recognition of a judgment shall be refused ... if such recognition is manifestly contrary to public policy (ordre public) in the Member State addressed'. Just like the exceptions to cooperation under the EAW framework, this ground for refusal must be interpreted strictly as applying only in 'exceptional cases'.[84] This is the case, if the judgment whose recognition or enforcement is sought violates a 'fundamental principle' or constitutes 'a manifest breach' of an essential rule or right in the executing Member State or the EU legal order.[85] This comes with an important caveat: individuals are required to use all legal remedies in the issuing Member State—including the preliminary reference procedure—to prevent a breach of public policy before it occurs. This caveat is based on the 'trust which the Member States accord to one another's legal systems and judicial institutions'.[86] It seems clear that this condition presupposes the existence of effective judicial protection in the issuing Member State. Further, it is out of the question that any violation of Articles 2 and 19 TEU or Article 47 of the Charter, in particular if they occur before the court rendering the judgment whose recognition or execution is sought, constitutes a manifest breach of fundamental principles. Against this backdrop, some have suggested extending the Court's EAW jurisprudence to cooperation in civil matters.[87]

Also beyond mutual recognition regimes in the AFSJ, there is room for horizontal review and suspension of cooperation. This is especially the case of so-called 'transnational administrative acts'.[88] One such example is Directive 2010/24 concerning mutual assistance for the recovery of tax claims. In *Donnellan*, the Court of Justice stressed that this system depends on the existence of mutual trust between the national authorities.[89] By implication, an affected person cannot raise

[83] See Art. 21 Regulation 593/2008 (Rome I); Art. 26 Regulation 864/2007 (Rome II); Art. 23 Regulation 2201/2003 (Brussels II bis). See Lenaerts (n 36) 824 ff; Eva Storskrubb, 'Mutual Trust and the Dark Horse of Civil Justice' CYELS 20 (2018), 179, 189 f; Eloisa Giorgi, *Il principio del mutuo riconoscimento nell'ordinamento dell'Unione europea* (Firenze Univ. Press 2020) 54 ff.

[84] With regard to the former Brussles I Regulation, see Case C-559/14 *Meroni* [2016] EU:C:2016:349, para 38; Case C-619/10 *Trade Agency* [2012] EU:C:2012:531, para 51; Case C-420/07 *Apostolides* [2009] EU:C:2009:271, para 55. See already with regard to the Brussels Convention Case C-7/98 *Krombach* [2000] EU:C:2000:164, para 37.

[85] *Meroni* (n 84) para 42; *Apostolides* (n 84) para 59.

[86] *Meroni* (n 84) paras 47 f; Case C-681/13 *Diageo Brands* [2015] EU:C:2015:471, paras 63 f.

[87] See e.g. Steffen Burrer and Dawid Marusczyk, 'Grenzüberschreitende Anerkennung und Vollstreckung polnischer Urteile nach der EuGVVO in Zeiten der polnischen Verfassungskrise' EuZW 33 (2022), 200; Monique Hazelhorst, 'Mutual Trust Under Pressure: Civil Justice Cooperation in the EU and the Rule of Law' *Netherlands International Law Review* 65 (2018), 103.

[88] On this, see Emilie Chevalier and Olivier Dubos, 'The Notion of "Transnationality" in Administrative Law: Taxonomy and Judicial Review' GLJ 22 (2021), 325.

[89] Case C-34/17 *Donnellan* [2018] EU:C:2018:282, para 41.

claims relating to the substance of a tax claim before the domestic authorities, whose assistance is requested. Such issues must be raised before the authorities of the applicant Member State.[90] By now it should be clear that this rule is subject to exceptions once the basis for mutual trust has been shattered. According to the Court, Member States can reject requests for assistance if the person concerned had no opportunity to raise the matter before the courts of the applicant Member States 'under conditions compatible with the fundamental right to an effective remedy'.[91] While *Donnellan* has remained an isolated case so far, it seems nonetheless possible to apply this exception to Member States, whose judicial system does not comply with essential guarantees of independence anymore.[92]

Admittedly, much of what has been proposed in this section remains a rough sketch. As they currently stand, mutual recognition regimes beyond the EAW framework are not developed enough to provide an instrument with bite against illiberal developments in the Member States. In this sense, much will depend on future academic work and the courts' willingness to rely on these mechanisms in order to set a respective development in motion. Taken individually, it seems that suspending cooperation under these regimes does not seem to exert much pressure on Member States who resist complying with Article 2 TEU. Yet, things might look different if such suspension takes place on several levels and in several regimes *at once*. The combined effect of such horizontal measures will certainly raise the costs of disregarding the Union's common values and might compel Member States to comply. Together they might thus constitute an important element in securing the constitutional homogeneity across the Verbund.

[90] See Art. 14(1) Council Directive 2010/24/EU of 16 March 2010 concerning mutual assistance for the recovery of claims relating to taxes, duties and other measures [2010] OJ L84/1.

[91] *Donnellan* (n 89) para 59. In detail Paolo Mazzotti and Mariolina Eliantonio, 'Transnational Judicial Review in Horizontal Composite Procedures' EP 5 (2020), 41.

[92] In this sense, see e.g. Sébastien Platon, 'Les fonctions du standard de l'État de droit en droit de l'Union européenne' RTDE 55 (2019), 305, 318 f.

11
Bottom-Up Review

I. Introduction

Constitutional homogeneity in the Verbund can be guaranteed not only through top-down or horizontal channels. As outlined in Chapter 8, the national level receives impulses from the European one and equally sends such impulses back. In this bottom-up context, the Member States' constitutional courts have an important role to play. Many national legal systems contain certain constitutional principles which must be respected at the EU level. As will be argued below, these requirements vis-à-vis the EU often correspond to those principles that make up the Member States' constitutional identities. Voicing these identities before the Court of Justice and assessing the Union's compliance with these principles can thus become an important tool to secure constitutional homogeneity across the Verbund.

At first sight, this might seem counterfactual. Recent developments demonstrate that constitutional identity conflicts have become an existential challenge for the Verbund. Instead of serving as a means of mutual stabilization, they have become a tool of contestation (Section II.A). At the same time, the central gateway for constitutional identity concerns under EU Law—Article 4(2) TEU—turned out to be a rather inadequate tool (Section II.B). Against this backdrop, the following chapter will suggest articulating identity concerns under the banner of Article 2 TEU (Section III.A). Indeed, the Member States' constitutional identities reveal surprising parallels to the common values. Addressing them under Article 2 TEU might not only help turn heated identity conflicts into a productive dialogue that stabilizes the constitutional homogeneity in the Verbund; it can also increase the role and relevance of national constitutional courts in the EU judicial space (Section III.B).

II. Tapping the Potential of Constitutional Identity Reviews

Before diving into these issues, the following sections will briefly introduce the instruments at issue. Over the past years, many national courts have established identity review mechanisms.[1] While the doctrines of the German

[1] For an attempt to compare and systematize these reviews, see e.g. Luke D. Spieker, 'Framing and Managing Constitutional Identity Conflicts' CML Rev 57 (2020), 361. For a detailed assessment, see the

EU Values Before the Court of Justice. Luke Dimitrios Spieker, Oxford University Press. © Luke Dimitrios Spieker 2023.
DOI: 10.1093/oso/9780198876717.003.0012

Bundesverfassungsgericht and the Italian Corte Costituzionale are probably the most influential examples, the concept has also emerged in Eastern European Member States, like Hungary, Poland, or Romania. Even seemingly weaker constitutional judiciaries, for instance, France or Belgium, have found the concept irresistible. Some even argue that constitutional identity has become 'the most successful legal transplant in the early twenty-first century'.[2] These instruments allow national courts to review whether a domestic transfer of competences to the EU or a Union act violates a set of constitutional core principles often but not necessarily summarized under the catchphrase of constitutional identity.

These mechanisms are usually derived from the domestic legal basis for conferring competences on the EU. Under these provisions, conferral is limited either explicitly or implicitly by certain constitutional principles. For example, pursuant to Article 23(1)(3) of the German Basic Law, any conferral must comply with the eternity clause enshrined in Article 79(3). That provision protects not only principles like human dignity, the rule of law, and democracy but also—through the latter—the order of competences between the domestic and the EU level. The democratic principle includes a right to be subjected only to public authority that has been legitimized by the voter.[3] This right can be violated when EU institutions assume new competences without any democratically mandated transfer or when they exceed already transferred competences in a manifest and structurally significant way (thereby committing an ultra-vires act). Hence, the ultra-vires review constitutes a 'particular case' of identity reviews.[4] In sum, identity review mechanisms can relate to the review of either certain *constitutional principles* or *competences*.

The former dimension seems well-suited to voice the Member States' homogeneity requirements towards the EU. If national constitutional courts express concerns in this respect, they can point to defects and trigger necessary reactions at the EU level.[5] Accordingly, these claims can serve as a bottom-up check to stabilize the constitutional homogeneity across the Verbund. In the course of European integration, this kind of interaction has been an important driving force. One only needs to think of the early *Solange* jurisprudence by the German BVerfG and its

individual contributions to Christian Calliess and Gerhard van der Schyff (eds), *Constitutional Identity in a Europe of Multilevel Constitutionalism* (CUP 2019) as well as Danielle Rojas, *L'utilisation de la notion d'identité constitutionnelle. Recherche axée sur les acteurs de la mobilisation de l'identité constitutionnelle nationale dans l'Union européenne* (IFJD 2021).

[2] Vlad Perju, 'Identity Federalism in Europe and the United States' *Vanderbilt Journal of Transnational Law* 53 (2020), 207, 211.

[3] See e.g. BVerfG, Judgment of 5 May 2020, 2 BvR 859/15, *PSPP*, para 98 ff.

[4] BVerfG, Judgment of 21 June 2016, 2 BvR 2728/13, *OMT*, para 153; Judgment of 2019, 2 BvR 1685/14, *Euroepan Banking Union*, para 205. On this relationship, see further Christian Calliess, 'Constitutional Identity in Germany' in Calliess and van der Schyff (n 1) 153, 175.

[5] On the strategic influence that national constitutional courts can exert on the CJEU, see e.g. Marco Dani, 'National Constitutional Courts in Supranational Litigation: A Contextual Analysis' ELJ 23 (2017), 189, 203.

Italian equivalent that pushed the development of fundamental rights at the EU level.[6] One could also point to Karlsruhe's decision in *Identitätskontrolle I* that arguably persuaded Luxembourg to allow the suspension of European Arrest Warrants in cases of grave fundamental rights violations in the issuing Member State.[7] Even if this dialogue will inevitably lead to conflicts, it can play an important role in guaranteeing the constitutional homogeneity in the Verbund—as long as it remains constructive.[8] In the current situation, however, the great potential of this bottom-up check remains largely untapped. Whereas many of these doctrines are still marked by a certain 'Europarechtsfreundlichkeit', some identity reviews have turned into highly conflict-prone instruments.[9] The German, Polish, Hungarian, and Romanian mechanisms, in particular, are increasingly geared towards contestation and conflict (Section A). At the same time, Article 4(2) TEU has proven to be an inadequate tool for voicing these concerns under EU law (Section B). Against this backdrop, the Verbund is in need not only of a more relational approach among the respective courts but also of more constructive channels to articulate identity concerns under EU Law.

A. Institutionally: Moving Towards a More Relational Approach

As indicated above, identity review mechanisms can bite in two kinds of situations.[10] First, constitutional courts can assess the initial transfer of competences to the EU level, respectively the act of ratification or consent (*ex ante or preventive identity review*). Second, these instruments allow the respective courts to review EU acts or their domestic implementation even after the transfer has taken place (*ex post or defensive identity review*).[11] If an EU act violates a Member State's

[6] The accuracy of this narrative is disputed, see Giacomo Delledonne and Federico Fabbrini, 'The Founding Myth of European Human Rights Law' EL Rev 44 (2019), 178 and William Phelan, 'The Role of the German and Italian Constitutional Courts in the Rise of EU Human Rights Jurisprudence' EL Rev 46 (2021), 175.

[7] BVerfG, Order of 15 December 2015, 2 BvR 2735/14, *Identitätskontrolle I*. See e.g. Matthias Hong, 'Human Dignity, Identity Review of the European Arrest Warrant and the Court of Justice as a Listener in the Dialogue of Courts' EuConst 12 (2016), 549.

[8] See e.g. Ana Bobić, 'Constructive Versus Destructive Conflict: Taking Stock of the Recent Constitutional Jurisprudence in the EU' CYELS 22 (2020), 60; Giuseppe Martinico, 'The "Polemical" Spirit of European Constitutional Law: On the Importance of Conflicts in EU Law' GLJ 16 (2015), 1343.

[9] In detail, Spieker (n 1) 373 f. Similarly Jiří Zemánek, Jordane Arlettaz, and Augustin Berthout, 'Droit de l'Union et noyau dur constitutionnel en France, Espagne, Italie, Allemagne et République tchèque' in David Petrlík et al. (eds), *Liber amicorum Jiří Malenovský* (Bruylant 2020) 231.

[10] For this systematization, see Mattias Wendel, 'The Fog of Identity and Judicial Contestation: Preventive and Defensive Constitutional Identity Review in Germany' EPL 27 (2021), 465, 472 f, 481 f.

[11] For instance, BVerfG, Order of 14 January 2014, 2 BvR 2728/13, *OMT* or *Identitätskontrolle I* (n 7). See also Corte Costituzionale, Ordinanza 24/2017 (IT:COST:2017:24); Trybunał Konstytucyjny, Judgment of 16 November 2011, SK 45/09, *Brussels I*; Conseil Constitutionnel, Décision n° 2006-540 DC, *Loi relative au droit d'auteur*.

constitutional identity, the respective court can decide to suspend its application in the domestic legal order.[12] As such, identity concerns constitute a permanent Damocles sword hanging over the primacy of EU law. This radically contradicts Luxembourg's mantra-like emphasis on primacy over any national law and the adamant interdiction of Member State courts to set aside Union law on their own motion.[13] In this sense, identity reviews give expression to a deeper conflict surrounding the final word on the application of EU law.[14]

Recently, this entrenched standoff has culminated in open confrontation. After several warning shots by other courts,[15] the BVerfG has put words into deeds and declared the CJEU's judgment in *Weiss* ultra vires.[16] The captured Polish Constitutional Tribunal followed suit and abused this precedent to undermine Luxembourg's intervention in the upheaval of the Polish judiciary.[17] The Court of Justice reacted with an unprecedented press statement emphasizing the primacy of EU law.[18] Even Commission President von der Leyen stressed in surprisingly blunt terms that '[t]he final word on EU law is always spoken in Luxembourg. Nowhere else.'[19] Still, concessions—let alone a surrender—seem highly unlikely. While national courts will hardly change course, the primacy of EU law remains unconditional for the Court of Justice.[20]

Ways to mitigate the conflict should thus not concentrate on *whether* national courts should exercise identity reviews but rather on *how* they articulate these concerns. Such adjustments require neither a decision on the final say nor a revocation of the established mechanisms. A promising path has been advanced by Marta Cartabia, former president of the Italian Corte Costituzionale. According to her, the Corte engages in a 'relational style' of constitutional adjudication.[21] This

[12] BVerfG, Judgment of 30 June 2009, 2 BvE 2/08, *Lisbon*, para 241.

[13] See only Case C-11/70 *Internationale Handelsgesellschaft* [1970] EU:C:1970:114 and Case C-314/85 *Foto-Frost* [1987] EU:C:1987:452.

[14] From the rich literature, see e.g. Ana Bobić, 'Constitutional Pluralism is not Dead' GLJ 18 (2017), 1395, 1417; Gertrude Lübbe-Wolff, 'Who Has the Last Word?' YEL 30 (2011), 86, 99; Mattias Kumm, 'Who is the Final Arbiter of Constitutionality in Europe?' CML Rev 36 (1999), 351, 384.

[15] See Højesteret, Judgment of 6 December 2016, 15/2014, *Ajos*; Ústavní soud, Judgment of 1 January 2012, Pl. ÚS 5/12, *Slovak pensions XVII*.

[16] BVerfG, *PSPP* (n 3).

[17] See Trybunał Konstytucyjny, Judgment of 14 July 2021, P 7/20 and Judgment of 7 October 2021, K 3/21.

[18] See CJEU, Press release following the judgment of the German Constitutional Court of 5 May 2020, No. 58/2020. Concerning the judgment of the Polish Constitutional Tribunal from 14 July 2021, see Case C-204/21 R-RAP *Commission v Poland* [Order of 6 October 2021] EU:C:2021:834, para 18.

[19] Statement by President von der Leyen (10 May 2020), STATEMENT/20/846. Concerning the judgment of the Polish Constitutional Tribunal from 7 October 2021, see 'European Commission reaffirms the primacy of EU law' (7 October 2021), STATEMENT/21/5142.

[20] For a recent emphasis, see Koen Lenaerts, José A. Gutiérrez-Fons, and Stanislas Adam, 'Exploring the Autonomy of the European Legal Order' ZaöRV 81 (2021), 47, 70; Thomas von Danwitz, 'Uniform Interpretation and Primacy of Union Law in the Dialogue of the Courts' *Verfassungsblog* (4 November 2022). For the general position, see Vassilios Skouris, 'Der Vorrang des Europäischen Unionsrechts vor dem nationalen Recht' EuR 56 (2021), 3

[21] Marta Cartabia, 'Courts' relations' I-CON 18 (2020), 3; Cartabia, 'Of Bridges and Walls: The Italian Style of Constitutional Adjudication' *Italian Journal of Public Law* 8 (2016), 37, 42; Cartabia

concerns especially the way in which courts interact with other institutions. The impact of such an approach can be illustrated by contrasting two examples. The Corte has been praised for its dialogical attitude throughout the *Taricco* saga.[22] Though flagging its constitutional identity concerns, it also affirmed the importance of primacy, demonstrated why the CJEU judgment in question was not in harmony with *European* standards, and made proposals for how to remedy the situation.[23] Obvious counterexamples are not only the *PSPP* judgment,[24] but also Karlsruhe's reference in *OMT*[25] or its non-reference in *Identitätskontrolle I*.[26]

The concept of relationality pertains not only to procedure, form, and style but also to substantive questions. Constitutional identity concerns emerge first and foremost under national constitutional law. To enter a dialogue with Luxembourg, these concerns need to be translated into EU law. What norms can facilitate such a translation? As noted above, identity reviews can operate both as a competence review and as a review of certain constitutional principles. Translating the former into the language of EU law seems relatively straightforward. As the BVerfG has already demonstrated with regard to measures taken during the financial crisis, these issues can be depicted as a dispute regarding the competences of EU institutions. With regard to constitutional principles, the first provision which comes to mind is Article 4(2) TEU. As will be discussed in the following section, however, that provision proves to be an inadequate gateway.

B. Substantively: Moving Away from Article 4(2) TEU

After Lisbon, many have read Article 4(2) TEU as heralding a new dawn in the relationship between the EU and its Member States. The provision was interpreted as overcoming the idea of absolute primacy, as giving expression to the national courts' caveats, and permitting them to set aside EU law if their constitutional identities are affected.[27] Article 4(2) TEU hardly fulfilled these high hopes. After

et al., *Italian Constitutional Justice in Global Context* (OUP 2016) 234 ff. See also Armin von Bogdandy and Davide Paris, 'Power is Perfected in Weakness' in Vittoria Barsotti et al. (eds), *Dialogues on Italian Constitutional Justice* (Routledge 2020) 263.

[22] See e.g. Daniel Sarmiento, 'Adults in the (Deliberation) Room. A Comment on M.A.S.' *Quaderni Costituzionali* 38 (2018), 228; Matteo Bonelli, 'The Taricco Saga and the Consolidation of Judicial Dialogue in the European Union' MJ 25 (2018), 357; Lucia S. Rossi, 'M.A.S. e M.B. e la torre di Babele: alla fine le Corti si comprendono ... pur parlando lingue diverse' in Chiara Amalfitano (ed.), *Primato del Diritto dell'Unione Europea e Controlimiti alla Prova della 'Saga Taricco'* (Giuffrè 2018) 153.

[23] See Davide Paris, 'Carrot and Stick' QIL 37 (2017), 5.

[24] In contrast to *Taricco*, see Joseph H.H. Weiler, 'Why Weiss?' I-CON 19 (2021), 179, 186.

[25] See e.g. Mattias Kumm, 'Rebel Without a Good Cause' GLJ 15 (2014), 203.

[26] See e.g. Julian Nowag, 'EU Law, Constitutional Identity, and Human Dignity: A Toxic Mix?' CML Rev 53 (2016), 1441, 1451.

[27] See e.g. Armin von Bogdandy and Stephan Schill, 'Overcoming Absolute Primacy' CML Rev 48 (2011), 1417, 1419, 1426 and, with regard to Art. I-5 of the Constitutional Treaty, Mattias Kumm and Victor Ferreres Comella, 'The Primacy Clause of the Constitutional Treaty' I-CON 3 (2005), 473, 476,

all, that provision has proven a rather insufficient mouthpiece for voicing constitutional identity concerns. This is due to three reasons.[28]

To start with, the status of national identities under Article 4(2) TEU does not correspond to the status of constitutional identities in the Member States. At first sight, both regimes seem to go 'hand in hand'.[29] Yet, in the rare occasions in which the Court has actually dealt with identity claims under Article 4(2) TEU, it has treated them as mere public policy exceptions stripped of any distinguishing value and as one of several components in the proportionality test.[30] This trivialization stands in stark contrast to the position constitutional identities occupy in the Member States. Their distinctive quality seems lost in translation. For this reason, the BVerfG departed from the doctrine of equivalence and stated in *OMT* that national identity under Article 4(2) TEU 'does not correspond to the concept of constitutional identity' under the Basic Law.[31] Recently, Advocate General Kokott suggested recalibrating the CJEU's jurisprudence. Where a 'fundamental expression' of a Member States' national identity is at stake, the Court should review only whether that expression respects the values enshrined in Article 2 TEU.[32] This recalibration would certainly raise the status of national identities under Article 4(2) TEU. At the same time, it significantly deviates from the current jurisprudential outlook.

Second, the CJEU has shown great reluctance to engage with national identities.[33] Even when outrightly asked, such as in *Taricco* or *Gauweiler*, the Court refrained from joining the identity tune. One can easily understand why. When operating with Article 4(2) TEU, the Court seems to walk a tightrope between Scylla

491 ff. Contrasting these expectations with the actual drafting history, Barbara Guastaferro, 'Beyond the *Exceptionalism* of Constitutional Conflicts' YEL 31 (2012), 263, 266.

[28] From very different perspectives, see also the critique of the identity concept by Federico Fabbrini and András Sajó, 'The Dangers of Constitutional Identity' ELJ 25 (2019), 457; Christoph Schönberger, 'Identitäterä: Verfassungsidentität zwischen Widerstandsformel und Musealisierung des Grundgesetzes' JöR 63 (2015), 41; Laurence Burgorgue-Larsen, 'L'identité constitutionnelle en question' in Burgorgue-Larsen (ed.), *L'identité constitutionnelle saisie par les juges en Europe* (Pedone 2011) 155.

[29] BVerfG, *Lisbon* (12) para 240. See also, Trybunał Konstytucyjny, Judgment of 24 November 2010, K 32/09, *Lisbon*, para 2.1.; Alkotmánybíróság, Decision of 30 November 2016, 22/2016 (XII.5.) AB, *Joint exercise of competences with the EU*, para 62.

[30] See e.g. Case C-673/16 *Coman* [2018] EU:C:2018:385, paras 42 ff; Case C-438/14 *Bogendorff* [2016] EU:C:2016:401, paras 64 f; Case C-208/09 *Sayn Wittgenstein* [2010] EU:C:2010:806, paras 83 f. For an overview, see François-Xavier Millet, 'Successfully Articulating National Constitutional Identity Claims' EPL 27 (2021), 571, 573–84; Ana Bobić, *The Jurisprudence of Constitutional Conflict in the European Union* (OUP 2022) 156 ff.

[31] BVerfG, Order in *OMT* (n 11) para 29.

[32] See Case C-490/20 *Stolichna obshtina, rayon "Pancharevo"* [2021] EU:C:2021:296, Opinion of AG Kokott, para 101. See also paras 82 f, 89 ff.

[33] For a systematization of the relatively limited case law, see Pablo Cruz Mantilla de los Ríos, *La identidad nacional de los estados miembros en el derecho de la Uníon europea* (Aranzadi 2022); Anita Schnettger, *Verbundidentität* (Mohr Siebeck 2020) 70 ff; Giacomo di Federico, *L'identità nazionale degli stati membri nel diritto dell'Unione europea. Natura e portata dell'art. 4, par. 2, TUE* (Editoriale Scientifica 2017) 74 ff; Elke Cloots, *National Identity in EU Law* (OUP 2015) 63 ff.

(a narrow interpretation that exposes the primacy of EU law to the risk of rejection by national constitutional courts) and Charybdis (a broad interpretation that likewise undermines the primacy of EU law). Accordingly, there are good reasons for the Court to keep Article 4(2) TEU a dead letter. This scarce use has led legal scholarship to examine cases in which the Court has expressed a 'silent sensitivity' towards national specificities.[34] Some have argued, for instance, that the judgment in *Omega* embraced the absolute concept of human dignity required by the BVerfG.[35] According to my understanding, however, the Court did not rely on a particular German conception of human dignity. To the contrary, it referred to a concept inherent in the EU legal order. 'There can ... be no doubt that the objective of protecting human dignity is compatible with Community law, it being immaterial in that respect that, in Germany, the principle of respect for human dignity has a particular status'.[36] This seems to follow a more general tendency in the CJEU's jurisprudence when dealing with specific interests of the Member States. Seldom does the Court allow national particularities to enter EU law in an unfiltered fashion.[37] Instead, it relies, as far as is possible, on conceptions inherent in the EU legal order before engaging with the permeability towards national specificities.

Finally, the notion of constitutional identity is inherently divisive. Although some hoped that Article 4(2) TEU would allow for a common European discourse on the sensitive issue of constitutional identity,[38] Article 4(2) TEU revealed to be more of an identity battleground than a platform for discourse. Identity has been compared to a shield and a sword pointed towards the EU or a *norme de résistance* at the discretion of national courts.[39] This has to do with the inherent nature of identities. Generally, the term identity has a twofold meaning. It can express commonality, convergence, equivalence, similarity, and sameness or—in total opposition to the former—distinctiveness, difference, individuality, idiosyncrasy, specificity, or selfhood.[40] In light of its very function, the notion of constitutional or national identity is attached to the latter meaning.[41] Understood as a trait that

[34] Cloots (n 33) 7. See also Loïc Azoulai, 'The European Court of Justice and the duty to respect sensitive national interests' in Mark Dawson et al. (eds), *Judicial Activism at the European Court of Justice* (Elgar 2013) 167, 176 ff.

[35] Jürgen Schwarze, 'Balancing EU Integration and National Interests in The Case-law of The Court of Justice' in Allan Rosas et al. (eds), *The Court of Justice and the Construction of Europe* (Asser 2013) 257, 260 f.

[36] Case C-36/02 *Omega* [2004] EU:C:2004:614, para 34. Similarly, Leonard Besselink, 'Case Note on C-208/09 Ilonka Sayn-Wittgenstein' CML Rev 49 (2012), 671, 680; Michael Goldhammer, 'Die Achtung der nationalen Identität durch die Europäische Union' JöR 63 (2015), 105, 114.

[37] See e.g. Floris de Witte, 'Sex, drugs & EU law' CML Rev 50 (2014), 1545, 1562 ff.

[38] von Bogdandy and Schill (n 27) 1440.

[39] Theodore Konstadinides, 'Constitutional Identity as a Shield and as a Sword' CYELS 13 (2011), 195; Xavier Millet, *L'Union européenne et l'identité constitutionnelle des États membres* (LGDJ 2013) 17. For a more positive take, see Christiaan Timmermans, 'Mediating Conflicts between National Identities and EU Law: The Potential of Article 4(2) TEU' CML Rev 59 (2022), 75, 85 f.

[40] Julien Sterck, 'Sameness and Selfhood' ELJ 24 (2018), 281; Alexandre Viala, 'Le concept d'identité constitutionnelle' in Burgorgue-Larsen (n 28) 7, 9.

[41] Kassandra Wetz, *Funktionen von Verfassungsidentität als gerichtliches Konzept in der Europäischen Union* (Mohr Siebeck 2022) 354.

sets apart, identity is defined in opposition to others; it is essentially constituted by negation.[42] In this sense, constitutional identities are inherently delineating.

III. The Potential of Article 2 TEU

Against this backdrop, articulating identity concerns under Article 4(2) TEU contributes little to stabilising the constitutional homogeneity in the Verbund. Whereas the notion of homogeneity denotes the sameness of constitutional structures across the Verbund, Article 4(2) TEU protects the Member States' specificities. This chapter suggests that as far as constitutional principles, such as democracy, the rule of law, or fundamental rights, are at stake, national courts should start relying on concepts that are common to the EU and its Member States. In fact, operating under such a 'common grammar' is a fundamental precondition for the functioning of any pluralist system.[43] Miguel Maduro, for instance, argued that national courts should reason in 'universal' terms when dealing with EU law. Only then can the Court of Justice internalize their views.[44] Such common concepts can be found in the common constitutional traditions under Article 6(3) TEU or the common values under Article 2 TEU. By definition, their key concern is to articulate convergence. As such, these notions can provide the basis for a more relational dialogue. While some have explored relying on common constitutional traditions,[45] this contribution argues that national courts should formulate their identity concerns under the banner of Article 2 TEU. The following sections will demonstrate that such reformulations are possible both substantively and procedurally (Section A) before outlining the advantages of the suggested approach (Section B).

A. Formulating Identity as Common Value Concerns

1. Substantive level

To start with, articulating constitutional identity as common value concerns presupposes the congruence of both concepts on a *normative*, *conceptual*, and *substantive* level. From a normative perspective, Article 2 TEU in fact requires a certain congruence of the EU's common values and the Member States' constitutional

[42] Michael Rosenfeld, 'Constitutional Identity' in Rosenfeld and András Sajó (eds), *The Oxford Handbook of Comparative Constitutional Law* (OUP 2012) 756, 759.

[43] See only Mireille Delmas-Marty, *Ordering Pluralism* (Hart 2009) 72 ff.

[44] On this 'universalisability', see Miguel Maduro, 'Contrapunctual Law' in Neil Walker (ed.), *Sovereignty in Transition* (Hart 2003) 501, 529 f. See also Bobić (n 30) 59–61.

[45] Oreste Pollicino and Massimo Fichera, 'The Dialectics Between Constitutional Identity and Common Constitutional Traditions' GLJ 79 (2019), 1097.

identities. As argued in Chapter 8, this claim is established in a twofold manner. On the one hand, the Member States' constitutional identities are the central point of reference when determining the content of Article 2 TEU (see Chapter 2, III.B.2). On the other hand, Article 2 TEU is not only a gateway for domestic constitutional law into the EU legal order,[46] but establishes a veritable value interaction (Chapter 8, III.A). Member States contribute the essential building blocks and are subsequently bound by a set of values that is common to the EU and its Member States. As long as the Member States are part of the Union, Article 2 TEU defines a common constitutional identity from which they cannot derogate. Such an understanding is indicated especially by Articles 7 and 49(1) TEU.

Eventually, this extends to the Member States' constitutional identities, which may not contradict the common values.[47] In this spirit, Advocate General Kokott argued in *Pancharevo* that 'only a conception of national identity which is consistent with the fundamental values of the European Union as enshrined inter alia in Article 2 TEU may be protected under Article 4(2) TEU.'[48] The Court embraced this position in one of its judgments on the rule of law conditionality regulation. Here, the Court stated that even though the national identities may vary in each Member State, they cannot deviate from the Union's common constitutional identity enshrined in Article 2 TEU. Put differently: only those claims can be accepted as legitimate expressions of national identities under Article 4(2) TEU that adhere to the values in Article 2 TEU.[49] This seems to be increasingly accepted in the national sphere too. In *Lisbon*, the German Constitutional Court still stressed that the values enshrined in Article 2 TEU may not claim primacy over the Member States' constitutional identities protected by Article 4(2) TEU.[50] In stark contrast, its former president, Andreas Voßkuhle, now emphasized that the values enshrined

[46] For some, this is the central purpose of Art. 4(2) TEU, see Mattias Wendel, *Permeabilität im europäischen Verfassungsrecht* (Mohr Siebeck 2011) 572 ff; Anita Schnettger, 'Article 4(2) TEU as a Vehicle for National Constitutional Identity in the Shared European Legal System' in Calliess and van der Schyff (n 1) 9, 13–6.

[47] Case C-156/21 *Hungary v Parliament and Council* [2022] EU:C:2022:97, paras 233 f. See also European Parliament, Resolution on the situation of fundamental rights: standards and practices in Hungary (3 July 2013), 2012/2130(INI), Rec. M; von Bogdandy and Schill (n 27) 1430; Darinka Piqani, 'In Search of Limits for The Protection of National Identities as a Member State Interest' in Marton Varju (ed.), *Between Compliance and Particularism* (Springer 2019) 21, 41 ff; Giuseppe Martinico, 'Taming National Identity' EPL 27 (2021), 447, 462.

[48] Case C-490/20 *Stolichna obshtina, rayon "Pancharevo"* [2021] EU:C:2021:296, Opinion of AG Kokott, paras 73, 116 ff. See also Case C-62/14 *Gauweiler* [2015] EU:C:2015:7, Opinion of AG Cruz Villalón, para 61 and Egils Levits, 'L'identité nationale des États membres selon l'article 4, § 2, du T.U.E. en tant qu'élément de la structure constitutionnelle de l'Union européenne' in *Liber amicorum Vassilios Skouris* (Bruylant 2015) 387, 395 f; Lucia S. Rossi, '2, 4, 6 (TUE) … l'interpretazione dell' "Identity Clause" alla luce dei valori fondamentali dell'Unione' in *Liber Amicorum Antonio Tizzano* (Giappichelli 2018) 858, 866; Marek Safjan, 'On Symmetry' dUE (2020), 673, 681.

[49] *Hungary v Parliament and Council* (n 47) paras 233 f. See also Case C-430/21 *RS (Effet des arrêts d'une cour constitutionnelle)* [2022] EU:C:2022:44, Opinion of AG Collins, para 64. On this, see Luke D. Spieker, 'Werte, Vorrang, Identität: Der Dreiklang europäischer Justizkonflikte vor dem EuGH' EuZW 33 (2022), 305, 313.

[50] BVerfG, *Lisbon* (12) para 332.

in Article 2 TEU already took up the central contents of the Member States' constitutional identities. 'Thus, appealing to the protection of national identity is ruled out where ... national measures contradict the fundamental values'.[51]

Conceptually, both the Union's values as well as constitutional identities reveal strikingly similar features. Appealing to constitutional identities often implies absolute constitutional limitations. Even if *PSPP* seems to break with this understanding,[52] constitutional identities generally comprise essential core guarantees[53] that are triggered only in exceptional situations.[54] The same holds true for Article 2 TEU. The previous part went to some lengths to establish that Article 2 TEU stands at the summit of the substantive hierarchies that pervade EU primary law (in detail Chapter 4). The Court's decision in *Kadi* already articulated this position with regard to former Article 6(1) TEU-Nice by stating that a provision of primary law cannot authorize any derogation from the principles enshrined therein.[55] In this light, Article 2 TEU can be understood as manifesting an untouchable core of EU law. One could even go so far as to interpret Article 2 TEU as an absolute limitation for future Treaty revisions (in detail Chapter 7). At the same time, Article 2 TEU cannot be understood as imposing very detailed standards. The Treaty drafters' intention to protect a 'hard core' of values,[56] the high thresholds that characterize Article 7 TEU as well as the obligation to preserve meaningful room for the Member States' constitutional autonomy support a restrained reading. In its Verbund dimension especially, Article 2 TEU can only guarantee a thin baseline of constitutional principles (in detail Chapter 3, III).

Finally, there is a high degree of substantial convergence between Article 2 TEU and constitutional identities.[57] It would go far beyond the scope of this chapter to undertake a comprehensive comparison between the content of the Union's common values and the Member States' constitutional identities.[58] It

[51] Andreas Voßkuhle, *The Idea of the European Community of Values* (Bittner 2018) 117. Similarly, Peter M. Huber, 'Art. 2 EUV als Grundlage des Staaten- und Verfassungsverbundes der EU' *Alkotmánybírósági Szemle* (2020), 20, 22.

[52] On its questionable necessity, see only Jürgen Basedow et al., 'European Integration: Quo Vadis?' I-CON 19 (2021), 188, 204 f.

[53] See e.g. BVerfG, *Lisbon* (12) para 240 ('inviolable core'); Trybunał Konstytucyjny, *Lisbon* (n 29) para 2.1 ('the heart of the matter'); Ústavní soud, Judgment of 3 November 2009, Pl. ÚS 29/09, *Lisbon II*, para 112 ('material core').

[54] See e.g. BVerfG, *Identitätskontrolle I* (n 7) para 45 ('in exceptional cases and under narrowly defined conditions'). Similarly, see Ústavní soud, Judgment of 26 November 2008, Pl. ÚS 19/08, *Lisbon I*, paras 84, 120, 139; Trybunał Konstytucyjny, *Brussels I* (n 11) para 2.7.

[55] Cases C-402 and 415/05 P *Kadi* [2008] EU:C:2008:461, para 303.

[56] Praesidium, Draft of Articles 1 to 16 of the Constitutional Treaty, CONV 528/03, Annex II, p 11.

[57] See e.g. von Bogdandy and Schill (n 27), 1432, 1436; Monica Claes, 'How Common are the Values of the European Union?' CYELP 15 (2018), VII, XI; Vlad Constantinesco, 'La confrontation entre identité constitutionnelle européenne et identités constitutionnelles nationales: Convergence ou contradiction?' in *Mélanges en l'honneur de Philippe Manin* (Pedone 2010) 79, 81.

[58] For a brief comparative assessment, see e.g. Stephan Schill and Christoph Krenn, 'Art. 4 EUV' in Eberhard Grabitz et al. (eds), *Das Recht der Europäischen Union* (75th edn loose-leaf C.H.Beck 2022) para 28.

seems, however, that Article 2 TEU as well as the constitutional identities of the Member States encompass—*en gros*—the same foundational principles: democracy, the rule of law, and the essence of fundamental rights. Several constitutional courts have expressly affirmed this 'identity of values'.[59] The Portuguese Tribunal Constitucional, for instance, assumes an equivalence of constitutional values at the EU and the national level, thereby generally excluding a conflict.[60] In a very similar manner, its Spanish counterpart noted that EU law could not violate the values and principles of the Spanish Constitution 'without a breakdown of the Treaty itself'.[61] Even the much-criticized Hungarian constitutional identity based on its 'historical constitution' generally mirrors, at least on paper, the values enshrined in Article 2 TEU.[62] Certainly, the new Hungarian Fundamental Law sets Hungary apart from the Union in many respects.[63] Still, many of the examples cited as parts of the Hungarian constitutional identity could equally be secured under Article 2 TEU.[64] Further, it should be reiterated that both Article 2 TEU and constitutional identities are limited to the protection of a hard core and not necessarily every specific concretization.

If it eventually appears that an element of a Member State's constitutional identity does not find expression under Article 2 TEU, Article 4(2) TEU still remains as an alternative option. In this sense, Article 4(2) TEU could acquire a subsidiary function. Inspiration could be drawn from the case law of the French Conseil Constitutionnel. While already foreshadowed by its previous jurisprudence,[65] the Conseil explicitly stated in a recent decision that it is only competent to review measures implementing EU law if they question 'une règle ou un principe qui, *ne trouvant pas de protection équivalente dans le droit de l'Union européenne*, est inhérent à l'identité constitutionnelle de la France'.[66] Thus, if a principle is shared

[59] See e.g. Ústavní soud, *Lisbon I* (n 54) paras 120, 208 f. See also Trybunał Konstytucyjny, *Lisbon* (n 29) para 2.2 ('full axiological compatibility') and *Brussels I* (n 11) para 2.10 ('axiological concurrence').

[60] Tribunal Constitucional, Judgment of 15 July 2020, No. 422/2020, para 2.6.4 ('valores paramétricos equivalentes'). See also Francisco Pereira Coutinho and Nuno Piçarra, 'Portugal: the impact of European integration and the economic crisis on the identity of the constitution' in Anneli Albi and Samo Bardutzky (eds), *National Constitutions in European and Global Governance* (Asser 2019) 591, 602.

[61] Tribunal Constitucional, DTC 1/2004 (ES:TC:2004:1D), Ground 3.

[62] Alkotmánybíróság, *Joint exercise of competences with the EU* (n 29) para 65: 'important components—identical with the constitutional values generally accepted today—can be highlighted as examples: freedoms, the division of powers, republic'.

[63] See only Editorial, 'Hungary's New Constitutional Order and "European Unity"' CML Rev 49 (2012), 871.

[64] See the Concurring Opinion of Judge Varga in Alkotmánybíróság, *Joint exercise of competences with the EU* (n 29) para 110 who lists as part of the Hungarian historical constitution 'freedoms and the limitation of power (the Golden Bull), respect for autonomies under public law (Tripartitum), freedom of religion (the Laws of Torda), lawful exercising of power (Pragmatica Sanctio), parliamentarism, equal rights (Laws of April 1848), separation of powers, acknowledging judicial power, protection of minorities (Laws of the Compromise)'.

[65] On this, see e.g. Xavier Millet, 'Plaider l'identité constitutionnelle de l'État devant la Cour de justice' *Quaderni costituzionali* 38 (2018), 831, 836.

[66] Conseil Constitutionnel, Decision n° 2021-940 QPC, *Société Air France*, para 13.

by both legal orders, it is for the EU to afford protection. Recently, the Portuguese Tribunal Constitucional took a very similar stance. As the EU legal order features an equivalent protection under Article 2 TEU, the Tribunal refrains from assessing the compatibility of EU law with the 'fundamental principles of a democratic state based on the rule of law' under Article 8(4) of the Portuguese Constitution. At the same time, it reserves its jurisdiction to review cases where constitutional principles are at stake that, due to their particular nature, can only be effectively guaranteed at the national level. That includes, for instance, the national territory or the unitary state (Articles 5 and 6 of the Portuguese Constitution).[67] Following such an approach, Article 4(2) TEU would have a subsidiary function by protecting only constitutional characteristics that are distinctive and unique to a Member State and not protected by the EU legal order,[68] like issues of territorial organization,[69] languages,[70] or laws abolishing nobility.[71] Strikingly, these are exactly the cases that the CJEU has approached under Article 4(2) TEU so far.

2. Procedural level

Generally, the preliminary reference procedure is the main avenue for raising identity concerns before the CJEU. In the last decade, constitutional courts have increasingly started to make use of this instrument and enter into a direct dialogue with Luxembourg.[72] Some of them have even made preliminary references an integral part of their identity review mechanisms.[73] At the same time, the CJEU has placed an increasing emphasis on apex courts' obligations to refer.[74] Nevertheless, articulating identity concerns under Article 2 TEU faces some procedural obstacles.

From the perspective of national constitutional courts, a crucial precondition is their capacity to embrace EU values as a yardstick. In many Member States, Union law is neither the object nor the yardstick of constitutional review.[75] Some courts face an exhaustive list of enumerated competences and Union law does not expressly feature therein.[76] Despite these constraints, most of them have sufficient

[67] Tribunal Constitucional, Judgment of 15 July 2020, No. 422/2020, paras 2.6.4, 2.8. See also Rui Medeiros, 'The Primacy of European Union law Over the Portuguese Constitution According to the Constitutional Court' *Católica Law Review* 5 (2021), 111.

[68] Alina Kaczorowska-Ireland, 'What is the European Union Required to Respect Under Article 4(2) TEU? The Uniqueness Approach' EPL 25 (2019), 57. For a 'weaker' reading, see also Matteo Bonelli, 'National Identity and European Integration Beyond "Limited Fields"' EPL 27 (2021), 537, 554 f.

[69] Case C-51/15 *Remondis* [2016] EU:C:2016:985; Case C-156/13 *Digibet* [2014] EU:C:2014:1756.

[70] Case C-391/09 *Runevič-Vardyn* [2011] EU:C:2011:291; Case C-202/11 *Las* [2013] EU:C:2013:239.

[71] *Bogendorff* (n 30); *Sayn Wittgenstein* (n 30).

[72] Monica Claes, 'Luxembourg, Here We Come?' GLJ 16 (2015), 1331. For empirical evidence, Arthur Dyevre et al., 'Who Refers Most?' JEPP 27 (2020), 912, 927, Appendix, Fig. 1C.

[73] See e.g. BVerfG, *Identitätskontrolle I* (n 7) para 46. See also Trybunał Konstytucyjny, *Brussels I* (n 11) para 2.6.

[74] Case C-416/17 *Commission v France* [2018] EU:C:2018:811, paras 105 ff.

[75] For a comparative assessment, see Davide Paris, 'Constitutional Courts as European Union Courts' MJ 24 (2017), 792, 795 ff; Daria Piqani, 'The role of national constitutional courts in issues of compliance' in Marise Cremona (ed.), *Compliance and Enforcement of EU Law* (OUP 2012) 132, 134 ff.

[76] See e.g. Art. 93 German Basic Law; Art. 55 French Constitution; Art. 88 Czech Constitution.

interpretative room to take EU law into consideration.[77] The BVerfG's decision on the *Right to be forgotten II* may serve as an illustration.[78] After its *Solange II* decision, the court distinguished whether EU law leaves discretion for its national implementation or not. Whereas the latter was excluded from review, the former was reviewed solely for its compliance with national fundamental rights.[79] This general separation has now been overruled.[80] The court expressly embraced EU fundamental rights as a yardstick if the case under review is governed by provisions that are fully harmonized under EU law.[81]

From the perspective of Luxembourg, identity concerns voiced by a court under Article 2 TEU will usually provide only one of twenty-seven potentially different perspectives. As such, the CJEU might face difficulties in placing these individual claims in their greater European context. Yet, such a view severely underestimates the comparative capacities of constitutional courts in the EU judicial space. Not only are these courts increasingly connected and in constant exchange;[82] they already conduct impressive comparative studies in their decisions.[83] In order to make a compelling case, the referring court will support its position with comparative arguments (on the problems that might arise from such comparisons, see Section III.B). The Court of Justice is a well-placed institution to review (and, if needed, complement) such assessments. In particular, the CJEU has an entire Documentation and Research Directorate at its disposal whose purpose is to draft research notes on approaches taken in the national legal systems.[84]

A further untapped potential is the involvement of national constitutional courts in CJEU proceedings that concern the Member States' constitutional identities. A group of constitutional judges recently suggested inviting national constitutional courts to act as interveners and submit written observations before the CJEU.[85] Such an involvement seems difficult to square with the law as it currently

[77] With much evidence Paris (n 75) 801, 809 ff.

[78] BVerfG, Order of 6 November 2019, 1 BvR 276/17, *Right to be forgotten II*, paras 50 ff.

[79] BVerfG, Order of 22 October 1986, 2 BvR 197/83, *Solange II*, para 132; Judgment of 2000, 2 BvL 1/97, *Bananenmarkt*, para 57; Judgment of 2007, 1 BvF 1/05, *Emissionshandel*, para 68.

[80] BVerfG, *Right to be forgotten II* (n 78) paras 50, 67.

[81] On the potential of embracing the Charter, see e.g. Editorial, 'Better In Than Out' EuConst 16 (2020), 1; Laurence Burgorgue-Larsen, 'La mobilisation de la Charte des droits fondamentaux de l'Union européenne par les juridictions constitutionnelles' *Titre VII* 2 (2019), 31; Alessandra Di Martino, 'Giurisdizione costituzionale e applicabilità della Carta dei diritti fondamentali dell'Unione europea' DPCE (2019), 759, 776 ff. Critically, Jan Komárek, 'Why National Constitutional Courts Should not Embrace EU Fundamental Rights' in Sybe de Vries et al. (eds), *The EU Charter of Fundamental Rights as a Binding Instrument* (Hart 2015) 75.

[82] See e.g. Maartje De Visser and Monica Claes, 'Courts United? On European Judicial Networks' in Antoine Vauchez and Bruno de Witte (eds), *Lawyering Europe* (Hart 2013) 75.

[83] For such comparative references, see e.g. BVerfG, Order of 23 June 2021, 2 BvR 2216/20, *Unified Patent Court*, para 74; *OMT* (n 4) para 142; *Identitätskontrolle I* (n 7) para 47. See also Mattias Wendel, 'Comparative Reasoning and the Making of a Common Constitutional Law' I-CON 11 (2013), 981.

[84] See <curia.europa.eu/jcms/jcms/Jo2_11968/>.

[85] Christoph Grabenwarter, Peter M. Huber, Rajko Knez, and Ineta Ziemele, 'The Role of the Constitutional Courts in the European Judicial Network' EPL 27 (2021), 43, 58 ff. See also Michal Bobek, 'Landtová, Holubec, and the Problem of an Uncooperative Court: Implications for the Preliminary Rulings Procedure' EuConst 10 (2014), 54, 83 f.

stands. Indeed, the Court has been quite adamant in its rejection of other third-party interventions, such as amicus curiae briefs.[86] Article 23(2) of the CJEU's Statute (together with Article 96 of its Rules of Procedure) authorizes certain actors to submit a written observation in preliminary reference proceedings, while Article 40 of the Statute allows for interventions in infringement proceedings in support of one of the parties. Both provisions mention only 'the Member States', which are usually represented by their governments. The representatives of a national government, however, are not necessarily interested in advocating the concerns of their constitutional court (in particular, if EU acts are at stake which were supported by them in the Council). Yet, this could easily be remedied. Even though the Statute is a part of EU primary law (Protocol No. 3), it can be changed at the Court's request through the ordinary legislative procedure (Article 281(2) TFEU).

B. What's In It for National Constitutional Courts?

Most certainly, any turn to values by national constitutional courts will be critically observed. Therefore, it seems necessary to clearly articulate the advantages and potential of such an approach. The most crucial question will be: what's in it for national constitutional courts? To start with, Article 2 TEU provides a stronger protection for the principles that come under its scope than Article 4(2) TEU (*substantive argument*). Further, taking an active role in fleshing out the Union's common values allows national constitutional courts to consolidate their institutional position in the EU judicial space (*institutional argument*). Moreover, by relying on common values instead of identity semantics constitutional courts can prevent abuses of their doctrines by captured constitutional courts in Poland or Hungary (*argument from abuse*). Finally, national courts might find a much more responsive counterpart in Luxembourg (*argument from dialogue*).

Starting with the first, Article 2 TEU corresponds much better to the paramount importance of constitutional identities in the national legal orders. Unlike Article 4(2) TEU, Article 2 TEU is not operated as a mere public policy exception that is balanced against other considerations. Since this provision stands at the top tier of its hierarchy, all EU law—even primary law—has to be interpreted in conformity with it (Chapter 5, III.B). As such, reformulating identity as EU value concerns leads to a considerably more effective expression and protection of constitutional identities at the EU level. If a national constitutional court aims at expressing a principle of *highest* constitutional authority, it can best do so by submitting its interpretation of the corresponding value under Article 2 TEU.

86 Cases C-403 and 429/08 *Murphy* [Order of 16 December 2009] EU:C:2009:789, paras 5 ff.

Second, engaging with Article 2 TEU would allow national courts to play a crucial role in constructing the Union's foundations. Since they are responsible for the authentic interpretation of their constitutional identities and, hence, for the individual building blocks of which Article 2 TEU is composed, national constitutional courts are an indispensable partner for the CJEU.[87] By embracing this role, they could actively participate in shaping the Union's common value basis, take ownership of these values, and have a significant impact on the further course of European integration.[88] This would provide them with a direct voice[89] and counter concerns regarding their increasing marginalization.[90] Admittedly, national courts cannot prescribe a specific interpretation of these values to the CJEU. Further, there is a risk—a strong likelihood indeed—that the referring court's input will amalgamate with the constitutional traditions of other Member States. Thus, it may change beyond recognition when the Court interprets Article 2 TEU. This does not mean, however, that engaging with common values instead of national identities constitutes an act of submission.[91] By referring to Luxembourg, national constitutional courts can influence the framing of a case and provide their provisional view on the respective issues. This might nudge the CJEU in a certain direction.[92] Further, empirical evidence suggests that the Court of Justice attaches great importance to references of peak courts.[93] In this spirit, power can be found not only in the 'final' but also in the 'first word'.[94]

Third, a turn from identity to values would prevent constitutional identity doctrines, e.g., by the German or Italian constitutional court, from becoming a template for captured courts in backsliding Member States. As can be observed in Hungary and Poland, appeals to national identity are key in justifying illiberal developments that violate European standards. Further, a doctrine of constitutional identity was recently established by the Hungarian Constitutional Court. While its reasoning is

[87] See already Case C-127/07 *Société Arcelor Atlantique* [2008] EU:C:2008:292, Opinion of AG Maduro, para 17.

[88] For this self-understanding, see Andreas Voßkuhle, '"European Integration Through Law": The Contribution of the Federal Constitutional Court' *European Journal of Sociology* 58 (2017), 145 and Grabenwarter, Huber, Knez, and Ziemele (n 85) 60 f. See also Bobić (n 30) 263: 'the shared values in Article 2 TEU are not the exclusive ownership of no single site of constitutional authority'.

[89] Michal Bobek, 'The impact of the European Mandate of Ordinary Courts on the position of Constitutional Courts' in Monica Claes et al. (eds), *Constitutional Conversations in Europe* (Intersentia 2012) 287, 305.

[90] See e.g. Jan Komárek, 'National Constitutional Courts in the European Constitutional Democracy' I-CON 12 (2014), 525.

[91] But see in this sense, Grabenwarter, Huber, Knez, and Ziemele (n 85) 57.

[92] For the considerable influence of such provisional views on the CJEU's interpretation, see the empirical study of references by U.K. courts in Gráinne de Búrca, 'The Mutual Judicial Influence of National Courts and the European Court of Justice through the Preliminary Rulings Mechanism' in Elizabeth Fisher et al. (eds), *The Foundations and Future of Public Law* (OUP 2020) 107, 115 ff.

[93] Michal Ovádek, Wessel Wijtvliet, and Monika Glavina, 'Which Courts Matter Most?' EJLS 12 (2020), 121.

[94] Daniel Thym, 'Friendly Takeover, or: the Power of the "First Word"' EuConst 16 (2020), 187, 204 ff; Nicola Lupo, 'The Advantage of Having the First Word in the Composite European Constitution' *Italian Journal of Public Law* 10 (2018), 186.

largely based on a comparative analysis, the construed identity review mechanism sharply dissonates with the instruments developed in other Member States.[95] Not only is the Hungarian Constitutional Court under the spell of the Hungarian government, but the established review mechanism is also based on a highly idiosyncratic, 'ethnocultural' conception of constitutional identity.[96] Therefore, many have argued that this review mechanism constitutes an abuse of the constitutional identity doctrine.[97] Similarly, the Polish Constitutional Tribunal[98] as well as the Romanian Constitutional Court referred 'mutatis mutandis' to the German doctrine to justify identity-based exceptions to the primacy of EU law.[99]

Despite futile attempts by German constitutional judges to underline the differences between Karlsruhe and Warsaw (or Budapest and Bucharest for that matter),[100] it seems that the German doctrine and, in particular, the *PSPP* judgment provide the essential building blocks to sharpen these instruments.[101] This chapter argues that the comparative basis for the abuse of identity review mechanisms would be considerably weakened if other constitutional courts started turning to common values. A continuing recourse to constitutional identity, however, might support and strengthen illiberal imitations and manipulations. In this context, the BVerfG's authority among European constitutional courts is of particular significance.[102] This authority comes with certain responsibilities. Some argue that dominant constitutional courts, such as those in Germany or Italy, carry

[95] See Alkotmánybíróság, *Joint exercise of competences with the EU* (n 29) paras 34–44, 49. On the questionability of these references, see Beata Bakó, 'The Zauberlehrling Unchained?' ZaöRV 78 (2018), 863.

[96] See e.g. Kriszta Kovács, 'The Rise of an Ethnocultural Constitutional Identity' GLJ 18 (2017), 1703, 1714. See also from the court's president, Tamás Sulyok and Gergely Deli, 'Perspektiven des Europarechts aus der Sicht des ungarischen Verfassungsgerichts' JöR 68 (2020), 721, 729 f.

[97] See e.g. Gábor Halmai, 'Abuse of Constitutional Identity' RCEEL 43 (2018), 23, 37 ff; R. Daniel Kelemen and Laurent Pech, 'The Uses and Abuses of Constitutional Pluralism' CYELS 21 (2019), 59, 65 ff; Giuseppe Martinico and Oreste Pollicino, 'Use and Abuse of a Promising Concept' YEL 39 (2020), 228, 244 ff; Pietro Faraguna, 'On the Identity Clause and Its Abuses' EPL 27 (2021), 427, 443 f. For a systematization of such abuses, see Julian Scholtes, 'Abusing Constitutional Identity' GLJ 22 (2021), 534.

[98] Polish Constitutional Tribunal, Judgment of 14 July 2021, P 7/20, paras 6.2–6.4.

[99] Curtea Constituțională, Decision No. 390 of 8 June 2021, para 81. See the country chapters on Romania in the Commission's 2021 (SWD(2021) 724 final, p 22) and 2022 Rule of Law Report (SWD(2022) 523 final, p 25).

[100] Andreas Voßkuhle, 'Applaus von der falschen Seite' in Voßkuhle, *Europa, Demokratie, Verfassungsgerichte* (Suhrkamp 2021) 334. See already Peter M. Huber, 'Art. 19 EUV' in Rudolf Streinz (eds), *EUV/AEUV* (3rd edn, C.H.Beck 2018) para 78.

[101] See e.g. the Commission's 2021 Rule of Law Report, COM(2021) 700 final, p 22. See also Stanisław Biernat, 'How Far Is It from Warsaw to Luxembourg and Karlsruhe' GLJ 21 (2020), 1104, 1114 f.

[102] Christoph Grabenwarter, 'The Cooperation of Constitutional Courts in Europe—Current Situation and Perspectives' XVIth Congress of the Conference of European Constitutional Courts (2014), <www.venice.coe.int/files/Bulletin/SpecBull-CECC-e.pdf>, p xxiv: 'Many national reports submitted by other constitutional courts ... mention the German Federal Constitutional Court as the most frequently cited foreign constitutional court, regardless of regional or linguistic factors'. See also Torben Ellerbrok and Robert Pracht, 'Das Bundesverfassungsgericht als Taktgeber im horizontalen Verfassungsgerichtsverbund' EuR 56 (2021), 188.

a 'special responsibility' to not infuse doctrines into the European legal discourse that are prone to abuse.[103]

Admittedly, nothing can prevent captured courts from pursuing the same aim, namely shielding their government's agenda from interventions by Luxembourg, through different channels. Julian Scholtes, for instance, argued that dismissing the concept of constitutional identity will not stop illiberal forces from bending and abusing the law to their own ends. Instead, there is a risk of being 'drawn into a game of "conceptual whack-a-mole", where cracking down on one concept might just provoke a similar concept in disguise to pop up elsewhere.'[104] Eventually, this might even put the values enshrined in Article 2 TEU at risk. In a gloomy version of this future, constitutional courts in Poland or Hungary could start repatriating the Union's common values and fuse their understanding into the European discourse. This might not only deepen the cleavages within the Verbund but also influence our own understanding of these values. However, the fact remains that Article 2 TEU lends itself much less to potential abuses than the notion of identity. Substantively, that provision is not about defending specificities but about establishing common ground. Accordingly, engaging with Article 2 TEU requires openness to comparison and compromise. Institutionally, national courts cannot unilaterally define the Union's common values. That is not to say that they cannot exert considerable influence. Eventually, however, it is the Luxembourg court that is tasked with making the Member States' constitutional traditions coalesce into a common whole. In this process, it can exclude illiberal understandings from tainting the interpretative development of Article 2 TEU.

Finally, national courts might find a much more responsive counterpart in Luxembourg. Shifting from Article 4(2) TEU to Article 2 TEU also means shifting the dialogue onto a more level playing field. As noted above, national courts claim an interpretative authority with regard to their constitutional identities. Indeed, the conflicts sketched above are less about identifying the 'right' interpretation of identity and more about the allocation of authority to interpret its meaning.[105] In this sense, the BVerfG noted that '[t]he protection of the latter is a task of the Federal Constitutional Court alone.'[106] To a certain extent, such a prerogative can hardly be considered unfounded. As Miguel Maduro noted, 'identity is lost if it is not self-determined.'[107] At the same time, there can be no absolute deference to national interpretations. Advocate General Cruz Villalón powerfully stressed that 'it seems … an all but impossible task to preserve *this* Union, as we know it today, if it is to be made subject to an absolute reservation, ill-defined and virtually at

[103] Stefania Ninatti and Oreste Pollicino, 'Identità costituzionale e (speciale) responsabilità delle Corti' *Quaderni Costituzionali* 40 (2020), 191.
[104] Scholtes (n 97) 550.
[105] In this sense, see Perju (n 2) 211.
[106] BVerfG, Order in *OMT* (n 11) para 29.
[107] Maduro (n 44) 526.

the discretion of each of the Member States'.[108] In any case, this tension makes the handling of Article 4(2) TEU rather difficult for the Court of Justice. Determining the Union's common values is structurally different from ascertaining identity under Article 4(2) TEU. National courts and the CJEU have an equally important role to play. In this spirit, perceiving the determination of the Union's common values as a joint exercise unburdens the dialogue from issues of final authority.

To sum up, constitutional identity reviews can be turned into a constructive tool by articulating them under Article 2 TEU. As noted above, justified challenges by constitutional courts can point to defects and trigger necessary reactions at the EU level. This might stabilize the overall constitutional homogeneity in the Verbund. Ultimately, articulating identity concerns under Article 2 TEU leads not only to a bottom-up check, but might also support the Court of Justice in countering the illiberal turn in the Member States. Given the developments in Hungary and Poland, but also in Romania, Malta, or Bulgaria, the consensus on European values seems to be crumbling. Yet, especially in times when the Union's value basis becomes shaky, it is of overarching importance to engage in a process that consolidates these foundations.[109] References by national courts concerning the meaning of the values enshrined in Article 2 TEU can foster this process.

[108] AG Cruz Villalón (n 48) para 59. See also AG Kokott (n 48) para 70; Case C-213/07 *Michaniki* [2008] EU:C:2008:544, Opinion of AG Maduro, para 33; Case C-53/04 *Marrosu and Sardino* [2006] EU:C:2006:517, Opinion of AG Maduro, para 40. Similarly, Vassilios Skouris, 'L'identité nationale: qui détermine son contenu et selon quels critères?' in *Liber Amicorum Tizzano* (n 48) 912, 916.

[109] Koen Lenaerts, 'New Horizons for the Rule of Law Within the EU' GLJ 21 (2020), 29.

IV
RISKS AND RECALIBRATION

12
Towards a Tyranny of EU Values?

I. Introduction

The last two parts attempted to unfold the vast potential of mobilizing Article 2 before the Court. Against this backdrop, we might answer the question 'Is it feasible?' with a confident 'yes'. But is it wise? This second question will be at the heart of the following two chapters. Placing an activated Article 2 TEU in the hands of the Luxembourg judges does not come without risks. Armin von Bogdandy raised the central concern: behind the serene wording of Article 2 TEU might loom a veritable 'tyranny of values'.[1] Article 2 TEU could develop into the central instrument of a militant EU democracy that destroys the very values it aims to protect.

Two values seem particularly at risk. First, the judicial activation of Article 2 TEU might endanger the rule of law (Section II). Due to its indeterminacy, the provision might become a gateway for the CJEU judges' political, moral, or ideological convictions and severely affect legal certainty (*the indeterminacy objection*). Similar concerns apply to the balancing of conflicting values (*the balancing objection*). At the same time, the judicial application of these indeterminate, yet highly significant values raises democratic concerns (Section III). For one, this relates to the judicial enforcement of EU values against Member State governments that enjoy a democratic mandate (*the counter-majoritarian objection*). Finally, the judicial mobilization of Article 2 TEU will reinforce the CJEU's powerful position in many fields and further tip the institutional balance towards the EU judiciary (*the judicial overreach objection*).[2]

Before engaging with these likely objections, two disclaimers are required. On the one hand, the concerns raised in this chapter essentially boil down to some of the evergreens of constitutional law. Our discussion will touch upon issues like the vagueness of law, the nature of balancing, the counter-majoritarian difficulty, and the general relationship of law and politics. There are certainly no straightforward answers to these issues. At times, this chapter might thus constitute rather a profession of faith than an elaborate refutation. Nevertheless, this approach allows us to situate the approach advanced in this book in a larger context and provides the

[1] Armin von Bogdandy, 'Towards a Tyranny of Values?' in von Bogdandy et al. (eds), *Defending Checks and Balances in EU Member States* (Springer 2021) 73, 75.

[2] For a detailed analysis of such arguments, see also Cassandra Emmons and Tommaso Pavone, 'The Rhetoric of Inaction' JEPP 28 (2021), 1611.

EU Values Before the Court of Justice. Luke Dimitrios Spieker, Oxford University Press.
DOI: 10.1093/oso/9780198876717.003.0013

reader with the underlying assumptions that carry these proposals. On the other hand, the rejoinders advanced in this chapter will hardly have an impact on the ground. It would be illusionary to believe that the following arguments will convince representatives of Member State governments that persistently disregard the Union's values. Yet, raising likely objections and refuting or mitigating them might persuade (or caution) members of the Court, European and national institutions, as well as the general public to follow (or refrain from) the paths outlined in this book.

II. Jeopardizing the Rule of Law: Article 2 TEU as a Gateway for CJEU Judges' Politics, Morality, or Ideology?

A first likely objection is that embracing Article 2 TEU might provide a gateway for the CJEU judges' political, moral, or ideological convictions. This could severely undermine legal certainty and the rule of law. Governments of recalcitrant Member States already try to shift the conflict on value compliance into the realm of 'ideological differences'[3] and accuse the EU institutions of pursuing an ideological agenda. Viktor Orbán's verbal attacks against the EU's 'moral judgement' passed over some Member States are evidence of this rhetoric.[4] In this sense, CJEU judges involved in cases concerning the enforcement of EU values might be discredited as 'ideological warriors' or 'guerrillas'.[5] At first glance, the value semantics seem to support such concerns. While it is generally accepted that certain values may be the basis for legal provisions (and thus, there can be a mediated value enforcement), their immediate judicial enforcement appears to be incompatible with the rule of law.[6] As values are subjective experiences, embracing them in adjudication might open the floodgates to the methodologically unconstrained preferences of judges.[7] This objection, however, would denote a severe misunderstanding of the

[3] See e.g. Letter of Zbigniew Ziobro to Frans Timmermans, Warsaw (11 Janaury 2016), BM-I-0830-2/16 p 3: 'may I ask you to exercise more restraint in instructing and cautioning the Parliament and Government of a sovereign and democratic state ... despite ideological differences that may exist between us, with you being of a left-wing persuasion'.

[4] Address by Prime Minister Viktor Orbán in the debate on the so-called Sargentini Report (Strasbourg, 11 September 2018).

[5] See e.g. the defamation of Commissioner Frans Timmermans, 'They want to make Soros's man the President of the Commission' (2 July 2019), <www.miniszterelnok.hu/they-want-to-make-soross-man-the-president-of-the-commission/>; Prime Minister Viktor Orbán's speech at the 30th Bálványos Summer Open University and Student Camp (27 July 2019), <abouthungary.hu/speeches-and-remarks/prime-minister-viktor-orbans-speech-at-the-30th-balvanyos-summer-open-university-and-student-camp>.

[6] Especially Carl Schmitt warned against the 'terror' of an immediate value enforcement by the judiciary, see *Tyrannei der Werte* (3rd edn, Duncker&Humblot 2011) 61 f. On such concerns, see also Giulio Itzcovich, 'On the Legal Enforcement of Values' in András Jakab and Dimitry Kochenov (eds), *The Enforcement of EU Law and Values* (OUP 2017) 28.

[7] See Schmitt (n 6) 55; Ernst-Wolfgang Böckenförde, 'Critique of the Value-Based Grounding of Law (1990)' in Mirjam Künkler and Tine Stein (eds), *Constitutional and Political Theory* (OUP 2017) 217.

values enshrined in Article 2 TEU. As explained earlier, Article 2 TEU should not be read as containing values but legal principles (Chapter 2). The Court's extremely broad discretion when engaging with them seems nonetheless problematic. To better address this challenge, the following sections will distinguish between two issues: the concretization of Article 2 TEU's content on the one hand (Section A) and the balancing of conflicting values on the other (Section B).

A. Value Concretization

1. The indeterminacy objection

Much of the critique centres on the indeterminacy of the values enshrined in Article 2 TEU.[8] The Polish and Hungarian challenge of Regulation 2020/2092 before the Court can serve as useful illustration. According to Article 4 of the Regulation, appropriate measures shall be taken where breaches of the rule of law in a Member State risk affecting the Union's financial interests. The Polish and Hungarian government invoked the indeterminacy of the 'rule of law' and claimed an infringement of the principle of legal certainty.[9] Before engaging with ways to deal with the risks flowing from Article 2 TEU's indeterminacy, two considerations might put this objection into perspective.

First, it seems that a judge's subjective views cannot be entirely excluded from adjudication. Today, it seems generally acknowledged that there is no such thing as a 'mechanical jurisprudence'.[10] A judge is neither the 'bouche qui prononce la loi' nor a 'Subsumtionsautomat'. One does not need to become a 'Freirechtler', a 'crit', or legal realist to accept the reality that judicial interpretation is not merely an act of cognition but always characterized by a certain degree of creation.[11] Even ardent positivists like Hans Kelsen acknowledged that legal interpretation has at its core an 'act of will'.[12] As such, a certain influence of presuppositions, personal opinions, convictions, or even ideologies on interpretative choices seems inescapable.[13] CJEU judges are certainly no exception in this regard.[14]

[8] The following part uses indeterminacy, ambiguity, vagueness, generality, or openness interchangeably. On their different facets, see Ralf Poscher, 'Ambiguity and Vagueness in Legal Interpretation' in Lawrence Solan and Peter Tiersma (eds), *Oxford Handbook on Language and Law* (OUP 2011) 128.

[9] See the grounds brought forward in Case C-156/21 *Hungary v Parliament and Council* and Case C-157/21 *Poland v Parliament and Council*.

[10] Borrowing from Roscoe Pound, 'Mechanical Jurisprudence' *Columbia Law Review* 8 (1908), 605.

[11] For a concise overview of reactions to this insight, ranging from resignation, through denial to endorsement, see Jan Komárek, 'Judicial Legitimacy in the European Union' in Claire Kilpatrick and Joanne Scott (eds), *New Legal Approaches to Studying the Court of Justice* (OUP 2020) 125, 145–9.

[12] Hans Kelsen, *Pure Theory of Law* (Univ. of California Press 1967) 354.

[13] From both ends of the spectrum, see H.L.A. Hart, *The Concept of Law* (3rd edn, Clarendon 2010) 272 ff and Duncan Kennedy, *A Critique of Adjudication* (Harvard Univ. Press 1997) 134 ff.

[14] See e.g. Tamara Capeta, 'Ideology and Legal Reasoning at the European Court of Justice' in Tamara Perišin and Siniša Rodin (eds), *The Transformation or Reconstitution of Europe: The Critical Legal Studies Perspective on the Role of the Courts in the European Union* (Hart 2018) 89. But see Thomas von Danwitz, 'Funktionsbedingungen der Rechtsprechung des Europäischen Gerichtshofes' EuR 43 (2008),

Second, indeterminacy is certainly not an issue which is particular to Article 2 TEU. Practically every legal order contains provisions of indeterminate, general, vague, or ambiguous meaning. One only needs to think of the German 'unbestimmte Rechtsbegriffe' and 'Generalklauseln' or notoriously ambiguous notions such as 'reasonableness', 'good faith', or 'ordre public'.[15] Some perceive such clauses as a delegation to the judiciary and an invitation for creative concretization.[16] In some legal orders, a judge might even feel compelled to do so. Article 4 of the French Code Civil, for instance, states that '[l]e juge qui refusera de juger, sous prétexte du silence, de l'obscurité ou de l'insuffisance de la loi, pourra être poursuivi comme coupable de déni de justice.' One could go even further and argue that indeterminacy is an inherent feature of the law. As generality is an important characteristic of legal provisions,[17] a certain open texture is inevitable.[18] Accordingly, some have argued that the rule of law—or more accurately: absolute legal certainty—is conceptually impossible.[19]

In addition, there are good reasons why a certain indeterminacy beyond the generality inherent in any legal rule may be *desirable*.[20] This applies especially to constitutions.[21] For one, it allows 'dilatory formal compromises'.[22] In constitution or Treaty making, vague notions may defer difficult questions on which no agreement was reached into the future. Moreover, indeterminate notions can foster a constitution's integrative potential (Chapter 3, III.B). For instance, the recourse to abstract values keeps dissent hidden and allows parallel processes of identification. In this sense, they enable what Cass Sunstein termed 'incompletely theorized agreements', agreements on abstract formulations (e.g. equality) accepted amidst disagreement on particular cases (e.g. equal rights for homosexual couples).[23] Finally, vague notions secure the constitution's openness to future evolutions.

769 ('das Grundverständnis der richterlichen Entscheidung als Erkenntnisakt, d. h. als ausschließlich rechtlich determinierter Erkenntnisvorgang, darf ... nicht in Zweifel gezogen ... werden').

[15] On such provisions, see e.g. Marietta Auer, 'Generalklauseln' in *Staatslexikon der Görres-Gesellschaft* (8th edn, Herder 2018); Agustín Luna Serrano, *Las normas que acogen conceptos elásticos o formulaciones abiertas* (Dykinson 2019) 123 ff; Chiara Amalfitano and Filippo Croci, 'Identificazione e ruolo delle clausole generali nell'ordinamento dell'Unione europea' dUE (2021), 9, 11 ff.

[16] See e.g. Anne Röthel and Florian Möslein, 'Concretisation of General Clauses' in Karl Riesenhuber (ed.), *European Legal Methodology* (2nd edn, Intersentia 2017) § 11, p 283.

[17] See only Lon Fuller, *The Morality of Law* (2nd edn, Yale Univ. Press 1969) 46.

[18] Hart (n 13) 123; Joseph Raz, *The Authority of Law* (2nd edn, Clarendon 2009) 180 ff; Neil MacCormick, *Rethoric and the Rule of Law* (OUP 2010) 14 f.

[19] Timothy Endicott, *Vagueness in Law* (OUP 2000) 185 ff. See also Alexandre Flückiger, 'Le principe de clarté de la loi ou l'ambiguïté d'un idéal' *Cahiers du Conseil Constitutionnel* 21 (2007).

[20] See e.g. Poscher (n 8) 143 f; Timothy Endicott, 'The Value of Vagueness' in Andrei Marmor and Scott Soames (eds), *Philosophical Foundations of Language in the Law* (OUP 2011) 14.

[21] See further Aaron Barak, 'Constitutional interpretation' in Ferdinand Melin-Soucramanien (ed.), *L'interprétation Constitutionnelle* (Dalloz 2005) 91, 97 ff.

[22] Carl Schmitt, *Constitutional Theory* (1928) (Duke Univ. Press 2008) 85 [p 32]. See also Michael Foley, *The Silence of Constitutions* (Routledge 1989) 9 ff.

[23] Cass Sunstein, 'Incompletely theorized agreements in constitutional law' *Social Research* 74 (2007), 1.

It seems that EU law is especially prone to indeterminacies.[24] Even though the depth and detail of EU law has considerably evolved, many Treaty provisions still reveal an open texture. This is exacerbated by the fact that the Treaties are equally authentic in each of the twenty-four official languages (Article 55 TEU).[25] While the Court insists on legal certainty as a fundamental principle of EU law,[26] it is generally accepted that the Court's mission under Article 19(1) TEU necessarily includes the creative development and concretization of indeterminate Treaty provisions. This is not only a position held within the Court but also shared by its national counterparts.[27] In sum, it seems that we have to accept that indeterminacy is simply a general characteristic of the law and that vague notions are essential features of almost every legal system, especially EU law. None of these considerations, however, implies that we should take indeterminate notions away from the courts.[28] The focus should rather lie on how to foster the rationality and transparency of judicial decision-making.

2. Rejoinders

These considerations indicate two ways to mitigate the tension between the indeterminate Article 2 TEU and legal certainty: rationalization (methodologically as well as institutionally) and transparency (stylistically). Starting with the first, the Court can rely on the rationalizing force of legal methodology. Some might argue that legal methods can easily be manipulated, allowing judges to arrive at almost any outcome.[29] For instance, an argument from analogy and an argumentum e contrario allow for opposite outcomes without there being any kind of hierarchy between them.[30] As such, legal methodology has been accused of merely concealing, as a kind of smokescreen, underlying political, moral, or ideological preferences.

[24] See e.g. Gunnar Beck, *The Legal Reasoning of the Court of Justice* (Hart 2013) 52 ff, 161 ff. See already Werner von Simson, 'Der Gerichtshof und unbestimmte Rechtsbegriffe' in *Zehn Jahre Rechtsprechung des Gerichtshofs der Europäischen Gemeinschaften* (Heymanns 1965) 396; Hélène Bauer-Bernet, 'Notions indéterminées et droit communautaire' in Chaim Perelman and Raymond Van der Elst (eds), *Les notions à contenu variables en droit* (Bruylant 1984) 269.

[25] See e.g. Elina Paunio, *Legal Certainty in Multilingual EU Law* (Routledge 2016) 20 ff.

[26] With regard to the clarity of legal provisions, see Case C-72/15 *Rosneft* [2017] EU:C:2017:236, para 161; Case C-308/06 *Intertanko* [2008] EU:C:2008:312, para 69; Case C-344/04 *IATA and ELFAA* [2006] EU:C:2006:10, para 69.

[27] See the sources cited in Chapter 9, n 74.

[28] This is the solution proposed by Hans Kelsen, 'Wer soll Hüter der Verfassung sein?' *Die Justiz* VI (1930/31), 576, 595 ff. For a more recent articulation, see Mark Tushnet, *Taking the Constitution Away from the Courts* (Princeton Univ. Press 1999) 9 ff.

[29] For a concise account of the U.S.-led debate among legal realists and critical legal scholars, see Lawrence B. Solum, 'Indeterminacy' in Dennis Patterson (ed.), *A Companion to Philosophy of Law and Legal Theory* (2nd edn, Wiley 2010) 479. For sceptical views from Europe, see e.g. Michel Troper, 'Une théorie réaliste de l'interprétation' in Troper, *La théorie du droit, le droit, l'État* (PUF 2001) 69; Riccardo Guastini, 'Rule-Scepticism restated' in Leslie Green and Brian Leiter (eds), *Oxford Studies in Philosophy of Law*, vol 1 (OUP 2011) 138, 148 f, 156 ff.

[30] See Kelsen (n 12) 352.

Even if one does not follow this view, it is reasonable to assume that choices among legal methods are determined by a judge's background assumptions.[31]

Certainly, legal methodology cannot completely remedy the issues arising from indeterminacy. Nevertheless, it exerts a *disciplining effect* on the interpreter.[32] Judges cannot simply base their interpretation on any kind of considerations but must translate them into a specifically legal reasoning. This process of translation leads to restraints and path dependencies that differ from reasoning based on morality, politics, or economics. Further, methodological reasoning has a *rationalizing effect* on the respective interpretation. It structures the reasoning, increases its persuasiveness, and may thus foster the decision's acceptability. As outlined in Chapter 2, the Court can employ a negative or a positive approach when fleshing out the values enshrined in Article 2 TEU. There are very good reasons to stick to a negative approach. Yet, at some point, the Court might feel compelled to flesh out the values enshrined in Article 2 TEU. When this point is reached, the CJEU might rely on the comparative method to render Article 2 TEU more specific without 'engaging in strategic behaviour to dispose ideological stakes'.[33]

Yet, the disciplining and rationalizing force of this method has its limits. When referring to external sources, like the common constitutional traditions, the Court employs an evaluative or critical legal comparison.[34] It does not draw on an arithmetical common denominator among the Member States but chooses the solution it deems to be best suited for the EU legal order.[35] Like the problematic relationship between analogy and argumentum e contrario, this tool may lead to completely opposite results. For instance, in *Mangold*, the CJEU recognized a general principle of discrimination on grounds of age although at that time practically no international instrument or Member State constitution referred to it. Conversely, it is not excluded that the Court will reject a general principle although there is a broad consensus among the Member States. As such, the Court will need to explain openly why it deviates from a commonly shared position.

In addition, the risk of pursuing ideological agendas can be further reduced from an institutional perspective. The Court consists of twenty-seven judges (not to mention the fifty-four judges at the General Court) with highly diverse personal, professional, cultural, and political backgrounds.[36] Thus, Article 2 TEU-related

[31] See e.g. Beck (n 24) 6. See Josef Esser, *Vorverständnis und Methodenwahl in der Rechtsfindung* (Athenäum 1970).

[32] See e.g. Poscher (n 8) 142. This is acknowledged even by sceptics, see Véronique Champeil-Desplats and Michel Troper, 'Proposition pour une théorie des contraintes juridiques' in Troper and Christophe Grzegorczyk (eds), *Théorie des contraintes juridiques* (Bruylant 2005), 11.

[33] Koen Lenaerts, 'Discovering the Law of the EU: The European Court of Justice and the Comparative Law Method' in Perišin and Rodin (n 14) 61, 62 f.

[34] Lenaerts calls this the 'teleological thrust of the comparative law method', ibid 82.

[35] See in particular Chapter 5, n 63 to 65.

[36] See e.g. Capeta (n 14) 107. But see on the 'transnational judicial esprit de corps', Antoine Vauchez, 'Keeping the Dream Alive: the European Court of Justice and the Transnational Fabric of Integrationist Jurisprudence' *European Political Science Review* 4 (2012), 51, 53.

decisions will be rendered by a rather heterogenous bench. Further, such cases are usually decided by the Grand Chamber in a changing composition. This makes it nearly impossible to trace the judges' personal convictions in the final decisions.[37] It might even be advisable for the CJEU to decide in full Court when fleshing out the values in Article 2 TEU. According to Article 16 of its Statute, the CJEU can decide to refer cases of 'exceptional importance' to the full Court. If this applies in cases like *Wightman* or *Pringle*, it might very well apply to Article 2 TEU-related decisions as well.

Finally, the Court's interpretation could benefit from the legitimizing force of transparency. It seems generally acknowledged that the reasoning that carries a decision is an essential part of judicial legitimacy.[38] Transparent reasoning allows for control by the public and may thus generate greater acceptance.[39] This concerns, in particular, the style of court decisions. The remarks by Jean Rivero are quite enlightening in this regard. He distinguished between two 'attitudes intellectuelles', putting an emphasis either on the court's and the law's authority or on the judgment's persuasiveness: 'l'une met l'accent sur son autorité ... l'autre sur son souci de convaincre'.[40] If a court's or the law's authority is precarious, it seems pertinent to follow the latter approach.

This applies especially to the Court of Justice.[41] Nevertheless, many argue that the Court's style is characterized by thin and poor, rather than fully developed, arguments.[42] In the words of Joseph Weiler, 'the CJEU is simply a terrible communicator.'[43] Anglo-American scholars have especially argued for the adoption of a more discursive or conversational style. Yet, such suggestions seem to fade out the fact that CJEU decisions are the product of and addressed to judges, scholars, and practitioners from twenty-seven legal cultures.[44] It seems impossible to square

[37] See Michal Bobek, 'What Are Grand Chambers for?' CYELS 23 (2021), 1.

[38] See e.g. Vlad Perju, 'Reason and Authority in the European Court of Justice' *Virginia Journal of International Law* 49 (2009), 307, 322 ff; Dominique Ritleng, 'The Independence and Legitimacy of the European Court of Justice' in Ritleng (ed.), *Independence and Legitimacy in the Institutional System of the European Union* (OUP 2016) 83, 120.

[39] Koen Lenaerts, 'The Court's outer and inner selves' in Maurice Adams et al. (eds), *Judging Europe's Judges* (Hart 2013) 13, 14; Mark A. Pollack, 'The Legitimacy of the European Court of Justice' in Nienke Grossman et al. (eds), *Legitimacy and International Courts* (CUP 2018) 143, 152.

[40] Jean Rivero, 'Le problème de l'influence des droits internes sur la Cour de Justice de la CECA' *Annuaire français de droit international* 4 (1958), 295, 298 f. From within the Court, see Maurice Lagrange, 'The Court of Justice as a Factor in European Integration' AJCL 15 (1966), 709, 721.

[41] From the bench, see e.g. Ulrich Everling, 'The Court of Justice as a Decision-Making Authority' *Michigan Law Review* 82 (1984), 1294, 1308; Ole Due, 'Pourquoi cette solution?' in Due et al. (eds), *Festschrift für Ulrich Everling*, vol 1 (Nomos 1995) 273, 275; Christiaan Timmermans, 'The European Union's Judicial System' CML Rev 41 (2004), 393, 398.

[42] Especially Joseph H.H. Weiler, 'Epilogue: The Judicial Après Nice' in Weiler and Grainne de Búrca (eds), *The European Court of Justice* (OUP 2001) 215, 219, 225; Mitchel Lasser, *Judicial Deliberations* (OUP 2004) 351 ff. See further Christoph Schönberger, '"Mi attendu, mi dissertation." Le style des décisions de la Cour de justice de l'Union européenne' *Droit et Société* 91 (2015), 505.

[43] Joseph H.H. Weiler, 'Why Weiss?' I-CON 19 (2021), 179, 185.

[44] Michal Bobek, 'Of Feasibility and Silent Elephants' in Adams (n 39) 197, 203 ff; Jan Komárek, 'Legal Reasoning in EU Law' in Damien Chalmers and Anthony Arnull (eds), *The Oxford Handbook*

them all. If a judgment tends to be overly terse and abstract, it risks being framed as apodictic or cryptic; if it tends to be more discursive and conversational, rest assured there will be voices claiming a 'surabondance' or 'excès de motivation'.[45]

What could be an alternative? This section suggests more transparency in respect to, first, the sources on which the Court's interpretation of Article 2 TEU values is based, and second, with regard to the arguments submitted by the parties (and especially the Member States). Indeed, the CJEU's jurisprudence is generally perceived as lacking a detailed engagement with the sources from which it draws its inspiration. Already in 1980, Pierre Pescatore noted with regard to the comparative method that 'les rares références à cette méthode dans les arrêts sont que ... la pointe visible de l'iceberg'.[46] When dealing with Article 2 TEU, the Court should make the hidden side of this iceberg visible. To provide just one example, the CJEU has an entire Documentation and Research Directorate whose purpose consists of drafting research notes on approaches taken in the national legal systems. Only recently did the Court make these comparative studies available.[47] A next step could consist of engaging with them in its judgments.

Second, the Court of Justice should attempt to sufficiently deal with and—if needed—refute the arguments brought forward by the parties. This applies especially to the observations submitted by the Member States. Some perceive an increasing negligence in this regard.[48] While the general impetus to provide short judgments might be a laudable effort in light of overall efficiency, the omission of dealing with the parties' arguments even in highly controversial cases seems sometimes astonishing. A good example is *Achmea*. Although fifteen Member States submitted their views, the CJEU did not mention or engage with one of their substantive arguments.

Several reasons might explain the CJEU's terse and at times opaque judicial style. To start with, the Court was modelled by drawing inspiration from the French administrative judiciary, the archetype of an authority-based model.[49] As French is also the Court's working language, it seems difficult to deny a certain institutional and linguistic influence on its style and reasoning.[50] Further, obscurity might result

of European Union Law (OUP 2015) 29, 49 f; Daniel Dittert, 'Art. 36 EuGH-Satzung' in Hans von der Groeben et al. (eds), *Europäisches Unionsrecht* (7th edn, Nomos 2015) paras 9 ff.

[45] In this sense, Jean-Claude Bonichot, 'Le style des arrêts de la Cour de justice de l'Union européenne' *Justice et Cassation* (2013), 253, 260; Laurent Coutron, 'Le styles des arrêts de la Cour de justice et normativité de la jurisprudence communautaire' RTDE (2009), 643, 644, 656 ff.

[46] Pierre Pescatore, 'Le recours, dans la jurisprudence de la Cour de justice des Communautés européennes, à des normes déduites de la comparaison des droits des États membres' *Revue internationale de droit comparé* 32 (1980), 337, 358. See also Hans Kutscher, 'Methods of Interpretation as Seen by the European Court of Justice' Judicial and Academic Conference (27–28 September 1976), I-28.

[47] These 'Notes and Studies' can be accessed here: <curia.europa.eu/jcms/jcms/p1_2170124/en/>.

[48] For examples, see Jan Komárek, 'In the Court(s) We Trust?' EL Rev 32 (2007), 467, 482.

[49] See e.g. Jean L'Huillier, 'Une conquête du droit administratif français. Le contentieux de la Communauté européenne du charbon et de l'acier' *Recueil Dalloz* (1953), Chronique XII, 63.

[50] See e.g. Anthony Arnull, 'The Working Language of the CJEU: Time for a Change?' EL Rev 43 (2018), 904; Michal Bobek, 'Epilogue' in Bobek (ed.), *Selecting Europe's Judges* (OUP 2015) 279, 309;

from the difficult deliberative processes and collegiate decisions within the Court. As it speaks with one voice (without dissenting opinions), it will often be easier to agree on a certain result than on the precise reasoning.[51] In light of these considerations, one may be tempted to argue that a certain obscurity is part of the Court's stylistic DNA.[52] Yet, there is much evidence demonstrating that even in its early case law the Court handed down judgments based on detailed comparative assessments.[53] In this sense, a thin reasoning should not be regarded as an inbuilt inevitability of CJEU judgments.

Certainly, the suggestions made above can sometimes prove contradictory. For instance, the more judges involved in a judgment, the more difficult it will be to reach a consensus on the interpretation of Article 2 TEU. As such, a decision by the Grand Chamber or even the full Court is likely to contain a thinner reasoning, thereby contravening the transparency advocated above. Further, Article 2 TEU-related cases will usually entail a certain urgency, especially when violations of EU values are litigated before the Court. Urgency does not foster a well-rounded reasoning. Even in such proceedings, however, there are ways to buy time. In infringement proceedings, for example, the CJEU might issue interim measures (if the Commission submits a respective application).

B. Value Conflicts

1. The balancing objection

Very similar concerns might also be raised with regard to the balancing of conflicting values. As discussed in the second Part of this book, the values enshrined in Article 2 TEU form a constitutional core of EU law. In relation to all other Treaty provisions, Article 2 TEU presents an untouchable set of core values that cannot be subject to any balancing. Instead, Article 2 TEU takes substantive precedence (see Chapters 4, IV). Among the values of Article 2 TEU the situation is quite different. While they can be regrouped under the banners of democracy, the rule of law, and fundamental rights, there are no abstract hierarchies between them—they are, in the words of Jürgen Habermas, 'co-original'.[54] In this context, Niklas

Federico Mancini and David T. Keeling, 'Language, Culture and Politics in the Life of the European Court of Justice' CJEL 1 (1995), 397, 399. Sceptical, Laure Clément-Wilz, 'Les Français, la France et la francophonie: réflexions sur la fabrique du droit européen' dUE (2020), 701, 716 ff. On the interplay of style and legal reasoning, see Ruth Weber, 'Le style, c'est la Cour même!' RFDC (126) (2021), 189, 200 f.

[51] See e.g. Eleanor Sharpston, 'Transparency and Clear Legal Language in the European Union' CYELS 12 (2009), 409, 416 f; Everling (n 41) 1295 ff, 1307 ff; Bonichot (n 45) 257.

[52] Brevity is indeed a central element of the CJEU's style guide, see Pierre Pescatore, *Vade-mecum—Recueil de formules et de conseils pratiques à l'usage des rédacteurs* (Bruylant 2008).

[53] Take, for instance, the detailed comparative considerations in Cases 7/56 and 3–7/57, *Algera* [1957] EU:C:1957:7, p 55 f.

[54] Jürgen Habermas, 'On the Internal Relation Between the Rule of Law and Democracy' *European Journal of Philosophy* 3 (1995), 12.

Luhman observed that a relationship of precedence exists only with regard to corresponding *counter*-values (e.g. peace is better than war) but not between *different* values.[55] By implication, such conflicts can be resolved only through balancing in the specific case. Yet, many question the rationality of such balancing processes. On the one hand, some have argued that balancing often requires the weighing of incommensurable values, such as fundamental rights and public security, that lack a common scale or metric.[56] As Antonin Scalia noted, balancing competing values is like assessing 'whether a particular line is longer than a particular rock is heavy'.[57] On the other hand, the lack of clear yardsticks increases the risk of methodologically unconstrained decisions that simply reflect the personal preferences of the adjudicator.[58] Due to their high level of indeterminacy, Article 2 TEU values might seem particularly problematic in this respect.

2. Rejoinders

It seems that these risks are already reduced with regard to Article 2 TEU. The interpretative scheme proposed in Chapters 4 and 5 serves exactly the purpose of reducing immediate value conflicts. To briefly recall the suggested approach, Article 2 TEU can be used to introduce a threefold substantive hierarchization into EU primary law: On the first level stands Article 2 TEU, on the second those provisions giving specific expression to a value enshrined in Article 2 TEU, and on the third the rest of primary law. This substantive hierarchization allows the Court to resolve more conflicts through substantive precedence rather than balancing. For instance, a clash between fundamental freedoms on the third level and Charter rights on the second level should be resolved by interpreting the former in conformity with the latter.

This led to the following objection: many provisions can be rearticulated on all three levels. For instance, fundamental freedoms (third level) can also be addressed as Charter rights, respectively Articles 15 and 16 CFR (second level), and thus give specific expression to the value of 'respect for human rights' enshrined in Article 2 TEU (first level). As previously noted, this might lead to a frequent regress to Article 2 TEU and eventually to highly abstract value conflicts. To avoid such a race to the top, the substantive hierarchies should be complemented with a layered scope of protection that becomes more constricted on each level (Chapter 4, IV). While a certain activity might be covered by fundamental freedoms, it could be less so under Articles 15 and 16 CFR. Ultimately, Article 2 TEU should protect only the

[55] Niklas Luhmann, *Gibt es in unserer Gesellschaft noch unverzichtbare Normen?* (C.F.Müller 1993) 20.

[56] See e.g. Cass Sunstein, 'Incommensurability and Valuation in Law' *Michigan Law Review* 92 (1994), 779.

[57] See *Bendix Autolite v Midweso Enterprises*, 486 U.S. 888, 897 (1998).

[58] For a concise overview of the critique, see e.g. Matthias Jestaedt, 'The Doctrine of Balancing–Strengths and Weaknesses' in Matthias Klatt (ed.), *Institutionalized Reason* (OUP 2011) 152, 159 ff.

very essence of these rights. This layering might help avoid a frequent recourse to Article 2 TEU and thus the immediate balancing of values (Chapter 5, III.B).

Certainly, the Court has a broad discretion to determine whether the essence of a right is affected. Indeed, EU law offers little guidance to distinguish between the essence and periphery of a value. As such, one may wonder whether we are simply exchanging one kind of unconstrained discretion (the balancing of competing values) with another one (the determination of what is part of the essence). It should be added, however, that elevating conflicts among competing legal provisions to the level of Article 2 TEU is not necessarily in the Court's interest. Indeed, balancing processes that involve highly abstract values are argumentatively challenging. By applying self-restraint in determining the content of Article 2 TEU, the Court can avoid a race to the top and resort to the easier tool of substantive precedence. In this sense, the CJEU would be well-advised to interpret Article 2 TEU as containing only a hard core of minimum guarantees (in detail, Chapter 13, III.A).

Nevertheless, balancing Article 2 TEU values cannot be completely excluded under this scheme. Take again our example of competing Charter rights: if *both* rights are affected in their essence, the conflict is raised to the level of Article 2 TEU and becomes one of competing values. Yet, this does not necessarily lead to completely unconstrained decisions by the Court. First, to say that balancing is devoid of *any* yardsticks seems exaggerated. Indeed, many scholars have attempted to rationalize balancing processes.[59] Admittedly, balancing establishes what Riccardo Guastini termed a 'gerarchia mobile',[60] a flexible precedence of one principle over the other in the specific case, that may undermine legal certainty. Over time, however, a certain stabilization seems very likely. Although not formally bound by its own precedent,[61] the CJEU usually sticks to its case law.[62] With regard to balancing, this may eventually lead to the development of relative weights among values that establishes a 'network of concrete preference decisions'.[63] These soft orderings are not absolute. Instead, they have a function similar to the burden of proof: The higher the weight accorded to a specific value, the less the permitted restriction or the greater the required reason in favour of the conflicting value.

Second, there seems to be a certain sense of inevitability. We live in an 'age of balancing'.[64] Once we start thinking in terms of balancing, once a court embraces this idea (method, principle, or whatever you may call it), it appears difficult to go

[59] See e.g. Robert Alexy, *A Theory of Constitutional Rights* (OUP 2010) 102 ff, 394 ff. See also Gustavo Zagrebelsky, *Intorno alla Legge* (Einaudi 2009) 102 ff; Aharon Barak, *Proportionality* (CUP 2012) 340 ff.

[60] Riccardo Guastini, *Interpretare e argomentare* (Giuffrè 2011) 206 ff.

[61] See e.g. Marc Jacob, *Precedents and Case-Based Reasoning in the European Court of Justice* (CUP 2014) 243 ff.

[62] Some even see a veritable 'originalism' at work, see Gareth Davies, 'Originalism at the European Court of Justice' in Sacha Garben and Inge Govaere (eds), *The Internal Market 2.0* (Hart 2020) 323.

[63] Alexy (n 59) 99. See also Duncan Kennedy, 'Proportionality and "deference" in contemporary constitutional thought' in Perišin and Rodin (n 14) 29, 52.

[64] Borrowing from T.A. Aleinikoff, 'Constitutional Law in the Age of Balancing' YLJ 96 (1987), 943.

back and perceive conflicts among competing values in any other way. This is more so as alternative approaches come with their own challenges.[65] Even ardent critics, like Bernhard Schlink, accept that balancing and proportionality more generally 'is part of a deep structure of constitutional grammar that forms the basis of all different constitutional languages and cultures. It comes to the surface sooner or later'.[66] This is supported by the global spread of balancing. Despite the considerable differences in each jurisdiction, it is safe to say that balancing is deeply rooted in the Member States' constitutional cultures.[67] Even though it sometimes glosses over this step,[68] the CJEU is no exception in this regard.

Against this backdrop, it might be possible to *reduce* the balancing of Article 2 TEU values by construing substantive hierarchies and relying on precedence. Nevertheless, it seems impossible to completely *exclude* it. For that reason, the discussion about balancing ultimately shifts to one about the role of courts in a democratic system.[69] Indeed, the hostility towards balancing often goes hand in hand with a certain scepticism vis-à-vis judicial lawmaking.[70] The critique by Martin Shapiro is exemplary in this regard: 'a court that admits it is balancing admits it is out of its assigned territory in a democracy'.[71]

III. Jeopardizing Democracy: Article 2 TEU as a Path to a European *Gouvernement des Juges*?

This leads us to the democratic concerns about the judicial mobilization of Article 2 TEU. Potential objections, based on the value of democracy, might be voiced in two distinct settings. On the one hand, there is a *horizontal* tension between the political EU institutions and the EU judiciary. On the other hand, there is a tension between European courts and national governments and legislatures. The latter reveals both an institutional, horizontal (courts vis-à-vis political branches) as well as a federal, vertical dimension (courts *at the EU level* vis-à-vis political branches *at the national level*). This leads to a kind of *diagonal* tension. In both relationships, diagonal and horizontal, democratic objections might be raised against the Court's

[65] See e.g. Barak (n 59) 487 f, 493 ff.

[66] Bernhard Schlink, 'Proportionality in Constitutional Law' *Duke Journal of Comparative and International Law* 22 (2012), 291, 302. See also Bernhard Schlink, 'Proportionality' in Michel Rosenfeld and András Sajó (eds), *The Oxford Handbook of Comparative Constitutional Law* (OUP 2012) 719, 739.

[67] For a comparative assessment, see BVerfG, Judgment of 5 May 2020, 2 BvR 859/15, *PSPP*, para 125.

[68] Critically, ibid para 126. See also Toni Marzal, 'From Hercules to Pareto' I-CON 15 (2017), 621; Verica Trstenjak and Erwin Beysen, 'Das Prinzip der Verhältnismäßigkeit in der Unionsrechtsordnung' EuR 47 (2012), 265, 269.

[69] Niels Petersen, *Proportionality and Judicial Activism* (CUP 2017) 8 f.

[70] Alec Stone Sweet and Jud Mathews, 'Proportionality Balancing and Global Constitutionalism' *Columbia Journal of Translational Law* 47 (2008), 78, 122.

[71] Martin M. Shapiro, 'Judicial power and democracy' in Christine Landfried (ed.), *Judicial Power* (CUP 2019) 21, 32.

engagement with Article 2 TEU. In the diagonal relationship, this concerns primarily the judicial protection of EU values. The respective Member State governments might ask: Why should a national government with a democratic mandate bow to the Court in Luxembourg, a court that seems far more remote and far less accountable than its national counterparts (Section A)? Also, in a horizontal perspective, one may wonder: Are the peoples represented in the Council and the Union citizens represented in the European Parliament not better placed to decide on the substance of the founding values? In this light, embracing Article 2 TEU might be perceived as an act of further judicial overreach (Section B).

A. Diagonal Tensions

1. The counter-majoritarian objection

The enforcement of EU values in recalcitrant Member States is already met with democratic objections. During the debate on the European Parliament's Sargentini report, Viktor Orbán stressed that 'Hungary's decisions are made by the voters in parliamentary elections'.[72] In a similar spirit, the Polish Prime Minister emphasized that his party 'gained the strongest democratic mandate in history' and that the Polish people is 'paternalistically lectured' about democracy and the rule of law.[73] Such objections are more likely to emerge where it is the Court of Justice that attempts to enforce Article 2 TEU values against the 'will of the majority'.

Ultimately, this critique harks back to a central tension in constitutional law: the counter-majoritarian difficulty.[74] This worn-out debate is not confined to academic circles but frequently finds expression in public discourse. An extreme example is the *Miller* case, in which the High Court of England and Wales ruled that—despite the referendum—an Act of Parliament was required before the UK government could initiate a withdrawal from the EU.[75] In response, several British tabloids, most prominently the Daily Mail, accused the court of blocking the peoples' democratic decision to leave the EU and targeted the respective judges as 'enemies of the people'.

The times when the CJEU largely escaped public crossfire—where it was blessed with 'benign neglect by the powers that be and the mass media' to employ the

[72] See n 4.

[73] Statement by Prime Minister Mateusz Morawiecki in the European Parliament (19 October 2021), <www.gov.pl/web/primeminister/statement-by-prime-minister-mateusz-morawiecki-in-the-european-parliament>.

[74] See only Alexander Bickel, *The Least Dangerous Branch* (2nd edn, Yale Univ. Press 1986) 16 ff, 49 ff. For a concise overview of the European debate, Victor Ferreres Comella, *Constitutional Courts and Democratic Values: A European Perspective* (Yale Univ. Press 2009) 86 ff. On the 'political' or 'popular' constitutionalism often underlying these claims, see Mark Tushnet, *Taking Back the Constitution* (Yale Univ. Press 2020) 241 ff; Richard Bellamy, *Political Constitutionalism* (CUP 2007) 15 ff.

[75] *R (Miller) v The Secretary of State for Exiting the European Union* [2016] EWHC 2768 (Admin).

formulation by Eric Stein—are long gone. Yet, Article 2 TEU-related cases might unleash a new dynamic in this respect. For a start, most of these cases deal with matters that not only pertain to the very core of state competences, but that are an integral part of the ruling party's political agenda (such as the overhaul of the Polish judiciary). Further, some recalcitrant Member State governments (especially in Hungary) started to pursue an extreme form of ultra-majoritarian democracy.[76] In this 'illiberal democracy', any checks and balances are considered to unduly constrain people's sovereignty.[77] Against this backdrop, it appears quite possible that CJEU judges find themselves one day discredited as 'enemies of the people' on the cover of a government-friendly Hungarian or Polish newspaper if they rule that an (arguably democratically mandated) government project violates Article 2 TEU.

2. Rejoinders

The issues raised above are an evergreen of constitutional law. There is not much new to add to this over-explored yet strikingly persistent debate. Nevertheless, the counter-majoritarian difficulty has not eased its grip on the imagination of legal scholars and political leaders.[78] As such, it seems that we have to repeat two well-established, often reiterated counter arguments.

First, Article 2 TEU has inscribed the model of constitutional democracy deeply into the Union's DNA. This understanding seems to be shared by all EU institutions. In this spirit, the 6th Recital of Regulation 2020/2092 notes that '[t]here can be no democracy and respect for fundamental rights without respect for the rule of law and vice versa'.[79] With regard to the Member States, this does not imply a specific system of government (how could it considering the extreme diversity among them?) but compliance with the outer limits that characterize constitutional democracies. The former Article F only mentioned that the Member State governments should be 'founded on the principles of democracy'. Orbán's vision of an ultra-majoritarian democracy might have been—at least textually—compatible with that provision. Article 2 TEU, however, explicitly posits democracy, fundamental rights, and the rule of law on an equal footing. Similarly, one could point to the 'rights of persons belonging to minorities' that were enshrined in Article 2

[76] On this 'extreme majoritarianism', see e.g. Nadia Urbinati, 'Populism and the Principle of Majority' in Cristóbal Rovira Kaltwasser et al. (eds), *The Oxford Handbook on Populism* (OUP 2017) 571; Paul Blokker, 'Populism as a Constitutional Project' I-CON 17 (2019), 536, 543 ff.

[77] Gábor Halmai, 'Does Illiberal Democracy Exist?' in Giuliano Amato et al. (eds), *Rule of Law vs Majoritarian Democracy* (Hart 2021) 171.

[78] Perceiving even a 'new' radicalization, see e.g. Dieter Grimm, 'Neue Radikalkritik an der Verfassungsgerichtsbarkeit' *Der Staat* 59 (2020), 321.

[79] Regulation 2020/2092 on a general regime of conditionality for the protection of the Union budget, Recital 6. See further e.g. European Commission, A new EU Framework to strengthen the Rule of Law, COM(2014) 158 final, p 4; Council, Presidency conclusions from the conference 'How to Ensure the Resilience of our Societies in a Changing European Landscape—the Interaction between Democracy, the Rule of Law and Fundamental Rights' (12 September 2019), 12128/19, para 6.

TEU (under the express demand of the Hungarian government, one should add).[80] Though originally aimed at ethnic minorities only, this provision appears to reject a purely majoritarian conception of democracy. Under such a vision of constitutional democracy, majority rule is not absolute but only *one* element in a complex balancing with competing values such as fundamental rights or the rule of law.

Second, the antagonism between non-accountable, counter-majoritarian courts with precarious democratic legitimacy and the democratically mandated political branches seems highly exaggerated. In constitutional democracies, constitutional courts are democratically legitimated in a twofold manner: they not only feed on *derived democratic legitimacy* by stabilizing the essential preconditions for democratic processes but also retain their very *own democratic legitimacy*.[81] In this sense, Pedro Cruz Villalón distinguished between active and passive legitimacy, meaning the democratic legitimacy that courts convey and the one they enjoy.[82] This applies to the CJEU as well.

On the one hand, constitutional courts (including the CJEU) can play a crucial role in securing the functioning of democratic decision-making. For instance, they guarantee the essential preconditions for democratic processes[83] and can correct what Niels Petersen called 'political market failures'.[84] This function is evidenced especially by the role of constitutional courts in many fragile democracies.[85] The CJEU's recent involvement in the Hungarian or Polish developments can be seen in this perspective. Many argued that these Member States have ceased to be fully-fledged democracies.[86] In 2016, Joseph Weiler noted that 'Orbán might be many things, but Dictator he is not: he gives perfect expression to the wishes of a majority of Hungarian citizens'.[87] The OSCE mission, however, noted that the 2022 election campaign was marked by an 'an absence of a level playing field' as media bias and

[80] Alain Pilette and Etienne de Poncins, 'Valeurs, objectives et nature de l'Union' in Giuliano Amato et al. (eds), *Genèse et destinée de la constitution européenne* (Bruylant 2007) 287, 301.

[81] On other traits of legitimacy, e.g. the constitutional courts' function as institutions of conflict resolution or the protection of individual rights, see among many others Christoph Möllers, *The Three Branches* (OUP 2013) 131 ff.

[82] See Pedro Cruz Villalón, 'Legitimidad activa y legitimidad pasiva de los tribunales constitucionales en el espacio constitucional europeo' *Teoría y Realidad Constitucional* 33 (2014), 141, 142.

[83] See e.g. Möllers (n 81) 127 ff; Dieter Grimm, 'Constitutional Adjudication and Democracy' in Grimm, *Constitutionalism* (OUP 2016) 213, 215 ff; Michel Troper, 'Justice Constitutionnelle et démocratie' in *Pour une théorie juridique de l'État* (PUF 1994) 329. See also John H. Ely, *Democracy and Distrust* (Harvard Univ. Press 1980) 73 ff, 105; Jürgen Habermas, *Between Facts and Norms* (Polity 1996) 264. For an account of the rich literature, see Christopher Scheid, 'Demokratieimmanente Legitimation der Verfassungsgerichtsbarkeit' *Der Staat* 59 (2020), 227.

[84] Petersen (n 69) 18 ff.

[85] See e.g. Samuel Issacharoff, *Fragile Democracies. Contested Power in the Era of Constitutional Courts* (CUP 2015) 241 ff. But see sceptically Tom G. Daly, *The Alchemists. Questioning our Faith in Courts as Democracy-Builders* (CUP 2017) 86 ff.

[86] Listing Hungary as an 'electoral autocracy', see V-Dem Institute, Democracy Report 2022, pp 33, 45.

[87] Joseph H.H. Weiler, 'Epilogue: Living in a Glass House' Carlos Closa and Dimitry Kochenov (eds), *Reinforcing the Rule of Law Oversight in the European Union* (CUP 2016) 313, 314.

campaign financing regulations constricted genuine political debate.[88] As such, it seems highly doubtful whether the election results are a well-suited indicator for the democratic nature of the Hungarian government.[89]

This applies even under Weiler's minimum conception of democracy. According to him, the most basic condition of representative democracy is that on election day the citizens 'can throw the scoundrels out'.[90] When the judiciary and parliamentary opposition are increasingly hollowed out, when free media, civil society, or academia are systematically silenced, when the laws governing elections, gerrymandering, party financing or campaigning are framed in favour of the ruling party, such a change in government becomes increasingly harder. If the Court of Justice mobilizes Article 2 TEU against such measures, it is not undermining but guaranteeing the essential preconditions for democracy. Recent examples in the CJEU's jurisprudence support this point. Value-related infringement proceedings concerned not only issues pertaining to the rule of law (e.g. against the overhaul of the Polish judiciary), but also measures such as the Hungarian transparency requirements for foreign funded NGOs.[91]

On the other hand, the CJEU enjoys its very own democratic legitimacy. It has both a *functional* as well as a *personal* democratic mandate.[92] Functionally, it discharges, when applying and interpreting the Treaties (and incidentally striking down national legislation), a task assigned to it by the Treaties (Article 19(1) TEU). As seen in Chapter 2, this includes the application and interpretation of Article 2 TEU. The Treaties have been adopted by all national Parliaments in democratic procedures, sometimes even with constitutional amendments. Granted, the personal chains of legitimation are much weaker at the EU level than at the national one. There is certainly much to improve in the appointment processes.[93] Nonetheless, the CJEU judges are appointed by common accord of the Member State governments (Article 253 TFEU). As such, each judge can rely on a chain of legitimation that connects him or her to the peoples of the Member States.

Finally, more recent conceptions of democracy started to challenge the often-assumed equation of an elected majority with 'the people', on which much of

[88] OSCE, Hungary, Parliamentary Elections and Referendum, 3 April 2022: Statement of Preliminary Findings and Conclusions. See also European Parliament, Resolution on a proposal calling on the Council to determine, pursuant to Article 7(1) of the Treaty on European Union, the existence of a clear risk of a serious breach by Hungary of the values on which the Union is founded (12 September 2018), 2017/2131(INL), Rec. 10.

[89] See with much evidence, Kim L. Scheppele, 'How Viktor Orbán Wins' *Journal of Democracy* 33 (2022), 45.

[90] Joseph H.H. Weiler, *The Constitution of Europe* (CUP 1999) 329.

[91] See Case C-78/18 *Commission v Hungary (Transparency of associations)* [2020] EU:C:2020:476.

[92] See Armin von Bogdandy, *The Emergence and Democratization of European Society* (OUP 2023) 4.5.A. See also Freya Clausen, 'In the name of the European Union, the Member States and/or the European citizens?' in Hélène Ruiz Fabri et al. (eds), *International Judicial Legitimacy* (Nomos 2020) 249.

[93] See e.g. Armin von Bogdandy and Christoph Krenn, 'On the Democratic Legitimacy of Europe's Judges' in Bobek (n 50) 162; Ezio Perillo, 'La justice européenne: au nom de qui?' RAE (2018), 319, 329.

the democratic critique of constitutional adjudication seems to hinge. Pierre Rosanvallon, for instance, argued for plural temporalities in democracy. In particular, he distinguished between the people that goes to the ballot box, the snapshot of a fleeting majority that might evaporate the day after the election, and the people in a long-term perspective.[94] This distinction places a question mark on the monopoly of elected majorities as representatives of the people and may allow us to perceive constitutional courts in a new light: *as representative institutions* complementing parliamentary majorities.[95] In particular, some have argued for the argumentative representativeness of constitutional courts.[96] In fact, procedures before these courts can often stir and improve the quality of public discourse, which becomes particularly important when the political process does not prove to be sufficiently discursive or inclusive.[97]

Applied to the illiberal turn in several Member States, one could argue that the Court can provide a forum for arguments that find no adequate expression in parliamentary debates, the media, or the general public at the national level. While individual access to the Court is certainly difficult, references to the CJEU may especially become a channel for citizen input.[98] Such a forum at the supranational level that is withdrawn from the reach of national majorities can be of increasing importance as the destruction of comparable fora at the national level advances.

B. Horizontal Tensions

1. The judicial overreach objection

Finally, the judicial activation of Article 2 TEU may also affect the horizontal relationship between the EU judiciary and other institutions, such as the Council or Parliament. On the one hand, Article 2 TEU is extremely indeterminate and provides the Court of Justice with practically unconstrained discretion. On the other hand, Article 2 TEU could apply extremely far-reaching constraints on EU institutions and Member States. As explored in the previous Chapters, Article 2 TEU can be used as yardstick for the judicial review of Treaty amendments (Chapter 7) and as a legal basis for the guaranteeing of a certain degree of constitutional homogeneity

[94] Pierre Rosanvallon, *Democratic Legitimacy* (Princeton Univ. Press 2011) 140 ff.

[95] See also Christopher Eisgruber, *Constitutional Self-Government* (Harvard Univ. Press 2001) 46 ff, 210. On the international plane, see Andreas von Staden, 'The Democratic Legitimacy of Judicial Review Beyond the State' I-CON 10 (2012), 1023, 1029.

[96] Mattias Kumm, 'On the Representativeness of Constitutional Courts' in Landfried (n 71) 281, 287; Robert Alexy, 'Balancing, Constitutional Review, and Representation' I-CON 3 (2005), 572, 578; Luís Roberto Barroso, 'Countermajoritarian, Representative, and Enlightened' AJCL 67 (2019), 109, 130.

[97] See e.g. Susanne Baer, 'Who Cares? A Defence of Judicial Review' *Journal of the British Academy* 8 (2020), 75, 95 f.

[98] See generally Bruno de Witte, 'Democratic Adjudication in Europe—How Can the European Court of Justice Be Responsive to the Citizens?' in Michael Dougan et al. (eds), *Empowerment and Disempowerment of European Citizens* (Hart 2012) 129, 131.

in the Member States (Chapter 9). Placing such a powerful tool into the hands of the Luxembourg judges seems to further tilt the institutional balance in their favour.

As noted earlier, constitutions usually strive to connect, separate, and balance law and politics. The constitution politicizes the creation of laws by connecting it to the political process and juridifies said processes by submitting them to constitutional constraints.[99] In order to police these constraints, many legal orders have set up constitutional courts. Due to the cases they are tasked to decide and the sometimes blurry line separating constitutional adjudication from legislation,[100] such courts are not only legal but also inevitably political institutions.[101] Despite this caveat, many will agree that a too 'activist' jurisprudence (whatever this means) may result in an overly constraining juridification of political processes and a politicization of the court overstretching its capacity and legitimacy. In case this asymmetry or imbalance becomes systemic, concerns of judicial overreach, a gouvernement des juges, a juristocracy, or Jurisdiktionsstaat emerge.[102] If pushed too far, this might result in an asphyxiation of political processes or—to the contrary—political hostility expressed in defiance, court curbing, or attempts to delegitimize the judiciary.[103]

The Court of Justice is all too familiar with such challenges. Despite the commonly assumed uncritical attitude of early EU legal scholarship,[104] it seems that similar allegations have accompanied the CJEU since its very foundation. Already in 1966, Jean-Pierre Colin observed that the Treaties failed in setting up an 'équilibre des pouvoirs'.[105] According to Colin, the high degree of indeterminacy of many Treaty provisions is the main source of the Court's 'immense pouvoir' and allowed the latter to develop a 'politique jurisprudentielle'.[106] Since then, the CJEU

[99] See only Niklas Luhmann, *Law as a Social System* (OUP 2004) 403 ff. From the rich literature, see e.g. Dieter Grimm, 'Types of Constitutions' in Rosenfeld and Sajó (n 66) 98, 124 f.

[100] On the elusiveness of this line, see e.g. Gérard Timsit, *Gouverner ou juger* (PUF 1995); Frank Schorkopf, 'Gesetzgebung durch Höchstgerichte und Parlamente' AöR 144 (2019), 202; Massimo Fichera, 'Constitutional Courts / Supreme Courts as Positive Legislators' in Rainer Grote, Frauke Lachenmann, and Rüdiger Wolfrum (eds), *Max Planck Encyclopedia of Comparative Constitutional Law* (OUP 2021).

[101] See e.g. Dieter Grimm, 'What Exactly is Political about Constitutional Adjudication' in Landfried (n 71) 307.

[102] These notions will be used interchangeably. Specific connotations by specific authors are left aside.

[103] For a colourful illustration of these scenarios, see e.g. Itzcovich (n 6) 38 f.

[104] See Editorial, 'The Critical Turn in EU Legal Studies' CML Rev 52 (2015), 881. Joseph Weiler criticized this as the 'Pescatore school', Joseph H.H. Weiler, 'Hjalte Rasmussen: Nemo propheta in patria sua' in Koch et al. (eds), *Europe: The New Legal Realism* (Djøf 2010) xiii. In Germany this has been criticized as 'EuGH-Positivismus', see Matthias Jestaedt, 'Luxemburger Richterrecht' in Christian Hillgruber (ed.), *Gouvernement des Juges—Fluch Oder Segen* (Schöningh 2014) 21, 39.

[105] Jean-Pierre Colin, *Le gouvernement des juges dans les communautés européennes* (LGDJ 1966) 511.

[106] ibid 37 f, 512 f. For caution when 'meddling in politics', see also A.M. Donner, 'The Constitutional Powers of the Court of Justice of the European Communities' CML Rev 11 (1974), 127, 129.

has been accused with remarkable persistency of disregarding its judicial role and engaging in judicial activism.[107]

This is not the place for a detailed analysis of these allegations. Suffice to say that this critique has recently gained new momentum. The Hungarian constitutional judge, Béla Pokol, for instance, observed a general rise of what he termed the 'juristocratic state'.[108] It comes as no surprise that Pokol transfers this critique to the EU level where he ascertains a veritable 'superjuristocracy'.[109] According to him, the gradual transition into a juristocracy is fostered in particular by the shift 'towards loose … thinking in legal principles and maxims'.[110] Without a doubt, embracing Article 2 TEU would—in Pokol's view—exacerbate this trend. But even beyond such a structural opposition there are legitimate concerns, especially with regard to the Court's involvement in the rule of law crisis. As these conflicts are of a highly political nature, there seems to be an imminent danger of dragging the Court into heated political conflicts.[111] This might lead to a politicization of the Luxembourg court overstretching its legitimacy. Further, an activist jurisprudence in the respective cases might damage the Court's credibility as a place for neutral conflict resolution.[112]

2. Rejoinders

The judicial overreach objection suggests that the Court goes beyond its proper judicial function. Generally, however, we must acknowledge that there is not *one* way of balancing the relationship between law and politics. Some States might opt for a fully-fledged constitutional court, others for a weaker form of judicial review, and yet others might trust the self-discipline of their Parliaments. In any case, this leads to a context-sensitive approach. The limits of courts ultimately depend on the respective context and on the choices spelled out in the constitutional framework.[113] Accordingly, it does not seem far-fetched to assume that German (Italian,

[107] For classic examples, see e.g. Hjalte Rasmussen, *On Law and Policy in the European Court of Justice* (Nijhoff 1986) or Patrick Neill, *The European Court of Justice: A Case Study in Judicial Activism* (European Policy Forum 1995). For a nuanced treatment, see Mark Dawson et al. (eds), *Judicial Activism at the European Court of Justice* (Elgar 2013) or Ulrich Haltern and Andreas Bergmann (eds), *Der EuGH in der Kritik* (Mohr Siebeck 2012). For a critical overview of the notion of 'judicial activism', see e.g. Takis Tridimas, 'The Court of Justice and Judicial Activism' EL Rev 21 (1996), 199; Gino Saccia, 'Cortes supranacionales de justicia y activismo judicial' *Teoría y Realidad Constitucional* 44 (2019), 177, 191 ff.

[108] Béla Pokol, *The Juristocratic State: Its Victory and the Possibility of Taming* (Dialóg 2017).

[109] See e.g. Béla Pokol, 'Az uniós jurisztokrácia hatalmi szerkezete' *Jogelméleti Szemle* (4)(2018), 126, 127. See also Béla Pokol, *Európai jurisztokrácia: Az Európai Unió jurisztokratikus szerkezetének kérdései* (Dialóg 2019).

[110] Pokol (n 108) 76.

[111] Filipe Marques, 'Rule of Law, National Judges and the Court of Justice of the European Union: Let's Keep It Juridical' ELJ 27 (2021), 228, 238 f.

[112] Mark Dawson, 'How Can EU Law Respond to Populism?' OJLS 40 (2020), 183, 211.

[113] Grimm (n 83) 217–19. See also Gertrude Lübbe-Wolff, 'Constitutional Courts and Democracy. Facets of an Ambivalent Relationship' in Klaus Meßerschmidt and A. Daniel Oliver-Lalana (eds), *Rational Lawmaking under Review* (Springer 2016) 19, 22.

Spanish ...) and Dutch (UK, Swedish, ...) legal scholars or practitioners will have very different views on what constitutes an acceptable limitation to constitutional adjudication.

What then is the constitutional context at the EU level? The Treaties contain the choice not only for a constitutional democracy but also for a strong constitutional court. Indeed, the CJEU's powerful position in the EU's institutional setting permeates the entire Treaty framework (see already Chapter 6). In this sense, Alec Stone Sweet observed that the Court 'has no rival as the most effective supranational judicial body in the history of the world, comparing favorably with the most powerful constitutional courts anywhere.'[114] Again, this is not solely due to the CJEU's allegedly activist jurisprudence, but flows from the institutional setting expressed in the Treaties. Despite ample opportunities (the European Single Act, Maastricht, Amsterdam, Nice, Lisbon ...), the Member States never aimed at correcting any real or perceived asymmetries. This choice for a powerful judiciary must be factored in when one attempts to determine whether the Court of Justice has overstepped its judicial constraints.

Seen in this light, what is the actual risk of an EU juristocracy emerging from the judicial mobilization of Article 2 TEU? Surely, many potentialities explored in this book may be understood as pushing the Court into an even more powerful position. While some of the propositions made in the previous chapters aimed at strengthening the legislative process (see Chapter 6), the judicial review of Treaty revision (Chapter 7) or the protection of EU values in the Member States (Chapter 9) are particularly problematic. While the former may lead to an overly constraining juridification of political processes, the latter could drag Luxembourg into heated political conflicts.

Generally, there are two strategies to counter these risks. The first is *self-restraint*, the second is a focus on the CJEU's *judicial role*. While strategies for self-restraint will be extensively assessed in the next chapter, the following sections will concentrate especially on the Court's judicial function. On the one hand, this role implies adhering to the constraints of legal discourse (see Section II.A.2). Submitting political issues to a constitutional court always goes hand in hand with a 'change of arena.'[115] In this arena, different logics and path dependencies apply. In particular, it can be distinguished from the political process by access to different sorts of reasons.[116] While the participants of political processes can resort to the entire spectrum of pragmatic or ethical reasons, courts are bound to the specific

[114] Alec Stone Sweet, *The Judicial Construction of Europe* (OUP 2004) 1. See also Karen Alter, *Establishing the Supremacy of European Law* (OUP 2001) 229.

[115] Grimm (n 101) 309.

[116] Habermas (n 83) 192. See also Armin von Bogdandy and Ingo Venzke, *In whose name?* (OUP 2014) 193 f.

constraints of legal discourse.[117] Eventually, this applies even to hard cases or the judicial development of the law. As Hart noted, 'judges do not just push away their law books and start to legislate without further guidance from the law'.[118]

On the other hand, the Court of Justice could apply a case-centred approach. Even if constitutional courts, including Luxembourg, are hybrids that straddle the legal and political sphere, they nonetheless are courts. First and foremost, they are tasked to decide specific cases. This requires contextualization, avoiding general obiter, or—with Cass Sunstein's minimalism—to remain 'narrow rather than wide'.[119] We have already made the argument for a negative red-line approach in Chapter 2. In this sense, the Court could flesh out the obligations stemming from Article 2 TEU in a very narrow manner and tailor them to the specific circumstances of the case.

There is one central objection to this focus on the CJEU's judicial function. It transforms the problem to an issue of judicial ethos, which essentially depends on the individual judge. It seems though that many judges, including those in Luxembourg, are well aware of the limits inherent in their judicial function.[120] As Judge Susanne Baer noted, 'courts are not suicidal' but usually follow a 'natural call for restraint'.[121] Still, we may argue that in order for methodological constraints to become actually constraining, the Court would need to be embedded in a broader context of control.[122] This leads to the age-old question, 'Who watches the watchmen'? At first glance, one could perceive the Court as a relatively unconstrained institution. Indeed, the options of formally overriding or politically influencing the Court of Justice are very limited (in detail, Chapter 6). Nevertheless, this does not mean that the Court escapes any control. First of all, it is subject to extensive scrutiny not only by a whole epistemic community of politicians, legal practitioners, and academia[123] but also increasingly by the public.

[117] Grimm (n 101) 307; Christine Landfried, 'Constitutional Review in the European Legal Space: A Political Science Perspective' in Armin von Bogdandy et al. (eds), *The Max Planck Handbooks in European Public Law*, vol 4 (OUP 2020).

[118] Hart (n 13) 274.

[119] Cass Sunstein, *One Case at a Time* (Harvard Univ. Press 1999) 10 f. In this sense, see also Christoph Möllers, 'Scope and Legitimacy of Judicial Review' in Hermann Pünder and Christian Waldhoff (eds), *Debates in German Public Law* (Hart 2014) 3, 23; Laurent Pech, 'Le remède au gouvernement des juges: le judicial self-restraint' in Sévérine Brondel et al. (eds), *Gouvernement des juges et démocratie* (Publications de la Sorbonne 2001) 63.

[120] See e.g. Guy Canivet, 'Les limites de la mission du juge constitutionnel' *Cités* 69 (2017), 41; Andreas Voßkuhle, 'Karlsruhe Unlimited? Zu den (unsichtbaren) Grenzen der Verfassungsgerichtsbarkeit' in Voßkuhle (ed.), *Europa, Demokratie, Verfassungsgerichte* (Suhrkamp 2021) 314; Jonathan H. Mance, 'The Role of Judges in a Representative Democracy' in Amato et al. (n 77) 335. From the CJEU, see e.g. Koen Lenaerts, 'Some Thoughts about the Interaction between Judges and Politicians' YEL (1992), 1; Tim Koopmans, *Courts and Political Institutions* (CUP 2003) 98 ff, 268 ff; Eleanor Sharpston, 'Legislating and Adjudicating' in Elizabeth Fisher et al. (eds), *The Foundations and Future of Public Law* (OUP 2020) 173.

[121] Baer (n 97) 91.

[122] In this sense, von Bogdandy and Venzke (n 116) 195 ff. Seeing a lack in this regard, Peter M. Huber, *Warum der EuGH Kontrolle braucht* (Sramek 2022) 20 ff.

[123] On these epistemic communities, see e.g. Komárek (n 11) 150.

Without going into detail, recent studies indicate that the Court is often receptive to public opinion, especially if the latter is combined with governmental pressure.[124] Further, the CJEU is in a more precarious situation than many of its critics realize. As Alexander Hamilton noted, judges have 'no power of purse or sword' (Federalist No. 78). This applies especially to the CJEU. Its judgments usually require enforcement by Member State institutions.[125] Even if there is a general 'habit of obedience',[126] this exerts a constant pressure to persuade.[127]

Recently this justificatory pressure has increased. As seen above, the German Constitutional Court has started monitoring whether its Luxembourg counterpart sticks to its judicial function. According to the BVerfG, this is the case 'as long as the CJEU applies recognised methodological principles'.[128] While certainly confrontational and highly questionable on merits, challenges like the recent *PSPP* judgment are not necessarily a 'mortal threat', a 'declaration of war', or a retour to the 'guerre des juges'.[129] Instead, they place additional justificatory constraints on the CJEU (see already Chapter 11). The confrontational, critical, and challenging relationship between Luxembourg and national constitutional courts can thus be perceived as a broader context of control. And indeed, contestations by national constitutional courts have their merits. As noted in the previous chapter, justified challenges by constitutional courts can point to defects and trigger necessary reactions at the EU level. While the CJEU should not be afraid to enter an open conflict with puppet courts like the Polish Constitutional Tribunal, it will definitely be aware of positions held in other, real constitutional and supreme courts within the EU legal space. These considerations should, if not refute, at least attenuate the judicial overreach objection and calm the critics.

[124] See e.g. Michael Blauberger and Dorte Sindbjerg Martinsen, 'The Court of Justice in Times of Politicisation' JEPP 27 (2020), 382, 388 f. On the CJEU's turn in its citizenship case law, see Michael Blauberger et al., 'ECJ Judges Read the Morning Papers' JEPP 25 (2018), 1422.

[125] On strategies of non-compliance with and containment of CJEU judgments in the Member States, see Andreas Hofmann, 'Resistance against the Court of Justice of the European Union' *International Journal of Law in Context* 14 (2018), 258; Lisa Conant, 'Compliance and What EU Member States Make of It' in Marise Cremona (ed.), *Compliance and the Enforcement of EU Law* (OUP 2012) 1, 26 ff.

[126] Joseph H.H. Weiler, 'The Political and Legal Culture of European Integration' I-CON 9 (2011), 678, 691.

[127] See e.g. Everling (n 41) 1308; Timmermans (n 41) 398.

[128] BVerfG, Judgment of 5 May 2020, 2 BvR 859/15, *PSPP*, para 112.

[129] See Ronan McCrea, 'German Constitutional Court is a bigger threat to EU than Brexit or Covid-19' *Irish Times* (16 May 2020); Interview with Franz Mayer, 'Es ist eine offene Kriegserkärung' *Süddeutsche Zeitung* (7 May 2020); Elvira Méndez-Pinedo, 'Une nouvelle "guerre des juges" en Europe?' *Revue des Affaires europénnes* (2022), 283.

13
Disrupting the Federal Balance?

I. Introduction

The judicial mobilization of Article 2 TEU, as outlined in the previous parts, implies a significant increase in the CJEU's powers. This concerns, in particular, the judicial protection of EU values in the Member States. As no part of their legal orders escapes Article 2 TEU and therefore Luxembourg's reach, such a protection has the potential to severely disturb the Union's federal balance. This general concern can be unravelled into four distinct objections. First, Member States could argue that reviewing compliance with Article 2 TEU—especially beyond the scope of other EU law—is not covered by the CJEU's competences (*ultra-vires objection*). Second, Article 2 TEU allows the Court to review fundamental constitutional structures and highly sensitive policy areas in the Member States. Depending on the case, this could touch upon their constitutional identities protected under Article 4(2) TEU (*identity objection*). Third, one could argue that enforcing a uniform understanding of Article 2 TEU values is normatively undesirable and incompatible with pluralist conceptions of the EU (*pluralist objection*). Finally, the existing diversity among the Member States could render the definition of 'common' values practically unattainable (*diversity objection*).

The following chapter will start by assessing these concerns (Section II). Even though many of them can be refuted or attenuated, they nonetheless advocate a cautious approach with respect to the judicial protection of Article 2 TEU. Such caution already flows from the dual character of Article 2 TEU outlined in Chapter 3. In its Verbund dimension, Article 2 TEU merely aims at a minimum of constitutional homogeneity. This conception must lead to judicial restraint, especially when reviewing the Member States constitutional structures for their compliance with Article 2 TEU. Hence, the last section will explore strategies that translate the idea of restraint into judicial practice (Section III).

II. Concerns for the Federal Balance

It is a truism that EU law as it currently stands reflects a complex trade-off between centralizing, centripetal and decentralizing, centrifugal forces. The outcome at which the Member States arrived is often described as federal balance.[1] This balance

[1] On this, see e.g. Signe Rehling Larsen, *The Constitutional Theory of the Federation and the European Union* (OUP 2021) 103 ff.

EU Values Before the Court of Justice. Luke Dimitrios Spieker, Oxford University Press. © Luke Dimitrios Spieker 2023.
DOI: 10.1093/oso/9780198876717.003.0014

has found a twofold expression. It is epitomized by provisions, such as Article 5(1) TEU or Article 4(2) TEU, shielding the Member States' autonomy (Section A). Moreover, the federal balance has repercussions for our understanding of the Union itself, namely as a legal order that strives for pluralism and diversity (Section B). Some argue that Luxembourg does not take these limitations seriously and tries to 'pave the way for its role as the Supreme Court of Europe'.[2] Similarly, many have observed a unitary, federalizing, or centralizing effect of the CJEU's jurisprudence, especially with regard to fundamental rights.[3] Operationalizing Article 2 TEU before the Luxembourg court could add fuel to the centralizing fire and force the Member States' constitutional structures into a Procrustean bed. The following sections will frame these objections and attempt to refute or attenuate them.

A. Competence and Identity

1. Article 5(1) TEU: the ultra-vires objection

Affected Member States argue that the CJEU acts ultra vires when it reviews their compliance with Article 2 TEU (especially beyond the scope of other EU law). In the words of the BVerfG, such objections are justified if the judicial activation of Article 2 TEU 'manifestly exceeds EU competences, resulting in a structurally significant shift in the division of competences to the detriment of the Member States'.[4] Without a doubt, assessing the Member States' constitutional structures against the values enshrined in Article 2 TEU constitutes a structurally significant shift.[5] Yet, the central question is whether it exceeds the CJEU's competences. According to the Polish government, Articles 2 and 19(1)(2) TEU do 'not alter the substance of the principle of conferral or the extent of the European Union's powers.'[6] Arguably, it is 'common ground' that the organization of the national judiciary is 'a competence reserved exclusively to the Member States.'[7]

[2] Christoph Grabenwarter, Peter M. Huber, Rajko Knez, and Ineta Ziemele, 'The Role of the Constitutional Courts in the European Judicial Network' EPL 27 (2021), 43, 58.

[3] See especially Peter M. Huber, 'The Unitary Effect of the Community's Fundamental Rights' EPL 14 (2008), 323, 330 f. See also Aida Torres Pérez, 'The Federalizing Force of the EU Charter of Fundamental Rights' I-CON 15 (2017), 1080; Luis I. Gordillo Pérez and Giuseppe Martinico, 'La jurisprudencia federalizante y humanizadora del Tribunal de Justicia' *Teoría y Realidad Constitucional* 32 (2013), 429, 430 ff.

[4] See only BVerfG, Judgment of 5 May 2020, 2 BvR 859/15, *PSPP*, para 110.

[5] Very critical in this respect, see Martin Nettesheim, 'Kompetenzkonflikte zwischen EuGH und Mitgliedstaaten' ZRP 54 (2021), 222, 223 f; Nettesheim, 'Die "Werte der Union": Legitimitätsstiftung, Einheitsbildung, Föderalisierung' EuR 57 (2022), 525, 533 ff. For such concerns, see also Andreas Voßkuhle, 'Werteorientierung in der EU: Gift oder Lebenselixier?' *Alkotmánybírósági Szemle* (2020), 13, 14.

[6] See the arguments raised in Case C-896/19 *Repubblika* [2021] EU:C:2021:311, para 63 and Case C-824/18 *A.B.* [2021] EU:C:2021:153, paras 67, 78.

[7] Case C-619/18 *Commission v Poland (Independence of the Supreme Court)* [2019] EU:C:2019:531, para 38. More recently, see e.g. Case C-487/19 *W.Ż.* [2021] EU:C:2021:798, paras 87 ff.

Based on this reasoning, the Polish government started to instrumentalize the captured Constitutional Tribunal[8] as a shield against potential EU intervention. So far, the Tribunal has fulfilled the government's expectations. For one, it declared the CJEU's interim order to suspend the activities of the Supreme Court's disciplinary chamber (Case C-791/19) to constitute an ultra-vires act.[9] In a second ruling, the Tribunal went even further. It explicitly rejected the primacy of EU law over the Polish constitution and reemphasized that EU institutions may not act beyond their competences. According to the Tribunal, the CJEU's interpretation of Articles 2 and 19(1)(2) TEU is incompatible with the Polish constitution insofar as it confers on Polish judges the power to review the independence of their peers.[10] Already before its capture, the Tribunal had established a sort of ultra-vires review. Yet, this doctrine was rarely used.[11] Despite the considerable differences between Karlsruhe and Warsaw in terms of institutional independence and constitutional doctrine,[12] it seems that the *PSPP* judgment has set a dangerous precedent.[13] This explains the rejoicing of Polish government officials in the aftermath of *PSPP*: 'The ruling of the German Constitutional Court shows that in the dispute regarding the judiciary system the Polish Government, the Polish Constitution and Member States ... are right.'[14]

However, we should not forget that doubts are harboured in some EU institutions as well (in detail Chapter 2, IV). In 2014, the Council's legal service noted that only Article 7 TEU 'provides for a Union competence to supervise the application of the rule of law, as a value of the Union, in a context that is not related to a specific material competence or that exceeds its scope.'[15] While the opinion concerned the Commission's rule of law framework, the litigation of Article 2 TEU violations beyond the scope of other EU law appears equally excluded. Even Commission

[8] See only Wojciech Sadurski, 'Polish Constitutional Tribunal Under PiS' HJRL 11 (2018), 63.

[9] Trybunał Konstytucyjny, Judgment of 14 July 2021, P 7/20.

[10] Trybunał Konstytucyjny, Judgment of 7 October 2021, K 3/21. For a blunt critique, see Marek Safjan, 'L'identité constitutionnelle polonaise' RDCE (72) (2022), 371; Aleksandra Gliszczyńska-Grabias and Wojciech Sadurski, 'Is It Polexit Yet?' EuConst 19 (2023) 163.

[11] See Anna Śledzińska-Simon and Michał Ziółkowski, 'Constitutional Identity in Poland' in Christian Calliess and Gerhard van der Schyff (eds), *Constitutional Identity in a Europe of Multilevel Constitutionalism* (CUP 2019) 243, 245; Regina Kiener and Ivan Gunjic, 'Das Prinzip des unbedingten Vorrangs von EU-Recht und der polnische Justizkonflikt' EuZ (2020), 112, 119; Krystyna Kowalik-Bańczyk, 'Should We Polish It Up? The Polish Constitutional Tribunal and the Idea of Supremacy of EU Law' GLJ 6 (2005), 1355.

[12] See e.g. Andreas Voßkuhle, 'Applaus von der falschen Seite' in Voßkuhle, *Europa, Demokratie, Verfassungsgerichte* (Suhrkamp 2021) 334.

[13] See e.g. Stanisław Biernat, 'How Far Is It from Warsaw to Luxembourg and Karlsruhe: The Impact of the PSPP Judgment on Poland' GLJ 21 (2020), 1104, 1114 f.

[14] Polish Ministry of Justice, 'The judgement of the German Constitutional Court confirms Poland's position in the dispute with the European Commission' (12 May 2020), <www.gov.pl/web/justice/the-judgement-of-the-german-constitutional-court-confirms-polands-position-in-the-dispute-with-the-european-commission>.

[15] Council, Opinion of the Legal Service: Commission's Communication on a New EU Framework to Strengthen the Rule of Law: Compatibility with the Treaties, 10296/14, para 17.

officials expressed their concerns: 'to interfere at such a level in domestic affairs would be possible if the EU were a federal state ... But we are not'.[16]

A central aim of this book is to dispel and counter these concerns. Although embracing Article 2 TEU in the CJEU's jurisprudence is certainly a bold move, the previous parts attempted to provide a legally and doctrinally sound path towards the judicial mobilization of EU values (see especially Chapters 2 and 9). Against this backdrop, we will only briefly reiterate the central arguments against the ultra-vires objection. First, it seems uncontested that the obligations flowing from Article 2 TEU apply also beyond the EU's competences and the scope of other EU law (Chapter 2, IV.B). The wording of Article 2 TEU does not feature any restrictions in scope, be they ratione tempore, materiae, or personae. This is an important difference not only with regard to the Charter (Article 51(1) CFR) but also with regard to the objectives of Article 3 TEU, which are linked to the EU's competences and policy areas. Moreover, it was the drafter's express intention that Article 2 TEU applies even 'in the field of the Member State's autonomous action (not affected by Union law)'.[17]

Second, there is simply no reason to assume that the Court of Justice lacks jurisdiction over Article 2 TEU—neither within nor beyond the EU's competences or the scope of other EU law. Nothing in the Treaties or the *travaux* suggests an exclusivity of the political Article 7 TEU procedure. Objections based on the CJEU's limited competences under Article 269 TFEU seem equally unconvincing. As demonstrated by Advocate General Bobek, Article 269 TFEU should rather be read as a provision *conferring* not *limiting* jurisdiction, namely, to review 'determinations' adopted under Article 7(1) and (2) TEU.[18] But even if we do not follow this interpretation, Article 269 TFEU seems like a rather weak argument to exclude the CJEU's general jurisdiction under Article 19(1) TEU. Further, the Court has repeatedly confirmed that although a certain issue falls within the Member States' competences, 'the fact remains that, when exercising that competence, the Member States are required to comply with their obligations deriving from EU law'.[19] Even beyond the EU's competences, these obligations remain subject to review by the Court (in detail Chapter 2, IV.B).

2. Article 4(2) TEU: the identity objection

The second objection boils down to the reproach that an enforcement of EU values in areas pertaining to the Member States' constitutional structures might encroach upon their constitutional identities protected under Article 4(2) TEU. The Polish

[16] See the interview with a Deputy Director-General conducted by Carlos Closa, 'The Politics of Guarding the Treaties' JEPP 26 (2019), 696, 709.

[17] Praesidium, Draft of Articles 1 to 16 of the Constitutional Treaty, CONV 528/03, p 11.

[18] Case C-650/18 *Hungary v Parliament* [2020] EU:C:2020:985, Opinion of AG Bobek.

[19] On the organization of the judiciary, see Cases C-585, 624, and 625/18 *A.K.* [2019] EU:C:2019:982, para 75.

government, for instance, relied extensively on constitutional identity arguments when justifying the overhaul of the Polish judiciary.[20] Similarly, the Hungarian delegation argued in the pending Article 7 TEU procedure that '[a]ccording to Article 4(2) TEU, the Union must respect essential State functions, which undoubtedly include what might be defined as the State's internal self-organisation.'[21] This line of defence has been reinforced by the Hungarian and Polish constitutional courts.

Several arguments may be advanced against the identity objection. As the Polish and Hungarian constitutional courts are instrumentalized by their respective governments, constitutional identity reservations raised by these institutions might be of an abusive nature. The identity review established by the Hungarian constitutional courts provides some evidence in this respect. Though the court's reasoning is largely based on a comparative analysis,[22] the established identity review sharply dissonates with the instruments in other Member States. Not only is the court composed of many judges that are close to the government's agenda; its review mechanism is also based on a highly idiosyncratic, 'ethnocultural' conception of constitutional identity. For that reason, many argued that this review constitutes an abuse of the constitutional identity doctrine (in detail, Chapter 11, III.B). Quite tellingly, Viktor Orbán is reported to have said: 'I threw my hat in the air when the Constitutional Court ruled that the government has the right and obligation to stand up for Hungary's constitutional identity'.[23] In response, some proposed a 'legitimacy test' by which one could assess whether certain instances of judicial opposition to the CJEU constitute a loyal and principled form of disagreement or abusive resistance.[24]

But also beyond these institutional issues, pitting national constitutional identities against the Union's common values seems hardly convincing. Importantly, there is a high degree of convergence between the constitutional identities of the Member States and the values enshrined in Article 2 TEU. National constitutional identities are an essential reservoir for the concretization of Article 2 TEU values (in detail, Chapter 2, III.B.2; Chapter 8, III.A; and Chapter 11, III.A.1). Whereas their specific realization can of course vary to a considerable extent, it should be

[20] See e.g. White Paper on the Reform of the Polish Judiciary (7 March 2018), <www.statewatch.org/media/documents/news/2018/mar/pl-judiciary-reform-chanceller-white-paper-3-18.pdf>, paras 168–74, 189, 206–7. See also Trybunał Konstytucyjny, Judgment of 14 July 2021, P 7/20, para 6.8.

[21] Hungarian Delegation to the European Council, Information on the Resolution on the situation in Hungary adopted by the European Parliament on 12 September 2018 (13 November 2018), 14225/18 p 5.

[22] Alkotmánybíróság, Decision of 30 November 2016, 22/2016 (XII.5.) AB, *Joint exercise of competences with the EU*, paras 34–44, 49.

[23] Quoted by Gabor Halmai, 'Abuse of Constitutional Identity' RCEEL 43 (2018), 23, 36.

[24] Tom Flynn, 'Constitutional Pluralism and Loyal Opposition' I-CON 19 (2021), 241, 245; Monika Polzin, 'Emotion and the Vertical Separation of Powers: Ultra-Vires Review by National (Constitutional) Courts, and EU and International Law' *ICL Journal* 16 (2022), 285, 308 ff.

kept in mind that both Article 2 TEU and constitutional identities are conceptually limited to the protection of core guarantees.

Several constitutional courts have expressly affirmed this equivalence and suggested that a violation of their constitutional identity would be a violation of Article 2 TEU and vice versa.[25] In this spirit, a group of constitutional judges, including well-known sceptics, openly acknowledged '[t]he fact that in recent times the CJEU has—quite trickily—assumed the task of examining the Member States adherence to the values laid out in Article 2 TEU—being (wholly or partially) part of many Member States' constitutional identity—may *contribute to safeguarding national constitutional identities*.'[26] Finally, it is widely accepted that Article 2 TEU constitutes a limit to what can be expressed as a justified constitutional identity claim under Article 4(2) TEU. As long as the Member States are part of the Union, Article 2 TEU defines a common constitutional identity from which Member States cannot derogate (Chapter 11, III.A).

B. Pluralism and Diversity

Intimately connected to the identity objection are arguments based on pluralism and the existing diversity within the EU. Viktor Orbán relied heavily on this rhetoric: 'European values are often mentioned, but frequently as though they were kept in a vault somewhere in Brussels. These, however, are not in Brussels, but in the hearts of European citizens … in each nation's own language, in line with its own culture.'[27] Similarly, the Polish government argued that the EU legal order is based on constitutional pluralism: 'Each country has specific constitutional solutions that are rooted in its history and legal traditions and these differences are protected by the treaty'.[28] Ultimately, these objections break down to two claims. *Normatively*, we should perceive different understandings of European values as legitimate. This claim underpins the idea of constitutional pluralism. *Factually*, one could claim that the existing diversity among the Member States renders the identification of common standards impossible.

[25] See Chapter 11, n 59–62.

[26] Grabenwarter et al. (n 2) 58 f (emphasis added). In this sense, see also Koen Lenaerts, 'EUdentity as a Way of Promoting National Identity' *Alkotmánybírósági Szemle* (2020), 9: 'far from supplanting the identity of its Member States, the Union's common identity is itself based on the values that are common to those national identities … our shared identity in fact underpins and reinforces respect for those common values, and thus for those national identities'.

[27] Viktor Orbán, Speech at the 11th Congress of the Slovenian Democratic Party (SDS) (20 May 2017).

[28] White Paper (n 20) para 169. See also paras 170 ff, 206.

1. Normative level: the constitutional pluralism objection

Starting with the first, pluralists perceive the relationship between the EU and its Member States not as one of vertical hierarchies but rather as one of horizontal heterarchy.[29] Leaving the issue of ultimate authority or final say unresolved, we should embrace the reality that each legal order operates on its own terms and maintains its authority.[30] As such, Article 2 TEU could neither be understood as imposing a unified set of values upon the Member States, nor could the Court of Justice claim final authority in conflicts between its understanding of Article 2 TEU and national conceptions. Eventually, it is left to judicial cooperation, dialogue, and spontaneous accommodation to keep this delicate and fragile system running.[31]

The *PSPP* judgment and the Polish and Hungarian developments especially triggered resistance against this pluralist account. Two key objections are usually advanced. First, pluralist conceptions arguably contradict the equality among Member States. To ensure this equality, EU law needs to apply in a uniform manner to all Member States, which can only be guaranteed by one court and under the premise of primacy.[32] Second, the concept of constitutional pluralism is inherently prone to abuse.[33] It heavily relies on the good faith of all judicial institutions involved and might thus prove unsustainable.[34] As this good faith seems to fade away increasingly, the nightmare of constitutional pluralism—that Member States might abuse it as a form of evasion[35]—seems to have materialized.

Even if one rejects these arguments and adheres to pluralism as a desirable normative concept for the EU, it should be acknowledged that constitutional pluralism is based on certain premises.[36] This is already expressed by the attribution

[29] Andreas Voßkuhle described this relationship as that of a mobile rather than a pyramid, see 'Pyramide oder Mobile?' in Voßkuhle (n 12) 305. See also Grabenwarter et al. (n 2) 49.

[30] See among many others Neil MacCormick, *Questioning Sovereignty* (OUP 1999) and Neil Walker, 'The Idea of Constitutional Pluralism' MLR 65 (2002), 317. For a mapping of the rich literature, see Klemen Jaklic, *Constitutional Pluralism in the EU* (OUP 2014) 11 ff and Orlando Scarcello, *Radical Constitutional Pluralism in Europe* (Routledge 2023) 40 ff.

[31] See e.g. Mattias Kumm, 'The Jurisprudence of Constitutional Conflict' ELJ 11 (2005), 262; Miguel Maduro, 'Contrapunctual Law' in Neil Walker (ed.), *Sovereignty in Transition* (Hart 2003) 520, 529.

[32] Koen Lenaerts, José A. Gutiérrez-Fons, and Stanislas Adam, 'Exploring the Autonomy of the European Legal Order' ZaöRV 81 (2021), 47, 70; Koen Lenaerts, 'L'égalité des États membres devant les traités' RDUE (2021), 7; Federico Fabbrini, 'After the OMT Case: The Supremacy of EU Law as the Guarantee of the Equality of the Member States' GLJ 16 (2015), 1003. But see Justin Lindeboom, 'Is the Primacy of EU Law Based on the Equality of the Member States?' GLJ 21 (2020), 1032.

[33] See R. Daniel Kelemen and Laurent Pech, 'The Uses and Abuses of Constitutional Pluralism' CYELS 21 (2019), 59.

[34] Julio Baquero Cruz, 'Another Look at Constitutional Pluralism in the European Union' ELJ 22 (2016), 356, 369 ff; R. Daniel Kelemen, 'The Dangers of Constitutional Pluralism' in Gareth Davies and Matej Avbelj (eds), *Research Handbook on Legal Pluralism and EU Law* (Elgar 2018) 392.

[35] Maduro (n 31) 526.

[36] See e.g. Matej Avbelj, 'Constitutional Pluralism and Authoritarianism' GLJ 21 (2020), 1023, 1029: 'A pluralist European integration assumes that its Member States are well-ordered societies'. Hence the 'fair-weather' critique by R. Daniel Kelemen, 'Is Differentiation Possible in Rule of Law?' *Comparative European Politics* 17 (2019), 246, 254.

'constitutional'. Neil Walker, for instance, conceded that a baseline of shared principles and values is essential to hold a pluralist system together.[37] The logic is hard to deny. If pluralist claims exert a centrifugal force, a centripetal counterforce is needed to hold the system together. Depending on the strength of these two forces, the outer frame is drawn either wider or narrower, granting more or less space for agreements to disagree. If these premises no longer hold, if their stabilizing and cohesive force fades away, constitutional pluralism collapses.

By implication, Member States can rely on arguments from constitutional pluralism only so far as the underlying premises carrying this conception are not shattered. The question then is, where we should draw this baseline.[38] Not surprisingly, this book argues for the values enshrined in Article 2 TEU.[39] Accepting this (or any other) baseline inevitably leads to the subsequent question of who should be tasked to police it. Again, it comes as no surprise that this chapter answers in favour of the Court of Justice. While this does not imply a general rejection of constitutional pluralism, the CJEU must have a final say concerning Article 2 TEU values. This raises the question of how to limit the impact of Article 2 TEU to preserve a meaningful degree of constitutional pluralism (see Section III).

2. Factual level: the diversity objection

This leads to the fourth and last objection presented in this chapter. The heterogeneity among the Member States renders any definition of the values enshrined in Article 2 TEU extremely difficult. Some Member States go so far as to assert that there are no shared understandings of the values of democracy, the rule of law, and fundamental rights. This argument was openly articulated by Judith Varga, Hungarian minister of justice: 'Is rule of law a set of universally applicable objective criteria? No. It lacks well-defined rules and remains the subject of much debate internationally and among national constitutional bodies and academia. Concern for the rule of law should pay greater respect to the specifics of Member States and not try to impose an artificial, one-size-fits-all framework.'[40] A common definition of the values enshrined in Article 2 TEU might thus prove unattainable.

[37] Neil Walker, 'Flexibility within a Metaconstitutional Frame' in Grainne de Búrca and Joanne Scott (eds), *Constitutional Change in the EU* (Bloomsbury 2000) 9, 14 ff. For similar claims, see Jessica C. Lawrence, 'Constitutional Pluralism's Unspoken Normative Core' CYELS 21 (2019), 24, 27 f; Richard Bellamy and Sandra Kröger, 'Countering Democratic Backsliding by EU Member States: Constitutional Pluralism and "Value" Differentiated Integration' *Swiss Political Science Review* 27 (2021), 619, 627; Ana Bobić, *The Jurisprudence of Constitutional Conflict in the European Union* (OUP 2022) 57–9.

[38] For an attempt, see Lawrence (n 37) 29 ff. Sceptical concerning the existence of such a common baseline, Signe Rehling Larsen, 'Varieties of Constitutionalism in the European Union' MLR 84 (2021), 477, 498 ff.

[39] Similarly, Bobić (n 37) 57; Ana Bobić, 'Constructive Versus Destructive Conflict' CYELS 22 (2020), 60, 69, 84. See also Julio Baquero Cruz, 'Minima moralia: el estado de derecho, el método comunitario y el presupuesto de la Unión Europea' RDCE (72) (2022), 431, 443 f. This comes also close to Kumm's demanding substantive baseline, see Kumm (n 31) 299 ff.

[40] Judit Varga, 'Facts You Always Wanted to Know about Rule of Law but Never Dared to Ask' *Euronews* (22 November 2019). See also Trybunał Konstytucyjny, Judgment of 7 October 2021, K 3/21, paras 347 f.

Such views are not entirely unfounded. As noted in Chapter 2, it is extremely difficult to arrive at a common understanding of the values enshrined in Article 2 TEU. This applies even to seemingly uncontroversial values like the rule of law. Terminologically, it is not clear whether notions such as the rule of law, 'Rechtsstaat', 'État de droit', or 'préemincence du droit' denote the same concept and can be treated as proxies. The Venice Commission observed that '[a]lthough the terminology is similar, it is important to note at the outset that the notion of "Rule of Law" is not always synonymous with that of "Rechtsstaat", "Estado de Direito", or "Etat de droit" '.[41] Conceptually, the rule of law provides an umbrella that may capture a plethora of different issues depending on whether one follows thin/formal or rather thick/substantive concepts.

Nevertheless, the Venice Commission arrived at a consensus on the 'core meaning of the rule of law'[42] and even established a checklist.[43] The latest attempts of the European Commission and the Court to flesh out the rule of law point in the same direction.[44] Such attempts should not be misunderstood as aiming at uniformity but rather at homogeneity at a more abstract level.[45] At this higher level of abstraction, it might be possible to speak of a common concept of the rule of law in Europe. Admittedly, abstract concepts lose explanatory value. Importantly, they cannot decide specific cases. As such, the CJEU will have to find ways to navigate between keeping Article 2 TEU values in an abstract form that preserves consensus and breaking them down to specific obligations providing orientation in specific cases. As will be demonstrated in the following sections, there are several strategies that might achieve this.

III. Limiting the Impact of Article 2 TEU in the Verbund Dimension

While it seems possible to attenuate the objections raised above, they nonetheless suggest caution. Even CJEU judges have emphasized a vigilant use of Article 2 TEU. Dean Spielmann, former ECtHR judge and now at the General Court, warned that Article 2 TEU has the potential to become an 'ultra-powerful tool'.

[41] Venice Commission, Report on the rule of law (4 April 2011), CDL-AD(2011)003rev, paras 4 f. On these terminological and conceptual differences, see also Martin Loughlin, The Rule of Law in European Jurisprudence, Study for the Venice Commission (29 May 2009), CDL-DEM(2009)006, p 1.

[42] Venice Commission (n 41) para 35. See also Laurent Pech, 'The Rule of Law as a Well-Established and Well-Defined Principle of EU Law' HJRL 14 (2022), 107.

[43] Venice Commission, Rule of Law Checkliste (18 March 2016), CDL-AD(2016)007rev.

[44] See only the European Commission's 2020 Rule of Law Report, COM(2020) 580 final, p 1: 'the core meaning of the rule of law is the same across the EU.'

[45] Luc Heuschling, 'État de Droit: Etude de linguistique, de théorie & de dogmatique juridique comparées' in Christian Calliess and Hartmut Bauer (eds), *Constitutional Principles in Europe* (Sakkoulas 2008) 103, 110.

The Court should resist the temptation of using these values exponentially.[46] Similar concerns have been raised by Advocate General Bobek. In his view, the obligations of judicial independence derived from Article 19(1)(2) and 2 TEU have become 'limitless', both area-based (application to all Member State courts) and seriousness-based (no de minimis rule).[47] He therefore warned against an 'over-extensive application' of Article 2 TEU.[48]

Such vigilance becomes even more pertinent when recalling the dual character of Article 2 TEU. Its limited role in the Verbund warrants *restraint*. The following sections will go beyond this commonplace and assess strategies that translate the idea of restraint into judicial practice. Instead of providing the CJEU with a definitive toolkit, this section will briefly discuss the merits and drawbacks of these strategies. Their interaction or compatibility will be left to further research. Though certainly overlapping, two broader approaches can be distinguished: limiting the *obligations* flowing from Article 2 TEU (Section A) and limiting their *enforcement* (Section B).

From the perspective of critics, recourse to judicial self-restraint might seem hardly reassuring. Indeed, prevalent narratives assume that the Court of Justice has always seized opportunities to enlarge its authority and power.[49] These past experiences may raise doubts about whether the Luxembourg judges will hold back when applying Article 2 TEU.[50] As discussed in the previous chapter, however, the Court is in a much weaker position than many critics think. It must not only fear for compliance with its judgments, but it is also embedded in a larger context of control. Both sources of pressure have significantly increased since Luxembourg's early jurisprudence, thus requiring greater restraint and responsiveness. Therefore, a cautious and restrained approach is commanded by what some Judges call 'Integrationsklugheit'.[51]

A. Limiting the Obligations in Article 2 TEU

The considerations outlined above strongly indicated that Article 2 TEU—especially in its Verbund dimension—can contain neither very demanding nor very detailed obligations (see Chapter 3, III.B). In this sense, the Court should

[46] Dean Spielmann, 'The Rule of Law Principle in the Jurisprudence of the Court of Justice of the European Union' in María Elósegui et al. (eds), *The Rule of Law in Europe* (Springer 2021) 3, 19.

[47] Cases C-83, 127, 195, 291, and 355/19 *Asociația "Forumul Judecătorilor din România"* [2020] EU:C:2020:746, Opinion of AG Bobek, para 207 f.

[48] Cases C-748 to 754/19 *Prokuratura Rejonowa w Mińsku Mazowieckim* [2021] EU:C:2021:403, Opinion of AG Bobek, para 131.

[49] See only Karen Alter, *Establishing the Supremacy of European Law* (OUP 2001) 37.

[50] Answering in the negative, see Nettesheim (n 5) 222 f.

[51] Thomas von Danwitz, 'Funktionsbedingungen der Rechtsprechung des Europäischen Gerichtshofes' EuR 43 (2008), 769, 785.

interpret the values enshrined in Article 2 TEU as a baseline of minimum obligations. As suggested in previous chapters, the Court could complement a narrow interpretation with a case-by-case approach that merely determines negative red lines without fleshing out the values in a positive manner.

1. Minimum obligations

Starting with the former, Article 2 TEU should be interpreted as containing minimum obligations only.[52] Such a minimum approach was at the heart of the drafters' considerations. In light of the far-reaching Article 7 TEU procedure, it was emphasized that Article 2 TEU can only contain a 'hard core' of values.[53] Accordingly, Article 2 TEU should remain an 'extraordinary remedy for extraordinary situations'.[54] This means, for instance, that the value of 'respect for human rights' in Article 2 TEU cannot encompass the entire Charter but only a qualified part. For that reason, it was proposed to operate with the concept of essence (Chapter 4, IV).[55] As far as a rights' essence is concerned, it is also protected as a value under Article 2 TEU, while Article 51(1) CFR continues to delimit the application of the full fundamental right acquis. This conception has recently been adopted by Advocate General Kokott: 'the examination under Article 2 TEU must be limited to observance of the essence of those principles and rights.'[56]

This cuts back to the problem of indeterminacy that was discussed in the previous chapter. Indeed, many have raised methodological concerns about the way in which the Court determines the essence of a right (Chapter 4, IV). Even though the concept has been somewhat neglected in EU law, both the Court as well as legal scholarship have been increasingly active in fleshing out this notion. In this sense, the essence under Article 52(1) CFR has become slowly operational in the CJEU's case law. This might explain why the Court has increasingly confirmed the link between the notion of essence and Article 2 TEU. For instance, it emphasized that judicial independence forms part of the essence of the right to a fair trial, which 'is

[52] For similar conceptions, see e.g. Werner Schroeder, 'The Rule of Law As a Value in the Sense of Article 2 TEU: What Does It Mean and Imply?' in Armin von Bogdandy et al. (eds), *Defending Checks and Balances in EU Member States* (Springer 2021) 105, 110; Andreas Voßkuhle, *The Idea of the European Community of Values* (Bittner 2018) 116 f; Gabriel Toggenburg and Jonas Grimheden, 'Managing the Rule of Law in a Heterogeneous Context' in Werner Schroeder (ed.), *Strengthening the Rule of Law in Europe* (Hart 2016) 221.

[53] Praesidium (n 17) 11.

[54] AG Bobek (n 48) para 147.

[55] See e.g. Armin von Bogdandy et al., 'Reverse Solange' CML Rev 49 (2012), 489, 509 ff; von Bogdandy and Luke D. Spieker, 'Protecting Fundamental Rights Beyond the Charter' in Michal Bobek and Jeremias Adams-Prassl (eds), *The EU Charter of Fundamental Rights in the Member States* (Hart 2020) 525, 531 f.

[56] Case C-490/20 *Stolichna obshtina, rayon 'Pancharevo'* [2021] EU:C:2021:296, Opinion of AG Kokott, para 118.

of cardinal importance as a guarantee ... that the values common to the Member States set out in Article 2 TEU ... will be safeguarded.'[57]

2. Red lines, regression, and results

As noted above, Article 2 TEU can hardly impose very detailed obligations on the Member States. This confronts the Court with a practical dilemma. When it intends to protect the values enshrined in Article 2 TEU, it is required to apply these vague notions to specific cases. At first glance, this requires a high degree of concretization. Three approaches can significantly reduce the necessary level of concretization. First, the Court can employ the negative, red-line approach outlined in Chapter 2 (III.B.1). This would require the Court to contextualize, tailor its reasoning to the case at hand, and avoid general obiter.[58] In this sense, it would largely refrain from providing a full-blown account of Article 2 TEU or establishing standards on a jurisprudential meta-level. Instead, the Court could merely determine whether a red line is crossed in the specific case.

Second, the Court can apply the regression test set out in its *Repubblika* judgment.[59] According to the CJEU, a Member State cannot 'amend its legislation in such a way as to bring about a reduction in the protection of the value of the rule of law, a value which is given concrete expression by, inter alia, Article 19 TEU'.[60] This assessment was already applied by the Court in the third value-related infringement procedure against Poland.[61] Instead of attempting to derive substantive yardsticks from Article 2 TEU, the Court merely provides a procedure for identifying violations. In this sense, the regression-test is essentially neutral with regard to substantive standards, such as judicial appointment processes. Instead, it concerns only a significant regression from pre-existing national standards. This relieves the Court of the burden to flesh out the values enshrined in Article 2 TEU and allows very different standards to coexist.

Certainly, the regression tests leave many open questions. Even though the judgment in Case C-791/19 seems to render the regression test operational in infringement proceedings, it remains extremely fuzzy. To start with, one may wonder about

[57] Case C-216/18 PPU *Minister for Justice and Equality (Deficiencies in the System of Justice)* [2018] EU:C:2018:586, para 48. More recently, see *Repubblika* (n 6) para 51; *A.B.* (n 6) para 116; Cases C-354 and 412/20 PPU [2020] *Openbaar Ministerie EU:C*:2020:1033, para 39.

[58] On such a minimalist approach, see only Cass Sunstein, *One Case at a Time* (Harvard Univ. Press 1999) 10 f, 68.

[59] Mathieu Leloup, Dimitry Kochenov, and Aleksejs Dimitrovs, 'Opening the Door to Solving the "Copenhagen Dilemma"? All Eyes on Repubblika v Il-Prim Ministru' EL Rev 46 (2021), 692; Oliver Mader, 'Wege aus der Rechtsstaatsmisere: der neue EU-Verfassungsgrundsatz des Rückschrittsverbots und seine Bedeutung für die Wertedurchsetzung' EuZW 32 (2021), 917; Nicola Canzian, 'Indipendenza dei giudici e divieto di regressione della tutela nella sentenza Repubblika' *Quaderni Costituzionali* (2021), 715.

[60] *Repubblika* (n 6) para 63 (emphasis added).

[61] Case C-791/19 *Commission v Poland (Régime disciplinaire des juges)* [2021] EU:C:2020:277, para 51.

the temporal point of reference for this exercise. Regression from what date? The accession? At least for the founding Member States, this would hardly be feasible. Which date then? The entry into force of the Treaty of Amsterdam, which established the Member States' obligation to adhere to the principles of democracy, fundamental rights and the rule of law in its Article 6(1)? Further, it is unclear whether this test captures—as the case law suggests—'any regression'[62] or only measures that cross a certain threshold of severity.[63] As noted before, the values in Article 2 TEU must be interpreted restrictively. In consequence, the regression test would necessarily be operated in form of a two-stage assessment. In a first step, the Court would be required to assess whether an Article 2 TEU value is generally concerned (e.g. are issues concerned that fall into the ambit of a Charter right's essence). In a second step, it would review whether there is a regression in this respect.

Finally, the Court indicated a third strategy to preserve the Member States' discretion when concretizing the values of Article 2 TEU. In its rulings on the rule of law conditionality regulation, it noted that the rule of law in Article 2 TEU constitutes an 'obligation as to the result to be achieved'.[64] This terminology suggests a parallel to directives.[65] According to Article 288(3) TFEU, directives are binding only 'as to the result to be achieved', while leaving the Member States discretion as to the form and method. In principle, the Member States remain free *how* they implement directives.[66] Admittedly, they are also under a duty to ensure their full effectiveness.[67] Even though this caveat has considerably limited the Member States' discretion,[68] directives are still deemed to better preserve national autonomy than, for instance, regulations.[69] The Court's formulation in the rule of law conditionality

[62] *Repubblika* (n 60) para 64; *Commission v Poland (Régime disciplinaire des juges)* (n 61) para 51.

[63] On these open questions, see also Julian Scholtes, 'Constitutionalising the end of history? Pitfalls of a non-regression principle for Article 2 TEU' EuConst 19 (2023), 59; Adam Łazowski, 'Strengthening the Rule of Law and the EU Pre-Accession Policy: Repubblika v. Il-Prim Ministru' CML Rev 59 (2022), 1803, 1814 f; Luke D. Spieker, 'The Conflict over the Polish Disciplinary Regime for Judges—An Acid Test for Judicial Independence, Union Values and the Primacy of EU Law' CML Rev 59 (2022), 777, 789 f.

[64] Case C-156/21 *Hungary v Parliament and Council* [2022] EU:C:2022:97, para 231.

[65] For a similar intuition, see Antonia Baraggia, 'The "Conditionality" Regulation under the ECJ's Scrutiny: A Constitutional Analysis' EL Rev 47 (2022), 687, 693.

[66] Grainne de Búrca and Paul Craig, *EU Law* (7th edn, OUP 2020) 139. See also Sacha Prechal, *Directives in E.C. Law* (2nd edn, OUP 2005) 73 ff; Antonio Tizzano and Roberto Adam, *Manuale di diritto dell'Unione Europea* (3rd edn, Giappichelli 2020) 182 ff; Matthias Ruffert, 'Art. 288 AEUV' in Ruffert and Christian Calliess (eds), *EUV/AEUV* (6th edn, C.H.Beck 2022) para 24.

[67] See e.g. Case C-303/20 *Ultimo Portfolio Investment (Luxembourg)* [2021] EU:C:2021:479, para 34; Case C-551/13 *SETAR* [2014] EU:C:2014:2467, para 37; Case 10/76 *Commission v Italy* [1976] EU:C:1976:125, para 12.

[68] Perceiving even a 'subcutaneous change of character' due to the ever more detailed content of directives, see Thomas von Danwitz, 'Rechtsetzung und Rechtsangleichung' in Manfred Dauses and Markus Ludwigs (eds), *Handbuch des EU-Wirtschaftsrechts* (55th edn, loose-leaf, C.H.Beck 2022) B.II. para 106. See also Jürgen Bast, 'Legal Instruments and Judicial Protection' in Bast and Armin von Bogdandy (eds), *Principles of European Constitutional Law* (2nd edn, Hart 2009) 345, 357; Robert Schütze, 'The Morphology of Legislative Power in the European Community' YEL 25 (2006), 91, 151.

[69] As more proportionate means under Art. 296 TFEU, see e.g. Paul J. Loewenthal, 'Art. 296 TFEU' in Manuel Kellerbauer et al. (eds), *The Treaties and the Charter of Fundamental Rights—A Commentary*

judgments seems to echo this particular feature of directives. Against this backdrop, Article 2 TEU should be read as containing only an 'obligation of result', namely the protection of certain minimum standards, while leaving the form and method to each Member State. This is further emphasized by the Court, when it states that Member States enjoy 'a certain degree of discretion in implementing the principles of the rule of law'.[70]

Some might object that the Court has used a very similar phrasing to justify the direct effect of specific provisions. In the context of directives, the CJEU noted that their provisions can only unfold direct effect (after the transposition period expired without implementation) if they are sufficiently precise.[71] This is the case, where the respective provision imposes on Member States 'in *unequivocal terms a precise* obligation as to the result to be achieved'.[72] With time, this formula has been developed into an integral part for the assessment of direct effect in general. For instance, the Court noted that Article 19(1)(2) TEU as well as Article 47 CFR impose such a clear and precise obligation as to the result to be achieved. As such, national courts must disapply any provision of national law conflicting with them.[73] Still, the crucial part—'in unequivocal terms' and 'precise'—are missing in the Court's characterization of Article 2 TEU.

In any case, these approaches have their limits. In many cases, the determination of a relevant regression or the result to be achieved will hardly be feasible without the establishment of substantive minimum standards. Similar concerns arise with regard to the negative red-line approach. For one, a thin reasoning limits the decision's persuasiveness, reduces a judgment's predictability, and sits uneasily with requirements of legal certainty.[74] Further, it seems impossible to completely prevent the gradual sedimentation and consolidation of certain negative standards. Over time, the accumulation of such negative standards will allow conclusions to be drawn about the positive content of the values enshrined in Article 2 TEU. As such, leaving the precise content of values in abeyance has its limits. Nonetheless, these three approaches may delay this process.

(OUP 2019) para 3. See also the former Protocol (No 30) on the application of the principles of subsidiarity and proportionality (1997), [2006] OJ C321E/308, para 6.

[70] *Hungary v Parliament and Council* (n 64) para 233.

[71] See only Case C-684/16 *Max-Planck-Gesellschaft* [2018] EU:C:2018:874, para 63.

[72] See e.g. Case C-205/20 *Bezirkshauptmannschaft Hartberg-Fürstenfeld (Effet direct)* [2022] EU:C:2022:168, para 19 (emphasis added). See also Case C-387/19 *RTS infra and Aannemingsbedrijf Norré-Behaegel* [2021] EU:C:2021:13, para 47; Case C-397/01 *Pfeiffer* [2004] EU:C:2004:584, para 104.

[73] *Hungary v Parliament and Council* (n 64) para 162; *W.Ż.* (n 7) para 159; *A.B.* (n 6) paras 142–6; Cases C-83, 127, 195, 291, 355, 397/19 *Asociația "Forumul Judecătorilor Din România"* [2021] EU:C:2021:393, para 250.

[74] See Cass Sunstein, 'Beyond Judicial Minimalism' *Tulsa Law Review* 43 (2008), 825, 836 ff.

B. Limiting the Enforcement of Article 2 TEU

A second strand of strategies could centre on a more limited enforcement of the obligations derived from Article 2 TEU. The following sections will distinguish between limitations applying to the EU's Verbandskompetenz (its competence as legal order) and those related to the Court's Organkompetenz for reviewing Article 2 TEU compliance in the Member States (its competence as an institution).[75]

1. Limiting enforcement by the EU

A first approach could consist of a restrained understanding of the EU's general competence to enforce Article 2 TEU in the Member States. The starting point for such a limitation is the scope of EU law, which provides an indicator for the primary responsibilities of either the EU or the Member States. As a rule of thumb, the more a situation falls within the scope of EU law, the more the EU and the less the respective Member States are responsible for remedying a violation of Article 2 TEU. At the same time, the more a situation is removed from the scope of EU law, the stronger the Member States' claim for autonomy becomes. Especially beyond the scope of the other EU law, Article 7 TEU is the only provision *explicitly* empowering the Union to protect Article 2 TEU. This might indicate that the Union's (and thus the Court's) competence is limited to the substantive thresholds triggering that procedure: a 'serious and persistent breach'.[76] This could provide the starting point for a workable restriction operating in the form of a scale. In case there is a clear link to EU law, any violation of Article 2 TEU values can be sanctioned by EU institutions. The more the situation departs from the scope of Union law and comes solely under Article 2 TEU, the greater is the need for a violation to reach the substantive thresholds of Article 7 TEU.

Under such a scheme, breaches of Article 2 TEU beyond the scope of other EU law can be vindicated only if they reach the substantive thresholds of Article 7 TEU. An applicant invoking such a violation before the Court must demonstrate that the alleged violation amounts to a serious and persistent breach. Certainly, there are several shades of grey between the scope of EU law and the areas that lie beyond. Some speak of 'penumbra cases'.[77] This is why the CJEU should apply the tool presented in this section not in an all-or-nothing fashion (either in or out) but rather in the form of a *sliding* scale (for an illustration, see Figure 13.1).

[75] On this distinction, see Armin von Bogdandy and Jürgen Bast, 'The Federal Order of Competences' in Bast and von Bogdandy (n 68) 275, 284. In French legal scholarship, the distinction between *compétence* and *pouvoir* is used, see Vlad Constantinesco, *Compétences et pouvoirs dans les Communautés européennes* (LGDJ 1974).

[76] See also Council of the European Union, Opinion of the Legal Service (n 15) para 17.

[77] Koen Lenaerts, 'The role of the EU Charter in the Member States' in Bobek and Adams-Prassl (n 55) 19, 21.

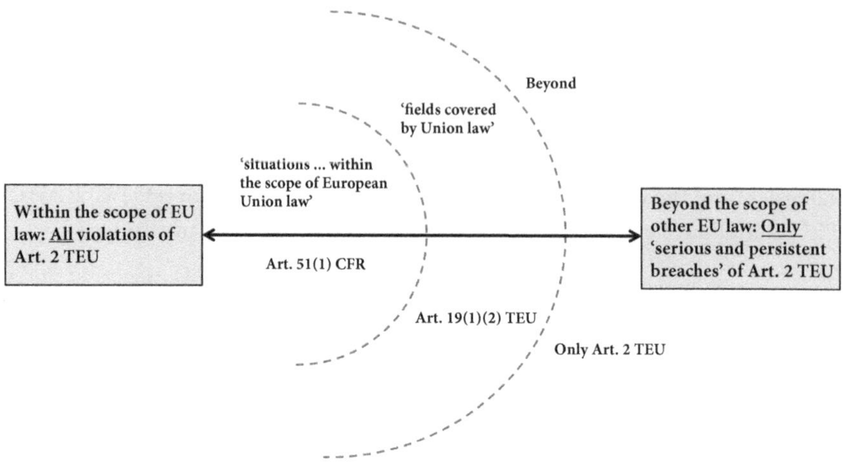

Figure 13.1 Sliding Article 2 TEU scale

2. Limiting enforcement by the Court of Justice

a) Reverse Solange *presumption*

When reviewing Article 2 TEU compliance in the Member States, the CJEU could apply a *Solange*-like logic. As proposed by the *Reverse Solange* doctrine,[78] the Court could make its review subject to a presumption of conformity. Though originally articulated by a national institution (the BVerfG) against a supranational institution (the European Community),[79] the *Solange* doctrine has been increasingly divested from its initial context. Today, the logic has been applied not only in the form of a *horizontal Solange* doctrine between the Member States (Chapter 10, III.A), but also between supranational and international organizations.[80] In this sense, the *Solange* doctrine has developed into a general judicial tool of cooperation between legal orders. Applied to our case, this means that the Court of Justice does not police Article 2 TEU in the Member States beyond the scope of other EU law as long as the presumption of general compliance holds.

i. Threshold: systemic deficiencies This leads to the threshold for refuting the said presumption. As noted above, any threshold should be guided by the high

[78] See von Bogdandy et al. (n 55). For an updated version, see von Bogdandy and Spieker (n 55).

[79] See BVerfG, Order of 29 May 1974, 2 BvL 52/71, *Solange I*, para 62; Order of 1986, 2 BvR 197/83, *Solange II*, para 132.

[80] Between the EU and the UN, Cases C-402 and 415/05 P *Kadi* [2008] EU:C:2008:461, para 256. Between the ECtHR and the EU, ECtHR, Judgment of 30 June 2005, App 45036/98 *Bosphorus v Ireland*, paras 155 f. Between the ECHR and the UN, ECtHR, Judgment of 21 June 2016, App 5809/08 *Al-Dulimi and Montana Management Inc. v Switzerland*, para 153.

substantive requirements of Article 7 TEU. When deciding the specific case, the Court seems to have two options. For one, it could employ a *micro-perspective* and look at the seriousness of the individual violation in a particular case. If the essence of fundamental rights is violated, even an isolated incident might suffice to refute the presumption of value compliance. In such a case, the seriousness of the violation—to employ the vocabulary of Article 7 TEU—might outweigh its lack of persistence. In other instances, the Court could apply a *macro-perspective*. Here, the threshold could be fixed at the level of systemic deficiencies.[81]

So far, the Court has applied this concept primarily as a ground for suspending the transfer of asylum seekers[82] and the surrender of individuals under the European Arrest Warrant regime.[83] Despite the increasing recourse to systemic deficiencies, the concept has remained remarkably under-theorized in the CJEU's jurisprudence.[84] Drawing on the work of Armin von Bogdandy and Michael Ioannidis, the attribution 'systemic' seems to comprise essentially two requirements.[85] On the one hand, it denotes infringements that affect the entire system (or an entire area of a system) and occur in a wide-spread manner. On the other hand, 'systemic' implies regularity and persistence. As such, systemic infringements are not an exception but a deeply-rooted characteristic of the system. Advocate General Bobek noted that this applies especially when the respective system lacks 'sufficient structural guarantees to self-correct the problem'.[86] Within the EU, the existence of a systemic deficiency can be particularly assumed when the deficiency starts to produce negative externalities and spill-over effects in other Member States.[87] Mutual recognition regimes have become a useful detector in this regard (see Chapter 10, III).

ii. Assessment: comprehensive, context-sensitive, and collective This leads to the second question: how should the Court assess systemic deficiencies? This chapter suggests a comprehensive, context-sensitive, and collective assessment.[88] From a methodological perspective, ascertaining a systemic deficiency in a specific case

[81] See Armin von Bogdandy and Luke D. Spieker, 'Countering the Judicial Silencing of Critics' EuConst 15 (2019), 391. With regard to Art. 2 and 19(1)(2) TEU, see AG Bobek (n 54) paras 140–8, 159 arguing in particular for a 'gravity and systemic nature' of the violation as a threshold (para 148).

[82] See especially Cases C-411 and 493/10 *N.S.* [2011] EU:C:2011:865, para 106. Recent case law indicates a departure from this requirement, see e.g. Case C-163/17 *Jawo* [2019] EU:C:2019:218, para 87.

[83] Cases C-562/21 PPU and C-563/21 PPU *Openbaar Ministerie (Tribunal établi par la loi dans l'État membre d'émission)* [2022] EU:C:2022:100; *Minister for Justice and Equality (Deficiencies in the system of justice)* (n 57) para 60. See also Cases C-404 and 659/15 PPU *Aranyosi and Căldăraru* [2016] EU:C:2016:198, para 89; Case C-220/18 PPU *Generalstaatsanwaltschaft* [2018] EU:C:2018:589, para 60.

[84] The European Commission remained equally vague on this point, see European Commission, A new EU Framework to Strengthen the Rule of Law, COM/2014/0158 final, para 4.1.

[85] See Armin von Bogdandy and Michael Ioannidis, 'Systemic Deficiency in the Rule of Law' CML Rev 51 (2014), 59. See also Mario Carta, *Unione europea e tutela dello Stato di diritto negli Stati membri* (Caducci 2020) 137 ff.

[86] AG Bobek (n 54) para 150.

[87] Armin von Bogdandy, 'Principles of a Systemic Deficiencies Doctrine' CML Rev 57 (2020), 705, 719.

[88] For the individual components, see ibid 734 ff.

will depend on a comprehensive, overall assessment concentrating not on a single act but on a plurality of measures and a high degree of context sensitivity. Some developments in the Member States present the particularity that they consist of a bundle of individual measures, which, when considered individually, do not transgress a critical threshold. Only when taken together do they constitute a violation of Article 2 TEU.[89] Some call this a 'cocktail effect'.[90] This is exacerbated by the fact that such developments are often cloaked as lawful measures that hide the underlying political agenda.[91] Further, the respective governments rely on comparisons with seemingly similar situations in other Member States. The Polish government especially went to great lengths to justify the overhaul of its judiciary with comparative considerations.[92] A comprehensive and contextual approach might help the Court navigate these issues. The case law provides some promising examples. In *A.K.*, the Court noted that, while certain measures escape criticism if taken individually, the picture changes when they are taken together.[93] Similarly, it stressed in *A.B.* the need to consider 'all the relevant factors ... in a specific national legal and factual context'.[94]

From an institutional point of view, the existence of a systemic deficiency could be established by having recourse to the congruent assessment of a plurality of independent institutions.[95] In this sense, the assessment should be understood as a process of collective evaluation.[96] Besides the CJEU, this collective would comprise the European Commission, the ECtHR, the Venice Commission, international organizations, and NGOs. This extends, in particular, to assessments conducted in the respective Member States themselves. The more institutions ascertain a problem, the greater the evidence pointing towards systemic deficiency. In this spirit, the CJEU referred not only to the findings of the Commission's reasoned proposals[97] but also to 'judgments of the European Court of Human Rights, judgments of courts of the issuing Member State, and also decisions, reports and other documents produced by bodies of the Council of Europe or under the aegis of the United Nations'[98] as relevant material for the determination of systemic deficiencies.

[89] See e.g. Kim L. Scheppele, 'Enforcing the Basic Principles of EU Law Through Systemic Infringement Actions' in Carlos Closa and Dimitry Kochenov (eds), *Reinforcing Rule of Law Oversight in the European Union* (CUP 2016) 105, 108.

[90] Sébastien Platon, 'Preliminary References and Rule of Law' CML Rev 57 (2020), 1843, 1864.

[91] See only Kim L. Scheppele, 'Autocratic Legalism' *University of Chicago Law Review* 85 (2018), 545.

[92] White Paper (n 20) paras 40 f. See also Jan Muszyński, 'Comparative Legal Argument in the Polish Discussion on Changes in the Judiciary' JöR 68 (2020), 705.

[93] *A.K.* (n 19) paras 142, 152.

[94] *A.B.* (n 6) para 129.

[95] See von Bogdandy (n 87) 735 ff.

[96] Armin von Bogdandy, 'Tyrannei der Werte?' ZaöRV 79 (2019), 503, 545 ff.

[97] See e.g. *Minister for Justice and Equality (Deficiencies in the system of justice)* (n 57) para 61.

[98] See Case C-128/18 *Dorobantu* [2019] EU:C:2019:857, para 52. See also *Aranyosi and Căldăraru* (n 83) para 89; *Generalstaatsanwaltschaft* (n 83) para 60

Such an approach has several advantages. To start with, it helps fend off reproaches of political bias and double standards. A CJEU decision establishing that certain measures violate Article 2 TEU while leaving a similar situation in other Member States untouched might be a target for such allegations. Relying on a comprehensive, context-sensitive, and collective assessment demonstrates the differences between the situations in recalcitrant Member States and countries with a—legally—comparable situation. This might prove useful, if, for instance, the Polish Minister of Justice delivers on his promise to bring the German system of judicial appointments before the Court of Justice.[99] In addition, the concurrent assessment of a plethora of independent institutions enhances the credibility of such distinctions and leads to burden-sharing. Eventually, this might also counter objections based on constitutional pluralism. As pluralism presupposes a 'plurality of epistemes',[100] it seems advisable to ground the identification of a systemic deficiency on a plurality of actors with different horizons.

b) A deferential approach

Finally, the Court of Justice could employ a deferential strategy. Generally, there are two avenues for such an approach: decentralized judicial review and margin of appreciation.[101] The former is usually applied in preliminary reference proceedings and relates to the leeway granted to the referring court. It thus concerns an institutional or procedural question, namely the *locus of scrutiny*. The margin of appreciation, by contrast, can be applied in any type of proceeding that involves the review of Member State acts. It is primarily a substantive question and relates to the degree or *intensity of scrutiny*.

i. Procedure: decentralized judicial review Starting with the former, it is commonplace that Article 267 TFEU is 'based upon a clear separation of functions between national courts and the Court of Justice'.[102] Yet, binary distinctions, such as the one between interpretation of law (for the Luxembourg court) and application to facts (for the referring court), can hardly do justice to the complex realities that characterize the judicial dialogue. Instead, the CJEU has applied varying degrees of specificity. Some have proposed to distinguish between outcome, guidance, and

[99] Press Release, The Ministry of Justice calls for an examination of the German model of judicial appointments (18 October 2021), <www.gov.pl/web/justice/the-ministry-of-justice-calls-for-an-examination-of-the-german-model-of-judicial-appointments>.

[100] Matej Avbelj, 'Pluralism and Systemic Defiance in the EU' in Dimitry Kochenov and András Jakab (eds), *Enforcing EU Law and Values* (OUP 2017) 44, 51.

[101] On these two 'deference routes', see Jan Zglinski, 'The Rise of Deference: The Margin of Appreciation and Decentralized Judicial Review in EU Free Movement Law' CML Rev 55 (2018), 1341, 1343 ff.

[102] Case 6/64 *Costa/ENEL* [1964] EU:C:1964:66, p 593. Recently, see e.g. *W.Ż. (Chamber of Extraordinary Control and Public Affairs of the Supreme Court—Appointment)* (n 7) para 78.

deference cases.[103] These variations are no random exercise but a conscious judicial choice. A higher degree of deference provides national courts with an opportunity to adapt the CJEU's interpretation to the specificities of their legal system. It may not only be more respectful towards national autonomy but also lead to a burden-sharing between the interacting courts. In light of the high sensitivity of value-related cases and the far-reaching implications for the Member States' constitutional structures, applying such a deferential approach appears to be a sensible strategy.

Still, deference is a two-edged sword. For one, it might overburden the referring courts. In the past, the Court did not shy away from identifying and fully assessing systemic deficiencies in the Member States.[104] As the *L.M.* judgment demonstrates, however, this determination is increasingly left to the referring courts.[105] The decision in *A.K.* may serve as another example. While providing detailed requirements for the assessment of judicial independence under Articles 2 and 19(1)(2) TEU, the CJEU left it to the referring court to determine whether the Polish Supreme Court's disciplinary chamber complies with them.[106] The Court's deferential stance in *A.K.* motivated both the Polish government as well as the affected judiciary to claim the judgment as a victory. The referring Supreme Court decided that the disciplinary chamber does not comply with the standards set out by the CJEU.[107] Instead of remedying the issues, the Polish government countered with a new bill aimed at preventing judges from questioning the independence of their peers.[108] Deference might thus show greater respect for national autonomy but risks leaving affected national courts with a burden too heavy to shoulder. In this sense, the Court of Justice will have to carefully assess the situation in the respective Member State as well as the position and authority of the referring court before determining the degree of deference.

At the same time, a high level of deference might frustrate referring courts, which are in need of orientation and expect the CJEU to provide sufficiently precise answers. National judges might think twice whether to invest considerable energy in referring a case to the Court. In the long term, this might even weaken the CJEU's institutional relevance.[109] Further, a decentralized judicial review might jeopardize the uniform application of EU law. If the CJEU does not provide

[103] Takis Tridimas, 'Constitutional Review of Member State Action: The Virtues and Vices of an Incomplete Jurisdiction' I-CON 9 (2011), 737, 739 ff. For further systematizations, see e.g. Zglinski (n 101) 1349.

[104] See e.g. *N.S.* (n 82); *Generalstaatsanwaltschaft* (n 83).

[105] See e.g. *Minister for Justice and Equality (Deficiencies in the system of justice)* (n 57).

[106] *A.K.* (n 19) para 140.

[107] Polish Supreme Court, Judgment of 5 December 2019, Case III PO 7/18.

[108] See Venice Commission, Poland—Urgent Joint Opinion on the amendments to the Law on organisation on the Common Courts, the Law on the Supreme Court and other Laws, CDL-PI(2020)002-e (16 January 2020); ODHIR, Urgent Interim Opinion, JUD-POL/365/2019 [AlC] (14 January 2020).

[109] Daniel Sarmiento, 'Half a Case at a Time' in Monica Claes et al. (eds), *Constitutional Conversations in Europe* (Intersentia 2012) 13, 33 ff.

sufficiently clear guidance, national courts might feel compelled to 'patriate' concepts of EU law.[110] As such, the Court of Justice should adopt a decentralized review with outmost caution.

ii. Substance: margin of appreciation A second option is to employ a margin of appreciation doctrine.[111] Such an approach could be construed in three different, albeit not mutually exclusive, ways. First, the Court could establish a link between the level of scrutiny and the *scope of EU law*.[112] This ties back to the sliding scale presented above and could lead to a layered margin of appreciation: the more a certain case is removed from the scope of other EU law, the wider the margin of appreciation. Within the scope of EU law, the Member States are subject to the highest level of scrutiny. In areas covered only by Article 2 TEU, Member States would have a wider margin of appreciation.

Second, the Court could apply a margin of appreciation doctrine corresponding to a *consensus among the Member States*. Such an approach can already be traced in the CJEU's jurisprudence. While the Court has never laid down a grand theory in this respect, bits and pieces of this approach are scattered throughout its case law.[113] For our purposes, two instances seem particularly relevant.[114] First, the Court has often granted national legislatures a margin of appreciation in sensitive policy areas. This approach can be observed especially with regard to the grounds justifying restrictions of fundamental freedoms, such as 'public morality' or 'public policy'. In *Omega*, for example, the Court stated that public policy justifications 'may vary from one country to another and from one era to another. The competent national authorities must therefore be allowed a margin of discretion'.[115] Second, the Court has connected a margin of appreciation to the consensus (or lack thereof) among Member States. In the area of gambling, for instance, the Court has argued that 'there are significant moral, religious and cultural differences' and that the Member States thus enjoy a wide discretion.[116]

Even if this case law remains very rudimental,[117] this second facet comes closest to the margin of appreciation established by the ECtHR. In this spirit, many have argued for a more open adoption of this doctrine, especially with regard to

[110] Tridimas (n 103) 755.

[111] For a first sketch, see Rainer Hofmann and Alexander Heger, 'Zur Zukunft der Europäischen Union als Werteunion' EuGRZ 49 (2022), 361, 368–71.

[112] In this sense, Armin von Bogdandy, *The Emergence and Democratization of European Society* (OUP 2023) 3.2.D; Jürgen Kühling, 'Fundamental Rights' in von Bogdandy and Bast (n 75) 479, 507.

[113] In this sense, see Jan Zglinski, *Europe's Passive Virtues* (OUP 2020) 67; Aude Bouveresse, *Le pouvoir discrétionnaire dans l'ordre juridique Communautaire* (Bruylant 2010) 57.

[114] For factors that might trigger a margin of appreciation, see Zglinksi (n 113) 68 ff; Janneke Gerards, 'Pluralism, Deference and the Margin of Appreciation Doctrine' ELJ 17 (2011), 80, 91 ff.

[115] Case C-36/02 *Omega* [2004] EU:C:2004:614, para 31.

[116] Case C-322/16 *Global Starnet* [2017] EU:C:2017:985, para 39.

[117] On its inconsistencies, see Zglinski (n 113) 82 ff.

fundamental freedoms[118] and fundamental rights.[119] Especially where there is no uniform European consensus, the ECtHR's review gives way to the 'choice of society' of the individual Member States.[120] In order to determine the existence of such a consensus, the Court usually resorts to an elaborate comparative analysis.[121] Several considerations justify the ECtHR's approach. Besides the claims that national institutions are better placed to decide certain issues (argument from expertise and proximity) and possess a stronger democratic pedigree (argument from democratic legitimacy), Protocol No. 15 indicates that the ECHR is primarily conceived as a subsidiary instrument (argument from subsidiarity).[122] These arguments apply to a lesser extent in the EU context. Although the EU legal order equally guarantees the diversity of its Member States, its transversal scope of competences together with primacy and direct effect lead to a higher degree of penetration into the domestic legal orders.[123]

Yet, the pull for diversity is greater when it comes to Article 2 TEU in its Verbund dimension. How then could a consensus-based approach be applied to Article 2 TEU? When there is a lack of consensus among the Member States on the concretization of the values enshrined in Article 2 TEU, the CJEU could reduce its level of scrutiny and apply Article 2 TEU as a negative red line only. By contrast, when it is possible to identify a consensus among the Member States (or a prevailing trend), the Court could apply a stricter scrutiny and even endeavour to flesh out the respective value in a positive manner. Eventually, establishing whether there is a consensus among the Member States would correspond to the comparative approach proposed for fleshing out the values in the first place (see Chapter 2, III.B). Against this backdrop, a margin of appreciation could be applied at two stages: first, when determining Article 2 TEU's content and, second, when a balancing of conflicting values is required.

It should be noted, however, that even a well-established margin of appreciation doctrine, such as the one developed by the ECtHR, does not escape criticism.

118 Sceptically, see Henrike Schulte, *Zur Übertragbarkeit der Margin-of-appreciation-Doktrin des EGMR auf die Rechtsprechung des EuGH im Bereich der Grundfreiheiten* (Nomos 2018) 375.

119 From different perspectives, see e.g. Huber (n 3) 333; Thomas von Danwitz, 'Gerichtlicher Schutz der Grundrechte' in Christoph Grabenwarter (ed.), *Europäischer Grundrechteschutz* (Nomos 2014) § 6, pp 255, 294. See also Gerards (n 114) 115 ff; Christopher Bilz, *Margin of Appreciation der EU-Mitgliedstaaten* (Mohr Siebeck 2020) 83 ff. Nuanced Kühling (n 112) 479, 508.

120 See e.g. ECtHR, Judgment of 1 July 2014, App 43835/11 *S.A.S. v France*, para 153.

121 On the ECtHR's methods, see e.g. Dean Spielmann, 'Allowing the Right Margin' CYELS 14 (2012), 381, 403 ff; Luzius Wildhaber, Arnaldur Hjartarson, and Stephen Donnelly, 'No Consensus on Consensus?' HRLJ 33 (2013), 248; Kanstantsin Dzehtsiarou, *European Consensus and the Legitimacy of the European Court of Human Rights* (CUP 2015) 38 ff, 78 ff.

122 For a similar systematization, see Andrew Legg, *The Margin of Appreciation in International Human Rights Law* (OUP 2012) 67 ff. For a reconstruction solely along the argument from democratic legitimacy, see Josephine Asche, *Die Margin of Appreciation* (Springer 2018) 215 ff.

123 For further differences, see also Oddný M. Arnardóttir and Dóra Guðmundsdóttir, 'Speaking the Same Language?' in Arnardóttir and Antoine Buyse (eds), *Shifting Centres of Gravity in Human Rights Protection* (Routledge 2016) 161, 168 ff.

Indeed, the consensus-based approach is probably one of Strasbourg's most controversial doctrinal innovations.[124] In this sense, many have argued that the margin of appreciation derived from the existence (or non-existence) of a consensus among the Member States is not only methodologically obscure[125] but also normatively undesirable. If the requirements for assuming a consensus are too high, it may lead to an increasing relativism. If the thresholds for consensus are too low (including e.g. looser trends), it might risk a hegemony of the majority.[126] Further, the ECtHR—like the CJEU—is a counter-majoritarian institution. Thus, it might miss the courts' function to allow a majority to decide what rights individuals should have in controversial cases.[127] Yet, such criticism seems to overestimate the force of a consensus-based margin of appreciation. It does not mean a complete absence of review but simply a reduced level of scrutiny that continues to go 'hand in hand with European supervision'.[128]

Third, the CJEU could apply a wider or narrower margin of appreciation corresponding to the *quality of legislative, administrative, or judicial procedures* that led to the adoption of the measures under review. Again, the ECtHR's innovative jurisprudence may serve as an example. With regard to legislative procedures, the ECtHR has been more lenient in granting a margin of appreciation if the respective processes satisfy a certain democratic quality.[129] Some have termed this a 'qualitative democracy-enhancing approach'.[130] While case law still lacks precise criteria for this assessment,[131] the ECtHR highlighted, for instance, the fact that the measure was 'the fruit of much reflection, consultation and debate'.[132] The underlying rationale for this kind of margin of appreciation can be found in the argument from democratic legitimacy mentioned above. National processes only reveal a stronger democratic pedigree warranting a wider margin of appreciation if they are

[124] In this sense, Christos L. Rozakis, 'Through the Looking Glass: An "Insider's" View of the Margin of Appreciation' in *Mélanges en l'honneur de Jean-Paul Costa* (Dalloz 2011) 527.

[125] From the plethora of contributions, see only Jan Kratochvíl, 'The Inflation of the Margin of Appreciation by the European Court of Human Rights' *Netherlands Quarterly of Human Rights* 29 (2011), 324, 351 ff.

[126] John L. Murray, 'Consensus: Concordance, or Hegemony of the Majority?' in *Dialogue between Judges* (Council of Europe 2008) 17, 30 f.

[127] On this, see e.g. George Letsas, *A Theory of Interpretation of the European Convention on Human Rights* (OUP 2007) 119; Dimitrios Kagiaros, 'When to Use European Consensus' in Panos Kapotas and Vassilis P. Tzevelekos (eds), *Building Consensus on European Consensus* (CUP 2019) 283, 288 f; Jens T. Theilen, *European Consensus Between Strategy and Principle* (Nomos 2021) 62 ff.

[128] ECtHR [GC], Judgment of 15 October 2015, App 27510/08 *Perinçek v Switzerland*, para 196.

[129] See e.g. ECtHR, [GC] Judgment of 22 April 2013, App 48876/08 *Animal Defenders International v United Kingdom*, para 108. See also Alejandro Saiz Arnaiz, 'Tribunal Europeo de Derechos Humanos y procesos políticos nacionales: democracia convencional y margen de apreciación' *Teoría y Realidad Constitucional* 42 (2018), 221, 231 ff; Thomas Kleinlein, 'The Procedural Approach of the European Court of Human Rights' ICLQ 68 (2019), 91.

[130] Robert Spano, 'The Future of the European Court of Human Rights Subsidiarity. Process-Based Review and the Rule of Law' HRLR 18 (2018), 473, 489.

[131] For a systematization, see e.g. Matthew Saul, 'The European Court of Human Rights' Margin of Appreciation and the Processes of National Parliaments' HRLR 15 (2015), 745, 762 ff.

[132] ECtHR [GC], Judgment of 10 April 2007, App 6339/05 *Evans v United Kingdom*, para 86.

actually free, representative, inclusive, transparent, and fair. It should be stressed that the procedural margin of appreciation does *not* impose specific requirements for parliamentary procedures. The ECtHR reviews the quality of domestic procedures not to find a violation but merely to determine the intensity of scrutiny. As such, the assessment should be understood as a carrot rather than a stick.

This approach is not entirely alien to the EU context.[133] Some have argued that the CJEU already applies a process-oriented review with regard to EU legislation.[134] Applied to the review of value compliance in the Member States, the Court could start by assessing the legislative or administrative procedures that led to the measures affecting Article 2 TEU. If they were of sufficiently democratic quality (e.g. free, representative, inclusive, transparent, and fair), the respective Member State could be granted a wider margin of appreciation. Arguably, the new Hungarian constitution[135] or the overhaul of the Polish judiciary would not fulfil these requirements.[136] Such an assessment could also take into consideration whether the aims, which are brought forward by the respective government to justify the measures, are pursued in a consistent manner.[137]

Such an approach might allow the Court to apply different levels of scrutiny to comparable legal situations. Take again the overhaul of the Polish judiciary. As noted above, the Polish government justified the respective measures by pointing to similar situations in other Member States. Suppose the Court is called to review the compliance of both the Polish and the German system with requirements of judicial independence. The CJEU could reason that the system in Germany was set up in an entirely unsuspicious context through sufficiently democratic procedures and, thus, apply a wider margin of appreciation. To avoid double standards, however, it is important to provide a detailed analysis that clearly articulates the factors that set the respective procedures apart. Admittedly, assessing the quality of democratic processes will be difficult, especially for a supranational court with practically no means to gather evidence on the ground. In addition, assessing the minutes or *travaux* of certain legislative acts would add to the CJEU's heavy workload. Yet,

[133] Arguing for a procedural proportionality review in case of sensitive moral issues, see Floris de Witte, 'Sex, Drugs & EU Law' CML Rev 50 (2014), 1545, 1570 ff; Tor-Inge Harbo, 'Introducing Procedural Proportionality Review in European Law' LJIL 30 (2017), 25, 33 ff.

[134] See Koen Lenaerts, 'The European Court of Justice and Process-Oriented Review' YEL 31 (2012), 3; Darren Harvey, 'Towards Process-Oriented Proportionality Review in The European Union' EPL 23 (2017), 93; Malu Beijer, 'Procedural Fundamental Rights Review by the Court of Justice of the European Union' in Janneke Gerards and Eva Brems (eds), *Procedural Review in European Fundamental Rights Cases* (CUP 2017) 177, 190 ff.

[135] On the lack of representation in the adoption process of the new Constitution, see e.g. Venice Commission, Opinion on the new Constitution of Hungary (17–18 June 2011), CDL-AD(2011)016, paras 11, 144.

[136] On the unconstitutional overhaul of the Polish judiciary, see only Wojciech Sadurski, *Poland's Constitutional Breakdown* (OUP 2019).

[137] It is established jurisprudence that national measures can only be justified by certain objectives if they pursue them in a consistent and systematic manner, see only Case C-400/19 *Commission v Hungary (Marges bénéficiaires)* [2021] EU:C:2021:194, para 48.

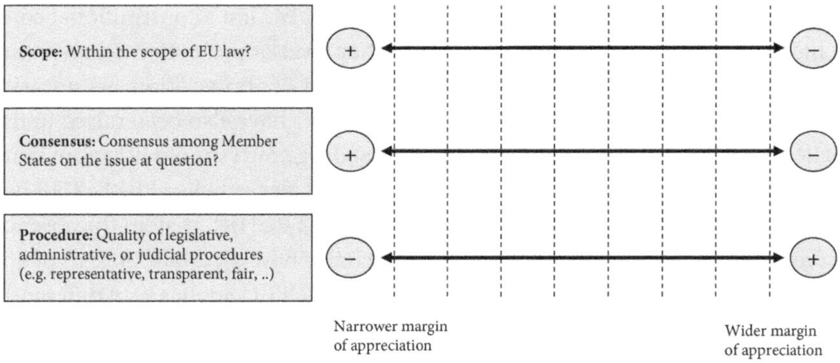

Figure 13.2 Margin of appreciation toolkit

it should be stressed that Article 2 TEU is a tool for extraordinary situations that transcend the Court's daily business. Such an assessments would therefore occur only in exceptional circumstances.

Eventually, such a procedural approach could also be applied to judicial proceedings. If a constitutional court is instrumentalized by the governing party, such as the Hungarian or Polish constitutional courts, decisions rendered by such a body would come under strict scrutiny. Beyond such institutional issues, one could further argue that the national court's reasoning—its persuasiveness, coherence, and anchoring in the European legal discourse—matters.[138] Eventually, this could lead to a filter for unmasking bad faith and abuses of legal procedures.

Together, these three factors might lead to a sophisticated toolkit (see Figure 13.2). While there is no room to assess the interaction and compatibility of these approaches in detail, there seems to be at least no immediately apparent reason why their cumulative application should be excluded.[139] In any case, the Court should start its assessment with the first factor as there is little room for wide margins of appreciation within the scope of EU law.

Nonetheless, two general objections could be raised against such a deferential approach. The first one boils down to the concern that a wide margin of appreciation threatens the uniform and coherent application of EU law. It should be reemphasized, though, that the suggested margin of appreciation would apply in exceptional situations. Moreover, it does not imply the complete absence of review. Second, it might seem flawed or counter-intuitive to apply a margin of appreciation to the very core issues enshrined in Article 2 TEU. The logic is usually reversed: the

[138] On such a 'legitimacy test', see Flynn (n 24) 245 f. On criteria for determining an 'abuse' of ultra-vires reviews, see Polzin (n 24) 308 ff.

[139] On such combinations, see e.g. Thomas Kleinlein, 'Consensus and Contestability: The ECtHR and the Combined Potential of European Consensus and Procedural Rationality Control' EJIL 28 (2017), 871, 891.

more salient an issue, the more it might form part of EU law's constitutional core, the higher the level of its protection. This higher level of protection corresponds to a higher level of judicial scrutiny. Thus, a margin of appreciation sits uneasily with constitutional core principles. Similar objections have also been raised in the ECHR context. Some have argued that the Strasbourg court should not grant margins of appreciation with regard to absolute rights.[140] Nevertheless, the ECtHR has recognized, for instance for the right to life (Article 2 ECHR), that 'in the absence of consensus among the member States . . . the latter have a certain margin of appreciation.'[141] We should also not forget that Article 2 TEU applies very differently in its EU and in its Verbund dimension. When applied beyond the scope of other EU law, it cannot impose the same kind of protection as in its EU dimension. Even if we would accept a sort of absolute protection of EU values that would exclude wider margins of appreciation in the EU dimension, Article 2 TEU follows different rationales in the Verbund.

140 See e.g. Javier García-Roca, 'International Deference, the Vague National Margin of Appreciation and Procedural Review' in Cristina Izquierdo-Sans et al. (eds), *Fundamental Rights Challenges* (Springer 2021) 245, 256; Jochen von Bernstorff, 'Kerngehaltsschutz durch den UN-Menschenrechtsausschuss und den EGMR' *Der Staat* 50 (2011), 165, 176 f; Johan Callewaert, 'Is There a Margin of Appreciation in the Application of Articles 2, 3 and 4 of the Convention?' HRLJ 19 (1998), 6.

141 See e.g. ECtHR [GC], Judgment of 5 June 2015, App 46043/14 *Lambert v France*, para 144 or [GC], Judgment of 8 July 2004, App 53924/00 *Vo v France*, para 82.

Conclusions

This book explored the rise of Article 2 TEU in the jurisprudence of the Court of Justice. First, it developed the practical, doctrinal, and theoretical foundations of this emerging jurisprudential edifice (Part I). In a second step, this book aimed at establishing a conceptual framework for the evolving jurisprudence, spelling out its potential, and charting possible ways ahead (Part II and III). The third step provided space for critical reflection and developed ways to recalibrate the jurisprudence (Part IV). The following conclusions will briefly summarize the central findings and proposals advanced in this study and provide an outlook for future research.

Since Lisbon, the Court of Justice has increasingly engaged with Article 2 TEU. In the past four years, it has laid the groundworks for a veritable Article 2 TEU-based jurisprudence. The judgment in *Associação Sindical dos Juízes Portugueses* constitutes a critical breakthrough. Despite these developments, many still question the judicial applicability of Article 2 TEU. These doubts boil down to doctrinal objections concerning the provision's legal normativity (values), its justiciability (indeterminacy), and the Court's jurisdiction (exclusivity of political procedures). None of these objections appear to be convincing. First, systematic considerations and the provision's drafting history strongly suggest that Article 2 TEU contains legal principles, not moral values. Second, the Court has found ways to overcome Article 2 TEU's indeterminacy by operationalizing these values through specific Treaty provisions. Further, this study explored strategies and sources that allow the Court to develop Article 2 TEU into a freestanding provision. Finally, there are no apparent reasons why the review of Article 2 TEU compliance in the Member States should be withdrawn from the Court's purview. This applies even to situations beyond the scope of other EU law or EU competences. In conclusion, Article 2 TEU can be anchored among the operative provisions of EU law.

Taking a step back, this book sought to develop a conceptual framework for the judicial mobilization of Article 2 TEU. Generally, the provision covers two different contexts: one relating to the EU legal system (the EU dimension) and another, broader context comprising the entirety of both the EU and the Member States' legal orders (the Verbund dimension). A closer look into the provision's drafting context suggests that these dimensions correspond to different forms of constitutionalism. While Article 2 TEU gives expression to a constitutive, thick constitutionalism in its EU dimension, it epitomizes a thinner, primarily restraining form in the Verbund. In this sense, the provision reveals a *dual character*. To grasp these

EU Values Before the Court of Justice. Luke Dimitrios Spieker, Oxford University Press. © Luke Dimitrios Spieker 2023.
DOI: 10.1093/oso/9780198876717.003.0015

two facets, this book proposed reading Article 2 TEU as the constitutional core of the EU legal order and as a constitutional frame of the Verbund.

The second Part explored the potential of Article 2 TEU in its EU dimension. Looking ahead, Article 2 TEU could serve as the basis for a profound reorganization of EU primary law. The Court has already started to distinguish a 'constitutional framework' from the plethora of Treaty provisions. This book suggested a different path. As the *constitutional core* of the EU legal order, Article 2 TEU could provide a starting point for the judicial construction of a substantive EU constitution. Such an Article 2 TEU-based constitution would consist of those provisions that give expression to a founding value (including, e.g., the Charter or the EU's democratic processes and institutions). This Article 2 TEU-based constitution can exert constitutional effects. Usually, constitutions take precedence over ordinary law. Drawing on this insight, the Court could introduce substantive hierarchies between those provisions that give expression to an Article 2 TEU value and those that do not. This would lead to a threefold, hierarchical division of primary law: Article 2 TEU at its summit (the EU's constitutional core), provisions giving expression to an EU value on the second level (the EU's substantive constitution), and the rest of EU primary law on a third one (incl. the EU's so-called 'economic constitution'). The potential of such a division has been assessed in three settings.

With regard to the Treaties, it can foster the coherence of primary law. In the past, the Court has relied especially on Community objectives and general principles to establish coherence among the vast array of Treaty provisions. Yet both concepts have lost much of their appeal. Article 2 TEU and the hierarchical division of primary law could provide a new tool. In consequence, Article 2 TEU could provide stronger guidance for the interpretation and application of primary law. Moreover, the threefold hierarchization would allow the Court to resolve many conflicts among Treaty provisions through substantive precedence rather than balancing.

With regard to EU legislation, the suggested division of primary law can encourage legislative processes. The extensive scope of primary law and the CJEU's strong institutional position considerably reduce the space for legislative decision-making. Some have even ascertained an over-constitutionalization of EU law. Though the Court's jurisprudence is already marked by a certain responsiveness, many policy choices are withdrawn from the legislature's reach. As such, it has been proposed to de-constitutionalize large parts of primary law and transfer these issues into the realm of secondary legislation. Based on the hierarchical division of primary law, the Court could achieve a similar result with less intrusive means. While retaining strict scrutiny of provisions that give expression to an Article 2 TEU value, the Court could relax constraints imposed by provisions from the third level and leave these issues to the legislature's discretion. This would reduce the constraining effects of its jurisprudence and broaden the space for legislative decision-making in important policy fields (e.g. the 'economic constitution').

Finally, *with regard to Treaty revisions*, Article 2 TEU could be turned into a justiciable limitation for amendments that affect the Union's founding values. In constitutional theory, the idea of implicit limits for constitutional amendments is based on the distinction between a primary and a secondary constituent power. The latter is empowered to amend but not to adopt a new constitution. The turning point is reached when a constitution's identity is affected. Article 2 TEU has been read by the Court as comprising the Union's constitutional identity. Certainly, there are difficulties in transferring this theory to the EU level. As the Member States created and amend the Treaties, the distinction between primary and secondary constituent power seems to collapse. The ordinary revision procedure, however, places procedural constraints on the Member States and involves several EU institutions. Accordingly, there is a difference between the unconstrained adoption of new and the revision of the current Treaties. Though procedurally tricky, such amendments could be reviewed by the Court for their compliance with Article 2 TEU.

In its Verbund dimension, Article 2 TEU should be read as a *constitutional frame* that guarantees only a minimum of homogeneity among the EU and the Member States' constitutional structures. Being an essential precondition of any federal system, the constitutional homogeneity across the Verbund is assured through a complex web of claims: top-down (EU → Member States), horizontal (among the Member States), and bottom-up (Member States → EU). Eventually, these claims converge in Article 2 TEU. The EU judicial system plays an important role in securing the required degree of constitutional homogeneity in the Verbund.

Top-down, the CJEU can review whether Member States respect the values in Article 2 TEU. The Court has already started assessing the compliance of certain Member States with EU values. Institutionally, there are solid arguments for involving Luxembourg. Judicial proceedings can depoliticize conflicts, guarantee procedural fairness, and have proven to be more efficient than the deadlocked political avenues. Substantively, however, upheavals of the Member States' constitutional structures seem to often escape the scope of EU law—except for Article 2 TEU. Instead of applying Article 2 TEU in a self-standing manner, the Court has found a way to operationalize it through specific Treaty provisions. While the specific provision translates Article 2 TEU values into applicable legal obligations, Article 2 TEU justifies an extensive reading of the specific provision. This construction allows the Court to review even the Member States' internal constitutional structures for their compliance with Article 2 TEU. This jurisprudence, developed in response to the overhaul of the Polish judiciary, could be extended to other values, such as democracy or the essence of fundamental rights.

Horizontally, Member State institutions can participate in this effort by policing the value compliance of their peers. First, national governments can hold other Member States accountable in infringement proceedings under Article 259 TFEU. In this sense, they can trigger a vertical review conducted by the Court of Justice. This path seems especially promising if willing Member States launch such procedures together. Second, national courts can review a Member State's value compliance through the gateway of mutual recognition regimes. The Court clarified that cooperation under these regimes must be suspended in case of demonstrated non-compliance with Article 2 TEU. This turns mutual recognition regimes into instruments for detecting and countering systemic deficiencies in the Member States. Still, this gateway is conceived in extremely narrow terms and proves difficult to handle in practice. So far, only the European Arrest Warrant regime has been operated in this sense. Still, this approach could be extended to other mutual recognition regimes as well and increase the pressure on Member States that disregard the values in Article 2 TEU.

Bottom-up, national constitutional courts can play an equally important role. Many Member State constitutions contain principles, often corresponding to their constitutional identities, which must be observed at the EU level. Voicing concerns in this respect and assessing the Union's compliance with these principles can become an important tool for securing the Verbund's constitutional homogeneity. Currently, however, constitutional identity doctrines seem rather geared towards contestation. To turn them into a constructive bottom-up check, this study suggested articulating identity concerns under the banner of Article 2 TEU. Conceptually, both contain core guarantees of the highest normative relevance and are confined to exceptional situations. Substantively, they boil down to the protection of the same fundamental principles, namely democracy, the rule of law, and fundamental rights. Addressing constitutional identities under Article 2 TEU instead of Article 4(2) TEU would raise their status under EU law, foster a more constructive dialogue, and actively counter abuses of identity doctrines by captured constitutional courts in Member States like Poland or Hungary.

This book ended with a call for caution. Placing Article 2 TEU in the hands of the Luxembourg judges does not come without risks. First, the indeterminacy of Article 2 TEU might provide a gateway for the judges' political, moral, or ideological convictions and jeopardize the rule of law. The Court could mitigate such concerns by deciding value-related cases in the Grand Chamber or full Court, by rigorously applying legal methods, and making the sources that inspire the concretization of Article 2 TEU more transparent. Second, the judicial enforcement of these indeterminate values might raise democratic concerns, especially when the Court reviews the value compliance of democratically mandated national governments. In such cases, however, the CJEU will usually intervene to protect the conditions for constitutional democracy. Such arguments are therefore hardly convincing. Third, enforcing Article 2 TEU values in the Member States could severely uproot the Union's federal balance. For one, it might be perceived as exceeding the Union's competences or as affecting the Member States' constitutional identities. Moreover, enforcing a uniform understanding of Article 2 TEU values might be normatively undesirable from a pluralist perspective and practically unattainable considering the diversity among the Member States.

Even if most of these objections can be refuted, they call for judicial self-restraint. A first strand of strategies concerns the obligations enshrined in Article 2 TEU, which should be interpreted as minimum standards. A second strand relates to the judicial enforcement of these obligations in the Member States. On the one hand, the Court could apply a *Reverse Solange* presumption that is refuted only in case of systemic deficiencies. To substantiate such deficiencies, the Court would be required to undertake a comprehensive, context-sensitive, and collective assessment that takes into consideration a larger set of national measures in their context and the opinions of other institutions (e.g. the ECtHR, Venice Commission, or independent national institutions). On the other hand, the CJEU could follow two deference routes: first, a decentralized review leaving the final say on Article 2 TEU violations to referring courts and, second, a margin of appreciation. The latter could be triggered when the respective case takes place beyond the scope of other EU law, by a lack of consensus among the Member States on the value at issue, or by the high quality of democratic procedures that led to the adoption of the act in question.

Coming to the end of this study, the readers might feel like they are sitting in a lighthouse whose lamp has completed merely a single rotation. The surrounding landscape has been briefly touched by the spotlight. Still, one rotation is hardly enough to complete the picture. Much remains hidden in the dark. Many more rotations will be necessary to fully illuminate this unknown territory. Against this backdrop, there might be two ways to proceed in future scholarship.

Zooming in, there is a need to accompany the Court of Justice in the development of its jurisprudence. Even though the Court has laid the groundworks of this new jurisprudential edifice, the building is far from complete. Further, this study had to leave many issues in the dark. Concerning the impact of Article 2 TEU in the Verbund, there are many procedural and substantive follow-up questions related to the enforcement of EU values. Having established the basic principles, the Court seems now to engage with the legal 'nitty gritty', such as the specific components of judicial independence under Article 19(1)(2) and Article 2 TEU.[1] Concerning the impact of Article 2 TEU in the EU legal order, many have argued that the Union itself does not live up to its values.[2] To them it might seem deeply unsatisfactory that this book treated the EU's own commitment to Article 2 TEU only in passing. Rather than concentrating on specific issues, this study aimed at laying groundworks. On this basis, future research can start tackling specific questions, such as

[1] In this sense, Michal Bobek, 'The Second and the Third Waves of the Rule of Law Cases in the Court of Justice: Looking at the Small Print' Keynote Speech at the Conference 'The Rule of Law in the EU' (Florence, 10–11 June 2021).

[2] See Theodore Konstadinides, *The Rule of Law in the European Union. The Internal Dimension* (Hart 2017); Dimitry Kochenov, Gráinne de Búrca, and Andrew Williams (eds), *Europe's Justice Deficit?* (Hart 2015); Joseph H.H. Weiler, 'Epilogue: Living in a Glass House' in Carlos Closa and Dimitry Kochenov (eds), *Reinforcing Rule of Law Oversight in the European Union* (CUP 2016) 313.

compliance with Article 2 TEU in the CFSP, at the European borders, or in the face of austerity measures.

Zooming out, there is equally a need to examine the broader implications of the Court's growing engagement with Article 2 TEU. Some interpret the CJEU's jurisprudence as a transformative step. Yet, it seems that we are still in the very middle of this transformative process. With regard to the EU legal order, it remains to be seen whether the Court will submit the Union's economic constitution to the values enshrined in Article 2 TEU and thus develop the Treaties into a more mature, constitutional system. This could include limiting the judicial review of EU legislation to genuinely constitutional constraints and referring in many important policy fields currently regulated by primary law to the legislature's discretion. With regard to the Verbund, Member State challenges to the common values are hardly overcome. If the Court of Justice succeeds in establishing Article 2 TEU as an uncontested, broadly accepted minimum standard for the entire Verbund, this would propel the integration project into a new, unknown dimension.

Bibliography

Aarnio A, *Essays on the Doctrinal Study of Law* (Springer 2011)

von Achenbach J, *Demokratische Gesetzgebung in der Europäischen Union. Theorie und Praxis der dualen Legitimationsstruktur europäischer Hoheitsgewalt* (Springer 2014)

Adam R and Tizzano A, *Manuale di diritto europeo* (3rd edn, Giappichelli 2020)

Adam S and Mena Parras FJ, 'The European Stability Mechanism through the Legal Meanderings of the Union's Constitutionalism: Comment on Pringle' *European Law Review* 38 (2013), 848–865

Adam S and Van Elsuwege P, 'L'exigence d'independance du juge, paradigme de l'Union européenne comme union de droit' *Journal de droit européen* (2018) 334–343

Adamovich LK, 'Juristische Aspekte der "Sanktionen" der EU-14 und des "Weisenberichts"' *Europäische Grundrechte-Zeitschrift* 28 (2001), 89–92

Adamovich LK, Funk BC, Holzinger G, and Frank SL, *Österreichisches Staatsrecht*, vol 1 (2nd edn, Springer 2011)

Aláez Corral B, *Los límites materiales a la reforma de la constitución Española de 1978* (Boletín Oficial del Estado 2000)

Albert R, Contiades X, and Fotiadou A, 'Imposition in Making and Changing Constitutions' in R Albert, X Contiades, and A Fotiadou (eds), *The Law and Legitimacy of Imposed Constitutions* (Routledge 2019) 1–12

Albert R and Emrah Oder B (eds), *An Unamendable Constitution?* (Springer 2018)

Albert R, 'The Expressive Function of Constitutional Amendment Rules' *McGill Law Journal* 59 (2013), 225–281

Aleinikoff TA, 'Constitutional Law in the Age of Balancing' *Yale Law Journal* 96 (1987), 943–1005

Alemanno A, 'À la recherche d'un juste équilibre ente libertés fondamentales et droits fondamentaux dans le cadre du marché intérieur' *Revue du droit de l'Union européenne* (2004), 709–751

Alexy R, *A Theory of Constitutional Rights*, trans. Julian Rivers (OUP 2010)

Alexy R, 'Balancing, Constitutional Review, and Representation' *International Journal of Constitutional Law* 3 (2005), 572–581

Alston P, 'Resisting the Merger and Acquisition of Human Rights by Trade Law' *European Journal of International Law* 13 (2002), 815–844

Alter KJ and Meunier S, 'Judicial Politics in the European Community: European Integration and the Pathbreaking Cassis de Dijon decision' in KJ Alter (ed), *The European Court's Political Power* (OUP 2009) 139–158

Alter KJ, *Establishing the Supremacy of European Law* (OUP 2001)

Amalfitano C and Croci F, 'Identificazione e ruolo delle clausole generali nell'ordinamento dell'Unione europea' *Il diritto dell'Unione europea* (2021), 9–42

Amalfitano C, *General Principles of EU Law and the Protection of Fundamental Rights* (Elgar 2018)

Ammann O, 'Language Bias in International Legal Scholarship: Symptoms, Explanations, Implications and Remedies' *European Journal of International Law* 33 (2022) 821–850

Anagnostaras G, 'Mutual Confidence is Not Blind Trust!' *Common Market Law Review* 53 (2016), 1675–1704

Andenas M and Chiussi L, 'Cohesion, Convergence and Coherence of International Law' in M Andenas and others (eds), *General Principles and the Coherence of International Law* (Brill 2019) 9–34

Andrés Sáenz de Santa María P, 'Mejorando la lex imperfecta: tutela judicial efectiva y cuestión prejudicial en la PESC' *Revista de Derecho Comunitario Europeo* 58 (2017), 871–903

Arato A, 'Forms of Constitution Making and Theories of Democracy' *Cardozo Law Review* 17 (1995), 191–231

Arendt H, *On Revolution* (Penguin 1965)

Arena A, 'The Wall Around EU Fundamental Freedoms: The Purely Internal Rule at the Forty-Year Mark' *Yearbook of European Law* 38 (2019), 153–219

Arnardóttir OM and Guðmundsdóttir D, 'Speaking the Same Language? Comparing Judicial Restraint at the ECtHR and the ECJ' in OM Arnardóttir and A Buyse (eds), *Shifting Centres of Gravity in Human Rights Protection* (Routledge 2016) 161–188

von Arnauld A, 'Harmonisation through General Principles of Law' in KS Ziegler, PJ Neuvonen, and V Moreno-Lax (eds), *Research Handbook on General Principles in EU Law* (Elgar 2022) 40–61

von Arnauld A, 'Normenhierarchien innerhalb des primären Gemeinschaftsrechts' *Europarecht* 38 (2003), 191–216

Arnull A, 'The Working Language of the CJEU: Time for a Change?' *European Law Review* 43 (2018), 904–919

Arnull A, 'The Principle of Effective Judicial Protection in EU Law' *European Law Review* 36 (2011), 51–70

Asche J, *Die Margin of Appreciation* (Springer 2018)

D'Atena A, *Lezioni di diritto costituzionale* (4th edn, Giappichelli 2018)

Auer M, 'Generalklauseln' in *Staatslexikon der Görres-Gesellschaft* (8th edn, Herder 2018)

Avbelj M, 'Constitutional Pluralism and Authoritarianism' *German Law Journal* 21 (2020), 1023–1031

Avbelj M, 'Pluralism and Systemic Defiance in the EU' in D Kochenov and A Jakab (eds), *Enforcing EU Law and Values* (OUP 2017) 44–61

Avbelj M, 'Theory of European Union' *European Law Review* 36 (2011), 818–836

Avbelj M, 'Questioning EU Constitutionalisms' *German Law Journal* 8 (2008), 1–26

Azébazé Labarthe D, 'À la recherche d'un patrimoine constitutionnel européen de la révision constitutionnelle' *Revue française de droit constitutionnel* (108) (2016), 769–806

Azoulai L, '"Integration Through Law" and Us' *International Journal of Constitutional Law* 14 (2016), 449–463

Azoulai L, 'The European Court of Justice and the Duty to Respect Sensitive National Interests' in M Dawson, B de Witte, and E Muir (eds), *Judicial Activism at the European Court of Justice* (Elgar 2013) 167–187

Azoulai L, 'The "Retained Powers" Formula in the Case Law of the European Court of Justice' *European Journal of Legal Studies* 4 (2011), 192–219

Azpitarte Sánchez M, 'Artikel 6 EU-Vertrag: Kodifizierung durch die Zeit, seine Bedeutung und Rechtsfolgen' *Jahrbuch des öffentlichen Rechts der Gegenwart* 51 (2003), 553–572

Babayev R, 'Duality of Economic Freedom Protection in the Interplay of Art.16 CFR and Art.102 TFEU' *European Law Review* 45 (2020), 694–712

Babayev R, 'Private Autonomy at Union Level: On Article 16 CFREU and Free Movement Rights' *Common Market Law Review* 53 (2016), 979–1005

Badet L, 'À propos de l'article 19 du Traité sur l'Union européenne, pierre angulaire de l'action de l'Union européenne pour la sauvegarde de l'État de droit' *Cahiers de droit européen* 56 (2020), 57–106

Badinter R, 'A European Constitution: Perspectives of a French Delegate to the Convention' *International Journal of Constitutional Law* 1 (2003), 363–372

Badura P, 'Bewahrung und Veränderung demokratischer und rechtsstaatlicher Verfassungsstruktur in den internationalen Gemeinschaften' *Veröffentlichungen der Vereinigung der Deutschen Staatsrechtslehrer* 23 (1966), 34–104

Baer S, 'Who Cares? A Defence of Judicial Review' *Journal of the British Academy* 8 (2020), 75–104

Bailleux A, 'Les récits judiciaires de l'Europe' *Revue de l'Union européenne* (2018), 5–17

Bajčić M, 'The Role of EU Legal English in Shaping EU Legal Culture' *International Journal of Language & Law* 7 (2018), 8–24

Bakó B, *Challenges to EU Values in Hungary* (Routledge 2023)

Bakó B, 'The Zauberlehrling Unchained? The Recycling of the German Federal Constitutional Court's Case Law on Identity-, Ultra Vires- and Fundamental Rights Review in Hungary' *Zeitschrift für ausländisches öffentliches Recht und Völkerrecht* 78 (2018), 863–902

Baldassarre A, 'Una risposta a Guastini' *Giurisprudenza costituzionale* 52 (2007), 3251–3296

Baldus M, 'Menschenwürdegarantie und Absolutheitsthese' *Archiv des öffentlichen Rechts* 136 (2011), 529–552

Banks K and von Rintelen G, 'Infringement Procedures and the Juncker Commission' *European Law Review* 45 (2020), 619–638

Baquero Cruz J, 'Minima moralia: el estado de derecho, el método comunitario y el presupuesto de la Unión Europea' *Revista de Derecho Comunitario Europeo* (72) (2022), 431–445

Baquero Cruz J, 'Another Look at Constitutional Pluralism in the European Union' European Law Journal 22 (2016), 356–374

Baquero Cruz J, *Between Competition and Free Movement: The Economic Constitutional Law of the European Community* (Hart 2002)

Baraggia A, 'The "conditionality" Regulation under the ECJ's scrutiny: a constitutional analysis' *European Law Review* 47 (2022), 687–698

Barak A, *Proportionality* (CUP 2012)

Barak A, 'Constitutional Interpretation' in Ferdinand Melin-Soucramanien (ed), *L'interprétation Constitutionnelle* (Dalloz 2005) 91–118

Baratta R, 'La "communauté de valeurs" dans l'ordre juridique de l'Union européenne' *Revue des affaires européennes* (2018), 81–91

Baratta R, 'Rule of Law "Dialogues" Within the EU: A Legal Assessment' *The Hague Journal on the Rule of Law* 8 (2016), 357–372

Barber NW, *The Principles of Constitutionalism* (OUP 2018)

Bárd P and van Ballegooij W, 'Judicial Independence as a Precondition For Mutual Trust? The CJEU in Minister for Justice and Equality v. LM' *New Journal of European Criminal Law* 9 (2018), 353–365

Barents R, 'EU Procedural Law and Effective Legal Protection' *Common Market Law Review* 51 (2014), 1437–1462

Barents R, 'The Fallacy of European Multilevel Constitutionalism' in M Avbelj and J Komárek (eds), *Constitutional Pluralism in the European Union and Beyond* (Hart 2012) 153–183

Barnard C, 'A Proportionate Response to Proportionality in the Field of Collective Action' *European Law Review* 37 (2012), 117–135

Barroso LR, 'Countermajoritarian, Representative, and Enlightened' *American Journal of Comparative Law* 67 (2019), 109–143

Barsotti V, Carozza PG, Cartabia M, and Simoncini A, *Italian Constitutional Justice in Global Context* (OUP 2016)

Bartoloni ME, *Ambito d'applicazione del diritto dell'Unione europea e ordinamenti nazionali* (ESI 2018)

Basedow J and others, 'European Integration: Quo Vadis? A Critical Commentary on the PSPP Judgment of the German Federal Constitutional Court of May 5, 2020' *International Journal of Constitutional Law* 19 (2021), 188–207

Basedow J, 'The Judge's Role in European Integration' in HW Micklitz and B De Witte (eds), *The European Court of Justice and the Autonomy of the Member States* (Intersentia 2012) 65–79

Bast J, 'Legal Instruments and Judicial Protection' in A von Bogdandy and J Bast (eds), *Principles of European Constitutional Law* (2nd edn, Hart 2009) 345–397

Bauer-Bernet H, 'Notions indéterminées et droit communautaire' in C Perelman and R Van der Elst (eds), *Les notions à contenu variables en droit* (Bruylant 1984) 269–295

Beaud O, 'Le cas français: l'obstination de la jurisprudence et de la doctrine à refuser toute idée de limitation au pouvoir de révision constitutionnelle' *Jus Politicum* 18 (2017), 93–115

Beaud O, *Théorie de la Fédération* (2nd edn, Presses Universitaires de France 2009)

Beaud O, 'La question de l'homogénéité dans une fédération' *Lignes* 13 (2004), 110–129

Beaud O, 'Propos sceptiques sur la légitimité d'un référendum européen ou plaidoyer pour plus de réalisme constitutionnel' in Andreas Auer and Jean-Francois Flauss (eds), *Le référendum européen* (Bruylant 1997) 125–180

Beaud O, *La puissance de l'État* (Presses Universitaires de France 1994)

Beck G, *The Legal Reasoning of the Court of Justice* (Hart 2013)

Beijer M, 'Procedural Fundamental Rights Review by the Court of Justice of the European Union' in J Gerards and E Brems (eds), *Procedural Review in European Fundamental Rights Cases* (CUP 2017) 177–208

Beladiez Rojo M, *Los princípios jurídicos* (Madrid: Civitas, 2010)

Bellamy R, *Political Constitutionalism* (CUP 2007)

Bellamy R and Kröger S, 'Countering Democratic Backsliding by EU Member States: Constitutional Pluralism and "Value" Differentiated Integration' *Swiss Political Science Review* 27 (2021), 619–636

Bengoetxea J, *The Legal Reasoning of the European Court of Justice* (OUP 1993)

Benlolo-Carabot M, 'La CJCE et la protection des valeurs fondamentales de l'ordre juridique communautaire' *Revue du marché commun et de l'Union européenne* (2009), 380–386

Benoît-Rohmer F, 'Valeurs et droits fondamentaux dans la Constitution' *Revue trimestrielle de droit européen* 41 (2005), 261–284

Bergel JL, *Théorie Générale du Droit* (5th edn, Dalloz 2012)

Bernhardt R, 'The Sources Of Community Law: The "Constitution" of the Community' in Commission of the European Communities (ed), *Thirty years of Community Law* (Office for Official Publ. of the EC 1983) 69–82

von Bernstorff J, 'Kerngehaltsschutz durch den UN-Menschenrechtsausschuss und den EGMR' *Der Staat* 50 (2011), 165–190

Besselink LFM, 'The Bite, the Bark, and the Howl' A Jakab and D Kochenov (eds), *The Enforcement of EU Law and Values* (OUP 2017) 128–144

Besselink LFM, 'Case C-208/09, Ilonka Sayn-Wittgenstein v. Landeshauptmann von Wien, Judgment of the Court (Second Chamber) of 22 December 2010, nyr' *Common Market Law Review* 49 (2012), 671–693
Besselink LFM, *A Composite European Constitution* (Groningen: Europa Law Publ., 2007)
Besselink LFM, Claes M, Imamović J, and Reestman JHM, *National Constitutional Avenues for Further EU Integration* (European Parliament, Legal Affairs, 2014)
Besson S and Utzinger A, 'Towards European Citizenship' *Journal of Social Philosophy* 39 (2008), 185–208
Bickel A, *The Least Dangerous Branch* (2nd edn, Yale Univ. Press 1986)
Bieber R, 'Les limites matérielles et formelles à la revision des Traités établissant la Communauté européenne' *Revue du marché commun* (1993), 343–350
Bieber R and Maiani F, 'Enhancing Centralised Enforcement of EU Law: Pandora's Toolbox?' *Common Market Law Review* 51 (2014), 1057–1092
Bieber R and Salomé I, 'Hierarchy of Norms in European Law' *Common Market Law Review* 33 (1996), 907–932
Biernat S, 'How Far Is It from Warsaw to Luxembourg and Karlsruhe: The Impact of the PSPP Judgment on Poland' *German Law Journal* 21 (2020), 1104–1115
Biernat S and Filipek P, 'The Assessment of Judicial Independence Following the CJEU Ruling in C-216/18 LM' in A von Bogdandy and others (eds), *Defending Checks and Balances in EU Member States* (Springer 2021) 403–430
Bifulco R, 'Federalism' in R Masterman and R Schütze (eds), *The Cambridge Companion to Comparative Constitutional Law* (CUP 2019) 312–332
Biltgen F, 'L'indépendance du juge national vue depuis Luxembourg' *Revue trimestrielle des droits de l'homme* (2020), 551–566
Bilz C, *Margin of Appreciation der EU-Mitgliedstaaten* (Mohr Siebeck 2020)
Bindi E and Perini M, 'Legal Effect of Constitutions' in R Grote, F Lachenmann, and R Wolfrum (eds), *Max Planck Encyclopedia of Comparative Constitutional Law* (OUP 2017)
Bitter S, *Die Sanktion im Recht der Europäischen Union* (Springer 2011)
Blanke HJ, 'Article 7' in HJ Blanke and S Mangiameli (eds), *The Treaty on European Union (TEU): A Commentary* (Springer 2013)
Blauberger M and others, 'ECJ Judges Read the Morning Papers. Explaining the Turnaround of European Citizenship Jurisprudence' *Journal of European Public Policy*, 25 (2018), 1422–1441
Blauberger M and Kelemen RD, 'Can Courts Rescue National Democracy?' *Journal of European Public Policy* 24 (2017), 321–336
Blauberger M and Sindbjerg Martinsen D, 'The Court of Justice in Times of Politicisation' *Journal of European Public Policy* 27 (2020), 382–399
Blokker P, 'Populism as a Constitutional Project' *International Journal of Constitutional Law* 17 (2019), 536–553
Bloks SA and van den Brink T, 'The Impact on National Sovereignty of Mutual Recognition in the AFSJ' *German Law Journal* 22 (2021), 45–64
Bluman C and Dubois L, *Droit institutionnel de l'Union européenne* (6th edn, LexisNexis 2016)
Bobek M, 'What Are Grand Chambers for?' *Cambridge Yearbook of European Legal Studies* 23 (2021), 1–19
Bobek M, 'The Effects of EU law in the National Legal Systems' in C Barnard and S Peers (eds), *European Union Law* (3rd edn, OUP 2020) 143–190
Bobek M, 'Epilogue. Searching for the European Hercules' in M Bobek (ed), *Selecting Europe's Judges* (OUP 2015) 279–309

Bobek M, 'Legal reasoning of the Court of Justice' *European Law Review* 39 (2014), 418–428

Bobek M, 'Landtová, Holubec, and the Problem of an Uncooperative Court: Implications for the Preliminary Rulings Procedure' *European Constitutional Law Review* 10 (2014), 54–89

Bobek M, 'Of Feasibility and Silent Elephants' in M Adams and others (eds), *Judging Europe's Judges* (Hart 2013) 197–234

Bobek M, 'The Impact of the European Mandate of Ordinary Courts on the Position of Constitutional Courts' in M Claes and others (eds), *Constitutional Conversations in Europe* (Intersentia 2012) 287–308

Bobić A, *The Jurisprudence of Constitutional Conflict in the European Union* (OUP 2022)

Bobić A, 'Constructive Versus Destructive Conflict: Taking Stock of the Recent Constitutional Jurisprudence in the EU' *Cambridge Yearbook of European Legal Studies* 22 (2020), 60–84

Bobić A, 'Constitutional Pluralism is not Dead: An Analysis of Interactions Between Constitutional Courts of Member States and the European Court of Justice' *German Law Journal* 18 (2017), 1395–1428

Böckenförde EW, 'The Constituent Power of the People: A Liminal Concept of Constitutional Law (1986)' in M Künkler and T Stein (eds), *Constitutional and Political Theory* (OUP 2016) 169–185

Böckenförde EW, 'Critique of the Value-Based Grounding of Law (1990)' in M Künkler and T Stein (eds), *Constitutional Theory* (OUP 2017) 217–234

Böckenförde EW, 'Fundamental Rights as Constitutional Principles (1990)' in M Künkler and T Stein (eds), *Constitutional and Political Theory* (OUP 2017) 235–265

Böckenförde EW, 'Conditions for European Solidarity' in K Michalski (ed), *What Holds Europe Together?* (CEU Press 2006) 30–41

Böckenförde EW, *Staat, Nation, Europa* (Suhrkamp 1999)

Boda JS, 'Bloc de constitutionnalité ou désordre constitutionnel?' *Revue française de droit constitutionnel* (130) (2022), 393–419

Boekestein TL, 'Making Do With What We Have: On the Interpretation and Enforcement of the EU's Founding Values' *German Law Journal* 23 (2021), 431–451

Boerger A and Rasmussen M, 'Transforming European Law. The Establishment of the Constitutional Discourse from 1950 to 1993' *European Constitutional Law Review* 10 (2014), 199–225

von Bogdandy A, *The Emergence and Democratization of European Society* (OUP 2023) (forthcoming)

von Bogdandy A, 'Towards a Tyranny of Values?' in A von Bogdandy and others (eds), *Defending Checks and Balances in EU Member States* (Springer 2021) 73–103

von Bogdandy A, 'Principles of a Systemic Deficiencies Doctrine: How to Protect Checks and Balances in the Member States' *Common Market Law Review* 57 (2020), 705–740

von Bogdandy A, 'Tyrannei der Werte? Herausforderungen und Grundlagen einer europäischen Dogmatik systemischer Defizite' *Zeitschrift für ausländisches öffentliches Recht und Völkerrecht* 79 (2019), 503–551

von Bogdandy A, 'Ways to Frame the European Rule of Law: Rechtsgemeinschaft, Trust, Revolution, and Kantian Peace' *European Constitutional Law Review* 14 (2018), 675–699

von Bogdandy A, 'European Law Beyond "Ever Closer Union". Repositioning the Concept, its Thrust and the ECJ's Comparative Methodology' *European Law Journal* 22 (2016), 519–538

von Bogdandy A, 'Deutsche Rechtswissenschaft im europäischen Rechtsraum' *JuristenZeitung* 66 (2011), 1–6 von Bogdandy A, 'Founding Principles' in A von Bogdandy and J Bast (eds), *Principles of European Constitutional Law* (2nd edn, Hart 2009) 11–54

von Bogdandy A, 'Constitutional Principles for Europe' in E Riedel and R Wolfrum (eds), *Recent Trends in German and European Constitutional Law* (Springer 2009) 1–35

von Bogdandy A, 'The Past and Promise of Doctrinal Constructivism' *International Journal of Constitutional Law* 7 (2008), 364–400

von Bogdandy A, 'Vergleich' in A von Bogdandy, P Cruz Villalón, and PM Huber (eds), *Handbuch Ius Publicum Europaeum*, vol 2 (C.F. Müller 2008) § 39

von Bogdandy A, 'The European Constitution and European Identity' *International Journal of Constitutional Law* 3 (2005), 295–315

von Bogdandy A, 'A Bird's Eye View on the Science of European Law' *European Law Journal* 3 (2000), 208–238

von Bogdandy A, 'The European Union as a Supranational Federation' *Columbia Journal of European Law* 6 (2000), 27–54

von Bogdandy A, 'The European Union as a Human Rights Organization?' *Common Market Law Review* 37 (2000), 1307–1338

von Bogdandy A, *Supranationaler Föderalismus als Wirklichkeit und Idee einer neuen Herrschaftsform* (Nomos 1999)

von Bogdandy A and Bast J, 'The Constitutional Approach to EU Law' in A von Bogdandy and J Bast (eds), *Principles of European Constitutional Law* (2nd edn, Hart 2009) 1–7

von Bogdandy A and Bast J, 'The Federal Order of Competences' in A von Bogdandy and J Bast (eds), *Principles of European Constitutional Law* (2nd edn, Hart 2009) 275–307

von Bogdandy A and others (eds), *Defending Checks and Balances in EU Member States* (Springer 2021)

von Bogdandy A and others 'A Potential Constitutional Moment for the European Rule of Law' *Common Market Law Review* 55 (2018), 983–995

von Bogdandy A and others, *German Legal Hegemony?* (MPIL Research Paper Series No. 2020-43)

von Bogdandy A, Huber PM, and Grabenwarter C (eds), *The Max Planck Handbooks in European Public Law*, vol 3 (OUP 2020)

von Bogdandy A and Ioannidis M, 'Systemic Deficiency in the Rule of Law: What It Is, What Has Been Done, What Can Be Done' *Common Market Law Review* 51 (2014), 59–96

von Bogdandy A and others, 'Reverse Solange. Protecting the Essence of Fundamental Rights Against EU Member States' *Common Market Law Review* 49 (2012), 489–519

von Bogdandy A and Krenn C, 'ECJ and ECtHR: Two Senates of Europe's Constitutional Jurisdiction' in A von Bogdandy, C Grabenwarter, and PM Huber (eds), *The Max Planck Handbooks in European Public Law*, vol 4 (OUP 2023) (forthcoming)

von Bogdandy A and Krenn C, 'On the Democratic Legitimacy of Europe's Judges' in M Bobek (ed), *Selecting Europe's Judges* (OUP 2015) 162–180

von Bogdandy A and Paris D, 'Power is Perfected in Weakness: On the Authority of the Italian Constitutional Court' in B Vittoria and others (eds), *Dialogues on Italian Constitutional Justice* (Routledge 2020) 263–280

von Bogdandy A and Schill S, 'Overcoming Absolute Primacy: Respect for National Identity under the Lisbon Treaty' *Common Market Law Review* 48 (2011), 1417–1453

von Bogdandy A and Spieker LD, 'Protecting Fundamental Rights Beyond the Charter. Repositioning the *Reverse Solange* Doctrine in Light of the CJEU's Article 2 TEU Case Law' in M Bobek and J Adams-Prassl (eds), *The EU Charter of Fundamental Rights in the Member States* (Hart 2020) 525–546 von Bogdandy A and Spieker LD, 'Countering the Judicial Silencing of Critics: Article 2 TEU Values, *Reverse Solange*, and the Responsibilities of National Judges' *European Constitutional Law Review* 15 (2019), 391–426

von Bogdandy A and Venzke I, *In Whose Name?* (OUP 2014)

Boháček L, 'Mutual Trust in EU Law: Trust "In What" and "Between Whom"?' *European Journal of Legal Studies* 14 (2022), 103–140

Bonelli M, 'Constitutional Language and Constitutional Limits: The Court of Justice Dismisses the Challenges to the Budgetary Conditionality Regulation' *European Papers* 7 (2022), 507–525

Bonelli M, 'Infringement Actions 2.0: How to Protect EU Values before the Court of Justice' *European Constitutional Law Review* 18 (2022), 30–58

Bonelli M, 'European Commission v Hungary (Transparency of Associations) (C-78/18): The "NGOs Case": On How to Use the EU Charter of Fundamental Rights in Infringement Actions' *European Law Review* 46 (2021), 258–271

Bonelli M, 'National Identity and European Integration Beyond "Limited Fields"' *European Public Law* 27 (2021), 537–557

Bonelli M, 'Intermezzo in the Rule of Law Play' in A von Bogdandy and others (eds), *Defending Checks and Balances in EU Member States* (Springer 2021) 455–476

Bonelli M, 'Effective Judicial Protection in EU Law: An Evolving Principle of a Constitutional Nature' *Review of European Administrative Law* 12 (2019), 35–62

Bonelli M, 'The *Taricco* Saga and the Consolidation of Judicial Dialogue in the European Union' *Maastricht Journal of European and Comparative Law* 25 (2018), 357–373

Bonelli M and Claes M, 'Judicial Serendipity: How Portuguese Judges Came to the Rescue of the Polish Judiciary' *European Constitutional Law Review* 14 (2018), 623–643

Bonichot JC, 'Le style des arrêts de la Cour de justice de l'Union européenne' *Justice et Cassation* (2013), 253–261

Borger V, 'Constitutional Identity, the Rule of Law, and the Power of the Purse: The ECJ Approves the Conditionality Mechanism to Protect the Union Budget' *Common Market Law Review* 59 (2022), 1771–1802

Boucon L, 'EU Law and Retained Powers of Member States' in L Azoulai (ed), *The Question of Competence in the European Union* (OUP 2014) 168–192

Bouveresse A, *Le pouvoir discrétionnaire dans l'ordre juridique Communautaire* (Bruylant 2010)

Bovis CH, 'Developing Public Procurement Regulation: Jurisprudence and its Influence on Law Making' *Common Market Law Review* 43 (2006), 461–495

Brenncke M, *Judicial Law-Making in English and German Courts* (Intersentia 2018)

Brkan M, 'The Concept of Essence of Fundamental Rights in the EU Legal Order: Peeling the Onion to Its Core' *European Constitutional Law Review* 14 (2018), 332–368

Broberg M and Fenger N, *Preliminary References to the European Court of Justice* (3rd edn, OUP 2021)

Brodocz A, 'Chancen konstitutioneller Identitätsstiftung. Zur symbolischen Integration durch eine deutungsoffene Verfassung' in H Vorländer (ed), *Integration durch Verfassung* (VS Verlag 2002) 101–119

Brown C, 'Case C-112/00, *Eugen Schmidberger, Internationale Transporte und Planzüge v. Austria*' *Common Market Law Review* 40 (2003), 1499–1510

Bugaric B, 'The Populist Backlash against Europe: Why Only Alternative Economic and Social Policies Can Stop the Rise of Populism in Europe' in F Bignami (ed), *EU Law in Populist Times. Crises and Prospects* (CUP 2020) 477–504

Bumke C and Voßkuhle A, *German Constitutional Law* (OUP 2019)

de Búrca G, 'Poland and Hungary's EU Membership: On Not Confronting Authoritarian Governments' *International Journal of Constitutional Law* 20 (2022), 13–34
Burchard D, *Die Rangfrage im europäischen Normenverbund* (Mohr Siebeck 2015)
Burgess M, *Federalism and the European Union. The Building of Europe, 1950–2000* (Routledge 2000)
Burgorgue-Larsen L, 'La mobilisation de la Charte des droits fondamentaux de l'Union européenne par les juridictions constitutionnelles' *Titre VII* 2 (2019), 31–40
Burgorgue-Larsen L, 'L'identité constitutionnelle en question' in L Burgorgue-Larsen (ed), *L'identité constitutionnelle saisie par les juges en Europe* (Pedone 2011) 155–168
Burgorgue-Larsen L, 'Article I-2' in L Burgorgue-Larsen, A Levade, and F Picod (eds), *Traité établissant une Constitution pour l'Europe*, vol 1 (Bruylant 2007)
Burley AM, 'Democracy and Judicial Review in the European Community' *University of Chicago Legal Forum* (1992), 81–91
Burrer S and Marusczyk D, 'Grenzüberschreitende Anerkennung und Vollstreckung polnischer Urteile nach der EuGVVO in Zeiten der polnischen Verfassungskrise' *Europäische Zeitschrft für Wirtschaftsrecht* 33 (2022), 200–207
Burrows N, 'The Risks of Widening without Deepening' *European Law Review* 17 (1992), 352–361
Bustos Gisbert R, *Independencia judicial e integración Europea* (Tirant lo Blanch 2022)
Bustos Gisbert R, 'La influencia de los textos no vinculantes del Consejo de Europa sobre independencia judicial en el TEDH y en la UE' *Teoría y Realidad Constitucional* 47 (2021), 61–98
Bustos Gisbert R, 'Communicación transjudicial en Europa en defesa de la independencia de los jueces' *Revista de Derecho Constitucional Europeo* 33 (2020)
Butler G, 'The Coming to Age of the Court's Jurisdiction in the Common Foreign and Security Policy' *European Constitutional Law Review* 13 (2017), 673–703
Butler G, 'The Court of Justice as an inter-state court' *Yearbook of European Law* 36 (2017), 179–208
Byberg R, 'The History of the Integration Through Law Project: Creating the Academic Expression of a Constitutional Legal Vision for Europe' *German Law Journal* 18 (2017), 1531–1556
Calahorro AA, 'La decisión Pringle en el proceso de constitucionalización de la Unión Europea' *Revista Española de Derecho Constitucional* (101) (2014), 337–380
Callewaert J, 'Is There a Margin of Appreciation in the Application of Articles 2, 3 and 4 of the Convention?' *Human Rights Law Journal* 19 (1998), 6–9
Calliess C and van der Schyff G (eds), *Constitutional Identity in a Europe of Multilevel Constitutionalism* (CUP 2019)
Calliess C, 'Constitutional Identity in Germany. One for Three or Three in One?' in C Calliess and G van der Schyff (eds), *Constitutional Identity in a Europe of Multilevel Constitutionalism* (CUP 2019) 153–181
Calliess C, 'Art. 2 EUV' in C Calliess and M Ruffert (eds), *EUV/AEUV* (6th edn, C.H.Beck 2022)
Calliess C, 'The Transnationalization of Values by European Law' *German Law Journal* 10 (2009), 1367–1382
Campos Sánchez-Bordona M, 'La protección de la independencia judicial en el derecho de la Unión Europea' *Revista de Derecho Comunitario Europeo* 65 (2020), 11–31
Canivet G, 'Les limites de la mission du juge constitutionnel' *Cités* 69 (2017), 41–58
Cannizzaro E, 'Il ruolo della Corte di giustizia nella tutela dei valori dell'Unione europea' in *Liber Amicorum Antonio Tizzano. De la Cour CECA à la Cour de l'Union: le long parcours de la justice européenne* (Giappichelli 2018) 159–169

Canor I, 'Suspending Horizontal *Solange*: A Decentralized Instrument for Protecting Mutual Trust and the European Rule of Law' in A von Bogdandy and others (eds), *Defending Checks and Balances in EU Member States* (Springer 2021) 183–206

Canor I, '*My Brother's Keeper?* Horizontal *Solange*: "An Ever Closer Distrust Among the Peoples of Europe"' *Common Market Law Review* 50 (2013), 383–421

Canzian N, 'Indipendenza dei giudici e divieto di regressione della tutela nella sentenza Repubblika' *Quaderni Costituzionali* (2021), 715–718

Capeta T, 'Ideology and Legal Reasoning at the European Court of Justice' in T Perišin and S Rodin (eds), *The Transformation or Reconstitution of Europe: The Critical Legal Studies Perspective on the Role of the Courts in the European Union* (Hart 2018) 89–119

Cappelletti M, Seccombe M, and Weiler JHH (eds), *Integration through Law. European and the American Federal Experience*, vols 1–3 (de Gruyter 1986)

Carcassone G, 'Un plaidoyer résolu en faveur d'un tel contrôle sagement circonscrit' *Cahiers du Conseil Constitutionnel* 27 (2010)

Caro de Sousa P, 'Catch Me if You Can? The Market Freedoms' Ever-Expanding Outer Limits' *European Journal of Legal Studies* 4 (2011), 162–191

Carrera S, Guild R, and Hernanz N, *The Triangular Relationship between Fundamental Rights, Democracy and the Rule of Law in the EU* (European Parliament, LIBE, 2013)

Carta M, *Unione europea e tutela dello Stato di diritto negli Stati membri* (Caducci 2020)

Cartabia M, 'Courts' Relations' *International Journal of Constitutional Law* 18 (2020), 3–11

Cartabia M, 'The Charter of Fundamental Rights of the European Union' in G Amato and others (eds), *The History of the European Union* (Hart 2019) 113–130

Cartabia M, 'Of Bridges and Walls: The Italian Style of Constitutional Adjudication' *Italian Journal of Public Law* 8 (2016), 37–55

Cartabia M, 'Ispirata alla volontà dei cittadini degli Stati d'Europa' *Quaderni costituzionali* 25 (2005), 9–38

Cartabia M, 'Riflessioni sulla Convenzione di Laeken: "come se" si trattasse di un processo costituente' *Quaderni costituzionali* 22 (2002), 439–447

Cattabriga C, 'Limiti materiali alla revisione comunitaria' *Rivista di diritto europeo* 34 (1994), 245–270

de Cecco F, 'Fundamental Freedoms, Fundamental Rights, and the Scope of Free Movement Law' *German Law Journal* 15 (2014), 383–406

Chalmers D and Barroso L, 'What *Van Gend en Loos* Stands for' *International Journal of Constitutional Law* 12 (2014), 105–134

Chamon M, 'Re-establishing the EU. Dissolution, Withdrawal or Succession' *EU Law Live* (10 October 2020)

Champeil-Desplats V, 'Hiérarchie des normes, principe justificatif de la suprematie de la constitution' in M Troper and D Chagnollaud (eds), *Traité international de droit constitutionnel*, vol 1 (Dalloz 2012) 733–764

Champeil-Desplats V and Troper M, 'Proposition pour une théorie des contraintes juridiques' in V Champeil-Desplats, M Troper, and C Grzegorczyk (eds), *Théorie des contraintes juridiques* (Bruylant 2005) 11–24

Chemerinsky E, *Constitutional Law* (6th edn, Kluwer 2019)

Chemerinsky E, 'Why Cases Under the Guarantee Clause Should Be Justiciable' *University of Colorado Law Review* 65 (1994), 849–880

Chevalier E and Dubos O, 'The Notion of "Transnationality" in Administrative Law: Taxonomy and Judicial Review' *German Law Journal* 22 (2021), 325–343

Cinnirella C, '"You cannot beat something with nothing": ossia la strategia della Corte di giustizia per tutelare l'indipendenza dei giudici nazionali (e lo Stato di diritto) nello spazio giuridico europeo' *Il diritto dell'Unione europea* (2020), 361–388

Claes M, 'How Common are the Values of the European Union?' *Croatian Yearbook of European Law and Policy* 15 (2018), VII–XVI

Claes M, 'Luxembourg, Here We Come? Constitutional Courts and the Preliminary Reference Procedure' *German Law Journal* 16 (2015), 1331–1342

Clausen F, 'In the name of the European Union, the Member States and/or the European citizens?' in H Ruiz Fabri and others (eds), *International Judicial Legitimacy* (Nomos 2020) 249–269

Clément-Wilz L, 'Les Français, la France et la francophonie: réflexions sur la fabrique du droit européen' *Il diritto dell'Unione europea* (2020), 701–728

Cloots E, *National Identity in EU Law* (OUP 2015)

Closa C, 'Institutional Logics and the EU's Limited Sanctioning Capacity Under Article 7 TEU' *International Political Science Review* 42 (2021), 501–515

Closa C, 'The Politics of Guarding the Treaties: Commission Scrutiny of Rule of Law Compliance' *Journal of European Public Policy* 26 (2019), 696–716

Closa C, 'Deliberative Constitutional Politics and the Turn Towards a Norms-Based Legitimacy of the EU Constitution' *European Law Journal* 11 (2005), 411–431

Closa C and Kochenov D (eds), *Reinforcing Rule of Law Oversight in the European Union* (CUP 2016)

Closa C and Kochenov D 'Reinforcement of the Rule of Law Oversight in the European Union: Key Options' in W Schröder (ed), *Strengthening the Rule of Law in Europe* (Hart 2015) 173–196

Closa C, Kochenov D, and Weiler JHH, 'Reinforcing Rule of Law Oversight in the European Union' EUI RSCAS 2014/25, pp 1–33

Cohen A, 'Constitutionalism Without Constitution: Transnational Elites Between Political Mobilization and Legal Expertise in the Making of a Constitution for Europe (1940s–1960s)' *Law & Social Inquiry* 32 (2007), 109–135

Colin JP, *Le gouvernement des juges dans les communautés européennes* (LGDJ 1966)

Coman R, *The Politics of the Rule of Law in the EU Polity: Actors, Tools and Challenges* (Palgrave Macmillan 2022)

Comparato G and Micklitz HW, 'Regulated Autonomy between Market Freedoms and Fundamental Rights in the Case Law of the CJEU' in U Bernitz and X Groussot (eds), *General Principles of EU Law and European Private Law* (Kluwer 2013) 121–154

Conant L, 'Compliance and What EU Member States Make of it' in M Cremona (ed), *Compliance and the Enforcement of EU Law* (OUP 2012) 1–30

Constantinesco V, 'La confrontation entre identité constitutionnelle européenne et identités constitutionnelles nationales: Convergence ou contradiction? Contrepoint ou hierarchie' in JC Masclet and others (eds), *L'Union européenne: union de droit, union des droits. Mélanges en l'honneur de Philippe Manin* (Pedone 2010) 79–94

Constantinesco V, 'L'intégration des principes constitutionnels nationaux dans le Traité: L'Article 6 § 1 du Traité sur l'Union' in H Gaudin (ed), *Droit constitutionnel, droit Communautaire. Vers un respect constitutionnel réciproque?* (Economica 2001) 299–311

Constantinesco V, *Compétences et pouvoirs dans les Communautés européennes* (LGDJ 1974)

Conzelmann T, 'Peer Reviewing the Rule of Law? A New Mechanism to Safeguard EU Values' *European Papers* 7 (2022), 671–695

Coppel J and O'Neill A, 'The European Court of Justice: Taking Rights Seriously?' *Common Market Law Review* 29 (1992), 669–692

Corthaut T, 'Plus ça change, plus c'est la même chose?' *Maastricht Journal of European and Comparative Law* 15 (2007), 21–34
Cotter J, 'To Everything There is a Season: Instrumentalising Article 10 TEU to Exclude Undemocratic Member State Representatives from the European Council and the Council' *European Law Review* 46 (2021), 69–84
Coutron L, 'La Cour de justice au secours de la forêt de Białowieska' *Revue trimestrielle de droit européen* 54 (2018), 321–330
Coutron L, 'Le styles des arrêts de la Cour de justice et normativité de la jurisprudence communautaire' *Revue trimestrielle de droit européen* (2009), 643–675
Crabit E, 'Upholding the Rule of Law for the Future of Europe' in W Heusel and JP Rageade (eds), *The Authority of EU Law* (Springer 2019) 261–270
Craig P, *EU Administrative Law* (3rd edn, OUP 2018)
Craig P, 'Institutions, power and institutional balance' in P Craig and G de Búrca (eds), *The Evolution of EU Law* (3rd edn, OUP 2021) 46–89
Craig P, 'Constitutions, Constitutionalism and the European Union' *European Law Journal* 7 (2001), 125–150
Craig P and de Búrca G, *EU Law* (7th edn, OUP 2020)
Cremer W, 'Art. 263 AEUV' in C Calliess and M Ruffert (eds), *EUV/AEUV* (6th edn, C.H.Beck 2022)
Cruz Mantilla de los Ríos P, *La identidad nacional de los estados miembros en el derecho de la Uníon europea* (Aranzadi 2022)
da Cruz Vilaça JL, 'Reflections on Judicial Review of the Constitutionality of EU Legislation' in JL da Cruz Vilaça, *EU Law and Integration* (Hart 2014) 44–54
da Cruz Vilaça JL and Piçarra N, 'Y a-t-il des limites matérielles à la revision des Traités instituant les Communautés européennes' *Cahiers de droit européen* 29 (1993), 3–37
Cruz Villalón P, 'El valor de posición de la carta de derechos fundamentales en la comunión constitucional europea' *Teoría y Realidad Constitucional* 39 (2017), 85–101
Cruz Villalón P, 'Legitimidad activa y legitimidad pasiva de los tribunales constitucionales en el espacio constitucional europeo' *Teoría y Realidad Constitucional* 33 (2014), 141–150
Cruz Villalón P, 'Grundlagen und Grundzüge staatlichen Verfassungsrechts: Vergleich' in P Cruz Villalón, A von Bogdandy, and PM Huber (eds), *Handbuch Ius Publicum Europaeum*, vol 1 (C.F. Müller 2007) § 13
Cruz Villalón P, *La Constitución inedita* (Trotta 2004)
Curti Gialdino C, 'Some Reflections on the Acquis Communautaire' *Common Market Law Review* 32 (1995), 1089–1121
Curtin D, 'The Constitutional Structure of the Union: A Europe of Bits and Pieces' *Common Market Law Review* 30 (1993), 17–69
Daly TG, *The Alchemists. Questioning our Faith in Courts as Democracy-Builders* (CUP 2017)
Dani M, 'Deconstitutionalising the Economic and Monetary Union' in *Continuity and Change—How the Challenges of Today Prepare the Ground for Tomorrow. ECB Legal Conference 2021* (ECB 2022) 282–308
Dani M, 'National Constitutional Courts in Supranational Litigation: A Contextual Analysis' *European Law Journal* 23 (2017), 189–212
Dann P, 'Thoughts on a Methodology of European Constitutional Law' *German Law Journal* 6 (2005), 1453–1473
von Danwitz L, 'Der Grundsatz des gegenseitigen Vertrauens zwischen den Mitgliedstaaten der EU' *Europarecht* 55 (2020), 61–89
von Danwitz T, 'Uniform Interpretation and Primacy of Union Law in the Dialogue of the Courts' *Verfassungsblog* (4 November 2022)

von Danwitz T, 'Rechtsetzung und Rechtsangleichung' in M Dauses and M Ludwigs (eds), *Handbuch des EU-Wirtschaftsrechts* (55th edn, loose-leaf, C.H.Beck 2022) B.II
von Danwitz T, 'Values and the Rule of Law: Foundations of the European Union—An Inside Perspective from the ECJ' *Revue du droit de l'Union européenne* (4) (2018), 263–270
von Danwitz T, 'The Role of the Court of Justice in Safeguarding the Rule of Law in Europe' in T von Danwitz, F Rinke, and C Bellmann (eds), *Current Challenges Facing the European Union–The Contribution of the Court of Justice,* 12th Berlin Legal Policy Conference (Konrad Adenauer Foundation 2018) 13–19
von Danwitz T, 'The Rule of Law in the Recent Jurisprudence of the ECJ' *Fordham Journal of International Law* 37 (2014), 1311–1347
von Danwitz T, 'Gerichtlicher Schutz der Grundrechte' in C Grabenwarter (ed), *Europäischer Grundrechteschutz, Enzyklopädie Europarecht*, vol 2 (Nomos 2014) § 6, pp 255–300
von Danwitz T, 'Funktionsbedingungen der Rechtsprechung des Europäischen Gerichtshofes' *Europarecht* 43 (2008), 769–786
Davies B, *Resisting the European Court of Justice. West Germany's Confrontation with European Law, 1949-1979* (CUP 2012)
Davies B, 'Resistance to European Law and Constitutional Identity in Germany: Herbert Kraus and *Solange* in its Intellectual Context' *European Law Journal* 21 (2015), 434–459
Davies G, 'Originalism at the European Court of Justice' in S Garben and I Govaere (eds), *The Internal Market 2.0* (Hart 2020) 323–333
Davies G, 'Does the Court of Justice Own the Treaties? Interpretative Pluralism as a Solution to Over-Constitutionalisation' *European Law Journal* 24 (2018), 358–375
Davies G, 'The European Union Legislature as an Agent of the European Court of Justice' *Journal of Common Market Studies* 54 (2016), 846–861
Davies G, 'Democracy and Legitimacy in the Shadow of Purposive Competence' *European Law Journal* 21 (2015), 2–22
Davies G, 'Legislative Control of the European Court of Justice' *Common Market Law Review* 51 (2014), 1579–1607
Dawson M, 'How Can EU Law Respond to Populism?' *Oxford Journal of Legal Studies* 40 (2020), 183–213
Dawson M, 'How Does the European Court of Justice Reason?' *European Law Journal* 20 (2014) 423–435
Dawson M, 'The Political Face of Judicial Activism: Europe's Law-Politics Imbalance' in M Dawson, B de Witte and E Muir (eds), *Judicial Activism at the European Court of Justice* (Elgar 2013) 11–31
Dawson M, 'Constitutional Dialogue between Courts and Legislators in the European Union' *European Public Law* 19 (2013), 369–396
Dawson M, Lynskey O, and Muir E, 'What Is the Added Value of the Concept of the "Essence" of EU Fundamental Rights?' *German Law Journal* 20 (2019), 763–778
Dawson M and Muir E, 'Hungary and the Indirect Protection of EU Fundamental Rights and the Rule of Law' *German Law Journal* 14 (2013), 1959–1979
Dawson M, de Witte B, and Muir E (eds), *Judicial Activism at the European Court of Justice* (Elgar 2013)
Dittert D, 'Art. 36 EuGH-Satzung' in H von der Groeben, J Schwarze, and A Hatje (eds), *Europäisches Unionsrecht* (7th edn, Nomos 2015)
de Boer NJ, 'Fundamental Rights and the EU Internal Market' *Utrecht Law Review* 9 (2013), 148–168
de Boer NJ and Van 't Klooster J, 'The ECB, the Courts and the Issue of Democratic Legitimacy after Weiss' *Common Market Law Review* 57 (2020), 1689–1724

de Búrca G, 'The Mutual Judicial Influence of National Courts and the European Court of Justice through the Preliminary Rulings Mechanism' in E Fisher, J King, and A Young (eds), *The Foundations and Future of Public Law. Essays in Honour of Paul Craig* (OUP 2020) 107–126

de Búrca G, 'After the EU Charter of Fundamental Rights: The Court of Justice as a Human Rights Adjudicator?' *Maastricht Journal of European and Comparative Law* 20 (2013), 168–184

de La Rosa S, 'The Directive on Cross-Border Healthcare or the Art of Codifying Complex Case Law' *Common Market Law Review* 49 (2012), 15–46

de Quadros F, 'L'identité constitutionnelle de l'Union européenne et les valeurs communs' in L Potvin-Solis (ed), *Les valeurs communes dans l'Union européenne* (Bruylant 2014) 165–169

de Quadros F, 'La Convention Européenne des Droits de l'Homme: un cas de ius cogens régional?' in U Beyerlin and others (ed), *Recht zwischen Umbruch und Bewahrung. Festschrift für Rudolf Bernhardt* (Springer 1995) 555–562

De Wet E, 'The Emergence of International and Regional Value Systems as a Manifestation of the Emerging International Constitutional Order' *Leiden Journal of International Law* 19 (2006), 611–632

Dehousse R, *Une Constitution pour l'Europe* (Presses de Sciences Po 2002)

Dehousse R, *The European Court of Justice: The Politics of Judicial Integration* (Macmillan 1998)

Deliège-Sequaris M, 'Révision des traités européens en dehors des procédures prévues' *Cahiers de droit européen* 16 (1980), 539–552

Dellavalle S, *Una costituzione senza popolo?* (Giuffrè 2002)

Delledonne G and Fabbrini F, 'The Founding Myth of European Human Rights Law' *European Law Review* 44 (2019), 178–195

Delledonne G, *L'omogeneità costituzionale negli ordinamenti composti* (Editoriale scientifica 2017)

Delledonne G, 'Homogénéité constitutionnelle et protection des droits fondamentaux et de l'État de droit dans l'ordre juridique européen' *Politique européenne* 53 (2016), 86–109

Delmas-Marty M, *Ordering Pluralism* (Hart 2009)

Dermine P and Markakis M, 'Bailouts, the Legal Status of Memoranda of Understanding, and the Scope of Application of the EU Charter: *Florescu*' *Common Market Law Review* 55 (2018), 643–671

Di Fabio U, 'Zur Theorie eines grundrechtlichen Wertsystems' in D Merten and HJ Papier (eds), *Handbuch der Grundrechte*, vol 2 (C.F.Müller 2006) § 46

Di Martino A, 'Giurisdizione costituzionale e applicabilità della Carta dei diritti fondamentali dell'Unione europea: profili comparativi' *Diritto Pubblico Comparato ed Europeo* (2019), 759–782

Díez-Picazo L, '¿Qué diferencia hay entre un tratado y una constitución?' *Cuadernos de derecho público* 13 (2001), 85–101

Dixon R, *Responsive Judicial Review. Democracy and Dysfunction in the Modern Age* (OUP 2023)

Donner AM, 'The Constitutional Powers of the Court of Justice' *Common Market Law Review* 11 (1974), 127–140

Dony M, 'Les valeurs, objectifs et principes de l'Union' in M Dony and E Bribosia (eds), *Commentaire de la Constitution de l'Union européenne* (Ed. de l'Université de Bruxelles 2005) 33–45

Dörr O, 'Art. 263 AEUV' in E Grabitz, M Hilf, and M Nettesheim (eds), *Das Recht der Europäischen Union* (75th edn, loose-leaf, C.H.Beck 2022)
Dougan M and Hillion C, 'The EU's Duty to Respect Hungarian Sovereignty: An Action Plan' *Common Market Law Review* 59 (2022), 181–202
Dougan M, 'Primacy and the Remedy of Disapplication' *Common Market Law Review* 56 (2019), 1459–1508
Drexl J, 'Competition Law as Part of the European Constitution' in A von Bogdandy and J Bast (eds), *Principles of European Constitutional Law* (2nd edn, Hart 2009) 659–698
Drinóczi T and Bień-Kacała A, *Illiberal Constitutionalism in Poland and Hungary* (Routledge 2021)
Dubout E, *Droit constitutionnel de l'Union européenne* (Bruylant 2021)
Dubout E, 'Integration Through the Rule of Law? La judiciarisation de l'État de droit dans l'Union européenne' *Revue des affaires europeennes* (2019), 51–66
Dubout E, 'Voyage en eaux troubles: vers une épuration des situations "purement" internes' *Revue des affaires européennes* (2016), 679–693
Dubout E, 'Les règles ou principes inhérents à l'identité constitutionnelle' *Revue française de droit constitutionnel* (83) (2010), 451–482
Due O, 'Pourquoi cette solution?' in O Due, M Lutter, and J Schwarze (eds), *Festschrift für Ulrich Everling*, vol 1 (Nomos 1995) 273–282
Duke G, 'European Constitutionalism and Constituent Power' *European Law Review* 44 (2019), 49–66
Dupré C, 'The Rule of Law, Fair Trial and Human Dignity: The Protection of EU Values After LM' in A von Bogdandy and others (eds), *Defending Checks and Balances in EU Member States* (Springer 2021) 431–442
Dutheil de la Rochère J, 'L'Espace économique européen sous le regard des juges de la Cour de justice' *Revue du marché commun* (1992), 603–612
Dworkin R, *Taking Rights Seriously* (Bloomsbury, repr. 2013)
Dyevre A and others, 'The Court of Justice and Treaty Revision: A Case of Strategic Leniency?' *European Union Politics* 19 (2018), 570–596
Dyevre A, Glavina M, and Atanasova A, 'Who Refers Most? Institutional Incentives and Judicial Participation in the Preliminary Ruling System' *Journal of European Public Policy*, 27 (2020), 912–930
Dyzenhaus D, 'The Politics of the Question of Constituent Power' in M Loughlin and N Walker (eds), *The Paradox of Constitutionalism* (OUP 2008) 129–146
Dzehtsiarou K, *European Consensus and the Legitimacy of the European Court of Human Rights* (CUP 2015)
Eck L, 'Faut-il constitutionnaliser la décision du Conseil constitutionnel du 16 juillet 1971?' *Revue française de droit constitutionnel* (130) (2022), 377–391
Eckes C, 'Protecting Supremacy from External Influences: A Precondition for a European Constitutional Legal Order?' *European Law Journal* 18 (2012), 230–250
Editorial, 'Not mastering the Treaties: The German Federal Constitutional Court's PSPP judgment' *Common Market Law Review* 57 (2020), 965–978
Editorial, 'The Critical Turn in EU Legal Studies' *Common Market Law Review* 52 (2015), 881–888
Editorial, 'Safeguarding EU Values in the Member States' *Common Market Law Review* 52 (2015), 619–628
Editorial, 'Hungary's New Constitutional Order and "European Unity"' *Common Market Law Review* 49 (2012), 871–883
Editorial, 'Protocology' *Common Market Law Review* 46 (2009), 1785–1793

Editorial, 'Better In Than Out: When Constitutional Courts Rely on the Charter' *European Constitutional Law Review* 16 (2020), 1–7

Edward D, 'Direct Effect: Myth, Mess or Mystery' *Il diritto dell'Unione europea* (2002), 215–227

Eisgruber C, *Constitutional Self-Government* (Harvard Univ. Press 2001)

Ellerbrok T and Pracht R, 'Das Bundesverfassungsgericht als Taktgeber im horizontalen Verfassungsgerichtsverbund—Ausstrahlungswirkungen der Rechtsprechung zum Integrationsverfassungsrecht in Europa' *Europarecht* 56 (2021), 188–209

Elster J, 'Deliberation and Constitution Making' in J Elster (ed), *Deliberative Democracy* (CUP 1998) 97–122

Ely JH, *Democracy and Distrust* (Harvard Univ. Press 1980)

Emmons C and Pavone T, 'The Rhetoric of Inaction: Failing to Fail Forward in the EU's Rule of Law Crisis' *Journal of European Public Policy* 28 (2021), 1611–1629

Endicott T, 'The Value of Vagueness' in A Marmor and S Soames (eds), *Philosophical Foundations of Language in the Law* (OUP 2011) 14–30

Endicott T, *Vagueness in Law* (OUP 2000)

Epiney A, 'La Cour de justice des Communautés européennes et l'Espace économique européen' *Swiss Review of International and European law* 2 (1992), 275–304

Esser J, *Vorverständnis und Methodenwahl in der Rechtsfindung* (Athenäum 1970)

Everling U, 'Justizielle Krisenbewältigung' in A Hatje (ed), *Verfassungszustand und Verfassungsentwicklung der Europäischen Union, Europarecht Beiheft 2/2015* (Nomos 2015) 86–103

Everling U, 'Überlegungen zum Verfahren vor den Gerichten der Europäischen Gemeinschaften' in N Colneric and others (eds), *Une communauté de droit. Festschrift für Gil Carlos Rodríguez Iglesias* (Berlin: BWV, 2003) 537–550

Everling U, 'Richterliche Rechtsfortbildung in der Europäischen Gemeinschaft' *JuristenZeitung* 55 (2000), 217–227

Everling U, 'Zur Stellung der Mitgliedstaaten der Europäischen Union als "Herren der Verträge"' in U Beyerlin and others (eds), *Recht zwischen Umbruch und Bewahrung. Festschrift für Rudolf Bernhardt* (Springer 1995) 1161–1176

Everling U, 'Sind die Mitgliedstaaten der Europäischen Gemeinschaft noch Herren der Verträge?' R Bernhardt (ed), *Völkerrecht als Rechtsordnung, internationale Gerichtsbarkeit, Menschenrechte. Festschrift für Hermann Mosler* (Springer 1983) 173–192

Everling U, 'The Court of Justice as a Decision-Making Authority' *Michigan Law Review* 82 (1984), 1294–1310

Fabbrini F, 'After the OMT Case: The Supremacy of EU Law as the Guarantee of the Equality of the Member States' *German Law Journal* 16 (2015), 1003–1023

Fabbrini F and Sajó A, 'The Dangers of Constitutional Identity' *European Law Journal* 25 (2019), 457–473

Fabbrini F and Maduro MP, 'Supranational Constitutional Courts' in R Grote, F Lachenmann, and R Wolfrum (eds), *Max Planck Encyclopedia of Comparative Constitutional Law* (OUP 2016)

Faraguna P, 'On the Identity Clause and Its Abuses: "Back to the Treaty"' *European Public Law* 27 (2021), 427–446

Favoreu L and others, *Droit Constitutionnel* (22nd edn, Dalloz 2020)

Favoreu L, 'L'injusticiabilité des lois constitutionnelles' *Revue française de droit administratif* 19 (2003), 792–795

Favoreu L, 'Les Courts de Luxembourg et de Strasbourg ne sont pas des cours constitutionnelles' in *Au carrefour des droits. Mélanges en l'honneur de Louis Dubouis* (Dalloz 2002) 35–45

Favoreu L, 'La constitutionnalisation du droit' in B Mathieu and M Verpeaux (eds), *La constitutionnalisation des branches du droit* (Economica 1998) 181–195

di Federico G, *L'identità nazionale degli stati membri nel diritto dell'Unione europea. Natura e portata dell'art. 4, par. 2, TUE* (Editoriale Scientifica 2017)

Feichtner I, 'The German Constitutional Court's PSPP Judgment: Impediment and Impetus for the Democratization of Europe' *German Law Journal* 21 (2020), 1090–1103

Fennelly N, 'The National Judge as Judge of the European Union' in A Rosas, E Levits, and Y Bot (eds), *The Court of Justice and the Construction of Europe* (Asser Press 2013) 61–79

Ferejohn J, 'Judicializing Politics, Politicizing Law' *Law and Contemporary Problems* 65 (2002), 41–68

Fernandez Esteban ML, 'La noción de Constitución Europea en la jurisprudencia del Tribunal des Justicia de las Comunidades European' *Revista Española de Derecho Constitucional* 40 (1994), 241–289

Fernández Soriano V, 'Las Comunidades Europeas frente al franquismo' *Cuadernos de Historia Contemporánea* 32 (2010), 153–174

Ferreres Comella V, *Constitutional Courts and Democratic Values: A European Perspective* (Yale Univ. Press 2009)

Ferri D and Martinico G, 'Revisiting the Ruiz Zambrano Doctrine and Exploring the Potential for Its Extensive Application' *European Public Law* 27 (2021), 685–706

Fichera M, 'Constitutional Courts / Supreme Courts as Positive Legislators' in R Grote, F Lachenmann, and R Wolfrum (eds), *Max Planck Encyclopedia of Comparative Constitutional Law* (OUP 2020)

Fioravanti M, 'Un ibrido fra "Trattato" e "Costituzione"' in E Paciotti (ed), *La Costituzione europea* (Rome: Meltemi, 2003) 17–27

Fioravanti M, 'Il processo costituente europeo' *Quaderni Fiorentini* 31 (2002), 273–297

Flückiger A, 'Le principe de clarté de la loi ou l'ambiguïté d'un idéal' *Cahiers du Conseil Constitutionnel* 21 (2007)

Flynn T, 'Constitutional Pluralism and Loyal Opposition' *International Journal of Constitutional Law* 19 (2021), 241–268

Foley M, *The Silence of Constitutions* (Routledge 1989)

Fossum JE and Jachtenfuchs M, 'Federal Challenges and Challenges to Federalism. Insights From the EU and Federal States' *Journal of European Public Policy* 24 (2017), 467–485

Fossum JE and Menéndez AJ, *The Constitution's Gift* (Rowman 2011)

Fossum JE and Menéndez AJ, 'The Constitution's Gift? A Deliberative Democratic Analysis of Constitution Making in the European Union' *European Law Journal* 11 (2005), 380–410

Frackowiak-Adamska A, 'Trust Until It Is Too Late! Mutual Recognition of Judgments and Limitations of Judicial Independence in a Member State: L and P' *Common Market Law Review* 59 (2022), 113–150

Franck JU, 'Striking a Balance of Power between the Court of Justice and the EU Legislature: The Law on Competition Damages Actions as a Paradigm' *European Law Review* 43 (2018), 837–857

Frankenberg G, 'The Return of the Contract: Problems and Pitfalls of European Constitutionalism' *European Law Journal* 6 (2000), 257–276

Franklin CNK, 'The Burgeoning Principle of Consistency in EU Law' *Yearbook of European Law* 30 (2011), 42–85

Franzius C, Mayer FC, and Neyer J (eds), *Die Neuerfindung Europas* (Nomos 2019)

Frischhut M, *The Ethical Spirit of EU Values* (Springer 2022)

Frischhut M, *The Ethical Spirit of EU Law* (Springer 2019)

Fritzsche A, 'Discretion, Scope of Judicial Review and Institutional Balance in European Law' *Common Market Law Review* 47 (2010), 361–403

Frowein JA, 'The European Community and the Requirement of a Republican Form of Government' *Michigan Law Review* 32 (1984), 1311–1322

Fuller L, *The Morality of Law* (2nd edn, Yale Univ. Press 1969)

Gabriel M, 'Justizfreie Hoheitsakte und die Unabhängigkeit des EuGH' *Zeitschrift für europäisches Wirtschaftsrecht* 31 (2020), 971–978

Gallo D, 'Rethinking Direct Effect and Its Evolution: A Proposal' *European Law Open* 1 (2022), 576–605

Gallo D, *L'efficacia diretta del diritto dell'Unione europea negli ordinamenti nazionali. Evoluzione di una dottrina ancora controversa* (Giuffrè 2018)

Gärditz KF, 'Europäisches Justizverfassungsrecht?' *Deutsche Richterzeitung* (2019), 424–427

Garben S, 'The "Fundamental Freedoms" and (Other Fundamental Rights)' in S Garben and I Govaere (eds), *The Internal Market 2.0* (Hart 2020) 335–369

Garben S, 'Restating the Problem of Competence Creep, Tackling Harmonisation by Stealth and Reinstating the Legislator' in S Garben and I Govaere (eds), *The Division of Competences between the EU and the Member States* (Hart 2017) 300–336

García-Roca J, 'International Deference, The Vague National Margin of Appreciation and Procedural Review' in C Izquierdo-Sans, C Martínez-Capdevila, and M Nogueira-Guastavino (eds), *Fundamental Rights Challenges* (Springer 2021) 245–275

Garrorena Morales A, *El Estado español como Estado social y democrático de derecho* (Tecnos 1984)

Gaudin H, 'Diversité et évolution des champs d'application en droit communautaire' *Revue des affaires européennes* (2003–2004), 7–20

Gaudin H, 'Amsterdam: l'échec de la hiérarchie des normes?' *Revue trimestrielle de droit européen* 35 (1999), 1–20

Gavison R, 'What Belongs in a Constitution?' *Constitutional Political Economy* 13 (2002), 89–105

Gerards J, 'Pluralism, Deference and the Margin of Appreciation Doctrine' *European Law Journal* 17 (2011), 80–120

Gerber DJ, *Law and Competition in Twentieth-Century Europe* (Clarendon 2001)

Gerken J and others, *"Mangold" als ausbrechender Rechtsakt* (Sellier 2009)

Gerkrath J, *L'émergence d'un droit constitutionnel pour l'Europe* (Éd. de l'Université de Bruxelles 1997)

Germelmann CF, 'Alternativen zum Rechtsstaatsverfahren nach Art. 7 EUV?' *Die Öffentliche Verwaltung* (2021), 193–204

Giegerich T, 'Die Unabhängigkeit der Gerichte als Strukturvorgabe der Unionsverfassung' *Zeitschrift für Europarechtliche Studien* 22 (2019), 61–112

Giorgi E, *Il principio del mutuo riconoscimento nell'ordinamento dell'Unione europea* (Firenze Univ. Press 2020)

Giorgi F, 'Le pouvoir constituant européen, "l'Arlésienne" du constitutionnalisme européen? Quel-ques réflexions à propos de l'arrêt Pringle' in V Kronenberger, M d'Alessio, and V Placco (eds), *De Rome à Lisbonne. Mélanges en l'honneur de Paolo Mengozzi* (Bruylant 2013) 275–278

Gliszczyńska-Grabias A and Sadurski W, 'Is It Polexit Yet? Comment on Case K 3/21 of 7 October 2021 by the Constitutional Tribunal of Poland' *European Constitutional Law Review* 19 (2023), 163–181

Goldhammer M, 'Die Achtung der nationalen Identität durch die Europäische Union' *Jahrbuch des öffentlichen Rechts der Gegenwart* 63 (2015), 105–127

Gordillo Pérez LI and Martinico G, 'La jurisprudencia federalizante y humanizadora del Tribunal de Justicia' *Teoría y Realidad Constitucional* 32 (2013), 429–478

Gormley LW, 'Judicial Review: Advice for the Deaf?' *Fordham Journal of International Law* 29 (2005), 655–689

Gourdet S, *Europäischer Grundrechtsschutz. Die Anwendung der Unionsgrundrechte in den Mitgliedstaaten der Europäischen Union und ihr Verhältnis zu den nationalen Grundrechten* (Nomos 2021)

Graf Vitzthum W, 'Form und Stil der Verfassung' in O Depenheuer and C Grabenwarter (eds), *Verfassungstheorie* (Mohr Siebeck 2011) § 10, pp 373–389

Grabenwarter C, 'Standard-Setting in the Spirit of the European Constitutional Heritage' in *Venice Commission. Thirty-Year Quest for Democracy Through Law* (Juristförlaget 2020) 257–280

Grabenwarter C, 'The Cooperation of Constitutional Courts in Europe—Current Situation and Perspectives' XVIth Congress of the Conference of European Constitutional Courts (2014), <www.venice.coe.int/files/Bulletin/SpecBull-CECC-e.pdf>, pp i-xxx

Grabenwarter C, 'Die Verfassung in der Hierarchie der Rechtsordnung' in O Depenheuer and C Grabenwarter (eds), *Verfassungstheorie* (Mohr Siebeck 2011) § 11, pp 391–416

Grabenwarter C, 'National Constitutional Law Relating to the European Union' in A von Bogdandy and J Bast (eds), *Principles of European Constitutional Law* (2nd edn, Hart 2009) 83–129

Grabenwarter C, Huber PM, Knez R, and Ziemele I, 'The Role of the Constitutional Courts in the European Judicial Network' *European Public Law* 27 (2021), 43–62

Griller S, Papadopoulou L, and Puff R (eds), *National Constitutions and EU Integration* (Hart 2022)

Grimm D, *Verfassungsgerichtsbarkeit* (Suhrkamp 2021)

Grimm D, 'Neue Radikalkritik an der Verfassungsgerichtsbarkeit' *Der Staat* 59 (2020), 321–353

Grimm D, 'What Exactly Is Political About Constitutional Adjudication?' in C Landfried (ed), *Judicial Power* (CUP 2019) 307–317

Grimm D, *Constitutionalism* (OUP 2016)

Grimm D, 'The Democratic Costs of Constitutionalisation: The European Case' *European Law Journal* 21 (2015), 460–473

Grimm D, 'Types of Constitutions' in M Rosenfeld and A Sajó (eds), *The Oxford Handbook of Comparative Constitutional Law* (OUP 2012) 98–132

Grimm D, 'Integration by Constitution' *International Journal of Constitutional Law* 3 (2005), 193–208

Grimm D, 'Verfassung–Verfassungsvertrag–Vertrag über eine Verfassung' in O Beaud and others (eds), *L'Europe en voie de constitution* (Bruylant 2004) 279–287

Grimm D, 'Does Europe Need a Constitution?' *European Law Journal* 1 (1995), 282–302

Groppi, Tania, 'Constitutional Revision in Italy' in X Contiades (ed), *Engineering Constitutional Change* (Routledge 2013) 203–228

Groussot X and Petursson GT, 'Balancing as a Judicial Methodology of EU Constitutional Adjudication' in X Groussot, GT Petursson, and S de Vries (eds), *Balancing Fundamental Rights with the EU Treaty Freedoms* (Eleven 2012) 43–69

Grzegorczyk C, *La théorie générale des valeurs et le droit* (LGDJ 1982)

Guastaferro B, 'Beyond the *Exceptionalism* of Constitutional Conflicts: The *Ordinary* Functions of the Identity Clause' *Yearbook of European Law* 31 (2012), 263–318

Guastini R, *Filosofia del diritto positivo* (Giappichelli 2017)

Guastini R, 'Gerarchie normative' *revus* 21 (2013), 57–69

Guastini R, 'Rule-Scepticism Restated' in L Green and B Leiter (eds), *Oxford Studies in Philosophy of Law*, vol 1 (OUP 2011) 138–161

Guastini R, *Interpretare e argomentare* (Giuffrè 2011)

Guastini R, *Le fonti del diritto: Fondamenti teorici* (Giuffrè 2010)

Haag M, 'Art. 10 EUV' in H von der Groeben, J Schwarze, and A Hatje (eds), *Europäisches Unionsrecht* (7th edn, Nomos 2015)

Habermas J, *The Lure of Technocracy* (Polity Press 2015)

Habermas J, *Zur Verfassung Europas* (Suhrkamp 2011)

Habermas J, *Between Facts and Norms* (Polity Press 1996)

Habermas J, 'On the Internal Relation Between the Rule of Law and Democracy' *European Journal of Philosophy* 3 (1995), 12–20

Halberstam D, '"It's the Autonomy, Stupid!" A Modest Defense of Opinion 2/13 on EU Accession to the ECHR, and the Way Forward' *German Law Journal* 16 (2015), 105–146

Halberstam D, 'Local, Global and Plural Constitutionalism' in JHH Weiler and G de Búrca (eds), *The Worlds of European Constitutionalism* (CUP 2012) 150–202

Halberstam D, 'Federalism: Theory, Policy, Law' in M Rosenfeld and A Sajó (eds), *The Oxford Handbook of Comparative Constitutional Law* (OUP 2012) 577–608

Hallstein W, *Die Europäische Gemeinschaft* (Econ 1973)

Hallstein W, *Der unvollendete Bundesstaat* (Econ 1969)

Halmai G, 'Does Illiberal Democracy Exist?' in G Amato, B Barbisan, and C Pinelli (eds), *Rule of Law vs Majoritarian Democracy* (Hart 2021) 171–188

Halmai G, 'Abuse of Constitutional Identity' *Review of Central and East European Law* 43 (2018), 23–42

Halmai G, 'The Case of the Retirement Age of Hungarian Judges' in B Davies and F Nicola (eds), *EU Law Stories* (CUP 2017) 471–488

Halmai G, 'Unconstitutional Constitutional Amendments: Constitutional Courts as Guardians of the Constitution?' *Constellations* 19 (2012), 182–203

Haltern U, 'Europarecht und ich' *Jahrbuch des öffentlichen Rechts der Gegenwart* 68 (2020), 439–469

Haltern U, 'Ultra-vires-Kontrolle im Dienst europäischer Demokratie' *Neue Zeitschrift für Verwaltungsrecht* 39 (2020), 817–823

Haltern U, *Europarecht. Dogmatik im Kontext. Vol. II: Rule of Law–Verbunddogmatik–Grundrechte* (3rd edn, Mohr Siebeck 2017)

Haltern U, 'Pathos and Patina: The Failure and Promise of Constitutionalism in the European Imagination' *European Law Journal* 9 (2003), 14–44

Haltern U and Bergmann A (eds), *Der EuGH in der Kritik* (Mohr Siebeck 2012)

Hanf D, 'Talking with the "pouvoir constituant" in Times of Constitutional Reform: The European Court of Justice on Private Applicants' Access to Justice' *Maastricht Journal of European and Comparative Law* 10 (2003), 265–290

Hanschmann F, *Der Begriff der Homogenität in der Verfassungslehre und Europarechtswissenschaft. Zur These von der Notwendigkeit homogener Kollektive unter besonderer Berücksichtigung der Homogenitätskriterien "Geschichte" und "Sprache"* (Springer 2008)

Haratsch H, Koenig C, and Pechstein M, *Europarecht* (11th edn, Mohr Siebeck 2018)

Harbo TI, 'The Criterion of "Consistent and Systematic Manner" in Free Movement Law' in M Andenas, T Bekkedal, and L Pantale (eds), *The Reach of Free Movement* (Asser Press 2017) 205–226

Harbo TI, 'Introducing Procedural Proportionality Review in European Law' *Leiden Journal of International Law* 30 (2017), 25–47

Harding C, 'The Identity of European Law: Mapping Out the European Legal Space' *European Law Journal* 6 (2000), 128–147

Harkin T, 'The Case Law of the Court of Justice of the European Union on "Judicial Authority" and Issuing European Arrest Warrants' *New Journal of European Criminal Law* 12 (2021), 508–530

Hart HLA, *The Concept of Law* (3rd edn, Clarendon 2012)

Hartley TC, *The Foundations of European Union Law* (4th edn, OUP 2014)

Hartmann N, *Ethik* (4th edn, de Gruyter 1962)

Harvey D, 'Towards Process-Oriented Proportionality Review in The European Union' *European Public Law* 23 (2017), 93–121

Hatje A, 'The Economic Constitution within the Internal Market' in A von Bogdandy and J Bast (eds), *Principles of European Constitutional Law* (2nd edn, Hart 2009) 589–622

Hatzopoulos V, 'Actively Talking to Each Other: The Court and Political Institutions' in M Dawson, B de Witte, and E Muir (eds), *Judicial Activism at the European Court of Justice* (Elgar 2013) 102–141

Hauriou M, *Précis du droit constitutionnel* (2nd edn, Sirey 1929)

Hazelhorst M, 'Mutual Trust Under Pressure: Civil Justice Cooperation in the EU and the Rule of Law' *Netherlands International Law Review* 65 (2018), 103–130

Hein M, 'Do Constitutional Entrenchment Clauses Matter? Constitutional Review of Constitutional Amendments in Europe' *International Journal of Constitutional Law* 18 (2020), 78–110

Heintzen M, 'Hierarchisierungsprozesse innerhalb des Primärrechts der Europäischen Gemeinschaft' *Europarecht* 29 (1994), 35–49

Heller H, 'Political Democracy and Social Homogeneity (1928)' in AJ Jacobson and B Schlink (eds), *Weimar. A Jurisprudence of Crisis* (Univ. California Press 2001) 256–265

Henze T and Jahn J, 'Die Gemeinsame Außen- und Sicherheitspolitik der EU unter der Kontrolle des EuGH' *Europäische Zeitschrift für Wirtschaftsrechts* 28 (2017), 506–511

Herdegen M, 'Art. 1 GG' in G Dürig, R Herzog, and R Scholz (eds), *Grundgesetz-Kommentar* (99th edn, loose-leaf, C.H.Beck 2022)

Herdegen M, 'General Principles of EU Law: The Methodological Challenge' in U Bernitz, J Nergelius, and C Cardner (eds), *General Principles of EC Law in a Process of Development* (Kluwer Law International 2008) 343–355

Herdegen M, 'Vertragliche Eingriff in das "Verfassungsystem" der Europäischen Union' in O Due, M Lutter, and J Schwarze (eds), *Festschrift für Ulrich Everling*, vol 1 (Nomos 1995) 447–461

Hesse K, *Grundzüge des Verfassungsrechts der Bundsrepublik Deutschland* (20th edn, C.F.Müller 1999)

Hestermeyer H, *Eigenständigkeit und Homogenität in föderalen Systemen* (Mohr Siebeck 2020)

Heuschling L, 'The Complex Relationship Between Administrative and Constitutional Law' in S Cassese, A von Bogdandy, and PM Huber (eds), *The Max Planck Handbooks in European Public Law*, vol 1 (OUP 2017) 493–556

Heuschling L, 'État de Droit: Etude de linguistique, de théorie & de dogmatique juridique comparées' in H Bauer and C Calliess (eds), *Verfassungsprinzipien in Europa–Constitutional principles in Europe–Principes constitutionnels en Europe* (Sakkoulas 2008) 103–155

Hilf M and Schorkopf F, 'Art. 2 EUV' in E Grabitz, M Hilf, and M Nettesheim (eds), *Das Recht der Europäischen Union* (75th edn, loose-leaf, C.H.Beck 2022)

Hillion C, 'Overseeing the Rule of Law in the EU' in C Closa and D Kochenov (eds), *Reinforcing Rule of Law Oversight in the European Union* (CUP 2016) 59–81
Hillion C, 'Enlargement' in P Craig and G de Búrca (eds), *The Evolution of EU Law* (2nd edn, OUP 2011) 187–216
Himmer RE, 'Die Geltendmachung der Nichtigkeitsgründe nach Art. 263 AEUV' *Neue Zeitschrift für Verwaltungsrecht* 41 (2022), 1512–9
Hirsch Ballin E, 'Mutual Trust: The Virtue of Reciprocity—Strengthening the Acceptance of the Rule of Law through Peer Review' in C Closa and D Kochenov (eds), *Reinforcing Rule of Law Oversight in the European Union* (CUP 2016) 133–146
Hirose I and Olson J, 'Introduction to Value Theory' in I Hirose and J Olson (eds), *The Oxford Handbook of Value Theory* (OUP 2015) 1–10
Hofmann A, 'Resistance against the Court of Justice of the European Union' *International Journal of Law in Context* 14 (2018), 258–274
Hofmann HCH, *Normenhierarchien im europäischen Gemeinschaftsrecht* (Duncker&Humblot 2000)
Hofmann HCH and Pantazatou K, 'The Transformation of the European Economic Constitution' in HCH Hofmann, K Pantazatou, and G Zaccaroni (eds), *The Metamorphosis of the European Economic Constitution* (Elgar 2019) 2–24
Hofmann R and Heger A, 'Zur Zukunft der Europäischen Union als Werteunion' *Europäische Grundrechte-Zeitschrift* 49 (2022), 361–378
Holterhus TP and Kornack D, 'Die materielle Struktur der Unionsgrundwerte' *Europäische Grundrechte-Zeitschrift* 41 (2014), 389–400
Hong M, 'Human Dignity, Identity Review of the European Arrest Warrant and the Court of Justice as a Listener in the Dialogue of Courts' *European Constitutional Law Review* 12 (2016), 549–563
Hooghe L, Lenz T, and Marks G, *A Theory of International Organization* (OUP 2019)
Höpner M and Haas C, 'Ist der Unionsgesetzgeber an die Grundfreiheiten gebunden?' *Europarecht* 57 (2022), 165–189
Höpner M and Schmidt SK, 'Can We Make the European Fundamental Freedoms Less Constraining?' *Cambridge Yearbook of European Legal Studies* 22 (2020), 182–204
Höreth M, 'Warum der EuGH nicht gestoppt werden sollte—und auch nicht gestoppt werden kann' in U Haltern and A Bergmann (eds), *Der EuGH in der Kritik* (Mohr Siebeck 2012) 73–112
Horsley T, *The Court of Justice of the European Union as an Institutional Actor* (CUP 2018)
Horsley T, 'Reflections on the Role of the Court of Justice as the "Motor" of European Integration' *Common Market Law Review* 50 (2013), 931–964
Huber PM, *Warum der EuGH Kontrolle braucht* (Sramek 2022)
Huber PM, 'The Constitutional Traditions Common to the Member States—Identification and Concretisation' in Court of Justice of the European Union (eds), *EUnited in diversity: between common constitutional traditions and national identities* (Luxembourg 2022) 55–72
Huber PM, 'Art. 2 EUV als Grundlage des Staaten- und Verfassungsverbundes der EU' *Alkotmánybírósági Szemle* (2020), 20–22
Huber PM, 'Constitutional Courts and Politics in the European Legal Space ' in PM Huber, A von Bogdandy, and C Grabenwarter (eds), *The Max Planck Handbooks in European Public Law*, vol 4 (OUP 2023) (forthcoming)
Huber PM, 'Art. 10 EUV' in R Streinz (ed), *EUV/AEUV* (3rd edn, C.H.Beck 2018)
Huber PM, 'Art. 19 EUV' in R Streinz (ed), *EUV/AEUV* (3rd edn, C.H.Beck 2018)

Huber PM, 'The Unitary Effect of the Community's Fundamental Rights' *European Public Law* 14 (2008), 323–333

L'Huillier J, 'Une conquête du droit administratif français. Le contentieux de la Communauté européenne du charbon et de l'acier' *Recueil Dalloz* (1953), Chronique XII, 63–66

Iglesias Sánchez S, 'The Scope of EU Fundamental Rights in the Area of Freedom, Security and Justice' in S Iglesias Sánchez and M González Pascual (eds), *Fundamental Rights in the EU Area of Freedom, Security and Justice* (CUP 2021) 21–38

Iglesias Sánchez S, 'Article 51: The Scope of Application of the Charter' in M Bobek and J Adams-Prassl (eds), *The EU Charter of Fundamental Rights in the Member States* (Hart 2020) 401–420

Iglesias Sánchez S, 'Purely Internal Situations and the Limits of EU Law: A Consolidated Case Law or a Notion to Be Abandoned?' *European Constitutional Law Review* 14 (2018), 7–36

Iliopoulou-Penot A, 'La justification de l'intervention de l'Union pour la garantie de l'Etat de droit au sein des pays membres' *Revue des affaires européennes* 24 (2019), 7–16

Iliopoulou-Penot A, 'Réflexions sur la codification de la jurisprudence par le législateur européen' in B Bertrand, F Picod, and S Roland (eds), *L'identité du droit de l'Union européenne. Mélanges en l'honneur de Claude Blumann* (Bruylant 2015) 187–201

Íñiguez G, 'The Enemy Within? Article 259 TFEU and the EU's Rule of Law Crisis' *German Law Journal* 23 (2022) 1104–20

Innerarity D, *Democracy in Europe* (Palgrave Macmillan 2019)

Ioannidis M, 'The Judicial Review of Discretion in the Banking Union: From "Soft"to "Hard(Er)" Look?' in C Zilioli and KP Wojcik (eds), *Judicial Review in the European Banking Union* (Elgar 2021) 130–145

Ipsen HP, 'Über Verfassungs-Homogenität in der Europäischen Gemeinschaft' in H Maurer (ed), *Das akzeptierte Grundgesetz. Festschrift für Günter Dürig* (C.H.Beck 1990) 159–182

Ipsen HP, *Europäisches Gemeinschaftsrecht* (Mohr Siebeck 1972)

Issacharoff S, *Fragile Democracies. Contested Power in the Era of Constitutional Courts* (CUP 2015)

Itzcovich G, 'On the Legal Enforcement of Values' in A Jakab and D Kochenov (eds), *The Enforcement of EU Law and Values* (OUP 2017) 28–42

Itzcovich G, 'The European Court of Justice' in G Itzcovich, A Jakab, and A Dyevre (eds), *Comparative Constitutional Reasoning* (CUP 2017) 277–322

Itzcovich G, 'The Interpretation of Community Law by the European Court of Justice' *German Law Journal* 10 (2009), 537–560

Jacqué JP, *Droit institutionnel de l'Union européenne* (9th edn, Dalloz 2018)

Jacqué JP, 'État de droit et confiance mutuelle' *Revue trimestrielle de droit européen* (2018), 239–243

Jacqué JP, 'Art. 2 EUV' in H von der Groeben, J Schwarze, and A Hatje (eds), *Europäisches Unionsrecht* (7th edn, Nomos 2015)

Jacqué JP, 'Le projet de traité établissant une constitution pour l'Europe. Constitutionnalisation ou révision des Traités?' in P Demaret, I Govaere, and D Hanf (eds), *Dynamiques Juridiques Européennes* (Peter Lang 2005) 41–52

Jacqué JP, 'The Principle of Institutional Balance' *Common Market Law Review* 41 (2004), 383–391

Jacqué JP, 'Cours générale de droit communautaire' *Collected Courses of the Academy of European Law* I-1 (1990), 237–361

Jacob M, *Precedents and Case-Based Reasoning in the European Court of Justice* (CUP 2014)

Jaeger T, 'Gerichtsorganisation und EU-Recht' *Europarecht* 53 (2018), 611–653

Jakab A and Kirchmair L, 'Two Ways of Completing the European Fundamental Rights Union: Amendment to vs. Reinterpretation of Article 51 of the EU Charter of Fundamental Rights' *Cambridge Yearbook of European Law* (2022), 1–23

Jakab A, 'Warum verliert die deutsche Verfassungsrechtswissenschaft an internationalem Einfluss und was kann dagegen getan werden?' *Zeitschrift für ausländisches öffentlices Recht und Völkerrecht* 82 (2022), 701–724

Jakab A, 'Application of the Charter of Fundamental Rights by National Courts in Purely Domestic Cases' in A Jakab and D Kochenov (eds), *The Enforcement of EU Law and Values* (OUP 2017) 252–262

Jakab A, 'The EU Charter of Fundamental Rights as the Most Promising Way of Enforcing the Rule of Law against EU Member States' in C Closa and D Kochenov (eds), *Reinforcing Rule of Law Oversight in the European Union* (CUP 2016) 187–205

Jakab A, *European Constitutional Language* (CUP 2016)

Jakab A, 'Judicial Reasoning in Constitutional Courts: A European Perspective' *German Law Journal* 14 (2013), 1215–1278

Jakab A and Kochenov D (eds), *The Enforcement of EU Law and Values* (OUP 2017)

Jaklic K, *Constitutional Pluralism in the EU* (OUP 2014)

Janse R, 'Is the European Commission a Credible Guardian of the Values?' *International Journal Of Constitutional Law* 17 (2019), 43–65

Janse R, 'The Evolution of the Political Criteria for Accession to the European Community, 1957–1973' *European Law Journal* 24 (2018), 57–76

Jellinek G, *Allgemeine Staatslehre* (3rd edn, Springer 1925)

Jennings R and Watts A, *Oppenheim's International Law*, vol 1 (9th edn, OUP 2008)

Jestaedt M, 'Luxemburger Richterrecht' in C Hillgruber (ed), *Gouvernement des Juges—Fluch Oder Segen* (Schöningh 2014) 21–44

Jestaedt M, 'The Doctrine of Balancing–Strengths and Weaknesses' in M Klatt (ed), *Institutionalized Reason* (OUP 2011) 152–172

Jestaedt M, 'Verfassungstheorie als Disziplin' in O Depenheuer and C Grabenwarter (eds), *Verfassungstheorie* (Mohr Siebeck 2010) § 1, pp 1–56

Joas H, *The Genesis of Values* (Univ. of Chicago Press 2000)

Joerges C, 'Integration through Law and the Crisis of Law in Europe's Emergency' in C Joerges, D Chalmers, and M Jachtenfuchs (eds), *The End of the Eurocrats' Dream* (CUP 2016) 299–338

Joppe A, 'EU Solidarity, Illustrated by the Covid-19 Crisis' *Utrecht Law Review* 17 (2021), 130–142

Kaczorowska-Ireland A, 'What is the European Union required to Respect under Article 4(2) TEU? The Uniqueness Approach' *European Public Law* 25 (2019), 57–82

Kadelbach S, *Zwingendes Völkerrecht* (Duncker&Humblot 1992)

Kadlec O and Kosar D, 'Romanian Version of the Rule of Law Crisis Comes to the ECJ: The AFJR Case Is Not Just About the Cooperation and Verification Mechanism' *Common Market Law Review* 59 (2022), 1823–1852

Kagiaros D, 'When to Use European Consensus' in P Kapotas and VP Tzevelekos (eds), *Building Consensus on European Consensus* (CUP 2019) 283–310

Kahl W, 'Dogmatik im EU-Recht' *Archiv des öffentlichen Rechts* 144 (2019), 159–207

Kalaitzaki K, 'The Application of EU Fundamental Rights During the Financial Crisis' *European Public Law* 27 (2021), 331–354

Kant I, *The Conflict of the Faculties* (Univ. Nebraska Press 1992)

Karpenstein U, 'Art. 259 AEUV' in E Grabitz, M Hilf, and M Nettesheim (eds), *Das Recht der Europäischen Union* (75th edn, loose-leaf, C.H.Beck 2022)
Karpenstein U, 'Art. 260 AEUV' in E Grabitz, M Hilf, and M Nettesheim (eds), *Das Recht der Europäischen Union* (75th edn, loose-leaf, C.H.Beck 2022)
Karpenstein U, 'Europa zeigt Zähne. Dreimal Polen, dreimal Neuland: Kommission und EuGH machen nun ernst' *Europäische Zeitschrift für Wirtschaftsrecht* 29 (2018), 97–98
Kelemen RD, 'Appeasement, Ad Infinitum' *Maastricht Journal of European and Comparative Law* 29 (2022), 177–181
Kelemen RD, 'Is Differentiation Possible in Rule of Law?' *Comparative European Politics* 17 (2019), 246–260
Kelemen RD, 'The Dangers of Constitutional Pluralism' in G Davies and M Avbelj (eds), *Research Handbook on Legal Pluralism and EU Law* (Elgar 2018) 392–404
Kelemen RD, 'The Political Foundations of Judicial Independence in the European Union' *Journal of European Public Policy* 19 (2012), 43–58
Kelemen RD and Pech L, 'The Uses and Abuses of Constitutional Pluralism: Undermining the Rule of Law in the Name of Constitutional Identity in Hungary and Poland' *Cambridge Yearbook of European Legal Studies* 21 (2019), 59–74
Kelsen H, *Pure Theory of Law* (Univ. of California Press 1967)
Kelsen H, *General Theory of Law and State* (Harvard Univ. Press 1945)
Kelsen H, 'Wer soll Hüter der Verfassung sein?' *Die Justiz* VI (1930/31), 576–628
Kennedy D, 'Proportionality and "Deference" in Contemporary Constitutional Thought' in T Perišin and S Rodin (eds), *The Transformation or Reconstitution of Europe: The Critical Legal Studies Perspective on the Role of the Courts in the European Union* (Hart 2018) 29–58
Kennedy D, *A Critique of Adjudication. Fin de Siècle* (Harvard Univ. Press 1997)
Kiener R and Gunjic I, 'Das Prinzip des unbedingten Vorrangs von EU-Recht und der polnische Justizkonflikt' *Zeitschrift für Europarecht* (2020), 112–125
Kilpatrick C, 'On the Rule of Law and Economic Emergency: The Degradation of Basic Legal Values in Europe's Bailouts' *Oxford Journal of Legal Studies* 35 (2015), 325–353
Kingreen T, 'Fundamental Freedoms' in A von Bogdandy and J Bast(eds), *Principles of European Constitutional Law* (2nd edn, Hart 2009) 515–549
Kirchhof P, 'Europa auf dem Weg zu einer Verfassung?' *Zeitschrift für Staats- und Europawissenschaften* 1 (2003), 358–382
Klamert M, 'Loyalty and Solidarity as General Principles' in KS Ziegler, PJ Neuvonen, and V Moreno-Lax (eds), *Research Handbook on General Principles in EU Law* (Elgar 2022) 118–135
Klamert M, 'Supremacy, the Uniformity of EU Law, and the Principle of Equality' *Austrian Law Journal* 9 (2022), 82–92
Klamert M, 'Article 48 TEU' in M Klamert, M Kellerbauer, and J Tomkin (eds), *The Treaties and the Charter of Fundamental Rights* (OUP 2019) 302–310
Klamert M, 'Article 7 TFEU' in M Klamert, M Kellerbauer, and J Tomkin (eds), *The Treaties and the Charter of Fundamental Rights–A Commentary* (OUP 2019) 380–382
Klamert M, 'Altes und Neues zur Harmonisierung im Binnenmarkt' *Europäische Zeitschrift für Wirtschaftsrecht* 26 (2015), 265–268
Klein C, *Théorie et pratique du pouvoir constituant* (Presses Universitaires de France 1996)
Klamert M and Kochenov D, 'Article 2 TEU' in M Klamert, M Kellerbauer, and J Tomkin (eds), *The Treaties and the Charter of Fundamental Rights—A Commentary* (2nd edn, OUP 2023)

Kleinlein T, 'The Procedural Approach of the European Court of Human Rights' *International and Comparative Law Quarterly* 68 (2019), 91–110

Kleinlein T, 'Consensus and Contestability: The ECtHR and the Combined Potential of European Consensus and Procedural Rationality Control' *European Journal of International Law* 28 (2017), 871–893

Knauff M, 'Ungeschriebenes Primärrecht' in PC Müller-Graff, S Schmahl, and V Skouris (eds), *Europäisches Recht zwischen Bewährung und Wandel. Festschrift für Dieter H. Scheuing* (Nomos 2011) 127–148

Kochenov D, 'Article 7: A Commentary on a Much Talked-About "Dead" Provision' *Polish Yearbook of International Law* 38 (2018), 165–187

Kochenov D, 'The *Acquis* and Its Principles' in D Kochenov and A Jakab (eds), *The Enforcement of EU Law and Values* (OUP 2017) 9–27

Kochenov D, 'Biting Intergovernmentalism: The Case for the Reinvention of Article 259 TFEU to Make It a Viable Rule of Law Enforcement Tool' *The Hague Journal on the Rule of Law* 7 (2015), 153–174

Kochenov D, *EU Enlargement and the Failure of Conditionality* (Kluwer Law International 2008)

Kochenov D and Bárd P, 'The Last Soldier Standing? Courts Versus Politicians and the Rule of Law Crisis in the New Member States of the EU' *European Yearbook of Constitutional Law* 1 (2020), 243–287

Kochenov D, de Búrca G, and Williams A (eds), *Europe's Justice Deficit?* (Hart 2015)

Kochenov D and Morijn J, 'Le rôle de la Charte dans la lutte pour l'État de droit au sein de l'Union européenne' in A Iliopoulou-Penot and L Xenou (eds), *La Charte des droits fondamentaux, source de renouveau constitutionnel européen?* (Bruylant 2020) 173–198

Kochenov D and Pech L, *Respect for the Rule of Law in the Case Law of the European Court of Justice. A Casebook Overview of Key Judgments since the Portuguese Judges Case* (SIEPS 2021:3)

Kochenov D and Pech L, 'Monitoring and Enforcement of the Rule of Law in the EU' *European Constitutional Law Review* 11 (2015), 512–540

Kokott J, 'Der *pouvoir neutre* im Recht der Europäischen Union' *Zeitschrift für ausländisches öffentliches Recht und Völkerrecht* 69 (2009), 275–288

Kolb R, *Peremptory International Law–Jus Cogens* (Hart 2015)

Komárek J, 'Judicial Legitimacy in the European Union' in C Kilpatrick and J Scott (eds), *New Legal Approaches to Studying the Court of Justice* (OUP 2020) 125–154

Komárek J, 'Legal Reasoning in EU Law' in D Chalmers and A Arnull (eds), *The Oxford Handbook of European Union Law* (OUP 2015) 29–51

Komárek J, 'Why National Constitutional Courts Should Not Embrace EU Fundamental Rights' in S de Vries, U Bernitz, and S Weatherill (eds), *The EU Charter of Fundamental Rights as a Binding Instrument* (Hart 2015) 75–92

Komárek J, 'National Constitutional Courts in the European Constitutional Democracy' *International Journal of Constitutional Law* 12 (2014), 525–544

Komárek J, 'In the Court(s) We Trust?' *European Law Review* 32 (2007), 467–491

König C, 'Zum Verfassungsrang der Grundfreiheiten und des europäischen Wettbewerbsrechts' *Europarecht* 57 (2022), 48–73

Konstadinides T, *The Rule of Law in the European Union. The Internal Dimension* (Hart 2017)

Konstadinides T, 'Constitutional Identity as a Shield and as a Sword: The European Legal Order within the Framework of National Constitutional Settlement' *Cambridge Yearbook of European Legal Studies* 13 (2011), 195–218

Koopmans T, *Courts and Political Institutions* (CUP 2003)

Koopmans T, 'Federalism: The Wrong Debate' *Common Market Law Review* 29 (1992), 1047–1052
Koskenniemi M, 'General Principles' in M Koskenniemi (ed), *Sources of International Law* (Dartmouth 2000) 359–402
Kosta V and Piqani D, 'Where Trade and Academic Freedom Meet: Commission v. Hungary (LEX CEU)' *Common Market Law Review* 59 (2022), 813–852
Kotzur M, 'Art. 20 GG' in I von Münch and P Kunig (eds), *Grundgesetz-Kommentar*, vol 1 (7th edn, C.H.Beck 2021)
Kovács K, 'The Rise of an Ethnocultural Constitutional Identity in the Jurisprudence of the East Central European Courts' *German Law Journal* 18 (2017), 1703–1720
Kowalik-Bańczyk K, 'Should We Polish It Up? The Polish Constitutional Tribunal and the Idea of Supremacy of EU Law' *German Law Journal* 6 (2005), 1355–1366
Krajewski M, 'The Many-Faced Court: The Value of Participation in Annulment Proceedings' *European Constitutional Law Review* 15 (2019), 220–246
Krajewski M, 'Who Is Afraid of the European Council? The Court of Justice's Cautious Approach to the Independence of Domestic Judges' *European Constitutional Law Review* 14 (2018), 792–813
Krappitz D and Kirst N, 'An Infringement of Democracy in the EU Legal Order' *EU Law Live* (29 May 2020)
Krastev I and Holmes S, *The Light that Failed* (Penguin 2019)
Kratochvíl J, 'The Inflation of the Margin of Appreciation by the European Court of Human Rights' *Netherlands Quarterly of Human Rights* 29 (2011), 324–357
Kraus H, 'Das Erfordernis struktureller Kongruenz zwischen der Verfassung der Europäischen Verteidigungsgemeinschaft und dem Grundgesetz' in *Der Kampf um den Wehrbeitrag*, vol 2 (Isar 1953) 545–554
Kress K, 'Coherence' in D Patterson (ed), *A Companion to Philosophy of Law and Legal Theory* (2nd edn, Wiley-Blackwell 2010) 521–528
Krisch N, *Beyond Constitutionalism: The Pluralist Structure of Postnational Law* (OUP 2010)
Kröll T and Lienbacher G, 'Art. 10 EUV' in J Schwarze and others (eds), *EU-Kommentar* (4th edn, Nomos 2019)
Krommendijk J, 'Wide Open and Unguarded Stand Our Gates: The CJEU and References for a Preliminary Ruling in Purely Internal Situations' *German Law Journal* 18 (2017), 1359–1394
Krommendijk J, 'The Use of ECtHR Case Law by the Court of Justice After Lisbon' *Maastricht Journal of European and Comparative Law* 22 (2015), 812–835
Küçük E, 'Solidarity in EU Law: An Elusive Political Statement or a Legal Principle with Substance?' *Maastricht Journal of European and Comparative Law* 23 (2016), 965–983
Kühling J, 'Fundamental Rights' in A von Bogdandy and J Bast (eds), *Principles of European Constitutional Law* (2nd edn, Hart 2009) 479–514
Kullak E, *Vertrauen in Europa. Entwicklung und Funktion als Verfassungsgrundsatz des Unionsrechts* (Mohr Siebeck 2020)
Kumm M, 'On the Representativeness of Constitutional Courts' in C Landfried (ed), *Judicial Power* (CUP 2019) 281–291
Kumm M, 'Rebel Without a Good Cause: Karlsruhe's Misguided Attempt to Draw the CJEU into a Game of "Chicken" and What the CJEU Might Do About It' *German Law Journal* 15 (2014), 203–215
Kumm M, 'Why Europeans Will Not Embrace Constitutional Patriotism' *International Journal of Constitutional Law* 6 (2008), 117–136

Kumm M, 'Who is Afraid of the Total Constitution?' *German Law Journal* 7 (2006), 341–369
Kumm M, 'The Jurisprudence of Constitutional Conflict' *European Law Journal* 11 (2005), 262–307
Kumm M, 'Who is the Final Arbiter of Constitutionality in Europe?' *Common Market Law Review* 36 (1999), 351–386
Kumm M and Ferreres Comella V, 'The Primacy Clause of the Constitutional Treaty' *International Journal of Constitutional Law* 3 (2005), 473–492
Kutscher H, 'Methods of Interpretation as seen by the European Court of Justice' Judicial and Academic Conference (27–28 September 1976)
Lachmayer K, 'Questioning the Basic Values. Austria and Jörg Haider' in A Jakab and D Kochenov (eds), *The Enforcement of EU Law and Values* (OUP 2017) 436–455
Ladenburger C, 'The Principle of Mutual Trust between Member States in the Area of Freedom, Security and Justice' *Zeitschrift für europarechtliche Studien* 23 (2020), 373–407
Ladenburger C, 'European Union Institutional Report' in J Laffranque (ed), *Reports of the XXV FIDE Congress Tallinn 2012. Vol. 1: The Protection of Fundamental Rights Post-Lisbon* (Tartu Univ. Press 2012) 141–215
Ladenburger C, 'Towards a Post-National Constitution—Federal, Confederal or Genuinely "Sui Generis"?' *European Review of Public Law* 16 (2004), 75–111
Ladenburger C and Rabourdin P, 'La constitutionnalisation des valeurs de l'Union. Commentaire sur la genèse des articles 2 et 7 du Traité sur l'Union européenne' *Revue des affaires européennes* (2022), 231–239
Lagrange M, 'The Court of Justice as a Factor in European Integration' *American Journal of Comparative Law* 15 (1966), 709–725
Landfried C, 'Constitutional Review in the European Legal Space: A Political Science Perspective' in A von Bogdandy, C Grabenwarter, and PM Huber (eds), *The Max Planck Handbooks in European Public Law*, vol 4 (OUP 2023) (forthcoming)
Langer J and Sauter W, 'The Consistency Requirement in EU Law' *Columbia Journal of European Law* 24 (2017), 39–73
Larik J, 'From Speciality to a Constitutional Sense of Purpose: On the Changing Role of the Objectives of the European Union' *International and Comparative Law Quarterly* 63 (2014), 935–962
Larsen SR, *The Constitutional Theory of the Federation and the European Union* (OUP 2021)
Larsen SR, 'Varieties of Constitutionalism in the European Union' *Modern Law Review* 84 (2021), 477–502
Larsson O, 'Political and Constitutional Overrides: The Case of the Court of Justice of European Union' *Journal of European Public Policy* 28 (2021), 1932–1949
Lasser M, 'Fundamentally Flawed: The CJEU's Jurisprudence on Fundamental Rights and Fundamental Freedoms' *Theoretical Inquiries in Law* 15 (2014), 229–260
Lasser M, *Judicial Deliberations* (OUP 2004)
Latzel C, 'Die Anwendungsbereiche des Unionsrechts' *Europäische Zeitschrift für Wirtschaftsrecht* 26 (2015), 658–664
Lavranos N, 'Protecting European Law from International Law' *European Foreign Affairs Review* 15 (2010), 265–282
Law S, 'The Rationales, Reasoning and Methodology Underpinning the Judicial Recognition of Principles of Union Law' *Cahiers de droit européen* 52 (2016), 11–38
Lawrence JC, 'Constitutional Pluralism's Unspoken Normative Core' *Cambridge Yearbook of European Legal Studies* 21 (2019), 24–40
Łazowski A, 'Strengthening the Rule of Law and the EU Pre-Accession Policy: Repubblika v. Il-Prim Ministru' *Common Market Law Review* 59 (2022), 1803–1822

Le Pillouer A, 'Le pouvoir de révision' in M Troper and D Chagnollaud (eds), *Traité international de droit constitutionnel*, vol 3 (Dalloz 2012) 34–65

Lecourt R, *L'Europe des Juges* (Bruylant 1976, repr. 2008)

Legg A, *The Margin of Appreciation in International Human Rights Law* (OUP 2012)

Leible S and Domröse R, 'Interpretation in Conformity with Primary Law' in K Riesenhuber (ed), *European Legal Methodology* (2nd edn, Intersentia 2021) § 8, pp 181–210

Leloup M, Kochenov D and Dimitrovs A, 'Opening the Door to Solving the "Copenhagen dilemma"? All eyes on Repubblika v Il-Prim Ministru' *European Law Review* 46 (2021), 692–703

Lenaerts K, 'The Constitutional Traditions Common to the Member States: The Comparative Law Method' in Court of Justice of the European Union (eds), *EUnited in Diversity: Between Common Constitutional Traditions and National Identities* (Luxembourg 2022) 35–43

Lenaerts K, 'Concluding Remarks' in Court of Justice of the European Union (eds), *EUnited in Diversity: Between Common Constitutional Traditions and National Identities* (Luxembourg 2022) 231–238

Lenaerts K, 'L'égalité des États membres devant les traités' *Revue du droit de l'Union européenne* (2021), 7–10

Lenaerts K, 'The Role of the EU Charter in the Member States' in M Bobek and J Adams-Prassl (eds), *The EU Charter of Fundamental Rights in the Member States* (Hart 2020) 19–36

Lenaerts K, 'New Horizons for the Rule of Law Within the EU' *German Law Journal* 21 (2020), 29–34

Lenaert K, 'EUdentity as a Way of Promoting National Identity' *Alkotmánybírósági Szemle* (2020), 9–12

Lenaerts K, 'Limits on Limitations: The Essence of Fundamental Rights in the EU' *German Law Journal* 20 (2019), 779–793

Lenaerts K, 'Upholding the Rule of Law through Judicial Dialogue' *Yearbook of European Law* 38 (2019), 3–17

Lenaerts K, 'Discovering the Law of the EU: The European Court of Justice and the Comparative Law Method' in T Perišin and S Rodin (eds), *The Transformation or Reconstitution of Europe: The Critical Legal Studies Perspective on the Role of the Courts in the European Union* (Hart 2018) 61–87

Lenaerts K, 'La Vie Après l'Avis: Exploring the Principle of Mutual (Yet Not Blind) Trust' *Common Market Law Review* 54 (2017), 805–840

Lenaerts K, 'Die Werte der Europäischen Union in der Rechtsprechung des Gerichtshofes der Europäischen Union' *Europäische Grundrechte-Zeitschrift* 44 (2017), 639–642

Lenaerts K, 'Les fondements constitutionnels de l'Union européenne dans leur rapport avec le droit international' in *La Cour de Justice de l'Union Européenne sous la présidence de Vassilios Skouris (2003–2015): liber amicorum Vassilios Skouris* (Bruylant 2015) 367–386

Lenaerts K, 'The Principle of Democracy in the Case Law of the European Court of Justice' *International and Comparative Law Quarterly* 62 (2013), 300–315

Lenaerts K, 'The Court's Outer and Inner Selves' in M Adams and others (eds), *Judging Europe's Judges* (Hart 2013) 3–60

Lenaerts K, 'The European Court of Justice and Process-Oriented Review' *Yearbook of European Law* 31 (2012), 3–16

Lenaerts K, ' "Civis europaeus sum": From the Cross-border Link to the Status of Citizen of the Union' in P Cardonnel, A Rosas, and N Wahl (eds), *Constitutionalising the EU Judicial System* (Hart 2012) 213–232

Lenaerts K, 'L'encadrement par le droit de l'Union européenne des compétences des États membres' in *Mélanges en l'honneur de Jean Paul Jacqué* (Dalloz 2010) 421–442

Lenaerts K, 'The Rule of Law and Coherence of the Judicial System of the European Union' *Common Market Law Review* 44 (2007), 1625–1659

Lenaerts K, 'Some Thoughts About the Interaction Between Judges and Politicians in the European Community' *Yearbook of European Law* 12 (1992), 1–34

Lenaerts K and Adam A, 'La solidarité, valeur commune aux états membres et principe fédératif de l'Union européenne' *Cahiers de droit européen* 57 (2021), 307–417

Lenaerts K and Corthaut T, 'Of birds and Hedges: The Role of Primacy in Invoking Norms of EU law' *European Law Review* 31 (2006), 287–315

Lenaerts K and Desomer M, 'New Models of Constitution-Making in Europe: The Quest for Legitimacy' *Common Market Law Review* 39 (2002), 1217–1253

Lenaerts K and Gutiérrez-Fons JA, *Les méthodes d'interprétation de la Cour de justice de l'Union européenne* (Bruylant 2020)

Lenaerts K and Gutiérrez-Fons JA, 'A Constitutional Perspective' in R Schütze and T Tridimas (eds), *Oxford Principles of European Union Law*, vol 1 (OUP 2018) 103–141

Lenaerts K and Gutiérrez-Fons JA, 'Epilogue on EU Citizenship: Hopes and Fears?' in D Kochenov (ed), *EU Citizenship and Federalism* (CUP 2017) 751–781

Lenaerts K and Gutiérrez-Fons JA, 'To Say What the Law of the EU Is' *Columbia Journal of European Law* 20 (2014), 3–61

Lenaerts K and Gutiérrez-Fons JA, 'The Constitutional Allocation of Powers and General Principles of EU Law' *Common Market Law Review* 47 (2010), 1629–1669

Lenaerts K, Gutiérrez-Fons JA, and Adam S, 'Exploring the Autonomy of the European Legal Order' *Zeitschrift für ausländisches öffentliches Recht und Völkerrecht* 81 (2021), 47–88

Lenaerts K and Gutman K, 'The Comparative Law Method and the Court of Justice of the European Union' in M Andenas and D Fairgrieve (eds), *Courts and Comparative Law* (OUP 2015) 141–176

Lenaerts K and Gutman K, '"Federal Common Law" in the European Union' *American Journal of Comparative Law* 54 (2006), 1–121

Lenaerts K, Maselis I, and Gutman K, *EU Procedural Law* (OUP 2014)

Lenaerts K and Van Nuffel P, *EU Constitutional Law* (OUP 2021)

Lenaerts K and Verhoeven A, 'Institutional Balance as a Guarantee for Democracy in EU Governance' in C Joerges and R Dehousse (eds), *Good Governance in Europe's Integrated Market* (OUP 2002) 34–88

Levits E, 'Die Europäische Union als Wertegemeinschaft' in T Jaeger (ed), *Europa 4.0* (Sramek 2018) 239–270

Levits E, 'L'Union européenne en tant que communauté des valeurs partagées' in *Liber Amicorum Antonio Tizzano. De la Cour CECA à la Cour de l'Union: le long parcours de la justice européenne* (Giappichelli 2018) 509–522

Levits E, 'L'identité nationale des États membres selon l'article 4, § 2, du T.U.E. en tant qu'élément de la structure constitutionnelle de l'Union européenne' in *La Cour de Justice de l'Union Européenne sous la présidence de Vassilios Skouris (2003–2015): liber amicorum Vassilios Skouris* (Bruylant 2015) 387–400

Lepsius O, 'The Standard Setting Power' in M Jestaedt and others (eds), *The German Federal Constitutional Court: The Court Without Limits* (OUP 2020) 70–130

Letsas G, *A Theory of Interpretation of the European Convention on Human Rights* (OUP 2007)

Lewandowski W, 'Pomiędzy Scyllą zawieszenia wzajemnego zaufania i Charybdą fragmentaryzacji standardu ochrony prawa podstawowego—dylematy Trybunału

Sprawiedliwości w wyroku C-216/18 PPU, LM' *Europejski Przegląd Sądowy* (2) (2019), 4–13

Ličková M and Oró Martínez C, 'Mutual Recognition in Civil and Commercial Matters: On Certified Mutual Trust' in S Iglesias Sánchez and M González Pascual (eds), *Fundamental Rights in the EU Area of Freedom, Security and Justice* (CUP 2021) 179–191

Lindahl H, 'Constituent Power and Reflexive Identity' in M Loughlin and N Walker (eds), *The Paradox of Constitutionalism* (OUP 2008) 9–24

Lindeboom J, 'Is the Primacy of EU Law Based on the Equality of the Member States?' *German Law Journal* 21 (2020), 1032–1044

Linderfalk U, *Understanding Jus Cogens in International Law and International Legal Discourse* (Elgar 2020)

Lippert A, *Der grenzüberschreitende Sachverhalt im Unionsrecht* (Mohr Siebeck 2013)

Loewenthal PJ, 'Art. 296 TFEU' in M Kellerbauer, M Klamert, and J Tomkin (eds), *The Treaties and the Charter of Fundamental Rights–A Commentary* (OUP 2019)

Loughlin M, 'The Concept of Constituent Power' *European Journal of Political Theory* 13 (2014), 218–237

Louis JV, 'Le Traité d'Amsterdam: Une occasion perdue?' *Revue du marché unique européen* 2 (1997), 5–18

Lübbe-Wolff G, 'Die Verfassung als Wertordnung—Was heißt das?' *Merkur* 70 (801) (2016), 47–54

Lübbe-Wolff G, 'Constitutional Courts and Democracy. Facets of an Ambivalent Relationship' in K Meßerschmidt and AD Oliver-Lalana (eds), *Rational Lawmaking under Review* (Springer 2016) 19–32

Lübbe-Wolff G, 'Who Has the Last Word?' *Yearbook of European Law* 30 (2011), 86–99

Luhmann N, *Theory of Society*, vol 1 (Stanford Univ. Press 2012)

Luhmann N, *Law as a Social System* (OUP 2004)

Luhmann N, 'Participation and Legitimation' in N Luhmann (ed), *Political Theory in the Welfare State* (de Gruyter 1990) 219–230

Luhmann N, *Gibt es in unserer Gesellschaft noch unverzichtbare Normen?* (C.F. Müller 1993)

Luna Serrano A, *Las normas que acogen conceptos elásticos o formulaciones abiertas* (Dykinson 2019)

Lupo N, 'The Advantage of Having the First Word in the Composite European Constitution' *Italian Journal of Public Law* 10 (2018), 186–204

Mac Amhlaigh CS, *New Constitutional Horizons: Towards a Pluralist Constitutional Theory* (OUP 2022)

MacCormick N, *Rethoric and the Rule of Law: A Theory of Legal Reasoning* (OUP 2010)

MacCormick N, *Questioning Sovereignty* (OUP 1999)

MacCormick N, *Legal Reasoning and Legal Theory* (Clarendon 1994)

MacCormick N, Bengoetxea J, and Moral Soriano L, 'Integration and Integrity in the Legal Reasoning of the European Court of Justice' in G de Búrca and JHH Weiler (eds), *The European Court of Justice* (OUP 2001) 43–85

Mader O, 'Wege aus der Rechtsstaatsmisere: der neue EU-Verfassungsgrundsatz des Rückschrittsverbots und seine Bedeutung für die Wertedurchsetzung' *Europäische Zeitschrift für Wirtschaftsrecht* 32 (2021), 917–922

Mader O, 'Enforcement of EU Values as a Political Endeavour: Constitutional Pluralism and Value Homogeneity in Times of Persistent Challenges to the Rule of Law' *Hague Journal on the Rule of Law* 11 (2019), 133–170

Maduro MP, 'Interpreting European Law: Judicial Adjudication in a Context of Constitutional Pluralism' *European Journal of Legal Studies* 1 (2007), 1–21

Maduro MP, 'The Importance of Being Called a Constitution' *International Journal of Constitutional Law* 3 (2005), 332–356

Maduro MP, 'Contrapunctual Law' in N Walker (ed), *Sovereignty in Transition* (Hart 2003) 501–537

Maduro MP, *We the Court* (Hart 1998)

Maduro MP and Menezes Queiroz B, 'A Hard Law Approach to States Systemic Violations of Article 2 of the Treaty of the European Union' in E Fisher, J King, and A Young (eds), *The Foundations and Future of Public Law. Essays in Honour of Paul Craig* (OUP 2020) 363–380

Maestro Buelga G, 'Poder constituyente, principio democrático y continuidad en el Tratado Constitucional de la Unión Europea' *Teoría y Realidad Constitucional* (2004), 133–158

Mancano L, 'Judicial Harmonisation Through Autonomous Concepts of European Union Law' *European Law Review* 43 (2018), 69–88

Mance JH, 'The Role of Judges in a Representative Democracy' in G Amato, B Barbisan, and C Pinelli (eds), *Rule of Law vs Majoritarian Democracy* (Hart 2021) 335–352

Mancini GF, 'The Making of a Constitution for Europe' *Common Market Law Review* 26 (1989), 595–614

Mancini GF and Keeling, DT, 'Language, Culture and Politics in the Life of the European Court of Justice' *Columbia Journal of European Law* 1 (1995), 397–413

Mangiameli S, 'The Union's Homogeneity and its Common Values' in HJ Blanke and S Mangiameli (eds), *The European Union after Lisbon* (Springer 2012) 21–46

Mangiameli S, 'La clausola di omogeneità nel trattato dell'Unione europea e nella costituzione europea' in S Mangiameli (ed), *L'ordinamento europeo*, vol 1 (Giuffrè 2006) 1–41

Markakis M, *Accountability in the Economic and Monetary Union: Foundations, Policy, and Governance* (OUP 2020)

Marques F, 'Rule of Law, National Judges and the Court of Justice of the European Union: Let's Keep It Juridical' *European Law Journal* 27 (2021), 228–239

Martenczuk B, 'Art. 7 EUV und der Rechtsstaatsrahmen als Instrument der Wahrung der Grundwerte der Union' in S Kadelbach (ed), *Verfassungskrisen in der Europäischen Union* (Nomos 2018) 41–59

Martens SAE, *Methodenlehre des Unionsrechts* (Mohr Siebeck 2013)

Marti G, *Le pouvoir constituant européen* (Bruylant 2011)

Martín y Pérez de Nanclares J, 'La Unión Europea como comunidad de valores' *Teoría y Realidad Constitucional* (43) (2019), 121–159

Martín y Pérez de Nanclares J, 'El proyecto de Constitución europea: reflexiones sobre los trabajos de la Convención' *Revista de Derecho Comunitario Europeo* 7 (2003), 530–572

Martín Rodríguez PJ, *El Estado de Derecho en la Unión Europea* (Marcial Pons 2021)

Martinico G, 'General principles of EU law and comparative law' in KS Ziegler, PJ Neuvonen, and V Moreno-Lax (eds), *Research Handbook on General Principles in EU Law* (Elgar 2022) 82–97

Martinico G, 'Taming National Identity: A Systematic Understanding of Article 4.2 TEU' *European Public Law* 27 (2021), 447–464

Martinico G, 'Building Supranational Identity: Legal Reasoning and Outcome in Kadi I and Opinion 2/13 of the Court of Justice' *Italian Journal of Public Law* 8 (2016), 235–267

Martinico G, 'The "Polemical" Spirit of European Constitutional Law: On the Importance of Conflicts in EU Law' *German Law Journal* 16 (2015), 1343–1374

Martinico G, 'Chasing the European Court of Justice: On Some (Political) Attempts to Hijack the European Integration Process' *International Community Law Review* 14 (2012), 243–272

Martinico G and Pollicino O, 'Use and Abuse of a Promising Concept: What Has Happened to National Constitutional Identity?' *Yearbook of European Law* 39 (2020), 228–249

Marzal T, 'Making Sense of the Use of Proportionality in the Bundesverfassunsgericht's PSPP Decision' *Revue des affaires européennes* (2020), 441–449

Marzal T, 'From Hercules to Pareto: Of Bathos, Proportionality, and EU law' *International Journal of Constitutional Law* 15 (2017), 621–648

Masing J, *Die Mobilisierung des Bürgers für die Durchsetzung des Rechts* (Duncker&Humblot 1997)

Mathieu B, 'Le respect par l'Union européenne des valeurs fondamentales de l'ordre juridique national' *Cahiers du Conseil Constitutionnel* (18) (2005)

Mayer FC, 'To Boldly Go Where No Court Has Gone Before' *German Law Journal* 21 (2020), 1116–1127

Mayer FC, 'Constitutional Comparativism in Action. The Example of General Principles of EU Law and How They Are Made—A German Perspective' *International Journal of Constitutional Law* 11 (2013), 1003–1020

Mayer FC, 'Die Rückkehr der Europäischen Verfassung?' *Zeitschrift für ausländisches öffentliches Recht und Völkerrecht* 67 (2007), 1141–1217

Mazák J and Moser MK, 'Adjudication by Reference to General Principles of EU Law: A Second Look at the Mangold Case Law' in M Adams and others (eds), *Judging Europe's Judges* (Hart 2013) 61–86

Mazzotti P and Eliantonio M, 'Transnational Judicial Review in Horizontal Composite Procedures' *European Papers* 5 (2020), 41–70

Medeiros R, 'The Primacy of European Union Law Over the Portuguese Constitution According to the Constitutional Court' *Católica Law Review* 5 (2021), 111–124

Méndez-Pinedo E, 'Une nouvelle "guerre des juges" en Europe? Analyse de la récente résistance judiciaire des cours constitutionnelles à la CJUE et au droit européen' *Revue des Affaires europénnes* (2022), 283–300

Menéndez A, 'The Guardianship of European Constitutionality: A Structural Critique of European Constitutional Review' in M Andenas, T Bekkedal, and L Pantale (eds), *The Reach of Free Movement* (Asser Press 2017) 173–204

Meng M, 'Art. 48 EUV' in H von der Groeben, J Schwarze, and A Hatje (eds), *Europäisches Unionsrecht* (7th edn, Nomos 2015)

Menzione S, 'The organization of the national judiciary: A Competence of the Member States within the Scope of EU Law' *Annuaire de droit de l'Union européenne* (2020), 361–376

Menzione S, 'Anything New under the Sun? An Exercise in Defence of the Reasoning of the CJEU in the ASJP Case' *Review of European Administrative Law* 12 (2019), 219–236

Meyer J, 'Präambel' in J Meyer and S Hölscheidt (eds), *Charta der Grundrechte der Europäischen Union* (5th edn, Nomos 2019)

Mezzetti L, 'Valori, Principî, Regole' in L Mezzetti (ed), *Principî Costituzionali* (Giappichelli 2011) 1–183

Miasik D and Szwarc M, 'Primacy and Direct Effect—Still Together' *Common Market Law Review* 58 (2021), 571–590

Miccù R, 'Il principio di omogeneità nel processo di costituzionalizzazione dell'Unione' in R Miccù and V Atripaldi (eds), *L'omogeneità costituzionale nell'Unione Europea* (Cedam 2003) 49–133

Michel S and Cofone IN, 'Credible Commitment or Paternalism? The Case of Unamendability' in R Albert and B Emrah Oder (eds), *An Unamendable Constitution?* (Springer 2018) 123–145
Miettinen S and Kettunen M, '*Travaux* to the EU Treaties: Preparatory Work as a Source of EU Law' *Cambridge Yearbook of European Legal Studies* 17 (2015), 145–167
Miglionico A and Maiani F, 'One Principle to Rule Them All? Anatomy of Mutual Trust in the Law of the Area of Freedom, Security and Justice' *Common Market Law Review* 57 (2020), 7–44
Millet FX, 'Successfully Articulating National Constitutional Identity Claims: Strait Is the Gate and Narrow Is the Way' *European Public Law* 27 (2021), 571–596
Millet FX, 'Plaider l'identité constitutionnelle de l'État devant la Cour de justice' *Quaderni costituzionali* 38 (2018), 831–853
Millet FX, *L'Union européenne et l'identité constitutionnelle des États membres* (LGDJ 2013)
Millns S, 'Unraveling the Ties That Bind: National Constitutions in the Light of the Values, Principles and Objectives of the Constitution for Europe' in J Ziller (ed), *L'européanisation des droits constitutionnels à la lumière de la constitution pour l'Europe* (Harmattan 2003) 97–120
Mitsilegas V, 'Autonomous Concepts, Diversity Management and Mutual Trust in Europe's Area of Criminal Justice' *Common Market Law Review* 57 (2020), 45–78
Modugno F, 'Divagazioni su "principi" e "valori"' in *Scritti in onore di Antonio D'Atena III* (Giuffrè 2015) 1995–2071
Molinier J, *Les principes fondateurs de l'Union européenne* (Presses Universitaires de France 2005)
Möllers C, *The European Union as a Democratic Federation* (Bittner 2018)
Möllers C, 'Scope and Legitimacy of Judicial Review' in H Pünder and C Waldhoff (eds), *Debates in German Public Law* (Hart 2014) 3–25
Möllers C, *The Three Branches* (OUP 2013)
Möllers C, 'Pouvoir constituant—constitution—constitutionalization' in A von Bogdandy and J Bast (eds), *Principles of European Constitutional Law* (2nd edn, Hart 2009) 169–204
Möllers C, 'The Politics of Law and the Law of Politics' in EO Eriksen, JE Fossum, and AJ Menéndez (eds), *Developing a Constitution for Europe* (Routledge 2004) 131–141
Möllers C and Schneider L, *Demokratiesicherung in der Europäischen Union* (Mohr Siebeck 2018)
Möllers T, *Legal Methods* (Hart 2020)
Monjal PY, 'Le projet de traité établissant une Constitution pour l'Europe' *Revue trimestrielle de droit européen* (2004), 443–475
Monjal PY, 'Le traité d'Amsterdam et la procedure en contestation politique de manquement aux principes de l'Union' *Revue du marché unique européen* (1998), 69–84
Montaldo S, Costamagna F, and Miglio A (eds), *EU Law Enforcement. The Evolution of Sanctioning Powers* (Routledge 2021)
de Secondat Baron Montesqieu C, *Esprit des Lois* (Garnier 1777)
Morijn J, 'Separate Charter invocation as a new enforcement method: The Lex NGO case' *Common Market Law Review* 59 (2022), 1137–1168
Mortati C, 'La Costituente' in *Raccolta di Scritti I: Studi sul potere costituente e sulla riforma costituzionale dello stato* (Giuffrè 1972) 3–347
Mortati C, 'Studi sulla costituzione e sulla revisione costituzionale' in *Raccolta di Scritti II: Scritti sulle fonti del diritto e sull'interpretazione* (Giuffrè 1972) 3–277
Möstl M, 'Regelungsfelder der Verfassung' in O Depenheuer and C Grabenwarter (eds), *Verfassungstheorie* (Mohr Siebeck 2011) § 11, pp 569–597

Mouffe C, *The Democratic Paradox* (Verso 2000)
Muir E, *EU Equality Law. The First Fundamental Rights Policy of the EU* (OUP 2019)
Müller F and Christensen R, *Juristische Methodik, Vol. II: Europarecht* (3rd edn, Duncker&Humblot 2012)
Müller JW, 'Should the EU Protect Democracy and the Rule of Law Inside Member States?' *European Law Journal* 21 (2015), 141–160
Müller-Graff PC, 'Europäisches Wirtschaftsordnungsrecht: Das System' in PC Müller-Graff (ed), *Europäisches Binnenmarkt- und Wirtschaftsordnungsrecht, Enzyklopädie Europarecht*, vol 4 (Nomos 2020) § 1, pp 53–128
Murray JL, 'Consensus: Concordance, or Hegemony of The Majority?' in *Dialogue between Judges* (Council of Europe 2008) 17–31
Muszyński J, 'Comparative Legal Argument in the Polish Discussion on Changes in the Judiciary' *Jahrbuch des öffentlichen Rechts der Gegenwart* 68 (2020), 705–720
Neill P, *The European Court of Justice: A Case Study in Judicial Activism* (European Policy Forum 1995)
Nettesheim M, 'Die "Werte der Union": Legitimitätsstiftung, Einheitsbildung, Föderalisierung' *Europarecht* 57 (2022), 525–46
Nettesheim M, 'Art. 10 EUV' in E Grabitz, M Hilf, and M Nettesheim (eds), *Das Recht der Europäischen Union* (75th edn, loose-leaf, C.H.Beck 2022)
Nettesheim M, 'Kompetenzkonflikte zwischen EuGH und Mitgliedstaaten' *Zeitschrift für Rechtspolitik* 54 (2021), 222–226
Nettesheim M, 'Normenhierarchien im EU-Recht' *Europarecht* 41 (2006), 737–772
Neyer J, *The Justification of Europe* (OUP 2012)
Ni Chaoimh E, *The Legislative Priority Rule and the EU Internal Market for Goods. A Constitutional Approach* (OUP 2022)
Nic Shuibhne N, 'The Social Market Economy and Restriction of Free Movement Rights: *plus c'est la même chose?*' *Journal of Common Market Studies* 57 (2019), 111–126
Nic Shuibhne N, 'Fundamental Rights and the Framework of Internal Market Adjudication: Is the Charter Making a Difference?' in P Koutrakos and J Snell (eds), *Research Handbook on the Law of the EU's Internal Market* (Elgar 2017) 215–238
Nic Shuibhne N, 'Free Movement of Persons and the Wholly Internal Rule: Time to Move On?' *Common Market Law Review* 39 (2002), 731–771
Nicolosi SF, 'The Contribution of the Court of Justice to the Codification of the Founding Values of the European Union' *Revista de Derecho Comunitario Europeo* 19 (2015), 613–643
Niedobitek M, 'Vertragliche Grundlagen, rechtliche Gestalt, Institutionen der Union' in M Niedobitek (ed), *Europarecht* (2nd edn, de Gruyter 2020) § 1, pp 3–203
Niedobitek M, 'Right and Duty to Pursue The "Wrongdoer" And a Possible Abuse of Art. 7 TEU' in A Hatje and L Tichý (eds), *Liability of Member States for the Violation of Fundamental Values, Europarecht Beiheft 1/2018* (Nomos 2018) 233–242
Ninatti S and Pollicino O, 'Identità costituzionale e (speciale) responsabilità delle Corti' *Quaderni Costituzionali* 40 (2020), 191–197
Nollkaemper A, 'The Duality of Shared Responsibility' *Contemporary Politics* 24 (2018) 524–544
Nowag J, 'EU Law, Constitutional Identity, and Human Dignity: A Toxic Mix?' *Common Market Law Review* 53 (2016), 1441–1454
Nußberger A, 'Gefahr für das europäische Erbe' *Internationale Politik Special* (4) (2022), 4–9
Nußberger A, 'La prise en compte de la Charte des droits fondamentaux de l'Union par la Cour européenne des droits de l'homme' in A Iliopoulou-Penot and L Xenou (eds), *La*

Charte des droits fondamentaux, source de renouveau constitutionnel européen? (Bruylant 2020) 69–76

Ohler C, 'Art. 48 EUV' in E Grabitz, M Hilf, and M Nettesheim (eds), *Das Recht der Europäischen Union* (75th edn, loose-leaf, C.H.Beck 2022)

O'Brien C, 'Civis capitalist sum: Class as the New Guiding Principle of EU Free Movement Rights' *Common Market Law Review* 53 (2016), 937–977

O'Leary S, 'Courts, Charters and Conventions: Making Sense of Fundamental Rights in the EU' *Irish Jurist* 56 (2016), 4–41

O'Neill R, 'Effet utile and the (Re)Organisation of National Judiciaries: A Not So Unique Institutional Response to a Uniquely Important Challenge?' *European Law Journal* 27 (2021), 240–261

Ondoua A, 'L'influence de la Cour dans l'elaboration des traités européens' in A Vauchez and P Mbongo (eds), *Dans la fabrique du droit européen* (Bruylant 2009) 199–215

Oppermann T, Classen CD, and Nettesheim M, *Europarecht* (9th edn, C.H. Beck 2021)

Ovádek M, 'The Making of Landmark Rulings in the European Union: The Case of National Judicial Independence' *Journal of European Public Policy* (2023) (forthcoming)

Ovádek M, 'Supranationalism, Constrained? Locating the Court of Justice on the EU integration dimension' *European Union Politics* 22 (2020), 46–69

Ovádek M, 'Has the CJEU Just Reconfigured the EU Constitutional Order?' *Verfassungsblog* (28 February 2018)

Ovádek M, Wijtvliet W, and Glavina M, 'Which Courts Matter Most? Measuring Importance in the EU Preliminary Reference System' *European Journal of Legal Studies* 12 (2020), 121–155

Palermo F, 'Annäherungen an den "Verfassungskern" der Europäischen Union. Die Homogenitäts- und Integrationsklauseln im integrierten Verfassungsrecht des Europäischen Verfassunsgsraumes' in K Weber and N Wimmer (eds), *Vom Verfassungsstaat am Scheideweg. Festschrift für Peter Pernthaler* (Springer 2005) 295–318

Palermo F, 'La prescrittività circolare dell'assetto ideologico. Le clausole di omogeneità e integrazione' in F Palermoand R Toniatti (eds), *Il processo di costituzionalizzazione dell'Unione europea* (Univ. Trento 2004) 115–177

Palermo F and Kössler K, *Comparative Federalism* (Hart 2017)

Paris D and Bifulco, Raffaele, 'The Italian Constitutional Court' in A von Bogdandy, C Grabenwarter, and PM Huber (eds), *The Max Planck Handbooks in European Public Law*, vol 3 (OUP 2020) § 9

Paris D, 'Carrot and Stick. The Italian Constitutional Court's Preliminary Reference in the Case Taricco' *Questions of International Law* 37 (2017), 5–20

Paris D, 'Constitutional Courts as European Union courts: The current and Potential Use of EU Law as a Yardstick for Constitutional Review' *Maastricht Journal of European and Comparative Law* 24 (2017), 792–821

Parodi M, 'Il ruolo degli Stati membri nella tutela dei valori dell'Unione europea: il ricorso agli strumenti giurisdizionali' *Diritti umani e diritto internazionale* (2021), 671–697

Passchier R and Stremler M, 'Unconstitutional Constitutional Amendments in European Union Law' *Cambridge Journal of International and Comparative Law* 5 (2016), 337–362

Passos R, 'Le système juridictionnel de l'Union' in G Amato, H Bribosia, and B de Witte (eds), *Genèse et destinée de la constitution européenne* (Bruylant 2007) 565–598

Patberg M, *Constituent Power in the European Union* (OUP 2020)

Patberg M, 'A Systematic Justification for The EU's *Pouvoir Constituant Mixte*: Principles of Constitutional Politics in Supranational Polities' *European Law Journal* 23 (2017), 441–453

Patberg M, 'Constituent Power' *Constellations* 24 (2017), 51–62
Patel KK, *Project Europe* (CUP 2020)
Paunio E, *Legal Certainty in Multilingual EU Law: Language, Discourse and Reasoning at the European Court of Justice* (Routledge 2016)
Peces Barba G, *Los valores superiores* (Tecnos 1986)
Pech L, 'The Rule of Law as a Well-Established and Well-Defined Principle of EU Law' *Hague Journal on the Rule of Law* 14 (2022), 107–138
Pech L, 'The Rule of Law in the EU' in P Craig and G de Búrca (eds), *The Evolution of EU Law* (3rd edn, OUP 2021) 307–338
Pech L, 'Le remède au gouvernement des juges: le judicial self-restraint' in S Brondel, N Foulquier, and L Heuschling (eds), *Gouvernement des juges et démocratie* (Publications de la Sorbonne 2001) 63–113
Pech L and Platon S, 'Judicial Independence under Threat: The Court of Justice to the Rescue in the *ASJP* Case' *Common Market Law Review* 55 (2018), 1827–1854
Pech L, Wachowiec P, and Mazur D, 'Poland's Rule of Law Breakdown: A Five-Year Assessment of EU's (In)Action' *Hague Journal of the Rule of Law* 13 (2021), 1–43
Peczenik A, *On Law and Reason* (Springer 2008)
Peers S, 'The Future of EU Treaty Amendments' *Yearbook of European Law* 31 (2012), 17–111
Peiffert O, 'Un possible malentendu en droit de l'Union européenne: le droit subjectif comme condition de l'effet direct' *Revue trimestrielle de droit européen* 53 (2017), 665–695
Pereira Coutinho F, 'Associação Sindical dos Juízes Portugueses: judicial independence and austerity measures at the Court of Justice' *Quaderni costituzionali* 38 (2018), 510–512
Pereira Coutinho F and Piçarra N, 'Portugal: The Impact of European Integration and the Economic Crisis on the Identity of the Constitution' in A Albi and S Bardutzky (eds), *National Constitutions in European and Global Governance* (Asser Press 2019) 591–639
Perillo E, 'Le decisioni collettive dei governi degli Stati membri e il rispetto dello Stato di diritto europeo: una competenza esclusiva della Corte di giustizia?' *Il diritto dell'Unione* (2021), 519–552
Perillo E, 'La justice européenne: au nom de qui?' *Revue des affaires européennes* (2018), 319–332
Perju V, 'Identity Federalism in Europe and the United States' *Vanderbilt Journal of Transnational Law* 53 (2020), 207–273
Perju V, 'Reason and Authority in the European Court of Justice' *Virginia Journal of International Law* 49 (2009), 307–377
Pernice I, 'Europäisches und nationales Verfassungsrecht (2001)' in I Pernice (ed), *Der Europäische Verfassungsverbund* (Nomos 2020) 481–529
Pernice I, 'Theorie und Praxis des Europäischen Verfassungsverbundes (2007)' in I Pernice (ed), *Der Europäische Verfassungsverbund* (Nomos 2020) 625–662
Pernice I, 'Verfassungsverbund (2010)' in I Pernice (ed), *Der Europäische Verfassungsverbund* (Nomos 2020) 663–682
Pernice I, 'Multilevel Constitutionalism and the Treaty of Amsterdam' *Common Market Law Review* 36 (1999), 703–750
Pernice I and Mayer FC, 'La Costituzione integrata dell'Europa' in G Zagrebelsky (ed), *Diritti e Costituzione nell'Unione europea* (Laterza 2003) 43–68
Pernice I and Mayer FC, 'De la constitution composée de l'Europe' *Revue trimestrielle de droit européen* 36 (2000), 623–647
Pescatore P, 'The Doctrine of Direct Effect: An Infant Disease of Community Law (1983)' *European Law Review* 40 (2015), 135–153

Pescatore P, *Vade-mecum—Recueil de formules et de conseils pratiques à l'usage des rédacteurs* (Bruylant 2008)

Pescatore P, 'Les principes généraux du droit en tant que source du droit communautaire (1986)' in F Picod (ed), *Études de droit communautaire européen* (Bruylant 2008) 691–730

Pescatore P, 'La carence du législateur communautaire et le devoir du juge (1983)' in F Picod (ed), *Études de droit communautaire européen* (Bruylant 2008) 613–636

Pescatore P, Les objectifs de la Communauté européenne comme principes d'interprétation dans la jurisprudence de la Cour de justice (1972)' in F Picod (ed), *Études de droit communautaire européen* (Bruylant 2008) 381–420

Pescatore P, 'La Cour en tant que juridiction fédérale et constitutionnelle (1963)' in F Picod (ed), *Études de droit communautaire européen* (Bruylant 2008) 61–96

Pescatore P, 'Foreword' in T Sandalow and E Stein (eds), *Courts and Free Markets. Perspectives from the United States and Europe*, vol 1 (Clarendon 1982)

Pescatore P, 'Die Gemeinschaftsverträge als Verfassungsrecht' in WG Grewe, H Rupp, and H Schneider (eds), *Europäische Gerichtsbarkeit und nationale Verfassungsgerichtsbarkeit. Festschrift zum 70. Geburtstag von Hans Kutscher* (Nomos 1981) 319–338

Pescatore P, 'Le recours, dans la jurisprudence de la Cour de justice des Communautés européennes, à des normes déduites de la comparaison des droits des États membres' *Revue internationale de droit comparé* 32 (1980), 337–359

Pescatore P, *Introduction à la science du droit* (Centre Univ. de l'Etat, repr. 1978)

Pescatore P, *Le droit de l'intégration* (Sijthoff 1972)

Peters A, 'The Constitutionalisation of the European Union—Without the Constitutional Treaty' in S Puntscher Riekmann and W Wessels (eds), *The Making of a European Constitution* (VS Verlag 2006) 35–67

Peters A, *Elemente einer Theorie der Verfassung Europas* (Duncker&Humblot 2001)

Petersen N, *Proportionality and Judicial Activism* (CUP 2017)

Petrić D, 'Game of Courts: A Tale of Principles and Institutions' *European Law Journal* 25 (2019), 273–291

Phelan W, 'The Role of the German and Italian Constitutional Courts in the Rise of EU Human Rights Jurisprudence' *European Law Review* 46 (2021), 175–193

Phelan W, 'The Troika: The Interlocking Roles of *Commission v. Luxembourg and Belgium, Van Gend en Loos* and *Costa v. ENEL*' *European Law Journal* 21 (2015), 116–135

Phelan W, *In Place of Inter-State Retaliation: The European Union's Rejection of WTO-style Trade Sanctions and Trade Remedies* (OUP 2014)

Piazza M, *I limiti alla revisione costituzionale nell'ordinamento italiano* (Cedam 2002)

Pignarre PE, *La Cour de justice de l'Union européenne, juridiction constitutionnelle* (Bruylant 2021)

Pilette A and de Poncins E, 'Valeurs, objectives et nature de l'Union' in G Amato, H Bribosia, and B de Witte (eds), *Genèse et destinée de la constitution européenne* (Bruylant 2007) 287–310

Pinelli C, 'Theories Concerning the Hierarchy of Norms' in R Grote, F Lachenmann, and R Wolfrum (eds), *Max Planck Encyclopedia of Comparative Constitutional Law* (OUP 2016)

Pino G, 'Costituzione come limite, costituzione come fondamento, costituzione come assiologica' *Diritto e Società* (2017), 91–120

Pino G, 'La gerarchia delle fonti del diritto' *Ars interpretandi* (2011), 19–56

Piqani D, 'In Search of Limits for the Protection of National Identities as a Member State Interest' in M Varju (ed), *Between Compliance and Particularism* (Springer 2019) 21–47

Piqani D, 'The Role of National Constitutional Courts in Issues of Compliance' in M Cremona (ed), *Compliance and Enforcement of EU Law* (OUP 2012) 132–156

Piris JC, *The Constitution for Europe* (CUP 2006)

Piris JC, 'Does the European Union have a Constitution?' *European Law Review* 24 (1999), 557–585

Platon S, 'The principle of institutional balance: rise, eclipse and revival of a general principle of EU constitutional law' in KS Ziegler, PJ Neuvonen, and V Moreno-Lax (eds), *Research Handbook on General Principles in EU Law* (Elgar 2022) 136–155

Platon S, 'Preliminary References and Rule of Law: Another Case of Mixed Signals From The Court of Justice Regarding the Independence of National Courts: *Miasto Lowicz*' *Common Market Law Review* 57 (2020), 1843–1866

Platon S, 'Les fonctions du standard de l'État de droit en droit de l'Union européenne' *Revue trimestrelle de droit européen* 55 (2019), 305–320

Pohjankoski P, 'Rule of Law with Leverage: Policing Structural Obligations in EU Law with the Infringement Procedure, Fines, and Set-Off' *Common Market Law Review* 58 (2021), 1341–1364

Pokol B, *Európai jurisztokrácia: Az Európai Unió jurisztokratikus szerkezetének kérdései* (Dialóg Campus 2019)

Pokol B, 'Az uniós jurisztokrácia hatalmi szerkezete' *Jogelméleti Szemle* (4) (2018), 126–190

Pokol B, *The Juristocratic State: Its Victory and the Possibility of Taming* (Dialóg 2017)

Poli S, 'The Common Foreign Security Policy after Rosneft: Still Imperfect but Gradually Subject To The Rule Of Law' *Common Market Law Review* 54 (2017), 1799–1834

Pollack MA, 'The Legitimacy of the European Court of Justice. Normative Debates and Empirical Evidence' in N Grossman and others (eds), *Legitimacy and International Courts* (CUP 2018) 143–173

Pollicino O and Fichera M, 'The Dialectics Between Constitutional Identity and Common Constitutional Traditions' *German Law Journal* 79 (2019), 1097–1118

Polzin M, 'Emotion and the Vertical Separation of Powers: Ultra-Vires Review by National (Constitutional) Courts, and EU and International Law' *ICL Journal* 16 (2022), 285–325

Popov A, 'La complémentarité entre les recours en annulation formés par les particuliers et les renvois préjudiciels en appréciation de validité' *Cahiers de droit européen* 48 (2012), 167–194

Pörksen U, *Plastic Words: The Tyranny of a Modular Language* (Penn. State Univ. Press 2004)

Poscher R, 'Theory of a Phantom: The Principles Theory's Futile Quest for its Object' in SL Paulson and others (eds), *Alexy's Theory of Law, Archives for Philosophy of Law and Social Philosophy, Sup. 144* (Steiner 2015) 129–148

Poscher R, 'Ambiguity and Vagueness in Legal Interpretation' in L Solan and P Tiersma (eds), *Oxford Handbook on Language and Law* (OUP 2011) 128–144

Poscher R, 'The Hand of Midas' in J Hage and D von der Pfordten (eds), *Concepts in Law* (Springer 2009) 99–116

Poscher R, 'Insights, Errors and Self-Misconceptions of the Theory of Principles' *Ratio Juris* 22 (2009), 425–454

Potacs M, 'Wertkonforme Auslegung des Unionsrechts' *Europarecht* 51 (2016), 164–176

Poulou A, 'Human Rights Obligations of European Financial Assistance Mechanisms' in A Poulou and U Becker (eds), *European Welfare State Constitutions after the Financial Crisis* (OUP 2020) 24–48

Pound R, 'Mechanical Jurisprudence' *Columbia Law Review* 8 (1908), 605–623

Prechal S, 'Effective Judicial Protection: Some Recent Developments' *Review of European Administrative Law* 13 (2020), 175–190

Prechal S, *Directives in E.C. Law* (2nd edn, OUP 2005)

Prete L, 'Infringement Procedures and Sanctions under Article 260 TFEU' in S Montaldo, F Costamagna, and A Miglio (eds), *EU Law Enforcement* (Routledge 2021) 71–92
Prete L, *Infringement Proceedings in EU Law* (Kluwer Law International 2017)
Prete L and Smulders B, 'The Coming of Age of Infringement Proceedings' *Common Market Law Review* 47 (2010), 9–61
Preuß UK, 'Is There a Constituent Power in the European Union?' in O Cayla and P Pasquino (eds), *Le pouvoir constituant et l'Europe* (Dalloz 2011) 75–92
Quermonne JL, 'Le traité constitutionnel européen est-il un acte refondateur?' *Politique étrangère* 70 (2005), 245–256
Ragone S, 'El control material de las reformas constitucionales en perspectiva comparada' *Teoría y Realidad Constitucional* 31 (2013), 391–406
Rasmussen H, *On Law and Policy in the European Court of Justice* (Brill 1986)
Raz J, *The Authority of Law* (2nd edn, Clarendon 2009)
Raz J, 'On the Authority and Interpretation of Constitutions: Some Preliminaries' in L Alexander (ed), *Constitutionalism* (CUP 2001) 152–193
Regan E, 'The Role of the Principles of Mutual Trust and Mutual Recognition in EU Law' *Il diritto dell'Unione europea* (2018), 231–247
Regan E, 'Are EU Sanctions Against Austria Legal?' *Zeitschrift für öffentliches Recht* 55 (2000), 323–336
Reimer F, *Verfassungsprinzipien* (Duncker&Humblot 2001)
Reuter P, *Introduction au droit des traités* (3rd edn, Presses Universitaires de France 1995)
Reynolds S, 'Explaining the Constitutional Drivers Behind a Perceived Judicial Preference for Free Movement Over Fundamental Rights' *Common Market Law Review* 53 (2016), 643–677
Reyns C, 'Saving Judicial Independence: A Threat to the Preliminary Ruling Mechanism?' *European Constitutional Law Review* 17 (2021), 26–52
Richard A, *Procédure en manquement d'État et protection des droits fondamentaux dans l'Union européenne* (Bruylant 2021)
Ritleng D, 'The Independence and Legitimacy of the European Court of Justice' in D Ritleng (ed), *Independence and Legitimacy in the Institutional System of the European Union* (OUP 2016) 83–124
Rivero J, 'Le problème de l'influence des droits internes sur la Cour de Justice de la CECA' *Annuaire français de droit international* 4 (1958), 295–308
Rivers J, 'Proportionality and Variable Intensity of Review' *Cambridge Law Journal* 65 (2006), 180–207
Rizcallah C, *Le principe de confiance mutuelle en droit de l'Union européenne* (Bruylant 2020)
Rizcallah C, 'The Challenges to Trust-Based Governance in the European Union' *European Law Journal* 25 (2019), 37–56
Rodríguez Iglesias GC, 'Der Gerichtshof der Europäischen Gemeinschaften als Verfassungsgericht' *Europarecht* 27 (1992), 225–245
Röhl KF and Röhl HC, *Allgemeine Rechtslehre* (3rd edn, Vahlen 2008)
Rojas D, *L'utilisation de la notion d'identité constitutionnelle. Recherche axée sur les acteurs de la mobilisation de l'identité constitutionnelle nationale dans l'Union européenne* (Institut francophone pour la justice et la démocratie 2021)
Röthel A and Möslein F, 'Concretisation of General Clauses' in K Riesenhuber (ed), *European Legal Methodology* (2nd edn, Intersentia 2017) § 11, pp 283–312
Rötting M, *Das verfassungsrechtliche Beitrittsverfahren zur Europäischen Union* (Springer 2009)
Rosanvallon P, *Democratic Legitimacy* (Princeton Univ. Press 2011)
Rosas A and Armati L, *EU Constitutional Law* (3rd edn, Hart 2018)

Rosen M, *Dignity* (Harvard Univ. Press 2012)
Rosenfeld M, 'Constitutional Identity' in M Rosenfeld and A Sajó (eds), *The Oxford Handbook of Comparative Constitutional Law* (OUP 2012) 756–775
Rossi LS, 'La valeur juridique des valeurs. L'article 2 TUE: relations avec d'autres dispositions de droit primaire de l'UE et remèdes juridictionnels' *Revue trimestrielle de droit européen* (2020), 639–657
Rossi LS, 'Autonomie constitutionnelle de l'Union européenne, droits fondamentaux et méthodes d'intégration des valeurs "externs"' in A Iliopoulou-Penot and L Xenou (eds), *La Charte des droits fondamentaux, source de renouveau constitutionnel européen?* (Bruylant 2020) 53–68
Rossi LS, '2, 4, 6 (TUE) … l'interpretazione dell'"Identity Clause" alla luce dei valori fondamentali dell'Unione' in *Liber Amicorum Antonio Tizzano. De la Cour CECA à la Cour de l'Union: le long parcours de la justice européenne* (Giappichelli 2018) 858–870
Rossi LS, 'M.A.S. e M.B. e la torre di Babele: alla fine le Corti si comprendono ... pur parlando lingue diverse' in C Amalfitano (ed), *Primato del Diritto dell'Unione Europea e Controlimiti alla Prova della "Saga Taricco"* (Giuffrè 2018) 153–168
Rossi LS, 'Fundamental Values, Principles, and Rights After the Treaty of Lisbon: The Long Journey Toward a European Constitutional Identity' in F Berrod and others (eds), *Europe(s), Droit(s) européen(s). Une passion d'universitaire. Liber amicorum en l'honneur du professeur Vlad Constantinesco* (Bruylant 2015) 511–524
Rossi LS, 'La "reazione commune" degli Stati membri dell'Unione europea nel caso Haider' *Rivista di diritto internazionale* (2000), 151–154
Roth WU, 'Verfassung und europäische Methodenlehre' *Rabel Journal of Comparative and International Private Law* 75 (2011), 787–844
Rozakis CL, 'Through the Looking Glass: An "Insider's" view of the Margin of Appreciation' in *La conscience des droits. Mélanges en l'honneur de Jean-Paul Costa* (Dalloz 2011) 527–537
Roznai Y, 'Necrocracy or Democracy? Assessing Objections to Constitutional Unamendability' in R Albert and B Emrah Oder (eds), *An Unamendable Constitution?* (Springer 2018) 29–61
Roznai Y, *Unconstitutional Constitutional Amendments* (OUP 2017)
Roznai Y, 'Legisprudence Limitations on Constitutional Amendments? Reflections on The Czech Constitutional Court's Declaration of Unconstitutional Constitutional Act' *ICL Journal* 8 (2014), 29–57
Roznai Y, 'Unconstitutional Constitutional Amendments—The Migration and Success of a Constitutional Idea' *American Journal of Constitutional Law* 61 (2013), 657–719
Ruffert M, 'Art. 10 EUV' in M Ruffert and C Calliess (eds), *EUV/AEUV* (6th edn, C.H.Beck 2022)
Ruffert M, 'Art. 288 AEUV' in M Ruffert and C Calliess (eds), EUV/AEUV (6th edn, C.H.Beck 2022)
Ruffert M, 'Art. 15 GRC' in M Ruffert and C Calliess (eds), *EUV/AEUV* (6th edn, C.H.Beck 2022)
Ruffert M, 'Eine Binnenperspektive auf die deutsche Europarechtswissenschaft' *Jahrbuch des öffentlichen Rechts der Gegenwart* 68 (2020), 515–525
Ruggeri A, 'Valori e principi costituzionali degli Stati integrati d'Europa' *Teoria del diritto dello Stato* (2009), 292–330
Ruiz Fabri H, 'Principes généraux du droit communautaire et droit comparé' *Droits* 45 (2007), 127–142
Saccia G, 'Cortes supranacionales de justicia y activismo judicial' *Teoría y Realidad Constitucional* 44 (2019), 177–207

Šadl U and Bengoetxea J, 'Theorising General Principles of EU Law in Perspective' in S Vogenauer and S Weatherill (eds), *General Principles of Law* (Hart 2017) 41–52

Sadurski W, *Poland's Constitutional Breakdown* (OUP 2019)

Sadurski W, 'Polish Constitutional Tribunal Under PiS' *Hague Journal on the Rule of Law* 11 (2018), 63–84

Sadurski W, *Constitutionalism and the Enlargement of Europe* (OUP 2012)

Safjan M, 'L´identité constitutionnelle polonaise' *Revista de Derecho Comunitario Europeo* (72) (2022), 371–391

Safjan M, 'On Symmetry: in Search of an Appropriate Response to the Crisis of the Democratic State' *Il diritto dell'Unione europea* (2020), 673–699

Safjan M, 'Prawo do skutecznej ochrony sądowej—refleksje dotyczące wyroku TSUE z 19.11.2019 r. w sprawach połączonych C-585/18, C-624/18, C-625/18' *Palestra* (5) (2020), 5–29

Safjan M, 'The Rule of Law and the Future of Europe' *Il diritto dell'Unione europea* (2019), 425–440

Safjan M, 'Domestic Infringements of the Rule of Law as a European Union Problem' *Osteuropa Recht* (2019), 552–560

Saiz Arnaiz A, 'Tribunal Europeo de Derechos Humanos y procesos políticos nacionales: democracia convencional y margen de apreciación' *Teoría y Realidad Constitucional* 42 (2018), 221–245

Sanfilippo Z, 'United, We Stand: Expelling Autocratic States from the European Union' *Duke Law Journal* 72 (2022), 675–722

Sarmiento D, 'The Juncker Presidency—A Study in Character' *European Journal of International Law* 31 (2020), 727–735

Sarmiento D, 'The Essential Content of EU Fundamental Rights' *Quaderni costituzionali* (2020), 851–854

Sarmiento D, 'Adults in the (Deliberation) Room. A Comment on M.A.S.' *Quaderni Costituzionali* 38 (2018), 228–231

Sarmiento D, 'Who's Afraid of the Charter? The Court of Justice, National Courts and the New Framework of Fundamental Rights Protection in Europe' *Common Market Law Review* 50 (2013), 1267–1304

Sarmiento D, 'The EU's Constitutional Core' in A Saiz Arnaiz and C Alcoberro Llivina (eds), *National constitutional identity and European integration* (Intersentia 2013) 177–204

Sarmiento D, 'Half a Case at a Time: Dealing with Judicial Minimalism at the European Court of Justice' in M Claes and others (eds), *Constitutional Conversations in Europe* (Intersentia 2012) 13–40

Saul M, 'The European Court of Human Rights' Margin of Appreciation and the Processes of National Parliaments' *Human Rights Law Review* 15 (2015), 745–774

Scarcello O, *Radical Constitutional Pluralism in Europe* (Routledge 2023)

Scarcello O, 'Preserving the "Essence" of Fundamental Rights under Article 52(1) of the Charter' *European Constitutional Law Review* 16 (2021), 647–668

Scarcello O, 'On the Role of Normative Hierarchies in Constitutional Reasoning' *Ratio Juris* 31 (2018), 346–636

Scharpf FW, 'De-Constitutionalization and Majority Rule: A Democratic Vision for Europe' *European Law Journal* 23 (2017), 315–334

Scharpf FW, 'De-Constitutionalisation of European Law: The Re-Empowerment of Democratic Political Choice' in S Garben and I Govaere (eds), *The Division of Competences between the EU and the Member States* (Hart 2017) 284–299

Scharpf FW, 'Legitimacy in the Multilevel European Polity' *European Political Science Review* 1 (2009), 173–204
Scheid C, 'Demokratieimmanente Legitimation der Verfassungsgerichtsbarkeit' *Der Staat* 59 (2020), 227–275
Scheppele KL, 'How Viktor Orbán Wins' *Journal of Democracy* 33 (2022), 45–61
Scheppele KL, 'Autocratic Legalism' *University of Chicago Law Review* 85 (2018), 545–583
Scheppele KL, 'Enforcing the Basic Principles of EU Law through Systemic Infringement Actions' in C Closa and D Kochenov (eds), *Reinforcing Rule of Law Oversight in the European Union* (CUP 2016) 105–132
Scheppele KL, Kochenov D, and Grabowska-Moroz B, 'EU Values Are Law, after All: Enforcing EU Values through Systemic Infringement Actions by the European Commission and the Member States of the European Union' *Yearbook of European Law* 38 (2020), 3–121
Schermers HG and Blokker NM, *International Institutional Law* (6th edn, Nijhoff 2018)
Schiek D and others, *EU Social and Labour Rights and EU Internal Market Law* (European Parliament, EMPL, 2015)
Schima B, 'Article 258 TFEU' in M Kellerbauer, M Klamert, and J Tomkin (eds), *The Treaties and the Charter of Fundamental Rights—A Commentary* (OUP 2019)
Schima B, 'Article 260 TFEU' in M Kellerbauer, M Klamert, and J Tomkin (eds), *The Treaties and the Charter of Fundamental Rights—A Commentary* (OUP 2019)
Schill S and Krenn C, 'Art. 4 EUV' in E Grabitz, M Hilf, and M Nettesheim (eds), *Das Recht der Europäischen Union* (75th edn, loose-leaf, C.H. Beck 2022)
Schlag P, 'Values' *Yale Journal of Law and the Humanities* 6 (1994), 219–232
Schlink B, 'Proportionality in Constitutional Law: Why Everywhere but Here' *Duke Journal of Comparative and International Law* 22 (2012), 291–302
Schlink B, 'Proportionality' in M Rosenfeld and A Sajó (eds), *The Oxford Handbook of Comparative Constitutional Law* (OUP 2012) 719–736
Schlink B, 'The Dynamics of Constitutional Adjudication' *Cardozo Law Review* 17 (1996), 1231–1238
Schmidt M, *Verfassungsaufsicht in der Europäischen Union* (Nomos 2021)
Schmidt M and Bogdanowicz P, 'The Infringement Procedure in the Rule of Law Crisis' *Common Market Law Review* 55 (2018), 1061–1100
Schmidt SK, *The European Court of Justice and the Policy Process* (OUP 2018)
Schmidt SK, 'Mutual Recognition as a New Mode of Governance' *Journal of European Public Policy* 14 (2007), 667–681
Schmidt-Aßmann E, 'Einheit und Kohärenz der europäischen Mehrebenenrechtsordnung' *Europäische Grundrechte-Zeitschrift* 43 (2016), 85–92
Schmidt-Aßmann E, 'Introduction: European Composite Administration and the Role of European Administrative Law' in O Jansen and B Schöndorf-Haubold (eds), *The European composite administration* (Intersentia 2011) 1–23
Schmitt C, *Tyrannei der Werte* (3rd edn, Duncker&Humblot 2011)
Schmitt C, *Constitutional Theory*, trans. Jeffrey Seitzer (Duke Univ. Press 2008)
Schnädelbach H, *Philosophy in Germany 1831–1933* (CUP 1984, repr. 2013)
Schnettger A, *Verbundidentität. Schutzgehalt, Funktionen und gerichtliche Durchsetzung des Art. 4 Abs. 2 S. 1 Var. 2 EUV* (Mohr Siebeck 2020)
Schnettger A, 'Article 4(2) TEU as a Vehicle for National Constitutional Identity in the Shared European Legal System' in C Calliess and G van der Schyff (eds), *Constitutional Identity in a Europe of Multilevel Constitutionalism* (CUP 2019) 9–38

Scholtes J, 'Constitutionalising the End of History? Pitfalls of a Non-Regression Principle for Article 2 TEU' *European Constitutional Law Review* 19 (2023), 59–87
Scholtes J, 'Abusing Constitutional Identity' *German Law Journal* 22 (2021), 534–556
Schönberger C, *Der "German Approach"* (Mohr Siebeck 2016)
Schönberger C, '"Mi attendu, mi dissertation." Le style des décisions de la Cour de justice de l'Union européenne' *Droit et Société* 91 (2015), 505–519
Schönberger C, 'Identitäterä: Verfassungsidentität zwischen Widerstandsformel und Musealisierung des Grundgesetzes' *Jahrbuch des öffentlichen Rechts der Gegenwart* 63 (2015), 41–62
Schönberger C, 'Die Europäische Union als Bund' *Archiv des öffentlichen Rechts* 124 (2004), 81–120
Schönlau J, 'New Values for Europe?' in EO Eriksen, JE Fossum, and AJ Menéndez (eds), *The Chartering of Europe* (Nomos 2003) 112–132
Schorkopf F, 'Art. 23 GG' in W Kahl, C Waldhoff, and C Walter (eds), *Bonner Kommentar zum Grundgesetz* (211th edn, loose-leaf, C.F. Müller 2021)
Schorkopf F, 'Der Wertekonstitutionalismus der Europäischen Union' *JuristenZeitung* 75 (2020), 477–485
Schorkopf F, 'Europäischer Konstitutionalismus oder die normative Behauptung des "European way of life". Potenziale der neueren Werterechtsprechung des EuGH' *Neue Juristische Wochenschrift* 72 (2019), 3418–3423
Schorkopf F, 'Gesetzgebung durch Höchstgerichte und Parlamente' *Archiv des öffentlichen Rechts* 144 (2019), 202–233
Schorkopf F, *Die Maßnahmen der XIV EU-Mitgliedstaaten gegen Österreich* (Springer 2002)
Schorkopf F, *Homogenität in der Europäischen Union: Ausgestaltung und Gewährleistung durch Art. 6 Abs. 1 und Art. 7 EUV* (Duncker&Humblot 2000)
Schroeder W, 'An Active EU Rule of Law Policy' in A Rosas, J Raitio, and P Pohjankoski (eds), *The Rule of Law's Anatomy in the EU* (Hart 2023)
Schroeder W, 'The Rule of Law as a Value in the Sense of Article 2 TEU: What Does It Mean and Imply?' in A von Bogdandy and others (eds), *Defending Checks and Balances in EU Member States* (Springer 2021) 105–126
Schroeder W (ed), *Strengthening the Rule of Law in Europe* (Hart 2016)
Schroeder W, *Gemeinschaftsrechtssystem* (Mohr Siebeck 2002)
Schulte H, *Zur Übertragbarkeit der Margin-of-appreciation-Doktrin des EGMR auf die Rechtsprechung des EuGH im Bereich der Grundfreiheiten* (Nomos 2018)
Schuppert GF and Bumke C, *Die Konstitutionalisierung der Rechtsordnung* (Nomos 2000)
Schuster U, *Das Kohärenzprinzip in der Europäischen Union* (Nomos 2017)
de Schutter O and Alston P, 'Introduction: Addressing the Challenges Confronting the EU Fundamental Rights Agency' in O de Schutter and P Alston (eds), *Monitoring Fundamental Rights in the EU* (Hart 2005) 1–22
Schütze R, *European Constitutional Law* (3rd edn, OUP 2021)
Schütze R, 'Constitutionalism(s)' in R Schütze and R Masterman (eds), *The Cambridge Companion to Comparative Constitutional Law* (CUP 2019) 40–66
Schütze R, 'Direct and Indirect Effects of Union Law' in R Schütze and T Tridimas (eds), *Oxford Principles of EU Law*, vol 1 (OUP 2018) 265–299
Schütze R, *From Dual to Cooperative Federalism* (OUP 2009)
Schütze R, 'The Morphology of Legislative Power in the European Community' *Yearbook of European Law* 25 (2006), 91–151
Schwarz M, 'Let's Talk About Trust, Baby! Theorizing Trust and Mutual Recognition in the EU's Area of Freedom, Security and Justice' *European Law Journal* 24 (2018), 124–141

Schwarze J, 'Balancing EU Integration and National Interests in the Case-Law of the Court of Justice' in A Rosas, E Levits, and Y Bot (eds), *The Court of Justice and the Construction of Europe* (Asser Press 2013) 257–278

Semmelmann C, 'General Principles of EU Law. The Ghost in the Platonic Heaven in Need of Conceptual Clarification' *Pittsburgh Papers on the European Union* 2 (2013), 1–30

Shapiro MM, 'Judicial Power and Democracy' in C Landfried (ed), *Judicial Power* (CUP 2019) 21–35

Sharpston E, 'Legislating and Adjudicating' in E Fisher, J King, and A Young (eds), *The Foundations and Future of Public Law. Essays in Honour of Paul Craig* (OUP 2020) 173–191

Sharpston E, 'Transparency and Clear Legal Language in the European Union. Ambiguous Legislative Texts, Laconic Pronouncements and the Credibility of the Judicial System' *Cambridge Yearbook of European Legal Studies* 12 (2009), 409–423

Sichert M, *Grenzen der Revision des Primärrechts in der Europäischen Union* (Duncker&Humblot 2005)

von Simson W, 'Der Gerichtshof und unbestimmte Rechtsbegriffe' in *Zehn Jahre Rechtsprechung des Gerichtshofs der Europäischen Gemeinschaften* (Heymanns 1965) 396–417

Sindbjerg Martinsen R and Blauberger M, 'The Court of Justice of the European Union and the Mega-Politics of Posted Workers' *Law & Contemporary Problems* 84 (2022), 29–57

Sindbjerg Martinsen D, *An Ever More Powerful Court?* (OUP 2016)

Skordas A and Spieker LD, 'Supranational Law' in A Peters (ed), *Max Planck Encyclopedia of Public International Law* (OUP 2021)

Skouris V, 'Der Vorrang des Europäischen Unionsrechts vor dem nationalen Recht. Unionsrecht bricht nationales Recht' *Europarecht* 56 (2021), 3–28

Skouris V, *Demokratie und Rechtsstaat. Europäische Union in der Krise?* (C.H.Beck 2018)

Skouris V, 'Erwartungen der gerichtlichen Praxis and die Wissenschaft des Europarechts' in A Hatje, PC Müller-Graff, and JP Terhechte (eds), *Europarechtswissenschaft, Europarecht Beiheft 2/2018* (Nomos 2018) 149–156

Skouris V, 'L'identité nationale: qui détermine son contenu et selon quels critères?' in *Liber Amicorum Antonio Tizzano. De la Cour CECA à la Cour de l'Union: le long parcours de la justice européenne* (Giappichelli 2018) 912–924

Skouris V, 'Fundamental Rights and Fundamental Freedoms: The Challenge of Striking a Delicate Balance' *European Business Law Review* 17 (2006), 225–239

Skouris V, 'Das Verhältnis von Grundfreiheiten und Grundrechten im europäischen Gemeinschaftsrecht' *Die Öffentliche Verwaltung* 59 (2006), 89–97

Śledzińska-Simon A and Ziółkowski M, 'Constitutional Identity in Poland' in C Calliess and G van der Schyff (eds), *Constitutional Identity in a Europe of Multilevel Constitutionalism* (CUP 2019) 243–267

Smulders B, 'Increasing Convergence between the European Court of Human Rights and the Court of Justice of the European Union in Their Recent Case Law on Judicial Independence: The Case of Irregular Judicial Appointments' *Common Market Law Review* 59 (2022), 105–128

Solum LB, 'Indeterminacy' in D Patterson (ed), *A Companion to Philosophy of Law and Legal Theory* (2nd edn, Wiley 2010) 479–492

Somek A, 'The Darling Dogma of Bourgeois Europeanists' *European Law Journal* 20 (2014), 688–712

Somek A, 'Constituent Power in National and Transnational Contexts' *Transnational Legal Theory* 3 (2012), 31–60

Somek A, 'The Argument from Transnational Effects I' *European Law Journal* 16 (2010), 315–344

Sommermann KP, 'Die gemeinsamen Werte der Union und der Mitgliedstaaten' in M Niedobitek (ed), *Europarecht* (2nd edn, de Gruyter 2019) § 3, pp 288–320

Sommermann KP, 'Art. 20 GG' in H von Mangoldt, F Klein, and C Starck (eds), *Kommentar zum Grundgesetz*, vol 2 (7th edn, C.H. Beck 2018)

Sommermann KP, 'Article 3' in HJ Blanke and S Mangiameli (eds), *The Treaty on European Union (TEU): A Commentary* (Springer 2013)

Sommermann KP, 'Herkunft und Funktion von Verfassungsprinzipien in der Europäischen Union' in H Bauer and C Calliess (eds), *Verfassungsprinzipien in Europa—Constitutional principles in Europe—Principes constitutionnels en Europe* (Sakkoulas 2008) 15–44

Sonnevend P, Jakab A, and Csink L, 'The Constitution as an Instrument of Everyday Party Politics: The Basic Law of Hungary' in A von Bogdandy and P Sonnevend (eds), *Constitutional Crisis in the European Constitutional Area* (Hart 2016) 33–109

Sørensen K, 'Reconciling Secondary Legislation with the Treaty Rights of Free Movement' *European Law Review* 36 (2011), 344–361

Spano R, 'The Rule of Law as the Lodestar of the European Convention on Human Rights: The Strasbourg Court and the Independence of the Judiciary' *European Law Journal* 27 (2021), 211–227

Spano R, 'The Future of the European Court of Human Rights Subsidiarity. Process-Based Review and the Rule of Law' *Human Rights Law Review* 18 (2018), 473–494

Spaventa E, 'Constitutional Creativity or Constitutional Deception? Acts of the Member States Acting Collectively and Jurisdiction of the Court of Justice' *Common Market Law Review* 58 (2021), 1697–1730

Spaventa E, 'Earned Citizenship' in D Kochenov (ed), *EU Citizenship and Federalism* (CUP 2017) 204–225

Spaventa E, *The Interpretation of Article 51 of the EU Charter of Fundamental Rights* (European Parliament, PETI-Committee, 2016)

Spaventa E, 'Federalisation versus Centralization: Tensions in Fundamental Rights Discourse in the EU' in M Dougan and S Currie (eds), *50 Years of the European Treaties* (Hart 2010) 343–364

Spielmann D, 'The Rule of Law Principle in the Jurisprudence of the Court of Justice of the European Union' in M Elósegui, A Miron, and I Motoc (eds), *The Rule of Law in Europe* (Springer 2021) 3–20

Spielmann D, 'Allowing the Right Margin: The European Court of Human Rights and The National Margin of Appreciation Doctrine: Waiver or Subsidiarity of European Review?' *Cambridge Yearbook of European Legal Studies* 14 (2012), 381–418

Spieker LD, 'The Conflict Over the Polish Disciplinary Regime for Judges—An Acid Test for Judicial Independence, Union Values and the Primacy of EU Law' *Common Market Law Review* 59 (2022), 777–812

Spieker LD, 'Werte, Vorrang, Identität: Der Dreiklang europäischer Justizkonflikte vor dem EuGH' *Europäische Zeitschrift für Wirtschaftsrecht* 33 (2022), 305–313

Spieker LD, 'Framing and Managing Constitutional Identity Conflicts: How to Stabilize the Modus Vivendi Between the Court of Justice and National Constitutional Courts' *Common Market Law Review* 57 (2020), 361–398

Spieker LD, 'Werteverteidigung im Binnenmarkt?' *Europäische Zeitschrift für Wirtschaftsrecht* 31 (2020), 854–858

Spieker LD, 'Breathing Life into the Union's Common Values: On the Judicial Application of Article 2 TEU in the EU Value Crisis' *German Law Journal* 20 (2019), 1182–1213

von Staden A, 'The Democratic Legitimacy of Judicial Review Beyond the State' *International Law Journal* 10 (2012), 1023–1049
Starck C, 'Idee und Struktur des Föderalismus im Lichte der Allgemeinen Staatslehre' in I Härtel (ed), *Handbuch Föderalismus*, vol 1 (Springer 2012) § 1
Starck C, 'Zur Notwendigkeit einer Wertbegründung des Rechts' in R Dreier (ed), *Rechtspositivismus und Wertbezug des Rechts, Archives for Philosophy of Law and Social Philosophy, Supp.* 37 (Steinerm 1990) 47–61
Stein E, 'Lawyers, Judges, and the Making of a Transnational Constitution' *American Journal of International Law* 75 (1981), 1–27
Steinbeis M, 'The EU has no National Guard' *Verfassungsblog* (31 January 2020)
Sterck J, 'Sameness and Selfhood: The Efficiency of Constitutional Identities in EU Law' *European Law Journal* 24 (2018), 281–296
Stolleis M, *Public Law in Germany. A Historical Introduction* (OUP 2017)
Stone Sweet A, 'The European Court of Justice' in P Craig and G de Búrca (eds), *The Evolution of EU Law* (2nd edn, OUP 2011) 121–153
Stone Sweet A, *The Judicial Construction of Europe* (OUP 2004)
Stone Sweet A and Mathews J, 'Proportionality Balancing and Global Constitutionalism' *Columbia Journal of Translational Law* 47 (2008), 78–164
Storskrubb E, 'Mutual Trust and the Dark Horse of Civil Justice' *Cambridge Yearbook of European Legal Studies* 20 (2018), 179–201
Streinz R, 'Principles and Values in the European Union' in A Hatje and L Tichý (eds), *Liability of Member States for the Violation of Fundamental Values, Europarecht Beiheft 1/2018* (Nomos 2018) 9–21
Streinz R, 'Art. 23 GG' in M Sachs (ed), *Grundgesetz* (8th edn, C.H.Beck 2018)
Stumpf C, 'Art. 6 EUV' in J Schwarze (ed), *EU-Kommentar* (2nd edn, Nomos 2009)
Šubic N, 'Resisting a European Arrest Warrant: A Social Rights Perspective' *New Journal of European Criminal Law* 11 (2020), 299–312
Sulyok T and Deli G, 'Perspektiven des Europarechts aus der Sicht des ungarischen Verfassungsgerichts' *Jahrbuch des öffentlichen Rechts der Gegenwart* 68 (2020), 721–733
Sunstein C, 'Beyond Judicial Minimalism' *Tulsa Law Review* 43 (2008), 825–842
Sunstein C, 'Incompletely Theorized Agreements in Constitutional Law' *Social Research* 74 (2007), 1–24
Sunstein C, *One Case at a Time* (Harvard Univ. Press 1999)
Sunstein C, 'Incommensurability and Valuation in Law' *Michigan Law Review* 92 (1994), 779
Suominen A, 'The Sensitive Relationship Between the Different Means of Legal Integration: Mutual Recognition and Approximation' in C Brière and A Weyembergh (eds), *The Needed Balances in EU Criminal Law* (Hart 2018) 165–184
Suteu S, *Eternity Clauses in Democratic Constitutionalism* (OUP 2021)
Sydow G, 'Die Europarechtwissenschaft europäisieren?' *Jahrbuch des öffentlichen Rechts der Gegenwart* 68 (2020), 545–559
Syrpis P, 'The Relationship Between Primary and Secondary Law in the EU' *Common Market Law Review* 52 (2015), 461–487
Szabados T, 'Conflicts Between Fundamental Freedoms and Fundamental Rights in the Case Law of the Court of Justice of the European Union' *European Papers* 3 (2018), 563–600
Terhechte JP, 'Art. 3 EUV' in E Grabitz, M Hilf, and M Nettesheim (eds), *Das Recht der Europäischen Union* (75th edn, loose-leaf, C.H.Beck 2022)
Terhechte JP, 'Prinzipienordnung der Europäischen Union' in JP Terhechte (ed), *Europäische Verfassungsstudien* (Nomos 2020) 217–260

Tesauro G, 'La sanction des infractions au droit communautaire' *Rivista di diritto europeo* (1992), 477–509

Teyssedre J, 'La judiciarisation du contrôle de l'État de droit: la Court de justice au chevet des juges nationaux' *Revue trimestrielle de droit européen* (2020), 23–52

Theilen JT, *European Consensus Between Strategy and Principle* (Nomos 2021)

Theuns T, 'The Need for an EU Expulsion Mechanism: Democratic Backsliding and the Failure of Article 7' *Res Publica* 28 (2022), 693–713

Thomas DC, 'Constitutionalization through Enlargement: The Contested Origins of the EU's Democratic Identity' *Journal of European Public Policy* 13 (2006), 1190–1210

Thornhill C, 'The European Constitution and the pouvoir constituant' in J Přibáň (ed), *Self-Constitution of European Society* (Routledge 2016) 13–36

Thym D, 'Friendly Takeover, or: the Power of the "First Word". The German Constitutional Court Embraces the Charter of Fundamental Rights as a Standard of Domestic Judicial Review' *European Constitutional Law Review* 16 (2020), 187–212

Thym D, 'The Limits of Transnational Scholarship on EU Law' EUI Working Paper LAW 2016/14, pp 1–27

Timmermans C, 'Mediating Conflicts between National Identities and EU Law: The Potential of Article 4(2) TEU' *Common Market Law Review* 59 (2022), 75–86

Timmermans C, 'The European Union's Judicial System' *Common Market Law Review* 41 (2004), 393–405

Timsit G, *Gouverner ou juger* (Presses Universitaires de France 1995)

Tinière R, 'Le contenu essentiel des droits fondamentaux dans la jurisprudence de la Cour de Justice de l'Union européenne' *Cahiers de droit européen* 57 (2021), 417–439

Toggenburg G and Grimheden J, 'Managing the Rule of Law in a Heterogeneous Context' in W Schroeder (ed), *Strengthening the Rule of Law in Europe* (Hart 2016) 221–240

Tomuschat C, 'Kampf oder diplomatischer Ausgleich?' *Verfassungsblog* (15 July 2021)

Tomuschat C, 'The (Hegemonic?) Role of the English Language' *Nordic Journal of International Law* 86 (2017), 196–227

Tomuschat C, 'Der Verfassungsstaat im Geflecht der internationalen Beziehungen' *Veröffentlichungen der Vereinigung der Deutschen Staatsrechtslehrer* 36 (1978), 38–63

Torres Pérez A, 'From Portugal to Poland: The Court of Justice of the European Union as Watchdog of Judicial Independence' *Maastricht Journal of European and Comparative Law* 27 (2020), 105–119

Torres Pérez A, 'The Federalizing Force of the EU Charter of Fundamental Rights' *International Journal of Constitutional Law* 15 (2017), 1080–1097

Tridimas T, 'The General Principles of EU Law and the Europeanisation of National Laws' *Review of European Administrative Law* 13 (2020), 5–31

Tridimas T, 'The General Principles of Law: Who Needs Them?' *Cahiers de droit européen* 52 (2016), 419–441

Tridimas T, 'Bifurcated Justice: The Dual Character of Judicial Protection in EU Law' in A Rosas, E Levits, and Y Bot (eds), *The Court of Justice and the Construction of Europe* (Asser Press 2013) 367–379

Tridimas T, 'Constitutional Review of Member State Action: The Virtues and Vices of an Incomplete Jurisdiction' *International Journal of Constitutional Law* 9 (2011), 737–756

Tridimas T, *The General Principles of EU Law* (2nd edn, OUP 2007)

Tridimas T, 'The Court of Justice and Judicial Activism' *European Law Review* 21 (1996), 199–210

Tridimas T and Gentile G, 'The Essence of Rights: An Unreliable Boundary?' *German Law Journal* 20 (2019), 794–816

Troper M, 'The Logic of Justification of Judicial Review' *International Journal of Constitutional Law* 1 (2003), 99–121
Troper M, *La théorie du droit, le droit, l'État* (Presses Universitaires de France 2001)
Troper M, *Pour une théorie juridique de l'État* (Presses Universitaires de France 1994)
Trstenjak V and Beysen E, 'The Growing Overlap of Fundamental Freedoms and Fundamental Rights in the Case-Law of the CJEU' *European Law Review* 38 (2013), 293–315
Trstenjak V and Beysen E, 'Das Prinzip der Verhältnismäßigkeit in der Unionsrechtsordnung' *Europarecht* 47 (2012), 265–285
Truchet D, *Droit administratif* (9th edn, Presses Universitaires de France 2021)
Tushnet M, *Taking Back the Constitution: Activist Judges and the Next Age of American Law* (Yale Univ. Press 2020)
Tushnet M, *Taking the Constitution Away from the Courts* (Princeton Univ. Press 1999)
Tuori K, 'European Constitutionalism' in R Masterman and R Schütze (eds), *The Cambridge Companion to Comparative Constitutional Law* (CUP 2019) 521–553
Tuori K, *European Constitutionalism* (CUP 2015)
Tzanakopoulos A, 'Judicial Dialogue in Multilevel Governance: The Impact of the Solange Argument' in OK Fauchald and A Nollkaemper (eds), *The Practice of International and National Courts and the (De-)Fragmentation of International Law* (Hart 2012) 185–216
Uerpmann-Wittzack R, 'Art. 23 GG' in I von Münch and P Kunig (eds), *Grundgesetz-Kommentar* (7th edn, C.H.Beck 2021)
Uitz R, 'The Perils of Defending the Rule of Law Through Dialogue' *European Constitutional Law Review* 15 (2019), 1–16
Unger S, '"Präzedenzlos zu denken"?—Unionsverfassungsrecht zwischen Abgrenzung und Analogie zum Staatsrecht' in A Hatje, PC Müller-Graff, and JP Terhechte (eds), *Europarechtswissenschaft, Europarecht Beiheft 2/2018* (Nomos 2018) 191–209
Urbinati N, 'Populism and the Principle of Majority' in C Rovira Kaltwasser and others (eds), *The Oxford Handbook on Populism* (Oxford; OUP, 2017) 571–589
Vajda C, 'Democracy in the European Union: What Has the Court of Justice to Say' *Cambridge Journal of International and Comparative Law* 4 (2015), 226–241
Van Drooghenbroeck S and Rizcallah C, 'Art. 52' in S van Drooghenbroeck and F Picod (eds), *Charte des droits fondamentaux de l'Union européenne* (2nd edn, Bruylant 2020)
Van Drooghenbroeck S and Rizcallah C, 'The ECHR and the Essence of Fundamental Rights' *German Law Journal* 20 (2019), 904–923
Van Elsuwege P and Gremmelprez F, 'Protecting the Rule of Law in the EU Legal Order' *European Constitutional Law Review* 16 (2020), 8–32
van den Brink M, 'The European Union's *Demoi*cratic Legislature' *International Journal of Constitutional* Law 19 (2021), 914–942
van den Brink M, 'Is It Time to Abolish the Substance of EU Citizenship Rights Test?' *European Journal of Migration and Law* 23 (2021), 13–28
van den Brink M, 'EU Citizenship and (Fundamental) Rights: Empirical, Normative, and Conceptual Problems' *European Law Journal* 25 (2019), 21–36
van den Brink M, 'Justice, Legitimacy and the Authority of Legislation within the European Union' *Modern Law Review* 82 (2019), 293–318
van der Schyff G, 'Constitutional Identity of the EU Legal Order' *Ancilla Iuris* (2021), 1–12
van Middelaar L, *The Passage to Europe* (Yale Univ. Press 2013)
Vauchez A, 'EU Law Classics in the Making' in B Davies and F Nicola (eds), *EU Law Stories* (CUP 2017) 21–34

Vauchez A, *Brokering Europe* (CUP 2015)
Vauchez A, 'Keeping the Dream Alive: The European Court of Justice and the Transnational Fabric of Integrationist Jurisprudence' *European Political Science Review* 4 (2012), 51–71
Vedel G, *Manuel élémentaire de droit constitutionnel* (1949) (Dalloz 2002)
Vedel G, Souveraineté et supraconstitutionnalité' *Pouvoirs* 67 (1993), 79–96
Vedel G, 'Schengen et Maastricht' *Revue française de droit administratif* 8 (1992), 173–180
Verdross A and Simma B, *Universelles Völkerrecht* (3rd edn, Duncker&Humblot 1984, repr. 2010)
Verellen T, 'Hungary's Lesson for Europe: Democracy is Part of Europe's Constitutional Identity. It Should be Justiciable' *Verfassungsblog* (8 April 2022)
de Vergottini G, *Diritto Costituzionale Comparato* (10th edn, Cedam 2019)
de Vergottini G, *Diritto Costituzionale* (9th edn, Cedam 2017)
Vesterdorf B, 'Le relevé d'office par le juge communautaire' in N Colneric and others (eds), *Une communauté de droit. Festschrift für Gil Carlos Rodríguez Iglesias* (BWV 2003) 551–568
Viala A, 'Le concept d'identité constitutionnelle' in L Burgorgue-Larsen (ed), *L'identité constitutionnelle saisie par les juges en Europe* (Pedone 2011) 7–24
de Visser M, 'Constitutional Courts Securing Their Legitimacy: An Institutional-Procedural Analysis' in A von Bogdandy, C Grabenwarter, and PM Huber (eds), *The Max Planck Handbooks in European Public Law*, vol 4 (OUP 2023) (forthcoming)
de Visser M and Claes M, 'Courts United? On European Judicial Networks' in A Vauchez and B de Witte (eds), *Lawyering Europe. European Law as a Transnational Social Field* (Hart 2013) 75–100
Volkmann U, *Grundzüge einer Verfassunsglehre der Bundesrepublik Deutschland* (Mohr Siebeck 2013)
Volpe V, 'Realizing European Identity. The Role of the Enlargement Process' in I Amodeo and others (eds), *Why Europe?* (Steiner 2017) 71–79
Voßkuhle A, 'Pyramide oder Mobile?' in A Voßkuhle (ed), *Europa, Demokratie, Verfassungsgerichte* (Suhrkamp 2021) 305–313
Voßkuhle A, 'Karlsruhe Unlimited? Zu den (unsichtbaren) Grenzen der Verfassungsgerichtsbarkeit' in A Voßkuhle (ed), *Europa, Demokratie, Verfassungsgerichte* (Suhrkamp 2021) 314–333
Voßkuhle A, 'Applaus von der falschen Seite. Zur Folgenverantwortung von Verfssungsgerichten' in A Voßkuhle (ed), *Europa, Demokratie, Verfassungsgerichte* (Suhrkamp 2021) 334–343
Voßkuhle A, 'Werteorientierung in der EU: Gift oder Lebenselixier?' *Alkotmánybírósági Szemle* (2020), 13–15
Voßkuhle A, *The Idea of the European Community of Values* (Bittner 2018)
Voßkuhle A, '"European Integration Through Law": The Contribution of the Federal Constitutional Court' *European Journal of Sociology* 58 (2017), 145–168
Voßkuhle A, 'The Cooperation Between European Courts: The Verbund of European Courts and its Legal Toolbox' in A Rosas, E Levits, and Y Bot (eds), *The Court of Justice and the Construction of Europe* (Asser Press 2013) 81–98
Voßkuhle A, 'Was leistet Rechtsdogmatik?' in G Kirchhof, S Magen, and K Schneider (eds), *Was weiß Dogmatik?* (Mohr Siebeck 2012) 111–114
Voßkuhle A, 'Multilevel Cooperation of the European Constitutional Courts: Der Europäische Verfassungsgerichtsverbund' *European Constitutional Law Review* 6 (2010), 175–198

Voßkuhle A, 'Verfassungsstil und Verfassungsfunktion: Ein Beitrag zum Verfassungshandwerk' *Archiv des öffentlichen Rechts* 119 (1994), 35–60

de Vries S, 'Balancing Fundamental Rights with Economic Freedoms According to the European Court of Justice' *Utrecht Law Review* 9 (2013), 169–192

Waelbroeck M and Oliver P, 'La Crise de l'État de Droit dans l'Union Européenne: Que Faire?' *Cahiers de droit européen* 53 (2017), 299–342

Wägenbaur R, 'Zur Nichtbefolgung von Urteilen des EuGH durch die Mitgliedstaaten' in in O Due, M Lutter, and J Schwarze (eds), *Festschrift für Ulrich Everling*, vol 2 (Nomos 1995) 1611–1623

Wahl R, 'Die Rechtsbildung in Europa als Entwicklungslabor' *JuristenZeitung* 67 (2012), 861–870

Wahl R, '*Lüth* und die Folgen' in T Henne and A Riedlinger (eds), *Das Lüth-Urteil aus (rechts-)historischer Sicht* (BWV 2005) 371–397

Walker N, 'Post-Constituent Constitutionalism?' in N Walker and M Loughlin (eds), *The Paradox of Constitutionalism* (OUP 2008) 247–268

Walker N, 'Postnational Constitutionalism and the Problem of Translation' in JHH Weiler and M Wind (eds), *European Constitutionalism Beyond the State* (CUP 2003) 27–54

Walker N, 'The Idea of Constitutional Pluralism' *Modern Law Review* 65 (2002), 317–359

Walker N, 'Flexibility within a Metaconstitutional Frame' in G de Búrca and J Scott (eds), *Constitutional Change in the EU* (Bloomsbury 2000) 9–30

Wasserfallen F, 'The Judiciary as Legislator? How the European Court of Justice Shapes Policy-Making in the European Union' *Journal of European Public Policy* 17 (2010), 1128–1146

Weatherill S, *Law and Integration in the European Union* (Clarendon 1995)

Weber F, 'The Pluralism of Values in an Identity-Framed Verbund: Federal Belonging in the European Union after the Rule of Law Conditionality Judgments' *European Law Review* 47 (2022), 514–533

Weber R, 'Le style, c'est la Cour même! Une analyse comparative du style de motivation du Conseil Constitutionnel et du Bundesverfassungsgericht' *Revue française de droit constitutionnel* (126) (2021), 189–205

Weiler JHH, 'Why Weiss?' *International Journal of Constitutional Law* 19 (2021), 179–187

Weiler JHH, 'Epilogue: Living in a Glass House' C Closa and D Kochenov (eds), *Reinforcing the Rule of Law Oversight in the European Union* (CUP 2016) 313–326

Weiler JHH, 'Van Gend en Loos: The Individual as Subject and Object and the Dilemma of European Legitimacy' *International Journal of Constitutional Law* 12 (2014), 94–103

Weiler JHH, 'Deciphering the Political and Legal DNA of European Integration' in J Dickson and P Eleftheriadis (eds), *Philosophical Foundations of European Union Law* (OUP 2012) 137–158

Weiler JHH, 'The Political and Legal Culture of European Integration' *International Journal of Constitutional Law* 9 (2011), 678–694

Weiler JHH, 'Hjalte Rasmussen: Nemo propheta in patria sua' in H Koch and others (eds), *Europe: The New Legal Realism* (Djøf 2010) xiii–xvi

Weiler JHH, 'On the Power of the Word: Europe's Constitutional Iconography' *International Journal of Constitutional Law* 3 (2005), 173–190

Weiler JHH, 'A Constitution for Europe? Some Hard Choices' *Journal of Common Market Studies* 40 (2002), 563–580

Weiler JHH, 'Epilogue: The Judicial Après Nice' in JHH Weiler and G de Búrca (eds), *The European Court of Justice* (OUP 2001) 215–226

Weiler JHH, *The Constitution of Europe* (CUP 1999)
Weiler JHH, 'Bread and Circus: The State of European Union' *Columbia Journal of European Law* 4 (1998), 223–248
Weiler JHH, 'The Transformation of Europe' *Yale Law Journal* 100 (1991), 2403–2483
Weinberg L, 'Political Questions and the Guarantee Clause' *University of Colorado Law Review* 65 (1994), 887–946
Wendel M, 'The Fog of Identity and Judicial Contestation: Preventive and Defensive Constitutional Identity Review in Germany' *European Public Law* 27 (2021), 465–496
Wendel M, 'Paradoxes of Ultra-Vires Review: A Critical Review of the PSPP Decision and Its Initial Reception' *German Law Journal* 21 (2020), 979–994
Wendel M, 'Auf dem Weg zum Präjudizienrecht? Zur Maßstabsetzung durch den Europäischen Gerichtshof' *Jahrbuch des öffentlichen Rechts der Gegenwart* 68 (2020), 113–145
Wendel M, 'Mutual Trust, Essence and Federalism—Between Consolidating and Fragmenting the Area of Freedom, Security and Justice after LM' *European Constitutional Law Review* 15 (2019), 17–47
Wendel M, 'Comparative Reasoning and the Making of a Common Constitutional Law: EU-Related Decisions of National Constitutional Courts in a Transnational Perspective' *International Journal of Constitutional Law* 11 (2013), 981–1002
Wendel M, *Permeabilität im europäischen Verfassungsrecht* (Mohr Siebeck 2011)
Wendel M, 'Renaissance der historischen Auslegungsmethode im europäischen Verfassungsrecht?' *Zeitschrift für ausländisches öffentliches Recht und Völkerrecht* 68 (2008), 803–827
Wennerås P, 'Saving a Forest and the Rule of Law: Commission v. Poland' *Common Market Law Review* 56 (2019), 541–558
Wetz K, *Funktionen von Verfassungsidentität als gerichtliches Konzept in der Europäischen Union* (Mohr Siebeck 2022)
Wheare KC, *Federal Government* (4th edn, OUP 1963)
Wildhaber L and Callewaert J, 'Espace constitutionnel européen et droits fondamentaux: une vision globale pour une pluralité de droits et de juges' in N Colneric and others (eds), *Une communauté de droit. Festschrift für Gil Carlos Rodríguez Iglesias* (BWV 2003) 61–85
Wildhaber L, Hjartarson A, and Donnelly S, 'No Consensus on Consensus?' *Human Rights Law Journal* 33 (2013), 248–263
Wilkinson MA, *Authoritarian Liberalism and the Transformation of Modern Europe* (OUP 2021)
Williams A, *The Ethos of Europe* (CUP 2010)
Williams RC, 'The "Guarantee" Clause' *Harvard Law Review* 132 (2018), 602–688
Willems A, 'The Court of Justice of the European Union's Mutual Trust Journey in EU Criminal Law: From a Presumption to (Room for) Rebuttal' *German Law Journal* 20 (2019), 468–495
de Witte B, 'Direct Effect, Primacy, and the Nature of the Legal Order' in P Craig and G de Búrca (eds), *The Evolution of EU Law* (3rd edn, OUP 2021) 187–227
de Witte B, 'Exclusive Member State Competences—Is There Such a Thing?' in S Garben and I Govaere (eds), *The Division of Competences between the EU and the Member States* (Hart 2017) 59–73
de Witte B, 'European Union Law: A Unified Academic Discipline?' in B de Witte and A Vauchez (eds), *Lawyering Europe. European Law as a Transnational Social Field* (Hart 2013) 101–116

de Witte B, 'Democratic Adjudication in Europe—How Can the European Court of Justice Be Responsive to the Citizens?' in M Dougan, N Nic Shuibne, and E Spaventa (eds), *Empowerment and Disempowerment of European Citizens* (Hart 2012) 129–144

de Witte B, 'Treaty Revision in the European Union' *Netherlands Yearbook of International Law* 25 (2004), 51–84

de Witte B, 'The Impact of Enlargement on the Constitution of the European Union' in M Cremona (ed), *The Enlargement of the European Union* (OUP 2003) 209–252

de Witte B, 'International Agreement or European Constitution?' in JA Winter and others (eds), *Reforming the Treaty on European Union* (Kluwer 1996) 3–18

de Witte B and Beukers T, 'The Court of Justice Approves the Creation of the European Stability Mechanism outside the EU Legal Order: *Pringle*' *Common Market Law Review* 50 (2013), 805–848

de Witte F, 'Sex, Drugs & EU Law: The Recognition of Moral and Ethical Diversity in EU Law' *Common Market Law Review* 50 (2014), 1545–1578

Wohlfahrt C, *Die Vermutung Unmittelbarer Wirkung des Unionsrechts* (Springer 2016)

Wright S, 'The Self-Restraint of the French Conseil Constitutionnel in 2003 and 2004' *European Public Law* 11 (2005), 495–500

Wunderlich N, 'Von der Wertegemeinschaft zur Verweigerungsunion?' *Europarecht* 54 (2019), 557–577

Wunderlich N, 'Art. 259 AEUV' in H von der Groeben, J Schwarze, and A Hatje (eds), *Europäisches Unionsrecht* (7th edn, Nomos 2015)

Yang N, *Die Leitentscheidung* (Springer 2018)

Yong A, *The Rise and Decline of Fundamental Rights in EU Citizenship* (Hart 2019)

Young EA, 'What Can Europe Tell Us About the Future of American Federalism' *Arizona State Law Journal* 49 (2017), 1109–1140

Zagrebelsky G, *Intorno alla legge* (Einaudi 2009)

Zagrebelsky G, *Il diritto mite* (Einaudi 1992)

Zagrebelsky G and Marcenò V, *Giustizia costituzionale, Vol. I: Storia, principi, interpretazioni* (Mulino 2018)

Zeh J, *Recht auf Beitritt?* (Nomos 2002)

Zemánek J, Arlettaz J, and Berthout A, 'Droit de l'Union et noyau dur constitutionnel en France, Espagne, Italie, Allemagne et République tchèque' in D Petrlík and others (eds), *Évolution des rapports entre les ordres juridiques de l'Union européenne, international et nationaux: Liber amicorum Jiří Malenovský* (Bruylant 2020) 231–260

Zglinski J, *Europe's Passive Virtues* (OUP 2020)

Zglinski J, 'The Rise of Deference: The Margin of Appreciation and Decentralized Judicial Review in EU Free Movement Law' *Common Market Law Review* 55 (2018), 1341–1385

Ziller J, 'Une Constitution courte et obscure ou claire et détaillé?' in G Amato, H Bribosia, and B de Witte (eds), *Genèse et destinée de la Constitution européenne* (Bruylant 2007) 957–993

Zimmerman MJ, 'Value and Normativity' in I Hirose and J Olson (eds), *The Oxford Handbook of Value Theory* (OUP 2015) 13–28

Zuleeg M, 'The Advantages of the European Constitution' in A von Bogdandy and J Bast (eds), *Principles of European Constitutional Law* (2nd edn, Hart 2009) 763–786

Zuleeg M, 'What Holds a Nation Together? Cohesion and Democracy in the United States of America and in the European Union' *American Journal of Comparative Law* 45 (1997), 505–526

Index

For the benefit of digital users, indexed terms that span two pages (e.g., 52–53) may, on occasion, appear on only one of those pages.

Figures are indicated by *f* following the page number